Mastering

Windows Server® 2003 Upgrade Edition for SP1 and R2

Mastering
Windows Server® 2003 Upgrade Edition for SP1 and R2

Mark Minasi

Rhonda Layfield

Lisa Justice

Wiley Publishing, Inc.

Acquisitions and Development Editor: Tom Cirtin

Technical Editor: James F. Kelly

Production Editor: Sarah Groff-Palermo

Copy Editor: Sally Engelfried

Production Manager: Tim Tate

Vice President and Executive Group Publisher:
  Richard Swadley

Vice President and Executive Publisher: Joseph B. Wikert

Vice President and Publisher: Neil Edde

Book Designers: Maureen Forys, Happenstance Type-O-Rama
  and Judy Fung

Compositor: Chris Gillespie, Happenstance Type-O-Rama

Proofreader: Ian Golder

Indexer: Ted Laux

Cover Designer: Ryan Sneed

Cover Image: © Pete Gardner/Digital Vision/Getty Images

For general information on our other products and services or
to obtain technical support, please contact our Customer Care
Department within the U.S. at (800) 762-2974, outside the U.S.
at (317) 572-3993 or fax (317) 572-4002.

Wiley also publishes its books in a variety of electronic formats.
Some content that appears in print may not be available in electronic books.

Library of Congress Cataloging-in-Publication Data is available from the publisher.

10 9 8 7 6 5 4 3 2 1

This book is dedicated to my dearest Rhonda. Many authors can thank their sweeties for being patient as they prepared their books. I am fortunate enough to be with someone whom I can trust to help *write* them!

—Mark

Acknowledgments

Lots of people sit down and write things, and some of those things are clever and insightful—but those insights never get to live between the covers of a book. The difference between "stuff that gets written" and "stuff that gets published and read by millions" is the small legion of people who get most of the work done.

Over the years, people have emailed me to say that the font's too small in the book, or they can't get an included CD to work, or the like. My answer is always a polite explanation that "I just write the books; I don't edit, typeset, lay out, print, bind, box, ship, or sell them." So here's a thank you to the people who do those things, or help with those things.

First, many thanks to my coauthors, Christa Anderson, Lisa Justice, Rhonda Layfield, Darren Mar-Elia, and C. A. Callahan. I knew I could cover most of the SP1-specific changes and provide some overview coverage of R2, but much of R2 called for very specific knowledge of particular areas, and I lacked the time to acquire that knowledge—so having these big brains shoulder their burdens cheerfully and with excellence freed me up to get the rest of the book done. If we managed to achieve any of the "clever and insightful" that I referred to in the opening of this page, then most of the credit goes to them.

Many thanks to our editors, Tom Cirtin, Sarah Groff-Palermo, and Jim Kelly, who shepherded this text into the readable form that you'll see in a page or two. They made the whole process easy, and so we got this book to you a bit sooner than we expected. Ditto for the production staff, Sarah Groff-Palermo, Sally Engelfried, Ian Golder, and Chris Gillespie, who turn the electrons in the document files into actual books.

Thanks go also to the folks at Waggener-Edstrom for their assistance in connecting us with the right people at Microsoft; in particular, I'd like to thank Rob Johnson of that outfit. The people we spoke with at Microsoft were friendly and helpful despite being quite obviously busy.

Finally, I wouldn't have had a chance to write this, my 25th book, if you readers didn't keep buying them. It is your continued faith in me that keeps these books coming out, so thank you very, very much for letting me continue to do what I enjoy more than almost anything: writing and explaining things. I hope you find this book of value, and a reason to come back for the next one!

Contents at a Glance

Contents

Introduction

Welcome to the Special Upgrade Edition of *Mastering Windows Server 2003: Upgrade Edition for SP1 and R2*. This book bridges the gap between the original April 2003 "release to manufacturing" or "RTM" version of Windows Server 2003, which we covered in *Mastering Windows Server 2003* (Sybex, 2003), and the two more recent versions of Server 2003 that you may encounter— either a copy of the RTM version Windows Server 2003 to which someone has installed Service Pack 1 (SP1), or a copy of Microsoft's interim and minor upgrade of Server 2003, Windows Server 2003 R2.

I have aimed this book, then, at two very nearly but not *quite* identical audiences: the people running Windows Server 2003 with SP1 installed, and the folks running Windows Server 2003 R2. Those audiences aren't quite identical because while adding SP1 and a bunch of downloads to an RTM copy of 2003 nearly makes it R2, it's only "nearly"—R2 contains a handful of features not found in 2003 with SP1. (And if you're thinking to yourself, "Hey! *That's* not true! R2's got a *lot* more features than 2003 does!" then I'm sorry to have to say while R2 *does* have some neat new features, there aren't many of them. Again, that's not to say that R2's handful of only-available-to-R2 features aren't cool—they are—but they're not as numerous as the Microsoft marketing folks would have you believe, as you'll see in the upcoming section entitled "The R2 Calculus.")

In this book, my co-authors and I have sought to achieve the same things that we've done in the past 13 years: to explain what new things these new versions of Server offer, and how to install, configure, manage, and troubleshoot those new things as easily as possible. You'll see that wherever possible we've first laid out the concepts, warned you about the pitfalls, and provided step-by-step examples demonstrating how to put the new stuff to work.

As I said above, this is an "upgrade" book, so it assumes that you already know how to work with the RTM version of Windows Server 2003, pre-SP1. If you're not fluent with 2003, then you'll still find this useful, but I'd ask you please to strongly consider getting a copy of the earlier *Mastering Windows Server 2003* to use in tandem with this volume. (Honest, I'm not trying to sell books; I'd just hate for you to find yourself constantly shaking your head in frustration as we refer to chapters from the earlier book.)

In other words, this book is for both the admin of the original Server 2003 software seeking to find out about the big changes wrought by SP1 and for the 2003-savvy admin who's upgraded to R2 and wants to know what *that* offers. For the person who's completely new to the Windows networking game, this book is still useful—but again, in that case please consider adding the original *Mastering Windows Server 2003* to fill out your 2003 networking references.

Why did I put together an upgrade book rather than just taking the original *Mastering* book and revising it to cover SP1 and R2? For a few reasons. First, every time I revise one of my books, I get emails from readers asking, "Do you have something that'll just cover the changes rather than making me comb through the new edition looking for the new stuff?" so I thought we'd give an upgrade book a try. (There's one exception to the "all new text" rule, the Terminal Services chapter, due to the volume of changes that SP1 wrought, but you'll find all of the other chapters to be completely new text.) Second, a lot of you have asked for a series of smaller books because the original *Mastering* book is, um, sort of large at almost 1800 pages, and once I heard the "this book is so big that it has its own weather system" joke for the hundredth time I figured that we needed to offer something smaller and yet useful. So, as the marketing types say, this is the book that you folks asked for, and I hope you like it.

Let's start out with the basics. In this Introduction, we'll look at

- What was the point of SP1 and how did it change 2003?

- Why did Microsoft come out with R2, given that it's a pretty minor upgrade, particularly given that there's a larger upgrade soon in the next version of Server?

- How exactly *do* 2003 RTM, SP1, and R2 all fit together?

After we're done with that, I'll give you a quick synopsis of what you'll find in the rest of the book.

Service Pack 1's Goals: Fix Bugs, Shore Up Security

Answering part of the question "why did Microsoft release an SP1 for 2003" is pretty easy: to fix bugs. As with every other version of the Windows NT family, Microsoft regularly finds and fixes bugs in their operating systems and periodically rolls all of those bug fixes into one big package, tests it a bit more thoroughly than they did the separate bug fixes, and calls the whole thing a service pack. As Microsoft released the original RTM version of 2003 in April 2003 and SP1 in April of 2005, that's two years of bug fixes.

A look at SP1 for 2003's size shows it to be the biggest service pack *ever*, weighing in at 329MB… and you thought XP's SP2 was a monster at 267MB! As SP1 contains a lot of those .CAB "file cabinet" files, does this suggest that Windows needs to go on a "low cab" diet? Nope (and sorry, that *was* a dumb pun), in fact XP's SP2 and 2003's SP1 are so hefty for the same reason: security. Which, by the way answers the question "what motivated Microsoft to create 2003's SP1?" Again, security.

I know, by now you're probably pretty tired of hearing about security. While computer networking has always involved security, it became a front-burner issue in 2001 with the Code Red and Nimda worms, leading to a directive from Bill Gates in early 2002 for everyone at Microsoft to stop any new coding so that everyone—and I mean *everyone*—at Microsoft could attend training about writing better code security-wise. For two months, in February and March 2002, no new code issued from Redmond. Microsoft delayed the release of Windows Server 2003 from its original ship date of early 2002 to the second quarter of 2003 to accommodate a fine-tooth-combing of the new version of Server's code. Gates's security epiphany also caused Microsoft to pretty much throw away all of their work to that date on a new service pack for XP, which eventually became XP SP2. That, in turn, eventually caused them to restart the application development project on Windows Vista, the late-2006 or early-2007 replacement for XP, essentially throwing away all of their previous Vista development and starting from scratch. Surely, they hoped, all new code from that point on would be as secure as secure could be.

Of course, it didn't work out that way, as Windows bugs that led to scary worms and Trojans kept (and, sadly, keep) popping up. 2003 saw a bug in SQL Server 2000 enable a worm that was so active that it slowed down the entire Internet for a few days in January, and August of that year saw a bug in XP that made possible the "Blaster" worm. Blaster embarrassed Microsoft so much that they went back to the Windows code *again* and looked it over from top to bottom. In the process XP SP2 was *again* delayed and Microsoft realized that any radical changes to XP via SP2—and it surely looked as if there would be some—would have to be retroactively included in Server 2003 and Windows 2000 Server via service packs.

In 2004, XP's SP2 finally shipped in August. One change in that service pack, something you'll read about in Chapter 3 called Data Execution Prevention, required that Microsoft recompile very nearly every single piece of the XP software, meaning that SP2 is essentially a complete new copy of XP, and of course that's why XP's SP2 is so large. XP SP2 also included not only bug fixes and security patches, but also a bunch of pretty useful new applications, mostly security-related. Furthermore, as you'll read in Chapter 5, SP2 changed the basic way that some of Windows' most fundamental communications systems worked, securing them and creating worries about compatibility. Microsoft needed to implement those changes in Server as well—meaning that they had to recompile nearly every piece of Server 2003 in SP1—and so, in 2005, SP1 for Server 2003's appearance heralded a huge download. Along the way, Microsoft decided not to offer an SP5 for 2000 with those changes, which is a shame but not that much of a surprise. Like most software vendors, Microsoft really hates the idea of "selling" software and would much prefer to liken its sales model more to that of beer—you don't buy it, you rent it. (They're not the only ones; check out how Red Hat sells Linux and you may be stunned to find that, at least based on the prices on their website, Red Hat has made Windows XP the low-cost desktop alternative.)

But Microsoft didn't stop with bug fixes and a few architectural realignments in XP SP2 and 2003 SP1. They also added about a dozen new features and yes, they're mainly security-related, but I think that you'll find them quite useful. Unfortunately about half of those features are essentially undocumented, and so, sadly, many admins are unaware that they're already the proud possessors of some neat new tools. That's another important reason for this book—to pass along the good news. And while this book isn't intended to be an XP SP2 book, it inevitably will be of some use to anyone with an XP SP2 desktop, as most of the new 2003 SP1 goodies are in XP SP2 as well.

2003 SP1 and XP SP2 are, then, a lot more than a lot of patches. They are quite significant upgrades of their respective OSes and deserve every administrator's attention from the point of view of understanding both how they can offer new features and how they sometimes can offer compatibility issues.

R2's Origins: Schedules and SA

Most people can easily understand what's up with SP1 because *all* service packs are basically big bunches of patches with the occasional extra program thrown in. SP1 is unusual only, as I've said, because of its sheer size and the number of new utilities. But what's the deal with this Windows Server 2003 R2 thing?

Once upon a time—between August 1993 and July 1996—Microsoft used to release a new version of NT Server annually. NT 3.1 Server appeared in 1993, 3.5 Server in 1994, 3.51 Server in 1995, and NT 4.0 Server arrived in 1996. Some were pretty minor upgrades, but they all brought new stuff and improvements to old stuff. But then Microsoft started working on NT 5.0. It took longer than expected, all the way to 2000, and, as you probably recall, got renamed to Windows 2000 in February 2000. Microsoft expected to quickly come out with a follow-up "1.1" version of 2000 Server but, as you've read, the security messes of the early 2000's slowed things down and eventually that 1.1 version appeared as Server 2003. As any veteran admin of 2000 Server knows, Server 2003 is indeed basically a 1.1 version of 2000 Server, but a welcome one—there are enough little grace notes in 2003 to make upgrading from 2000 to 2003 a worthwhile endeavor. But the 38 months between the two made a lot of customers wonder whether Microsoft knew how to manage large software projects.

What exactly were those customers concerned about? Well, to understand that, you've got to understand that Microsoft's main focus, like most big companies' main focus, is on their big customers. I'd guess that they probably make the vast majority of their revenue from their fellow Fortune 500 firms and a few large governments. So those are the folks that they listen to most closely. I mean, don't get me wrong, it's not like they don't *care* about the rest of us but, um, hey, will you *look* how the time's just flown! Better get back to the original point…

Those big customers all like to do budget planning, and long-term budget planning at that. They don't want to discover in May of 2008 that in September of 2008 the electric company's changing over to direct current and thus all of a sudden they'll have to throw out all of their AC-based electrical appliances and buy ones running on DC. Of course, concerns about something like that would be true of an organization of any size—but what's different about the really big ones is that it honestly may be simply *impossible* to get those funds approved; it may be the case that the only kind of money that can get spent in September 2008 is money asked for in the spring of 2007. Folks like this need to and want to be able to see what's coming cost-wise, preferably a year or two in advance. Which brings us back to the 2000 Server and Server 2003 issue. From 1997 through 2000, organizations heavily dependent on Windows software were saying to Microsoft, "When's the new desktop software coming? When is that new server coming?" and Microsoft just wasn't sure. That annoyed customers, and so Microsoft has tried to cook up a schedule of regular software releases.

NOTE Now, I'm a guy who's written a lot of books, magazine articles, columns, newsletters and the like about Microsoft and who never stints at picking on them when they deserve it. But on the issue of "tell us exactly when the product's going to be available, and tell us a year and a half in advance," I've got to side with the folks in Redmond. Software is research, all brain-work. It's hard to schedule that kind of stuff. Personally I'd rather they shipped any given version of Windows later without bugs, than that they ship it on time *with* bugs.

The first thing Microsoft did to "regularize" software shipments was to realize that putting out a new version of Server every year just plain wasn't happenin', and that's probably a good thing. NT's role in most large networks was pretty small until around 1998, so no one really noticed that for a while Microsoft was popping out a new version of NT every year or so.

This decade, in contrast, has seen Microsoft networks take a much more center-stage role, and most firms aren't interested in ripping up their software infrastructure every 12 months, no matter *how* much cooler the GUI has become in that time. Microsoft's big customers seem to be saying, "Yeah, we need software innovation, but not *that* often."

Second, it's not clear that a new version every year of Server or, for that matter, the desktop version of Windows makes any sense technologically. Why? Well, you're about to read some heresy, so make sure that the door's closed and no one's looking over your shoulder. Go ahead, I'll wait… Ready? Great, then here's the secret:

The pace of technological change in computers has slowed down tremendously.

Don't think so? Stop and think about it. As I write this sentence in early 2006, there are people, lots of people, still running Windows NT 4.0 domain controllers because they still haven't gone to Active Directory. Windows NT 4.0 was released in 1996, ten years ago as I write this in 2006. Heck, you may know someone still using Windows *95*! That would be like someone running Windows 3.1 in the year 2000, or, to choose a more ancient example, MS-DOS 3.3 in 1992—examples that would have been practically impossible to find in those days. While I personally wouldn't want to have to live in 95-land, I can understand why people do—it still gets the job done. They can surf the Web, get email, play a lot of games. That would, again, not be a possibility in the past: someone using Windows 3.1 in the year 2000 would find that virtually not a single application on the shelf would run on 3.1. But computing is tending to plateau these days, as hardware vendors are hitting limits in at least two ways. First, Intel has said that it's not possible to create a Pentium chip faster than 3.8 GHz and, second, hard drive vendors claim that they've nearly hit the wall on data density.

When hardware hits a wall, that affects software because hardware change has often been the *driver* for software change. People thirsted for a version of DOS that could easily handle hard disks bigger than 32MB in size, and so Microsoft sold a lot of DOS 5. A bit later on, they liked the idea of not having to learn the command line and to use the full potential of their neat new graphics boards, and so Microsoft sold a lot of Windows 3.*x*. After that, they wanted networking and so people bought Windows 95, with its built-in support of Internet software. USB support partially drove buyers to Windows 98, although in smaller numbers. As the flow of new hardware dried up, so did the "gotta have it" urgency for new software.

Don't get me wrong, it's not that there's nothing new left to do in computing, not by any means: I'm still looking forward to being able to stick a FireWire cable in my ear and either back up my brain or learn something new in a second. There will always be innovation in computing, but it'll be slower. (Consider, by way of analogy, technological change in cars; in the '50s, when the modern car first appeared—one with air conditioning, automatic everything, long-lived tires—then people talked a lot about how cars could keep innovating, and so we heard a lot about flying cars, computer-managed highways that would handle the driving, and so on. Those things might happen one day, and they might not. There are still innovations to come in cars, they just don't come as quickly as they did in the '20s through the '50s.)

Anyway, the combination of big customers wanting some advance notice on new versions, unwillingness to upgrade every single year, and a slowed pace of hardware change seemed to Microsoft to suggest a four-year cycle of operating system change. Microsoft now intends to release a major version of its server operating system every four years. Windows Server 2003 eponymously (and don't think I haven't been looking for a chance to use that word for a few books) appeared in 2003, so the next one's arriving in 2007 or 2008 and will be called Windows Server 2007 or 2008. (I'll just refer to it as "Windows Server 2007/8" in this book, as my crystal ball's out for repair.)

But, thought Microsoft, four years is a long time. I mean, *something* big could come along and they might not want to wait two or three years to offer that new big thing. And, more important, there's the matter of those Software Assurance customers.

Software Assurance (SA), also known as Licensing 6.0, is Microsoft's latest way of charging for software. Back in the old days, you'd buy a computer and pay for an operating system on it. (You still do that.) If Microsoft came up with a newer OS a year or two later, then they'd offer two versions of it. The first version was the basic distribution, the kind that you'd get on a new machine. It cost a fair amount of money. The second version was essentially the same thing as the first—a CD, a little manual, and a box—but it cost far less, as it was the "upgrade" version. It would only install if you could prove that you owned the old version.

In 2001, Microsoft introduced a new approach, SA. Under SA, Microsoft stopped offering upgrade versions. Instead, they offered customers who'd just purchased one of their operating systems a kind of "upgrade insurance" that went something like this: pay Microsoft a fee equal to about two-thirds of what you just spent for the new operating system and that buys you a "free" upgrade to the next version of that operating system…so long as they ship that OS in the next three years. (The "three years" varies but as far as I can see, that's the standard term.) Now, this "let's do an OS every four years" decision came a bit after the "let's offer 'upgrade insurance' with a three-year term" decision, and so Microsoft had already sold a lot of SA licenses to XP and 2003 buyers.

A simple arithmetic comparison of "three-year SA licenses" and "four-year software cycle" leads one to the conclusion that, well, this whole business *had* to annoy a few customers. Buy a copy of 2003 Standard Edition for about $1000 in 2003 and pay Microsoft another $600 or $700 for the right to get any new versions of server up to 2006…only to find out that yup, there's another version of Server coming, but in 2007.

Now it's easy to see the second reason for R2's existence. It offered Microsoft the chance to right any grievous wrongs in 2003 without having to wait for the next version of Server, as I suggested before, but it also gave the SA folks something for their money. In some senses, this small revision of Server 2003 should be called "Server 2003 SA" rather than "Server 2003 R2." Microsoft also decided not to offer the original Server 2003 any more; if you buy a copy of Server now, you're getting Windows Server 2003 R2.

Overall R2 Details: Future, Licensing, Support, AD Impact

Windows Server 2003 R2, as I suggested earlier, will not be the only R2, at least according to Microsoft's plans. This R2 notion will continue for future versions of Server. For example, assuming that Microsoft ships the next major version of Server, Windows Server 2007/8 in 2007 or 2008, then there won't be another major Server release until around 2011, and around 2009 we'll see a "Windows Server 2007/8 R2" release.

Anyone buying a piece of software nowadays has to wonder, "What sort of support will I get if I buy this?" Microsoft offers a wide array of support…but it doesn't last forever. You may know that Microsoft has paired the schedule of regular releases of software that I mentioned earlier to a schedule for *supporting* that software. For example, Server 2003's "mainstream support" (the Microsoft website's phrase) goes away on June 30, 2008, at least according to http://support .microsoft.com/lifecycle/?LN=en-us&p1=3198&x=14&y=9. Now, you might think that would imply that they'd support R2 for an extra two years after that, but that's not the case; when the regular old RTM original version of Server 2003's support disappears, so does 2003 R2's, in mid-2008.

What are all of the costs of moving to R2? First, of course, if you didn't pay for Software Assurance, then you'll have to buy entirely new software licenses for Windows Server 2003 R2. As with Server 2003, there are four varieties of R2—Web Edition, Standard Edition, Enterprise Edition, and Datacenter Edition. Prices for Standard and Enterprise R2 appear unchanged from 2003's Standard and Enterprise, as they list at $1000 and $4000, respectively. But anyone who's ever priced out a Windows server-based network knows that its largest cost component is the so-called "client access licenses" or CALs, essentially per-user add-on fees. Will you have to buy new CALs? Good news— if you already have 2003-variety CALs, you do not have to upgrade any 2003 CALs to R2 CALs, as both types of CALs are apparently identical, according to http://www.microsoft.com/ windowsserver2003/howtobuy/licensing/priclicfaq.mspx#EVF. So adding a Windows Server 2003 R2 system to your network won't require new CALs. Yay!

Another cost that R2 will exact is a change in your Active Directory. If you've added a 2003-based domain controller to an existing 2000-based AD then you may recall that you can't add that first 2003-based DC without first modifying your forest's schema with the adprep command, as we explained in Chapter 8 of *Mastering Windows Server 2003*. Similarly, you cannot add any R2-based DCs to any existing Active Directory domains without pumping up the AD schema—the structure of the Active Directory—first. As with adding the first 2003-based DC to the 2000-based domain, you find the adprep.exe file and run it from the command line with the /forestprep option. (The R2 adprep is on the second installation CD—yes, R2 ships on two CDs—in the \cmpnents\r2\adprep folder.) You can add simple R2-based member servers without a schema change, however.

NOTE As you'll see in the later R2 chapters, R2's two-disc installer leads to some interesting things. I installed my first R2 server without bothering with the second disc and was able to DCPROMO the new R2 server with no trouble and use it as a DC with no troubles. But when I realized that I'd forgotten to fire up the second Setup disc, then that disc complained to me that it couldn't continue until I'd upgraded my schema.

Summarizing, then, you don't need new CALs to add an R2 server (which is good), but if you want to add an R2-based domain controller or use about half of R2's new features, then you'll have to modify your AD's schema (which may worry your IT staff, as people tend to be twitchy about modifying AD schemas).

Who Might Move to R2?

Don't take any of that as a criticism of R2. In essence, if you like Server 2003, then you'll like R2. You'll move to R2 if you fall into one of four categories.

◆ If you're running Windows 2000 Server and want to upgrade, particularly as Microsoft is gradually withdrawing support for 2000, then 2003 RTM would have been a good move. But you can't buy 2003 RTM any more; Microsoft doesn't sell it. For the same price that 2003 RTM would have cost you, you get Server 2003 R2, which is 2003 RTM and more. So you latecomers to the 2003 party got some benefit from waiting, even if you *do* end up with a fairly short support lifetime.

◆ If you're new to the Windows networking world, then your first Server purchase will be R2 because, again, that's what Microsoft's selling at the moment. Welcome to the club!

◆ There is a small list of features that R2 contains that Server 2003 lacks. Microsoft aimed at least one of them—the Active Directory Federation Service—at its big customers, and a few of those larger organizations tell me that they've adopted R2 quickly because of these new features.

◆ If you did pay for Software Assurance, then you've got R2 coming to you free of (further) charge. If it offers anything that looks useful, anything at all, then you might consider upgrading, as the incremental software cost is zero, and you needn't buy new CALs.

Who *wouldn't* upgrade to R2? Well, if you've already got your systems running the RTM version of Server 2003 and added SP1 to those systems but don't see an R2-specific benefit compelling enough to make you part with the cost of entirely new Server licenses, then you'll stay with 2003.

Note that even if there's nothing in R2's bag of goodies that makes you want to upgrade *now*, Microsoft might manage to change your mind in the near future, as they keep adding subtle incentives to move to R2. As I write this, I can think of two of those incentives.

First, they've changed the software license for R2's Enterprise Edition to allow you to put one software license on up to four different virtual machines. Given that Standard Edition costs about a quarter of what Enterprise Edition costs, *and* taking into account the fact that R2 Standard Edition's license does *not* allow you to create four virtual machines with it, then Enterprise R2's four-for-one deal might not be of value. But for those needing Enterprise and working in environments using virtual machines, it's pretty tempting.

Second, Microsoft has released a free download called the Identity Integration Feature Pack (IIFP, soon to be renamed something like the "Windows Metadirectory Service"). IIFP is a tool that greatly simplifies managing a network with multiple independent and separate forests. And the price is right…*but* it only runs on R2, and only on *Enterprise* Edition.

The R2 Calculus: What's in R2

I've been saying that R2 is different from 2003 with SP1 added, but I really haven't said how, and oddly enough it's not extremely simple to figure out what is the difference between an RTM copy of 2003 with SP1 added and a copy of 2003 R2—at least, *I* had trouble at first sorting it all out from Microsoft's marketing material. But now that I've worked with 2003 RTM, 2003 SP1, and R2, I can offer you what I call the "R2 calculus."

R2 = new SP1 features + downloadable stuff + "R2-only" features

"New SP1 features" just refers to things that you get when you add SP1 to an RTM copy of 2003, like Windows Firewall or the Security Configuration Wizard. They're both nice things…but you can get 'em without buying R2. In the "New SP1 features" category, I'd include things like (and don't worry, I'll explain them all later)

◆ Access-based enumeration

◆ Data execution prevention

◆ IP stack improvements

◆ More secure program-to-program communications

◆ Per-user auditing

◆ Group policy whitelisting/blacklisting of ActiveX and browser helper objects

◆ Windows Firewall

◆ Forcing USB devices to read-only

◆ Terminal server upgrades

◆ Security Configuration Wizard

These are things that, while they *can* be called R2 features, they're also available to any 2003 RTM owner who installs SP1. (And given the security benefits, I'm hoping that all of you using 2003 have added SP1.)

"Downloadable stuff" refers to things that Microsoft has previously released as freely downloadable applications since 2003 RTM's release. For example, Microsoft released something called "Windows SharePoint Services" as a free download back in March 2003. (In case you're wondering what SharePoint does, we've got a chapter on it in this book.) According to Microsoft's website, it'll only install on a copy of Server 2003 or R2, making Windows SharePoint Services one of those "free" things that also provide just a bit of upgrade-arm-twisting—"C'mon, don't you want to upgrade? You can use SharePoint if you do!" In the "downloadable" category I'd include

◆ Group Policy Management Console

◆ Windows SharePoint Services

◆ NFS server support

◆ NIS server support

◆ Unix/Active Directory password synchronization

◆ Active Directory Application Mode (ADAM)

◆ Microsoft Management Console 3.0

◆ The .NET Programming Framework 2.0

In each of those cases, pieces of software—and sometimes quite extensive pieces of software—are available for free download and would work just fine atop a 2003 RTM server with or without SP1, and, in some cases, those software run fine atop 2000 Server or even XP. The main difference with R2 is that they're now packaged, as I've mentioned earlier, on R2's two CDs. (And before you ask: no, for some reason Microsoft doesn't offer a one-DVD version.) As these pieces of software come on the CDs, you needn't download the software. A convenience, even if not a large one.

Finally, there's the "R2-only" stuff, typically features borrowed from the next upcoming major release. These are really the only features that can honestly be said to be only available to those who own an R2 license. They include

- Print Management Console
- Folder screens and quotas
- Storage Reports Manager
- DFS Namespaces and DFS-R Replication
- Active Directory Federation Service
- Hardware IPMI Manager
- Storage Area Network Manager
- Common Logging File System

In this book, we cover almost all of the SP1-specific stuff, downloadable doodads, and new-to-R2 features. That's "almost" because we're mostly covering things of general value to administrators. That lets out the programmer-centric stuff like .NET 2.0 and the Common Logging File System, and we don't cover the SAN or IPMI managers because they're very hardware-specific. But I think you'll find the rest of those doodads easy to learn and of value to use—even if they just get you ready for Server 2007/8!

Meet the Authors

Of the roughly two dozen chapters in this book, I wrote all but 11. For the others, I turned to some friends, all of whom I've worked with before. Permit me to introduce my co-authors.

Christa Anderson and I have worked together on the *Mastering Server* books since their first edition back in 1994. She's done tons of things since then, including recently taking a temporary position at Microsoft where she got to help shape the direction of Terminal Server in very positive ways. She's written or co-authored a ton of articles, columns, and books. Christa explains how SP1 improves Terminal Services in Chapter 10 and covers R2's all-new Print Management Console (perhaps the niftiest new-to-R2 feature) in Chapter 14.

Lisa Justice and I have worked together on and off around 1996, when we taught seminars together and she wrote extensively on user support technologies in Windows. Much of her writing in the user support tools area has been about user profiles, which turn out to be far more complex than you'd imagine at first glance, but Lisa took them apart and made them understandable for the NT 4 version of the Server book. Since 1998, she's been an NT/Windows techie, a SQL type, a Solaris administrator, an AD designer and more, making her the perfect candidate to cover the Unix/Windows integration tools in R2 in Chapters 19–21.

Darren Mar-Elia has done things ranging from being "the" NT guy at Charles Schwab to his current job as CTO of Quest, and along the way has written things like the group policies book in

Microsoft's Windows Resource Kit and several e-books about group policies and contributed to the first edition of the 2000 Server book. Oh, and how could I forget that he took a sabbatical in the middle of all this to go spend several months working at a winery? There's no better go-to guy when you want deep insights and clear explanations about enterprise-level things, so I asked him to explain ADAM and ADFS in Chapters 22 and 23.

C.A. Callahan, whom I met at a Windows conference about four years ago, is another one of those dying breed, the freelance IT person who teaches, consults, and speaks on, well, just about anything that interests her. She wrote three well-received chapters for the *Mastering Windows Server 2003* book. She's only with us for one chapter in this book, but it's an important one—the Windows SharePoint Services coverage in Chapter 18.

Last but not least, Rhonda Layfield got started with computers back in the early '80s while serving in the Navy. That experience led her, after leaving the service seven years later, to alternate between IT consulting and teaching, including a stint as a Microsoft Product Support Specialist in networking, so she not only knows how this stuff works, she can explain it as well. Rhonda is also one of the few people on the planet that I know who understands and can explain the File Replication Service (FRS) in 2000 Server and Server 2003, which made her the perfect person to cover the *new* File Replication Service named "DFS-R" in R2, in Chapter 17. She also agreed to take on the other new storage-related tools, storage management reports in Chapter 15, and folder screens and quotas in Chapter 16.

What's in This Book

Here's a quick synopsis of what you'll find in this book. Chapter 1 explains how to get and install SP1, in case you haven't done that yet or, in the unlikely event that you've got to get rid of it, how to do that.

Chapter 2 covers something called Access-Based Enumeration, or ABE. Ever wished you could create a file share and prevent people from seeing folders in that share that they don't have access to? It's an obvious way to deter people from trying to get into places that they're not supposed to be, and it's a great way to simplify what a user sees in a given share. Besides, anyone who's ever used a Novell NetWare network wonders why Novell's had this feature for years and Microsoft hasn't. At least, Microsoft *hasn't* had that feature until now, that is, as ABE is one of SP1's neatest undocumented (until Chapter 2) features.

Ever wonder why XP SP2 and 2003 SP1 are so huge? Chapter 3 explains that Data Execution Prevention (DEP) is why. DEP is an aspect of SP1 that affects every piece of code in Windows, which, again, made SP1 and SP2 so large. It is *also* the thing that may save you from the next Windows worm, even if you haven't had time to patch.

TCP/IP, the language of the Internet, is a great way to build networks that are big, flexible, compatible…and easy to attack. Learn in Chapter 4 what nonobvious (but important) changes SP1 brought to 2003's networking software. You'll also learn about a neat feature that can undo the damage that spyware sometimes does to your system when you remove the spyware.

Chapter 5 explains what I call SP2, SP1, and R2's "de-anonymizers." When XP's SP2 and 2003's SP1 first appeared, they met with a lot of fear, as some people said that they caused a lot of applications to stop working, and so many said not to install XP SP2 and 2003 SP1. But there's no real need to worry, because once you understand how 2003 SP1 seeks to better secure your system, then you'll see how to resolve almost any incompatibility.

One of SP1's basically undocumented features is the notion of "per-user" auditing. This takes an old but not always useful NT technology—security auditing—and increases its value significantly. Chapter 6 shows you how per-user auditing can help you fine-tune what your network looks after.

The job of securing a network isn't an unchanging one, unfortunately. Just when we almost had the virus threat in hand, spyware appeared. It spreads in a manner similar to viruses, but it's much scarier. Where viruses just want to spread quickly and either annoy you or damage your data, spyware wants to stay nice and inconspicuous as it *steals* your data and possibly your identity. Two favorite methods for bad guys to install spyware on your system are through ActiveX controls and Browser Helper Objects (BHOs). But Service Pack 1 includes a bunch of new group policy settings to allow you to cut bad ActiveX and BHOs off at the knees, and Chapter 7 shows you how to use those group policy settings.

Chapter 8 takes up one of SP2 and SP1's most complex pieces, Windows Firewall. This chapter covers Windows Firewall in detail, as well as explaining another not-well-documented SP1 feature—IPsec bypass. A quick read will show you how this tool might save you money.

Nowadays, it's dead easy for a thief to make off with your data, assuming he's got physical access to one of your computers. He can pop a USB "thumb drive," "jump drive," "memory stick" or even one of the many small solid-state MP3 players into your computer's USB ports, copy the data, and walk away. Unless you've got 2003 SP1, that is. Chapter 9 explains how another of SP1's basically undocumented options lets you restrict any USB storage devices plugged into a 2003 system to be read-only. In other words, the attacker can copy data from the USB memory to your PC, but not the other way around.

Terminal Services got a quiet but important makeover in 2003 SP1, and Christa Anderson explains that makeover in Chapter 10 by revising the Terminal Services chapter from the *Mastering Windows Server 2003* book. (Every other chapter in this book is all-new material, but the changes in Terminal Services were so important that we decided to include one revised, rather than completely new, chapter.) For one thing, SP1's Terminal Services helps work around one of Terminal Services' biggest pain points: printers. With SP1 it's possible to create "printer driver failovers." SP1 also enables Terminal Services to use Secure Sockets Layer (SSL) to encrypt Terminal Server sessions, as you'll learn in that chapter. You'll also learn about new group policy settings to simplify central control of your terminal servers…including one that addresses one of the most common support issues in all of Windows Server: licensing mode mismatches.

System "hardening"—disabling services, blocking particular ports, requiring digital signing on certain kinds of communications—was once the province of only the very paranoid. But nowadays it's a job for every network administrator. Microsoft's made it easier for us with a 2003 SP1/R2 tool called the Security Configuration Wizard. Most wizards can be a bit scary—what exactly *did* it do, why did it do it, and how can I undo it?—but not SCW, particularly after you've read Chapter 11.

In Chapter 12, we move to the next part of the book: what's new to R2 only. R2's first chapter discusses how to prepare for and install R2. It's very similar to a 2003 setup but with a few differences—hey, that extra CD's got to have *some* effect on an install!

From there, we'll introduce you to R2's changes to an old friend. Chapter 13 discusses Microsoft Management Console version 3.0. To be truthful, most of the changes evidenced in MMC 3.0 apply only to programmers, but there are a few things that you'll see that'll make life a little different for admins.

Christa then returns in Chapter 14 to showcase what may be my favorite new-to-R2 feature: the Print Management Console (PMC). It's a neat new tool that lets you view all of your print servers and printer shares all in one screen, as well as easily deploy printers via group policy objects that PMC creates for you.

In Chapter 15, Rhonda Layfield joins us to explain Storage Reports Management. The steady growth in affordable disk size has given even the smallest organizations so many bytes to keep track of that server administrators need tools to find out what's on those disks and, often, which files to get rid of to free up some space! (After all, we all know that the email server's hunger for disk space is *never* satisfied.) R2 offers a basic disk usage reporting tool that, while it probably won't put Veritas out of business any time soon, is a nice addition to R2's list of goodies.

Rhonda then walks us through the next new-to-R2 storage feature: folder screens and folder quotas. Windows has had quotas in the past since Windows 2000, but they only apply to entire volumes and so can be of limited use. R2, in contrast, lets an administrator set quotas on an entire folder. R2 also lets an administrator ban files with particular extensions so that one could, for example, block any files with the extension "MP3" from a given folder and thereby keep such files out of a share. It's all built atop a new snap-in called the File Server Resource Manager, covered in Chapter 16.

If you thought that some new reports and folder screens and quotas was all that R2 had to offer that was new storage-wise, then get ready for a surprise called DFS Namespaces. You may recall that Server 2000 introduced a tool that lets you organize many file shares into a neat, hierarchical system, changing a process of doing a scavenger hunt among dozens of file servers into a one-click operation. That tool also allowed you to make those file shares reliable and highly available even over a geographically disparate organization. Its name was the Distributed File System or DFS, and it was built atop another new-to-2000 service called the File Replication Service or FRS. DFS and FRS were nice but didn't quite do the job in some situations, causing Microsoft to completely rewrite FRS for R2. But DFS isn't the only thing that depends on FRS—FRS is also an invaluable tool for Sysvol, an essential part of any Active Directory domain. Microsoft decided, however, not to let Sysvol use the new-and-improved FRS (as they're apparently saving that for the next version of Server). R2, then, contains two completely *different* file replication services: the original, which is still called File Replication Service, and the updated version, which Microsoft called the Distributed File Service Replicator, or DFS-R. And, since the Distributed File Service on R2 now uses the new-and-improved file replication service (DFS-R), DFS itself needed a new name: DFS Namespaces. Confused? You won't be, after Rhonda explains it all in Chapter 17.

A few years ago, Bill Gates said to his programmers, "It's too darn hard to communicate and collaborate with corporate partners via the Web!" So Redmond's coders created something called SharePoint Portal Services, a moderately pricey tool to fill that bill. Microsoft liked what SharePoint Portal Services could do so much, however, that they decided to create a free downloadable "SharePoint Lite" called Windows SharePoint Services or WSS. They then took things a bit further and decided to include WSS right in R2. WSS is, to hear the Microsoft folks talk, Big Stuff; for example, it's not unusual to hear a Microsoft SharePointer say that "departmental file servers are obsolete; WSS is the way to go." SharePoint lets you create a website wherein people can carry on threaded discussions and share things like contact information, things-to-do lists, announcements, pictures, documents, meeting announcements, and the like. You can create surveys with WSS and customize it quite a bit, all without any need to do any HTML coding—it's all click by click. C.A. Callahan joins us in Chapter 18 to make it all clear.

Chapter 19 starts off a three-chapter series by Lisa Justice highlighting R2's Windows/Unix tools. For years, Microsoft has offered a series of tools that make it easier to run both Windows and Unix (or its cousin Linux) on the same network. Those tools were all packaged together as something called Services for Unix (SFU) and it used to be a separate for-pay product. A bit back, however, Microsoft decided to give it away—you can find it still at Microsoft's site as Services for Unix 3.5—and incorporated it on the R2 CDs. One of the major pieces of SFU that R2 inherits is the ability to act both as a client and server for Network File System or NFS. First invented at Sun Microsystems in 1984, NFS is a file sharing system much like the Server Message Block (SMB) file sharing system built into every copy of Windows. Like SMB, NFS is mostly an intranet, inside-the-firewall solution; most of us wouldn't employ either NFS or SMB across the Internet. Including an NFS server module in every R2 server will simplify communicating with Unix clients, because virtually every copy of Unix or Linux includes an NFS client. Similarly, allowing any R2 server to be able to communicate with Unix boxes hosting NFS shares makes accomplishing the Windows-Unix connection a bit simpler.

In Chapter 20, Lisa explains that before there was Active Directory, Sun Microsystems built an application that could let a bunch of Unix (or, later, Linux) systems share a centralized list of users and passwords called Network Information Service or NIS. NIS is, then, a very simple directory service. It's not used as much as it once was, mostly because it's not very scalable or secure, but in some networks it makes perfect sense. R2 supports NIS in two ways, and the first is its NIS support. Any R2-based domain controller can "speak NIS." More specifically, a 2003 R2 DC can act as something called a "master NIS server," which then can provide authentication/logon services to Unix/Linux workstations and/or "slave NIS servers." (R2 cannot act as a slave NIS server.)

If you're running a mixed Windows/Unix/Linux network and want to simplify managing all of those accounts, then making your R2 DC a master NIS server may be the answer. But alternatively, if your network already has a set of NIS servers, then your users probably have two user accounts—a Windows account and an NIS account. In that case, R2 can keep these two different accounts' passwords synchronized with a tool called Identity Management for Unix, as Lisa explains in Chapter 21.

Since its advent in February of 2000, Active Directory has become the most popular directory service in the world. But that success has created new demands, the most common of which is, "How do I make my AD forest talk to someone else's AD forest, and how do I do it without having to relax my forest's security to an unacceptable level?" Active Directory Federation Service (ADFS) is one of Microsoft's answers, and, according to some folks at Microsoft, ADFS is the most-requested thing in all of R2! Darren Mar-Elia joins us in Chapter 22 to explain how it works and to offer some step-by-step examples to get you started ADFSing.

Darren returns for Chapter 23 to explain that a part of Active Directory that we tend not to think much about is the fact that it's built atop a database engine and a somewhat interesting engine at that. That led Microsoft to decide to create a version of Active Directory that lacks built-in support for user accounts, group policies, and the like. That's called Active Directory Application Mode, or ADAM. Basically, ADAM lets developers build AD-aware applications while still allowing customers to run those apps without requiring that the customers have an AD. ADAM also allows developers to write AD-aware applications that require changes to the "schema," the structure of AD. Knowing that installing a given AD-aware app will require modifying an organization's AD schema usually gives buyers pause—but ADAM lets developers write AD-aware apps that can store their schema changes separately in ADAM, offering customers the benefits of an AD-aware app without the worry of schema modification. ADAM is mostly of interest to developers, so administrators don't usually have to worry too much about it. But if you purchase an application built atop ADAM then it is almost certain that you'll have to install ADAM.

Contacting Us and Keeping Up-to-Date

Got a question about something that we didn't make clear? A suggestion for the next book, perhaps? Or might you have stumbled across one of those once-in-a-hundred-years errors? (Sure it's a one-in-a-hundred-years event…I didn't say which *planet*'s years I was referring to.) Then drop us a line! You can find me at help@minasi.com, although before mailing me there please take a moment to see if my FAQ at www.minasi.com/gethelp might answer your question. You can find Christa at christa.anderson@gmail.com, Callahan at callahan@callahantech.com, Darren at darren@gpoguy.com, Lisa at ljustice1968@yahoo.com, and Rhonda at rhonda@minasi.com.

Please also visit www.minasi.com to get access to two great (and free) resources: my roughly-monthly newsletter and my online forum, a place where a bunch of really smart folks hang out and help others. Come join us!

Well, now that we've got the Introduction part out of the way—"Reader, may I introduce Book?; Book, I'm pleased to introduce Reader"—let's dig in and see how to get, install, and sometimes *uninstall* SP1.

Part 1

Windows Server 2003 Service Pack 1

In this part:

Chapter 1

Getting and Installing SP1

As you've already read, you can get an awful lot of the features ascribed to R2 free of charge; just install SP1. And while I'm sure that many of you have already installed SP1, I *also* know that unfortunately some of you have been waiting to take the plunge. (And yes, I *additionally* know that it's more than a year since SP1's release—but I'm constantly amazed when I visit clients that so many of them are still leery of SP1. Install it, I say!)

In this chapter, I'll try to eliminate one of the reasons for the holdouts not to install SP1: the fear that installing SP1 will be difficult. You'll learn where to get SP1, how to install it, how to preinstall when creating new 2003 servers, and—just in case!—how to uninstall it. (Not that I've ever needed to.)

Do I Have SP1 Already?

As you're about to read, Microsoft's got a couple of systems in place that may have installed SP1 on your server so quietly that you may not have noticed that you *have* SP1. So here's a pretty reliable way to find out whether you're running the original year-2003 version of Windows Server 2003—the Release To Manufacturing or RTM version—or 2003 with SP1 installed.

Whenever Microsoft ships an operating system, they set the time and date of almost all of that OS's files to some particular date. They time-and-date stamped the RTM files as March 25, 2003, and the SP1 files as March 25, *2005*. So find out your system files' dates like so:

1. Open a command prompt.

2. Type `dir %windir%\notepad.exe` and press Enter.

3. The date on the Notepad file will indicate whether you're RTM or SP1.

There's another just-as-easy way: right-click the My Computer icon, and choose Properties. Under the text System in the resulting page, you'll see the name of your operating system. If you see the line "Service Pack 1" under the OS's name, then you've got SP1; if you don't see any references to service packs, then you're probably RTM. I say "probably" and gave you two ways to figure out your SP level—there are others, like looking at Help/About on most Windows utilities—but occasionally I need more than one "corroborating witness," as sometimes I'll be working at a client's machine trying to fix something, and the client doesn't tell me that the reason the server is messed up is that the client started installing SP1, decided to reboot in mid-stream, and now things aren't working out the way the client would have preferred.

Getting SP1

Assuming that you need SP1, you can get SP1 in a number of ways:

◆ Automatically via Microsoft Update

◆ Automatically through Windows Server Update Services

◆ Order it on CD from Microsoft

◆ Download it from Microsoft

Anyone who's used a computer in the past few years knows by now that (1) Microsoft code has bugs, (2) some of those bugs can enable bad guys to write programs that enable those bad guys to control our computers, and (3) sadly, this isn't just a remote possibility, it happens a few times a year. Worms with names like Code Red, Nimda, Spida, SQL Slammer, Blaster, Sasser, and Zotob have, at various times between early 2000 and now, caused havoc amongst Microsoft users and the Internet as a whole. So most of us know by now that Security Rule Number One is "patch!" The second Tuesday of every month, Microsoft releases announcements of discoveries of various security bugs and patches to fix those bugs so that the worms stay away. This monthly event, known as "Patch Tuesday" to us already overworked administrator types, means that we've got to get the latest patches and get them on our systems.

Most of us get and deliver those patches in one of two ways. First, we can have every one of our servers and workstations connect daily to a special website run by Microsoft called Microsoft Update.

TIP   Despite the fact that the website in question is probably one of the ten most visited and well known websites in the universe, let me offer its URL for the sake of completeness: http://update.microsoft.com. (And I do mean "universe"—I've heard rumors that Microsoft's web server logs indicate some patch downloads occurring to clients using IPv35!)

Any system running Windows 2000 (Server or Pro) with SP3 or later, Windows XP with SP1 or later, and any copy of Server 2003 have built into them some web tools that can be configured to automatically hook up to Microsoft Update. It's a nice, convenient way to get patches without thinking about it. But it *can* be a bit of a pain in the neck, as there have been a few Patch Tuesdays when I left a file unsaved on my Desktop only to stumble into my office the next morning with a hot mug of Earl Grey (Twinings or Stash, of course) in my hand and see the Windows "Please press Ctrl-Alt-Del" Welcome screen on my monitor. (I'm such a Boy Scout that I configured Microsoft Update to reboot my system automatically if it deems it necessary, so it's really my fault, not Microsoft's.)

Microsoft Update's not a bad answer for patching, but if you've got a bunch of systems, then it can be horribly inefficient in terms of download bandwidth. For example, a while back Microsoft released a service pack for Internet Explorer 6 that ran around 10MB. Now, that may not seem like much, but consider what happened on the evening of Patch Tuesday at a company with 1000 workstations. In total, that firm would have downloaded that same 10MB 1000 times, turning a small 10MB download into a bandwidth-squandering 10 GB. Ugh.

So Microsoft offers Windows Server Update Services (WSUS), an application that you can run on a 2000 or 2003 server. WSUS acts as a kind of "local Microsoft Update." Whatever server you've installed WSUS on sucks down the patches from Microsoft's Microsoft Update servers, and then you configure your internal systems to no longer check with Microsoft's servers for patches but instead to look to your WSUS server.

TIP WSUS is a big topic and not one we're covering in this book, but you can find more information and download links at www.microsoft.com/windowsserversystem/updateservices/default.mspx. If you don't currently have a tool to make patching easier, consider WSUS. It's free and pretty good.

If you've set your system up to automatically draw patches from Microsoft Update, or if you've got it configured to get patches from your WSUS server, then you've probably got SP1 already. But if not, then you may want to either order a CD with SP1 on it from Microsoft, or just download it. Why not just download it? Well, SP1 is over 300MB in size, and if your Internet connection is at a low speed, then you might not get the download done before, say, the release of 2003 SP2. If you do want to order SP1 on a CD, Microsoft charges $5.25 per CD, and you can find the links to order it at www.microsoft.com/technet/downloads/winsrvr/servicepacks/sp1/default.mspx.

To download SP1 instead of getting it shipped to you, just go to the above URL and click the Downloading it from Download Center hyperlink, or go to www.microsoft.com/downloads and search on "Microsoft windows server 2003 service pack 1"—2003 SP1 will be one of the hits the search engine will return. (Note that if you're using Small Business Server 2003, SBS 2003 has its own separate set of SP1 files; look down the list of files offered by Microsoft's web server and you'll see them.) Start it downloading, and it'll be done in no time, geologically speaking. The file you'll get will have a name representing the language that the service pack is built to support. As I'm doing this for the U.S. English version of SP1, the file I ended up downloading was named WindowsServer2003-KB889101-SP1-x86-ENU.exe, where the ENU means "United States English"; you'll see a different code if you're downloading a version localized to another place.

Before we go any further, do yourself a favor: rename the file to something short like sp1.exe. For brevity's sake, that's how I'll refer to it for the rest of this chapter. Next, let's install it.

Installing SP1

Assuming that you're not letting Microsoft Update or WSUS install SP1 for you, you've got a few options at this point to get SP1 on one or more of your systems:

◆ Just put SP1 on a CD, walk around to your 2003 servers and run sp1.exe on each server from the GUI.

◆ Put sp1.exe somewhere on the network where all of your 2003 servers can access it, and use the command-line options to kick off the SP1 install.

◆ If you have an Active Directory, then extract sp1.exe to its component files and deliver it as a group policy.

SP1 from the GUI

Assuming that you want to install SP1 by just double-clicking the WindowsServer2003-KB889101-SP1-x86-ENU.exe file (which, recall, I suggested that you rename sp1.exe), then you'll first see a dialog box labeled Extracting Files like Figure 1.1.

Sp1.exe creates a temporary file with a random name like b0bda746128 or the like and unpacks SP1's heft to about 413MB of files. After a bit, you'll see a typical wizard greeting page like Figure 1.2.

Click Next and you get to agree to the SP1 software license as in Figure 1.3.

FIGURE 1.1
Unpacking SP1

FIGURE 1.2
"Hello!" from SP1

FIGURE 1.3
SP1's software license

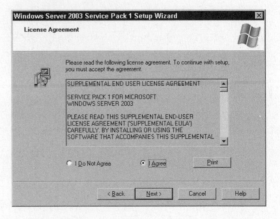

I find agreeing to software licenses of all kinds sort of liberating, you know? I mean, when I go to install a piece of software, I'm usually a little anxious about whether it'll break something and cause me trouble. But once I've read the license and clicked I Agree, then I've pretty much surrendered all of my goods to that software company. (Read a license some time and you'll see what I mean.) That causes a wonderful Zen-like feeling of freedom from material wants to gently wash over me. Anyway, click the I Agree radio button and click Next to see the "Where shall we backup before installing?" page, as in Figure 1.4.

The idea here is that in the unlikely event that you find yourself suffering from "updater's remorse" and want to restore your server to its pre-SP1 state, then you can: as you'll see in a bit, sp1.exe will let you uninstall SP1. This step tucks away the RTM files so that the uninstaller can function if necessary.

Now, personally I have not experienced a single problem with 2003 SP1. Yes, I've run into trouble with some NT 4 service packs, but not with any of the 2000, XP, or 2003 service packs, so I'm inclined to trust SP1 and not bother with the backups. Notice, however, that the SP1 install wizard doesn't offer you the option not to back up, which is one reason why I don't install SP1 with the GUI much. Many of my clients like to create a small C: partition so that they can devote the rest of their storage to separate drives for data, databases, logs, and the like. As a result, I've found that many people have installed Server 2003 on C: drives as small as 4 GB. Now, understand please that I don't *recommend* it, but people have done it because of reasons that made sense back in the NT 4 days. Those folks soon find that 2003 has a much bigger appetite for disk space than 2000 or NT 4 did, and so their systems can run into out-of-space problems, and skipping the pre-SP1-install backup saves about 400MB of space. So if you find yourself applying SP1 to a system with less than, say, 2 GB or so of free space on whatever drive contains the operating system, then I recommend that you skip the GUI and look to the next section, where I'll show you how to install SP1 without making sp1.exe back up a lot of files and thereby put your system in a free space squeeze. But if you've got plenty of free space on your operating system's partition and want to finish running the wizard, then click Next and you'll see something like Figure 1.5.

After a bit, SP1's installed and the wizard offers you a Finish button. Click it, reboot your system, and you've got SP1 installed.

FIGURE 1.4
Where to backup
for an uninstall?

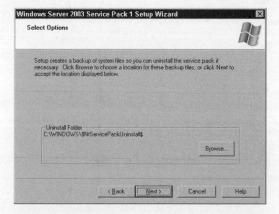

FIGURE 1.5
SP1 installation
under way

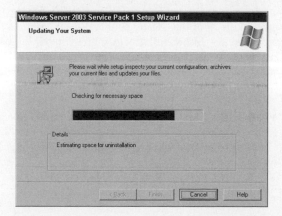

SP1 from the Command Line

As I've already said, many folks will choose to start up sp1.exe and run the SP1 installation from the GUI because it's simple. But if you have some special needs, then consider running SP1 from the command line with one or more of its options. Those options fall into a few rough categories:

- /quiet, /passive, and /o reduce the amount of information that the SP1 installer shows and causes it to ask you fewer questions.

- /norestart, /forcerestart, and /f let you control whether or not your system immediately reboots after SP1's installed, and how.

- /n and /d: let you control the amount of space that the SP1 installation process takes up on your disk by letting you skip the backup part of the SP1 install (/n), or telling sp1.exe to store the backup on another drive (/d:).

- /x lets you pre-extract the files from sp1.exe to a folder.

- /uninstall uninstalls SP1.

- /integrate preinstalls SP1 onto an I386 directory so that you can do fresh installs of 2003 with SP1 already included.

- /l tells sp1.exe to list the hotfixes that you've got on this system.

And note that sp1.exe, the SP1 installer, doesn't care about uppercase or lowercase; /forcerestart and /FORCERESTART get the same results.

MAKE THE SP1 INSTALLER QUIETER

Let's consider these options in the order that I've already listed them. First, /quiet tells sp1.exe not to show you any input, *including* error messages. That's good if you want to kick off sp1.exe and have it just do its job without splashing things on the screen *and* if you're sure that you've got SP1's syntax down correctly. It's *bad*, in contrast, if you're *not* so sure about the sp1.exe syntax, as it can be pretty puzzling to try to start up SP1 with some options, leave the service pack to install itself, and then return a bit later only to find that nothing's installed, and SP1's not produced an error message that offers any clues to why it didn't work.

If you'd like SP1 to install without asking you any questions, as /quiet does, but to have it still provide you some feedback, as /quiet *doesn't*, then use /passive. /passive installs SP1 in a hands-off manner but shows SP1's installation progress bar. For example, to tell sp1.exe to just install with all of the default settings—back up the RTM files, install SP1, and do not reboot until told to do so—but to still show progress on the screen, you could open up a command prompt and type

```
sp1 /passive
```

WARNING This will only work if you've put sp1.exe somewhere on your system path, or if you have changed your current directory to wherever sp1.exe is using the CD command. That advice applies to any of the examples in the rest of this chapter. (And, of course, as with any command-line command, you've got to press the Enter key to activate the command.)

LETTING THE SP1 INSTALLER OVERWRITE NON-MICROSOFT FILES

The /o option tells you to automatically overwrite any existing files that *didn't* come with 2003 RTM. Wait a minute—why would a 2003 service pack, which should only contain updated files for Windows Server 2003 RTM, have to overwrite a file that *didn't* come with Windows Server 2003 RTM? Because your hardware manufacturer may have created their own customized versions of some file or files to replace some of the files in the RTM version. For example, suppose HP shipped 2003 Server on some of their server computers but with a rewritten version of some SCSI driver, replacing Microsoft's version. (Or consider the Help files—every computer manufacturer seems to tweak them a bit from the original Microsoft files.) In that case, when 2003 SP1 tried to overwrite that SCSI driver, it would notice from the driver's digital certificate—or lack of one—that this copy of 2003 Server has a file on it that's not a Microsoft-created file. By default, sp1.exe *won't* overwrite the non-Microsoft file with a Microsoft file because Microsoft figures that if your hardware manufacturer—your "OEM" in computer sales lingo—replaced Microsoft's SCSI driver with one of their own, then that OEM probably had a pretty good reason, and so if sp1.exe were to overwrite that customized-to-HP's-hardware driver, then things *could* turn out badly, as in "Auuggh! I installed that stupid service pack and now my system won't boot!!!!" If, however, you have reason to believe that SP1 contains files that will work fine on your server hardware, then you might not want to have to click OK every time sp1.exe stumbles across an OEM file and asks, "Is it okay to overwrite this file?" particularly as the SP1 installer might have to do that oh, say, 364 times. In *that* case, add /o to the sp1.exe command line, and you won't wear out your mouse button and give yourself carpal tunnel by having to click Yes 3,811 times.

CONTROLLING THE POST-SP1 REBOOT

/norestart and /forcerestart are options that tell the SP1 installer sp1.exe to do just what the options sound like—either finish installing SP1 and then do *not* automatically restart, or finish installing SP1 and then automatically restart. (The default behavior is to not restart.) /f works in conjunction with /forcerestart and says "when restarting, force any open programs to close." That would mean that *if* while you were waiting for SP1 to install you were running Word on the server's Desktop, *and* perhaps if you were using Word to write the Great American Novel, *and* if you hadn't saved your work in a while, then when SP1 finished installing, it'd close Word without so much as an, "Are you sure?" and reboot, dropping your literary brilliance in a black hole. (And no, I'm not suggesting that you should use your server's Desktop to run personal productivity applications, it's just an example. And while I'm at it, I guess I'd also suggest not bothering to write the Great American Novel anyway, as when last I'd heard Samuel Clemens had already accomplished it.) If, on the other hand, you'd started up sp1.exe without the /f option, then SP1 wouldn't reboot until you'd responded to Word's Save changes to document? dialog box.

NOTE   On a slightly more serious note, I should point out that some applications are programmed to care more about the operating system's wants (that is, 2003 saying, "I want to reboot and you're getting in my way by refusing to close, Wordpad!") than the user's wants (that is, you saying, "Oh no, don't close, just let me save thi... auugh!"). Such applications will close with files open even *if* you've omitted the /f option. Two examples of apps like that are Notepad and Word-Pad. I've never actually installed Word on a server to find out if it cares more about me or about the server OS. (As they say, There Are Things That Man Is Not Meant To Know.)

Here's another command-line example. To tell `sp1.exe` to install SP1 with the defaults (back up RTM files) and to automatically restart the system, but not to offer any kind of feedback about the progress of the installation and not to reboot if any applications reported unsaved files, you'd type

```
sp1 /quiet /forcerestart
```

TELLING THE SP1 INSTALLER NOT TO BACKUP RTM FILES

As I mentioned before, I tend to skip backing up the RTM files, as it saves disk space and speeds up the install process. You can tell `sp1.exe` to skip backups with the `/n` option.

WARNING   I said that *I* don't do RTM backups, but that doesn't necessarily mean that it's a good idea for you. Let me reiterate this: if you forgo backups then there's no way to return your server to its pre-SP1 state without a complete wipe and reinstall.

Skipping backups also means that you'll save just under 400MB worth of space on the operating system's partition, which might be important to those working on a system with a small amount of space on that OS partition drive. (Here I'm again referring to the folks who I run into now and then who've unadvisedly installed Server 2003 on a 4 GB C: drive.) And as long as I'm discussing saving space on a fairly full C: drive, what about the unpacking process? When `sp1.exe` unpacks its 413MB of files, where does that go? Well, I guessed that if I ran `sp1.exe` from the C: drive then `sp1.exe` would automatically put the unpacked files into a folder on the C: drive—but I was wrong. A bit of experimentation with `sp1.exe` shows that it apparently tries to unpack itself onto a drive that is *not* the one holding the operating system—a nice touch on Microsoft's part.

So, for example, to install SP1 so that it does not back up the RTM files (`/n`), doesn't ask any questions but does show us progress (`/passive`), and reboots the system automatically when SP1's installed (`/forcerestart`) but holds off on the reboot if there are applications with open files (leave off the `/f`), you could open up a command prompt and type

```
sp1 /n /passive /forcerestart
```

As you can imagine, this is a nice "type this, press Enter, and walk away" method of installing SP1. But, again, SP1 might still not install automatically, as it might want to prompt you if it can overwrite OEM files, or it might stop because of an application that refuses to close itself. The truly "damn the torpedoes, full steam ahead!" command would be

```
sp1 /n /passive /forcerestart /o /f
```

SAVING SPACE BUT *STILL* DOING BACKUPS

But suppose you like the idea of backups but are short of space on your OS's drive? That's a toughie. It's quite improbable that you'll need those backups, but it's a complete certainty that the backup will suck up 400MB of disk space on your OS's drive. What to do? Use the `/d:` option.

Normally, the SP1 installer creates the backup in the Windows directory of your operating system, in a folder called `$ntservicepackuninstall$`. But if you add the option "`/d:path`" to an `sp1.exe` invocation, then the SP1 installer will instead do the backup to *path*. For example, if your C: drive is low on free space but your E: drive has 400MB free, you could tell the SP1 installer to put the RTM backups in a folder named e:\rtmbackups, along with the other options that we used in the last example, like so:

```
sp1 /d:e:\rtmbackups /forcerestart /passive /o /f
```

You needn't even create the e:\rtmbackups directory; the SP1 installer will do it for you.

PREUNPACKING SP1 WITH THE /X OPTION

Consider this scenario: you need to put SP1 on a number of servers, but for some reason don't want to use WSUS or Microsoft Update. So you burn sp1.exe onto a CD-ROM disc and walk it around your servers. After installing SP1 on a couple of servers, you notice that every time you pop that disc into a server's drive and start up SP1, you have to spend 10 minutes twiddling your thumbs while sp1.exe unpacks itself. You could save time, you reason, if you could first unpack the whole thing, converting it from one big EXE file to a folder full of files, and *then* burn that folder to a CD-ROM. Then—somehow—you'd figure out how to get all of those SP1 files to install themselves. Once you figure that out, you could walk that CD-ROM around to your remaining servers, saving precious time on the SP1 install. But how to unpack sp1.exe? With the -x option. Just type

```
sp1 -x:path
```

Where *path* is a drive and folder name, like sp1 -x:d:\unpackedsp1files. That causes sp1.exe to create the d:\unpackedsp1files folder if it's not already created, and to put a folder *inside* that one called i386. (If you alternatively leave the :path off the option and just type a simple -x, then sp1.exe will prompt you for a location to save the unpacked files to.) The resulting folder contains about 413MB of files and folders. Inside i386 is a folder called update that contains a few files, one of which is named *update.exe*, and it's the program that we'd use to tell this already-unpacked copy of SP1 to install itself. And controlling update.exe is easy—it uses the exact same options as sp1.exe does. So, for example, suppose I'd unpacked SP1 to some folder on my hard disk, and then took the resulting i386 folder and burned it to a CD-ROM disc. Then suppose I pop that disc into the CD-ROM drive of one of my servers, and that the CD-ROM's drive letter is D:. I could then start up an SP1 install that skipped backups, showed the progress bar, and automatically rebooted despite apps with open files. To do this, I'd type

```
d:\i386\update\update.exe /n /passive /forcerestart
```

UNINSTALLING SP1

As I've said, I've never had the occasion to uninstall SP1. But if you do, then as far as I can see there's only one way to do it—with the SP1 installer program and the /uninstall option. Just type

```
sp1 /uninstall
```

And in a few minutes, you'll be back to RTM-ness. When uninstalling, SP1 will accept the /forcerestart, /passive, /quiet, and /f options. (And by the way, if you've been avoiding the command line so far, then in this case resistance is futile; there's no choice!)

Rolling Out SP1 with a GPO

In *Mastering Windows Server 2003*'s Chapter 12, we showed how to create a domain-based group policy object (GPO) that would deploy software to domain members. You can use software deployment GPOs to roll out SP1 as well, quite simply. There are just a few steps.

1. Extract the files in the SP1 installer with the -x option, as you've already read.

2. Create a share accessible by your 2003 servers, and put the extracted i386 folder in that share.

3. Create a software-deploying group policy object. Use the *computer* Software Installation category, not the *user* Software Installation category.

4. Look in the i386\update folder and you'll see a file named update.msi. As its extension suggests, it is a Microsoft Installer package file. Configure the GPO to deploy this file to your 2003 servers. Assign the file, do not publish it, or it won't work.

How do you ensure that this only gets to your 2003 Servers, and not your 2000, XP, or Vista systems? Simple—2000 and later are smart about service packs. 2000, XP, and Vista will not even try to install 2003's SP1.

Preinstalling SP1: "Integrating"

As you probably know, the folder that contains the Server 2003 installation files on 2003's Setup CD is called i386, the same name as the folder in the unpacked SP1. You may also know that it's been possible in every version of NT since NT 4.0 to take a service pack and incorporate it into the i386 folder of an existing Setup CD. When you do that, you end up with an i386 folder that contains all of the files needed to install a brand-new copy of NT that starts out life with the service pack already installed. That's nice for two reasons: first, it saves you the time of first installing the OS and then installing the service pack, as now you need only install the OS and, second, you end up with a more secure system from the very beginning. And if the reason for *that's* not clear, try installing the RTM version of Windows XP on a computer directly connected to the Internet. RTM XP is vulnerable to a number of vicious worms, and it's a pretty good bet that between the time that you boot up this freshly installed RTM copy of XP and when you get the XP Service Pack 2 CD into the computer's drive, your new system will have already caught something nasty. That's why it's nice to do all new XP installs from a Setup disk that has SP2 incorporated into it; all of a sudden, XP setup isn't a footrace between the worms and the poor guy installing the XP patches. It's the same story with Server 2003.

How to take SP1 files and incorporate them into an i386? With a few simple steps.

1. Copy the i386 folder from a Server 2003 Setup disk to your computer's hard disk. (After all, you can't modify files on a CD-ROM.) For the sake of example, I'll say that we've copied it to e:\I386. The folder must have the name i386, no matter how deeply buried it is in your disk's folder structure. In other words, e:\i386 is fine, e:\myfiles\i386 is fine, e:\files\setup\project\i386 is fine—but e:\2003setupfiles would not be. You will not be able to "integrate" — SP1's new word for what it used to call "slipstreaming"— SP1 files into a Server 2003 i386 unless the folder's name is i386.

2. Extract the SP1 files to a folder somewhere.

3. Tell the SP1 installer to integrate the new SP1 files in your i386 folder like so:

```
sp1.exe /integrate:folder-location
```

Be aware that *folder-location* is the name of the folder that contains the i386 folder. So, for example, if the i386 folder with the Setup programs is in e:\i386, then you'd type

```
sp1.exe /integrate:e:\
```

This is what I meant when I said that the folder must be named i386—the /integrate option expects it. You *cannot* convince the SP1 installer to integrate its files with RTM 2003 Setup files unless you call the folder i386, oddly enough.

Once the integration's done, you get a confirmation dialog box telling you that "Integrated install has completed successfully." Now you've got an up-to-date I386 setup folder ready to roll out servers sporting SP1 right out of the maternity ward!

Now that you've got SP1 on your system, let's see what it can do. Turn the page, and you'll learn about its first neat tool—Access-Based Enumeration.

Summary

SP1 may be the biggest patch in history (at least until 2003 SP2), but it's worth getting and installing. As you saw in this chapter, Microsoft's offered us a pile of options to both acquire and apply SP1. If you've not rolled it out yet, I'd recommend considering it.

Chapter 2

Hiding Folders from Prying Eyes: Access-Based Enumeration (ABE)

Over the years, I've gotten literally tens of thousands of pieces of email from readers, so of course there are a few *very* frequently-asked questions. Here's the single most common question from ex-Novellians:

"In Novell, users couldn't even *see* folders that they had no access to. If you couldn't read the folder, then it was invisible. How do I do that in Microsoft networking?"

I always had to answer the same way: "Sorry, we can't do anything like that in Windows. If a user doesn't have access to a folder, however, then she can't really do anything to that folder except see that it exists. But it *is* a shame." An accurate answer but a lame one—but fortunately I don't have to give that lame answer any more. Windows Server 2003 SP1 and R2 have a new feature that lets you tell a server, "When you're listing the files and folders in a share, check that whoever asked to see that list of files and folders has at least read access to each object. If he doesn't have read access to a file or folder, then don't show that file or folder." This new feature might have been called "Novell Invisible Folders: Terrific! Yes!" or NIFTY but is instead called Access-Based Enumeration and is abbreviated ABE.

How ABE Works

ABE is a feature of the Server service, the Windows service that provides file and printer sharing. It works by modifying a feature of the Server service called "enumeration," which basically means how the server service answers the question, "What files and folders exist in a given share?" Windows Explorer does the same thing when you open up a folder. You know that flashlight that shines around the folder for a second—well, a second on a *good* day—when you open a folder? That's Explorer entertaining you while it *enumerates* the folder contents.

ABE boils down to just a simple change in how the Server service handles an enumeration request from your client computer. Suppose you're sitting at a client computer called Client and you've connected to a share named Stuff on a file server named Bigserver. You want to see what's in the \\bigserver\stuff share, and so to do that from your client computer Client, you either open a command prompt and type a **DIR** command to see the share \\bigserver\stuff's contents, or you open up a folder in Explorer to see \\bigserver\stuff's contents, and that gets translated by your computer into a request along the lines of, "Hey, Bigserver across the network, would you please enumerate the Stuff share?" Prior to ABE's appearance, the Server service on Bigserver *used* to just look in a file share for the share's contents and report everything that it saw in that folder to your computer. But now with ABE enabled, a file server service looks at the NTFS permissions on each file and folder sitting in the share and compares that to whatever user account you used to connect to the share. Then the Server service says for each file or folder in the share, "Does this person have permission to read this file or folder?" If you do have the permission, then the enumerator tells you the file exists. If not, the enumerator is silent about the file's existence.

NOTE   Every wonder why the file server service is called the "Server" service rather than the "file server" service? After all, we don't call the DNS server service or Internet Information Server (the web server software) the "Server" service, so what makes the file server special? It's not arrogance on the file server service's part, it's just that way back when Microsoft started writing network software, their servers did just one thing—file and print serving. So back in the old days, "server" meant "file and print server." The name just stuck. That also explains the odd name for the *client* software for the file and print server; it's called the "Workstation" service.

Does ABE Matter?

While this *will* warm the hearts of some, it's worth stepping back and asking, "Is ABE *really* useful?" I mean, the first time that a Novell guy explained the hide-the-folders-you're-not-authorized-to-see feature, I thought, "Dang, that's cool—I wish *we* had that!"

But then I thought about it. I'd thought that hiding inaccessible folders would be a nice feature for reasons of security, and so did just about everyone who asked me about how to accomplish it in Windows. The main argument went something like this.

Many network administrators offer home directories to their users, folders that are only accessible to the user and, perhaps, the administrator. It's a pain to have to create a separate share for every single user, though, so most folks put all of the home directories in one folder and then share that folder. So, for example, a network might have a share called Homedirs that contains a folder for every user. But that means that when the user connects to the Homedirs share, then she sees not just her folder, but a folder for every other user. (In actuality this behavior changes if the user logs onto the domain from a 2000 or XP box, but let's ignore that for the purposes of this discussion.) Having users see a whole pile of folders rather than just their own folders troubled a lot of admin types.

But is it really bad for one user to be able to see, but not access, the home directory folders of all other users? It's a matter of opinion. If the administrator's done his job, then he's set the NTFS permissions on each folder so that, again, no one can get to that folder save for the person who uses it as a home directory. But administrators don't like that Sally can see that there's a folder for Larry and Paul and Jane and so on. *Why* don't they like it? Well, there's an argument that it's something of a security breach, as any user can pretty much get the list of all user accounts by just looking at the names of the folders in the Homedirs share besides the user's personal folder. That sounded good at first, but upon a bit of reflection I have to say that I don't buy it. You see, every user in an Active Directory has read access to all of the AD. That means that any user who wanted to could just cook up a quick VBscript program to dump the names of all of the user accounts anyway. So arguing that hiding inaccessible folders in the Homedirs share is a security measure is specious— just something that provides the *illusion* of security, not actual security.

So is ABE pointless? No. While it may not be all that big a deal security-wise, it may get some security auditor with a silly checklist off your back. Furthermore, what you'll like about ABE is that it *simplifies* things for users.

Forget the scenario about the evil user writing down the names of his fellow users. The more likely scenario is the perfectly honest user in a firm of 500 people who logs onto the home directory share for the first time…only to be greeted with the vision of *five hundred folders*. With ABE, he would only see one folder…his personal home directory folder.

So in the end analysis, ABE *is* useful. But it's useful less as a security tool and more as a productivity tool.

Isn't ABE the Same As Hiding a Folder with "$"?

When I talk about ABE, sometimes people will comment to me that it's always been possible to put a "$" at the end of a file share's name and thereby to hide that share from people. For example, if I created a share with my games on it for my convenience—perhaps to be able to easily install those games on other systems without making them obvious to others—then I might create a share called not \\myserver\games but instead \\myserver\games$. Then, when people browsed MYSERVER's shares from either Network Places or the NET VIEW command, then they would not see the games$ share.

There are two reasons why this is different from ABE.

First, ABE does not hide entire shares. ABE hides folders *within* shares. So, for example, if I had a folder inside my hypothetical games share named markscreditcards then I just might not want people to be able to get to that folder. I might not have a problem with them finding the games, or the games share itself, but \\myserver\games\markscreditcards—no way I want them to even *see* that exists. So I just yank out everyone's NTFS read access to the markscreditcards folder except mine. Now, anyone opening up the \\myserver\games folder will see whatever folders are in the games share—*except* the markscreditcards folder. (And yes, this is a silly example—I'm just trying to underscore what ABE does.)

Second, that "$" thing at the end of a share isn't very good security. I was quite surprised years ago when I did a network trace to see what happens when I browse a server via what was then called Network Neighborhood. As it turns out, your workstation says to a server, "Tell me the names of all of your shares," and the server sends them all along—even the ones with the "$" on the end. It is the software on your workstation, not the server, that filters out the ones with the "$" on the end of their share names, meaning that a bad guy could just write some revised Network Neighborhood software that *didn't* hide the shares whose names were suffixed with "$." In contrast, ABE does the filtering *on the server*, so the workstation never sees the hidden files.

If that's still not clear, try following along with the example that I'll build here to see the difference before and after ABE.

ABE Details

That's the big picture. But there's more to know:

- ABE only works on Server 2003 SP1 and later systems; XP, 2000, and the rest need not apply.

- The actual programming code to make ABE work is installed on a 2003 SP1 or later system, but it's not enabled by default; you need a separate small program to turn ABE on or off.

- You can choose to turn ABE on for all shares on a system or just a few.

- To see an ABE-protected file, you need a specific set of permissions.

Here are the details.

ABE Must Be Enabled

Any system including 2003 SP1 or later—which means any R2 or, for that matter, any upcoming Server system—has the ABE code sitting on it, but it's not enabled. To make it work, you need a tool to turn it on. You can find that tool at Microsoft's site, as I'll discuss in a bit.

Again, it's 2003 only; you *cannot*, and probably will never be able to make ABE work on a 2000- or XP-based system. But don't misunderstand; 2000, XP, even Windows 98 users can see the effects of ABE, as all of the work of hiding the share's files and folders is done by the file server holding the share, not the client operating system. So, for example, if that file server Bigserver holding the share named Stuff was running Server 2003 with SP1 installed, and the client named Client was running Windows 2000 Professional, then that user on Windows 2000 Professional would still not see folders on the Stuff share for which the user lacked read access. When I say that 2000 will never use ABE, I mean that a file server running Windows 2000 Server cannot hide files and folders in shares from users based on their NTFS permissions.

ABE Works on Both Files and Folders, and Only in Shares

I've mentioned this before, but I wanted to clarify that ABE will not only hide an entire folder, it can also hide particular files. As with folders, the question of whether or not ABE shows a given file is all a matter of the NTFS permissions on that file.

Furthermore, ABE only affects the way that users see the contents of file *shares*. Someone actually sitting at a computer and using Explorer to browse the files and folders on a system would still see files and folders that she can't read, as has been the case for ages in the Windows world.

ABE Works On All Shares, or *Some* Shares

In my experience, in general people don't usually care about being able to hide files and folders in shares based on those objects' NTFS permissions, with one exception. If someone creates an Accounting share, then they just set the folder permissions so that only folks in the Accounting department can connect to the share in the first place, and so do not need to hide particular objects in that share.

But, as I've suggested earlier in the "Does ABE Matter?" discussion, there is one exception to the "if you're here, you should probably be able to see everything" rule, and it's a big one—home directories. I suspect that most folks will find ABE most useful for just the home directory share.

The bottom line here is that ABE doesn't make sense for a lot of shares, and it *does* slow things down a trifle. So some folks will want to tell their file servers not to bother ABEing some shares and to ABE others. You'll see how soon, when we see how to install and configure ABE.

What ABE Needs for Permissions

ABE hides files and folders from people who don't have the NTFS read permission, says Microsoft's documentation. But what exactly does that mean? As you probably know (or can remind yourself of by reviewing Chapter 11 of *Mastering Windows Server 2003*), looking at the Security tab of any object gives you a kind of high-level view of permissions. But click the Advanced button in the Security tab, and then click the View/Edit button to see the lowest-level permissions. A bit of experimentation shows that to show you a file or folder, ABE wants to see that you have the following four specific permissions:

- ◆ List folder/read data
- ◆ Read attributes
- ◆ Read extended attributes
- ◆ Read

Of course, someone could have more permissions than these and see a file or folder via ABE. But lacking any of those four will make the file or folder disappear.

An ABE Example, Part 1

Before we continue, let's set up an example system to use to play with ABE. (If you're not interested in a step-by-step example, then just skip this section and go to "Installing and Configuring ABE," the next section.) First, we'll need a system running either Server 2003 with SP1 or an R2 system. Give it any name you like; I called mine R2STD because it's Windows Server 2003 R2, Standard Edition. My intention in this example is to first create a home directory folder on R2STD, then create two folders inside that folder—one for a user named Paul and one for a user named Sally. I'll set the NTFS permissions so that only Paul and Sally can access their folders (well, we'll let the Administrator account work with the folders as well), share the home directory folder, and then install the ABE UI. We'll enable ABE on the home directory share, and then log on as Paul and look in the home directory share. If all goes well, we'll only see the Paul folder; Sally's folder will be invisible.

Now, it'd probably take a dozen pages of click-by-click explanation to set all of this up, so let's make this a bit more concise by just using the command line. (Besides, it's a great example of how much you can get done with just a few commands.) Make sure you're logged onto your server as an administrator. Then open up a command prompt and type in these commands:

```
md c:\homedirs
md c:\homedirs\paul
md c:\homedirs\sally
net user paul Paulie1 /add
net user sally Sallie1 /add
net share Homedirs=c:\homedirs /grant:"authenticated
users",full /remark:"Home directories share"
echo y|cacls c:\homedirs\paul /g administrators:f paul:f
echo y|cacls c:\homedirs\sally /g administrators:f sally:f
```

What's all that do? If you're not a command-line black belt, here's the preceding, dissected.

The first three commands use the md or "make directory" command to create a folder named Homedirs, and then to create subfolders of Homedirs named Paul and Sally. The next two commands create local user accounts called paul and sally with passwords Paulie1 and Sallie1, respectively. Uppercase or lowercase doesn't matter in either the md or net user commands, except of course for the password text itself—if Paul tries to log on with password paulie1 he won't succeed, as we typed it in Paulie1 with a capital "P."

The next command, the `net share` command, is a long one and wrapped on the printed page but should be typed as one long line. `Net share` says that you're going to create a new shared folder. `Homedirs=c:\homedirs` means to give the new share the name Homedirs and that the actual directory to share is the one at `c:\homedirs`. The `/grant...` option says to set the share permissions on Homedirs to Full Control for the Authenticated Users group, and the `/remark:` option lets you put a comment on the share.

Thus far, we've created the folders, the users, and the share, as well as setting the share's permissions. But we've still got to set the NTFS permissions, and for that we can use the CACLS ("Change ACLS") command. I know, the lines don't start with `cacls`, they start with `echo y|` but that's only because of an annoying feature of `cacls`—it always stops and asks, "Are you sure?" The beauty of prefixing the statement with the echo command is that the echo command automatically answers the "are you sure?" question with y, and so `cacls` does its work. The `cacls` commands break down like this:

```
cacls directory-to-work-on /G username:permission username:permission...
```

The `/G` stands for "grant," as it grants permissions. It removes any existing NTFS permissions on, for example, `c:\homedirs\paul` and installs the ones in the command. `administrators:f` means "grant the Administrators group Full Control," and of course, `paul:f` grants Paul full control of his directory. The following command does the same thing for Sally. Now that the stage is set, let's return to our discussion of ABE.

Installing and Configuring ABE

Ready to see ABE in action? Let's see how to get the ABE user interface, install it, and configure ABE.

Download ABE from Microsoft.com

As I said before, all of the machinery for ABE is in your 2003 SP1 or R2 system, but Microsoft chose not to throw the switch. To do that, you need a file called `ABEUI.MSI`. Surf over to Microsoft's Downloads site at `www.microsoft.com/downloads` and type into the Search field "**access-based enumeration**." (It'll work with or without the quotes.) As I write this, you'll only get one hit, one with the title "Windows Server 2003 Access-based Enumeration" dated April 8, 2005. I *would* give you a specific URL rather than have you search, but for some reason it appears that there's some guy at Microsoft whose job it is to rearrange the website every two weeks—so searching Microsoft.com/downloads by keywords works better then URLs in my experience. If it doesn't, try another search, but this time type in the name of the file that we're looking for—**abeui.msi**.

Click the link, and you'll end up at a page that offers a brief explanation of ABE and three download hyperlinks: one for systems using standard 32-bit Intel processors, one for people using Itanium-based servers—and wasn't it thoughtful of Microsoft to create a whole new version of `abeui.msi` for the six guys in the world with an Itanium server?—and finally, a version for systems using either AMD or Intel's 64-bit processors. Choose the one that's right for your system and download that `abeui.msi` to your system.

Install ABEUI.MSI

Double-click `abeui.msi` and that'll start up a wizard that installs ABE's user interface. The first panel shows you a paragraph that basically explains ABE; click Next and you'll get the obligatory software license; accept it and click Next. That'll take you to the screen that asks where you want to install the ABE user interface files (the default is fine) and who should be able to use the ABE user interface—either just you or everyone. Choose whichever option works for you and click Next. That leads you to a screen like the one in Figure 2.1.

Just take the default; in a moment I'll show you how to turn ABE on or off. Click Next and it'll ask you to confirm that you actually want to install the ABE UI. Click Next, it'll install, and then click Close at the Installation Complete page.

If you're following along on the example, go ahead and get the version of the ABE UI for your system and install it. Go with all of the defaults except to click the I accept radio button on the license page.

FIGURE 2.1
Turn on ABE
now or later?

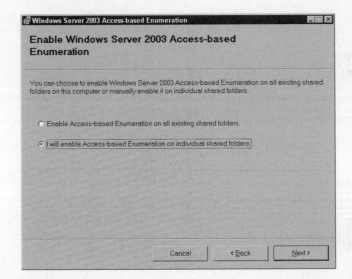

Configuring ABE

Now that you've got ABE's UI installed, you can do several things:

◆ You can turn ABE on for all shares.

◆ You can turn ABE off for all shares.

◆ You can turn ABE on for particular shares.

◆ You can turn ABE off for particular shares.

You've also got both a command-line and a GUI tool. First let's look at the GUI. If you've got the ABE UI installed on a system with a shared folder, then right-click that shared folder in Explorer and choose Properties. You should see a new tab, Access-based Enumeration. Click it and you'll see a dialog box like Figure 2.2.

FIGURE 2.2
Initial ABE tab

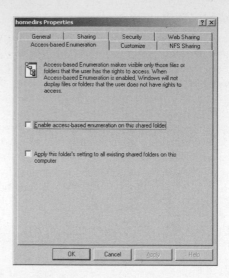

Now, GUIs are supposed to be easier to use than command-line tools, but this one's a little odd. I would have expected a check box *somewhere* that would let you just check the box and cause ABE to be turned on for all shares or, for that matter, to cause ABE to be *disabled* for all shares, but it doesn't really work like that. The first check box lets you enable ABE for the particular share that you've clicked, as a casual read of the label next to that check box will show. But look at the second one—Apply this folder's setting to all existing shared folders on this computer. Hmmm. Oh, *now* I get it—to turn on ABE for all shares, go to any *one* share and enable ABE for that share, *then* check the box that applies that folder's ABE setting to all shared folders. Kinda awkward, yes—you'd think that there would be a Control Panel applet or the like that would let you turn it on or off universally. But no matter; the command line makes it easier.

After installing the ABE UI, you'll have a new command-line tool abecmd. It looks like

```
abecmd [/enable|/disable]{/all|sharename} [/server servername]
```

Or, when rephrased from the Geekish:

1. Type **abecmd** followed by a space.

2. Then you must type either **/enable** if you're enabling ABE, or **/disable** if you're disabling it.

3. Then you must either type **/all** if you want this enable or disable command to apply to all shares, or type the name of the share to have it apply just to that share.

4. You may optionally type **/server** followed by the name of a server to assert control of ABE across a network. For example, abecmd /enable/ all would tell ABE to enable itself for all shares on a system. abecmd /disable /all would universally disable it. To tell the system to only enable ABE for the Homedirs share, type **abecmd /enable homedirs**.

An ABE Example, Part 2

Time to return to our example. Let's turn on ABE for the Homedirs share and demonstrate that Paul will only be able to see his folder…but the administrator will be able to see both Paul and Sally's folders. As you just saw, you can turn on ABE for Homedirs by opening a new command prompt and typing

```
abecmd /enable homedirs
```

You'll get a response like

```
Access Based Enumeration enabled on share "homedirs"
```

If you like, or if you're naturally skeptical, then right-click the Homedirs share in Explorer, choose Properties and the Access-based Enumeration tab, and you'll see that the Enable access-based enumeration on this shared folder check box is now checked. At this point, if Paul looks in \\r2std\homedirs then he'll only see a Paul directory, not a Sally directory. We could see that in action by logging off from the Administrator account and logging on as Paul, but that's too much work. Instead, we'll open up another command prompt and we'll use the runas command to open up that command prompt as Paul. Any commands in the "Paul" command prompt will run as if Paul typed them. We'll have two command prompt windows, then—the one we've already opened as Administrator, and another as Paul. Better yet, let's open up Paul's command prompt window with a blue background so that we can keep track of which command prompt window is which. To accomplish this, type this in the current (Administrator) command prompt:

```
runas /noprofile /user:paul "cmd /k color 1f"
```

You'll be prompted for Paul's password, which, recall, is Paulie1, and then press Enter. You should get a second command prompt window with a blue rather than a black background.

Now, in Paul's (blue) command prompt window, type

```
dir \\r2std\homedirs
```

And press Enter. You should see a paul directory but no sally directory. *Now* go to the old command prompt window, the one where you're logged in as Administrator, and try that command again. You'll see both directories. Neat, eh?

Summary

ABE's a nice SP1 freebie. By keeping prying eyes from seeing shared files and folders that those eyes aren't supposed to see, ABE helps reduce the temptation to play internal hacker. And by reducing the clutter of files and folders presented to the average user, ABE can help make your network more productive.

Chapter 3

De-Worming Windows with Data Execution Prevention (DEP)

August 11, 2003, was, I'm told, a pretty rough day for Microsoft executives and PR folks. It surely wasn't a picnic for us administrator types. That was the day that the Blaster worm exploded onto the Internet. All of a sudden, Internet-connected XP systems that hadn't already installed a patch named MS03-026 would start counting down from 30 and then shut themselves down.

By the late summer of 2003, most of us were pretty familiar with the term "worm." We knew how worms could ride rampant through the Internet astride Windows systems afflicted with software bugs exploitable through something called a *buffer overflow* attack, as they had with Code Red, Nimda, Spida, and SQL Slammer. But the first two worms affected only servers running Internet Information Services (IIS), and the latter two affected only systems running some version of SQL Server and there weren't really all that many of either of those kinds of systems. Or, to be more precise, there weren't all that many SQL and web servers when compared to the number of systems running Windows XP, either in the Home or Professional variety. So when an XP-loving worm like Blaster appeared, it was never at a loss for a fresh horse as it galloped from network to network.

As Blaster found more and more systems to infect, and every newly infected system tried to find even more systems to infect, XP owners found their systems unusable, and Internet users of all types found their formerly useful worldwide network brought to its knees. Of course, summer's always a slow time for journalists, so they had plenty of time to descend on Microsoft in droves, asking Microsoft execs repeatedly, "How will you keep this from happening ever again?"

Which brings us to this chapter.

Microsoft's answer to the worm-weary-world was to give the XP, 2003, and Vista operating systems a sort of basic immune system, whereby an OS could, in some circumstances, detect a worm trying to plant itself in the OS and thereupon take some remedial measures. (I like to say that they "de-wormed" Windows.) That basic immune system is called Data Execution Prevention (DEP), and SP1 installed it in Server 2003. It's enabled by default, so many of you already enjoy its protection.

If DEP's a good thing and it's on by default, then why bother with this chapter? Because while biological immune systems are great, they tend to sometimes do more harm than good by attacking their hosts, producing *autoimmune* behaviors, as is unfortunately the case with some unlucky humans. And while DEP doesn't visit our systems with anything as bad as autoimmune ailments like lupus, multiple sclerosis, or rheumatoid arthritis, it can bring on the occasional attack of "Windows psoriasis," and I'll show you how to treat that. I'll also show you where you would actually *disable* DEP and how to do that.

A Different Kind of Malware

To understand the motivation for DEP, let's return to what must be called DEP's seminal event. How *did* the Blaster worm infect XP systems, and how did it spread so quickly? To see how, let's review some of the many ways that a system gets some kind of *malware*, the word for malicious, criminal, or just plain unwanted software.

A lot of malware delivers itself as email attachments. Whether masquerading as pictures, PIFs, videos, or the like, these types of malware can only infect you if you open the attachment carrying them. Other malware appears as hyperlinks on web pages which, when clicked, cause your browser to ask you if it may download and run a file. A third malware delivery mechanism appears in the form of specialized applications, which can't run by themselves but can only run inside Internet Explorer, called ActiveX controls and Browser Helper Objects (BHOs). Not all ActiveX and BHO apps are malware, of course, but much of what we call spyware is implemented as either ActiveX controls or BHOs.

Notice that in each case, whoever's using the computer must decide to click on a web page, run a program, allow Internet Explorer to download and run a file, or the like—the malware must trick you into some deliberate action in order to get itself installed on your system. Yes, some malware's pretty good at fooling people—click here and get to see some naked people or get a cheaper mortgage or find out your IQ or whatever—but in each of these situations the user has the chance to say, "Hmmm, this sounds fishy," forego the click, and thereby skip getting infected. That's why one of the things that I tell folks when discussing computer security is that while antivirus and antispyware applications are nice to have, in the end analysis the most effective antimalware tool is an alert user possessed of a bit of caution and common sense. In fact, in the late '90s, I was only exaggerating a bit when I told my security classes that all they needed for security was smart users.

Put another way, malware may stand outside your front door offering you all kinds of goodies if you'll just invite it in…but there's no way that it can open the door for itself, and it can't come in without being invited. So if we're attentive, then we can avoid malware…or at least, that was true until the spring of 2001, when Code Red came around. If you were running IIS 5.0 without the proper patches, then you didn't *need* to click anything for your web server to be infected. All you had to do was connect the server to the Internet, and the worm did the rest, sneaking into your web server and seizing control of it via what is called a *buffer overflow*. In other words, the malware had figured out how to open the door for itself. In another word, "Yikes!"

Where the Worm Lives: Pieces of a Program

To understand buffer overflows and how they work, let's back up a bit and see a little bit of how programs work inside so that we can then see how a program like IIS can be attacked by a buffer overflow exploit. (I'm going to get a little techy, but you won't have to be a programmer to understand this explanation.)

We store programs on our computers as files on the computer's hard disk. When our computers start up a program, they must copy the information on those files into the computer's RAM; no program that I know of can run directly from hard disk.

For example, let's look at what happens when you start up the Windows Notepad program. Notepad is contained in a file called `notepad.exe` in the Windows directory. When you tell Windows to start Notepad, the Windows Explorer program finds the `notepad.exe` file and—I'm simplifying a bit—looks to `notepad.exe` to find out how much RAM Notepad needs. The OS allocates that much RAM and loads `notepad.exe` into that allocated RAM. Most programs divide their RAM into four areas:

◆ Space to store the actual program, the executable part of the program

◆ Space to store the program's static data

◆ Space to store the program's stack

◆ Space to store the program's dynamic data area, also called the *heap*

Those four areas are usually arranged in a particular order, as you see in the following graphic.

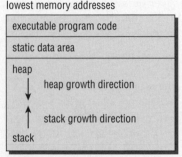

lowest memory addresses

executable program code
static data area
heap

heap growth direction

stack growth direction

stack

highest memory addresses

Those four areas need a bit of explaining before their role in our story will make sense. First is the executable part of the program, and that's easy to understand. That area contains the actual instructions to the CPU to make the program work.

Static Data and the Heap

The *static data* and *dynamic data* areas refer to the two ways that application programs store the data manipulated by the program. The static data area is a space where a program stores data of a predetermined, rather than variable, size. Most programs have at least a little of each type.

For example, among the many pieces of information that Notepad stores is almost certainly a space in memory holding the size of the currently edited file in bytes. While Microsoft doesn't seem to document the size of the largest file that Server 2003's copy of Notepad can handle, the limit seems to be about 630MB. Microsoft doesn't let me see Windows source code, but I would guess that the size of the currently loaded file is stored in an area of memory four bytes long, as that's about how much space you'd need to store a number as large as 630 million.

But consider: while setting aside four bytes of RAM is convenient in that it allows us to potentially edit a text file a half-gigabyte in size, the fact is that the vast majority of text files are under 65,535 bytes in size. I picked that number because there's enough space in just *two* bytes to hold a number as large as 65,535. Now, if most of the time we only need two bytes to store a file's size, isn't it a terrible waste to preallocate a static, unchanging four bytes? Wouldn't it make better sense to redesign Notepad to store a document's size in some kind of variable-sized space in RAM?

No, not really. First of all, two bytes is nothing compared to the amount of RAM that systems have nowadays. Additionally, static-length data structures are far easier to manage and debug than variable-length data, so most simple, small pieces of data like our document length example get stored statically, even if that sometimes seems to lead to a little bit of wasted space.

Static fixed-length data contrasts with variable-length or *dynamic* data, which, as its name suggests, can take up more or less space in RAM depending on what the program's doing at the time. For example, Notepad needs to read whatever text file it's editing into RAM. Would a programmer design Notepad to put the contents of the currently edited file into a static or dynamic data area? Well, to put the document into a static data area, Notepad's programmer would have had to choose some maximum possible text file size and allocate that much space statically. Suppose he'd chosen a static, fixed-size data area of 630MB in which to store the document that you're editing. Putting that into *static* data areas would mean that Notepad would chew up 630MB of RAM every time you fired it up to edit a 4-line text file! For the sake of keeping Notepad's RAM requirements reasonable for most jobs, dynamic data would be the way to go for storing the currently edited document. Understand, however, that even data in the heap has limits, as in the case of Notepad's 630MB document ceiling. It's just that while static data has limits enforced automatically, keeping track of the multiplicity of data objects in the heap is more the programmer's job.

The Stack

In addition to code, static, and dynamic data areas, every program has an area for something called the *stack*. The stack is an area of memory that helps a program keep track of what it's doing. You see, if we could view Notepad's actual program code, we'd probably see that Notepad is not one big monolithic set of programming instructions but many *sub*programs. There might be one subprogram to delete a character, one to save the file, one to load the file, the one that prints, and so on. Why chop a program up into lots of subprograms? Because it lets programmers break down their coding tasks into small, manageable chunks. It also means that a very big program can be created more quickly by delegating different sets of subprograms to different people instead of relying on one overworked programmer.

But there's a small price to pay for being able to write a program as a lot of small subprograms: there's got to be a way for the program to keep track of where it is in among all of these subprograms. For example, here's an extremely simple version of the main Notepad program:

Step One: Go to the subprogram that listens for the user to press a key or click the mouse.

Step Two: Take that mouse click or keystroke and hand it to a different subprogram that actually performs whatever command the user indicated that she wants.

Step Three: Go back up to Step One.

The main program, then, is a short three-command loop, and two of the commands are nothing more than "drop what you're doing here, go run some subprogram, and when you're done with that subprogram, then come back here to the main program *where you left off*." The important part is the piece in italics—somehow remembering where you were before jumping to the subprogram, which is where the stack comes in. The stack is the part of a program's memory that lets the computer say, "Now, where *was* I before…?" Put in bad meter, you could say:

Keeping *track* of how to get *back* is the job of the *stack*.

Catchy, eh? Yup, I know, geek rap's just never going to make it, but the point, simplified, is that the stack is basically a part of an application's memory that lets a program remember where it left off—and there's a surprising amount of need for that kind of remembering. It's not unusual for a program to start off in the main routine of the program, where it's told to go run subprogram 1 and, while running subprogram 1, the program's told to go run subprogram 2. Then, when it's done with subprogram 2, it's got to remember where it was in subprogram 1 so it can return there and, when it's done with subprogram 1, then it must remember where it was in the main routine to return *there*. That small example showed two levels of *nesting*, but in fact real-life programs may end up dozens of levels deep with subprograms calling subprograms calling subprograms and so on. As a result, the stack may require quite an amount of RAM.

Summarized, the stack is a third area of data storage besides the static data area and the heap. The data that it stores, however, are addresses or, more exactly, *return* addresses—where to return to one subprogram after finishing another subprogram.

An Example Server Software: ICMP

Criminals don't launch buffer overflow attacks against just *any* kind of software; no, unfortunately buffer overflows are typically aimed at *server* software—software that lets a computer sit on a network and listen for requests, and then respond to those requests. I'm just about ready to tell you exactly what a buffer overflow *is*, but before I do I'll need one more thing: a useful piece of server software to serve as the basis for an illustrative example.

The simplest example that I can think is some software built into Windows that implements something called the Internet Control Message Protocol (ICMP) stack. Never heard of it? Sure you have—it's the software that makes ping possible. You probably have used the ping command to test IP connectivity, as when you type something like **ping 70.168.214.165**. Ping exists because a guy named Mike Muus realized in 1983 that he could use the ICMP software already built into what would become the Internet to build a simple connectivity test program. ICMP's the railroad, Mike built the ping "train." (And by the way, according to Mike's page on the subject, he named the program "ping" after the sound of a sonar pulse; someone else cooked up that "packet internet groper" stuff later.)

Let's take a moment and consider exactly what happens when you issue a ping request with the `ping.exe` command. As with virtually all network software, ping requires two components —a piece of client software, which starts the conversation by making requests, and a piece of server software, which constantly listens for requests from clients. ICMP is the protocol that ping's built atop. The ICMP client is the `ping.exe` command. The ICMP *server* is a bit of software living inside the main program that implements TCP/IP itself, a file called `tcpip.sys`. Consider that so long as there're no firewalls in the way, you can ping just about any machine on the Internet, whether it's a desktop client machine or a server and expect a response. *That* means that just about *every* machine on the Internet is technically a server; at least from the ICMP point of view. As a matter of fact, I'd guess that there are more ICMP servers than any other kind of server…so our friend ping makes for a pretty good example of how a buffer overflow might attack a piece of server software.

Let's imagine that we don't have an OS that already contains an ICMP stack, and that we're looking over the shoulder of a somewhat sloppy programmer writing an ICMP stack. We'll see that a few simple programming errors can create an avenue of attack of that ICMP stack, an attack of the buffer overflow variety.

As you've just read, most programs partition out the RAM that they receive into four parts, the first of which is the actual executable code itself. The other three—static data, the stack, and dynamic data—may change from second to second. The first part, the executable, doesn't change. Or at least, it *shouldn't* change.

Watching What You Eat: Input Validation

So what exactly is a buffer overflow? Well, simplified, every program does the same thing: it takes some kind of input data, processes it, and produces some kind of output data. Input data comes in many varieties from many sources. It could be mouse clicks, keystrokes, video from a camera, sound from a microphone, information from a data file or, more and more commonly, a stream of data transmitted over a network from a client to server or vice versa. Computers store input data in areas of application memory—often *dynamic* data areas—called *buffers*. As with any data object, buffers have a particular length, and it's up to the programmer to make sure that his program isn't stuffing more data into a buffer than the buffer's got space for. But if the programmer goofs and lets the application put more data into the buffer than there's room for, that's called a *buffer overflow*. As to why that's so dire, read on.

Programmers have to be very careful when writing the part of the program that accepts input because not only is the old "garbage in, garbage out" cliché right, and so bad input leads to bad output, it is also true that in some cases *really* bad input leads to *really* bad output. For example, asking Calculator to divide something by zero isn't nice, as dividing things by zero is meaningless math-wise and asking earlier pre-Windows operating systems to divide something by zero literally crashed the OS. Try it with Calculator now, however, and Calc will just scold you with a "Cannot divide by zero" answer. That's because someone added extra programming code to Calculator to look for a user's request to divide by zero. Code like that is called "input validation" code, and programs need *lots* of it. For example, input data can be of the wrong type (answering age with "forty-eight" instead of "48"), wrong format (telephone number as "(757) 555-1212" instead of "7575551212" or "+17575551212") or, in the case of a buffer overflow, input data can be of the wrong length.

To see how too much data might cause problems, let's look into how the ping command works in a little more detail. When requesting a response from a remote computer, ping doesn't just say, "Tell me that you're alive" because recall that Mike Muus built ping atop existing capabilities of the already-extant ICMP stack. The particular capability that Muus used was something called an "ICMP echo" which, as you've probably guessed, lets a program on one computer say to a program on another computer, "Here's some data; please echo this data back to me." Ping, then, sends a remote computer's ICMP stack some number of bytes of data and expects that remote computer to send the same bytes back to it. But for ICMP to repeat ping's data back to ping, ICMP must store the data that ping sent.

Let's look at how a programmer creating an operating system might approach writing the code to implement the ICMP echo. Basically the code for ICMP echo says, "As an ICMP echo request comes in, store the incoming data from ping. Then create a message back to the pinging computer and include the data saved from the incoming ping." So part of the ICMP program must set aside some space in memory to hold the incoming data to be echoed. But where? Let's say that our imaginary programmer decides to put it in the heap. He writes a bit of computer code that says, "Set aside this many bytes in the heap to store the incoming data from an ICMP echo request." That space in RAM, the place where ICMP will temporarily store incoming data, is called a buffer.

How much space should the programmer set aside? There's no fixed rule about how many bytes of data a ping packet should include, although most ping programs include either 32 or 64 bytes by default and usually let you specify if you'd like to send more or less than the default. But in theory the data in a ping packet could be as much at 65,507 bytes. So our programmer should plan on his incoming data buffer growing to potentially 65,507 bytes.

But what happens if someone deliberately sends a ping with a larger data block, like one with 65,508 bytes? Well, that depends on how our programmer wrote his ping program. If he just designed the ping command to take the incoming data and store it in a buffer living in RAM starting at X address, then the ping program will dutifully copy all 65,508 bytes…into a space with only 65,507 bytes allocated. What happens to the 65,508th byte? To see, take a look at how many programs organize their RAM.

Once a program has been written, it is trivial for its compiler to calculate how much space the executable and the static data parts are, as those things don't change from one run of the program to another. But there's no way to know beforehand how much space the stack will take up, nor the heap, as the heap and stack sizes will vary from run to run. So the most flexible way to arrange the memory is to just start the heap right after the static data and have it grow toward higher memory addresses and to have the stack start at the highest memory address and have it grow downward to the lowest memory addresses. Careful programming keeps the stack and heap from colliding. But programming isn't always careful, as we'll see.

Returning to the question, "What happens to the 65,508th byte?", the *right* answer and the one that we hope is the actual answer is, "The programmer wanted to be extra careful that the program never accepted more data than he'd set aside space for, and he wrote the program so that it checked to see if ICMP were sent more than 65,507 bytes, and *if* that happened, then the program knows to discard the extra bytes." But checking to see that the volume of incoming data doesn't exceed the space set aside for that data involves writing a bit more code, which takes programmer time, and the actual process of checking slows down the program a trifle, so some programmers are a bit lazy and allowed their programs to just accept byte after byte after byte, dutifully putting them into the buffers allocated for them, even if there are more bytes of data than allocated space in the buffer. The result? You guessed it—a "buffer overflow." Whatever was in that location overwritten by the 65,508th incoming ping byte has now been overwritten. And what if the data in the ping packet were much, much larger than 65,607 bytes? A look at the memory layout shows that with a large enough set of data, the ping packet could overwrite the rest of the heap as well as the stack.

Launching the Buffer Overflow

What would that mean, in a concrete sense? Well, assuming the issuer of the big ping packet was acting in ignorance rather than malice, then the data filling up the heap and possibly the stack would just be a repetition of the lowercase letters a-w, the data that every implementation of ping that I know uses as its data. If the overflow only overwrites the heap, then some of the heap's data would end up nonsensical, which would probably cause the ICMP stack to issue some kind of fatal error and crash. If the data overflows into the stack, then things get uglier. Recall that the stack is mainly a list of memory addresses for a program to return to once it's finished with some subprogram; stuffing random letters in there might crash the computer.

Now let's consider a worse situation—a buffer overflow being used to inject malware into a system. Supposing that we had an ICMP stack that didn't check the size of the data in an ICMP echo request, then an attacker could insert new code into the middle of ping with a single ICMP echo request with a particular set of data. With a little research, the attacker could figure out how to create a buffer overflow attack that overflowed both the heap and the stack. The heap would be a convenient place to install whatever new code he wanted on the victim computer. But how to get the victim to execute this new code, especially when that code's sitting in what the computer thinks is an area for data? Simple—by overflowing the heap entirely so as to overflow the stack, and *then* stuff onto the stack a return address that points to the new code.

What would this new code do? Anything that the attacker wanted. Steal data from the victim computer, format its hard disk, cause the victim computer to launch buffer overflow attacks on other computers, or all of the above.

Reviewing this scenario:

◆ We start with a computer running an ICMP stack.

◆ The ICMP stack has a programming error whereby the programmer has neglected to check that the amount of bytes being sent by a remote system asking for an ICMP echo does not exceed the maximum possible amount, 65,507.

◆ An attacker then writes some code that he wants to inject into our (or anyone else's) computer.

◆ He pads out the space after the new code so that the overflow will overflow not just the heap but also the stack, and when overflowing the stack places a return address on the stack that points to the entry point of the new code.

Then comes the particularly evil point:

◆ How does the attacker force the computer to accept this new code? Answer: the attacker just creates a version of the ping program that lets him specify exactly what data to put in the ICMP echo request. Then all he's got to do is to ping the victim computer.

I call this pernicious because, again, the person who runs the victim computer may be completely up to date on his virus pattern files, his antispyware stuff, you name it, but he's still going to get infected. His only "mistakes" were leaving his ICMP stack open to the Internet and running an operating system that, unknown to him, had a buggy ICMP stack.

NOTE And by the way, I wasn't completely honest with you when I said that this was a hypothetical attack. Believe it or not, most circa-1995 operating systems either did no input-length checking on ICMP echoes, or had only recently acquired input length checking. Millions of computers could be remotely crashed with what became known as "the ping of death," a simple ping with a payload longer than 65,507 bytes. I don't know of anyone using this as a worm delivery system.

Buffer Overflows in Perspective

Lest I end up costing you sleep over fear that your servers are actually gardens of buffer overflows waiting to be harvested by evildoers, let me stress that buffer overflows are *not* normal or expected software behavior; they are *always* programming errors. Now and then I'll hear a security expert type say that "bad guys can always attack you via buffer overflows (so buy our product or hire us)," but that's nonsense. Buffer overflows are caused by programmer error; no well-written program can be attacked via a buffer overflow. Buffer overflows are by no means a certainty of life.

Where do worms come into the buffer overflow story? A buffer overflow exploit is, as we've said, just some arbitrary code, a program that does something or another and that can be installed and activated on a machine without the permission of the machine's owner. A worm, as you may know, is a program that seeks to spread itself automatically.

So now take those two concepts—server software with a bug that leaves it susceptible to buffer overflows, and software that seeks to replicate itself—and you've got a difficult situation. For example, suppose some dirtbag wrote a program that generated millions of random IP addresses and then used something like our ICMP echo overflow to install itself on any random IP address. In most cases, the worm would come up with an IP address that was either unused or attached to a machine that had been configured to ignore ICMP echo requests (many people think ignoring ICMP is a good security measure; I disagree, but it's a matter of taste) or attached to a machine listening for ICMP echo requests but *not* running an operating system whose ICMP stack had the buffer overflow bug. But computers and networks can work quickly, and worms are patient. Even if the worm were successful only once in a thousand times, that'd still mean an awful lot of successes. As each success means another computer searching random IP addresses looking to infect still more systems, the power of compound interest soon takes over, and you get a *very* fast-moving worm indeed. For example, the SQL Slammer worm of January 2003 reached 90 percent of all of the servers that it would infect *globally* in just seven minutes. Talk about the world getting smaller!

NOTE   I should stress that Code Red, Nimda, Spida, SQL Slammer, and Blaster did not spread through any ICMP bugs but instead in the Index Service, IIS, the SQL Discovery Service, and the Remote Procedure Call service.

Handling Buffer Overflows Before DEP

Any server program can, potentially, contain a bug with a buffer overflow. Given how vulnerable that might make your system, then, it's fortunate that we've seen as few buffer overflow exploit opportunities as we have. But, again, there's no way to create bug-free software, so how can we ever hope to secure our systems from some future buffer overflow?

To answer that, consider how we've protected ourselves from Code Red, Nimda, SQL Slammer, Blaster, Sasser, and the rest. The sequence of events goes something like this

1. Someone—usually not someone at Microsoft, sadly—figures out that some component of Windows has a buffer overflow error.

2. That someone tells Microsoft about the bug.

3. Microsoft looks over its source code and finds the bug. (I'm sure there's more here, like "heads roll, adult managers scream at overworked programmers, said programmers get reassigned to Microsoft's North Pole office," and the like, but I'm not sufficiently privy to Microsoft insider details to know.)

4. Microsoft comes up with a fix to the bug.

5. Microsoft announces the bug and the fix on the next Patch Tuesday unless the bug is *really* scary, in which case they release it immediately.

6. Bad guys—dang, I meant security researchers, I seem to get that wrong a lot—look at the code *before* the patch and the code *after* the patch and deduce where the error is and how to exploit the error.

7. Meanwhile, people get the patch via Microsoft Update or wherever and wonder, "Will applying this patch cause something on my system to break?" Admin types look at the "buffer overflow" part and say "Hmm… so there's a very small chance that this patch might break something, and a very large chance that in the next three weeks or so some hacker dirtbag will exploit this and seize control of my server. Some admin types think, "There's probably nothing worse than having criminals take control of my server," and apply the patch. Other admins decide to wait a few weeks to hear if any of their friends apply the patch and experience bad things.

8. Within a few weeks, the dirtbags write a worm that exploits the vulnerability that Microsoft has already provided a patch with which to avoid.

9. The guys who patched are okay but can't use the Internet because all of the other guys' servers—who are now infected—are chewing up the Internet bandwidth trying to find other servers to infect.

10. Eventually guys infected with the worm get rid of it…they think.

As you can see, there are two problems with this system. First, what if the person who found the buffer overflow *didn't* report it to Microsoft? He could then create his own worm and turn it loose on the completely unprotected world of Microsoft servers.

NOTE   Something close to that happened in September 2005 when Moroccan Farid Essebar paid Turkish citizen Atilla Ekici to quickly write and disseminate the Zotob worm. It stole bank card information to allow Essebar to run a bank card forgery scam.

Second, as the preceding note shows, hackers are exploiting buffer overflows faster and faster; what happens when Microsoft announces a bug and a patch on Patch Tuesday but the bad guys have a worm running by 2 A.M. Wednesday, before almost anyone has the patch? And, finally, what about those people who are required by law or fear of termination to test a patch thoroughly—perhaps over weeks and months—before implementing it?

Beyond Patching: How DEP De-worms Windows

To see how Microsoft built what I've called an "immune system" for Windows, consider the salient points of a buffer overflow attack:

- ◆ The attack is only possible on systems with some kind of buffer overflow bug. (And yes, they've got to be attached to a network, but that's kind of a necessity these days so I'll take it for granted.)

- ◆ The attack stores malware in an area of memory intended for a program's heap, one of its data areas.

- ◆ Merely storing the code isn't enough; the attack must be created "just right," so that it lands just the right return address on the stack.

We've already discussed the first requirement—a system with a bug. The answer to that is patching, and we've just discussed that.

Is there a way to detect when someone's been fooling around with the heap? Yes: two ways, in fact: marking the heap as *nonexecutable*, and putting markers called *cookies* into the heap to indicate where blocks of data begin and end.

64-Bit Heap Protection: the NX Bit

Intel's Itanium and EM64T and AMD's 64-bit processors all grew up in the age of worms, so their designers built into them a tool to help operating system creators de-worm their OSes, something called the *NX bit*. (Intel has added NX support to most of its post-2004 32-bit Pentium processors as well.)

Modern processors all help an operating system keep track of its memory with memory management hardware. OSes chop your system's memory up into 4096-byte blocks called *pages*, and tables inside the computer's RAM keep track of information about each page. Since the dawn of time (1981, that is), Intel processors have allowed an operating system to mark any given page as "read-only." Once marked as read-only, any attempt by any instruction to write data to that 4K block of memory would cause the CPU to say, "Hey, that's not right"—*trigger an exception* is the actual term—and report that behavior to the operating system, which could deal with it as it liked.

The new NX bit works sort of like that. When XP SP2, Server 2003 SP1, or Vista load an application into memory, they set all of the pages that contain the executable code so that the NX bit is disabled. The pages containing the static data, heap, and stack areas get their NX bits set. Then, when a buffer overflow stuffs code into the heap and the victim computer is eventually tricked into running that code, the CPU will note that it's trying to execute code from a "no execute" page, and it will then tell the operating system, "Hey, that's not right"—and Windows then stops the program that tried to run code from an NX page. The error looks like Figure 3.1.

FIGURE 3.1
"You tried to execute code from a page marked NX!"

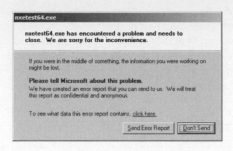

32-Bit Heap Protection: Cookies

The NX stuff is nice, but it only works on systems running 64-bit CPUs or the relatively small number of 32-bit Prescott Intel CPUs. For the rest of us 32-bit user types (can you believe Microsoft's calling our brand-new 32-bit servers "legacy hardware" already in early 2006?), there's no hardware support, so Microsoft added a couple of workarounds. One tries to protect the heap, the other the stack. Let's first look at the heap's protection, something that Microsoft calls *cookies*.

Under DEP, the operating system takes an extra step whenever an application stores data to the heap. It puts a few distinctive bytes that Microsoft calls "cookies" at the beginning and end of each data object in the heap. Then, whenever that data gets read, the system checks for the presence of those distinctive bytes and, if they're not there, then the OS terminates the program.

Saving the Stack

Initially, all a buffer overflow accomplishes is the corruption of heap data by replacing that data with the soon-to-be executed malware. But that malware's no more than corrupted data in RAM until it gets executed. And it gets executed via a corrupted stack.

DEP exploits an option in Microsoft's C/C++ compilers called the */gs switch*. Code compiled with the /gs switch inserts another cookie (it is also sometimes called a "canary," as in when miners used canaries to warn them of rising levels of toxic gases in a mine shaft) between the heap and the stack. A buffer overflow that dumps some new code and new stack values into RAM without placing a canary between the new evil "heap data"—the code—and the new address in the stack causes the application to detect that the stack's been monkeyed with, and to stop the application. To make this work, Microsoft had to recompile virtually every program in XP and Server 2003 with the /gs switch. That's why XP SP2 and 2003 SP1 are so huge!

The actual value of the cookie is apparently randomized in some way that the application will recognize—Microsoft's not talkin' on how it's done—and so every app could have a different cookie, making it difficult for future would-be buffer overflow exploiters to craft a "canary-embedded exploit."

Does All of This Stop Buffer Overflows?

The idea behind DEP is, again, to catch buffer overflow exploits before they succeed in executing their dangerous code. So the buffer overflow ends up modifying the server program's data in RAM but not affecting anything on disk. DEP makes it far more difficult, then, to plant malware on-disk and corrupt system files and thereby operating system security. And it does it even if you haven't first installed a given patch to fix a given buffer overflow-causing bug.

But DEP doesn't, and can't, stop the initial data injection that a buffer overflow exploit tries to use. And DEP responds to discovering that an application's been attacked by shutting the application down. That means that while DEP makes it harder for malware to use buffer overflows to infect systems, DEP can't stop malware from producing denial of service attacks on software vulnerable to buffer overflows. (Having loaded the patch would, in contrast, stop the exploit from getting to square one.)

Controlling DEP

By default, DEP is enabled on all XP SP2, 2003 SP1, and Vista systems. But DEP supports two levels of protection. At the first level, it watches out only for problems with Windows itself and doesn't watch to see if third-party applications are under attack. At the second level, DEP watches *everything*. By default, XP SP2 and Vista run DEP level 1; Server 2003 and R2 run DEP level 2. You can change that by going to Control Panel ➤ System ➤ Advanced ➤ Performance and then clicking the Settings button. In the Performance Options dialog box that appears, click the Data Execution Prevention tab. You'll see something like Figure 3.2.

The first option, Turn on DEP for Essential Windows…, is what I've called "DEP level 1." The second option, DEP level 2, which you can see is selected by default for this copy of Server 2003, watches all applications. Now, turning on full DEP can give some applications heartburn. That's because some applications are *designed* to create code and stuff it into the heap, so DEP wouldn't let those apps run. So, in that case, you can tell DEP to make an exception for that app. I can add an application *not* to watch by clicking Add and when I do, I get a dialog box that lets me browse the hard disk for a given EXE file. You see that my screen shot refers to a program `nxetest`, which is an application written specifically to trigger DEP. I've run it before and DEP's offered to ignore `nxetest` if I check the box next to it.

FIGURE 3.2
DEP tab in
Performance
Options
property page

TIP If your DEP tab looks like mine but includes a note that starts "your computer's processor does not support hardware-based DEP…," then don't worry. I took that screen shot on a 64-bit system, which by definition has hardware DEP. Remember, you still get software DEP on all 32-bit systems.

I've said that DEP's a good thing, and it is, but it exacts a price: speed. DEP watches accesses to the stacks and heaps, as you've already read, and there are a *lot* of stack and heap accesses, so the bad news about 2003 SP1 and XP SP2 is that your system gets a bit slower. That seems a fairly reasonable price to pay, at least to my mind, but there are times when I'd like to squeeze the most out of a machine *and* I'm sure that the machine is in no danger of being attacked. Here I'm talking about running virtual machines, or running older hardware on a test network. Assuming that a VM or a test machine is running on a disconnected network, then I'd say that it's perfectly reasonable to turn DEP off and get somewhat better performance.

But you can't do that from the GUI. Instead, you've got to disable DEP from `boot.ini`. Take a look at your current `boot.ini` by opening Control Panel ➢ System ➢ Advanced and then find the Startup and Recovery section and click the Settings button next to it. Under System Startup, you'll see an option that says To Edit the Startup Options File Manually, Click Edit, and an Edit button. Click that button and Notepad will start up with your current `boot.ini` in it. Look for your default startup setting and it'll probably look something like mine:

```
multi(0)disk(0)rdisk(0)partition(1)\WINDOWS="Windows Server 2003, Standard" /
fastdetect /NoExecute=OptOut
```

The first part's familiar up to and including the … `/fastdetect` part, but look at the end—`/NoExecute=OptOut`. In addition to installing a bunch of new code on your system, SP1 also edited your `boot.ini`! The `/NoExecute boot.ini` parameter takes four possible values.

◆ `/NoExecute=AlwaysOn` turns on DEP and tells DEP to track *everything*—the OS, third-party apps and all, with no exceptions possible. The field that you saw in Figure 3.2 that lets me specify apps not to check with DEP just grays out, as do the two radio buttons that let you enable DEP.

◆ `/NoExecute=AlwaysOff` completely disables DEP. As I've already said, this can be a useful way to speed up a slow system but *only* on a nonproduction system. I think it's a very bad idea to disable DEP on a production system at any time. If you choose `AlwaysOff` then, once again, the Data Execution Prevention tab in the Performance Options property page grays out, as with `AlwaysOn`.

◆ `/NoExecute=OptIn` turns on DEP level 1 but offers you the option to enable level 2. If you enable level 2, then as you saw before it allows you to choose applications to tell DEP to ignore. This is the default setting for XP and Vista.

◆ `/NoExecute=OptOut` is the same as `OptIn`, except it turns on DEP level 2 instead of level 1. This is the default setting for Server 2003.

Summary

In this chapter, I gave you a long look and, I hope, a good understanding of buffer overflows, the things that led to Data Execution Prevention. If you didn't already, you now know that DEP makes your system more secure but at something of a price in terms of speed. But that's not such a bad thing; I'll take slow and smart over fast and sloppy any day.

Chapter 4

Stacking the Deck Against the Bad Guys...the IP Stack, That Is

2003 SP1, XP SP2, and R2 all include two changes to the software that supports and implements TCP/IP to greatly reduce the ability of a worm to spread and make it hard for someone to launch an attack against another system and remain anonymous. But that's not all; a third change affects something called WinSock and lets you recover from a particularly nasty side effect of removing spyware from your system.

What's Wrong with TCP/IP?

TCP/IP is the protocol upon which most of the Internet rests. It's clearly robust, reliable, and, best of all, scaleable; so far as I know, no one's ever built a network as big as the Internet, so that's got to be a vote of confidence for TCP/IP. (After all, any testbed called "Planet Earth" is pretty impressive.)

But let's remember what problem TCP/IP was supposed to solve. In the '80s, the U.S. government found itself the proud owner of at least one piece of every kind of computer and network made in the USA. (If it's not clear to you how it got into that state, recall that every American computer and network manufacturer has at least two Senators and at least one Congressional representative, and those guys all get a say in the Federal budget.) The U.S. government needed a way to make all of these things work together in a large, diverse network that included government offices, government contractors, and university researchers. A large network, yes, but something of a big private club. No one ever imagined that they'd eventually let, well, *everyone* into the club.

TCP/IP was a "solve it now" answer while waiting for the ultimate answer. In the mid-'80s *everyone* knew that network interoperability was a problem that would ultimately be solved by groups like the International Telecommunications Union, the Comité Consultatif International Télégraphique et Téléphonique, and the International Standards Organization. These international standards organizations were slowly shaping a set of standards collectively called the Open Systems Interconnection or OSI model.

I'll bet that some teacher bored you to death at some point with a discussion of the seven-layer OSI model, constantly calling it a "model" to underscore the fact that it wasn't an actual set of products that you could buy, but instead was just an intellectual framework for thinking about different networks. And yes, that's all it's good for now. But back in the '80s? In those days, *everyone* knew that eventually we'd be using real, honest-to-God software running a transport protocol not called Transmission Control Protocol (TCP), but Transport Protocol Class 4 (TP4). And use IP as a layer-three protocol? Nope; we were all working toward a world using something called X.25.

So what happened to all of that? Where are those worldwide standards today? They fell victim to an old truth: "The worst enemy of perfect is 'good enough.'" While we were waiting for the OSI guys, all of us folks with PCs and modems were jealously eyeing all of the cool stuff on the Internet, gazillions of files for the downloading from FTP sites. And then in 1989, a high-energy research lab in Europe invented something called the World Wide Web, and from that point on, it was "game over" for anything that didn't run TCP/IP. All of us American taxpayers said, "We want in," and we were in. Websites sprouted by the millions, the rest of the world said, "Hey, there's a lot of content there," and soon what was once essentially a large "corporate network" for the U.S. government became the world's network...which brings us to the problem.

Although the government-only Internet was large, it wasn't so large that it was impossible to track down an evildoer. Determine that someone launching a denial of service attack against someone else was at IP address such-and-such, and you've pretty much identified the bad guy. I'm simplifying a bit, but back in 1989 you could fairly easily establish the identity of a network criminal, given his IP address. That made the early Internet a safer place than it is now. And even *if* there weren't a loose association between IP addresses and people in those days, the old Net would *still* have been a better-behaved place than it is now for a simple reason: it was, in general, a network of people with jobs. Getting caught messing with the Net often meant losing not only access to the Net, but losing a *job*. Quickly. Or even possibly going to jail.

There are so many Internet standards that it's strange to realize that there *is* no standard way to connect network *actions* like launching a worm or directing a denial-of-service attack at someone to the network *actors*—the dirtbag starting the trouble. It is because the early Internet was small enough that its administrators *could* smoke out bad guys; we don't have an easy way in the modern Internet to close the loop. That's led to an anonymity that provides security for people creating worms, spyware, and the like, making the modern Internet an ideal platform for bad guys.

2003 SP1, XP SP2, and R2 try to slow the bad guys down by changing two aspects of the TCP/IP stack. First, they remove an attacker's ability to employ something called "raw sockets" to handcraft IP packets that deliberately deceive their recipients in manners calculated to attack those recipients while leaving the attacker impossible to trace. Second, Microsoft's updated TCP/IP stack restricts TCP/IP activity patterns that almost always point to a worm program rather than a person. But that's only *almost* always, as that second change will get in the way of some security monitoring programs.

Raw Sockets and the New Stack

You've already read that the first change greatly restricts "raw sockets." What's a raw socket?

Network protocols are complex and exacting things, far more complex than most of the users of those networks can understand, *including* most of the folks who write programs that use those networks. Building a program that could compute which byte goes in what order so as to manage even the simplest TCP/IP conversation is a significantly difficult task, and if every single network-enabled application required that kind of programming, then there would be very few network-aware apps. For that matter, if I had to sit down and build a telephone from scratch in order to call people on the phone, then I'd never bother even trying to use a phone. So I let someone else do that work—I go to the store, buy a phone, and plug it into one of those nice RJ11 phone jacks that the telephone vendors and the phone company have been so nice to standardize on. No matter what brand of phone I buy and no matter who provides my phone service, all I've got to know is to pick up the phone, wait for the dial tone, and then punch in the number of the phone that I want to call.

Yeah, there's that occasional complexity, like, "Do I have to punch in ten digits to call someone a few miles away, or will seven do it?" but if I get it wrong then the phone company is excellent about conditioning me to the proper action by having my phone emit irritating screeches when I make the wrong choice.

In the same way, people wanting to write programs that take advantage of the Internet don't have to understand all the details of how an IP packet is assembled or how to manage a TCP/IP communication. Instead, operating systems come with the software equivalent of a standard phone jack: something called the "socket" programming interface. It's a set of prebuilt subprograms that any programmer can call upon to handle the ugly details of getting two computers to talk across the Internet. That way, someone wanting to write something like an instant messaging program that lets John and Mary talk over the Internet need only worry about grabbing John's keystrokes and then giving them to the operating system's prebuilt routines, saying only, "Send this to IP address such-and-such and port such-and-such." An applications programmer like this could be blissfully ignorant of how an IP packet is laid out.

But what if a programmer *wanted* to control how an IP packet is laid out? For example, every IP packet contains two addresses: the IP address of the machine that originated the packet, the *source address*, and the IP address of the machine that the packet is intended for, the *destination address*. Without a destination address, of course, the packet doesn't get anywhere useful. But why does every IP packet have a source address? So that the receiver machine knows where to send its response to the sender's request. Again, when a programmer uses an operating system's built-in socket routines, she needn't remember to insert the source and destination addresses into the IP packet in the right place because the socket routines do that automatically. Most operating systems, however, offer the programmer the ability to handcraft the IP packet.

Why would a programmer want to do that? In many cases, to write a piece of code that attacks another system. What if I were a bad guy and wanted to bring down some website? I'd write a program that says, "Hi, I'd like to establish a web connection with you, can we do that?" Web servers are polite systems and they always respond to requests to talk, and so whenever I ask a web server if it will talk with me, then I'm forcing it to spend a little CPU power and a bit of RAM to respond to me.

Now suppose I write a program that sends a given website millions of "can we talk?" requests. I could, in theory, overload that web server, effectively shutting down the website. Ah, but then the managers of the attacked network could just look inside the IP packets that I sent to the web server, see my IP address, and track me down.

Unless, of course, I do a bit of raw socket coding. If my operating system allows, I can bypass the nice, high-level socket routines and build my own IP packet byte by byte. And if I do that, then I can craft my attack-the-web-server packets so that they include *a fake source address*.

Consider how pernicious this can be. First of all, I machine-gun bazillions of, "Hi! Let's talk!" packets at the poor web server, and the web server then dutifully sends, "Sure, I'd love to!" packets…at someone else. In one fell swoop, I've not only covered my tracks, I've also managed to get the victim web server to pepper some poor fool with packets responding to an offer that the poor fool didn't make in the first place. In fact, I've engineered it so that the website may well appear to be attacking the poor fool whose IP address I used in the "source address" field of my handcrafted packet. Overall, a bad thing.

So what do XP SP2, 2003 SP1, and R2 do about this? Their revised TCP/IP stack refuses to send any raw socket-created packets via the UDP protocol and refuses any raw socket-created packets via TCP unless those packets contain a truthful source address.

Is this a good idea or a bad idea? Well, from one point of view, it's annoying not to be able to build any arbitrary IP packet because some security software is built atop raw sockets. From another point of view, Microsoft has drawn a line in the sand and said, "From this point on, people using various raw socket–based tools to attack others by faking a source address won't be able to do it from Windows XP, Server 2003, or Server 2003 R2." (Earlier Windows did not have any raw socket support, so falling back to 2000 won't provide a platform for fake-return-address attacks either.) Overall, it's probably a good thing.

WARNING   Oh, and one more point: you'll see web pages saying that if you need raw sockets then all you have to do is download their `tcpip.sys` file (the file in Windows that implements much of TCP/IP) and install it on your system. Please don't do this under any circumstances; I've seen versions of `tcpip.sys` floating around the Web with various kinds of malware in them.

Incomplete Connections and the New Stack

The new TCP/IP stack not only eliminates a lot of raw socket support, it also includes a new restriction intended to make life harder for worms. Unfortunately, this new change renders some security scanning products much less effective.

Review: Worms and Propagation

As I explained in the last chapter, worms are program code that seek to quickly exploit some bug in an operating system. First, something pops up like the hole in the Index Service that led eventually to Code Red. A bad guy figures out how to exploit the hole to seize control of your computer and writes a tool to exploit said hole. But the bad guy knows that merely attacking a few computers doesn't do much; no, he wants to infect a lot of systems. (This was the plan for Code Red, where Chinese hackers sought to use infected web servers to attack the White House's website.) So the dirtbags have the key to the back door; how to quickly get to millions of back doors before people hear about the attacks and start patching?

Answer: with a worm. The attack exploits some buffer overflow to install a bad program that does something—attack the White House website or whatever. The bad program *also* contains, of course, the code to attack other web servers. But how to find a web server? Well, one way is to just randomly generate an IP address and try to infect that address. If there's no one there or if there isn't an unpatched IIS 5.0 system, then nothing happens; but if that random IP address happens to have an unpatched IIS 5.0 system, then not only have the bad guys infected another web server, but *that* web server will now try to find and infect other web servers. So if the bad guys write the code so that every web server generates one million random IP addresses and tries every one of them, and if out of those million IP addresses a mere one hundred of those addresses yield vulnerable IIS 5.0 systems, well, if you consider how quickly computers work, then in no time you'll find that many, many systems are infected. Most worms work in a similar fashion: blindly generate a pile of IP addresses and try to contact them.

Again, if a worm were to just pick one random IP address to try to infect, then it's not likely to get very far, as most IP addresses are either not used or are firewalled. You'd need to try a *lot* of random IP addresses, and most of the initial "can we talk?" requests would go unanswered. *That's* how this change to the TCP/IP stack tries to stop worms dead in their tracks.

When SQL Slammer appeared in January 2003, it too adopted the approach of "generate random IP addresses in search of a potentially vulnerable system and try to infect it." But the percentage of IP addresses on the Internet that actually ran an unpatched SQL server was pretty small. No problem, said the dirtbag who wrote SQL Slammer—I'll have my infected systems just generate literally hundreds of millions of IP addresses and try to contact them all.

The result was that even though an infected SQL Server had about a 0.001 percent chance of actually finding a likely victim, that infected system generated so many random IP addresses and tried so hard to get a response from each of them that it could swamp not only the Internet, but many *intranets* with the sheer volume of its communication.

Throttling the Worms

What to do to confound software like this? The key is in remembering that the vast majority of the IP addresses that a worm tries to infect either don't have systems attached to them or are firewalled and won't respond. In other words, when the worms says, "Hi, can we talk?" the answer is usually a stony silence.

The revised TCP/IP stack in XP SP2, 2003 SP1, and R2 helps slow down worms with a new rule:

NOTE You are only allowed to have ten "open"—unanswered—requests for a TCP/IP conversation extant at any moment.

So suppose you had an R2 system that was running an unpatched version of SQL Server 2000 and it became infected with SQL Slammer. (Yes, I know, R2's got DEP working to protect it and that would probably stop Slammer dead in its tracks even if the copy of SQL Server on the R2 system weren't unpatched, but let me ask you to imagine for a bit, it's just an illustrative story.) It'd spin up a bazillion IP addresses and start probing them…

…Only to be stopped in its tracks after launching its tenth "probe." Every TCP/IP stack that I know of works like this when making a connection: first offer a connection and wait about 20 seconds for a response. If no response after 20 seconds, then forget it. So where a system running the old stack could unwittingly host a worm probing literally millions of systems in a minute, a worm running on XP SP2, 2003 SP1, or R2 could probe a big *30* systems. Heh heh.

Even better, a look at the Event Viewer reveals that you're hosting a worm who's tried and failed to annoy tons of people. A new event ID, 4226, alerts you to the fact that something on your system has tried to contact more than ten systems that do not respond to it. It looks like

```
Event Type:Warning
Event Source:Tcpip
Event Category:None
Event ID:4226
Date:5/20/2006
Time:5:56:56 PM
User:N/A
Computer:FERRARI64
Description:
TCP/IP has reached the security limit imposed on the number of concurrent TCP
connect attempts.

For more information, see Help and Support Center at http://go.microsoft.com/
fwlink/events.asp.
Data:
0000: 00 00 00 00 01 00 54 00  ......T.
0008: 00 00 00 00 82 10 00 80  ....,.._
0010: 01 00 00 00 00 00 00 00  ........
0018: 00 00 00 00 00 00 00 00  ........
0020: 00 00 00 00 00 00 00 00  ........
```

TIP   This might be a fruitful candidate for the `eventtriggers.exe` program that you can find in XP, 2003, and R2! "If we get an event ID 4226 from source TCP/IP, then alert an admin," for example.

The Bad News

This is a change to the TCP/IP stack that's troubled many people because a number of excellent and useful security scanning programs work by scanning a range of IP addresses looking for vulnerabilities. Clearly they won't work all that well when launched from a system running XP SP2, 2003 SP1, or R2, as probing a range of IP addresses will almost certainly yield a fair number of unresponsive systems, leading to event ID 4226s and slowdowns.

This is certainly a downside to the recent TCP/IP changes. Can those changes be ameliorated? Well, you could always just run the scanners from Linux, but of course that's not that easy if you don't have Linux-savvy people. Or you could be careful about running the scanners from Windows systems, but to configure the scanners to only check IP addresses that you know have systems attached to them. Yes, that's a labor-intensive system, but I don't know of another way.

Clearly Microsoft made a trade-off here. Was it a good one? It's a tough question. On the one hand, I understand the irritation of the folks who've worked hard to build security scanners. On the other hand, the fact is that most people who set up servers are generally unfortunately overworked and short on time, so many of them might not know how to properly secure their systems from attack.

Permit me, if I may, to weigh in on whether or not this was a good balance. In a few words, well, this is war. There are jerks, scumbags, miscreants, thieves, and malcontents seeking to parasitize the—in my opinion—wonderful public good that is the Internet. They have created an environment where we must, I feel, adopt measures that not only protect ourselves, but also that slow down the bad guys. One day, and I hope it's one day soon, we'll have an operating system that's settled down in terms of its feature set and goals, and at that point it will, with hope, be a fairly clean and bug-free OS. But until then, I think that an ounce of sometimes-irritating prevention is worth a ton of cure.

Did Installing an Antispyware Program Kill Your IP Networking?

Speaking of cures, sometimes the cure is worse than the disease. (Consider that "cures" and "curse" are just one letter transposition apart!) But XP SP2, 2003 SP1, and R2 include a bit of anticure that I guarantee you'll find useful eventually.

A good friend installed Microsoft's Anti-Spyware beta—it's now called Windows Defender—at my recommendation. (I can't stress how much you need this or some other antispyware tool. I've liked Ad-Aware as well.) Anyway, he had a terrible reaction to the antispyware tool—his IP stack no longer worked. I was puzzled until I ran across this feature of XP's SP2 and 2003's SP1 and R2. Just type this command:

```
netsh winsock reset catalog
```

As it turns out, many things insert themselves between your IP stack and the rest of your system. Most are benign or outright helpful. But because something that sits between the rest of the OS and the IP stack may not be the *only* thing between the OS and the IP stack, these in-between programs must play well with one another—they all sit in a line and must be aware of who's ahead of them and who's behind them in line. That way, if one in-between program exits, it knows to link the program behind it in line to the one in front of it in line. (This "line" is the "catalog" in the preceding command.) But some poorly written browser helper objects (one type of these in-between programs often used in spyware) aren't good at cleaning up after themselves and, when those kinds of browser helper objects are removed by antispyware tools, then the line of in-between programs may get messed up, with the result that you can't do anything on IP. Or maybe they're *not* poorly written; perhaps the whole goal of the spyware author was, "If I go, your network connection goes."

In any case, the bottom line is that if installing some kind of antispyware tool has made it impossible for you to network, open up a command line and try typing `netsh winsock reset catalog`. Then reboot your system. You may have to follow that up with a `netsh int ip reset c:\iplog.txt` if you're still having trouble.

Summary

The changes that the 2004 and later versions of the TCP/IP stack bring are subtle, and many people may never even notice them. But the bottom line is this: recent versions of Windows are considerably harder to use as launching platforms for worms…and that, on balance, is a good thing.

Chapter 5

Solving SP1/R2 Incompatibilities: Understanding the "De-anonymizers"

When XP's SP2 and 2003's SP1 first appeared, they were greeted with a lot of fear, as some people said that they caused a lot of applications to stop working, so many chose not to install XP SP2 and 2003 SP1, or later to install R2 so as to avoid application compatibility problems.

In general, I felt those concerns to be largely fear mongering on many of the naysayers' parts. We seem to have this "cyclical amnesia" about service packs. Service Pack X for some version of Windows comes out and people say, "No, no, it breaks things, don't use it, it's not reliable..." until Service Pack X+1 arrives, and all of a sudden those same people say, "No, no, Service Pack X+1 is bad, use Service Pack X, it's well -understood and doesn't present the new SP's problems." Hmmm, say I. Maybe Microsoft should deliberately release service packs in pairs: release the real Service Pack Number such-and-such, then wait a month and rerelease it with a new number. Then people can feel good about the "old" service pack. Okay, I'm kidding...

Anyway, yes, in fact XP SP2, 2003 SP1, and R2 can cause some applications to break. But I've run into very few of those breakages, and most of those are something simple, like, "Oh, no! I can't ping my computer any more," which is incredibly simple to fix, as you'll see in the Windows Firewall chapter. (If you can't wait, the short answer is: enable the ICMP echo on the firewall.) Furthermore, most of the incompatibilities are caused by a small group of changes that I call the *de-anonymizers*. By those I mean a set of changes that target and either eliminate or ameliorate certain long-standing security holes in Windows.

In this chapter, you'll first understand what those security holes were, how the changes in SP2/SP1/R2 seek to plug them, and why those changes cause the occasional incompatibility. Then you'll learn how to, when necessary, nullify those changes to solve a compatibility problem.

Why De-anonymize?

Why did Microsoft bother with these changes? Heck, it seems as if Windows has worked okay in the past. What needed fixing? Well, lots, actually, as you'll see. Permit me to try to explain that with an analogy. Think of an operating system as being a large office building; after all, they're both places where things get done.

In this analogy, each room in the office building is a program. You probably already know this, but permit me to review the fact that operating systems aren't built from just one program. Instead, they're a collection of hundreds, thousands, or even tens of thousands of smaller component programs. Some programs are the applications that we recognize—things like Notepad. Some are device drivers like the files that let you use your video card, and others are programs that we as users never see but are essential in that they support other programs. In the rooms of our imaginary office building, imagine that there are people working and that they represent the effort that the CPU expends working on each program.

Now, the workers in those rooms need to communicate with workers in other rooms, as programs have to be able to talk to other programs to get anything done. For example, every time you press a key in Notepad, then Notepad needs to show you, the user, that new keystroke. But Notepad doesn't put characters on the screen; something called the Graphical Device Interface (GDI), the video driver, and a bunch of other programs do that, so Notepad's got to be able to talk to those programs in order to get anything done. In my office building story, we'd visualize Notepad's request to GDI as a few guys from the Notepad room walking over to the GDI room, walking through the GDI room's doorway, and asking some of the folks in the GDI room to put a few characters on the screen in Notepad's window.

Clearly in order to get from Room Notepad to Room GDI, there's got to be some way to get in and out of the rooms—that is, doorways. (Yeah, I know, pointing out that each room has at least one doorway falls in the "duh" category, but please stay with me, this'll be useful.) Operating systems folks would call these methods for one program to communicate with another *interprocess communications* or IPCs.

Let me pause the analogy discussion for a moment and make a couple of important points about IPCs. First, there are many types of IPCs in the computer world. Why not just one? Some are focused at doing communication between very specific types of programs, as is the case with IPCs focused on letting database client applications talk to their database server programs, and some are there for historical reasons. We're going to meet a few in this chapter with names like RPC (Remote Procedure Call), MSDTC (Microsoft Distributed Transaction Coordinator), and others. Second, many IPCs don't just let two programs in the *same* computer communicate; they can let two programs running on two *different* computers—clearly computers networked in some way—talk to one another. For example, if you use Outlook as a client application to talk to Exchange Server, then Outlook and Exchange talk via an IPC called the Remote Procedure Call or RPC. So if an operating system is like an office building, then we can think of a network of computers as being like a city full of office buildings. It is, then, sometimes possible that the guys from the Notepad room might have to walk out of the building and down the street to ask some other folks to do something for Notepad, like, "Hey, we're from Notepad in a building that doesn't have a printer, and we need to print some things. We see that you've got a sign in the front of your building labeled 'we print stuff for other people'; can you print this document for us?"

You can probably see where this story is going: security. For years, some of those IPCs had no security at all, or only very minimal security. We can extend this to our building analogy by looking more closely at those doorways I talked about before. What's in them or, more specifically, what's sometimes *not* in those doorways?

Answer: doors with locks.

Modern operating systems were born in a day when everyone trusted everyone. (Well, almost all modern OSes: NetWare was a bit forward-thinking by today's standards, security-wise, and has been safely paranoid since its 2.0 days, when I first encountered it.) That's not true any more, and so over the past 15 years Unix, Linux, Windows, and just about every other OS has had to undergo changes to make them more appropriate in the modern networking world—what might be called "the big scary Internet." Not too many years ago, most operating systems could be described as office buildings with bezillions of doorways, the vast majority of which lacked doors and locks, or that had doors with locks that could be picked by the average five-year-old with a paperclip. A lot of the "hardening" that's been built into OSes in the past decade-and-a-half involves refitting minimal-security IPCs with lockable doors, or replacing the lame existing locking mechanisms on many doors with something that'll hold up to a serious attack.

But what happens when we take some given program in an OS and install a door with a useful lock on its formerly-open-or-easily-opened doorway? Well, some older applications won't look where they're going and will just run into the door—or perhaps "crash" into the door is a better term, because that's what the apps do: crash, when presented with an unexpected lock. Now we're ready to understand what's going on, and what to do about it.

What did XP SP2, 2003 SP1, and R2 *do* that's upset so many programs? Well, first, it installed lockable doors in many formerly doorless doorways. Second, they changed Windows' out-of-the-box configuration by locking some doors by default. Some of those doors were ones that have had locks for a long time but that weren't locked by default, and others locked some of the newly installed lockable doors.

What can we do about it? Well, as I've said, in fact there's often nothing to worry about, as it may affect nothing. But if we come across some old-timer or poorly written application that just plain refuses to check to see if there's a locked door ahead of it before barreling on through, then we'll have to take an extra step and unlock the door. That's not optimal, as we sort of hate to leave any doors open that needn't be, but if your apps need it, then your apps need it.

In the remainder of this chapter, you'll learn about new locks, or newly locked-by-default settings in four systems:

◆ The Remote Procedure Call (RPC) IPC

◆ The Microsoft Distributed Transaction Coordinator (MSDTC) RPC

◆ The Distributed Common Object Model (DCOM) and, finally,

◆ The Web Development and Versioning (WebDAV) system in Windows

Remote Procedure Call (RPC) Changes

As network-enabled IPCs go, RPC is one of the oldest around, if not *the* oldest. As with all networkable interprocess communication systems, RPC allows Program A in Computer 1 to reach across the network and ask Program B in Computer 2 to do something for Program A. Now, if you think about it, that's a generic way of describing everything that happens on a network, except we'd more commonly describe it as "a client program on one computer makes requests to a server program on another computer, and the server program eventually sends the client back the results of the client's request." The phrase *remote procedure call* is so basic and so generic that virtually every operating system that I've ever worked with that was network-aware included its own sort of RPC, from Univac Exec8 to Xenix to Digital's VMS to Sun Solaris, other Unixes, Linux, and, of course, Windows. (But that doesn't mean that they can interoperate—if you want a Sun server process to handle requests from a Windows client process, then you'd probably use some other form of IPC.) There are many kinds of IPCs, as I mentioned before.

Windows' particular flavor of RPC allows programmers building something with Windows RPC (which I'll just call "RPC" from here on in instead of "Windows RPC") to require the client to authenticate itself to the server. As I mentioned earlier, Outlook asks Exchange for your email via an RPC, and Exchange is designed to require authentication before it'll cough up your personal e-missives. Because RPC's so old, however, it allowed programmers the option to design server software that used RPC but didn't require authentication; such a use of RPC is called *anonymous RPC*. I don't know of many legitimate apps that use anonymous RPC offhand (Microsoft BizTalk Server is one, oddly enough), but I *can* name a not-so-legitimate application that used it: the Blaster worm. So the Microsoft security folks said, "Let's just get rid of that anonymous RPC thing."

But there are probably legitimate apps out there that need anonymous RPC, so Microsoft created a new Registry entry that lets you configure a system's handling of anonymous RPC in one of three ways. The Registry hack is in `HKEY_LOCAL_MACHINE\SOFTWARE\Policies\Microsoft\Windows NT\RPC`, and the entry's name is called RestrictRemoteClients. It's a REG_DWORD entry, and can take three values—0, 1, or 2. These values work as follows:

- Setting RestrictRemoteClients to 0 makes the system behave as it did before this SP2/SP1/R2 change.

- Setting RestrictRemoteClients to 1 makes RPC require authenticated connections, unless the application knows to specifically request an anonymous connection. Microsoft says that some Distributed Common Object Model (DCOM) apps require this setting to work.

- Setting RestrictRemoteClients to 2 makes RPC require authenticated connections, but unlike setting 1 this will not allow anonymous connections, even if the app requests one.

Which setting is right for you? Well, in XP SP2 Microsoft set RestrictRemoteClients to 1, but in Server 2003 SP1 and R2 Microsoft set it to 0. Their reasoning ran something like this. RestrictRemoteClients is a setting for *servers*, not *clients*, and it creates potential incompatibilities with older clients. So while setting RestrictRemoteClients to 1 or, better, 2 offers the positive result of a harder-to-attack server, it also creates the negative possibility of a secure server that people may not be able to connect to. Microsoft figured that XP systems aren't usually servers, and so erring on the side of caution wouldn't cause too much pain. On the other hand, 2003 SP1 and R2 servers *are* usually used as servers (I know, that's another "duh" moment), and so the out-of-the-box setting for those two was 0.

Therefore, if you're running some kind of server software on XP and clients can no longer connect to it after SP2, then set RestrictRemoteClients to 0. If, on the other hand, you're running mainly modern software on your network and would like to tighten up security on your 2003 SP1 and R2 servers, consider bumping RestrictRemoteClients up to 1 or 2. The change requires a reboot to take effect.

Once you tell your servers that they expect authentication, then you'll want to warn your client systems that they should offer authentication. You can do that on XP SP2, 2003 SP1, and 2003 R2 systems with another Registry entry, EnableAuthEpResolution in the same key as RestrictRemoteClients. It too is a REG_DWORD and takes two possible values: 0, which means "don't try to authenticate when connecting to an RPC service," and 1, which means "try to authenticate when connecting to an RPC service."

Clearly both RestrictRemoteClients and EnableAuthEpResolution are Registry settings that you may want to apply wholesale across your network, so it's nice that there are group policy settings that correspond to them. They're both located in the Computer node of Group Policies, in Administrative Tools ➢ System ➢ Remote Procedure Call. The Restrictions for Unauthenticated RPC Clients offers, not surprisingly, three options: None, Authenticated, and Authenticated without Exceptions, which set RestrictRemoteClients to 0, 1, or 2, respectively. You can configure EnableAuthEpResolution through group policies with the setting RPC Endpoint Mapper Client Authentication, which takes either the Disabled or Enabled settings, corresponding to 0 or 1 in the Registry.

Before moving along to the next IPC, let me summarize what you probably need to do:

Nothing. Honest, so relax. Again, this won't affect the majority of you.

In most cases you will not run across an incompatibility, as I've said. But if you've tightened up your security by setting RestrictRemoteClients to 1 or 2 on a 2003 server, then either roll it back, or try setting EnableAuthEpResolution to 1 on your clients. If you're running some kind of server on an XP box, and clients can't get to that server, consider rolling RestrictRemoteClients back to 0 on that XP box.

Microsoft Distributed Transaction Coordinator (MSDTC) Changes

RPC's an old-timer among IPCs and its simplicity means that it gets used a lot for a variety of purposes. But some IPCs are much higher-level and specialized; one such is the Microsoft Distributed Transaction Coordinator or MSDTC.

What MSDTC Does

As a close look at its name suggests, MSDTC does two things for programmers. First, it assists programmers who are trying to build client-server systems that must do database transactions by making the whole process or database updates simple. But the job of just doing a database transaction can be handled by a number of IPCs. What MSDTC adds to that is in the word *distributed*. Many databases are distributed, which means that there is more than one database server holding copies of the databases. And *that* means that every time the database changes, then whoever's doing that change had better make sure that all of the database servers holding all of the copies of the database all get and post those changes. That's what MSDTC's good at.

Despite the fact that MSDTC can help juggle updating a lot of different database servers simultaneously, its usefulness in doing database things in general means that many coders, including Microsoft's own developers, have ended up using it for much simpler tasks, like just managing a database transaction between a client and a server on the same machine, with nary a "distributed" in sight. As I suggested in my introductory discussion of IPCs, MSDTC can act as a go-between either for a client and server on different systems or on the same system…and that's where the security aspect comes in.

Inasmuch as MSDTC comes on every copy of XP, 2003, and R2, and given that it is turned on automatically, it's a way for one computer to ask another computer to do something, and so that might become a doorway for a worm to attack a system. (Again, I don't want to adopt the stance of "security hysteric" here. Just because your building has a door that lets folks on the outside come in doesn't mean that the door isn't secure or can't be trusted. But if you were looking to harden your building then you'd logically look first at the outside doors. Sure, the bad guys could use sledgehammers to knock down the walls and enter that way, but it's less likely, unless your building's made of balsa wood.) Microsoft observed that most of the MSDTC-using apps *don't* actually employ a client program in one computer talking to a server program on another computer, but instead support a conversation between client and server programs on the same machine.

As a result, SP2, SP1, and R2 all keep MSDTC enabled for clients and servers on the same computer but disable it for cases where the client and server live on different boxes. As with RPC, you can undo this if it causes compatibility problems and, again, I've never seen a case where this happened (or at least, I've never seen one where it happened save where I *made* it happen).

Addressing MSDTC Compatibility Issues

But, if you've got a database-oriented application that worked before 2003 SP1 or worked on 2000 or 2003 RTM but that fails on R2, then it's time to do some diving into MSDTC. Here's how.

First, bring up the Components snap-in. The easiest way is to just click Start ➤ All Programs ➤ Administrative Tools ➤ Components. That'll yield an MMC console like Figure 5.1.

Click the plus sign next to Component Services and underneath that you'll get an object named Computers. Click the plus sign next to *that* and you'll see an icon that looks like a 1992 computer that is labeled My Computer. (Maybe it's *your* computer, Mr. Programmer, but *we* started buying more laptops than desktops back in 2002. Perhaps it's time to update that icon, hmmm?) Right-click the My Computer icon and choose Properties and, by the way, don't be surprised if you've got to give your computer a minute or two between these steps. The Components snap-in seems to be a thoughtful one and takes some time to respond between clicks. You'll see a property page like Figure 5.2.

That's an important page, because we'll return to it for the next IPC, DCOM. To address MSDTC issues, however, just click the MSDTC tab and you'll see a page like Figure 5.3.

I know, there's a lot of stuff in there, but we don't need to worry about it all because we're not programmers. Instead, just click the Security Configuration button to see the Security Configuration dialog box, as in Figure 5.4.

The only important thing here to notice is the Network DTC Access check box. This is the switch that says, "MSDTC, you can let clients and servers talk across the network." Notice that it's *not* checked. That's the main difference with XP SP2, 2003 SP1, and R2. XP SP1 and 2003 RTM had pretty much the same Security Configuration screen, but the Network DTC Access check box was checked by default. If you need to restore MSDTC's network privileges, then check the box and click OK until all of the dialogs and property pages are cleared.

FIGURE 5.1

Components snap-in

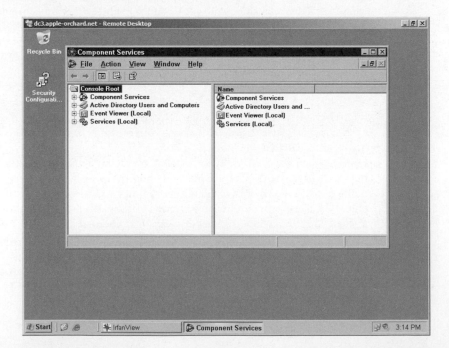

FIGURE 5.2
Properties page
for several IPCs

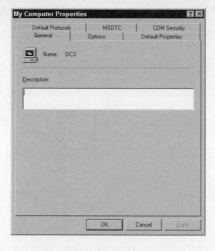

FIGURE 5.3
MSDTC property page

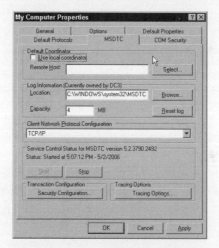

FIGURE 5.4
MSDTC Security
Configuration dialog

Distributed Common Object Modem (DCOM) Changes

We saw that RPC was an old IPC for generic uses and that MSDTC was a newer one with more specific uses. DCOM is a high-level way for modern applications to talk to one another, and it has a wide-reaching set of uses. (For example, it can handle database functions—but it relies upon MSDTC for many of them!) Like MSDTC, DCOM allows programs to talk to one another regardless of whether those programs are in the same computer or running on different computers. And, like MSDTC, prior to XP SP2, 2003 SP1, and R2, DCOM's permissions made no significant distinction between intracomputer and intercomputer communication. That's all changed now.

To see that, return to the My Computer Properties page that you saw in the last section, but this time, click the COM Security tab to see a screen like Figure 5.5. (The dialog refers to *COM* rather than *DCOM* for reasons known only to Microsoft; COM is simply *Common Object Model*, and, again, DCOM is *Distributed COM*.)

As their labels say, this tab lets you control who can access or launch (start, that is) an application. Just for comparison, though, take a look at the corresponding dialog box *before* the service packs. Here's the same dialog box from a pre-SP1 2003 system, as you see in Figure 5.6.

FIGURE 5.5
DCOM Permissions

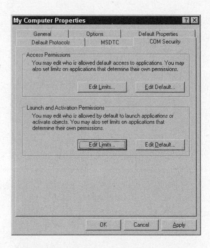

FIGURE 5.6
Pre-SP1 DCOM
Permissions

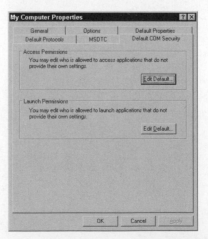

Notice that the old dialog let you set the "default" permissions, but not the "limits." These refer to the fact that anyone building a DCOM-based application—*DCOM object* is the more exact phrase—can build permissions into the application, and in general that makes sense, as the coder is probably the person who understands the DCOM program the best and knows who it's intended for. (For example, if you start up Active Directory Users and Computers and right-click a user account, then you'll see the Reset Password option—but *only* if you have the power to reset passwords.) But if the developer doesn't set permissions, then the Default buttons set the defaults for any DCOM objects on a given system whose coders did not embed permissions in them.

But what if the person who coded the DCOM object built it not to benefit you, but himself; what if some DCOM object had a complete set of built-in permissions, but those permissions were either inimical to your system, or perhaps the coder wasn't a bad guy, just a dumb guy, and built in a set of far too loose permissions? That's where "limits" comes in. In the pre-SP1 days, you could say, "Well, if a DCOM object doesn't have built-in permissions, then I'll set them from the Permissions area in Components." Now you can take it a step further and say, "Heck, I don't *care* if the DCOM object has a complete built-in set of permissions. I don't want *anything* on my system looser than such-and-such level of permissions."

But that's not where the DCOM tightening ends. To see how much more things have changed, take a look at Figure 5.7.

It's a pretty simple permissions dialog. No Full Control, Read, Delete, or any of the other stuff that we're used to seeing in NTFS permissions. Just "Yes, you can run this," or, "No, you can't run this." But now look at the corresponding permission dialog box from a 2003 SP1 system, as you see in Figure 5.8.

See the difference? As with other 2003 SP1 changes, you now have the ability to distinguish between permissions for local users and remote users.

What will this mean for you? Again, for most of us it'll mean nothing. For others, we'll open up these dialog boxes and tweak things when directed to by a software vendor—"In order to make GreetingCardMaster work, you must open up the Component snap-in…," that sort of thing. But for those of us dealing with some kind of home-grown application, or an old app whose developer isn't available any more and whose application isn't working on an XP SP2, 2003 SP1, or R2, we can always open up these permissions dialogs and loosen them up a bit to see if the problem goes away.

FIGURE 5.7
Access Permission
dialog pre-SP1

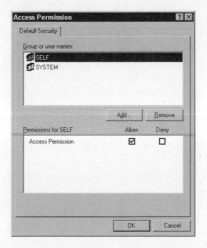

FIGURE 5.8
Access Permission
dialog post-SP1

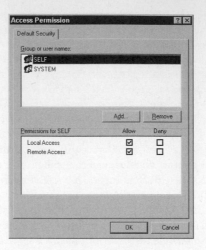

WebDAV Changes

Ever run a website that someone else hosted? Then you know that the biggest pain about doing that is updating your content. The web hosting vendor gives you a folder on one of their servers, and your website goes there. To update it, you usually log onto the hosting vendor's server via FTP. But gosh, is FTP clumsy or what? It'd be really neat if that folder on the hosting vendor's server just showed up as drive W: or something like that.

Well, that's the idea with the Web Development and Versioning system, or WebDAV. In February 1998, RFC 2291 described how an HTTP-based system could allow file and folder updates over the Web. In other words, RFC 2291 describes something very much like the Server Message Block (SMB) file sharing that we're familiar with in the Microsoft world but based on standards and running over port 80 or, potentially, SSL's port 443. I'm not a FrontPage fan, but I'm told that you can edit your web pages and save them straight to your hosting vendor with FrontPage…and a bit of setup.

Microsoft has supported WebDAV for quite some time. If you've ever noticed the WebFolders feature that's been around since (if I recall right) Windows 2000, then you've seen WebDAV in action, or at least Microsoft's implementation of it. There is also a client piece for WebDAV built into XP, 2003, R2, and Vista, called the WebClient Service.

What's that you say, you don't use WebDAV and so don't care about it? You might be surprised, as Microsoft has quietly built a number of tools atop WebDAV. For example:

◆ If you've ever used Outlook Express to access an Exchange account, you've used WebDAV.

◆ If you've ever interacted with other people through MSN Communities, you've used WebDAV.

◆ If you've ever used SharePoint, then you've used WebDAV.

As you've probably guessed, you need IIS to run WebDAV, but as you also probably know, Exchange and SharePoint both run IIS; that's where their WebDAV connections come in. But Microsoft noticed something of a hole in their WebDAV implementation: cleartext authentication traffic.

Deep within the bowels of its configuration screens, IIS has always offered three levels of authentication. The simplest is anonymous, which just means, "You needn't log in." It's the default for 99.9 percent of the IIS servers out there because 99.9 percent of the web servers that you visit don't make you log on.

The other .1 percent, however, *does* make you log on because they contain data that you own and you don't want other people to see without your permission. For example, Outlook Web Access would be a pretty lame web front-end to email if just anyone could fire up a web browser and read your mail. So IIS offers the other two levels of authentication: Basic and Windows Integrated. Basic is nice because it's platform-independent. Secure any website with Basic Authentication and people will be able to get to it regardless of whether or not they're running Windows or some browser besides IE. The only problem with Basic is that it passes your name and password in a barely obscured text format called *base 64*. It's trivial to decrypt, but, again, it's compatible. Windows Integrated Authentication, in contrast, is secure but can present problems to some client operating systems and browsers.

Making a website function can be a complex task, and by the time we actually get the thing running many of us might be excused for simply saying, "I don't want to have to figure out authentication, so I'll just turn on all of the options." Don't misunderstand, I'm not saying that it's the *right* answer…just a common one.

WebDAV seeks to keep that from happening with a new default behavior. By default, any IIS server running atop the XP SP2, 2003 SP1, or R2 system will not allow Basic Authentication when doing WebDAV. So now IIS has two new Registry entries that control Basic Authentication on WebDAV.

The first rolls back WebDAV's behavior to pre-SP1 days, allowing Basic Authentication. Located in `HKEY_LOCAL_MACHINE\SYSTEM\CurrentControlSet\Services\WebClient\ Parameters`, just create a new REG_DWORD entry called UseBasicAuth and give it a value of 1, then restart IIS, and you'll be able to log onto WebDAV with Basic Authentication.

Now, it could be that the reason that you enabled Basic Authentication was because your application simply needed it, but you'd still like to see those Basic Authentications a bit more secure. A moment's thought may reveal to you how to allow cleartext logons that are still relatively secure: use SSL! To encourage that, Microsoft's added a new Registry setting not to IIS, the web server, but instead to IE, the web *client*. This Registry entry that says in effect, "Okay, so maybe you'll hook up to some WebDAV site via this cleartext Basic stuff; fine—but not unless you're logging on via SSL." You can do that by going to `HKEY_CURRENT_USER\SOFTWARE\Microsoft\ Windows\CurrentVersion\Internet Settings`, then creating a new REG_DWORD entry called DisableBasicOverClearChannel. Set it to 1, reboot, and your client system will refuse to do WebDAV without SSL. Now, you'll need to make this setting on your *client* systems, which is a bit of a pain given that there is for some incomprehensible reason no group policy setting to do this. (And you could always create a custom group policy to do that.)

Summary

In this chapter, we've gotten a bit esoteric and talked about things are usually more relevant in developer-land than in administrator-land. But if you find that SP2, SP1, or R2 give you a few headaches when trying to run old apps, I think you'll find knowing this stuff pretty useful!

Chapter 6

Fine-Tuned Security Monitoring: Per-User Auditing

We all know that we should adjust the Audit Policy section of our group policies' Windows Settings ➤ Local Policies ➤ Audit Policy component and look at our Security event logs regularly, right? Okay, how many of you do it? C'mon, now, tell the truth… Many of us don't bother with either Audit Policy settings or Security log because there's *so much darn stuff in the Security log*. For example, I like having the wealth of information that I get from auditing both success and failure in logon and account logon events, but finding useful stuff by looking through the logs even on a small network like mine is often about as easy as finding an honest politician. I don't really care if and when Janie or Johnny logged on; I want to see when someone's tried to log on as Administrator, or perhaps as one of those worrisome service accounts. But turning on auditing of success and failure in group policies offers no fine-tuning: either the fire hose is on, or it's off.

So it's deluge or drought…unless you're running XP SP2, 2003 SP1, or R2, that is. Because they include a command-line utility called `auditusr.exe` that lets you pick and choose what to audit on a per-user basis.

Auditusr Overview

Auditusr lets you turn on security auditing for just some small set of accounts or, inversely, it allows you to audit everything *except* some small set of accounts. Basically, here's how it works.

◆ To only audit a small set of accounts, leave auditing turned off in group policies, but then use auditusr to tell your system to audit particular user accounts (not groups, unfortunately).

◆ To audit everyone *except* for some small set of accounts, turn on auditing in group policies, which normally audits every user account, and then use auditusr to exempt particular user accounts.

It's a pretty neat tool and I'm already finding uses for it. But before you get too excited about auditusr, let's understand its limitations.

◆ This only works on XP SP2 and 2003 SP1 or later; you can't make it work on earlier OSes.

◆ As I mentioned before, it only works on user accounts, not user groups. (Ever noticed that more and more things in the Windows world don't support groups, like quotas? Seems like a bad trend, y'know?) On the plus side, however, it *can* track machine accounts.

◆ As far as I can see, there is no easy way to deploy this across an enterprise short of login batch scripts.

Auditusr Syntax

That's not so bad a set of limitations. Here's the syntax for auditusr:

```
auditusr function accountname:what-to-audit
```

Where

◆ *function* is what you want auditusr to do: audit successes regardless of the group policy auditing settings, audit failures regardless of group policies, *not* audit successes regardless of group policies, to audit failures regardless of group policy, to import or export per-user settings, or to remove per-user settings. We'll see auditusr's functions in detail in just a moment.

◆ *accountname* is, not surprisingly, an account name (computer or user). It'll take simple names like "Jane" if they are local accounts, or names like mydomain\Joe if you need to specify where Joe's account is, or Active Directory logon names like sally@bigfirm.com.

◆ *what-to-audit* is one or more of the familiar auditable things—system events, logons, policy change, and so on.

Auditusr supports eight functions:

◆ /is: audit a success for a particular account even if it's generally disabled in GPOs. For example, to say that I want the mydomain\mark account's logon successes audited whether the GPO setting turns on logon auditing or not, I'd type

```
auditusr /is "mydomain\mark":"Logon/Logoff"
```

And I'll tell you what works besides "Logon/Logoff" in a bit.

◆ /if does the same thing as /is, but for auditing failures—/if says to audit a failure for a particular account even if it's generally disabled in GPOs—/is and /if are, then, "include successes" and "include failures."

◆ /es: do not audit a success for a particular account even if it's generally enabled in GPOs. So, for example, if I had my GPO settings arranged so that I was tracking account management success but didn't care about any account management referring to a local account "Mary" then I would type

```
auditusr /es mary:"Account Management"
```

Notice that I did not have to surround Mary's name with quotes, as it didn't contain any spaces, backslashes, or the like.

◆ /ef: do not audit a failure for a particular account even if it's generally enabled in GPOs— /es and /ef are "exclude successes" and "exclude failures."

◆ /e *filename* exports all per-user auditing settings so that you can then use…

◆ /i *filename* imports per-user settings. This first wipes out any existing per-user auditing setting. The export/import files are simple ASCII, so I guess that one way to spread per-user settings would be through an `auditusr /i` command in a login batch file, although that'd be a bit clumsy to set up.

◆ /r *accountname* removes all per-user audit settings that refer to a given account.

◆ /ra removes all per-user audit settings. Really — *all* of them, and there's no "are you sure?" prompt.

◆ And I should mention that specifying *no* function causes auditusr to just display every per-user audit setting on the system.

What can you audit? The same as you see in the Audit Policy folder of group policies:

◆ System Event

◆ Logon/Logoff

◆ Object Access

◆ Privilege Use

◆ Detailed Tracking

◆ Policy Change

◆ Account Management

◆ Directory Service Access

◆ Account Logon

You've got to type those audit targets exactly as you see them here and surround them with double quotes, although the case doesn't matter. And if you've forgotten what any of those things *do*, then check back to pages 604-606 in the *Mastering Windows Server 2003* book for a quick summary.

Auditusr Example Applications

Let's take auditusr out for a spin to see how it works. We've already seen a couple of simple examples; let's look at few more complete ones.

Audit Just One User

Suppose I want to audit logons and logoffs as well as account logons for a user named Mark; let's also suppose that his account is a local account on a machine named X1000. I'd like to audit logon successes and failures for Mark, even if I've got logon/logoff and account logons disabled in general via group policies. Breaking this down, then, I want to do four things:

◆ Audit logon/logoff successes for x1000\mark

◆ Audit logon/logoff failures for x100\mark

◆ Audit account logon successes for x1000\mark

◆ Audit account logon failures for x1000\mark

I can accomplish this with four separate commands. The first one looks like

```
auditusr /is "x1000\mark":"logon/logoff"
```

Note the /is option, which says "audit successes even if the group policy settings says not to bother." Note also that I've typed Mark's account as "x1000\mark". Let's assume, however, that I'm typing these auditusr commands right on the X1000 system, so from this point on I'll skip the x1000\ prefix. Next, there's the command to audit logon/logoff failures for Mark even if group policies says not to bother with auditing logon/logoff failures. That looks like

```
auditusr /if mark:"logon/logoff"
```

Notice that the only difference is that the /is—"include successes"—option becomes /if, or "include failures." To finish, I just create the same commands again, substituting "account logon" for "logon/logoff":

```
auditusr /is mark:"account logon"
auditusr /if mark:"account logon"
```

But actually I needn't have typed four lines; auditusr lets you stack up more than one area to audit. So I could have alternatively typed just two commands:

```
auditusr /is mark:"account logon","logon/logoff"
auditusr /if mark:"account logon","logon/logoff"
```

See Your System's Current Per-User Audits

That all seemed good, but auditusr's idea of feedback is *not* to produce any output at all when things are fine. On the one hand I appreciate its close-lipped nature, as I often find garrulous applications annoying, but on the other hand there's often what might be called a *Cool Hand Luke* aspect to computing: "What we've got here. . .is a failure to communicate." (In case you've never seen the movie, the line is most effective when spoken in a slow, intimidating, obnoxious drawl.) So it's always nice when you can ask a computer, "What do you *think* we just did?" We can do that with auditusr by just typing **auditusr** without any options. That'll spit back all of the per-user auditing options that it knows of, like so:

```
C:\>auditusr
Auditusr 1.0
X1000\Mark:include:success:Logon/Logoff,Account Logon
X1000\Mark:include:failure:Logon/Logoff,Account Logon
C:\>
```

Notice that auditusr already knew about that "put more than one thing to audit on the same line" thing. Unfortunately, that's all that you can do to reduce your work with auditusr—you can't put, for example, /is /if on the same line, nor can you stack up a lot of user accounts on one line (which makes the fact that you can't use this with groups even more annoying).

Export Per-User Settings

Now suppose I'm decommissioning this system because I've got a new computer, but I like my per-user settings. Here's how to export them to an ASCII file for easy importing to the new system.

1. First, run auditusr with the /e option followed by the name of a file to export the per-user settings to:

   ```
   auditusr /e c:\pesettings.txt
   ```

2. Once that runs, take a look at the file and you'll see that it's formatted identically to the output that you got from just typing **auditusr** all by itself. Copy the file to the new system and import the settings like so:

   ```
   auditusr /i c:\pesettings.txt
   ```

   You can then erase the pesettings.txt file.

Remove All User-Specific Settings

Finally, suppose you want to remove all per-user auditing settings. That's easily done with just one line:

```
auditusr /r
```

Typing **auditusr** all by itself will show that there aren't any per-user settings now.

Tracking Per-User Audit Settings

Before I leave per-user audit settings, I should answer the question that may be on your mind right now: "Hey, wait a minute—so you're telling me that someone with some administrative power could choose to 'fly under the radar' and opt out of being tracked by security audits? Yikes!"

No need to worry, however. Every time that someone creates a per-user audit entry, the Security log in Event Viewer shows it. For example, if I were to exclude my successes from logon/logoff events, I'd find this Event 807 in my Security log:

```
Per user auditing policy set for user:
 Target user:%{S-1-5-21-3595350925-105542128-2184560269-1012}
 Policy ID:(0x0,0x7BC64)
 Category Settings:
  System:0x0
  Logon:0x2
  Object Access0x0
  Privilege Use:0x0
  Detailed Tracking:0x0
  Policy Change:0x0
  Account Management:0x0
  DS Access:0x0
  Account Logon:0x2
```

In the above Event Viewer entry, note that some of the entries have a zero in front of them and some have a one in front of them. The zero entries mean, as you've probably already guessed, that Windows shouldn't audit those things, and the ones mean that it should audit those items.

Summary

While auditusr isn't an earth-shattering addition to Windows, it fulfills a need that I've seen for a long time, and it's a welcome addition. Now you can use your event logs to track security in as focused a manner as you like, greatly improving what might be called the "signal to noise ratio" in your logs.

Chapter 7

Stopping Spyware: Controlling ActiveX and Browser Helper Objects

Worried about spyware? If you're not, then your computer is either never connected to the Internet, or, um, you need to start worrying. Old-style malware like viruses existed mainly to prop up the egos of the maladjusted; spyware exists so that criminals can gather your user IDs, passwords, and the like so that they can steal your money. As money is a fairly powerful motivator, expect spyware to be the vast majority of your malware problems in the future, if it isn't already.

Spyware is different from old-style email attachment viruses, the previous most-common kind of malware, in that it gets on your system in the form of some kind of program added by a user to Internet Explorer. The two most common are called ActiveX controls and Browser Helper Objects (BHOs). You've probably heard of ActiveX controls, but BHOs may not sound familiar. You have almost certainly worked with them, though—the Google Toolbar is an example of a nonmalware BHO. If you've ever had a user complain that every time he tried to go to *one* site on the Web but always ended up at *another* site on the Web, then you've tilted with a BHO of the *bad* variety. So spyware can live in either ActiveX controls or Browser Helper Objects, but "ActiveX controls and Browser Helper Objects" takes an awfully long time to say. That's probably why Microsoft calls ActiveX controls and Browser Helper Objects collectively "add-ons."

Spyware and the Service Packs

XP SP2, 2003 SP1, and R2 all make finding and stopping spyware a bit easier, between Microsoft's free download Windows Defender, a spyware scanner, and some new IE features. (By the time you read this, IE 7 may have shipped and it's got even more antispyware stuff, but I'll just be talking here about the IE 6 that comes with XP SP2, 2003 SP1, and R2.)

One improvement that you may have already noticed is that in IE you can select Manage Add-ons from the Tools menu, which results in a dialog box like the one in Figure 7.1.

This one shows that this particular system only uses three add-ons. The last one is the simplest, so I'll consider it first. It's an ActiveX control, the Macromedia (now part of Adobe) Flash ActiveX control that lets you see all of those cutesy time-wasting animated home pages. The first two comprise the Google Toolbar; apparently it needs both an ActiveX control *and* a BHO. Note to the right of the table that you can even see the particular file that is the actual ActiveX control or Browser Helper Object, a convenient touch. Windows doesn't come with the Flash Player or the Google Toolbar by default, so you've got to go to the Adobe and Google websites to get them. Now, the Adobe and Google folks are good about making it entirely clear that you're downloading a new ActiveX control, but other websites aren't always so clear; for instance, I've been to a few sites that, when visited, pop up a dialog box saying something like, "To enhance your viewing experience at this site, click here," which then downloads and installs some kind of IE-based spyware. (This is a great example of how common sense is the best antimalware tool. When I get that "enhance your viewing pleasure" stuff, I just say, "Hey, it's HTML, dodo—I've already *got* a web browser," and don't let IE load them.) It used to be tough to find all of the IE add-ons on any given client's troubled system, but Manage Add-ons really helps. But the SPs and R2 do even more to let you block the bad stuff from installing in the first place, which is the subject of this chapter.

FIGURE 7.1
Manage Add-ons
dialog box

Add-On Group Policy Settings Overview

One problem with XP SP2 and 2003 SP1, as I've already suggested, is that while they've got some nice features, figuring out how to *use* them isn't always easy.

Of those features, one of my favorites is the ability to create a group policy that lets you define whose ActiveX controls and Browser Helper Objects to install into Internet Explorer and whose to never install.

WARNING The Gator people don't want people referring to their Gator add-on as spyware, so let me be clear that I'm not mentioning Gator at this point, although it'd be an *obvious* example. (Heh heh.)

Now, I knew that the feature existed back when XP SP2 appeared, but I hadn't gotten around to actually figuring out what clicks would make that happen.

And then I *tried* it.

When I sat down to map out the step-by-step methods that would allow me to block a given ActiveX control, I discovered that using the add-on blocking feature is not intuitive at all. (Well, not intuitive unless you know what a CLSID is.) So in this chapter, I'll walk you through the specific steps in blocking and then unblocking a popular add-on, the Google Toolbar. (Please note that I'm not suggesting to anyone that you actually block the Google Toolbar; it's a fabulously useful tool and is definitely not malware. It's just that I need an easy example, and the Google Toolbar is so easy to find.)

If you'd like to follow along, I suggest that you try this out on a test machine. In this example, I'm not going to create a *domain-based* group policy object to accomplish the add-on restrictions; instead, I'll show you how to create the restrictions on that test machine's *local* group policy object (GPO). I'm doing that because it's easier to try group policy settings on the local GPO, and besides, I don't want to tempt anyone into testing out such a powerful setting in their production environment. Once you're comfortable with it on the local GPO, then of course it's simple to re-implement it on a live AD's domain-based GPOs. (And if you're not comfortable with group policies, then take a look back in Chapters 8 and 9 of the *Mastering Windows Server 2003* book.)

First, Get the Class ID

Before we dive into the Group Policy Editor, we need one fairly obscure bit of information: the Class ID of the particular ActiveX control or Browser Helper Object. As you'll see, the group policy settings that let you block a particular add-on identify the add-on not by its name, but by one or more long strings of hexadecimal called *CLSIDs*, which is computerese for *class ID*. For example, the Google Toolbar has two CLSIDs, 2318C2B1-4965-11D4-9B18-009027A5CD4F and AA58ED58-01DD-4D91-8333-CF10577473F7.

How did I get *them*, I hear you cry? There are actually four different ways to discover the CLSID(s) of a renegade add-on (or, for that matter, any add-on):

1. Search the Internet for it/them.

2. Install the add-on on a test system and use Manage Add-ons to show the CLSID(s).

3. View the HTML source on the page that the add-on is loaded from, searching for the phrase "CLSID."

4. Read Microsoft Knowledge Base article 555235, which lists some CLSIDs of internal Microsoft add-ons.

Let's cover those in some more detail.

Search the Internet

I know, the acronym STFW (Search The, uh, *Friendly* Web) has become as common a derisive response to a user question as RTFM (Read the *Friendly* Manual), but in this case it's the way to go. I Googled "clsid spyware list" and got several web pages with useful (and, sadly, plentiful) lists of bad add-ons and their CLSIDs.

In this case, then, the lazy person's way may be the best way!

Ask Manage Add-ons

Here's another way to get the CLSID of a baddie. Set up a test system that you will immediately wipe when done—it's times like this that I must repeat that Microsoft's Virtual Server and VMWare's VMWare Server are *free* and both include image snapshot/undo features, which make cleanup after the kind of not-so-safe surfing that we'll be doing a lot easier.

On your test machine, surf to the page where you can install the bad add-on, and install it. Then open Tools ➤ Manage Add-ons. I know, there's no CLSIDs there, *but* now right-click anywhere on the headings of the Manage Add-ons dialog—the row containing Name, Status, Type, and the like. You'll see that you get a drop-down rectangle overlaying the list of installed add-ons, as in Figure 7.2.

This section of the Manage Add-ons dialog shows that you can get the dialog to cough up a lot more than just name and the like; you can display the CLSID. Once you've done that, you can also grab the CLSID heading with the mouse and drag it right over to the left, so you end up with the name of the add-on right next to the CLSID. Manage Add-ons then looks like Figure 7.3.

The only bad news is that, um, well, you can't click the CLSIDs and copy them to the Clipboard. Yes, it's silly, but IE makes you retype the blasted things. (This is how I got the two CLSIDs for the Google Toolbar.) Or just use the next method.

FIGURE 7.2
Optional columns in Manage Add-ons

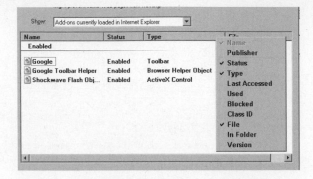

FIGURE 7.3
The CLSIDs revealed!

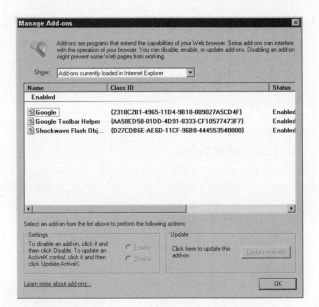

Find the CLSID in the HTML

No matter how dark the intentions of the spyware-wielding web page, it's got to include right in its HTML text the CLSID of the add-on that it's trying to get you to install. If the CLSID on the web page and the CLSID embedded in the add-on don't match, then IE will never try to download the add-on. (This is how I found Flash's CLSID the first time I looked for it.)

Again, surf to the page that the bad add-on loads from, but decline to install it. Instead, right-click that page near the spot on the page where you see the button, hyperlink, or graphic that's saying "click me to install" or whatever it says. If there is a pop-up offering you the add-on, then right-click that instead. If you see in the resulting menu the words View Source then choose that; if not, then click nearby it until View Source appears. The HTML source will appear in Notepad.

From Notepad, find the phrase "CLSID" and, following it, you will find the CLSID of the offending add-on.

Look Up the "Mystery" CLSIDs in KB555235

As you'll see soon, you can use these Knowledge Base settings in either a *blacklist* mode, where your users can install any add-ons *except* a list of baddies that you create, or a *whitelist* mode whereby all add-ons will be blocked except for a list of trusted add-ons that you create. Clearly the second approach, the whitelist, is the more secure approach, although it involves a bit more work. In particular, you will find that things like Outlook Web Access stop working. So you think to yourself, "Hmmm…OWA must be an add-on; I wonder what its CLSID is?" But you don't install it from a web page, and it doesn't show up on Manage Add-ons.

As it turns out, there are a couple of dozen things in IE that have CLSIDs, but those CLSIDs are embedded in the IE program itself. The only way to get them is by asking Microsoft—and KB555235 is the answer.

Creating a Whitelist via Group Policy

With the Google Toolbar's CLSIDs safely in hand, let's put group policy to work. First, we'll set things up so that *only* the Google Toolbar can run, blocking all other add-ons. As I've already said, my example will walk you through the process of controlling add-ons on just one machine through that machine's local group policy object. The process is nearly identical if you decide that you like the add-on control and decide to implement it domain-wide via a domain-based group policy object (GPO).

Locate the Add-on Management GP Settings

First, let's find the relevant settings for controlling add-ons in the welter of group policy settings. XP SP2 introduced *619* new types of group policy settings, 2003 SP1 added a bunch more, and R2 threw in some of its own, so you'd be forgiven for feeling a bit befuddled when searching for the setting that will get any job done. (Before XP SP2, the total number of group policy settings that let you control Internet Explorer was 11. SP2 added about 600 settings. Makes you wonder why there isn't a Ctrl-F (Find) item in the Group Policy Editor.) Open Group Policy Editor and navigate to the category that holds the relevant settings like so:

1. Log onto a freshly installed test system running XP SP2, 2003 SP1, or R2. Make sure you're logged on as a local administrator. (By the way, if you're not sure if you're currently logged on as an administrator, open up a command line and type `whoami /all|find "Administrators"`—if you get no output then you're not an admin, if you get a line that starts with `BUILTIN\Administrators`, then you're an admin.)

2. Click Start ➢ Run.

3. In the Run dialog, type **gpedit.msc** and click OK.

4. In the Group Policy Microsoft Management Console that appears, open Computer Configuration, then the folder (*category* is the more exact group policy word), Administrative Tools, then Windows Components, Internet Explorer, Security Features, and finally Add-on Management.

NOTE   And yes, if you're wondering why this stuff that lets you restrict downloading and running ActiveX controls isn't found in the categories (folders) that actually *do* exist and are specifically named Restrict ActiveX Install or Restrict File Download, then that makes two of us. But remember what I always say: Hey, if this stuff gets easy, we'll all have to go find jobs.

The particular group policy looks like Figure 7.4.

5. In that category/folder, you'll see just four settings: Deny all add-ons unless specifically allowed in the Add-on List, Add-on List, Process List, and All Processes. We're going to work with the first two.

As I said before, you can either set this up in whitelist or blacklist mode. Under the new XP and 2003 service packs and under R2, IE's default behavior is the same as it has always been: any user can download and install any ActiveX control or Browser Helper Object. (In other words, a blacklist—everything's fine except for the things that are specifically disallowed.) You name those specifically disallowed things in a list under the group policy setting named Add-on List.

IE can also act in a whitelist mode, whereby the Add-on List isn't a list of the few disallowed add-ons but instead a list of the few *allowed* add-ons. You control whether it's a blacklist or a whitelist with the group policy setting Deny all add-ons unless specifically in the Add-on List; enable Deny all add-ons and the Add-on List becomes a whitelist. Disable it or leave it in its default state, and the Add-on List is a blacklist.

FIGURE 7.4
Add-on Management
group policy category

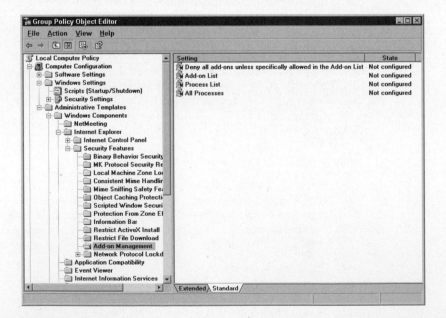

Actually, you can name add-ons and then either designate them as acceptable *or* unacceptable. Why name something as unacceptable when Deny all add-ons unless specifically allowed in the Add-on List makes everything unacceptable by default? Because you might have a different approach to controlling add-ons: maybe you don't mind what people download and use, so long as it's not (to pick an infamous example) Xupiter. In that case, you wouldn't bother with the Deny all policy. So you can either blackball everything and create exceptions, or allow everything and veto a few exceptions.

Block 'Em All: Make the List a Whitelist

Let's start with the "nothing's okay unless I approve it" or whitelist approach. To do that, you'd start with the Deny all policy setting. Double-click the Deny all add-ons unless specifically allowed in the Add-on List setting and check the Enabled radio button, then click OK. You needn't log off and back on, and you needn't even run gpupdate; apparently IE rereads the effect of this group policy setting every time it's refreshed. A simple F5, then, will cause IE to realize that it's no longer supposed to allow any add-ons. (A nice feature, but it makes you wonder how much it slows IE down, y'know?)

Try it out: go to the toolbar's site at `www.google.com/toolbar`, click Download Google Toolbar and try to install the Google Toolbar. The installation will seem to run fine, but when it's done, the final installation web page will say "Google Toolbar is now installed on your browser," and there's even an arrow pointing to where the Toolbar is supposed to be...but isn't. No error messages, no complaints that you tried to do something wrong, just a straightforward blocking of the toolbar and, for that matter, all other add-ons—including things like Microsoft Update.

TIP   Normally when I talk about the add-on management feature of group policies, I use Macromedia Flash as my example, as it's probably the best-known add-on. But when as I write this in May 2006, I find that if I disable all add-ons and go to the Macromedia site intending to download Flash, something odd happens. Clicking the link to download Flash or, for that matter, Shockware, causes the Macromedia Downloads Web page—which, again, is *now* run by Adobe—to offer me the *Macintosh* Flash player. Returning to the page without add-ons disabled offers the Windows version of the Flash add-on. Clearly IE with restrictions looks Mac-ish to Adobe. That's why my example here is the Google Toolbar rather than my first choice, Flash.

Now Permit Google Toolbar to Run

Clearly we're not going to get very far with a copy of IE that cannot use ActiveX controls like Shockwave, Flash, Windows Update, Trend's free housecall.antivirus.com scanner, or browser helpers like the Google Toolbar. So, while it's nice to know that we're protected from all of the bad add-ons out there, we *do* need the good add-ons. We can override the "don't allow anything" setting, adding in exceptions with the next group policy setting, Add-on list. Let's see how to allow the Google Toolbar.

1. Open up Group Policy Editor again (Start ➢ Run ➢ gpedit.msc).

2. Return to the Computer Configuration/Administrative Templates/Windows Components/Internet Explorer/Security Features/Add-on Management category.

3. This time, double-click the Add-on List setting and click Enabled, then Show to see the Add-on List. It'll look like Figure 7.5.

4. When you first open that list, you'll see two columns, Value Name and Value. Click Add and you'll get a dialog box like Figure 7.6.

I have already filled in the things that the Add Item dialog needs, but I think you'd agree that it's not the clearest dialog box in Windows—what's an "item" and a "value" of the item?

FIGURE 7.5
Dialog box that
allows you to control
the add-on

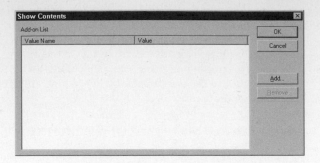

FIGURE 7.6
First Google Toolbar
add-on specified
in the Add Item
dialog box

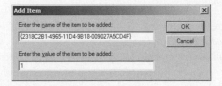

Item refers to the add-on that you want to allow (as the list is currently a whitelist) or disallow (when it's a blacklist). *Value* is one of three possible numbers:

◆ 0 means "don't run this add-on."

◆ 1 means "let this run."

◆ 2 means "let the user control this add-on."

The name of the item refers to how Windows wants you to identify a particular ActiveX control or browser helper; as you've probably guessed by now, it's the CLSID of the add-on that you want to allow or disallow. (The first, actually, as the Google Toolbar requires two add-ons.) Type or cut and paste that CLSID into the Value Name field, and enclose it in braces—don't enter 2318C2B1-4965-11D4-9B18-009027A5CD4F, enter {2318C2B1-4965-11D4-9B18-009027A5CD4F}.

TIP I've forgotten those stupid braces many times, leading me to scratch my head, reboot the system a half-dozen times and wonder why the silly Add-ons Management group policies aren't working…and then I remember the braces. So be smarter than me, and remember the braces.

Once you've got the value name and the value—1, recall—then click OK to return to the Show Contents dialog.

1. Next, we'll add the second add-on for the Google Toolbar. Again, click Add to raise the Add Item dialog.

2. In the Enter the name of the item to be added field, fill in the CLSID of the second Google Toolbar add-on, **{AA58ED58-01DD-4D91-8333-CF10577473F7}**, braces and all, and in the Enter the value of the item to be added field, enter a **1**, signifying that you want this add-on to be able to run.

3. Click OK to close the Add Item dialog box, then OK to close the Show Contents dialog box, then OK to close the Add-on List Properties dialog box.

Close any open copies of IE—a simple refresh won't do the job because the toolbar lives in the frame of IE—and you'll see the toolbar. (Interestingly enough, you *did* just install the Google Toolbar before; you just didn't see it because the Add-on List blocked it.) No other add-ons will run, however. To allow other add-ons, just repeat the process.

But the group policy setting is just the high-level interface; what's happening in the Registry? Inside the HKEY_LOCAL_MACHINE\SOFTWARE\Microsoft\Windows\CurrentVersion\ policies\Ext key, you'll find a new key, CLSID. In that key you'll find a REG_SZ entry whose name is the CLSID of one of the Google Toolbar components, and whose value is either 0, 1, or 2.

Similarly, there's a direct Registry hack to make the Add-on list a whitelist or blacklist. Enabling the Deny all add-ons unless specifically allowed in the Add-on List works by setting a Registry entry in HKEY_LOCAL_MACHINE\SOFTWARE\Microsoft\Windows\CurrentVersion\ policies\Ext named RestrictToList, a REG_DWORD. When set to 1, this value entry disallows all browser add-ons except for the ones listed in the Add-on List; 0 has the effect of either disabling the policy or leaving it as not configured.

Now Turn the Tables—Everything *but* Toolbar Runs

I think what I've presented so far covers the way that most people would use this—reject all ActiveX controls and browser helpers *except* for the small group of acceptable ones. But for some the story will different; for those folks, it might make more sense to allow every single ActiveX control, except for a few bad eggs. How can the new add-on control serve their needs? Simple: with a blacklist. First, do not enable the Deny all add-ons unless specifically allowed in the Add-on List setting; either disable it or leave it as not configured. Second, for any add-ons that you want to prohibit, first find their CLSIDs as before and add them to the Add-on List, but set their values not to 1 (allow add-on to run) but to 0 (disallow add-on). Anyone trying to install or use those add-ons will fail, but anything else will run.

WARNING   And here's an irritating note: if you want to change the 1 to a 0 or vice versa in the Show Contents dialog box, you've got to retype the whole CLSID. You can't just edit an existing entry in Show Contents. Nor can you copy and paste the CLSID from the existing group policy setting. Of course, now that you know where it's hiding in the Registry, you can copy and paste from there.

I've found these new group policy settings that provide add-on blocking pretty useful, and so have my clients. But before I go, let me suggest that you go back to the Group Policy Editor and remove all of the settings that we did. Trying to get to Microsoft Update, only to find that you've been blocked by some mysterious force can be frightening and time-consuming!

Summary

The numbers of spyware masters and their foul myrmidons are growing, as are their deceptive tactics as they try to socially engineer your users into installing some truly bad software. There is no one tool to fend them all off, but this one, built into XP SP2 and 2003 SP1, should have a place in your arsenal.

Chapter 8

Locking Up the Ports: Windows Firewall

One of Microsoft's strongest responses to the ongoing buffer-overflow-worm threat was a complete rewriting of the software firewall incorporated into XP, 2003, and R2. They renamed the firewall from Internet Connection Firewall (ICF) to Windows Firewall (WF). They also added something called IPsec bypass that extends the firewall's ability to allow you to easily require a secure server to authenticate not just incoming users, but *machines*. In this chapter, you'll see what WF does, what issues it can raise, and how to configure it so that it suits your security needs best.

What Is Windows Firewall?

How can an operating system have a firewall, anyway? Isn't a firewall a box with blinking lights and a bunch of cables coming out of it? The answer is that the term *firewall* refers to any of a number of ways to shield a computer network from other networks, networks rife with untrustworthy people—you know, networks like the Internet. Let's dig down a bit further, however, and start with a look at what a firewall is, basically.

What Firewalls Do

With the advent of the Industrial Revolution, people started building things driven by steam power, such as locomotives, ships, and the like. Creating steam required fire, and fire's a scary thing, at least when it gets out of hand. To protect against fire-related problems, those locomotives, ships, and the like were designed so that a thick, sturdy, nearly fireproof wall existed between wherever the fire was kept—usually a boiler—and the rest of the vehicle. That way, if something caught fire in the boiler's compartment, then the onboard engineers would have a bit more time to put out the fire without having to worry about the fire immediately spreading to the rest of the craft. Later on, we started using internal combustion engines and they, too, can catch fire, so things like automobiles and private aircraft have firewalls designed into them. (In fact, the "wall" referred to when people say that something is running "balls to the wall" is the firewall. You control a small aircraft's engine speed by moving a ball-shaped control called the *throttle*. Pulling it back toward you reduces the engine's speed; pushing the ball forward—"to the firewall"—increases engine speed.)

Basically, then, a firewall's job is to contain bad stuff. But where engine firewalls contain a relatively small space so as to contain a fire, computer network firewalls attempt to contain a truly huge space: the Internet. Firewalls exist to make it harder for dirtbags to attack our networks.

How Firewalls Work

Firewall is one of those words that sounds so good—just put one box between your network and the Internet, and you're safe from all of the baddies—that people use the term to mean a lot of things.

PORT-FILTERING FIREWALLS

The earliest kind of firewall was a box that sat between an internal network and the Internet. Now, if you think about it, what sort of box *normally* sits between our network and the Internet? Probably a router and, in fact, many firewalls are just routers with a bit of intelligence added.

Consider what an IP router does, as you see in the following figure.

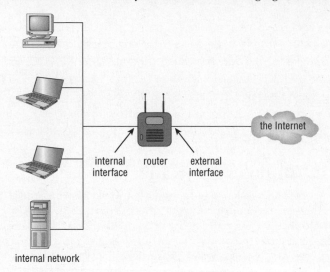

On the left you see the internal network (including PCs, laptops, and servers), on the right the Internet. In between is the IP router, which has at least two interfaces—the one that connects to the Internet (which may be an Ethernet cable, a wireless connection, a modem, an ISDN connection, a DSL connection, a frame relay, or perhaps a cable modem), and the one that connects to the internal network (which is usually an Ethernet connection). The router is a very simple computer that listens to messages sent to it from either the internal or external interface.

Yes, that's right—a router is a computer running a very simple program; here's how it works. Suppose the IP addresses that you use in your network are ones in the range of 200.100.7 to 200.100.7.254. (Yes, that is a range of routable addresses. Nonroutable addresses didn't appear in the Internet originally; we'll get to that in a minute.) Here are the instructions that essentially capture a router's entire program:

♦ Listen to IP packets sent to either the internal or external interface.

♦ If a packet needs to go to an address in the range of 200.100.7.1 to 200.100.7.254, then resend the packet onto the internal network.

♦ If a packet needs to go anywhere else, assume that address is on the Internet, and resend the packet on the external interface.

That's all there is to it. Sure, routers can actually handle more complicated sets of, "If I get a message destined for IP range *X* then I should resend it on interface *Y*," but my example encapsulates enough for our firewall discussion.

Now let's make the router a bit smarter. Suppose you've got some jerk trying to connect to your server—the big PC in your network—via TCP port 139, one of the ports you use when you do a NET USE command. You don't want them doing that because it ties up the server, and if they try logging on with enough user names and passwords, they might figure out one of your accounts. (This is a simple example, so imagine that there are no account lockouts.) So you (somehow) hack the program in your router and give it an extra rule:

If a packet appears on the *external* interface destined for an address on the internal network, *and* if that packet is destined for TCP port 139, just discard the packet; don't transmit it.

Here, then, is an example of a working firewall. A very simple one, to be sure, but a working firewall. Because the firewall's program (called the firewall *rules* by most) decides what to pass and what not to pass based on the destination port, such a firewall is called a port-filtering firewall.

Now, in my example I only blocked one port. But you may know that in the real world, people tend to configure port-filtering routers with rules like "block all incoming traffic on all ports *except* for such-and-such port ranges." Additionally, consider that the one rule that I've shown you—"block all traffic destined for an internal IP address on TCP port 139"—refers only to *incoming* traffic. Port-filtering firewalls can, however, usually filter *outgoing* traffic as well. For example, your firm might have discovered at some time that employees were running websites of their own that featured, well, content of questionable legality and taste, and so you want to keep people from running web servers on every computer except for your official web server. If the official web server had address 200.100.7.33, then you could create a firewall rule that said, "If a packet appears on the internal interface destined for some address on the Internet, and if the packet originated from port 80, and if the packet's source does *not* have the IP address 200.100.7.33, then discard it." You'll see, however, that WF does not offer you the option to block outgoing traffic, just incoming traffic.

NAT FIREWALLS

For almost anyone who first started doing Internet networking after about 1996, that example might have seemed odd. Put routable addresses to every desktop machine? Crazy, you might think. But the notion of creating an internal network of IP addresses in the range of 10.x.x.x, or 192.168.x.x, or the range of IP addresses from 172.16.0.0 through 172.31.255.255 first appeared in March 1994 with RFC 1597, "Address Allocation for Private Internets." The idea was that people might need IP addresses to run a TCP/IP-based network but might not need access to the public Internet. Of course, that's not the case for most of us. You want lots of IP addresses, so the three ranges of "private network addresses" are widely used, but you also want to be able to have those networks talk to the public Internet, which is where May 1994's RFC 1631, "The IP Network Address Translator," fills the bill.

NAT routers have at least two interfaces, as did the simple router, but NAT routers contain a somewhat more complex routing program. A single NAT router may have only one routable IP address on its external interface, but that router's also clever enough to be able to allow all of those "private"—*non*routable—addresses to carry on conversations with systems on the Internet by sharing that one routable IP address. (This was covered in more detail in Chapter 6 of *Mastering Windows Server 2003*.) The toughest part of NAT routing is that notion that the router can carry on a bunch of different conversations between its internal computers and various servers out on the public Internet. For example, suppose ten systems behind the NAT router were all talking to Microsoft's web server. When Microsoft's web server responds to one of the ten systems, how does the NAT router know which of its internal systems this is destined for? The answer is that every system talking to Microsoft's web server talks to that web server on port 80, but the web server responds to each of those systems on different ports. So, for example, if the web server were to respond to all ten systems at the same time, then the IP packets that comprise those responses would all specify a source IP address of whatever Microsoft's web server is, and port 80. But while the *destination* IP addresses would all be the same—the routable IP address of the NAT router—each of them would be destined for a different TCP port number. The NAT router must, then, keep track of the fact that X machine on the inside intranet is having a conversation with Y machine on the Internet, and that conversation uses Z port number. That information is called the *state*, and any router that keeps track of states of conversations is said to be a *stateful* router. That'll be useful later.

But how do Internet conversations *start* on a NAT system? In every case, a system on the intranet must initiate the conversation by contacting a server on the Internet. That's worth highlighting:

NOTE   In client-server communications, which is pretty much the only kind of communications we do on the Internet, the client *starts* the conversation by sending an *unsolicited* request to the server. We'll return to this notion a bit later, but for now, remember that client requests are seen as unsolicited packets to a server, and server packets are always responses of some kind.

This leads to an interesting side-effect of NAT: it's a kind of firewall. Inasmuch as all of those systems attached to the inner interface of the NAT router have nonroutable addresses, it is flatly impossible for a system on the public Internet to initiate a conversation. It can only respond, which means that a NAT router says to the Internet, "Internet, I love you but I don't trust you—so do me a favor and only speak to me when I first speak to you."

Let me not, however, leave you with the idea that a NAT router's "firewallish" nature is great protection for your network. Remember that any internal computer can start up a conversation, so all a bad guy needs to attack your network is one computer on the inside to "invite it in." How would that happen? If someone visited a website and downloaded a malicious ActiveX control. Or if someone opened an email attachment that included some malware.

SOFTWARE FIREWALLS

Now I've explained enough firewall background to start telling you how WF works. You've already read that a simple NAT router without any official firewall features acts as something of a firewall in passing because of its stateful nature. That leads us to *software* firewalls.

The idea of a software firewall isn't a new one. In fact, some of the earliest firewalls were actually just complex pieces of software that you installed on a regular old computer. You'd then put two Ethernet cards in the computer—one connected to the intranet, one to the Internet—and that was your firewall. Nor is that an outdated notion; one of the most popular firewalls among Windows users is Microsoft's Internet Security and Acceleration Server, or ISA Server.

But I'm not talking here about something like ISA Server, which lets you create the computer that stands between your network and the Internet. I'm talking instead about something called a "personal firewall," a piece of software that you might run on every single computer in your network. It is a program that runs on a computer and that acts in some way to restrict the flow of IP traffic into or, in some cases, out of the computer so as to keep bad programs out.

Loads of personal firewalls have appeared over the years. The first one that I recall hearing of was called Black Ice. One that's been around for almost as long but seems well-known is something called Zone Alarm that many people like but I've found annoying. The big "security suites" offered by Trend, Grisoft, Panda Software, McAfee, and others tend to include a personal firewall as well.

While WF is relatively new, Windows has contained at least some of the rudiments of a software firewall for a long time. For example, ever since at least NT 3.5 it's been possible to go to TCP/IP Advanced Properties and block all ports except for those specified in a list—a crude firewall, but, if you're willing to do some typing to enter all of the allowed ports, you could create a very simple port-filtering firewall on your computer. And, since February of 2000, Windows has included IPsec, a quite powerful method for securing TCP/IP stacks that lets you create a series of firewall rules as flexible as any you might want, like "block all incoming traffic on TCP port 1433 unless it's from IP address 34.11.98.7." You could, with some work, create a monster batch file full of IPsec commands that would be the software-based firewall envy of your friends. But it'd be a lot of work.

TIP   By the way, did you notice in the last paragraph that I spelled "IPsec" with a little "s" instead of "IPSec," as might make more sense given that it's short for "Internet Protocol Security?" A look at the IPsec-related RFCs—there are a dozen, from RFC 2401 through 2412—shows that IPsec's inventors choose to spell it with the small "s" and, well, they get to define how to spell the thing, so I'm following that convention here and in my other writing. Note that this puts me at odds with most of Microsoft, as their GUI stuff all spells it with the cap "S."

CONTENT FILTERING FIREWALLS

Before I leave this brief discussion of firewalls, I should mention a newer sort of firewall: the content filtering firewall. Building firewalls solely out of rules constructed from ports and IP addresses is helpful but less and less effective in today's world. The people who want to provide server services in an organization are often not the same people as the ones charged with network security and firewall operation, and so the folks who want to provide some new network service sometimes come into conflict with the firewall folks. But, many clever content and service providers realize, there's a way around the firewall people… port 80. HTTP port 80 is, you probably know, the standard port for communicating with a web server and, well, there are very few firewall people who can deny a server guy's request that they open port 80.

As a result, more and more types of developers of various types of network services have crafted their services so that they live atop HTTP itself. Terminal Services, when run as the TSWEB tool, needs only port 80 open. Many online chat programs run entirely on port 80. Web-based email clients like Outlook Web access mean that you can access not just email but public folders, mail handling rules, and the like, all over port 80. By stacking everything atop port 80, the network world both avoids firewalls and, unfortunately, makes them considerably less useful. That led to a tongue-in-cheek RFC 3093 dated 1 April 2001—yes, that was April Fool's Day 2001—called the "Firewall Enhancement Protocol" that details what I've said in the paragraph, but in a much techier way.

Well, those firewall guys aren't going to take *this* lying down, no siree. So firewalls like ISA Server not only let you control the firewall via ports and IP addresses; ISA server also has intelligent filters that look at the particular HTTP traffic, letting you block not only a given port, but a given kind of data stream. It does more than just watch ports—it looks inside the data packets for suspicious-looking data. Such a firewall is called a *content filtering firewall*. (And no, Windows Firewall doesn't include such behavior. At least, not yet.)

Windows Firewall Basics

Writing that batch file might be impressive, but, again, it'd be a lot of work. Fortunately, you needn't do that, because of the things that WF does. Put briefly, here's an overview of what kind of firewall services it offers and what else might be appealing about it.

◆   Basically, WF is a stateful packet filter; by default, all packets trying to enter a system with WF enabled will be discarded unless those packets are responses to queries from that system. Unsolicited packets never get past the TCP/IP stack.

◆   WF lets you create exceptions for particular ports from particular ranges of IP addresses; for example, it's possible to say, "Accept unsolicited packets on port 25, but only from the range of addresses from 192.168.0.1 through 192.168.0.254." When paired with IPsec on Server 2003 and R2, WF can do some impressive things via something called *IPsec bypass*.

◆ Windows lets its firewall behave in two different ways ("profiles"): one where the system is inside the corporate firewall, and another when outside the firewall. (Clearly having two different behaviors for WF is of more interest to XP users—XP SP2 introduced WF—than to server users, as most of us don't carry our servers outside the building.)

◆ WF may not be the most full-featured of firewalls, but it may have the most broad-spectrum means of control of almost any Windows feature. First, you can control it from a fairly comprehensive command-line interface via the `netsh` command. Second, WF has near-complete group policy setting-based control. Finally, it's got a GUI.

◆ Unlike its predecessor ICF, Windows Firewall starts up *before* the TCP/IP stack does. ICF had the troublesome aspect that it started after the TCP/IP stack did, leaving the stack unprotected for a few seconds on bootup.

A good, but not great, list of abilities. Still, a great improvement over the ICF firewall originally shipped with XP and 2003.

The Specific WF "Firewall Rules"

Still wondering if WF is worth looking at? Then let's get very specific about what it blocks and what it can't block, why Microsoft took the time to create this newer WF, and whether or not you should consider enabling it on your 2003 or R2 system (it's disabled by default) or whether to disable it on your XP boxes (it's enabled by default).

First, let's more exactly answer the question, "How does WF decide whether to block or pass information?" With just a few rules.

WF MUST BE ENABLED TO DO ANYTHING

First, of course, it's got to be enabled before it'll monitor packets. It is, again, off by default on Server 2003 SP1 and R2 and on by default on XP SP2.

WF NEVER BLOCKS OUTGOING TRAFFIC

If your computer wants to send out an IP packet of any kind to any system on the Internet, then WF couldn't give a hoot. Now, this turned out to be a fairly controversial issue at Microsoft, and an early version of WF in XP SP2 could block outgoing traffic. The idea was that if the buffer overflow worm *du jour* entered your system via port 515 (I'm making that up) and, after infecting your system, it tried to communicate with other systems on port 515, then it might be nice to be able to write a group policy that would block any outgoing messages destined for port 515, caging the worm until all of the infected systems could be found and disinfected. It didn't seem like a bad idea at the time, but some folks had an argument against it, and so WF will always pass outgoing packets. (And, in an interesting Part 2 to the story, Vista's version of WF will supposedly allow you to block outgoing packets. We'll see.)

WF BLOCKS ALL INCOMING PACKETS *EXCEPT* ONES THAT ARE RESPONSES TO REQUESTS, OR IF THE PACKET IS DESTINED FOR A PORT THAT YOU HAVE MADE AN EXCEPTION FOR

For example, suppose you're sitting at a Server 2003 SP1 system with WF enabled. You start up IE to visit Microsoft Update. WF does not block the outgoing initial request to Microsoft Update, as I've already said. But it also remembers that there's an outstanding HTTP request to Microsoft Update.

Eventually Microsoft Update's web server sends a packet back to your 2003 SP1 system. WF is by nature suspicious of any incoming packet and so examines this one with the full intention of just dropping it on the floor. But then it consults its state table, which reminds it that this packet is from Microsoft Update, and we're *expecting* a response from Microsoft Update, so it passes.

Alternatively, suppose that Server 2003 system that I just said you accessed Microsoft Update from also runs server software of some kind; suppose it's running some SMTP/POP3 software and so acts as an Internet email server. SMTP uses TCP port 25 and POP3 uses TCP port 110. Thus, if this server is your firm's email server, then whenever anyone outside of your organization tries to send you some email, they (well, their email server, actually) will do that by sending a request to your 2003 server on its port 25. If the firewall's up, then what happens? Well, a request from some outsider that your 2003 server receive some email looks to WF like an unsolicited communication. Now, recall my note from a few pages back: *clients solicit, servers respond*. Put that together with what you've seen about WF's packet filtering rules, and I hope you'll see that turning on WF on a server of any kind presents a big potential problem:

NOTE   Because the requests that get client-server computing going are by their nature unsolicited, installing a stateful firewall on a server will make that server useless…unless you get the firewall to relax a bit.

By "relax a bit," I mean that a purely stateful firewall wouldn't work on a server; instead, stateful firewalls must also let you make what Microsoft calls *exceptions*. There are two kinds of exceptions: *port exceptions* and *program exceptions*. A port exception is just WF's way of acting like an old-style port-filtering router. Using the command line, GUI, or group policy, you'll see a bit later that you can say, "Hey, WF, let in any traffic on port 25, whether it's solicited or not." A program exception, in contrast, is where you say to WF, "Hey, whatever ports XYZ program needs you to open for unsolicited communications, just open." Once you open port 25 on the 2003 server, the mail can arrive.

So you've seen how WF would allow a response to pass because of WF's state table, and how it might allow a piece of Internet email to pass because of an exception. Now let's consider a situation where you *wouldn't* want WF passing a packet. Suppose there were some buffer-overflow-exploiting worm floating around, knocking on port 515 of every system that it meets to see if that system has the imaginary "port 515 vulnerability" that I supposed earlier. In this case, WF would see the incoming packet, examine its state table, and say, "Hey, we didn't initiate a conversation with that system; discard the packet," and the packet never gets to port 515 on our Server 2003 system.

Those three cases are, in a nutshell, examples of what WF does most of the time: pass all outgoing traffic, pass incoming responses, pass incoming exceptions, and reject all other incoming traffic.

WF's Role = DEP's Worm-Fighting Cousin

So why would Microsoft put a software firewall in Windows? Partly because most of the competitors all cost money (Zone Alarm's the exception, although you've got to do a bit of hunting to find the free one on their site), but mostly because the people who need personal firewalls most are the people who'd be the least likely to go buy one, so making it a default item in Windows is intended to slow down the growth of the next worm. In many ways, WF's in Windows for the same reason that Data Execution Prevention is there: as a sort of generic defense against buffer-overflow-exploiting worms.

Recall how a worm like Blaster attacks a system. There's a program listening on port 135 called RPCSS.DLL with a bug allowing a possible buffer overflow attack. RPCSS.DLL runs as LocalSystem, an account that can do *anything* on your computer, and so any worm successfully injecting code into RPCSS.DLL would then run as LocalSystem (because the new code looks to the computer like the regular old RPCSS.DLL program). To attack a computer would not, recall, require any user intervention; instead, all the worm would need to attack a system would be for the worm to be able to "see" port 135.

Of course, by default computers expose all of their ports; it's only with some kind of firewall technology that they do *not* expose them. That's where WF might have greatly reduced the spread of Blaster. You may recall that a major reason for DEP was its generic ability to combat worms because of the sequence of events that occur leading up to a new worm: first someone finds a potential buffer overflow, and then Microsoft releases a patch. After Microsoft releases the patch, there's a race between the bad guys, who try to create a worm that exploits the buffer overflow *on the unpatched systems*, and the systems administrators who must first speedily test the patch to ensure that it won't crash their systems, and then roll out the patch. Given the millions and millions of systems that were infected by Blaster, it's clear that it's a race that the bad guys often win. The beauty of DEP, then, is that it can detect many attempts at buffer overflows, making systems more generically buffer-overflow-resistant. That's nice because it may buy us overworked systems admins a few more days or weeks to test those patches before rolling them out.

Windows Firewall is similar to DEP because if used properly it, too, can shift the odds in the bad-guys-versus-good-guys race. Remember the two ingredients that Blaster needed: first, a buffer overflow possibility, and, two, access to port 135. (I'm simplifying, as it was theoretically possible to use a *number* of ports to exploit the buffer overflow bug that Blaster used.) DEP tries to detect and block the first ingredient; WF blocks the second. If everyone running an XP system (the target of Blaster) had *not* been patched but *had* a working firewall in place blocking unsolicited transmissions to port 135, then Blaster wouldn't have ever made it out of the starting gate.

As far as I can see, and from what I've heard from Microsoft people, the largest motivation for completely rewriting Internet Connection Firewall into the vastly different Windows Firewall was the Blaster worm. Microsoft released patch MS03-026 in July 2003 and about three weeks later, Blaster appeared, exploiting the bug that MS03-026 patched on unpatched XP systems. Now, it's not like Microsoft was secretive about this patch and the importance of deploying it. Dozens of journalists like me told millions of readers that MS03-206 was a huge gaping hole that the bad guys would be completely unable to resist, and believe me, we didn't need to be prescient to know that: the weakness exposed by MS03-026 was so *prima facie* that anyone reading the description of the security bulletin announcing the patch would come to the same conclusion. Here in the U.S., the Office of Homeland Security actually issued announcements telling people to get the patch. Anyone using Windows Update would get the patch automatically. But despite all that, literally millions of people had their unpatched systems infected. Antivirus vendors reported as late as *two years* after the Blaster outbreak that they saw hundreds of Blaster infections around the globe a day. Put simply, not patching against Blaster was very unwise, and apparently there are many, many unwise users. But the problem with unwise users is that they don't just affect themselves; their infected systems clog the Internet by constantly scanning for more vulnerable systems to infect. To repurpose an old phrase, when it comes to Internet worms, "If you're not part of the solution, you're part of the problem."

Here, then, is one of the major motivators for WF: Microsoft believed, probably correctly, that there are enough people out there using Windows who don't know and/or don't care about system security. Folks like that would be, again, certainly welcome to expose themselves to the malware of the week, *if* it weren't for the fact that their inattention affects others. So Microsoft built a vastly improved software firewall, put it in XP SP2, and *turned it on by default*. Their reasoning seems to be, "If a user wants to skip caring about keeping their system safe, no problem—but that person will probably also not choose to spend the time to turn off the firewall." Thus, WF as a default on XP (and Vista, actually) protects the rest of us on the Internet from the clueless. Probably not a bad answer.

NOTE On the other hand, Microsoft assumes that anyone running Server 2003 has at least something of a clue, and so it's not enabled by default on Server 2003 SP1 or R2.

When To Use (or Not Use) WF

Enabling Windows Firewall doesn't make sense on every machine, but I think it's a good idea for many. I think that there are factors that people might consider when deciding whether or not to enable WF on a given system:

- Does your network have a hardware firewall already, and is the system inside that firewall's area of protection?

- Are you already using another software firewall on the system?

- Does the system primarily act as a server, or instead as a client?

- Is the system directly connected to the Internet?

Let's consider each in turn.

If the System is Protected with a Hardware Firewall, Use WF Anyway

At first glance, it might seem silly to have two levels of firewalls—a hardware router between the intranet and the Internet, what is sometimes called a *perimeter firewall*, and a software firewall on every workstation. But it makes good sense because of, again, our friend the buffer-overflow-exploiting worm.

Once again, a worm needs two things to attack a system: a bug that's not been patched and access to the port "connected to" that bug. So, returning to the Blaster example, wouldn't a perimeter firewall protect systems inside that perimeter?

The answer is no, probably not. So long as the worm is running around on the Internet then yes, the perimeter firewall protects the systems *inside* that perimeter, because I don't know of anyone who lets a firewall pass port 135; it's one of the few dozen "what are you, *crazy*?" ports—ones that most of us don't expose to the Internet. But suppose there's a leak in that perimeter? When discussing this with clients, I like to ask two questions:

Question 1: "Do you let people take laptops outside of the office? You do? Great. But you don't let people bring them back in, do you?"

What I'm saying here is that if the worm gets past the firewall and is on your intranet, then the perimeter firewall no longer stands between the worm and port 135. (Again, remember that I'm just using 135 as a common example. Other worm exploits have targeted bugs attached to other ports.) In other words, once you're past the front gate, there's no security and, if anything, many people are more lax than usual about security on their intranet because "we have a firewall." This has led to security types observing over the years that many networks have what they call "candy bar" security because it's "hard and crunchy on the outside, but soft and chewy on the inside."

Suppose your employee Felix takes an unpatched company laptop out of the building on the afternoon before Blaster hits. He takes it home and plugs it into his cable modem, which directly connects him to the Internet. Blaster hits and his system is infected. Felix returns to work the next day, plugs into the company intranet, and in no time, the worm has found worm food by the cubic yard in your company's network.

Question 2: "Do you have any wireless networks in your organization…*that you know of*?"

Anybody with $75 can become the proud owner of a Linksys WRT54G wireless-G router. They're great, I use 'em all the time, albeit with encryption and with a modified administrator password. But not everyone takes those precautions. Think of the convenience, our friend Felix muses, of being able to put my laptop anywhere in my office, or even down the hall, instead of needing these annoying Ethernet cables! So Felix picks up a wireless router in Wal-Mart, brings it into the office, plugs it in to the power and the network jack, runs the wizard that sets that router up, and now he—and your organization's network—are "on the air." And I'll bet that Linksys router's still got the password "admin," the default out of the box. Result? Anyone in the parking lot can get onto the router…and therefore inside your firewall's perimeter. Just think: drive-by worms, just another convenience (sigh) that computers offer.

Until worms become a thing of the past, it's better to think of the perimeter firewall as a good idea but not a complete solution. I mean, there's a *reason* why NASA has astronauts keep their spacesuits on when their rockets are doing dangerous stuff like taking off or re-entering.

If Already Using a Software Firewall, Don't Use WF Usually

As I mentioned earlier in this chapter, lots of folks offer software firewalls, and several of the big security suites include them, so you might just already *have* a software firewall on your system. If that's the case, and if you're happy with what that software firewall does, then stay with it, and forgo WF.

Why? Because WF's fairly minimal set of features is probably improved upon in every way by a third-party software firewall. That might, however not be the case entirely, as WF's ability to be administered centrally through group policy might save you a lot of time over some of the third-party software firewalls. I suggest that you look at the features of WF and the alternative, and choose one. Running two software firewalls can lead to all kinds of unexpected behaviors, like network lockups or inexplicable inabilities to talk to some server.

Workstations Always Need Firewalls, Servers *Almost* Always

Part of your decision criteria is whether or not you're considering turning WF on at a system that's primarily a client—that is, a workstation system—or primarily a server—that is, a server system. (And yes, I know, this is a server book, but WF appears on both 2003 Server and XP with SP2, so it's worthwhile taking up a workstation topic briefly.)

I believe that you'd be wise to enable WF (or some other firewall) on all of your XP systems. Recall that the main foundation of WF's firewall functionality is stateful inspection, which says, "I reject incoming packets unless they're server responses to a request from this client." As workstations mostly act as clients in the client-server world, they'll be largely unaffected by enabling the firewall, and of course they'll get some protection from any future worms.

Now, let me be very clear here: there is one very significant and troubling side effect of turning on WF on a workstation: remote control tools stop working. You can't use an MMC to remotely control a firewalled workstation; you can't use Remote Desktop to run a session on it; and the like. This isn't an insoluble problem, but it *does* mean that you may have to create some exceptions to allow those remote control tools to work, and you'll have to think long and hard about which exceptions to allow, as the ports you'll have to open to enable remote control are often the very same ones that have been the favorites of worms throughout the ages. (We'll take up the question of which ports to open a bit later.)

Servers require the same kind of analysis, and more of it. Inasmuch as servers mainly host the server side of client-server applications, and inasmuch as servers don't start conversations, they respond to them, then servers must open the ports needed to let client requests through. Again, this will require a bit of study before it's safe to enable WF on your servers. But I would argue that enabling WF or some other firewall on each of your 2003 SP1 and R2 servers is overall a good idea.

Won't Enabling the Firewall Kill Domain Membership?

When Microsoft announced that they were going to not only install a new firewall on every XP, 2003, and later system, *and* that the firewall would be enabled by default on desktop OSes, the whole idea struck me as insane at first. *All* systems, I wondered? What about domain memberships? Wouldn't a system running on an intranet with domain controllers become unable to "hear" those domain controllers?

No, I eventually realized, firewalls don't get in the way of domain membership because, recall, anything gets through the firewall, as long as the conversation is initiated by the client. So, for example, when an XP box wants to log on, then it does so with the help of a domain controller. The XP box acts as what might be called a "logon client," and the domain controller acts as the "logon server." The XP box started the conversation by saying, "Please log me on," and when the DC responds, that response passes through the firewall. When the XP box requests your roaming profile, the response is unaffected by the firewall because the XP box started the conversation, and when the XP box requests group policy information every hour and a half or so, the response passes through the firewall because of the XP box's having spoken first.

That's not to say that raising a firewall on workstation OSes wouldn't cause a few support headaches. Domain membership isn't affected, but remote control tools stop working in a firewall scenario unless you noodle with the firewall settings, as you'll see later.

If Connected Directly to the Internet, Enable a Firewall

As I travel a lot, and my laptop runs XP (x64 Edition, actually), I end up plugging my system into a lot of different Internet hookups—hotels, conferences, airports, and so on. Who's running those networks? Heck, I have no idea. But I do know that when I connect to one of these public Internet providers, I often end up with a routable IP address. In other words, there's nothing between me and the big, scary old Internet. So turning on WF is a great idea in that case.

Yes, I know, that was a workstation example, and this is a server book. Who directly connects their *servers* to the Internet? Some people do, and I don't think it's a terrible idea, as long as the system is firewalled. Servers directly on the Internet are often *on* the Internet because they're offering some specific set of services across the Net, and in most cases that's a pretty small set of services— web, email, and DNS are a common triad. In that case, the prescription for better security is simple. First, turn on WF. Second, collect the ports that people use to communicate with the server (probably TCP ports 80, 443, 25, and 53 and UDP port 53 in this case), and only open those ports. And if you're wondering how you'd know which ports to open, we're going to discuss the Security Configuration Wizard in a few chapters. It will examine the services that you're offering and suggest which ports to open.

By now, I've covered "how it works" and "why and when to use it," and I hope that I've convinced you that WF's got some value. Next, let's move along to the nuts and bolts of getting it working and configuring it.

Enabling and Disabling Windows Firewall

Let's start by seeing how to turn WF on or off. Like most of WF, you can control its on/off switch either from the command line, the GUI, or a group policy setting.

Example/Demonstration Setup

In order to offer examples of how Windows Firewall works, I'll work with two systems. If you'd like to follow along, set them up like so:

- The first system, web.bigfirm.com is a 2003 SP1 server, although an R2 server would work just as well. Install Internet Information Services's World Wide Web Service on it and, in c:\inetpub\wwwroot, create a simple file called default.htm that just contains the line "Hello!" Give web.bigfirm.com the IP address 10.50.50.39. (If you don't recall how to set up an IIS server, look at Chapter 17 in the *Mastering Windows Server 2003* book.)

- The second system, client.bigfirm.com, is an XP SP2 system. Give it IP address 10.50.50.37. (Actually, names won't matter much; we're going to keep this simple to set up by mostly using web.bigfirm.com's IP address to connect to it.)

Once you've got that set up, test out a few things. First, ensure that from the XP box you can ping the server: type **ping 10.50.50.39**. Then open up IE on the XP box and surf to 10.50.50.39. You should see "Hello!" on your browser. Close IE.

Ensuring WF's Off

Before you try to actually *mess* with WF's configuration, let's see what the heck it's currently doing. From Web, the 2003 SP1 server, you can easily see what WF's up to like so:

1. Open a command prompt.

2. Type **netsh firewall show state**.

3. Press Enter.

WARNING   I'm only going to say to "press Enter" this once; it's just a reminder. From this point on, whenever I offer a command-line firewall command, it'll always start with netsh firewall and end with Enter.

I get a response of The service has not been started, which is what you expect from Server. (Again, XP will have it enabled by default.)

Turning WF On... and Off

So let's fire it up, from the GUI, command line, and group policy editor.

ENABLING/DISABLING WF FROM THE GUI

To start WF from the GUI, click Start ➤ Control Panel ➤ Windows Firewall. You'll get a dialog box like figure 8.1.

Now, security can be confusing and scary, so it's kind of scary when the dialog boxes associated with security are confusing. This just says, "Hey, you wanted to configure Windows Firewall, but it's not on. Do you want to turn it on?" Click Yes, and you'll soon see a property page like Figure 8.2.

FIGURE 8.1

So you wish to play
with firewall, eh?

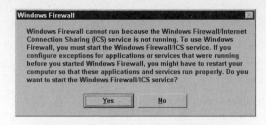

FIGURE 8.2

Windows Firewall's
main on/off switch

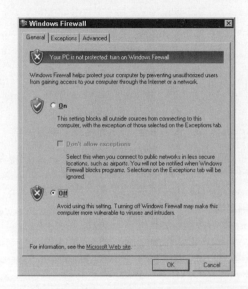

As you've already figured out, click the radio button next to On and then click OK, and the property page disappears. But is the firewall doing anything? Open up a command prompt (in case you don't still have one hanging around) and try that `netsh firewall show state` command again. You'll see something like

```
Firewall status:
-------------------------------------------------------------------
Profile                          = Standard
Operational mode                 = Enable
Exception mode                   = Enable
Multicast/broadcast response mode = Enable
Notification mode                = Enable
Group policy version             = None
Remote admin mode                = Disable


Ports currently open on all network interfaces:
Port   Protocol  Version  Program
-------------------------------------------------------------------
No ports are currently open on all network interfaces.
```

There's lots to see there, and we'll talk about all of it before the chapter's over, but the main thing we're looking for here is `Operational mode = Enable`. That's Microsoft-ese for "The firewall's turned on."

Try it out to see if you do indeed have a working firewall. From the XP box, try pinging 10.50.50.39; you'll get just timeouts. Try visiting 10.50.50.39 via IE, and you won't get any response.

Let's move along to command-line control, but before we do, disable WF from the GUI by returning to the same property page that enabled it, but this time click Off and OK. Try the ping and the web access, and they'll work.

ENABLING/DISABLING WF FROM THE COMMAND LINE

From the command prompt, start up WF by typing

```
netsh firewall set opmode enable
```

You'll get a laconic `Ok.` from the firewall. Try the pings and web access from the XP box, and again they'll fail. Do a `netsh firewall show state` and you'll see that it's enabled. To disable WF from the command line, type

```
netsh firewall set opmode disable
```

Once you do, the Web and pings will work again.

ENABLING/DISABLING WF FROM GROUP POLICY SETTINGS

We're working from a couple of computers in a workgroup rather than a domain, so I'll demonstrate WF enable and disable with local group policies. Start up the Group Policy Editor (Start ➢ Run ➢ **gpedit.msc**) and navigate to Computer Configuration ➢ Administrative Tools ➢ Network ➢ Network Connections ➢ Windows Firewall ➢ Standard Profile. You'll see a list of group policy settings like the ones in Figure 8.3.

FIGURE 8.3
The 14 main group
policy settings for WF

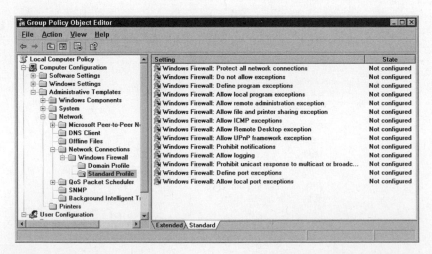

You'll see these settings again and again throughout the rest of this chapter. The one you want now is Windows Firewall: Protect all network connections, which is Microsoft-ese for "turn on the firewall." Double-click it, choose the Enabled radio button in the resulting dialog box, and click OK. Try a ping or a web access from the XP box, or do a `netsh firewall show state`, and you'll see that the firewall's been enabled by group policy editor—and no `gpupdate` commands required! To undo it, just return to the group policy setting and either choose Disable or Not configured… but don't do that right now; let's leave the firewall up.

By the way, what if you've configured WF one way in the GUI and another from the command line or group policy setting? If it's GUI versus command line, then whichever command applied most recently wins. But if the command line or the GUI try to conflict with the group policy setting, then that command line or GUI is ignored. The firewall's General tab grays out on the On and Off radio buttons, and any `netsh firewall set opmode disable` commands are received with an `Ok`. but actually are ignored. The quickest way to see if WF's being controlled at least in part by group policy settings is by looking at the output from a `netsh firewall show state`; you'll see `group policy version = Windows Firewall` if WF's being controlled by group policy settings, or you'll see `group policy version = None` otherwise.

Making Server Applications Work with Windows Firewall

While raising a firewall makes a server more secure, it can also make it useless, as you've seen—take a web server and turn on WF and it's not a web server anymore. But fear not, you needn't forgo a firewall. Just open up a few ports.

By "open up a few ports," I mean to tell the firewall to continue to discard unsolicited incoming packets, *unless* those packets are destined for a particular port—TCP port 80, in this case. In Windows Firewall-ese, this is called creating an *exception*. WF lets you do that in two ways:

◆ You can specify a particular port to open, creating a *port exception*, or

◆ You can tell Windows Firewall, "Look, I don't know what ports XYZ server program needs, so just let XYZ server program open whatever ports it wants." That's called creating a *program exception*.

Here's how to create each type.

Creating Port Exceptions

To create a port exception, just do two things. First, find out what port or ports your server application uses. Second, use the GUI, group policy, or the command line to tell WF to open those ports.

WHICH PORTS TO OPEN? (PART ONE)

How do you know what ports your server application uses? Sometimes it's relatively easy, as when your server implements some standard protocol. For example, let's return to your web server. What ports would it need opened? Simple: ports 80 and 443. How'd I know that? It's in the documentation of most kinds of web server software, or you could Google "list of standard internet service ports," a search that will yield many answers. Sometimes it makes sense to create what WF calls a *program exception*, which we'll talk about in a few pages, whereby you don't need to open port numbers at all; instead, you just tell WF the name of the program and direct WF, "Open whatever ports that application wants."

Another approach is to use `netstat`. Set up your server application on a computer and connect a client to the server application so that you know the server app is active. Then open a command prompt and type

```
netstat -ano
```

You'll see an output like this, which I've shortened to simplify reading it:

```
c:\>netstat -ano

Active Connections

  Proto  Local Address  Foreign Address  State      PID
  TCP    0.0.0.0:42     0.0.0.0:0        LISTENING  1820
  TCP    0.0.0.0:53     0.0.0.0:0        LISTENING  1584
  TCP    0.0.0.0:80     0.0.0.0:0        LISTENING  2028
```

"Listening" means "I'm watching this port for incoming requests." Servers listen, clients don't. To read the Local Address and Foreign Address columns, translate 0.0.0.0 to "any IP address." So you could read the first line's components as "Local Address = any data coming into port 42 from any one of my IP addresses," and "Foreign Address = I'll take data from any address on the Internet." PID stands for Process ID, and it's the internal identifier that the operating system uses to name each running process. So you know that process number 1820 listens on port 42, process 1584 listens on port 53, and process number 2028 listens on port 80.

But what are those processes? To answer that, type **tasklist**, and you'll get an output that looks like this (which, again, I've shortened for clarity):

```
c:\>tasklist

Image Name     PID    Session Name   Mem Usage
============== ====== ============== =========
dns.exe        1584 Console         4,540 K
inetinfo.exe   1680 Console         8,624 K
wins.exe       1820 Console         5,700 K
svchost.exe    2028 Console         5,176 K
```

Here, you see that something called dns.exe has PID 1584. That makes sense, as DNS's standard ports are TCP and UDP 53. Similarly, you see that wins.exe—the WINS server, obviously—runs on port 42, and something called svchost.exe runs on port 80.

I threw in that last one to demonstrate that while this can be useful, it's not perfect. Svchost.exe is an application that acts as something called a *wrapper* for services. One svchost.exe can hold one or more services, so merely saying that a given svchost uses port 80 doesn't tell you all that much. As Microsoft has implemented IIS inside a svchost, then, you lack an easy way to figure out what ports are associated with IIS, and in that case you would, as I've already suggested, either look up the ports on the Web or look in the IIS documentation to discover that IIS needs TCP ports 80 and 443 open.

Now that you've got the particular port or ports, let's open 'em up! For my example, I'll open up TCP port 80.

OPENING PORT 80 FROM THE GUI

To create a port exception, return to the Windows Firewall property page (Start ➢ Control Panel ➢ Windows Firewall) and click the Exceptions tab. It'll look like Figure 8.4.

WF tries to be smart and detect what exceptions you might want to create; file and print is pretty common amongst servers, as is remote desktop. But it hasn't anticipated the web server, so you'll have to create one of your own. To do that, click Add Port to see a dialog box like Figure 8.5.

The dialog box asks for a label for the exception, and as you can see I've filled in **Web Server**. It also wants to know the port number, and whether it's a TCP or UDP port. You *could* click OK, but then you'd be missing one of the neater things that WF does: it lets you be *very* picky about who gets to use a port. Click Change Scope to see a dialog box like Figure 8.6.

FIGURE 8.4
Exceptions tab in Windows Firewall

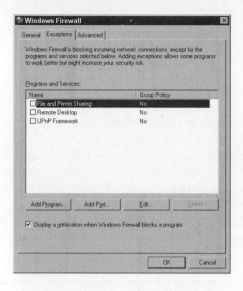

FIGURE 8.5
Opening port 80 in Add a Port

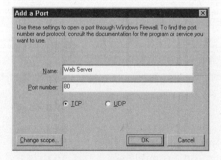

FIGURE 8.6
Limiting the exception to just the 10.50.50.x subnet

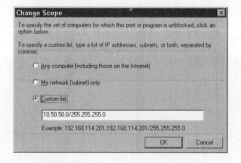

While much of WF is sort of basic, I think this is pretty neat—more than I expected. (Actually that's true for two reasons. The first is, as I said, I didn't expect Microsoft to offer something this useful in a free tool. The second is that the first time WF appeared, in XP SP2, this feature did not exist in even the near-final betas. But enough of us beta testers said, "Hey, we need better fine-tuned control of exception scopes!" and, *mirabile dictu*, they answered our prayers!) This lets me say, "This web server should only be available on this subnet."

More specifically, this lets you tell WF, "I want you to open up port 80, but *only* to packets from IP address 10.50.50.0 through 1050.50.255." That's what the 10.50.50.0/255.255.255.0 means— network number followed by subnet mask. Note, by the way, that I didn't have to type all of that out, because there's a My Network (Subnet) Only radio button. The Custom List option even lets you specify a list of addresses or address ranges, separated by commas.

OPENING PORT 80 FROM THE COMMAND LINE

If you return to the Exceptions tab, you'll see that there's now, in addition to the three optional exceptions, a new one named Web Server, and it's checked. Click it and then click the Delete button so you can rebuild the exception from the command line. (It'll ask if you're sure; tell it that you are.)

You create a port exception with the `netsh firewall` command. A basic port exception looks like

```
netsh firewall add portopening protocol=tcp|udp port=n name=descriptive name
scope=all|subnet|custom
```

Yeah, I know, that looks ugly, but it'll make more sense with a few examples. If you remember that the command line just does the same thing as the GUI, which you've already seen, then it gets a bit easier. To simply open up port 80 to the entire Internet, you'd type

```
netsh firewall add portopening protocol=tcp port=80 name="Web Server"
```

As with all `netsh` commands, that's all one line, even if it broke on the printed page. Make sure that you type all of the `netsh` commands in this chapter as one big line, even it wraps—only press Enter once, at the end of the line. If you typed it right, then you'll get `netsh`'s normal laconic response—Ok.—and all of the world will be able to see your web page. But this is supposed to be a *secure* web server, only available to folks on the same subnet. So you could instead type

```
netsh firewall add portopening protocol=tcp port=80 name="Web Server"
scope=subnet
```

And you could get even more specific with the `scope=custom` format. To show custom IP ranges, you add `scope=custom addresses=` followed by a list of either IP addresses, and/or IP address ranges. For example, if I wanted to block port 80 to every system on the Internet except for a system at 10.50.50.37, I'd type

```
netsh firewall add portopening protocol=tcp port=80 name="Web Server"
scope=custom addresses=10.50.50.37
```

Or, to only allow the entire A-class 10.x.x.x network and the C-class 192.168.1.x network, I'd type

```
netsh firewall add portopening protocol=tcp port=80 name="Web Server"
scope=custom addresses=10.0.0.0/255.0.0.0,192.168.1.0/255.255.255.0
```

As you can probably see, the format for identifying a network is the network's number, a forward slash and a subnet mask in dotted quad notation, with multiple ranges separated by a comma. (Review Chapter 6 in *Mastering Windows Server 2003* if you're unclear on any of that.)

You can remove a port exception with the `netsh firewall delete portopening` command, which looks like

```
netsh firewall delete portopening protocol=udp|tcp|all port=portnumber
```

In this case, I'd lock port 80 back up with

```
netsh firewall delete portopening protocol=tcp port=80
```

OPENING PORT 80 WITH GROUP POLICY SETTINGS

Using the GUI to configure WF on a few systems is quick, easy, and efficient. But to configure WF on a whole domain's worth of servers and/or workstations, there's nothing like group policy. That's why Microsoft included 15 new group policy settings to control WF.

Understanding the WF Settings Area: Standard versus Domain

Open up `gpedit.msc` and navigate to Computer Configuration ➤ Administrative Tools ➤ Network ➤ Network Connections ➤ Windows Firewall ➤ Standard Profile. That's where you'll find 14 of the 15 settings (see Figure 8.3) and yes, I'll show you the fifteenth later. But for now, let me briefly touch on an initially confusing element about this particular bunch of group policies: the `Standard Profile` and `Domain Profile` folders. A look in them will show that they contain the same 14 settings. So what's the difference?

Microsoft's original reason, the *real* reason why they built WF, was, as I've suggested, so that they could have an acceptable-quality firewall for XP that they could turn on by default and reduce the chances that the clueless would leave an unpatched system on the Internet, ripe for exploitation by future worms. I think they saw WF on a server as something of an afterthought, although I may be wrong and, in any case, I'm a big fan of using WF on a Windows-based server.

Running WF on XP, however, presented one big problem: many XP systems are mobile. I'd guess that there are more laptops running XP than any other operating system. Many of those laptops spend about half of their time inside corporate firewalls, at the office, and the rest of their time at an employee's home, a client site, on a hotel Internet connection, or hooked up to the Internet wirelessly at Starbucks. So, in the XP SP2 beta process, a lot of people complained to Microsoft that while they liked the idea of having a firewall handy while their XP systems were out of the office, they didn't really want the firewall enabled while they were *in* the office. (As you've already read, I don't agree with this, but it's easy enough to understand the point of view.)

Microsoft addressed their question by constructing WF to be able to store and recognize two completely different sets of configuration information: a *domain profile* to be used when inside the corporate network and a *standard profile* to be used at all other times. I really haven't talked all that much about standard and domain, mainly because this is a book about Server, and I'm guessing that you don't move your servers into and out of your buildings all that much.

Configuring Standard versus Domain Profiles

Okay, it's not an XP book, but since I'm here, let me add that both the command line and group policies let you separately configure the standard and domain profiles. In command lines, just add the phrase `profile=standard` to tell WF that whatever you're telling it should only happen in standard mode, or `profile=domain` to tell WF that whatever you're telling should only happen in domain mode. Not adding any `profile=` parameters tells WF, "Do what I'm telling you in both standard and domain mode."

With group policies, in contrast, there are those two folders `Standard Profile` and `Domain Profile`. There isn't a folder named `Both Profiles` so to accomplish something in both profiles, just adjust your group policy settings in both folders. My demonstrations here work on a server that is *not* in a domain, but rather in a workgroup, so my examples all belong in the `Standard Profile` folder. But most of you will be configuring things via domain-based group policy objects. In that case, just do your work in the `Domain Profiles` folder.

How Does It Know?

How does a system know whether it's in standard or domain mode? Microsoft accomplished that by employing an already-existing XP service, the Network Location Awareness (NLA) Service, and configured WF to ask the NLA, "Are we inside the corporate firewall, or not?" Here's exactly how it works.

◆ By default, every system sees itself as being in standard profile. Domain members are the only possible systems in domain profile.

◆ A computer's NLA remembers the full DNS name of the last domain controller that the computer got domain policies from.

◆ NLA removes the DNS suffix and remembers that. So, for example, if a system last got its group policy settings from a machine named dc1.bigfirm.com, then NLA on that system would remember the DNS suffix bigfirm.com.

◆ Any time that NLA needs to know whether it's in domain mode or not, NLA examines all of the network adapters on the system. It then examines the DNS names on those network adapters to see if any of the DNS names on the network adapters have a domain suffix that matches "bigfirm.com." If there's a match, then NLA assumes that the system is inside its domain's corporate network.

Thus, if your XP laptop is a member of a domain called bigfirm.com, but it finds that the only DNS name currently associated with any of the laptop's network cards is temporaryname653.akronairportnet.com, it presumes that it's been taken out of the office.

To see if your system thinks it's in standard or domain profile, just open up a command prompt and type `netsh firewall show state`. You'll see something like this:

```
Firewall status:
-----------------------------------------------------------------
Profile                               = Standard
Operational mode                      = Enable
Exception mode                        = Enable
Multicast/broadcast response mode = Enable
Notification mode                     = Enable
Group policy version                  = Windows Firewall
Remote admin mode                     = Disable

Ports currently open on all network interfaces:
Port   Protocol  Version  Program
-----------------------------------------------------------------
No ports are currently open on all network interfaces.
```

Notice up top the line `Profile=Standard`; that's where you find out your system's current WF profile.

Opening a Particular Port with Group Policies

Let's return to opening up your web server to the local subnet. Looking in the `Standard Profile` folder, there's a setting called `Windows Firewall: Define port exceptions`. That leads to a sort of scary-looking settings page like the one in Figure 8.7.

When you bring this up, the Enabled radio button won't be clicked; I did that to make the screen shot easier to read. To actually create this policy, click the Show button to see the Show Contents dialog box, as you see in Figure 8.8.

Sorry to have you have to dive down levels of dialog boxes, but one more click and you'll be ready to specify your port exception. Click Add to get the very simple Add Item dialog box, as you see in Figure 8.9.

FIGURE 8.7

Creating a custom port exception via group policies

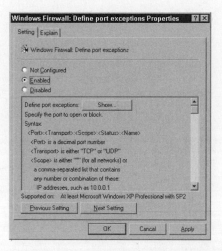

FIGURE 8.8

Dialog containing port exceptions

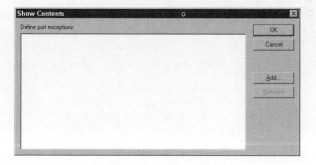

FIGURE 8.9

Entering the specifics of the exception

Now, *your* Add Item dialog box won't include 80:tcp:*:enabled:WebException; I added that to mine and I'll explain it in a minute. If you want to try it out now, enter **80:tcp:*:enabled:WebException**, and then click OK three times to clear the dialog boxes and get you back to the Group Policy Editor. You'll see that your XP box can once again access the "Hello!" page.

Now, what was that string thing all about? It's how you specify which port to open, and to whom to open them. The string looks like

portnumber:**TCP** | **UDP**:*scope*:**enabled** | **disabled**:*exceptionname*

Where *portnumber* is the port that you want to open, then either TCP or UDP, depending on which protocol you want to open that port on, then a list of subnets to open this port on (in my first example, I used "*" which means "the entire Internet," but I'll show you how to get more specific in a moment), then either enabled or disabled, depending on whether you want it open or closed, and then finally a descriptive name that can be anything. Picking 80:tcp:*:enabled:WebException apart, then, it says to

◆ Open port 80…

◆ On TCP…

◆ To the entire Internet…

◆ And enable this port opening… (and in case you're wondering, you might use disabled to block the exception from some small range of addresses inside a larger set of addresses for which you've allowed the exception)

◆ And finally, call this exception WebException.

That's a pretty complete example, except for one thing: the scope. You can specify the scope, which is nothing more than the range of IP addresses to allow this port exception for, with a list of one or more networks separated by commas. You can specify networks in three ways:

◆ As you've already seen, "*" means "the entire Internet."

◆ You may recall that when creating a custom port exception from the command line that you could specify the local subnet with the phrase subnet. This group policy string works in a similar way, but instead of the phrase subnet you'd use localsubnet. Thus, a group policy string of "80:tcp:localsubnet:enabled:WebException" would open up port 80 only for the local subnet which was, recall, our original goal here.

◆ Finally, you can specify particular networks by writing them in CIDR "slash" notation, as I covered in Chapter 6 of *Mastering Windows Server 2003*. For example, you could specify the entire 10.x.x.x network as 10.0.0.0/8, or the 256-address network starting at 192.168.0.0 as 192.168.0.0/24.

Here are a few examples:

3389:tcp:*:enabled:RemoteDesktopOpening lets TCP port 3389 (Remote Desktop Protocol) arrive from anywhere on the Internet.

110:tcp:localsubnet:enabled:PostOffice opens port 110 (POP3 requests) to arrive from any system on the local subnet.

139:tcp:10.0.0.0/8,192.168.1.55,localsubnet:enabled:WebException allows file server requests (NET USE) from anyone on the 10.x.x.x network, the specific IP address 192.168.1.55, and the local subnet.

OPENING OTHER PORTS WITH PREBUILT GROUP POLICY SETTINGS

Now, I've been using port 80, the Web, as my example, and admittedly the command-line and group policy syntaxes are a little ugly, but central control of opening ports is worth a little effort.

Microsoft knows, however, that there are certain ports that many people will want to open, and so there are a few group policy settings that simplify doing that. They are

◆ Allow Remote Administration Exception opens TCP ports 135 (RPC, recall) and 445 (the Common Internet File System, a newer version of the SMB file system that's been around for ages; CIFS was discussed in the *Mastering Windows Server 2003* book in Chapter 11) and also allows ICMP to respond to ping requests. The setting, and the others in this list, let you control which incoming IP addresses to accept 135 and 445 traffic from.

◆ Allow File and Printer Sharing Exception allows, as its name suggests, the ports needed to NET USE to a file share or connect to a shared printer. That means opening UDP ports 137 and 138 and TCP ports 139 and 445. This setting also throws in ICMP echo response, allowing pings.

◆ Allow Remote Desktop Exception lets the Terminal Services applications Remote Assistance and Remote Desktop work by opening TCP port 3389.

◆ Allow UPnP Framework Exception allows universal Plug and Play requests to come into your system via TCP port 2869 and UDP port 1900.

Each of the settings dialogs looks similar. For example, if you open the Allow Remote Administration Exception settings dialog, it looks like Figure 8.10.

The only ugly part is the text field where you specify Allow Unsolicited Incoming Messages From. In that field, you'd type a list of acceptable sources of requests in the same format as you used to create a scope on a custom port opening. As before, "*" just means "the entire Internet," 10.50.50.0/24 means "the range of 256 addresses starting at 10.50.50.0," and so on. As with custom ports, you can also enter more than one range, separated by commas, as in

```
10.50.50.0/24, 192.168.0.0/28, localsubnet
```

FIGURE 8.10
Configuring Remote Administration Exception

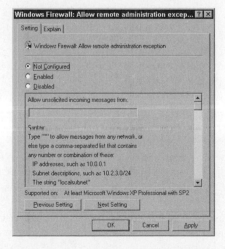

There's just one more GP setting worth looking at here in reference to port exceptions: Allow Local Port Exceptions. This really means "allow the administrator to use the GUI to configure port exceptions on a given machine." If the setting's set Enabled, or Not Configured, then a local administrator can use the Exceptions tab to configure exceptions. If the setting is set to Disabled, then bringing up the GUI will show that any ability to modify the Exceptions settings is grayed out.

WHICH PORTS TO OPEN? (PART TWO: THE BAD NEWS)

Those were the geeky details, but let's take a moment now and reconsider: what ports to allow open? It's a tough question, honestly. A very simple examination of the firewall might make someone say, "Heck, there are over 60,000 ports, and in a few clicks WF closes 'em all. In a few more clicks I can open just the half-dozen or so that I need to get the job done. How insecure could *that* be?"

I've already said that servers that don't respond on any port at all *aren't* servers. And, to an extent, every system is a server, even XP workstations., or at least they are if they don't want to drive their support staff crazy: again, as I've already said, every time you use a remote control tool of any kind on an XP system, whether it be an MMC that works remotely or Remote Desktop or the like, then you are starting an unsolicited conversation with an XP box, and so, as you know, WF will block it. So, while it might seem at first blush that the folks supporting XP workstations have an easier time determining how to configure WF for their XP boxes, they've got the same basic issue as do Server admins configuring WF: which ports to open?

Okay, so you decide to allow a handful of ports left open on your servers so that they can, well, *serve*. And you decide to allow a handful of ports open on your XP boxes for remote administration. But you want to keep as many ports closed as possible, in the event that a worm gets loose in your intranet before you've rolled out the patch to block the worm.

Well, here's the bad news. The fact is that all buffer overflow exploit opportunities aren't created equal. Most of the scary bugs pop up in the really old code, the code that Microsoft's certainly improving over time, but that they dare not simply wipe clean and start all over again, because so many existing things rely upon them. For example, consider RPC and file sharing. They need just a handful of ports:

- ◆ TCP ports 135, 139, and 445
- ◆ UDP ports 137 and 138

Unfortunately, I've just named the ports that have suffered the most attacks. It would be a great irony for us to lock up every port on our systems, causing us a potential raft of low-grade compatibility headaches, only to find that our networks are no more secure because we've left open the doors most popular with bad guys.

So what to do? First, exploit DEP and stay on top of patches. Remember that in theory a system can be left open and unfirewalled on the Internet itself if its code is well written and it's kept up to date on patches and may still be immune to worms. (I'm *not* recommending that.)

Second, when it comes to XP, I suggest leaving the preceding ports blocked but to open port 3389, which allows remote administration via Remote Desktop. No, it's not a perfect answer, but RDP has not seen a buffer overflow exploit that I know of, and the others have seen several.

Third, look closely at what your server needs. If it's a web server, then it's theoretically just fine to block every single port but 80 and 443. (You can even block 443 if you're not using SSL.)

Fourth, avoid enabling Universal Plug and Play if you can. Unless your computer is running as your network's firewall itself, I've not found a must-have need for it. And UPnP is particularly worrisome because its whole job is to tell the world about your system's configuration. Ugh.

Fifth, look seriously at IPsec bypass; we'll cover it later in this chapter. It creates a system whereby you can somewhat simply create port exceptions that apply not to networks but to groups of particular machines.

AN IMPORTANT WINDOWS FIREWALL LIMITATION: ONE PORT AT A TIME

If you've ever played with firewalls before, you may be wondering something. I've been talking here about how to open particular ports, but in many real-world situations you might want to open large ranges of ports. (For example, the RPC service that I've discussed a number of times earlier in this book needs at least 100 ports open, according to Microsoft's KB 154596.) But there's no way to do that in WF, short of writing a script to generate numerous `netsh firewall add portopening` commands. That's a shame, as it kind of excludes WF from some uses.

On the other hand, though, I suppose that a bit of fancy command-line work could work around that. You could, for example, open up, say, ports 300 through 309 by opening up a command prompt and carefully typing this command:

```
for /L %p in (300,1,309) do netsh firewall add portopening protocol=tcp port=%p name=port%p
```

That command broke on the page, but again it's important to type it at the command prompt without pressing Enter until you're done typing! This exploits a built-in Windows command `for` that lets you take a single command like `netsh firewall` and loop through it for some number of times. The `%p` is a placeholder for a number that changes as the `for` command loops. The (300,1,309) tells `for` which numbers to use: this means to start at 300 and count up to 309, and to count up by one. After `do` is the actual command to execute. See the two places where there's a `%p`? `for` doesn't actually execute the command

```
netsh firewall add portopening protocol=tcp port=%p name=port%p
```

Instead, it takes the current value in `%p` and substitutes that, so that, for example, the first time `for` executes a `netsh firewall` command, the command is, after the substitution,

```
netsh firewall add portopening protocol=tcp port=300 name=port300
```

But I don't think Microsoft ever intended us to do this with their free firewall; I think they want to sell you ISA server. In any case, that `for` trick might get you out of a tight spot.

WINDOWS FIREWALL AND DOMAIN CONTROLLERS

That leads me to digress a bit about something that most people get around to asking at some point about Windows Firewall and, indeed, about any firewall in the Windows world:

"If I wanted to set up a firewall between my domain controllers and their client systems, which ports should I leave open?"

This is a simple question to answer in a simple environment, where all you're using AD for is file and print, there's just one DC and no sites to worry about and no AD-aware apps like Exchange Server. So I can't answer the question for every network in the world, but I have tested the following in a dual-DC environment with XP clients and 2003-based member servers in a single-forest, single-site operation. But this will probably be enough information to let you experiment with WF and domain controllers in test labs.

NOTE For details on more complex arrangements, search the Microsoft site for a white paper called "Active Directory in Networks Segmented by Firewalls."

TABLE 8.1: First, create port exceptions for these ports:

SERVICE	TCP PORT	UDP PORT
DNS	53	53
Kerberos	88	88
NetBIOS name service		137
NetBIOS datagram service		138
SMB file sharing	139	
CIFS file sharing	445	
LDAP	389	389
LDAP SSL	636	
GC (global catalog)	3268	
GC SSL	3269	
RPC	135	
WINS	42	
Windows time service	123	
Kpassword	464	464

Then allow "ICMP inbound echo request" and "output packet too big" (covered in the next section on ICMP exceptions), and you're almost done.

The final piece requires setting aside ports for RPC. I'll spare you the long description, but RPC assists other server services to find ports for themselves, and those ports are fluid from one day to another. That means that if any given service were to ask RPC for a port one day, then RPC might assign that service port 2000 one day (RPC only assigns port numbers above 1023) and 3017 the next day. Hmmm…if RPC might grab *any* port above 1023, then that means that you'd have to open every single port from 1024 through 65535…ugh. Fortunately, there's a better way, although it's still not perfect. You can, with some Registry fiddling, restrict RPC to a range of ports. But how many ports to give away? Microsoft says that about 100 will do, so let's leave some room and set aside 201, in the range of port 50000 through 50200. Here's how.

1. Open regedit.exe.

2. Navigate to HKEY_LOCAL_MACHINE\Software\Microsoft\Rpc.

3. Under that key, create a new key—not an entry, a whole new key—named Internet. Do the following Registry changes in that key; you'll have to create each entry, as they don't currently exist.

4. Create a REG_MULTI_SZ ("multi-string value" in Regedit terms) called Ports. In it, put 50000-50200.

5. Create a REG_SZ entry PortsInternetAvailable and put "Y"—just a capital "Y"—in it.

6. Create a REG_SZ entry UseInternetPorts, another REG_SZ, and fill it with "Y," as with the previous entry.

7. Close Regedit.

8. Reboot the domain controller.

Now you've restricted RPC to ports 50000 through 50200. But that means you'll have to create 201 new open ports. That's a lotta clicking! Well, it is, but not if you open up a command prompt and type one long line very carefully, taking for out for a spin:

```
for /L %p in (50000,1,50200) do netsh firewall add portopening protocol=tcp
port=%p name=port%p
```

Again, that's all one line. It'll scroll a few hundred lines of text on the screen and *voila*! you'll have 201 new opened ports. And at this point, you can connect clients to your firewalled DC.

Permitting Ping: ICMP Exceptions

When Windows Firewall first appeared in XP SP2, I started getting odd questions on email. They all went something like, "Hey, something's weird on my system now that I'm running SP2. I've got two computers, A and B. A can ping B, but B can't ping A. What's going on?" What was going on was that system A was running XP SP2 with Windows Firewall enabled by default, and system B was a Windows 2000 system without any firewalls.

When A pinged B, then the firewall on A said, "Ah, we're pinging B; when the response comes back, I'll let it through," but when A pings B, then B says "Auugh! An unsolicited transmission! No doubt it's some blackguard worm, I'd better block it!"

Ping's the most basic troubleshooting tool in many a networker's arsenal, and it's a pain to try to do network troubleshooting in a network that's blocked all pings, as I discussed back in the DEP chapter. But pings are useful to more than folks trying to troubleshoot; several network protocols *need* ping to operate correctly. For example, part of group policy processing on a client needs an answer to the question, "Am I dialed up or directly connected via a high-speed network to my domain controller?" If the client's dialed up, then the client skips software installation (installing Word over a 56 Kbps connection wouldn't be fun), folder redirection (ditto), and login scripts. But how to know whether a system's dialed up or LAN-connected? Well, believe it or not, your system pings the domain controller, times how long it takes for the response, and guesses the connection speed from there. Of course, a DC with a ping-ignoring firewall in place never responds, and so every system in the network thinks it's dialed up, and that's not good, so let's see how to allow ICMP messages through WF.

ALLOWING PING FROM THE GUI

To open the door for pings from the GUI, bring up the Windows Firewall applet in Control Panel as you've done before: Start ➢ Control Panel ➢ Windows Firewall, and then click the Advanced tab; it'll look like Figure 8.11.

Click the Settings button in the ICMP section, and you'll see a dialog box like the one in Figure 8.12.

You see several different settings to allow different things in ICMP with check boxes next to them. You may have to check them all in some cases, but in my experience the only thing I tend to need is ICMP's incoming echo request. I've checked that box in the screen shot. To allow ping responses, check Allow Incoming Echo Request and click OK, then click OK to clear the WF property page. You'll then be able to ping the web server from the XP box, if you're following along in the examples.

FIGURE 8.11
Windows Firewall Advanced property page

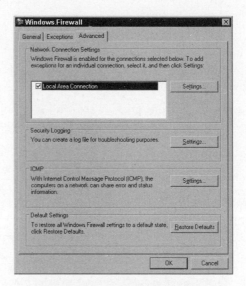

FIGURE 8.12
ICMP Settings dialog box

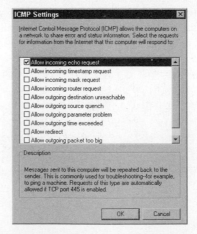

Once you've opened up ICMP responses, a `netsh firewall show state` won't reflect any changes. But add `verbose=enable`, and you'll get a *lot* more information, including this:

```
ICMP settings for all network interfaces:
Mode    Type  Description
------------------------------------------------------------------
Disable 2     Allow outbound packet too big
Disable 3     Allow outbound destination unreachable
Disable 4     Allow outbound source quench
Disable 5     Allow redirect
Enable  8     Allow inbound echo request
Disable 9     Allow inbound router request
Disable 11    Allow outbound time exceeded
Disable 12    Allow outbound parameter problem
Disable 13    Allow inbound timestamp request
Disable 17    Allow inbound mask request
```

Notice the line with `Enable 8 Allow inbound echo request`; that's the one that shows you that this system will respond to pings.

ALLOWING PING FROM THE COMMAND LINE

Next, let's see how to allow ICMP echoes from the command line. (If you're following the examples, then go back to the Advanced tab and uncheck the box in ICMP Exceptions that allowed ICMP echoes.) To enable ICMP echoes from the command line, you'd type

```
netsh firewall set icmpsetting 8 enable
```

The 8 means "ICMP echo"; to see all of the other numeric values and what they correspond to in ICMP-ese, type `netsh firewall set icmpsetting /?`. (Again, I've never found a use for them.) Alternatively, you can open up the whole set of ICMP responses with

```
netsh firewall set icmpsetting all enable
```

After executing either command, the web server will again respond to pings. To disable either ICMP echo or all ICMP responses, just replace `enable` with `disable` on the command line. To stop ICMP echo so as to be able to reopen it again with a group policy setting, then, you'd type

```
netsh firewall set icmpsetting 8 disable
```

ALLOWING PING FROM GROUP POLICY SETTINGS

To allow ICMP echoes from group policy, return to the Group Policy Editor and the Standard Profile folder under Windows Firewall. Open up the setting Windows Firewall: Allow ICMP Exceptions and you'll see a dialog box like Figure 8.13.

Yours will probably have the Not Configured radio button clicked; I've clicked the Enabled radio button so you can more easily see the options. (Oddly enough, there's a scroll bar in this dialog box, but scrolling up or down doesn't show any more options, so you're not missing anything!)

FIGURE 8.13
All of the possible
ICMP settings

The setting you're looking for here is Allow Inbound Echo Request. After clicking Enabled in your dialog box, check the box next to Allow Inbound Echo Request and then click OK. Again, the pings will flow freely. As before, `netsh firewall show state` won't show any difference without the `verbose=enable` parameter except to reveal in the `Group policy version = Windows Firewall` that group policy settings are somewhere afoot. As before, any attempts to override the group policy setting via command line or GUI will be ignored.

Creating a Program Exception

Sometimes you want to open the ports necessary for a particular server program to run but don't know what ports the program needs. In that case, you can just point to the program and tell WF, "Please open any ports that application requests." Such an exception is called a *program exception*.

I have honestly never needed to create a program exception with WF, for two reasons. First, I am extremely leery of offering *carte blanche* to any application when it comes to a firewall. Look, turning on firewalls introduces new annoyances in the name of security; why jeopardize that by blindly letting some app open up whatever ports it wants? But that's just my paranoia talking; certainly we all trust *some* software vendors, and so program exceptions could make some sense. But even then I've never had to set one up, as many modern applications' Setup programs say, "I need to punch a hole or two in the firewall, would you like to make me a program exception?"

WHICH APPLICATION TO EXCEPT?

Just as you previously had to ask, "How do you know what port numbers to open?" when creating port exceptions, with program exceptions you've got to ask, What *application* do I create exceptions for? While that seems like a simple task, it can get a bit ugly. For example, let's consider two server applications:

◆ The copy of Internet Information Server that ships with Server 2003 and R2, and

◆ An inexpensive piece of FTP server software that I found on the web, RhinoSoft's Serv-U FTP server. (Yes, Windows comes with an FTP server of its own, but this is a bit more flexible and I needed a third-party server example.) They've got five different levels of the product, and we'll be using the most basic, Serv-U Personal. You can download the tool from `www.serv-u.com`'s Downloads link. The application downloads as a file called `ServUSetup.exe`.

IIS: An Ugly Character Program Exception-Wise

I first examined the copy of IIS that I installed on my test Server 2003 SP1 system named web.big-firm.com with the intention of creating a program exception for it instead of opening ports 80 and 443. You've already read that I used a combination of information from netstat and tasklist to determine that IIS actually ran inside a wrapper called `svchost.exe`. But `svchost.exe` is just a program that, again, developers tuck their services *into* to simplify the task of writing a secure service. A quick look at the output of tasklist on any XP, 2003 SP1, or R2 system would show that there are quite a number—nine on the test Server 2003 SP1 system that I've been working from in this chapter. Telling WF, "Just open anything that `svchost.exe` wants," yields an error message, and it'd be a dumb thing to do anyway, as opening the door for `svchost.exe` opens it for *all* copies of `svchost.exe`, and in the process ends up telling WF to open any port that almost any service wanted which, again, would kind of negate the whole point of the firewall.

We can go a bit deeper, however, with a great tool from www.sysinternals.com called Process Explorer. With it, I was able to find out that the application *inside* the particular `svchost.exe` that runs IIS is a file called `c:\windows\system32\inetsrv\iisw3adm.dll`. Creating a program exception (you'll see how in a moment) did not open up a port for IIS. Nor did creating a program exception for another program running on the server that was clearly connected with IIS, `inetinfo.exe`. At that point, I just cried "uncle!" and decided that if there's a way to name the process that IIS uses that actually talks out ports 80 and 443, I wasn't smart enough to figure it out. Moral of the story: it's not always clear what program to make a program exception for.

Trying Out Program Exceptions with FTP

Then I tried the RhinoSoft U-Serv FTP server application. It's free for personal use, so no licenses to worry about and no cost if you'd like to follow along with my example for this section, which focuses on U-Serv. Running the `ServUSetup.exe` installation program, I immediately got a message from WF looking like Figure 8.14.

This is WF's way of telling me that some application's trying to open up a port, and should I allow it? WF has already blocked the program, it's just asking if I'd like to unblock it. Now, choosing to "unblock" has the effect of telling WF to create a permanent program exception for U-Serv FTP's Setup program. This demonstrates what I said before about you perhaps never needing to create a program exception: as WF detects any application's attempt to open an incoming port and pops up a dialog box asking you if it should unblock the application, then in many cases you'll just click Unblock and the program exception's created. But you might want to create the program exception *beforehand*, so you needn't have to click the Unblock button, which is why I included this section.

FIGURE 8.14
Let Setup have
its way?

By the way, I kept the Setup program blocked. As it was trying to create an opening on port 1900—that scary old Universal Plug and Play thing—it seemed wise to keep the block in place, and the installation ran fine without the need to open 1900 to the world.

On the other hand, clicking Unblock on a test system yields some useful information—the actual name of the program that needs the program exception. I reran U-Serv's Setup program and then did a `netsh firewall show state`, and here's what I got:

```
Firewall status:
-----------------------------------------------------------------
Profile                        = Standard
Operational mode               = Enable
Exception mode                 = Enable
Multicast/broadcast response mode = Enable
Notification mode              = Enable
Group policy version           = Windows Firewall
Remote admin mode              = Disable


Ports currently open on all network interfaces:
Port   Protocol  Version  Program
-----------------------------------------------------------------
1900   UDP       IPv4     C:\Documents and Settings\Administrator\Local Settings
\Temp\is-7MAKI.tmp\is-7L9D2.tmp
```

That last line's the interesting one. It's the one that shows me that the Setup program was asking to open up port 1900 UDP, and that the application trying to do it was `C:\Documents and Settings\Administrator\Local Settings\\Temp\is-7MAKI.tmp\is-7L9D2.tmp`. That's of limited use in this case, as I'm interested in knowing how to make the *FTP server* work, not the *setup program* for the FTP serve, but in other situations, installing an app on a test system and letting WF unblock that app could save a lot of detective work.

NOTE   It also points to something that puzzles me: WF's new-found reticence when telling me that it's blocking an app. It offers to let me Keep Blocking, Unblock, and Ask Me Later, when what I really need is a button that says Explain Exactly What the Stupid Thing Is Trying to Do, which in the perfect world would pop up a dialog telling me exactly what app we're talking about and what port it's trying to open.

Understanding the FTP Protocol's Ever-Changing Port Needs

Again, we're not that interested in opening ports for U-Serv FTP's Setup program; we're interested in opening ports for the U-Serv FTP server itself. How hard is it to figure out what ports *it* needs?

Well, it's sort of difficult, actually. Downright complicated.

If you've ever studied how FTP works port-wise, then you know that it's a mite protean, which to be honest is why I chose an FTP server for my example. There are basically *two* modes for FTP to transfer data from an FTP server to a client, modes called *active* and passive. I don't want to turn this into a chapter on FTP internals, but it's worth spending a little time examining both modes.

Active FTP: Expose the Clients   In active FTP file transfer, a client like your XP box first picks a port on itself with a number above 1023; let's say in this example that your XP box picks port 1400. (The more accurate phrase for "port above 1023 that changes from session to session" is *ephemeral port*.) The FTP client then says to the FTP server, "Hey, when I ask you to send me data, send it to my port 1400." So far, so good, but here's where the freaky part starts. When your FTP client asks the FTP server to send it data, then the FTP server approaches your client's port 1400 from the server's port 20 by starting a whole new TCP/IP conversation. It essentially knocks on your XP box's door at port 1400, saying, "Hey, I'd like to send you something."

WARNING   In other words, when transferring data from an FTP server to an FTP client in active mode, the FTP server behaves like a *client*, and the FTP client behaves like a *server*. As the communication is an unsolicited one, then your XP firewall will reject it.

Can you fix this? Well, the main trouble with fixing this would be telling the copy of Windows Firewall on the XP box to allow incoming transmissions on port 1400. Oh, but remember—the incoming FTP port was 1400 in this one example. Start up XP's FTP client the next day, and it could turn out to use port 1208, and so on. What to do about this? Well, you could create a *program exception* for the FTP client software. That way, XP would open the port required for incoming FTP data, even as the port number changes. That's about the best example that I can think of where you'd want to use a program exception rather than a port exception, but it's still a bit messy to have to configure WF on a bunch of clients. Yes, there are group policies, but this might be a publicly available FTP server, and you can hardly do group policy on random Internet denizens. (And come to think of it, automatically configuring nonconsenting clients goes by some name…wait a minute, I'll get it…backing? Sacking? Something like that.)

Passive FTP: Expose the Server   Seems sort of odd that FTP would require the *client* to open up a port, doesn't it? It's just a remnant of the prehistoric Internet, where everyone trusted everyone. Alternatively, FTP can transfer data in what's called *passive mode*. Passive mode *also* requires picking a random port number above 1023, but in this case it's the FTP *server* that has to pick the high port.

Here's how it works. As before, a client contacts an FTP server on the server's port 21 to log on and issue commands ("please download X file, please let me upload Y file, show me what files are in the directory," that kind of stuff). The FTP server chooses a random port on itself, again one numbered above 1023. This port number will vary from client to client and session to session. The FTP server tells the FTP client what this ephemeral port is, and the FTP client uses that port to receive or send data.

It's fairly simple, except for the fact that the ephemeral port changes, and so we can't really tell WF which ports to keep open. Here's where a program exception makes good sense, presuming that we trust the server application: as the FTP server accepts sessions, it temporarily grabs ports and reports that to WF, which opens them to the outside world…but only for as long as the FTP server uses them.

You Might Not Have to Create the Program Exception

Now, I'm about to show you how to create a program exception, using U-Serv FTP Server as my example, but it's worth pointing out that you may not ever have to create a program exception.

In the case of U-Serv, the RhinoSoft guys have added a page to their Setup wizard that says in effect, "I see you've got Windows Firewall running; may I create a program exception for U-Serv FTP?" If you don't agree, once you've actually got U-Serv FTP Server running, Windows Firewall pops up another of those, "I'm blocking this FTP server program, do you want me to unblock it?" In any case, it's clearly pretty simple to create a program exception for this particular third-party server with or without knowledge of WF's GUI, command-line interface, or group policy settings, and in my experience most third-party server apps offer the same convenience.

Let me finish this section by summarizing the answer to the question, "How do you know which program to create a program exception for?" First of all, the program's Setup program may do the job for you, in which case you needn't do anything more. If it doesn't, then the warning notifications that Windows Firewall pops up will give you more clues, and you can always install the new server app on a test machine, tell Windows Firewall that it's okay to unblock it, and then do a `netsh firewall show state` to find the actual application name so that you can then use that information in creating a program exception. But despite all that, you may not be able to isolate a particular application to make an exception for, as in the case of IIS. In that case, look to port exceptions.

DIGRESSION: STOPPING NOTIFICATIONS

Let me pause my FTP store here and briefly point out that those boxes that WF pops up to tell you that it's blocked something and do you want it to stop blocking it can be sort of annoying. Worse yet, they're downright confusing for regular old users. So you might want to disable them. You can, easily.

◆ From the GUI, go to the Exceptions tab. At the bottom is a check box Display a Notification When Windows Firewall Blocks a Program. Uncheck it, and the notifications go away.

◆ From the command line, type **netsh firewall set notifications disable** to stop them, or **netsh firewall set notifications enable** to restart them.

◆ From group policies, it's the Windows Firewall: Prohibit Notifications setting. Click Enabled to stop notifications, Disabled to restore them.

CREATING PROGRAM EXCEPTIONS FROM THE GUI

In the case of U-Serv FTP Server, I installed it on a test machine, let its Setup program create the program exception, and then ran `netsh firewall show state` to get an output ending with this line:

```
Ports currently open on all network interfaces:
Port   Protocol Version  Program
-----------------------------------------------------------------
21     TCP      IPv4     C:\Program Files\RhinoSoft.com\Serv-U\ServUDaemon.exe
```

So now I know the name—actually the file specification—of the program to create the exception for: `c:\program files\rhinosoft.com\serv-u\servudaemon.exe`.

How would I create such an exception from the GUI? As always, open up the Windows Firewall Control Panel applet and click the Exceptions tab, as you saw back in Figure 8.4. Mine looks a little different, however, as you see in Figure 8.15.

Recall that the FTP server got there because I let its Setup program create a program exception automatically. I can look at that by clicking once on the Serv-U FTP Server line and then the Edit button. That shows the Edit a Program dialog, as you see in Figure 8.16.

I merely point this out because it's another way of discovering the exact program for which the program exception's been made. Click Cancel to remove the dialog, and then click Delete to remove the already-built program exception. (It'll ask for confirmation; click Yes to agree to remove the exception.)

Now let's create a program exception from scratch in the GUI. From the Exceptions tab, click the Add Program button to reveal the Add a Program dialog, as you see in Figure 8.17.

FIGURE 8.15
Exceptions with
Serv-U FTP Server
added

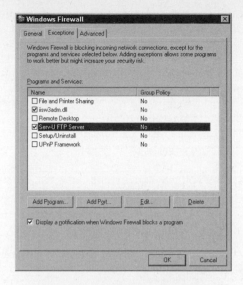

FIGURE 8.16
Edit a Program dialog
box showing Serv-U
FTP Server

FIGURE 8.17
Dialog box to create a
program exception

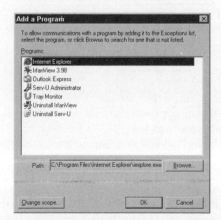

To enter the path to ServUDeamon.exe, click Browse and navigate to c:\program files\ rhinosoft.com\serv-u\servudaemon.exe, then click Open to create the program exception. (Why Open instead of Choose or Create Exception? I'm guessing someone just reused an existing dialog box to save time.) But now that you're back in the Add a Program dialog, don't click OK to clear it. Notice that there's a Change Scope button. It's identical to the one that you saw in the port exceptions section and lets you rein in the range of IP addresses that can make use of a program exception. Adjust it if you like, and click OK to clear the Change Scope dialog. Click OK to clear the Add a Program dialog, and your exception's in place.

When Serv-U FTP Server installed, it asked you where to put anonymous users. Put a file in whatever directory you chose. Then go to your XP client and start up Internet Explorer, and in the address bar type **ftp://10.50.50.39**. You'll see whatever files you've put in the anonymous users' directory back on web.bigfirm.com.

Close IE on the XP box, return to the Exceptions tab on the web.bigfirm.com server, and delete the program exception for `servudaemon.exe` so we can take the command line out for a spin.

CREATING PROGRAM EXCEPTIONS FROM THE COMMAND LINE

The syntax to create a program exception is very similar to creating a port exception, except the command is `netsh firewall set allowedprogram` instead of `netsh firewall set portopening`. Basically, the command looks like

```
netsh firewall set allowedprogram programpath exceptionname enable|disable
scope=all|subnet|custom
```

So, for example, to allow `ServUDaemon.exe` to open ports to the entire Internet, you'd type

```
netsh firewall set allowedprogram "c:\program files\rhinosoft.com\serv-
u\servudaemon.exe" "Serv-U FTP Server" enable
```

And despite the fact that the line is indeed long and ugly and broke on the printed page, it must be typed as all one line. To add a `scope=` clause, just do the same thing that we discussed in the port exceptions section.

To remove the program exception, type

```
netsh firewall program=program filespec
```

In this case, you'd type

```
netsh firewall program="c:\program files\rhinosoft.com\serv-u\servudaemon.exe"
```

CREATING PROGRAM EXCEPTIONS WITH GROUP POLICIES

The GUI and command lines are useful, but as you've learned, the uber-tool is group policies, as it can override and lock out the GUI and the command line. In the Standard Profile folder of the Windows Firewall section of group policies, take a look at Windows Firewall: Define Program Exceptions. Double-click it to bring up its dialog box and you'll see a page like Figure 8.18.

This works similarly to port exceptions; you click the Enabled radio button, which I've clicked here to show the Show button, which is the next thing that you click. That leads to a Show Contents dialog that is identical to the one that you saw for creating a port exception, and just like the port exception, there's an Add Item dialog box with a field for a text string.

That text string is a list of information separated by colons, as with port exceptions, except that the string has a different set of items in it:

*program filespec:scope of exception:***Enabled | Disabled:***name of exception*

FIGURE 8.18

Creating a program exception in group policies

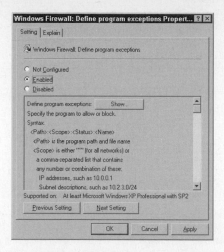

As with port exceptions, the scope of exception is a comma-separated list of networks in either CIDR notation, "*" for the entire Internet, or the word "localsubnet" for the local subnet. (And in case you're wondering, they use `all` for the command line versus "*" in group policies and `subnet` for the command line versus "localsubnet" in group policies, as well as `enable` for the command line versus "enabled" for group policies, just to see if you're paying attention.) It appears that you need not surround strings with double quotes to make this work. To create a program exception for Serv-U for the entire Internet, then, you'd enter a string in this Add Item field looking like

```
c:\program files\rhinosoft.com\serv-u\servudaemon.exe:*:enabled:Serv-U FTP Server
exception
```

Click OK until the dialog boxes all disappear, and once again the XP box will be able to see the contents of wherever you put your Anonymous users.

As with the Allow Local Port Eexceptions rule in group policy settings, "Allow Local Program Exceptions controls how much a local administrator can do to change the program exceptions created by a group policy object.

Temporarily Halting All Exceptions

As I've said before, opening ports is a convenience sometimes and a necessity others, but no matter what ports you open, there's always the chance that a worm will appear that can plant itself in an unpatched system (assuming that it can get past DEP), if given access to a particular port.

At times that some new worm's loose on the Internet, you can bet that it's just a matter of days, maybe hours, before some dodo drags it into your intranet. But you can prepare for it by temporarily shutting down all exceptions, whether port or program, with a GUI, command line, or group policy setting. Now, disallowing exceptions doesn't cause systems to forget what exceptions they're supposed to grant; it just temporarily suspends all exceptions until you lift the ban. In the meantime, systems not only remember what exceptions to allow, they will actually accept new exceptions—they just won't put them into action until the exception halt is removed.

Exceptions are useful in one other place: workstations taken out of the organizational intranet. With an XP laptop inside the company firewall, you may feel safer exposing a handful of ports; at an airport waiting lounge, you might not. Of course, you could more easily tell WF to skip exceptions altogether by employing the different standard and domain profiles, but simply suspending exceptions may be a better answer for you.

Here's how to suspend exceptions.

DISABLING EXCEPTIONS FROM THE GUI

From the Windows GUI, open up the Windows Firewall applet in Control Panel, as you saw in Figure 8.2. Note the check box between the On and Off radio buttons labeled Don't Allow Exceptions. If the check box is grayed out, then exceptions have been either enabled or disabled from group policies.

DISABLING EXCEPTIONS FROM THE COMMAND LINE

To temporarily suspend all exceptions on a computer from the command line, type

```
netsh firewall set opmode mode=enable exceptions=disable
```

Note that you must include the `mode=enable` parameter even if the firewall is already running. (And also please note that the online Help for `netsh firewall` claims that you can just type `netsh firewall set opmode exceptions=disable`, but this is a case where the Help is wrong.) To re-enable exceptions, just type

```
netsh firewall set opmode mode=enable exceptions=enable
```

To find out whether exceptions are enabled or not, just do a `netsh firewall show state`.

DISABLING EXCEPTIONS FROM GROUP POLICY

In the Standard Profile and Domain Profile folders in group policy, you can enable or disable exceptions with the Windows Firewall: Do Not Allow Exceptions setting. It's one of those group policies with just three settings: not configured, enabled, and disabled.

Automatic Exceptions: IPsec Bypass

I know, this has been a long chapter, but if you're still with me, then I'll let you in on a secret: I saved the best for (almost) last. Quietly embedded in Windows Firewall, which first shipped with XP SP2 in August of 2004, is a pretty neat technology, and one that also offers a look at some of the new version of Windows Server's upcoming surprises.

What IPsec Bypass Can Do for You

The technology that I'm talking about is called *IPsec bypass*. To understand it, let's review some of the main principles comprising Windows Firewall:

◆ When you enable WF on a given computer, then by default no outside systems can initiate communications with your computer.

◆ This makes it secure, but *too* secure. If it's a server, then servers that you can't approach are kind of useless. A raised firewall without exceptions makes even workstations more trouble, as we, at minimum, want to ping workstations and usually want to do some kind of remote control on them, which requires a small amount of server-like behavior. Trying to connect to a workstation via a remote control tool is essentially an unsolicited conversation, which the firewall would reject.

◆ In the real world, then, virtually every software firewall needs exceptions. A good firewall lets you be very specific about those exceptions. Having the ability to open just a few ports is better than having to open or close them all. Having the ability to open a given port to a specific set of IP addresses is better than having to open the port to every IP address on the Internet, and WF lets you do that.

That about summarizes what you've seen about WF so far. Given that information, what can you do to really control which systems could access a given server?

For most of this chapter, I've been suggesting that WF's main value is to slow down a worm set loose inside an organization's intranet, inside the organization's perimeter firewall. But now let's take the question, "What can software firewalls on my servers and workstations do to secure my network?" a bit further.

Around 1999, I was doing some work for a large corporation. They asked if I'd like to see their data center, and so I took the tour of their racks and racks of servers, switches, and the like. Then they took me to a separate room with a smaller group of servers. Waving their hands around this separate-from-most-of-the-data-center room, they said with a smile, "*This* is our perimeter fire-walled area." They explained to me that the growth of wireless networks, the number of people VPNing into the company from unsecured laptops, and the increasing number of outside "partner" firms to whom they were opening their network in a limited way led them to realize that more and more their intranet was looking about as safe as the Internet. As a result, they were experimenting with creating an inner perimeter which would enclose some of their most important servers.

That seemed a trifle paranoid in 1999 but doesn't seem quite so goofy today. For example, I've often been asked by people, "How do I ensure that only the accounting people get to the accounting servers?" Fifteen years ago, my answer would be, "Secure the NTFS, share, and database permissions on the accounting servers to just people in the Accounting group," and that's still not a *bad* answer. But what if you could say, "To access the accounting server, you've got to be a member of the Accounting group, *and* you've got to be sitting on a machine that's a member of that Accounting Computers group?"

With IPsec bypass, you can require that a prospective client of a given server must authenticate not only herself, but her computer as well. And sure, there are other ways to do this; Microsoft programmers surely weren't the first to think of this. But now they've made it a free add-on to some software— Server 2003 and XP—that you've already paid for.

How IPsec Bypass Works, in Short

More specifically, here's what IPsec bypass does.

1. First, you need an Active Directory. AD is different from earlier Windows domains, you may recall, because AD allows for groups that contain not just user accounts, but machine accounts.

2. With IPsec bypass, you first create a group that contains the machines that you want to be the only ones that can communicate with a given server.

3. Next, create IPsec policies that connect these acceptable clients to the server. These IPsec policies must either cause IPsec to do digital signing of the communications between the client and server (AH, in IPsec-ese), or that encrypt those communications (ESP, in IPsec-ese). (If you're rusty on IPsec, look back at Chapter 6 of *Mastering Windows Server 2003*.) While IPsec policies can employ either shared secrets, certificates, or Kerberos to authenticate the client to the server and vice versa, IPsec bypass requires Kerberos authentication.

4. With the machine group created and the IPsec policies in place, use the group policy setting Windows Firewall: Allow Authenticated IPsec Bypass, identifying the machine group.

5. Finally, enable Windows Firewall on the server, but do not create any exceptions.

Yes, you read that last part right. You're enabling Windows Firewall on a server but not creating any port or program exceptions, which until now has meant that no client can access the server. So how *does* a client get to the server when the firewall's set to "maximum cranky?" Simple; it just *bypasses* the firewall. To activate the Windows Firewall: Allow Authenticated IPsec Bypass group policy setting, you must tell Windows Firewall the name of one or more AD groups and/or machine accounts. This tells Windows Firewall, "Hey, listen, WF, I know that up to this point *you've* been the first player to examine incoming packets, but now that's changed. If there's an incoming packet and you find that it meets two criteria: it is either signed or encrypted by IPsec *and* it comes from a machine that's on that list that I just gave you, then just let it through—don't worry about it, don't even look at it."

This is what I meant when I said that IPsec bypass lets you set up a server so that it required both the user and the machine to authenticate. The user authentication is old hat; we've been doing it since NT 3.1 with file, directory, and database permissions. But the machine authentication's new. Your client machines must have AD machine accounts, and those accounts must be members of some group, and you configure IPsec bypass on a server to allow any machine using an authenticated IPsec connection *and* who is a member of that designated group to have access to the server.

TIP You can, of course, also still create exceptions in WF on the server so that non-IPsec-connection clients can get to particular services, as you've seen in the rest of this chapter.

How to Set Up IPsec Bypass

That's the overview. As always, the specifics can get a bit uglier. Let's look at the steps in some more detail.

YOU NEED ACTIVE DIRECTORY

IPsec bypass needs AD because configuring IPsec bypass on a given server requires that you specify the name of a group (I'm simplifying when I say "group," because in actuality it's a list of groups and machines, but I'll fill in the details on that in a bit; for now, it's just easier to say "group") containing the client systems that you want to be able to bypass the firewall in talking to the server. Local machine groups, however, can't contain machine accounts, just user accounts.

IPsec bypass also requires AD because IPsec bypass requires an authenticated IPsec relationship between the client and the server, and IPsec bypass is extra picky about that authentication in that it insists on Kerberos authentication. Kerberos authentication on IPsec relationships in the Microsoft world only works between members of the same Active Directory forest.

A minimum client-server configuration that can exploit IPsec bypass, then, must have at least one client and at least one server who are members of the same domain. (I found it easiest to do my initial IPsec bypass experiments by testing IPsec bypass on a member server, which required a three-machine setup rather than playing with IPsec bypass on a domain controller, but either arrangement works.)

For the sake of example, suppose you've got a slightly different setup than the one we've been using so far in this chapter. Let's suppose that you've got three systems in a test domain called big-firm.com:

- A domain controller name dc1.bigfirm.com at 10.50.50.100. It's also a DNS server and hosts the bigfirm.com zone for the AD. dc1.bigfirm.com as well as the two other systems point to this DNS server for their DNS needs. It needn't have Windows firewall enabled for this example, although if you did want it firewalled, then you'd have to make the changes to WF discussed in the previous section, "Windows Firewall and Domain Controllers."

- A member server called web.bigfirm.com at 10.50.50.39. It hosts a secure website that you want only someone sitting at xpclient.bigfirm.com, your next system, to be able to access. (If you want to test this out, then you don't need anything fancier than to put a file in `c:\inetpub\wwwroot` on web.bigfirm.com that contains the words "Welcome to the secure website!") It is a domain member and, obviously, has IIS running. When setting IPsec bypass up on any server, I find it easier testing-wise to keep WF disabled until I've tested my IPsec policies, as you'll see as you go along. Recall that web.bigfirm.com points to dc1.big-firm.com for DNS.

- An XP client called xpclient.bigfirm.com, the privileged system who will be the only one to be able to view web.bigfirm.com's website. It is also a domain member and sits at 10.50.50.37. It really doesn't matter whether its firewall is up or down. xpclient.bigfirm.com points to dc1.bigfirm.com for DNS.

CREATE A GROUP OF TRUSTED CLIENT MACHINES IN AD

If you're going to use IPsec bypass to restrict which machines can access a given server, than you must create a domain group and make those machines members of that group. I've used global groups in my experience with IPsec bypass, but I'd imagine that domain local groups would work fine, provided that the clients and the server were all in the same group.

You might run into one problem, however, when adding a machine to that group. When you want to add a member to a group, of course, then you open up the group in Active Directory Users and Computers, where you're presented with a property page with tabs labeled General, Members, Member Of, and Managed By. If you click the Members tab, then you add a member by clicking the Add button, which offers you the Select Users, Contacts, or Computers dialog box that you've no doubt seen many times. In the Enter the Object Names to Select field, you type the name of the machine, and click OK or Check Names, and that's where the fun starts.

If you've never added a machine to a group before, then you may not notice that in the Select Users, Contacts, or Computers dialog is a field called Select This Object Type, and it says by default Users or Other Objects. Apparently, "other objects" don't include computer accounts. Next to the field is a button labeled Object Types which, if clicked, will show you a list of the kinds of things that the dialog box will accept, and by default you'll see check boxes next to Other Objects and Users…but not next to Contacts and, significantly for us in this case, Computers. Just check the box next to Computers to return to Select Users, Contacts, and Computers, and now it'll accept your machine names.

If you intend to use IPsec bypass to protect more than one server, you'll probably want to create a separate group for each server.

WARNING   And remember that whenever a user or machine becomes a member of a group, then that user or machine doesn't actually get the benefits of being a member of that group until the user or machine logs off, then on. *That* means that if you were, for example, to create a group that you decided to call "trusted" and put a machine named xpclient in that group, then xpclient would not look to the rest of the network like a member of trusted *until you rebooted xpclient*. I figured that a simple `netdom reset` command would do the trick, but as far as I can see, adding a machine to a group or deleting a machine from a group doesn't really take effect until you reboot the machine.

If you're following along in my example then at this point you should start up Active Directory Users and Computers and create a new global group in bigfirm.com called trusted, and add xpclient to it. Then reboot xpclient to make the membership change actually happen.

CREATE AND TEST IPSEC POLICIES LINKING THE CLIENT MACHINES AND SERVERS

Next, examine how the client systems communicate with the server, and create IPsec policies on both the clients and the server to allow them to communicate either with signed (*integrity* in the lingo of the Windows IPsec interface, or *AH* in IPsec RFC-speak) or encrypted (*integrity and encryption* in the Windows UI, *ESP* in RFC-speak) communications. If all you're interested in is the IPsec bypass, than either signing or encrypting will do fine because IPsec bypass is interested only in seeing the client machine authenticate to the server machine, and signing and encrypting are the only two of the four IPsec filter actions that require authentication. (The other two IPsec filter actions are permit and block.) If your main interest in IPsec is as a vehicle to IPsec bypass, then remember that signing takes a lot less CPU power than encrypting and therefore signing might be preferable.

Let's quickly review IPsec. (It's covered in more detail in Chapter 6 of *Mastering Windows Server 2003.*) Recall that IPsec policies are composed of one or more IPsec rules, and that IPsec rules incorporate two main mandatory parts and a sometimes-mandatory one:

IP Filter List   This tells the IPsec policy agent running on every 2000, XP, and 2003 system when to wake up and do something. More specifically, IP filter lists look like "use this rule when you see traffic coming from X to Y from port A to port B." X and Y can be very general, as in "from any IP address to any IP address"; a bit more specific, as in "from any IP address to my IP address"; very specific, as in "from 10.50.50.37 to 10.50.50.42"; or anything in between. The source and destination ports can be either "any port" or a particular port. IP filter lists also specify whether a communication is TCP, UDP, or another protocol. So, for example, if one of your clients were at 10.50.50.37 and the server were at 10.50.50.39 and you only needed the client to be able to access the web service on 10.50.50.39, then you could build an IP filter list along the lines of "this filter kicks in when there's traffic from 10.50.50.37, any port, to 10.50.50.39 on port 80, protocol TCP." Alternatively, someone just liking IPsec's ability to, say, digitally sign traffic might create an IP filter list that says "any data coming from any IP address on the Internet to my IP address." Such a filter would *always* kick in for any IP traffic. Filter lists can also be "mirrored" to save time in creating them. The idea behind mirroring is that if you want, for example, your data to be encrypted when A talks to B, then you probably also want encryption when B replies to A. An IPsec rule can incorporate as many IP filter lists as you like.

Filter Action   This says, "Now that the criteria for the IP filter list's criteria have been met, what do we do?" There are four possible actions: permit the traffic to pass untouched, block the traffic from arriving, sign the traffic, or encrypt it. Thus, you could use IPsec as a means to block some arbitrary port 107 by first creating an IP filter list that says, "Employ this rule whenever there is data coming from any IP address, any port to my IP address, TCP port 107," and the resultant action would be, "Block the traffic." By writing many of these rules, one could create a software firewall on any IPsec-aware system. If signing or encrypting, then there are many different cryptographic algorithms, and both sides of the conversation would have to agree on an algorithm.

Authentication   If the filter action is either signing or encrypting, then both sides of the conversation must authenticate to each other. Windows IPsec supports three ways of authenticating. First, both sides might know the same text password, like "open sesame" or the like. Second, both sides might offer certificates to prove their identity. (Note again that when IPsec says "authentication," it wants one *machine* to authenticate itself to another *machine*—there are no user accounts involved here.) Finally, Windows IPsec supports using Active Directory's Kerberos protocol to authenticate between the two parties to the conversation. As mentioned before, IPsec bypass requires Kerberos authentication; shared secrets or certificates will not work.

Putting it together, then, to allow a client at 10.50.50.37 to always sign any communications with the web server on the system at 10.50.50.39, then you'd build two IPsec policies: one for the client and one for the server.

The server policy would look like

◆ IP filter list: "This filter activates when data originates from anywhere on the Internet on any port to my IP address, TCP port 80. This filter is mirrored, so whatever action we take on receiving this incoming data we should also do to my replies."

◆ Filter action: "Digitally sign all traffic, using SHA-1." (SHA is Secure Hashing Algorithm, and it's commonly used for digital signatures.)

◆ Authentication: "Let's use Kerberos."

You create IPsec policies on a computer either by working in the GUI interface of the local Group Policy Editor, or by creating a domain-based group policy object containing an IPsec policy, or from the command line with either `ipseccmd` on XP or `netsh ipsec` on 2003. (And please forgive me for not taking you through the process click by click, but it's not the focus of this chapter and besides, if I did, then I'd have to reproduce about 25 pages from Chapter 6 of the earlier book.)

The client would also need an IPsec policy. It might look like

◆ IP filter list: "This filter activates when data originates from my IP address on any port to 10.50.50.39 on TCP port 80. It is mirrored." Thus, the client has a fairly specific filter that only kicks in when doing web communication with a particular system.

◆ Filter action: "Digitally sign all traffic, using SHA-1."

◆ Authentication: "Let's use Kerberos."

Once you've got these policies in place, I highly recommend testing them. I'd fire up a copy of IE on the client and point it at the server to ensure that the IPsec relationship ("security association" is the RFC-ese for "relationship") can be established. While I'm at it, here are a few notes on testing and troubleshooting an IPsec security association.

Use XP and 2003's IP Security Monitor

Sometimes it's difficult to figure out if IPsec is doing *anything*. So XP and 2003 have an MMC snap-in called the IP Security Monitor, but most people just call it "ipsecmon." It's a quite different animal from the Windows 2000 ipsecmon, in case you've ever used that.

You start it up by just opening up an MMC and choosing File ➢ Add/Remove Snap-in, and then Add and IP Security Monitor. It'll show you two or three folders. If you're running 2003, then you get a first folder Active Policy, but you won't get that folder in the XP version of ipsecmon. Both XP and 2003 have folders named Main Mode and Quick Mode. Once you've got IE running on xpclient and have got the message "Welcome to the secure server!" or whatever message you put in the `default.htm` file on web.bigfirm.com, then you can quickly check whether or not you have a security association with web.bigfirm.com.

Open the Quick Mode folder and you'll see a folder inside of it called Security Associations. Inside it, you'll see one or more lines describing each of your IPsec connections to other systems. If xpclient's talking to the web, then you'll see a line saying that the source address is 10.50.50.37, the destination address is 10.50.50.39, the protocol is TCP, and so on. If the folder's blank, press F5, as ipsecmon sometimes needs to be refreshed.

Add a Bogus GP Setting

Can't see any security association in ipsecmon, or perhaps IE just sat there for a bit and finally gave up with a "cannot find server" error message? Then you may have fallen prey to something that I see now and then: an ignored local group policy.

When setting up an ad hoc testing platform like the one I've described here, I find that the quickest and easiest way to set up the IPsec policies on the client and server are just to open up `gpedit.msc`, the Group Policy Editor, and just create the IPsec policy in the local group policy object. But now and then XP—it doesn't seem to happen in 2003—will simply ignore its local group policy object altogether. I have no idea why, but it only happens if the *only* settings in the local group policy object are IPsec policies.

My workaround was to find an innocuous setting in Administrative Templates and enable it. All of a sudden XP noticed that its local GPO had settings in it, and I got my IPsec policy enabled. By the way, the innocuous policy setting that I've used is Computer Configuration ➢ Administrative ➢ Templates ➢ System ➢ Internet Communication Management ➢ Internet Communication settings, and I enable the Turn Off the "Order Prints" Picture Task.

Load Group Policy Management Console (GPMC)

I banged my head against the wall for a few hours trying to figure out why my blasted xpclient system couldn't set up an IPsec communication with the web machine. Then I realized that hey, this is a question of what and why group policy's doing what it's doing, and the best tool for that is… GPMC. I downloaded it onto the xpclient box, ran a Resultant Set of Policies report, and that's how I found out that the local group policy object was being ignored because the XP box thought that the local GPO was "empty."

If You're Using Virtual Machines, Force a Time Synchronization

Once I was playing with IPsec security associations between a client and a server and nothing, I mean *nothing* could make it work. But then I looked more closely and noticed two things. First, the client and server were virtual machines running on my laptop. Second, *their clocks were 18 minutes apart*. In order for Kerberos to work, all systems in an AD must have their clocks synchronized to no more than about five minutes apart, and clocks on VMs tend to drift. I opened up a command prompt on the client and server and typed `net time /set /yes` on each. They then had the same time as the domain controller, and everything started working. (Remember that `w32tm /resync` also works and is a more modern command, as you read in Chapter 8 of *Mastering Windows Server 2003*.)

When You Modify an IPsec Policy, Unassign and Assign It

If you find that you've made a mistake in the settings of your IPsec policy, then you may find that your system doesn't always take notice of it. I find that explicitly unassigning, then reassigning the policy in Group Policy Editor can give IPsec the kick in the pants that it sometimes needs.

ENABLE IPSEC BYPASS AND ENTER THE GROUP'S SID

With confidence in your IPsec security associations, it's time to go to the server and enable IPsec bypass. Remember, this is an instruction to the *server's* firewall; you needn't fiddle with IPsec bypass on every system, just the servers that you want to use IPsec bypass.

There's only one way that I know of to enable and configure IPsec bypass: through a group policy setting. It works both with the local group policy object or a domain group policy object. No GUI or command options here. You find the group policy setting in Computer Configuration ➤ Administrative Tools ➤ Network ➤ Network Connections ➤ Windows Firewall, Windows Firewall: Allow Authenticated IPsec Bypass. When opened and configured, it looks like Figure 8.19.

Basically, this dialog box has to do two things. First, it's got to say to the computer, "Do IPsec bypass—any systems in this group with IPsec security associations get to skip the firewall rules." That's easy; just clicking the Enabled radio button accomplishes that. But the second thing is to actually *name* the group. That's what goes in that field labeled Define IPsec Peers to be Exempted from Firewall Policy.

You'll notice from the screen shot that the field is not filled with something like "trusted," which you'll recall was the name that I gave to the group that I created in AD for the clients that I wanted my web server to trust. Anyway, I'm not sure why Microsoft did this, but you don't name the group; instead, you type in this string:

```
O:DAG:DAD:(A;;RCGW;;;sid-of-group)
```

Yes, it's strange-looking, formatted in something that Microsoft calls the Security Descriptor Definition Language, or SDDL, but you needn't worry about that. You just need to find the SID of the group containing the trusted machines. For example, the SID of "trusted" on my domain is S-1-5-21-1630122595-2559777985-2744330755-1109, so my completed SDDL string for the IPsec bypass policy setting is

FIGURE 8.19
IPsec bypass group
policy setting

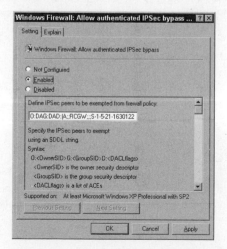

O:DAG:DAD:(A;;RCGW;;;S-1-5-21-1630122595-2559777985-2744330755-1109) How, though, to get the SID of a group? Probably the easiest way is to surf over to www.sysinternals.com and get Mark Russinovich's command-line tool psgetsid.exe. Once you've got it, just open up a command prompt and type **psgetsid trusted**. The result I get is

```
PsGetSid v1.42 - Translates SIDs to names and vice versa
Copyright (C) 1999-2004 Mark Russinovich
Sysinternals - www.sysinternals.com

SID for BIGFIRM1\trusted:
S-1-5-21-1630122595-2559777985-2744330755-1109
```

You can actually include more than one group, and you can use SIDs of individual machine accounts instead of groups. Just repeat the sequence in parentheses right after the first parenthesized sequence with no spaces, commas, or other punctuation in between them. For example, if I had another client named mypc with a SID of S-1-5-21-1630122595-2559777985-2744330755-1110, then I could tell my web server to trust both the members of the group trusted and the particular machine mypc with this SDDL string:

O:DAG:DAD:(A;;RCGW;;;S-1-5-21-1630122595-2559777985-2744330755-1109) (A;;RCGW;;;S-1-5-21-1630122595-2559777985-2744330755-1110)

TIP If you want to use psgetsid to get the SID of a computer/machine account, don't type psgetsid *machinename*; instead, add a $ to the end of the machine name, as in **psgetsid** *machinename***$**.

RAISE THE SHIELDS!

Once you've got the AD in place, the group or groups built, the members in the groups, the IPsec security associations working, and the IPsec bypass group policy setting enabled and configured, then it's time to turn on Windows Firewall on the server that you want to protect. If you've followed these instructions, then you'll now have a server that in general accepts *no* incoming communications except for those from its favored guests.

TIP Wondering how the IPsec security association gets created on a system with no firewall exceptions? If you assign an IPsec policy to a system, then WF automatically creates exceptions for 500 UDP and 4500 UDP, allowing the IPsec negotiation.

Watching WF

Finally, let's consider firewall logging. Don't you want to know what WF's doing? Well, sometimes you'll need to. So WF will create a nice ASCII log for you of its success in its ongoing battle between you and the worms.

Configuring Logging From the GUI

From the GUI, go to the Advanced tab and look for the area labeled Security Logging. Click Settings and you'll see a dialog box like the one in Figure 8.20.

As you can see, this lets you control the location, name, and size of the firewall log. It also lets you specify whether to log passed packets, blocked packets, or both.

FIGURE 8.20
Configuring the
firewall log

Configuring Logging from the Command Line

From the command line, you can control the same things as the GUI, with this line:

```
netsh firewall set logging [filelocation=path] [maxfilesize=size in Kbytes]
[droppedpackets=Enable|Disable] [connections=Enable|Disable]
```

Notice that there's not a global "turn the logging on" or "turn the logging off" setting. Instead, you decide independently whether to log successes (`connections`) or failures (`droppedpackets`). For example, to completely turn on logging, you'd type

```
netsh firewall set logging droppedpackets=enable connections=enable
```

Configuring Logging from Group Policies

To control firewall logging from group policies, look in either the Standard Profile or Domain Profile folders for the Windows Firewall: Allow Logging Properties, and you'll see a dialog like the one in Figure 8.21.

As you can see, the dialog box is nearly identical to the one presented in the GUI from the Advanced tab.

FIGURE 8.21
Group policy firewall
logging settings

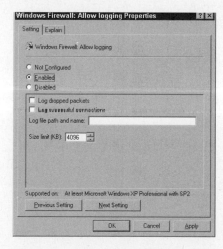

Summary

Windows Firewall is not only an improvement over the Internet Connection Firewall, it's, well, the first version of Windows' built-in firewall that passes the "laugh test." But it does quite a lot more, as you've seen, including its powerful IPsec bypass feature that, if tweaked a bit, can provide a whole new level of security to an intranet. If you haven't checked it out yet, it's worth examining more closely and, as I always say, the price is right.

Chapter 9

Thwarting Mobile Thieves: Blocking USB Memory Sticks

In the 2003 movie *The Recruit*, a bad guy steals data from a supposedly secure CIA computer. (Don't bother watching the movie unless you enjoy Al Pacino when he's in over-the-top mode.) This CIA computer has no CD or DVD drives and no floppy drive, and even if it *did*, then the bad guy would have been discovered as his stuff was searched and scanned on the way out. So how'd he steal the data? Simple: he plugged a small USB memory drive into a USB slot on the computer, copied data onto the USB device, and walked out the door. As USB devices can be as small as key fobs or even watches, the highly trained guards never noticed the device. (Okay, in reality the guards didn't notice it because they read the script, and the script said that they shouldn't notice it.)

Unfortunately, theaters let all kinds of people into their establishments, and so, unbelievably, nontechnical people saw this (jargon check: *nontechnical people* means *managers*) and panicked. Some folks thought that the answer to this would be—I'm not kidding—to simply squeeze epoxy into the USB slots on their computers.

Actually, being concerned about small, easily interfaced devices isn't panic. Anyone running an organization whose data is of value and who lets people sit down at modern computers runs the risk that those people could copy that data onto some small and either inconspicuous or easily concealed device, and most of those devices interface to a computer via a USB port. There are the familiar rectangular USB memory devices called "jump drives," "stick drives," "memory sticks," or the like. There is also the ever-growing legion of small portable and personal music and video playback devices. In the past three years, I've purchased three different digital cameras, and they all look, when plugged into an XP or 2003 computer, just like a removable drive. There's a wristwatch available that has an inconspicuous cable incorporated into it with a USB plug at the end and some memory in the watch. In short, USB devices are both ubiquitous and hard to detect. On top of that, XP, 2003, and to an extent, 2000-based systems ship with USB memory-device drivers already installed. That means that by default most of the computer world is ready, willing, and able to let people steal your data in a matter of minutes and stealthily take that data away physically.

What's to be done about it? Well, Vista and the new version of Windows Server have a neat feature whereby you can, using centralized group policies, ban entire classes of hardware. You could, for example, instruct a network of Vista client machines and Server 2007/8 systems to refuse to recognize USB memory drives, joysticks, and digital cameras entirely. But as I write this in June 2006, neither of those operating systems are available.

XP SP2, 2003 SP1, and R2, however, offer at least a little help: the ability to flick a switch in the Registry and render all USB memory devices read-only. Once you flick that switch, then people can still plug USB memory devices into your USB ports, but they can then only copy data from the USB device to your computer, not the other way around.

Making USB Devices Read-Only

I am told that a branch of the U.S. military—the one for which the unit of length "fathom" might make sense—asked Microsoft to do something to give them some leverage over USB data thieves, and this XP SP2, 2003 SP1, and R2 feature appeared. Here's how to make it work.

1. Open Regedit.

2. Navigate to `HKEY_LOCAL_MACHINE\SYSTEM\CurrentControlSet\Control`.

3. In the key, create a new key by right-clicking the HKEY_LOCAL_MACHINE\ SYSTEM\CurrentControlSet\Control key and choosing New/Key.

4. Call the new key StorageDevicePolicies.

5. In the new key, create a REG_DWORD entry called WriteProtect.

6. To enable the USB read-only feature, set WriteProtect to 1; to disable it, set WriteProtect to 0.

This change takes effect the next time that you plug a USB memory device into a USB port. If you set WriteProtect to 1 and try to create a new file on that USB memory device, you'll get an error dialog box that says `Unable to create the file 'filename.' The media is write protected`. (Then it offers just one button labeled OK. You have to wonder where the "not okay" button is.)

Is This of Any Value?

Could a bad guy get around this? Sure, in a number of ways.

◆ First, this feature only applies to USB devices that use the generic, built-in USB memory device driver. Were someone to connect something that required its own driver to a computer, then of course the read-only restriction would not apply to that device.

◆ Second, the would-be thief could always just modify the Registry to set WriteProtect back to zero, disabling the feature. Just pulling out the USB device and re-inserting it would then restore the device to read/write status.

◆ Third, the thief could always open up the computer's case and steal the hard disk in the computer. Desktop hard disks are smaller than most paperbacks, and notebook hard disks are smaller than a deck of cards. Neither presents a great physical burden to carry away, and a notebook hard disk could probably be put into one's pocket and remain unnoticed.

◆ Fourth, a thief could burn data onto a CD or DVD, assuming that there is a burner drive on the computer.

Are these critical flaws in the USB read-only feature? Yes and no. Let's look into them in more detail, but first, let me pass along some background. When I first learned of this feature, I thought it was pretty neat. So I was surprised when some of my contacts in the Microsoft security group were very disparaging of this feature. "What's wrong with this?" I asked. They replied with the four bullet points that you just read. They're smart guys, but I don't agree with them, so let's look more closely into these objections.

First, it is certainly true that any USB device using a driver other than the built-in storage would be read/write. But then the thief would have to have the privileges necessary to load a new driver. In other words, the thief would have to be an administrator.

Well, if that's the case, then it's pretty much "game over," security-wise, no matter what you do. Admins can do anything because they're admins. If you give someone both physical access to one of your systems and give that person administrator-level rights, then all of the security in the world won't help you—that person's got the ability to do anything to that machine. So if we're talking about a situation where a consultant or guest needed access to a machine, then I'd give her user-level permissions. Or watch her, because, again, there's no way to protect your computer from someone with that level of power. And let me take that point one bit further by pointing out that while Vista does indeed have the ability to ban certain classes of hardware, once again, a local administrator could override that.

Second, it's also true that a thief could modify the Registry but, then, again, he'd have to be an administrator to do that, and we've already considered that issue. Third, a bad guy could indeed open up a computer and steal a hard disk, given a lack of supervision. That's why I recommend putting guest-available machines in some open, public place where anything someone did would be obvious. Finally, you can restrict CD burning and DVD burning ability by keeping burners off your guest-available machines.

Is the USB read-only setting a perfect answer? No. But, if you assume physical access by people with local administrator powers, then there will never be a perfect answer. But if something like this can slow down one of the bad guys then hey, it's better than nothing. I mean, he *would* have to know what Registry bit to flip before he could steal data, and not everyone's smart enough to own this book, right?

Summary

Small, portable USB devices do indeed constitute a threat of data theft. Vista and Server 2007 will offer a fairly solid countermeasure in a set of new group policies that let you lock out entire classes of hardware (like USB stick drives), but until then we've got at least partial help in this Registry entry. Try it out and, with the cautions enumerated in this chapter, you may find that it offers your organization a bit of peace of mind.

Chapter 10

Supporting Clients with Windows Terminal Services

Multiuser Windows, server-based computing, thin client computing—whatever you call it, it's part of the core Windows Server OS. Multiuser Windows has been around for quite a while. Citrix created MultiWin, the set of extensions to Windows NT that enables it to run multiple user sessions from the same machine. The first MultiWin product was multiuser NT 3.51, Citrix's WinFrame. Starting in July 1998, Microsoft began shipping its Terminal Server Edition of NT 4 (TSE). Terminal Services first became part of the core OS with Windows 2000, and in Server 2003 it is installed (but not enabled, for security reasons) by default. Even Windows XP has the same multiuser core required for Terminal Services, manifest in both Remote Desktop and in Fast User Switching. And in Server 2003, Terminal Services has gained a number of new client- and server-side features that make the service attractive even without using the once unavoidable Presentation Server—in smaller environments, anyway.

Installing Terminal Services is easy. Creating a working terminal server capable of supporting multiple users, all running different applications and wanting to use their client-side resources, may not be. You'll need to do a fair amount of tweaking once you get past the basic step of running Notepad from the terminal server. If you're serious about administering a terminal server, I *highly* recommend you make the Terminal Services section of the Microsoft Knowledge Base your favorite pleasure reading because this is relatively new territory to Microsoft and they're still working the bugs out. This chapter will do the basic legwork for you, however.

Why Care about Terminal Services?

Terminal Services gives you secure remote access to a computer and requires little enough bandwidth that you can use it over low-speed connections. So?

The first reason to care about Terminal Services applies to anyone using Windows Servers, not just people wanting to support an application server. Terminal Services has two modes: Remote Administration (the default, discussed at the end of this chapter) and Application Server (which I'll concentrate on in this chapter). Remote Administration enables you to manage Windows Server computers from across a network, without limiting your access to tools within the Microsoft Management Console (MMC) or even requiring you to use Windows Server 2003 or 2000 as the managing operating system. If you don't use Terminal Services for anything else, use it for managing servers without having to physically move from console to console. Turn to the section "Using Remote Administration Mode" to read more about the requirements for remote management access, how to enable it, how to connect, and what you should know about it.

In this chapter, however, I'll focus on how you can use Application Server mode—the "terminal server" part of Terminal Services—to support clients. If any of the following are important to you, then seriously consider how you could use Application Server mode:

◆ Deploying and managing applications only on a few terminal servers instead of on hundreds or thousands of client computers.

◆ Providing applications to end-users whom you cannot easily support because they're in another office—or another country.

◆ Reducing the impact of client hardware failures by keeping all applications on a central server. If a client's computer dies, plug in a new one and they're back to work.

◆ Avoiding misconfigured computers.

◆ Getting out of the hardware rat race that constantly requires more updates to support the latest and greatest software.

◆ Using computers in environments that are not compatible with desktop computers.

◆ Simplifying help desk and training support.

WHAT'S NEW IN SERVICE PACK 1?

Windows Server 2003 Terminal Services was a major improvement over Windows 2000's. Similarly, SP1 makes some really necessary changes. These changes aren't new client features but server-side modifications that should make your life easier. These changes are discussed in detail in this chapter.

GENERIC PRINTER DRIVER SUPPORT

Quite a few companies make a good business out of printer driver support for Terminal Services because the support built into it can take a lot of work to get set up, and if you don't set it up properly Bad Things (like crashed terminal servers) can happen. (Luckily, these days this isn't as much of a problem. Windows Server 2003 has a group policy enabling you to permit only user-mode drivers, and printer companies got enough bad press from the terminal server crashes that they wrote better drivers.) One solution to this printer driver problem is to support a generic printer driver that may not look great, but will produce a decent print job if nothing else is available—and it won't crash the terminal server. Citrix introduced a generic printer driver in its product years ago. Now in SP1, Microsoft has got its own generic printer driver. At 300 dpi and black and white it's not beautiful, but as a fallback it works for printing text.

LICENSING IMPROVEMENTS

Licensing remains a headache for Microsoft for two reasons: it wasn't developed from a plan so much as it "just growed" and it's enforced, meaning that a licensing problem can prevent users from working. Licensing isn't fixed in SP1, but some incremental improvements will help you.

Better License Server Discovery This change isn't well documented, but it's important. Anyone who's tried loading the terminal server and license server on the same server may have noticed that the terminal server couldn't find the license server via discovery and it would only appear if you explicitly pointed the terminal server to the license server. The problem was that the terminal server's search algorithm didn't include looking at *itself* for the license server. This is now fixed.

Group Policy Support for Choosing a License Mode   I used to be a program manager on the Microsoft Terminal Services team. One of the two problems that people most often called in about had as its root cause that the terminal server was in the wrong mode—it was set up for per-device licensing when all that were available were per-user licenses. This group policy at least makes it easier to apply a global fix if you discover that you retained the default setting but bought per-user licenses.

UI and Group Policy Support for Specifying a License Server   The *other* main problem that people called Microsoft about was license server discovery problems. One way to just avoid the whole problem is to point the terminal server to a license server. You've always been able to do this by editing the Registry, but now you can do it through Terminal Services Configuration or through group policy.

SSL Authentication and Encryption for RDP Connections

SP1 allows you to configure the Remote Desktop client to use SSL security. This authenticates the server so an unwitting user doesn't provide sensitive information through a rogue server spoofing a real one. It also provides another level of encryption for the connection.

Group Policy Support for Starting a Single Application

It's always been possible to configure RDP to display only a single application on connection, but doing this has been a laborious process. With SP1, you can specify the starting application using group policy.

Centralized Deployment of Applications

One great benefit to Terminal Services is how it simplifies application deployment to the clients. Windows Server 2003 has some application deployment tools in the form of group policy objects (GPOs), and Chapter 9 of *Mastering Windows Server 2003* discusses those tools in detail. If you use GPOs to deploy applications to the Desktop, you can create packages that enable you to run applications on the client computer while making those applications "maintainable" from a central point. GPOs have their failings, however. First, you can't use GPOs with just any Win32 operating system; instead you must use Windows 2000 Professional or Windows XP clients—and you will need to check the version information for the GPOs, as some require Windows XP clients. Second, setting up GPOs effectively is not necessarily a simple matter. Third, you can't always use GPOs to deploy applications across a low-bandwidth network connection well—the application packages may not be small. Finally, all these factors make GPOs a questionable method of application deployment for any applications that need to be updated frequently (as some database clients do). The more often you need to deploy an application across the network, the greater the chance something weird will happen along the way.

Using Terminal Services to deploy applications has its own difficulties—namely, getting all the applications and all the users to play nicely in the same space and keeping users connected to the server—but it avoids the problems and limitations associated with GPOs. For example, when you update an application installed on a terminal server, it's instantly updated for everyone using that server. Any operating system that has a Remote Desktop Protocol (RDP) client (and, these days, that can include Macintosh and Linux clients as well as Win32) can use the terminal server, so you're not limited to deploying applications to the higher-end clients. A Terminal Services connection requires little bandwidth to get core functionality, so you can use it on busy or slow network connections. And, because you're not actually sending applications or data across the network or installing applications on the clients, once an application starts working it typically keeps working.

Running applications on a terminal server is not a trouble-free process; getting things set up properly and keeping people from fiddling with the terminal server is important. Some older or badly designed applications won't work at all in a multiuser environment. (Generally, though, if it's certified for Windows XP it will work on a terminal server.) And in case you thought installing applications on a terminal server meant you could support many users with a single license, think again—you'll still need to pay for application licensing for each user or computer connecting to the applications published on the terminal server. However, this basic fact remains true: Set a compatible application up once on the terminal server, and its updates are available to everyone who has access to the terminal server, without the need for any changes to the client.

Supporting Remote Users

I live and work just south of Washington, DC. The company I work for is based in Frankfurt, Germany. If I ran into a problem with one of my applications or needed to update its computer, we'd need to either fly someone three thousand miles to fix my computer or I'd need to do it myself. I'm kind of busy, so I don't like the second option. Everyone else is also kind of busy, so they don't like the first option. Therefore, every application I use at work is available to me on a terminal server. Accessing my applications remotely also means that, when I get a new work computer, I don't need to rebuild much of anything, just connect to the application portal.

This isn't an unusual situation. More and more people are telecommuting at least a couple of days a week. Many U.S. government agencies have a legal *requirement* to support telecommuters. They don't even have offices or desks for all their staff. Rather than trying to maintain desktop computers, they're giving the users computers to take home and providing their applications on terminal servers.

Supporting PC-Unfriendly Environments

The dream of "a PC on every desktop" will remain a dream, if for no other reason than in some environments the conditions are bad for the PC or the PC is bad for the conditions. In other words, you can't run a PC everywhere.

Some environments are bad for PCs. PCs do not like dust, excessive heat, or vibration, and *you* will not like maintaining the PCs if you try to use them in an environment that has any of these characteristics. PCs are also a commodity item; if you leave them unattended and unguarded where just anyone can get to them, they will disappear. For these reasons, Windows terminals are a popular choice in environments that are PC-unfriendly but still need access to Windows applications. Warehouses and unattended trucker kiosks (where the truckers can log in to display and print their shipping orders from a terminal) are two good examples of how to use Windows terminals in PC-unfriendly environments. I've also seen terminals in health club cafes and coffeehouses set up so that only the monitor is visible, thus reducing the chances of someone dropping a strawberry-banana low-fat smoothie with a shot of wheatgrass juice down the vents. For that matter, if someone does drop said smoothie down the terminal's vents, then, because the applications are installed on and running from the terminal server, replacing the device to provide an identical environment is as simple as unplugging the sticky terminal and plugging in a new one. If you drop the smoothie down a computer's vents, then restoring an identical working environment is significantly more complicated.

What about PCs being bad for the conditions? Clean rooms where chips and boards are made are good candidates for Windows terminals. You can't have dust in a clean room, and the fans in a PC kick up dust. Additionally, becoming sanitized to enter a clean room is neither simple nor inexpensive; you don't want to put devices that need care and feeding from the IT staff in there. Another factor applies to many situations, not just clean rooms: anyplace where space is at a premium is a good candidate for Windows terminals.

This section isn't to sell you on the idea of Windows terminals but to point out that sometimes they're useful, even required—and you can't use them without a terminal server.

POWER STRUGGLES

Another aspect of the environment-unfriendly PC applies to the power a desktop PC uses. Inspired by the California energy crises of 2000 and 2001, my cohort Steve Greenberg and I did a couple of lab and real-world studies to see how desktop-centric computing and server-based computing compared in terms of power usage. What we found was sobering: A server-based computing network required less power to provide application support than did a desktop-centric environment, even when the client computers for accessing the terminal server were desktop computers instead of terminals. In fact, the Windows terminals used so little power that the use of terminals increased the difference dramatically.

If you're interested in the results of our research, you can download the main study at www.thinclient.net (look in the "What's New" section for the link), but here are the highlights: The desktop PCs we tested had a constant power draw of about 85 watts when running applications locally (excluding a 15-inch CRT monitor, which drew an additional 85 watts). Running applications from a terminal server, the desktop PC power usage dropped to 69 watts—not a big difference on a small scale, but this difference increases as the network grows. The terminals we tested drew less than 10 watts, or 24 watts with a built-in LCD display. If you're assuming (as many did) that the power use of the terminal server was great enough to offset the gains realized by using server-based computing, think again. Although a terminal server used an average of 141 watts in our testing (the power draw fluctuated depending on how many people were using it), a terminal server can support many clients, so its greater power draw is offset by the number of people it's supporting.

The power savings realized become more dramatic as the network gets larger—and as power gets more expensive. If you'd like to figure out how much you're spending on power, then calculate the result of $n*p*h*52$ to get the number of kilowatts (kW) your client computers use each year, where n is the number of desktop devices, p is the power (in kW) used by each device, h is the number of hours each week that the devices are turned on, and 52 is the number of weeks in a year. For example, say your network has 5,000 client computers, each powered on 50 hours a week. If the 5,000 clients are PCs with CRT displays running applications locally (.17kW), then they'll use 5000*1.7kW*50*52, or 2,210,000 kW each year. If the 5,000 clients are thin clients with integrated LCD panels (.024kW), they'll use 5000*.024kW*50*52, or 31,200kW each year. Say those 5000 thin clients need 200 servers (.141kW) to support them, and those servers are on 24/7. In that case, the calculation is 200*.141kW*168*52, or 246,355.2, giving you a total of 277,555.2kW.

Based on these calculations, at 0.20 per kW, serving applications with the PC network costs $442,000 to run each year. Serving applications via a thin client network—with servers on all the time—costs $55,511.04. And we haven't even begun to talk about other aspects of Total Cost of Ownership or the investment required to keep IT hardware up and running. Nor have we talked about how reducing power usage reduces power costs because dissipating two units of heat (generated by power-sucking devices) requires one unit of energy.

Saving on power costs is not the only reason to use Windows terminals, but, if you're tossing around the idea of replacing PCs with terminals, it's a compelling argument in favor of it.

Fewer Hardware Refreshes

First, about those ever-more-powerful computers: does it take a 2GHz Pentium with 1GB of RAM installed to check email, do accounting, and poke around on the Web a bit? Of course it doesn't, but, as of mid-2006, that's not an unusual hardware profile for a desktop computer. Not that these computers are too expensive in absolute terms; I'm wryly amused that every time I buy a new computer, I pay less for a system more powerful than the last one I bought. But although they're not too expensive in absolute terms, the new computers aren't always worth it because what you're doing doesn't demand all that much from your hardware. Ironically, unless your job is something demanding such as computer-assisted design, you're often more likely to need a powerful computer at home than at work because game hardware requirements are so high. It takes more computing power to play a few swift rounds of WarCraft III than it does to write this chapter. (Fighting orcs is hard work!)

The trouble is, sometimes you do need those more powerful computers if you're planning to keep up with existing software technology. True—you don't need the world's fastest computer to do word processing. You may, however, need a computer faster than the one you have if you're going to keep up with the latest and greatest word processing package that everyone's using. If you want to be able to read all those charts and graphs, you can't always do it when the word processor you're using is six years old, even if it still suits your in-house needs. And you can't always run that new word processor if your computer is six years old.

If you're using Terminal Services to support applications, however, the client only displays applications running on the terminal server, rather than running them locally—you don't have to concern yourself with whether the applications will run on the client computer, just the server. If the application will run on the terminal server and the client can get to the terminal server, then the application will display on the client. As I'll discuss in this chapter, you may need to tweak an application to make it run *well* on the terminal server, and a few applications won't run well at all, but you can use Terminal Services to get an application to a computer that would not normally support it, thus lengthening your client upgrade cycle.

Simplifying the User Interface

Another potential benefit to Terminal Services is it can simplify the user interface (UI). Using a computer isn't as easy as the marketing would have you believe. Experienced users find it easy to customize their interface, but those who are less experienced find all sorts of pitfalls when it comes to using their computers: so many options that they get confused, and too many ways to break something. Colorful icons with rounded corners do not a simple UI make.

Terminal Services does not automatically make the UI simpler. But, as I'll explain later in this chapter, it's possible to run either a complete desktop from a terminal server or a single application. With third-party products such as Presentation Server, you can present applications in a web browser. If the people you're supporting only need a single application, then you can save yourself and them a lot of grief by providing a connection that runs it and nothing else. This is particularly true with Windows-based terminals, which are little more than a monitor, a box, a keyboard, and mouse.

Providing Help Desk Support

Finally, Terminal Services can make application support easier, not just in terms of installing new applications and applying fixes, but in helping people learn to use those applications. Remote Control lets administrators connect to another person's terminal session either to watch what they're doing or to interact with the session. (This isn't the security hole it may seem—you must have permission to do this, and by default the person to whom you're connecting has to permit the connection before you can see their screen.) When you have remote control of another user's session, you can either watch what they're doing and coach them (perhaps over the telephone) or actually interact with the session so that you can demonstrate a process. This beats standing over someone's shoulder saying, "Click the File button at the top left. No, *File*. The FILE button," or trying to figure out what they're doing when your only information comes from their description of the screen. I'll talk more about how to use Remote Control later in this chapter.

The Terminal Server Processing Model

I mentioned the many versions of Terminal Services earlier in this chapter. Regardless of which one you're using, in a broad sense they all work pretty much the same way. *Thin client networking* or *server-based computing* (same thing, different emphasis) refers to any computing environment in which most application processing takes place on a server enabled for multiuser access, instead of a client. The terms refer to a network by definition, so it leaves out stand-alone small computing devices such as personal digital assistants (PDAs) or handheld PCs, although you can add thin client support to some of these devices. What makes thin client networking and computing "thin" is neither the size of the operating system nor the complexity of the apps run on the client, but how processing is distributed. In a thin client network, all processing takes place on the server, instructions for creating video output travel from server to client, mouse clicks and keystrokes pass from the client to the server, and all video output is rendered on the client.

Son of Mainframe?

You may have heard thin client networking described as *a return to the mainframe paradigm*. (I have heard this less politely phrased as "You just reinvented the mainframe, stupid!") This comparison is partly apt and partly misleading. It's true that applications are stored and run on a central server, with only output shown at the client. However, the applications being run in the thin client environment are different from those run in a mainframe environment; mainframes didn't support word processing or slideshow packages, and the video demands on the graphical Windows client are necessarily greater than they were with a text-based green-screen terminal. Yet the degree of control that thin client networking offers is mainframe-like, and I've heard one person happily describe thin client networking and the command it gave him over his user base as "a return to the good old mainframe days."

Why the move from centralized computing to personal computers and back again? Business applications drove the development of PCs—the new applications simply couldn't work in a mainframe environment. Not all mainframes were scrapped, by any means, but the newer application designs were too hardware-intensive to work well in a shared computing environment. But those applications came back to a centralized model when it became clear that the mainframe model had some things to offer that a PC-based LAN did not:

♦ Grouping of computing resources to make sure none are wasted

♦ Centralized distribution and maintenance of applications

♦ Clients that don't have to be running the latest and greatest operating system with the latest and greatest hardware to support it

♦ Client machines that don't require power protection because they're not running any applications locally

All in all, reinventing the mainframe has its advantages. Just as PCs didn't replace mainframes, server-based computing isn't replacing PCs. However, it's nice to have the option to use server-based computing when it makes more sense than installing applications on the Desktop.

Anatomy of a Thin Client Session

A thin client networking session has three parts:

◆ The *terminal server*, running a multiuser operating system

◆ The *display protocol*, which is a data link layer protocol that creates a virtual channel between server and client through which user input and graphical output can flow

◆ The *client*, which can be running any kind of operating system that supports the terminal client

THE TERMINAL SERVER

Terminal Services is one of the optional components you can choose to install during Setup, similar to Transaction Services or Internet Information Services. If you've enabled Terminal Services, when the server boots up and loads the core operating system, the terminal service begins listening at TCP port 3389 for incoming client connection requests.

TIP Because Terminal Services is essential to the operation of a terminal server, you can't shut this service down. If you try it from the command line with the net stop termserv command, you'll get an error. Click the service in the Services section of the Computer Management tool, and you'll see that the options to pause or stop the service are grayed out in the context menu. If you want to keep people from logging onto the terminal server for a while (perhaps while you're doing maintenance on it), then open the Terminal Services Configuration tool and disable RDP or go to the command prompt and type **change user disable**. This will end any current connections and prevent anyone else from logging on until you enable the display protocol again.

Understanding Sessions

When a client requests a connection to the server and the server accepts the request, the client's unique view of the terminal server is called its *session*. In addition to the remote sessions, a special client session for the console (that is, the interface available from the terminal server itself) is created.

NOTE Some have asked if there's any way to make Windows XP into a multiuser server (of sorts). Nope—no Microsoft desktop operating system includes full-fledged Terminal Services, and there is no way to add it. Windows XP, which has the Remote Desktop feature that allows someone to connect to the computer via the RDP display protocol, can only support one connection at a time—console or terminal session. The Terminal Services I discuss in this chapter is solely a server-class feature.

All sessions have unique Session IDs that the server uses to distinguish the processes (processes are roughly equivalent to executable files) running within different terminal sessions on the same computer. The console session is assigned Session ID 0. When a client connects to the terminal server, the Virtual Memory Manager generates a new Session ID for the session and passes it to the Session Manager once the SessionSpace for that session has been created.

Every session, whether displaying an entire Desktop or a single application, runs the processes shown in Table 10.1.

NOTE In Windows operating systems, an executable file is internally known as an *image*. This is because, technically speaking, an application isn't the piece getting processor cycles but instead is a collection of commands called *threads* that get processor time to do whatever they need to do. The threads have an environment called the process that tells them where to store and retrieve their data. The part of the process that does something is collectively called the image or executable. For the sake of consistency with the interface, I'll refer to programs running on the terminal server as processes.

TABLE 10.1:   Processes Common to Terminal Services Sessions

COMPONENT	FUNCTION
Win32 Subsystem	Win32 subsystem required for running Win32 applications (including the Win2K GUI).
User Authentication Module	Logon process responsible for capturing user name and password information and passing it to the security subsystem for authentication.
Executable Environment for Applications	All Win32 user applications and virtual DOS machines run in the context of the user shell.

The other processes in the session will depend on the applications the user is running. The crucial points to be learned from this are that every session has its own copy of the Win32 subsystem (so it has a unique Desktop and unique instances of the processes that support the Desktop) and its own copy of the WinLogon application that authenticates user identity. In practical terms, what this means is that every separate session a single person runs on the terminal server is using memory to support these basic files. I said earlier that you could set up terminal sessions that display only single applications—no Desktop. The flip side of this convenience is that supplying a full suite of applications connected separately requires a lot more memory on the terminal server than supplying all those applications from a single Desktop in a terminal session. That is, if you create one session to use Microsoft Word, one session to use Outlook, one session to use AutoCAD, and one session to use Solitaire, this will place a heavier strain on the server than running all those applications from a single Desktop session. You'll also be opening multiple copies of your profile, which opens the door to other problems.

NOTE With each generation, Terminal Services has become more frugal with memory allocation, so a single server can support more users. The amount of memory reserved for the Session-Space and the memory required for supporting per-session mapped views have both fallen dramatically. Server 2003 has changed the way that it reads user Registry information into memory, reducing one serious crunch on another area of memory outside SessionSpace.

The terminal session keeps per-session processes from corrupting each other or viewing each other's data. However, although the sessions are allowed to ignore each other, they still have to coexist. All sessions use the same resources—processor time, memory, operating system functions—so the operating system must divide the use of these resources among all of the sessions while keeping them separate. To do so, the terminal server identifies the processes initiated in each session not only by their Process ID but by their Session ID as well. Each session has a high-priority thread reserved for keyboard and mouse input and display output, but ordinary applications run at the priority they'd have in a single-user environment. Because all session threads have the same priority, the scheduler processes user input in round-robin format, with each session's input thread having a certain amount of time to process data before control of the processor passes to another user thread. The more active sessions, the greater the competition for processor time.

The number of sessions a terminal server can support depends on how many sessions the hardware (generally memory but also processor time, network bandwidth, and disk access) can support and how many licenses are available. When a client logs out of his session, the virtual channels to that client machine close and the resources allocated to that session are released.

Memory Sharing on a Terminal Server

The terminal server does not necessarily have to run a separate copy of each application used in each session—in fact, ideally it does not. When you start an application, you're loading certain data into memory. For example, say that running WordMangler loads files A–E into memory. If you start a second instance of WordMangler, is it really necessary to load a second instance of all those files into memory? You could do this, but as more and more sessions started up on the terminal server, the duplicated DLLs and EXEs would cause the server to quickly run out of memory. But if you let all instances of WordMangler use the same copies of A–E, then if one instance needs to change a file that's in use, all other instances will be affected by that change. To get around the wasted-space/data-corruption dilemma, the server uses *copy-on-write* data sharing. "Helper files" are available on a read-only basis to as many applications that need them and are able to reference them. Let an application *write* to that data, however, and the memory manager will copy the edited data to a new location for that application's exclusive use. Copy-on-write works on any NT-based operating system, not just a terminal server, but because terminal servers are likely to be running multiple copies of the same application simultaneously, they greatly benefit from this memory-sharing technique.

The catch to copy-on-write is that only 32-bit applications can benefit from it. The reason for this has to do with how 16-bit applications run in a 32-bit operating system. Namely, they don't: to run a 16-bit application, NT-based operating systems have to create a 32-bit operating environment called a *NT virtual DOS machine* (NTVDM) that contains the 16-bit application. The NTVDMs can do copy-on-write data sharing, but the 16-bit applications they're hosting cannot. Therefore, all else being equal, Win16 and DOS applications will use more memory than Win32 applications. (Also, not all applications can use copy-on-write, especially if they're not written to support it.)

With the advent of 64-bit Windows on the horizon, it's reasonable to ask how a larger memory space will affect terminal servers. At this point, it appears that the results will depend on the hardware. One of my fellow MVPs, Bernhard Tritsch, researched the performance benefits and confirmed that, *on the same hardware*, 64-bit Windows will support *fewer* users than 32-bit. It's not thunking of 32-bit applications onto a 64-bit operating system that's the problem. The new version of 64-bit windows actually handles that mapping pretty well. No, the problem is the processes themselves: the 64-bit processes use quite a bit more memory. Therefore, if you go to 64-bit, you will be able to get many more users onto one box because you won't have the memory constraints in 32-bit—CPU or disk I/O are more likely to be bottlenecks. However, you'll need to throw a lot more memory at the box to support the OS.

THE REMOTE DESKTOP PROTOCOL

You can run all the sessions you like on the terminal server, but that won't do you any good unless you can view the session output from a remote computer and upload your input to the terminal server for processing. The mechanism that allows you to do both is the *display protocol.*

How RDP Works

A display protocol downloads instructions for rendering graphical images from the terminal server to the client and uploads keyboard and mouse input from the client to the server. Terminal Services natively supports the Remote Desktop Protocol (RDP), and with Citrix's Presentation Server add-on to Terminal Services, it supports the Independent Computing Architecture (ICA) protocol. RDP was originally based on the T.120 protocol originally developed for NetMeeting, and as such has some theoretical capabilities that aren't realized in the release product. The way it's implemented now, RDP provides a point-to-point connection dependent on TCP/IP that displays either the Desktop or a single application on the Desktop of a client running RDP.

The processing demands placed on the client are reduced by a feature called *client-side caching* that allows the client to "remember" images that have already been downloaded during the session. With caching, only the changed parts of the screen are downloaded to the client during each refresh. For example, if the Microsoft Word icon has already been downloaded to the client, there's no need for it to be downloaded again as the image of the Desktop is updated. The hard disk's cache stores data for a limited amount of time and then eventually discards data using the Least Recently Used (LRU) algorithm. When the cache gets full, it discards the data that has been unused the longest in favor of new data.

NOTE The image on the screen is updated at very short intervals when the session is active. If the person logged in to the session stops sending mouse clicks and keystrokes to the server, then the terminal server notes the inactivity and reduces the refresh rate until client activity picks up again.

Note that in addition to each client session, there's also a session for the server's use. All locally run services and executables run within the context of this server session.

Understanding RDP Channels

The way that the Desktop or single application in a terminal session look and interact with the client's computer depends on the *channels* used in the display protocol. Channels work like roads between two locations in that they must be open on both sides to work. For example, Route 29 in Virginia presents a straight shot between two cities: Charlottesville and Gainesville. If either Gainesville or Charlottesville shut down their end of the road—in other words, if the road became unavailable on either side—then traffic could no longer travel along that road. It doesn't matter that Gainesville's end is open if Charlottesville is closed. Channels work the same way: They're like roads between the terminal server and the client. If the road is not available on one side, it's closed—it does not matter if it's available on the other.

The capabilities of any one version of RDP are entirely dependent on what channels that version exploits. RDP has room for lots of channels for doing different things, and each version of RDP enables more of them. However, channels must be enabled on both the client and on the server to be useable, as shown in Figure 10.1. That's why, even though the Remote Desktop Connection tool downloadable from Microsoft's website can map client-side drives to terminal sessions, this feature does not work when you use this client to connect to a Windows 2000 terminal server. The virtual channel required to support this feature is not enabled on Windows 2000 Server.

FIGURE 10.1
RDP is a collection of channels conveying data between the terminal server and terminal client.

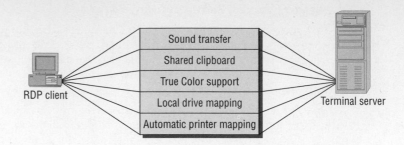

NOTE   Although you can update the RDP client component by downloading the latest client from the Microsoft website or getting it from the Setup CD for Windows XP, you cannot update the RDP server component that goes on the terminal server. There is no way to make a TSE terminal server or a Windows 2000 terminal server as capable as a Server 2003 terminal server.

Notice something about channels: The more capable the RDP version—that is, the more channels it uses—the more bandwidth is required to support those channels. It's not the channels themselves that are the problem, it's the data being passed. That is, if you print through RDP, or listen to sound from an application running on the terminal server, then these capabilities will need bandwidth to support them. Depending on the speed of your connection, this could slow down application responsiveness. Enabling some channels can also be a security risk—client drive mapping being the best example of this.

Therefore, you will not always want to enable all these channels. I'll show you how to selectively enable and disable them in the course of this chapter.

THE CLIENT

So you've got a terminal server running sessions and a display protocol to pass information to and from the sessions. All you're missing now is someone to use the sessions.

A client session is connected when a client computer chooses a terminal server from the RDP interface and gets far enough to see the login screen. The session becomes *active* when the user successfully logs onto the domain or onto the terminal server's local account. During this session, client input in the form of mouse clicks and keystrokes is uploaded to the server via a virtual channel. The commands to render bitmaps showing the interface are downloaded to the client via another virtual channel. If client-printer mapping is enabled for the connection, the communication between terminal server application and client-printer takes places along yet another channel. A buffer supports the shared clipboard data for local and remote sessions, too.

NOTE   Session 0—the console session—does not use the same keyboard and video drivers that client sessions use. Whereas Session 0 uses the normal video and keyboard drivers, the client sessions use drivers based in the RDP.

Once the graphics-rendering instructions download to the client, the client resources create the images for display. During the course of the session, the user can work on the terminal server as though she were physically at the terminal server, using the client machine's keyboard and mouse. As the client runs applications, loads data into memory, and accesses shared resources on the network as though logged on directly (clients are not restricted to accessing the terminal server but can access any available network resources), the client uses the hardware on the server. The only restrictions on the client are those defined by security settings.

Server and Client Requirements

The computing model for thin client networking means that the horsepower is concentrated on the server end, not the client end. Because the server will be supporting dozens of people—maybe more—this is not the time to skimp on power.

Server Hardware

The notion of using a bigger server so that you can skimp on client-side hardware isn't new. That's all a file server is: a computer running a big, fast hard disk so that you don't have to buy big, fast hard disks for everyone in the office. Terminal servers are designed on a similar principle: If most of the processing takes place in a single location, you can concentrate the hardware resources needed to support that processing in a single location and worry less about power on the client end.

CORE HARDWARE RECOMMENDATIONS

For the purposes of running an efficient terminal server, the bare minimum required to run Server 2003 won't cut it. It was technically possible to run a TSE session from a terminal server with a Pentium 133 and 32MB of RAM—I've done it. It worked fine so long as only one person wanted to use the terminal server. Although there are no hard and fast specifications for a terminal server, some general guidelines for server sizing follow.

Processor Faster is better to a point. More important than a fast processor is one with enough cache so that it doesn't have to reach out to the (slower) system memory for code and data. Faced with a choice between more cache and more speed, go with more cache. Most terminal servers these days have multiple processors. Although only multithreaded applications will actually use more than one processor, if there are two processors, then threads needing execution can line up at both. At this point, however, I'd stick with two processors. Processor time is not the main bottleneck in a terminal server and using more servers instead of fewer removes some of the other bottlenecks. When you move to 64-bit Windows, 4-ways or 8-ways will make more sense then.

Memory Terminal servers tend to be memory bound, not processor bound. Get high-speed, error-correcting memory, get plenty of it, and be prepared to add more as you add more users or applications to the terminal server. The amount of memory you'll need depends on the applications that people use, the number of concurrent sessions, and the memory demands of the files opened in those sessions—CAD programs will stress the system more than, say, Notepad. Because memory is relatively inexpensive these days, most terminal servers I've seen use at least 2 GB of RAM.

Disk Use SCSI disks on a terminal server if at all possible. A SCSI disk controller can multitask among all the devices in the SCSI chain, unlike an EIDE disk controller that can only work with one device at a time. This is an important capability in any server, and especially so in a terminal server.

Network On a busy terminal server, consider load-balancing high-speed network cards, which can assign multiple NICs to the same IP address and thus split the load of network traffic. Another alternative is a multihomed server with one NIC dedicated to terminal session traffic. So far as network *speed* goes, sending application output and client-side input back and forth requires little bandwidth, but client-print jobs sent to mapped printers can take quite a bit. Mapped drives may also increase the load by making it possible to copy files back and forth across the RDP connection. Be sure to only support client-mapped printers and other bandwidth-intensive features over networks that can handle it, or get helper software to compress print jobs sent to mapped printers.

USING THE SYSTEM MONITOR

The System Monitor discussed in Chapter 18 of *Mastering Windows Server 2003* can help you get an idea of how test terminal sessions are stressing the server. Server load will scale linearly with the number of people using the server, so as long as you pick a representative group of around five people, you should be able to extrapolate your needs for larger groups. The key objects and counters for measuring general server stress introduced in that chapter will help you size terminal servers, too. But a couple of Terminal Services–specific System Monitor objects are worth examining.

First, the Terminal Services object has counters representing the number of active sessions (sessions where the user has connected to the terminal server and successfully logged on), inactive sessions (where the user is still logged onto the terminal server but has stopped using the session), and the total combined. Mostly, this object is useful for keeping track of how many sessions a terminal server has to support. Chapter 18 discusses performance logging and alerts; if you find that a terminal server functions best below a certain number of connections, you could set up an alert log with that threshold and then, if the server breaches that tolerance, use the `change logon / disable` command to disable the server for new connections and send you a message to alert you. (Do disable connections at the upper limit, or else you'll go mad intercepting the alert messages telling you that the threshold has been breached.)

Although you can get some session-level information from the Terminal Services Manager, a performance object called Terminal Services Session provides quite a bit more. Use the Terminal Services Manager to find the session you want to monitor (because they're identified to System Monitor by their session numbers, not user login name) and then add counters to monitor that session. Each session object has processor and memory counters that should look familiar to anyone who's used System Monitor, but it's also got session-specific counters such as the ones in Table 10.2. I haven't included all the counters here, just the ones to show you the kind of information that will be useful when you're calculating the load on the server and looking at the kind of performance the sessions are getting.

WARNING   When experimenting with terminal sessions to find out how many users you'll be able to support for each session, do not set up a license server; let the terminal server issue its temporary 120-day licenses for this purpose. Although this sounds counterintuitive, using the temporary licenses prevents you from unwittingly assigning per-device licenses to test equipment. See the "Terminal Services Licensing" section for an explanation of how licensing and license allocation works.

TABLE 10.2:   Key Terminal Services Session System Monitor Counters

COUNTER	DESCRIPTION	SEE ALSO
% Processor Time	Percentage of time that all of the threads in the session used the processor to execute instructions. On multiprocessor machines the maximum value of the counter is 100 percent times the number of processors.	
Total Bytes	Total number of bytes sent to and from this session, including all protocol overhead.	Input Bytes, Output Bytes

TABLE 10.2:   Key Terminal Services Session System Monitor Counters *(CONTINUED)*

COUNTER	DESCRIPTION	SEE ALSO
Total Compressed Bytes	Total number of bytes after compression. Total Compressed Bytes compared with Total Bytes is the compression ratio.	Total Compression Ratio
Total Protocol Cache Hit Ratio	Total hits in all protocol caches holding Windows objects likely to be reused. Hits in the cache represent objects that did not need to be re-sent, so a higher hit ratio implies more cache reuse and possibly a more responsive session.	Protocol Save Screen Bitmap Cache Hit Ratio, Protocol Glyph Cache Hit Ratio, Protocol Brush Cache Hit Ratio
Working Set	Current number of bytes in the Working Set of this session.	Virtual Bytes, Page Faults/Sec

Client Hardware

When connecting to a terminal server via a native RDP client, you'll most often use a PC with a Win32 operating system loaded, a Windows terminal, or a handheld PC using Windows CE.

NOTE   In this context, a native RDP client means one available from Microsoft and thus implies Win32. Although Microsoft does not support other platforms (except for their OS X Macintosh client, available for download from the website), Hoblink sells a cross-platform (Windows, Mac, Linux, DOS) Java client at www.hob.de/www_us/produkte/connect/jwt.htm, and there is a free Linux RDP client available at www.rdesktop.org.

WINDOWS TERMINALS

In its narrowest definition, a Windows terminal is a network-dependent device running Windows CE that supports one or more display protocols such as RDP or ICA, the display protocol used to connect to Presentation Server servers. Many Windows terminals also support some form of terminal emulation.

NOTE   In this section, a Windows terminal is any terminal device designed to connect to a Windows terminal server; it can run any operating system that's got an RDP client. A Windows-based terminal (WBT) is such a device that's running a Windows operating system locally—CE or (more rarely) Embedded XP—and follows the Microsoft system design requirements for WBTs.

The main thing defining a Windows terminal is its thin hardware profile: because the main job of most Windows terminals is to run a display protocol, they don't need much memory or processing power, and they don't use any storage. A Windows terminal includes a processor; some amount of memory, network, and video support; and input devices: a keyboard (or equivalent) and mouse (or equivalent). The terminals don't generally have hard disks, CD-ROMs, or DVD players. The operating system (these days, PocketPC, one version or another of XP Embedded, or Linux) is stored in local memory. Beyond those similarities, Windows terminals range physically from a "toaster" form factor to a pad to a small box that can attach to the back of a monitor—or even be part of the monitor itself. Some models of Windows terminals are wireless tablets, intended for people (such as doctors and nurses) who would ordinarily use clipboards and folders to store information.

Although most Windows terminals are entirely dependent on their terminal server, a small set of them can run applications locally. The devices still don't have hard disks; the applications are stored in ROM like the operating system. The types of applications available depend on the terminal's operating system since locally stored applications must run locally instead of just being displayed. Generally speaking, however, it's more common for Windows terminals to depend on a terminal server for applications.

Windows terminals are most popular in environments where people are using a single application, where supporting PCs would be logistically difficult, or anywhere else that PCs aren't a good fit. However, PCs still outnumber Windows terminals as thin clients. Part of this is because many environments can't depend totally on server-based computing. Companies already have PCs, and unless they're refreshing the desktop entirely, taking away a powerful PC to replace it with a less-powerful terminal doesn't really make sense.

PC CLIENTS

At this point, people are using more than twice as many PCs as Windows terminals for terminal server client machines. This isn't surprising. First, unless they're starting afresh, people already have the PCs. Even though WBTs are a little less expensive than low-end PCs (not much, though), they're still an added cost. Second, not all applications work well in a terminal server environment. It's often best to run some applications from the terminal server and some locally. Unless you're buying new hardware and don't anticipate any need to run applications locally, you're likely to have to work with PCs for at least some of your terminal clients.

To work with Terminal Services, the PCs must be running a Win32 operating system, have the RDP display protocol installed, and have a live network connection using TCP/IP and a valid IP address.

HANDHELD PCS

I'm surprised that handheld PCs (H/PCs) aren't more popular than they are, given how handy they are and how much time I spend explaining to curious people what mine is. They're a terrific substitute for a laptop—inexpensive, lightweight, and thrifty with their power so that you can actually use them during the entire flight instead of having to give up two hours after takeoff. (You can also use one on a plane without worrying that the person in front of you will suddenly recline their seat and crack your laptop's display.) Usually, they run PocketPC and, thus, only compatible applications such as Pocket Office. But by downloading and installing the Terminal Services client for handheld PCs and getting network support if it isn't already built in, you can use wired, wireless LAN, or dial-up connections to connect to a terminal server.

NOTE Because Microsoft rearranges its website regularly, there's no use providing a link to the RDP client—it'll be outdated by the time you read this. Look in the Downloads section of the Windows Mobile area on www.microsoft.com; you should be able to find it there.

What a H/PC looks like depends on who makes it. Some (mine among them) look like a laptop's baby brother. Others fold into a little portfolio shape or are a flat tablet. Some devices known as H/PCs are small pocket-sized deals that are, in my personal opinion, too small to really work on. Some—the ones I prefer—have keyboards; others have only pointers. What all this comes down to is that a H/PC isn't really in a position to replace a desktop PC. Instead, it's usually used in cooperation with a desktop machine with which it's partnered.

Installing (or Removing) Support for Terminal Services

Terminal Services is preinstalled on Server 2003, but you still need to set the server up to be an application server. The easiest way to do that is by assigning the appropriate role to the server, using the Manage Your Server tool. Doing so will permit the server to accept incoming connections and tweak the server to make it perform well as a terminal server.

Assigning the Application Server role is dead simple. From the Manage Your Server tool, click the Add or Remove a Role button near the top. You'll see a short checklist of things to make sure of before adding a role (network's connected, path to installation media in case you need it, Internet connection if it will be necessary—by this point you've probably seen this screen a few times). Click Next to open the dialog box displaying the available roles (see Figure 10.2). Select that role, and click Next.

Confirm that you want to assign the selected role to the server, as in Figure 10.3.

FIGURE 10.2

List of available roles for the server

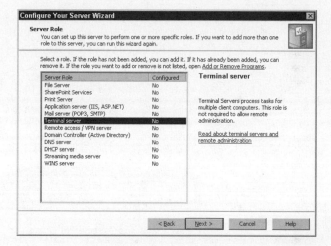

FIGURE 10.3

Confirm the role you selected.

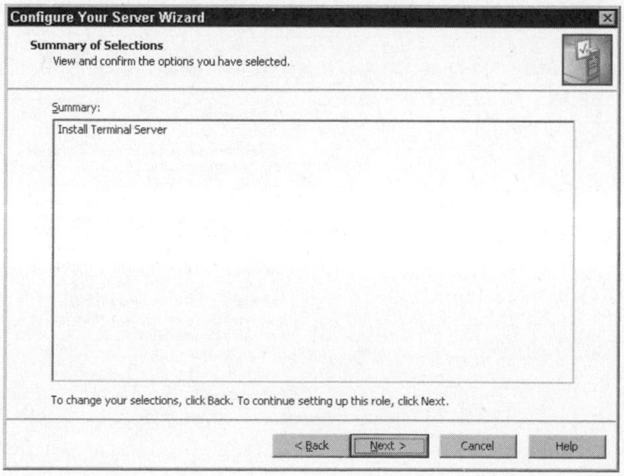

When you click Next, you'll see the status bar begin chugging away and a dialog box warning you that the Configure Your Server Wizard will restart the computer. Click OK and close any open dialog boxes. In a minute or two, the server will automatically restart and display an informational dialog telling you that the server is now a terminal server. After it's rebooted, it's ready to be an application server. You can click a link to view the change log, which will show an entry like this:

```
(5/14/2006 12:58:24 PM)
Configurations for a Terminal Server
Terminal Server installed successfully.
A Terminal Services Licensing Server must exist on the network. If no licensing
server exists, this server will stop accepting connections from unlicensed
clients 120 days after the Terminal Server installation. For more information,
read the Terminal Services Licensing Overview in Windows Help.
```

The log is stored in \%systemroot%\debug.configure your server.log.

The Manage Your Server page will display information about the roles you've got installed. Read it. You'll be able to determine here whether a license server is installed and what the current IIS security settings are. As you can see from Figure 10.4, you'll also have quick links to the tools you'll need.

To remove the role and make the server function like an ordinary server, run the wizard again and select the enabled role. When confirming that you want to remove the role, you'll need to check a box confirming its removal. When you do so, the wizard will remove that role and restore the normal Server 2003 performance.

FIGURE 10.4

The Manage Your Server page displays information and important links for installed roles

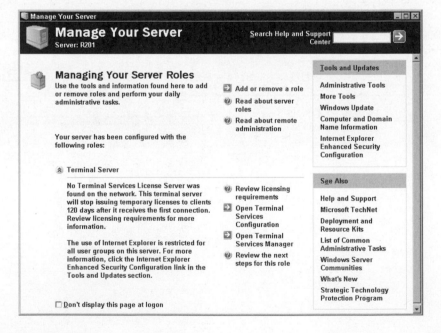

Creating a New Terminal Server Client

The procedure for connecting a client to the terminal server varies slightly depending on whether you're talking about PC clients, handheld PCs, or WBTs.

PC-Based RDP Clients

To connect a PC-based client to Terminal Services, you have to run a short installation program on the PC to install client support for RDP. This process is quite simple and does not require that you reboot the computer afterward.

If that client is a Windows XP or Server 2003 computer, then you're done—the client is preinstalled on both operating systems. Other Win32 clients that can use the Remote Desktop Connection (which I strongly recommend, as it is not only required for the richest client environment but is also noticeably faster than the older versions of the RDP client) will need it installed. The client files are no longer installed with Terminal Services, but you can get them off the Server 2003 installation CD. Better yet, download `msrdpcli.exe`, currently available from the Microsoft website (look in the Downloads section) and run the executable to install Remote Desktop Connection on any Win32 computer.

Once you run the EXE and start the installation wizard, follow these steps:

1. Agree to the terms of the EULA.

2. Enter your name and company if Setup does not populate these fields for you and indicate whether you want the Remote Desktop available to anyone who uses the computer or just you.

3. Click Install to let the Setup Wizard copy the files, and the Remote Desktop icon will be added to Programs ➢ Accessories ➢ Communications.

You don't need to reboot when you're finished.

Setting Up and Connecting a Windows-Based Terminal

Setting up a WBT for the first time is pretty simple. It's largely a matter of plugging everything in (power supply, monitor, network connection, mouse, and keyboard) and supplying the information the WBT needs to interact with the terminal server. For this example, I'll set up a Windows CE–based Windows terminal on a LAN. Although some Windows have different options from others, the basic setup information required is the same on all CE-based Windows terminals.

NOTE Setting up Linux-based Windows terminals gets a bit more complicated because the UI is not necessarily consistent across terminal manufacturers. You'll need to peruse your Linux terminal's documentation for instructions. You'll be providing much the same information to the Linux-based terminal that you're providing to the Windows-based terminal. In some Linux-based terminals, the setup is similar to the CE-based setup I'm describing here, using the same tabbed configuration tools.

SETTING UP THE TERMINAL

Once everything is plugged in and you've powered on the unit, choose to begin creating a new connection. The Setup Wizard walks you through the following steps:

1. First off, accept the terms of the EULA, which states that use of the unit with Terminal Services is predicated upon your having a valid Terminal Services user license and that you must follow the licensing for any applications run from the terminal server.

2. Indicate whether the WBT is connecting to the terminal server via a LAN (the default) or a dial-up connection.

3. Choose the display protocol that should be used to make connections. You have the option of the Microsoft Terminal Server Client (the default, which I'll use here) or the Citrix ICA client, which you'd choose if connecting to a terminal server running Presentation Server. Most modern Windows terminals also offer some kind of terminal emulation support, but you will not use this to connect to a Windows terminal server.

4. The Setup Wizard will attempt to locate a DHCP server on your network. If it can't find one, the wizard will tell you so. You'll have the option of telling the wizard to use the IP information supplied by DHCP or supplying a static IP address.

TIP If you have a DHCP server and the wizard doesn't detect it, make sure the DHCP service on the server is up and running properly and that the server is connected to the network. If they are, then restart the wizard to see whether it finds the DHCP server. Don't tell the wizard to use DHCP information if it's not able to find it, or you may run into problems in getting an IP address assigned to the terminal. No IP address, no connection to the terminal server.

5. If you choose to supply a static IP address, you'll be prompted for it, the subnet mask, and (if applicable) the default gateway. The IP address, recall, is the identifier for the network node, and the subnet mask identifies the network segment that the node is on. The default gateway is only necessary if the network is subnetted and the terminal will need to connect to another subnet.

6. Next, you'll be prompted to supply the servers used for name resolution: WINS, DNS, or both. You'll need to know the IP addresses of the servers, as there is no browse function. If you're using one of the name resolution services, be sure to check the box that enables that service. Otherwise, the connection won't work, and you'll have to edit it to use the IP address instead of the NetBIOS name. To establish support for WINS, you'll need to reenter the unit's network setup.

7. Choose a video resolution. One possible option is Best Available Using DDC. DDC, which stands for Display Data Channel, is a VESA standard for communication between a monitor and a video card. If it supports DDC, a monitor can inform the video card about its capabilities, including maximum color depth and resolution.

When you click the Finish button in the final screen, you'll be prompted to restart the terminal to make the settings take effect. After restarting the system, you'll begin the second half of the terminal setup: the connection.

TIP To manually restart a WBT, turn the unit off and back on again. If you're one of those people (like myself) who normally leave a PC on, don't worry. Turning off a WBT is equivalent in seriousness to turning off a printer. Doing so will disconnect any current sessions you have open, but it's not like rebooting a computer.

CREATING A NEW CONNECTION

To create a new connection, follow these steps:

1. Choose a name for the new connection and the name of the terminal server to which you're connecting. If you're using a dial-up connection instead of a LAN, be sure to check the Low-Speed Connection box so that RDP will compress the data a little further.

2. To configure the terminal for automatic logon to the terminal server session, fill in the name, password, and domain of the person using the terminal. If you leave this section blank, you'll have to explicitly log in each time you connect to the terminal server. For tighter security, leave it blank; if it doesn't matter whether someone can log in to the terminal server, you can set it up for automatic login.

3. Choose whether you want the terminal server session to display a Desktop or run a single application. Once again, there's no browse function, so you need to know the name and path (from the server's perspective) of any application you choose. If you don't provide correct path information, the connection will fail.

At this point, the connection is set up and you're ready to go. The Connection Manager displays a list of the available connections. To use one, select it and click the Connect button. You'll see a logon screen (assuming you didn't set up the connection for an automatic login). Type your name and password, and you're in.

Setting Up a Handheld PC

To use a handheld PC (H/PC) to connect to a terminal server, you must install the RDP client on the H/PC and then create a session on the client.

First, you must get the RDP client. Go to the Microsoft website and navigate to the Downloads section of the Windows Mobile section. You'll have to go through some screens where you agree that you understand that having the RDP client installed does not imply that you're licensed to access a terminal server. (There's also a link to a place where you can buy more licenses if needed.) Download the 1MB-client setup program (`hpcrdp.exe`) to the desktop partner of the H/PC.

To install the RDP client on the H/PC, follow these steps.

1. Turn on the H/PC and connect it to the desktop partner. Make sure that they're connected.

2. Run the installation program to start the installation wizard.

3. Click Yes to agree to the EULA.

4. Choose an installation folder for the client on the desktop partner. The default location is a subfolder of the `Windows CE Services` folder, which you'll have installed in the course of partnering the desktop machine and the H/PC.

5. The installation program will start copying the files to the H/PC. This may take a few minutes if you're using the sync cable instead of a network connection—a sync cable is a serial connection.

6. Once the files have been copied, click Finish on the desktop side to end the Setup program.

To set up a connection, go to the H/PC and look in Start ➢ Programs ➢ Terminal Server Client. There are two options here: the Client Connection Wizard and the Terminal Server Client.

To use the default connection settings, click the Terminal Server Client and type in the name or IP address of the terminal server to which you want to connect. Click the Connect button, and the client will search for that terminal server. You'll need to log in as if you were logging into the server or domain.

For a little more control over the connection settings, run the Client Connection Wizard. You don't have as many options as you do when running the similar wizard for the PC client, but you can specify a connection name, provide your user name and password for automatic logon, and choose whether to run an application or display the entire Desktop. Click the Finish button, and the wizard will put a shortcut to that connection on your H/PC's Desktop.

Creating, Deleting, and Modifying Connections

Now that the client is installed, you're ready to connect to the terminal server. Let's take a look at how to do this from a PC.

To set up a connection on the Remote Desktop client, open it (Programs ➢ Accessories ➢ Communications ➢ Remote Desktop). When you first run the tool, no servers will be selected, but you can either type a server's name or browse for them by clicking the down-arrow button in the Computer box and choosing Browse for More.

When you've found the terminal server to connect to, double-click it or click OK to return to the main login window, which should now have a server selected, as shown in Figure 10.5. To connect to this server with the default settings, just click the Connect button. This will connect you to the selected terminal server and prompt you to log in. When you have successfully logged in, by default the session will run in full-screen mode with a sizing bar at the top so that you can easily minimize or resize the window to show the local Desktop.

Notice that I didn't touch the Options button in Figure 10.5. If you're using the default settings, you'll never need to touch it. Let's take a look at what those settings involve.

When you first click the Options button, you'll see the General tab, as shown in Figure 10.6. From here, you can choose user credentials to log in with, to save or open shared connection settings, and, if you like, pick another server to log into. The only part that might cause confusion (and with reason) is the box prompting you for your user password. Even if you supply this information, you'll still be prompted for your password when you connect to the terminal server.

The Display tab controls all session settings relating to display. The default settings shown in Figure 10.7 may not apply to the terminal session, since the maximum color depth on the terminal server will override the color depth you specify on this tab, but the full-screen mode will. The connection bar at the top of the terminal session window is useful for full-screen sessions, as it offers an easy way to minimize the session and reach the local Desktop. The resolution for the setting will depend on the local client settings—the settings for Remote Desktop size apply only to the window's size.

FIGURE 10.5
To use the selected terminal server with the default settings, click the Connect button.

FIGURE 10.6
Use the General tab to supply user credentials and save connection settings to a file.

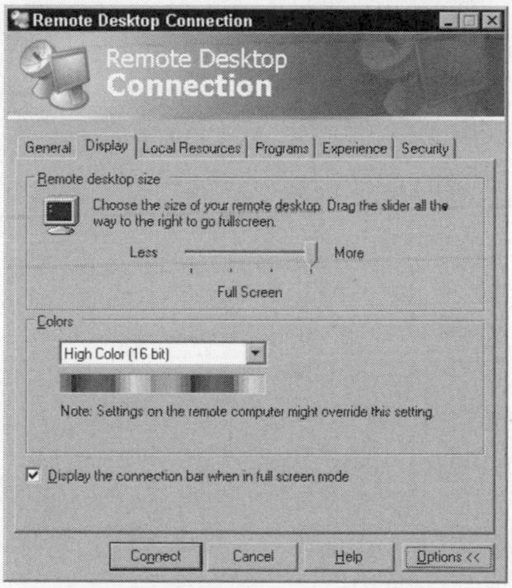

FIGURE 10.7
The Remote Desktop display settings are intended to mimic a user's local Desktop.

The Local Resources tab shown in Figure 10.8 is a little more in-depth, containing some options that have not been previously available to people using RDP. Most of the settings are fairly self-explanatory, however. RDP's sound channel is enabled in Server 2003, so you can control where sound initiated in terminal sessions (perhaps from a training video) is played: on the user's computer, on the terminal server, or not played at all. In a terminal server environment, the two options that make sense are Bring to This Computer and Do Not Play. The option to leave sounds at the remote computer really applies only to a Windows XP computer whose Desktop you were connecting to, and even then it seems like a bit of a stretch.

The key combinations settings specify whether standard Windows key combinations should apply to the remote session only in full-screen mode, all the time, or if they should always apply to the local session. This is something new, and I really like it. Before Windows 2003, to use key combinations to navigate around the Desktop of a terminal session, you had to memorize a new set of key combinations—for example, rather than pressing Ctrl+Esc to open the Start menu, you had to press Alt+Home. Now you have the option of using the standard key combinations in terminal sessions. I like the default option of sending the key combinations to the Desktop when it's in full-screen mode, as that way the key combinations always go to the most prominent work area. You can still use the nonstandard key combinations listed in Table 10.3 when a session is running in a window.

NOTE One nonstandard keyboard combination still applies even if the session is in full-screen mode and you've chosen to send key combinations to the terminal session. To bring up the Task Manager in a terminal session, you must press Ctrl+Alt+End. Pressing Ctrl+Alt+Del still opens the Task Manager on the local computer.

FIGURE 10.8
Edit local resource settings to determine how the local and remote sessions will work together.

TABLE 10.3: Keyboard Shortcuts in Terminal Services Client Sessions

FUNCTION	LOCALLY USED COMBINATION	SESSION-SPECIFIC COMBINATION
Brings up application selector and moves selection to the right	Alt+Tab	Alt+PgUp
Brings up application selector and moves selection to the left	Alt+Shift+Tab	Alt+PgDn
Swaps between running applications	Alt+Esc	Alt+Insert
Opens the Start menu	Ctrl+Esc	Alt+Home
Right-clicks the active application's icon button in the upper left of the application window	Alt+spacebar	Alt+Del
Brings up the Windows NT Security window	Ctrl+Alt+Del	Ctrl+Alt+Esc

One last thing about Local Resources: look at the options for port mapping. I answer Terminal Services questions for Tech Target (`http://www.techtarget.com/`), and recently got a reader question asking me why their HP 4L mapped, but a newer printer—I think it was a 1320—didn't work. My first thought was that there was something weird about the 1320 or there was a permissions problem, but then I checked the specs. Sure enough, that printer supported only USB 2.0, which means that its port won't map. To use that printer from within a session, the reader would have to share that printer with the network or get a third-party print utility that enables USB port mapping.

The Programs tab displayed in Figure 10.9 is pretty self-explanatory if you've used Terminal Services before. If you choose a program to run here, then that program will be the only one available—if the user closes it, then they'll end their session. The starting folder settings supply a working directory for the program if you don't want to use the default (often My Documents), but this is an optional setting.

FIGURE 10.9
Choose a single program for terminal sessions.

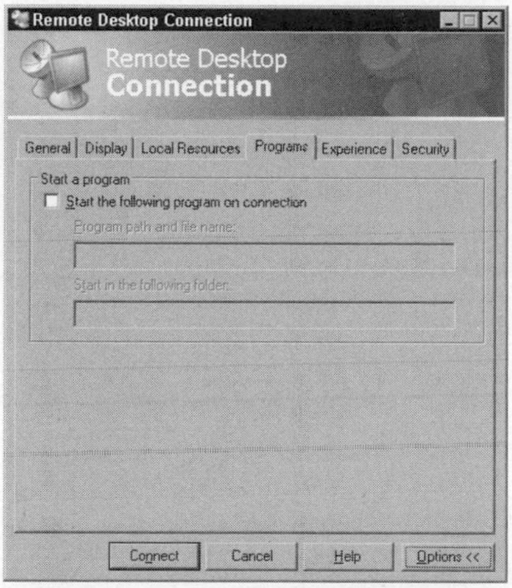

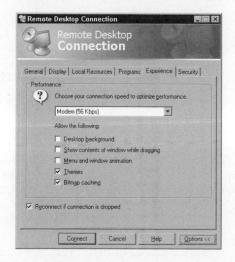

FIGURE 10.10
Enable or disable session features depending on the network speed the connection will be using.

Choosing to run only a single application isn't a security feature, it's a convenience. Even if the initial session displays only a single application, it's still possible for a user to get to Run through the Ctrl+Alt+End sequence.

The Experience tab determines some features to enable based on Microsoft's guesses about what will work best on the selected connection speed (see Figure 10.10). Although you can manually check or uncheck boxes to enable and disable features, for each network speed offered Remote Desktop will have some default settings.

TIP   When creating a connection to work over a slow network, seriously consider disabling printer mapping. Sending print jobs down the slow connection will impact the rest of the session's performance.

Finally, the Security tab (see Figure 10.11) is new in SP1. This tab prevents an exploit in which a malicious user sends you an RDP file purporting to be a work server, when it's really a trip to collect your credentials. This tab just allows you to require this setting. For this to work fully, the server will need a certificate installed on it.

FIGURE 10.11
Choose an authentication level for the connection.

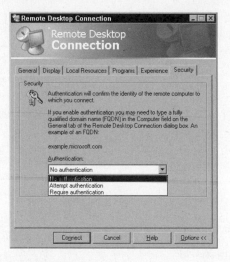

Editing Client Account Settings

Everything's ready to go on the client side, but you may still have some work to do to get the server side configured. The following are optional—but useful—settings that allow you to define how long a session may last, whether someone can take remote control of a user's terminal session, how the RDP protocol is configured, and client path and profile information. The location of these settings depends on whether you've set up the member accounts on the terminal server itself (as a member server) or are editing the main user database on a domain controller for the Active Directory. If the accounts are local to the server, the settings will be in the Local Users and Groups section of the Computer Management tool in the `Administrative Tools` folder. If the accounts are in the domain, the settings will be in the Active Directory Users and Computers tool in the `Administrative Tools` folder.

In this example, I'll use the Active Directory Users and Computers tool, shown in Figure 10.12. The settings for user accounts in the Local Users and Groups option are the same as the ones in the user accounts stored in the Active Directory, the only difference being that the Active Directory account properties have tabs related to user contact information.

Open the Users folder, find the user you want, then right-click it and choose the Properties item. This properties page controls all user settings, so I'll concentrate on the settings that apply to Terminal Services.

NOTE Although per-user account properties normally control if you configure settings from the user account properties, computer-based GPOs control if a policy may be set for both users and computers and is set for both.

FIGURE 10.12
Edit account properties from the Users folder in Active Directory Users and Computers.

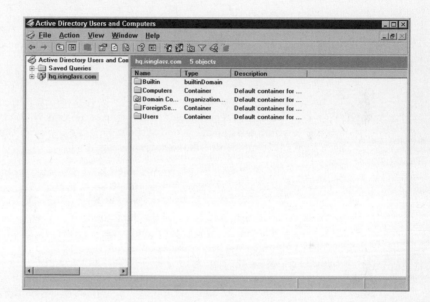

Remote Control

The ability to take remote control of a user's session comes in handy when troubleshooting time comes. Rather than trying to blindly talk someone through a series of commands ("Okay, find the Programs folder. Got it? Now look for the icon that says 'Microsoft Word'"), you can take over the session, manipulating it from your session while displaying it also for the user. The person whose session you're controlling will be able to see exactly how to complete the task and will have it done for them.

The settings for the kind of remote control that you can take are defined on the Remote Control tab of each user's properties pages, shown in Figure 10.13.

First, you must specify whether remote control is even permitted for the session (by default, you can take control of any session, no matter what rights the owner of the session has). Specify also whether the user whose session is being shadowed must permit the action before the remote control can begin. If you choose this option, the person who originated the session will see a message box telling them that such and such person of such and such domain is attempting to control their session, offering the chance to accept or refuse the control.

FIGURE 10.13
Setting remote control
options for taking over
user sessions

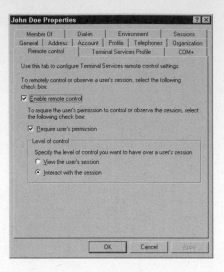

NOTE If permission is required, and a user refuses the remote control connection (or doesn't agree to it within the timeout period of about a minute), you can't control or view the session even from an account with Administrator privileges.

The final option on this tab determines what kind of control you can have over this user's session. For troubleshooting purposes, you'll find it most useful to be able to interact with the session, so you can actually show the user how to do something (or just do it for them). Choosing this option means that both the original user and the person with remote control over the session can send mouse clicks and keystrokes to the terminal server for interpretation. Graphical output is displayed on both the original session and the remote control view of the session.

If you're choosing the option to view the user's session, the person remotely controlling the session isn't really controlling it but is only able to watch and see what the original user is doing. The person who set up remote control can't use the mouse or keyboard with the remotely controlled session. This could potentially be a troubleshooting tool if you're trying to find out exactly what someone's doing wrong and help them correct it, while making sure that you can't interfere. Most often, however, I find the option to take control of the session more useful than the ability to watch.

To control remote control settings via GPOs, turn to User Configuration ➤ Administrative Templates ➤ Windows Components ➤ Terminal Services and enable Set Rules for Remote Control of Terminal Services User Sessions. When you do, you'll be able to choose options from the drop-down menu visible in Figure 10.14.

Once you've permitted administrators to use remote control, the options here are divided into two main groups: full control, which lets the administrator interact with the user's session, and View Session, which lets the administrator only watch what the user is doing. Within those two main groups, you can specify whether the user must explicitly permit the administrator to take remote control of his session. All five options are listed in this drop-down list.

NOTE These settings are also available from the same path in the Computer Configuration section of the Group Policy Editor. If you set policies in both places, then the computer policies apply.

FIGURE 10.14
Remote control
settings

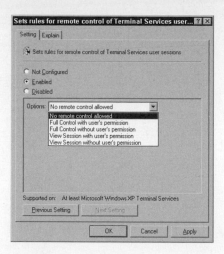

Session Time-Outs

The status of a client session isn't a binary proposition. Rather than on/off, the state of a client session may be active, disconnected, or reset. An *active* session is what it sounds like: a session that's actively in use. In a *disconnected* session, the client has shut off the client interface to the session, but the session—and all its applications—is still running on the server. If the client connects to a disconnected session, he's right back where he left off. When a client *resets* or *terminates* a session with the Logoff command, the session ends and all applications in the session are shut down. Although the distinction may not sound significant at first, it's important. When clients disconnect from their sessions, all their data is still loaded into memory and their applications are running, exactly as they left them. This means that a client can disconnect while going to lunch, and thus secure the session without having to start over.

The only catch to a disconnected session is that it still uses up processor cycles and some memory because the session thread still gets its crack at the processor and because all the user data is still active. However, as the data stops being accessed, the server will swap it out to the paging file on the hard disk and replace it in physical memory with more recent data; when the client reconnects to the session and tries to use the data, the data will be paged back in. The still-running client session also won't impact available network bandwidth much because the terminal server will detect that the session is idle and stop sending video updates to the client machine. You'll need to train users to make sure that they don't just close session windows and inadvertently disconnect when they mean to log off. If a user attempts to reconnect to the terminal server with more than one disconnected session running, a dialog box will display the disconnected sessions, their resolution, and the time that they've been disconnected. The user can then pick the session to reconnect. If the user doesn't pick a session in a minute or so, the highlighted session will be reestablished. The other session will remain on the terminal server, still in its inactive state.

You can control how long a session may stay active, how long it may stay disconnected without being terminated, how long active but idle sessions may stay active before they're disconnected—and even whether a particular user may connect to the server at all. These settings are controlled from the Sessions tab, shown in Figure 10.15.

FIGURE 10.15
Configuring session
connection settings

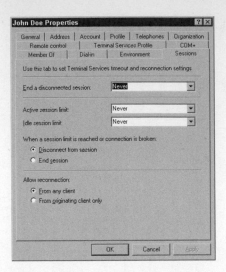

You can control how long the setting may remain active before being disconnected or terminated. If you want to prevent people from forgetting to log out from their terminal session at the
end of the day or at lunch, use this setting.

As I already discussed, a disconnected session is still using up terminal server resources—in the
page file if nowhere else. This is by design, so that users can reconnect to a session and have all their
applications and data still loaded, but if a session is permanently abandoned, there's no point in
leaving it up. Choose a time-out period that reflects the amount of time you're willing to give a user
to get back and use their connection before their applications are all closed.

You can also determine how long a session can be idle before being disconnected or terminated.
This isn't quite the same setting as the first one, which limits connection time whether or not the session is still getting input. Rather, this setting limits the amount of time that a session can be idle
before being shut down. This setting is a little more useful in most cases, given that the session must
be unused for a certain period before it is shut down.

The default for all three settings is Never, meaning there's no restriction on how long a session
may be running, disconnected, or idle. The maximum time-out period is two days.

TIP   If you want to gather some statistics about how long people are staying logged in, or how long
disconnected sessions are remaining idle on the server, you can get this information from the
Terminal Services Manager. System Monitor can tell you how many active or inactive sessions
are currently running on a given terminal server.

The settings on the bottom of the tab determine how disconnected and reestablished connections should be handled. You may have noticed that two of the time-out options give you the choice
of disconnecting or terminating the session at the end of the time-out session, but no option for
specifying which it should be—disconnection or resetting the connection. The answer depends on
whether you pick Disconnect from Session (the default) or End Session (which resets the connection) for broken or timed-out connections. The other option controls how users may reconnect to
disconnected sessions. RDP sessions can reconnect to their client session from any client machine.
Only ICA sessions can be forced to reestablish the connection from the same machine from which
they started, and then only if you set up the ICA client to identify the computer it's running on. If
a user has more than one disconnected session running on the same terminal server, when they

reconnect they'll have a choice of which session they want to use. The session(s) not chosen will continue to run on the terminal server.

To configure these settings with GPOs, turn to User Configuration ➢ Administrative Templates ➢ Windows Components ➢ Terminal Services ➢ Sessions. You'll see the available policies in Figure 10.16.

The editing for each policy works the same way in all cases: enable a policy and then pick the timeout period that you want, exactly as you would if configuring the setting on a per-user basis as described already in this section. The only policy in this area that might cause you difficulty is the one about only permitting people to reconnect from the same computer. Again, this setting is only available to those using properly configured ICA clients, but this isn't obvious unless you scroll down to the very bottom of the explanation.

NOTE These settings are also available from the same path in the Computer Configuration section of the Group Policy Editor. If you set policies in both places, then the computer policies apply.

FIGURE 10.16
Session timeout GPOs for user accounts

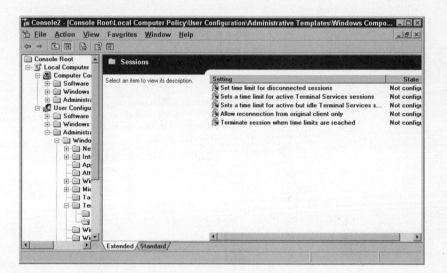

Setting Client Path Information

Unless you specify otherwise, user home directories are in subfolders of the terminal server's `Profiles` folder and are identified by user name. Their temporary directories are subfolders of the terminal server's temporary directory and identified by Session ID. To keep all per-user information in a single place, you may want to specify a new home directory—a home directory located on a file server. This will give you a fighting chance of applying per-user system quotas and keeping all files in one place for easier recovery.

PROFILE PATHS AND HOME DIRECTORIES

Roaming profiles are stored on a profile server instead of a local machine, so the user can log in with the same settings wherever she connects to the network. The other option is locally stored profiles, stored on the computer where they're displayed. When a profile is applied, it makes per-user changes to the Registry of the computer the person is logged in to that apply only to that user. So far, this is just like NT profiles have been for years.

Terminal Services still works more or less the same way. The profiles may still be stored either locally or on a profile server—but in this case *locally* means on the terminal server. As you probably know, you can't *not* use a profile—if you don't specify one, then you'll get the Default User profile.

You have a couple of options when it comes to profiles and Terminal Services. If you only provide a path for the user profile, then that path applies to both "normal" user settings and settings for terminal sessions that the user starts up. Filling in only the information the Profile tab in a user's profile will have this effect—the person will have the same profile path and home directory for terminal sessions as they do normally.

This may sound like a good plan, but in most cases it's not. First off, what works well for local use may not work well when logging onto a terminal session. For one example, the screensaver you might use on a Desktop without a second thought is a resource-draining vanity in a terminal session. For another, using the same profile for both ordinary sessions and terminal sessions leaves you exposed to lost profile changes. Consider how profiles work. When you open a profile and make changes to it, those changes are stored locally and don't get written back to the profile server until you log out. So what happens if you have two copies open, make a change in one and then log out, then make a change in the other copy and then log out? Right—you lose all the changes made to the first one because the copy you saved last to the profile server overwrote the copy you saved first. This can happen any time you open a profile more than once—it's not just a problem with Terminal Services—but you're not likely to log in two or more times when you're logging in to the domain from a fat client. Log in to both the fat client (since you needed to log in to the domain to get to a computer from which you could run the terminal session) and to the terminal server, and you immediately have two copies open. For these reasons, it's probably best to use different profiles for terminal sessions and fat client sessions.

How about roaming profiles for terminal sessions, if those profiles are different from the ordinary user profiles? This is still not a good idea because of the possibility that you'll have multiple copies of your profile open at once. Particularly if your terminal session is set up to only serve applications and you use more than one application, you're likely to open multiple copies of your profile at the same time.

So does this mean that local profiles are the way to go? Nope—not if you have many users to support and those users won't always log in to the same server. When you use local profiles, they're stored on the terminal server. If you have 60 users, each with her own profile, and you can't predict which of four servers those 60 users will connect to, then that means that you've got to store those 60 profiles on each server. That's a lot of room to munch up on the terminal server's system drive. It can also lead to inconsistency in the user environment if a user changes his profile on one server and not on another. It's especially important to not keep user profiles locally if you're using load balancing of any kind because doing so would mean that people would never know which profile they'd get.

For this reason, the best plan might be to use mandatory profiles, which are just ordinary profiles with a .man extension. Users can edit mandatory profiles to the degree their system policies allow them to, but those changes don't get saved to the server. Limiting to the user experience, perhaps, but if you use mandatory profiles with terminal sessions, then you avoid the problems of lost profile edits from multiple copies of the profile being opened. To specify a profile location, set the path location for the Terminal Services profile from each user's properties pages, as shown in Figure 10.17.

TIP Combine mandatory profiles with third-party profile management tools to get the flexibility of roaming profiles but the predictability of mandatory profiles.

The Deny This User Permissions to Log on to Any Terminal Server check box controls whether the person is permitted to log in to the terminal server at all. By default, anyone with an account on the domain or server may do so.

User profile and home directory information are configured in computer group policies located in Computer Configuration\Administrative Templates\Windows Components\Terminal Services. The policies you're looking for are Set Path for TS Roaming Profiles and TS User Home Directory. Just include the computer name and path to the profile directory; the policy will fill in the user name automatically. If the path you provide does not exist (or the server can't reach it) then it will create a local profile.

The same goes for setting up the home directory—type the UNC name for the network share and assign a local drive letter if necessary (for applications that demand a drive letter), as I've done in Figure 10.18. I do not recommend putting the user home directory on the local terminal server unless you really have no other options, as doing so will give users separate home directories depending on which server they're connected to.

FIGURE 10.17
Specify the path to the user profile and home directory in the Terminal Services Profile tab.

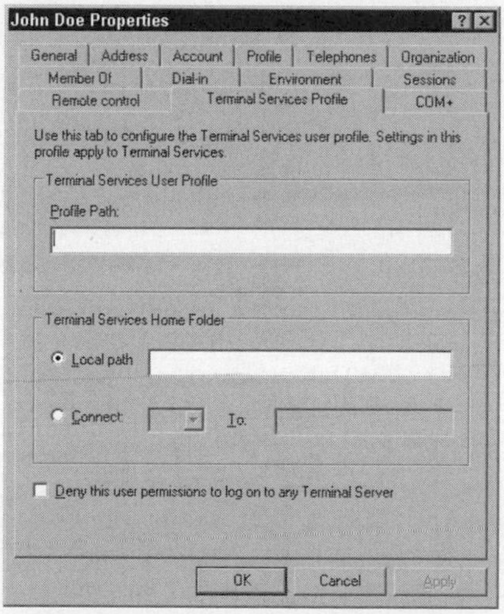

FIGURE 10.18
You can set home directory paths through group policies.

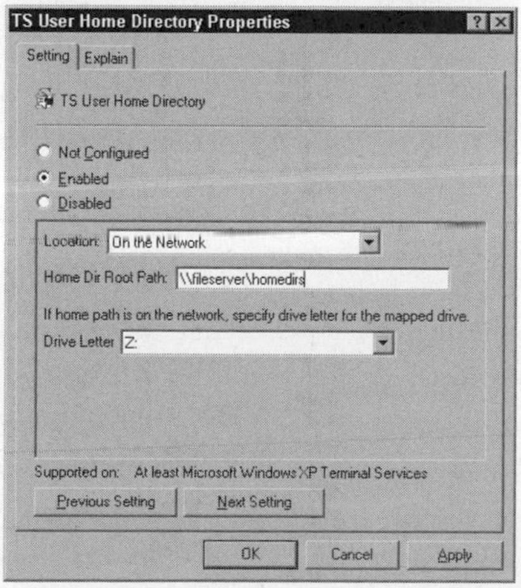

PROGRAMMATIC UPDATES TO PROFILE INFORMATION

To change or set user profile information for one user account is no big deal: open Active Directory Users and Computers, open the user account's properties sheet, turn to the Terminal Services Profile tab, and make the change. Multiply this procedure by 50, 500, or 5000 users, however, and it gets less easy. But all is not lost: You can make these edits through ADSI (the profile path is now exposed as a property of the object representing the terminal server—this wasn't an option in previous versions of Terminal Services) or, if you're VBScript-challenged, with the tsprof command-line tool.

Tsprof supports three actions: You can update account profile information, you can copy it to another user account, or you can query a user account to make sure your changes took or see what the current profile settings are. The basic syntax for these commands looks like this:

```
TSPROF /UPDATE [/DOMAIN:domainname|/LOCAL] /PROFILE:<path> username
TSPROF /COPY   [/DOMAIN:domainname|/LOCAL] [/PROFILE:<path>] sourceuser
destinationuser
TSPROF /Q      [/DOMAIN:domainname|/LOCAL] username
```

Make sure you don't include extra spaces in the command, or you could accidentally query the domain name as though it were a user name.

For example, say that my Terminal Services users don't have session-explicit user accounts; they're using the same accounts they typically use to log on to the domain. The profile settings that work well for a full-color session on a single-user computer might not translate well to a terminal session, so I want to edit that account information to C:\profiles. I can do so from the command line, like this:

```
tsprof /update /domain:redroom /profile:c:\profiles\profile.man christa
```

In this example, the user account is in the REDROOM domain, the profile path is C:\profiles, and the user account I'm editing is named Christa. This command will spit back the following information:

```
Terminal Services Profile Path for redroom\christa is { c:\profiles\profile.man }
```

If the curly brackets don't contain any information, you haven't set a Terminal Services profile for that user account. The /update argument doesn't tell you what the profile path information was *before* you changed it, so if you want to ensure that it needs to be updated, query the account. To perform the query, use the /q argument, like this:

```
tsprof /q /domain:labrynth christa
```

If you used tsprof with TSE, notice that the command now is /q, not /query. The command changed in Windows 2000 and retains that change in Server 2003.

Finally, you can copy profile-path information from one account to another. The /copy command works similar to /update, except you must provide the source and destination account names, in this case, Christa and Vera, respectively:

```
Tsprof /copy /domain:redroom christa vera
```

The system will now copy Christa's profile account information to Vera's user account; if I query Vera's account, the profile information will be there.

Be careful when you use these tools. Tsprof can't tell whether a profile path is valid any more than the graphical user account management tools can; tsprof will enter whatever information you give it. If the account name is invalid, tsprof will generate an error when it attempts to update the information— Failed Setting User Configuration, Error = 1332 (0x534)—but won't show any problems when you perform a query.

DEFINING THE SESSION ENVIRONMENT AND MAPPING CLIENT RESOURCES

The Environment tab in the properties pages (see Figure 10.19) sets the Terminal Services environment for the user, replacing any related settings (such as an application to run at logon) that might already appear in a user's client logon settings. If you want to automatically run an application at logon, type its path in the Program File Name box (sadly, there's no browse function). The working directory goes in the Start In box. Supplying the name of an application does not limit the terminal server session to only running that application and then ending when the application is terminated. All this does is run the application when the session starts—the main Desktop still remains available. If you want to provide a terminal session running only a single application and then closing when that application closes, you'll need to set that up when configuring the client connections, as described earlier in this chapter.

The settings in the Client Devices section at the bottom of this tab apply to clients using Remote Desktop Connection. The first one, Connect Client Drives at Logon, applies only to sessions where remapping client drives for use in terminal server sessions is enabled (and it may confuse users as to whether they're saving files to their local drives or to the terminal server, so this may be an option to give only to experienced users). Mapped drives will show up as "Other" drives in My Computer, retaining their original drive letters but without colons (that is, drive C: on your local computer will be drive C when mapped to a terminal session). Checking Connect Client Printers at Logon specifies that any printers mapped from the terminal server session should be reconnected. Default to Main Client Printer specifies that the client should use its own default printer, not the one defined for the terminal server.

To specify a program to run in the terminal session via group policies, go to Computer Configuration\Administrative Templates\Windows Components\Terminal Services and enable Start a Program on Connection. (You can also edit this setting in user GPOs, but if the policies conflict then the per-computer settings take control.) As when editing the setting for individual users, you'll need to know the path and working directory—you can't browse for it here.

All decisions about client resource mapping are set with policies in Computer Configuration\Administrative Templates\Windows Components\Terminal Services\Client/Server Data Redirection (see Figure 10.20).

FIGURE 10.19

Tuning the user environment and mapping client resources

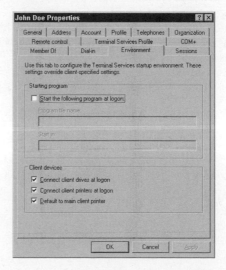

FIGURE 10.20
Many policies
control client
resource mapping.

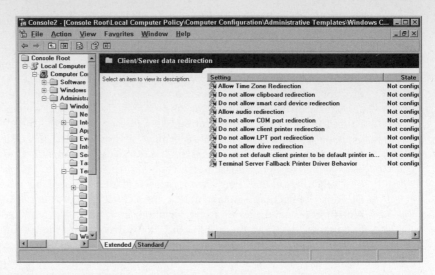

Most of these settings are easy to associate with their counterparts in the user account properties. One that you might not recognize (both because it's not on the Environment tab—it's a protocol configuration setting, not a user setting—and because it's new to Terminal Services in Server 2003) is Allow Time Zone Redirection. This policy pertains to how time zones work in terminal sessions. Prior to Windows Server 2003, terminal sessions displayed the time zone of the terminal server, and if this time zone was different from that of the person connected to the terminal session, that was just too darn bad. (Some third-party utilities fixed this problem, but Microsoft had no built-in fix for it.) Server 2003 allows time zone redirection, which is off by default. You must enable this setting to turn it on.

Configuring Terminal Services for All Connections

You can configure general settings for all Terminal Services connections from the Terminal Services Configuration tool in the `Administrative Tools` folder. If you're running Terminal Services alone, you'll have only the RDP connection in this folder; if you have other multiuser Windows components added (like Presentation Server's ICA protocol or direct video support), they'll be in the folder as well.

What can you do here? The `Server Settings` folder contains settings that apply to all connections made to the server. The `Connections` folder shows all installed display protocols.

NOTE Server 2003 only supports one RDP connection per network adapter. If your terminal server has more than one NIC installed and you're using RDP with both of them, you can configure the RDP protocol for each adapter separately.

THE *SERVER SETTINGS* FOLDER

The `Server Settings` folder (see Figure 10.21) contains options that control the creation and deletion of per-session temporary files and the types of access permitted to the terminal server. The options here are identical whether the server is set up to be an ordinary server with remote administration capabilities or an application server.

FIGURE 10.21
Server Settings
folder for a terminal
server in Application
Server mode

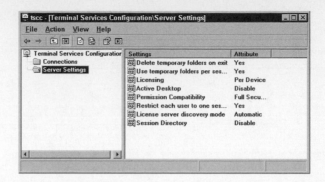

Licensing

On an application server, the licensing may be either Per Device (the default) or Per User. (On a server using RDP only for remote administration, the licensing information here will read Remote Administration.) Per User licensing is new in Server 2003. To change the licensing mode, just double-click Licensing to open the dialog box in Figure 10.22. Don't choose Per Device licensing unless you have per-device licenses installed or definitely plan to do so. Per-device licensing is enforced and having no per-device licenses can easily lead to users being locked out. If you're unsure of the right license type or are using another licensing mode, put the terminal server into Per User mode.

Service Pack 1 introduced a new license server discovery feature. As noted earlier, it fixed one search algorithm that prevented a terminal server from finding a license server installed on itself. However, to prevent other problems caused by failure of automatic discovery, it also added a simple way to avoid license server discovery and just specify the servers, as in Figure 10.23.

Choosing specific license servers will change the discovery mode to As Specified.

TIP Always check server names before clicking OK, as this option disables automatic discovery.

Temporary Folder Settings

Ordinarily, a terminal server stores temporary files for each session as a subfolder to each user's profile in *%userprofile%\Local* Settings\Temp*sessionID* (the SessionID folders are necessary in case a user has more than one session open at a time). For applications that can't deal with per-user temporary directories, you can force all temporary files to be written to the same folder on the server: *%userprofile%\Local Settings\Temp* on the server.

FIGURE 10.22
Always configure the
license mode to the
kind of licenses you
have installed.

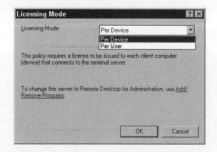

FIGURE 10.23
To avoid bugs in the automatic discovery process, specify a license server.

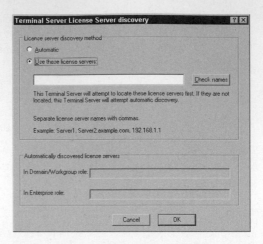

Deleting the temporary folders on exit means that when a user logs out of a terminal server session, the temporary folder they used—and all the TMP files in it—is deleted. This setting, set to Yes by default, keeps the terminal server from getting cluttered with TMP files and ensures that those files are only deleted when they're no longer needed.

You can also apply these settings to temporary directories using GPOs, using the policies in Computer Configuration\Administrative Templates\Windows Components\Terminal Services\ Temporary Folders. There are two policies here. Do Not Use Temp Folders Per Session and Do Not Delete Temp Folder Upon Exit, which you can enable or disable as appropriate. If you leave them unconfigured, then the default settings (to use temporary folders per session and delete those folders when the session ends) apply.

Active Desktop Use

Another option lets you turn off the Active Desktop on the terminal server sessions. Unless you really need it for some reason, I'd turn it off and save the resources.

User Connection Restrictions

This is something new in Windows Server 2003—the ability to allow each person connecting to a particular server only one connection. If you have only one terminal server, then using this setting prevents the I-have-three-copies-of-my-profile-open problem. On multiple servers, this setting makes it easier for users to reconnect to disconnected sessions by giving them only one possible choice. The default setting limits users to one session per server.

To configure this setting using GPOs, you'll need the Restrict Terminal Services Users to a Single Remote Session setting, found in Computer Configuration\Administrative Templates\Windows Components\Terminal Services.

Security Settings

Finally, you can choose the type of permissions you want to apply to this terminal server. Relaxed Security file access is compatible with all applications (but may leave some system folders vulnerable to changes from user applications) or Full Security file access may not work with older applications (because it denies permissions to some system folders) but does not allow applications to tamper with system folders. Always start out using Full Security, and only use Relaxed Security if a vital application simply won't run without it. Newer applications should work with Full Security.

The *Connections* Folder

Use the `Connections` folder to configure protocol-wide settings. First, you can disable RDP so that no one can connect to the server, something you might want to do if you know you're going to be taking the server down for maintenance and don't want to have to bother with kicking new people off. Since you can't turn off the terminal server service, this is the easiest way to keep people off the server while still keeping it running. To do so, just right-click the protocol and choose Disable Connection from the All Tasks part of the pop-up menu. The command to re-enable the connection is in the same All Tasks section.

NOTE This setting does not end existing sessions. To end all sessions—ungracefully and at once— you can reset a RDP listening session from Terminal Services Manager.

For more detailed control of RDP, choose the Properties option from the pop-up menu. Most settings in the RDP-Tcp dialog box work the same way as their counterparts in the per-user connection settings, which normally take precedence. For a more uniform set of protocol configurations, you may edit the settings here and check the boxes that tell the protocol properties not to inherit their settings according to the user. The two settings that aren't configurable on a per-user basis control security are found on the General and Permissions tabs.

The General Tab

The General tab shown in Figure 10.24 controls the degree of encryption used with RDP. The encryption can protect both logins and the stream of text, but at a minimum protects the information passed during the login process.

By default, the client's level of encryption determines the level of encryption between client and server, which means that all communications between client and server are encrypted with a 56-bit algorithm. High encryption forces 128-bit encryption, which means that clients incapable of supporting this encryption level won't be able to connect to the terminal server. FIPS Compliant security encrypts all traffic between server and client with Triple DES.

Figure 10.24
Configuring RDP
access security

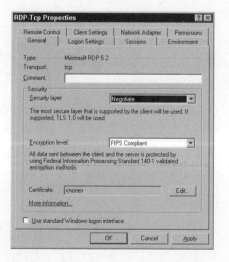

You don't have to worry about the Use Standard Windows Authentication Logon Interface check box unless you've installed a third-party authentication package on the server. In that case, checking this box tells the terminal server to use its native authentication scheme to validate terminal session user logons, rather than using the third-party package.

SP1 introduced Transport Layer Security (TLS, the most recent version of SSL) support for server authentication and to provide a greater level of encryption than is possible with RDP's native encryption. To set this up on the terminal server, in the Security Layer choose to Negotiate (and configure the client Security tab appropriately. SSL support both adds some further encryption to the connection and validates that a server can be trusted—that it's really the server it claims to be. To use it, you'll need to install a certificate on the terminal server.

SSL security requires:

◆ At least Windows Server 2003 SP1 on the terminal server and Windows XP on the client

◆ A certificate installed on the terminal server and configured for FIPS compliance

◆ The client running at least RDP 5.2

PERMISSIONS

Those familiar with the Windows Server security model will remember that you secure a network by defining user rights for what people can *do* on the network and setting permissions for the resources that people can *use*. Terminal Services security is controlled with permissions, on a per-group or per-user basis.

To set or edit the permissions assigned to terminal server sessions, turn to the Permissions tab. You'll see a dialog box like the one in Figure 10.25. From here, you can edit the basic permission sets of the groups for whom some kind of access to terminal server functions has been defined.

Not sure how to interpret the check boxes? If a permission is checked, then it's explicitly enabled or disabled, depending on which box is checked. If a permission is clear on both sides, then it's implicitly enabled. You can explicitly enable or disable the permission by checking the appropriate box.

FIGURE 10.25
Default terminal
server permissions

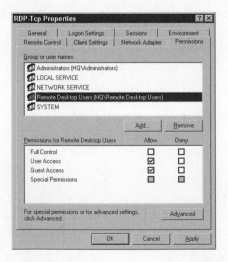

Fine-Tuning Access to Terminal Server Functions

The first page shows only the default groups and the basic permissions they've been assigned. For more control over the permission process, click the Advanced button to open the dialog box shown in Figure 10.26.

From here, you can see the state of the defined permissions. The Inherited From field indicates the level at which the permissions were set—here, or at a higher level.

You can adjust these permissions either by adding new users or groups to the list (getting them from the domain controller) or by editing the permissions of the groups already there. To define permissions for a new user or group, click the Add button. You'll open a dialog box where you can choose the name of the account to edit. Type the name of a user or group, then click the Check Names button to confirm that you got it right. When you've got the right user or group account name, click OK to open the dialog box in Figure 10.27.

FIGURE 10.26
Setting advanced permissions

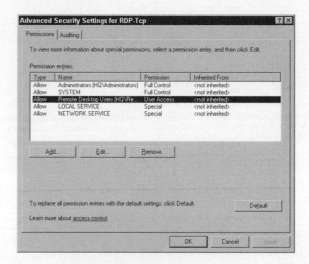

FIGURE 10.27
Defining the permissions for a new user

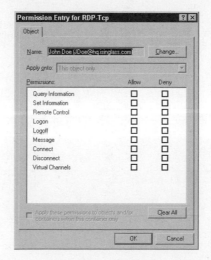

By default, new users and groups (even domain administrators) have no permissions at all. You will need to specify the access you'd like to grant or deny to the groups and users you're adding to the list.

The permissions listed here have the characteristics outlined in Table 10.4. I'll talk more about how to *use* these functions in the later section "Managing Terminal Sessions."

Changing permissions for an existing user or group works in much the same way as adding permissions for a newly defined group: Select a name, click the Edit button, and you'll see the same set of options to explicitly grant or deny permissions.

TIP   If you want to cancel all permission changes for a user or group and start over, click the Cancel button. If you want to remove every granted or denied permission associated with a user or group, click Clear All, or just select them in the list on the Permissions tab of the RDP Properties sheet and click the Remove button—this will have the same effect.

TABLE 10.4:   Terminal Services Permissions

Access Type	Effect	Included In
Query Information	Allows users to gather information about people using the terminal server, processes running on the server, sessions, and so forth	Full Control, Service Permissions
Set Information	Allows users to set the level of control other users have over the session	Full Control
Remote Control	Allows users to take control of or view other user sessions	Full Control
Logon	Allows users to log on to the terminal server	Full Control, User Access, Guest
Logoff	Allows users to log off from the terminal server	Full Control, User Access, Guest
Message	Allows users to send messages to other terminal server clients	Full Control, Service Permissions, User Access
Connect	Allows users to connect to other terminal servers	Full Control, User Access
Disconnect	Allows users to disconnect from other terminal servers	Full Control
Virtual Channels	Enables virtual channels for that group	Full Control

Terminal Services Licensing

Licensing single-user computers is complicated enough. Bring terminal servers into the equation, and the complications increases. Do you have to pay for only the operating system? Only the client sessions active at any given time? Only some client sessions? What about applications—an application is only loaded on one machine, so you should only have to pay for one license, right? And who's in charge of keeping track of all these licenses, anyway?

Licensing is never fun and it's not glamorous, but it's part of the cost of doing business. Read on to make some sense of the Terminal Services licensing model.

The Terminal Services Licensing Model

First, let's take a look at how the licensing model works in Win2K. In TSE, licensing was handled by a license manager service that came with TSE. You told the license manager how many Terminal Services licenses you had, and it kept track of how they were used. Windows 2000 added a license server, which might or might not be the terminal server—depended on the security model you were using. Beginning with Windows 2000, you also had to activate the licenses through Microsoft. You can't just tell the license server how many TS licenses you have, you must get official licenses from Microsoft and activate them.

As shown in Figure 10.28, several players cooperate to make Terminal Services licensing work in Server 2003:

- ◆ The terminal servers
- ◆ The license servers
- ◆ The Microsoft clearinghouse that enables the license servers and the access licenses

FIGURE 10.28
The Terminal Services licensing model

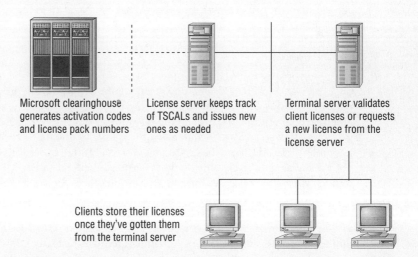

Microsoft clearinghouse generates activation codes and license pack numbers

License server keeps track of TSCALs and issues new ones as needed

Terminal server validates client licenses or requests a new license from the license server

Clients store their licenses once they've gotten them from the terminal server

Understanding Session Licensing

When Microsoft first released Windows NT, Terminal Server Edition, it made a terrible marketing decision. Any client connecting to the terminal had to have a valid NT Workstation license. At $400 a pop, NTW licenses weren't cheap, so a lot of people looked at TSE and said, "Nice, but not worth the money." This didn't do much to promote the use of Terminal Services by anyone not already using NTW. In an effort to win those people back, in February 1999 Microsoft revamped their licensing structure, giving NT Workstation clients a built-in license to access the terminal server but requiring you to purchase terminal server licenses (which cost approximately $150 per device instead of $400) for computers running any other operating system. However, by default access to the server running Terminal Services is licensed on a per-device basis, not per user—computers are licensed, not people.

The licensing structure includes three license types:

◆ Terminal Server Client Access Licenses (TSCALs)

◆ Built-in licenses

◆ Temporary licenses

NOTE   Not all Terminal Services functions use licenses. When you're running Terminal Services capabilities in Remote Administration mode you don't need TSCALs because Remote Administration mode comes with two administrator's licenses. You cannot use this licensing mode on a server configured with the Application Server role.

TERMINAL SERVER CLIENT ACCESS LICENSES

Terminal Server Client Access Licenses (TSCALs) are for named user accounts in the domain and issued on a per-device basis. Anyone in a company who's using the terminal server must have a TSCAL, regardless of whether they're connecting to the terminal server via Microsoft's RDP display protocol or Citrix's ICA display protocol (which they will if you install Presentation Server). To access a terminal server at all, of course, a client also needs a Client Access License (CAL).

The Unlimited pool no longer exists in Windows Server 2003 and later. Each user or device accessing the terminal server must have a license, regardless of the generation of the client operating system.

License Packaging

The way you buy TSCALs determines how you pay for them and how much flexibility you have in the purchase. Most people who buy small volumes of Microsoft products will buy their TSCALs as part of a 5-CAL or 20-CAL Microsoft License Pak (MLP). Physically, an MLP is a thin cardboard envelope that contains the EULA denoting the number of CALs purchased. The MLP for TSCALs also includes a license code, a 25-character alphanumeric code that indicates what the license is for and how many TSCALs it purchases (so that you can't fudge the entries and say that you bought 20 TSCALs when you really only bought 5). You can only install an MLP once. Small to medium customers will get their licenses through a program called Microsoft Open License, which allows you to purchase a user-specified quantity of licenses, after which Microsoft issues you an Open License Authorization and license numbers for the licenses, which you can install as many times as you need to. Select and Enterprise Agreements for large customers work like open licenses, except that the customer provides their Enrollment Agreement number instead of the Open License numbers.

Reclaiming TSCALs

Once allocated to a computer, a TSCAL belongs to that computer and is identified as such in the license server's database. You cannot manually reclaim TSCALs from a computer, so the visiting consultant who logs in to the terminal server once leaves with a TSCAL. Not only that, but if you wipe a computer's hard disk and reinstall, then there's no record of that TSCAL on the computer and it will have to request a second one. Unused TSCALs will eventually revert to the license pool on their own, but the process takes a while.

Rather than permanently assigning TSCALs to clients, the license server will give first-time requesters a TSCAL with a time-out period (a randomly assigned interval between 52 and 89 days). When the user logs onto the terminal server, the terminal server tells the license server that the license has been validated (used by someone with permission to log onto the terminal server). The TSCAL is then assigned to that machine. Every time someone connects to the terminal server from that machine, the terminal server will check the expiration date on the TSCAL. When the expiration date is less than 7 days, the terminal server renews the TSCAL assignment to that machine for another 52 to 89 days. Should the client machine not log into the terminal server before its TSCAL expires, its TSCAL will return to the pool of available licenses.

This applies only to per-device licenses, by the way. As you'll see, per-user licenses in Windows Server 2003 and R2 aren't assigned or tracked. They can't be reclaimed because they're never issued.

TEMPORARY LICENSES

Temporary licenses expire after a short time, unlike the permanent licenses stored on a client computer. A client device gets a temporary license under one of two circumstances: at first logon and when a license server is unavailable but the terminal server is in its grace period. I'll explain the mechanics of this in more detail in "How Licenses Are Assigned."

HOW LICENSES ARE ASSIGNED

How does a user or computer get a license? How and whether this works depends on the type of license you're talking about and whether the terminal server can get one.

Per-Device Mode

Let's take a terminal server using per-device licensing first. This terminal server has a license server with per-device licenses available.

The first time a user logs onto a terminal server from a new computer, the process goes like this.

1. The client computer connects to the terminal server and gets a temporary license allowing them to stay connected to attempt a login.

2. The user logs on at the Windows Security screen.

3. When the user has successfully logged in, the temporary license on the computer is replaced with a permanent license stored in the Registry. This permanent license is associated with that computer's hardware ID in the license server database.

4. When the user logs off, the device they used retains that license and will present it the next time someone logs on from that machine.

I want you to come away with a couple of things here. First, the client device does not get a permanent license until the user has successfully logged on. If the user's logon is denied, that device doesn't have a license assigned to it. This prevents (or at least complicates) a denial of service attack based on failed attempts to log into a terminal server. Second, the client device keeps its license and presents it the next time someone logs onto the terminal server from it.

What happens if the terminal server can't find a license server? Or if the license server doesn't have per-device licenses available (either because they're all assigned or none are installed? What happens then depends on a few factors:

◆ If the terminal server has not yet discovered a license server and it's still in its grace period, the terminal server will provide a temporary license to the device.

◆ If the terminal server has discovered a license server but no licenses of the right type are available, the license server will provide a temporary license to the device.

◆ If the device has an expired temporary license already installed on it, it cannot get a new one.

◆ If the device had a license previously but you formatted the operating system, it will get a new license. Yes, this means that one computer can use up two—or more—licenses before they automatically revert to the license pool.

◆ If the device already has a license but the terminal server can't find a license server, the user can log in normally.

Per-user Mode

This all becomes moot when the terminal server is in per-user mode. In Windows Server 2003 and R2, putting the terminal server into this mode turns off the logic that makes the terminal server ask for a license. The terminal server will still need a license server to keep operating past its grace period, but it will never run out of licenses because it never assigns them.

This *doesn't* mean that it's legal to under license, just that per-user licensing isn't tracked or enforced in this version. For this reason, put the terminal server into per-user mode when using any kind of licenses other than per-device.

The Terminal Server Licensing Tool

The Terminal Server Licensing tool, found in the Administrative Tools program group of any Server with the Terminal Server Licensing service running on it, helps you keep track of license usage.

TIP To add Terminal Services Licensing, open the Add/Remove Programs applet in the Control Panel and click the Add Windows Components icon. Follow the Windows Components Wizard and just pick the component from the list of available options. In a purely Active Directory domain, this license server must be on a domain controller. In a Mixed domain, the license server may be on a member server.

When you first start the licensing tool, it will browse for license servers on the network and then report back with the ones it found, as shown in Figure 10.29.

FIGURE 10.29
Use the Terminal Server Licensing tool to manage license usage.

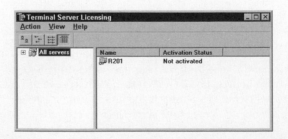

Creating a license server is a two-step process: you need to install the service, and you need to activate the license server. Although the temporary licenses will function for a limited time (120 days), to fully enable the terminal server licenses, you'll need to activate the server and download the license key.

INSTALLING TERMINAL SERVER LICENSING

For some reason, Terminal Server Licensing is not a role, but a Windows component. Go to Add/Remove programs and choose Add/Remove Windows Components from the left-hand pane to start the wizard. Click through the opening page and you'll see a dialog box like the one in Figure 10.30.

The next page (see Figure 10.31) isn't entirely clear. The license server database is okay—that's a path where the database is stored, and in this location it's part of System State data and so will be backed up as part of a normal System State backup.

FIGURE 10.30
Terminal Server Licensing is a Windows component.

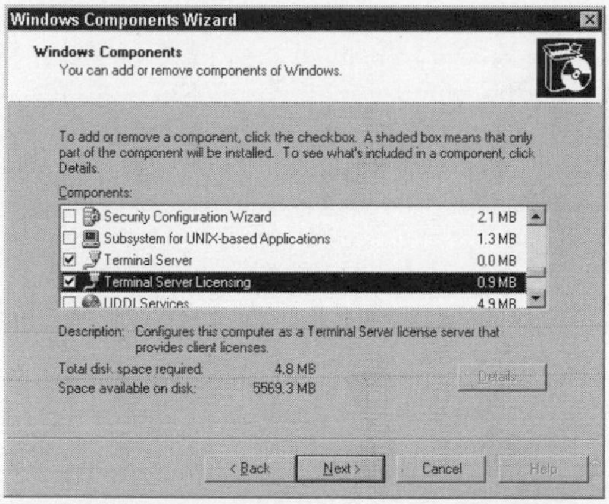

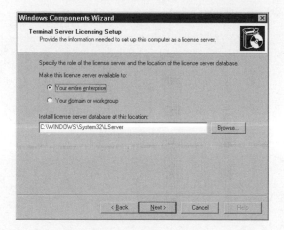

FIGURE 10.31
Choose the scope of the license server and the location of the license server database.

The scope of the license server's ability to issue licenses isn't super clear, however. To clarify, Your Domain or Workgroup restricts the license server to issuing licenses to terminal servers in the same domain or workgroup. The enterprise option allows the license server to issue licenses to a terminal server in any trusted domain…except that a bug in the license server discovery algorithm restricts the search to a single site. If you have more than one site, you'll need a different license server for each one. In fact, that's worth a note.

NOTE An enterprise-wide license server is restricted to a single site, so organizations with more than one site will need more than one license server.

Once you've chosen the scope, Setup will configure the license server.

ACTIVATING THE LICENSE SERVER

Activating the license server firmly associates the licenses you install with that license server. It's really an antipiracy measure, but it also means that there's a record of the licenses you've bought in the Microsoft clearinghouse. If you did lose your license server, you could get the installation information back from them if you had to. When you activate a license server, you're providing your product number to Microsoft. Microsoft then runs an encryption algorithm on it and sends you back the results as your activation code. You then give Microsoft back the activation code, they run another encrypting algorithm on it, and they send you a license code that corresponds to that activation code. You can't install licenses on a license server that isn't activated.

When you first open the Terminal Services Licensing tool, it looks like Figure 10.29, which showed an unactivated license server. As you can see, the licensing server is present but not yet activated, as indicated by the red dot. To make the license server ready to issue and track TSCALs, you'll need to activate the server and install the license pack assigned to that server. To do so, connect the server to the Internet (easiest, as otherwise you'll need to recite license numbers and activation codes over the telephone) and follow these steps:

1. Right-click the server and choose Activate Server from the context menu. Click through the opening screen, but read it—this tells you how long you have to set up a valid license server and what will happen if you do not.

2. Choose a method of contacting Microsoft to get a license. You have three options for contacting Microsoft to give them your product number. Automatic Connection, the default option, gives you a direct connection to Microsoft but requires that the license server have an Internet connection. Other options include the Web (whether from the license server or another computer with an Internet connection) or telephone. For this example, choose the Automatic Connection (see Figure 10.32) and click Next to display the screen shown in Figure 10.33.

NOTE If you choose to contact the licensing people via telephone, the next screen of the wizard will display a list of countries to choose from so that you've got a shot at making a toll-free call.

3. Next, fill out the form identifying yourself, as shown in Figure 10.33.

4. Next, the wizard will prompt you for some further contact information (see Figure 10.34).

5. The wizard will contact the Microsoft licensing clearinghouse and activate the server, then show you the confirmation screen in Figure 10.35.

FIGURE 10.32
Choose a way of contacting the Microsoft clearinghouse to get an activation code and valid license packs.

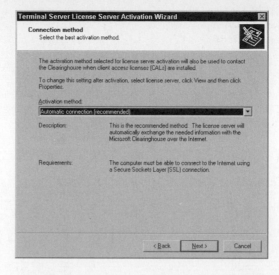

FIGURE 10.33
Fill in your name and company.

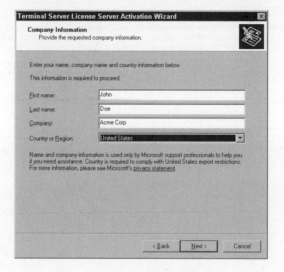

6. You'll need client licenses, so you might as well continue. Click Next to move to the next screen of the licensing tool (see Figure 10.36), where you'll need to fill in the codes of all the license packs you have (the MLP number, or your Open License or Enrollment Agreement number, depending on what kind of customer you are). Again, confirm the information that you've entered and click Next to submit it.

7. In the next page of the wizard, you'll need to provide the license pack numbers. You can add more than one at a time—just click the Add button to add them to the list.

Once you install the license pack, the license server is ready to go.

FIGURE 10.34
Other contact information is optional.

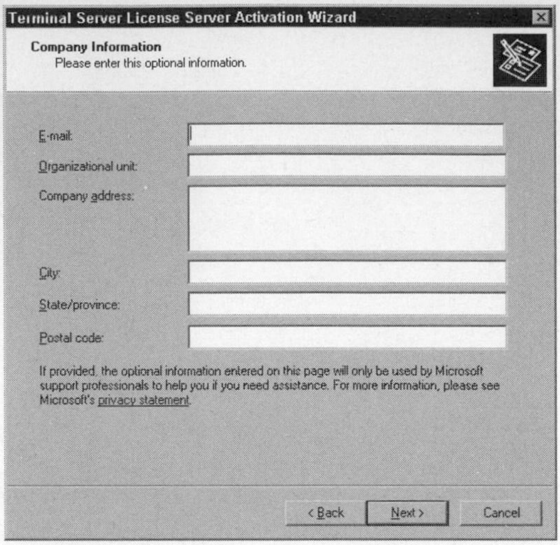

FIGURE 10.35
Completed license server activation

TIP   If the license server won't accept a license pack and you're sure you typed it correctly and have selected the right type, the database might be damaged. If it is, you can rebuild by uninstalling the licensing service, reinstalling it, and then reactivating the server.

All that said, here's a warning: You have 120 days to activate a TSCAL license server. Use those 120 days to make sure you're running the licensing service on the computer that you want to take the job. The client licenses you create will only work on the server you've activated, and the activation code is based on the product ID and server ID.

FIGURE 10.36
Installing a
license pack

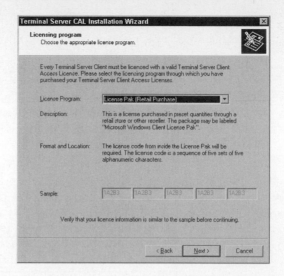

Application Licensing

Application licensing in a terminal server environment is very simple: whatever licensing applies to a product in a single-user environment applies to the terminal server environment. For example, Microsoft Office XP is licensed on a per-device basis. If you install Microsoft Office onto the terminal server, then every computer that will ever run a Microsoft Office application will need to have an Office license, even if the application only runs once a year, because the application is *apparently* running on the client workstation. However, because Office is licensed on a per-device basis, if you already have a licensed copy of Office installed on a PC client running terminal services, that client may use Office in the terminal session (perhaps when dialing into the terminal server from home) without purchasing an additional Office license because that computer is already licensed to run the application suite. Be sure to get familiar with the licensing a given application requires so you can see how it will work in the multiuser environment.

Configuring Applications for a Multiuser Environment

Not all applications work well in a thin client environment—at least not without a little help. Some use up too many processor cycles or too much memory; some can't tell the difference between a user and a computer; some store information in locations inappropriate to a multiuser operating system. Sometimes you're stuck with these problems, and if you really need to run those applications, you'll need to do it from the client Desktop, not on the terminal server. However, some problems are fixable, if you take a little time.

Choosing Applications

First, which applications should you be trying to run at all? An application suitable for a terminal server environment fits the following profile:

- ◆ Undemanding of processor cycles and memory
- ◆ Modular in video output for better caching

◆ Stores user data in per-user spaces, not in per-machine spaces

◆ Identifies users by user name, not computer name

◆ Stores global data in global locations, not local ones

WARNING   Poorly designed applications that can function in a single-user environment will bring a terminal server to a screeching halt. For example, the effect of memory leaks in an application is exponentially increased because multiple instances of the application—all leaking—may be running.

In addition to these traits, consider the operating system for which the application was originally designed. Although some Win16 and DOS applications can work in a multiuser environment, Terminal Services works best for Win32 applications. The reason for this has to do with how the terminal server runs Win32 and Win16 applications. As a Win32 operating system, Windows 2000 can't run Win16 applications on its own. Instead, it creates a Virtual DOS Machine (VDM), which is a 32-bit application, and runs the Win16 application within the context of that VDM. Whereas Win32 applications running normally on the server can share files and structures among themselves, so long as they're not changing those files or structures, applications running within VDMs can't "see" each other to share files. The practical upshot of this, combined with the fact that translating 16-bit calls to the operating system into 32-bit calls takes some overhead, means that Win16 applications perform less well in this environment than Win32 applications. They'll work—a good thing because you may not have a choice about running them if that's what you're using—but they'll use more memory than Win32 apps.

DOS applications present another kind of problem. Actually, they present two other kinds of problems. First, DOS applications were written for a single-user, single-tasking environment. To be as responsive as possible, some DOS applications constantly poll the keyboard buffer, looking for input that's meant for them. This means that a DOS application in the foreground, even when not doing anything, is using up an astounding amount of processor time. This is acceptable in a single-user environment but won't work when that processor time has to be shared with a dozen people.

TAMING DOS APPLICATIONS

Windows NT, Terminal Server Edition (TSE), included a utility called DOSKBD that modifies a program's keyboard polling to improve system performance when you run DOS-based programs. Essentially, DOSKBD puts a program to sleep when it polls the keyboard buffer too often and negatively affects server performance. Server 2003 doesn't include a copy of DOSKBD, and the TSE version doesn't work with later versions of Terminal Services. However, there's another option. Go to www.tamedos.com and check out Tame, a tool for tuning DOS applications in an Windows Server environment. That's the advice you'll get from Microsoft Support if you ask about tuning DOS applications.

Also, DOS applications with a graphical UI don't use Windows graphics rendering instructions, but bitmaps. Bitmaps take much longer to download to the client than GDI rendering instructions, so session responsiveness will suffer. Bitmap-displaying applications are jerky at best in a terminal server environment and more often are completely unusable, particularly on slower connections. Another problem with DOS applications in a multiuser environment is that you can't run them in full-screen mode. Because full-screen mode requires loading a different font set from the Windows one used for DOS applications running in a window (and thus increased memory overhead), Microsoft decided not to permit this.

You *can* run DOS and Win16 applications in a terminal server environment. They just won't cooperate with other applications as well as Win32 applications will. DOS applications in particular probably won't look as good as they would running locally.

However, you can often tweak an application to make it work better in a multiuser environment than it would if left to its own fell devices. Installing applications in a multiuser environment takes a little more care than does installing them for a single-user environment, but that's part of the price of thin client networking.

Making Your Applications Play Well with Others

Even if an application doesn't need any massaging to make it work right when shared among multiple people, you can't install it in the same way you would if installing it for a single person's use.

To work properly in a multiuser environment, applications should edit the HKCU branch of the Registry to add user-specific information, rather than HKLM. Otherwise, those settings apply to the machine, not to the user. This means that not only are per-user settings available to everyone using that particular machine, but the settings will only be available at that machine—if the user logs in to another machine, the settings won't be available. If you've only got one terminal server in your network, it won't matter for this reason if application settings are machine specific, but a single terminal server will generally only serve a few dozen people, tops, and maybe fewer than that if client demands are high. Even if you do only have one terminal server, you've still got the problem of trying to keep user-specific information limited to the people who set it up. For example, say that web browser bookmarks are stored in a machine-specific area. In a terminal server environment, that means everyone will have the same bookmarks—and will overwrite each other's settings at will.

Point being: User-specific settings should go into HKCU, not HKLM. However, you can't *install* applications into HKCU. HKCU applies only to the current user, not all users, and the identity of the current user will change depending on who's logged in—the contents of HKCU are different for each terminal server session. To get around this dilemma you need some user-specific settings, but you need to keep them someplace all users can get to, at least at first. The terminal server manages this by providing a global installation mode that exploits the machine-wide settings of HKLM.

INSTALLING APPLICATIONS FOR MULTIPLE USERS

Each Terminal Services session has two operating modes: Execute and Install. The names are descriptive of what the modes are for: Execute mode is for running applications or installing for single users, and Install mode is for installing applications to be available to multiple users. The mechanics of installing an application depend on which mode you're in when running the application's Setup program.

If you install an application while in Execute mode, it installs and edits the Registry as it would if you installed it for use on a single-user computer. When a session is in Install mode, all Registry entries created during that session are shadowed under HKLM\Software\Microsoft\Windows NT\CurrentVersion\Terminal Server\Install. Any edits that an application makes to HKCU or HKLM are copied to HKLM\Software\ Microsoft\Windows NT\CurrentVersion\Terminal Server\Install\Machine. You don't have to know all this to install applications. What you *do* have to know is that when the session is in Execute mode, if an application attempts to read an HKCU Registry entry that doesn't exist, Terminal Services will look in HKLM\Software\Microsoft\ Windows NT\CurrentVersion\Terminal Server\Install for the missing key. If the key is there, Terminal Services will copy it and its subkeys to the appropriate location under HKCU and copy any

INI files or user-specific DLLs to the user's home directory. For users without home directories, the files go to their profile folder. In short, the server makes the basic settings for each application machine specific, then copies these base settings into the user Registry entries so that the user can customize the application. Notice that this doesn't mean the application keeps returning to its pristine state every time the user runs it—the keys are only copied from their Install mode location to their user location if the keys don't already exist under HKCU.

Well, that's mostly true. The keys are timestamped, so that the newest version wins. If you add capacity to a server farm, then the new servers (which you just installed) will have a newer timestamp, so HKLM will overwrite HKCU again. This can lead to random settings disappearing. Brian Madden has a couple of utilities available for download that you can use to set the timestamp properly, so you can make new servers without having to manually change the system time or create servers only from images. You can download the tools from www.brianmadden.com/content/content.asp?ID=238.

NOTE Unfortunately, there's no way to spoof a user's identity to install an application for an individual while logged in with another account (if you logged in as Administrator and wanted to install an application for a particular user, for example). Some third-party products can help you set up applications for large numbers of users, so you don't need to log in as everybody to set up their Outlook, for example.

So how do you put the server into Install mode? On a terminal server, it's easy: if you attempt to install an application from its Setup program (named Setup.exe) without using the Add/Remove Programs applet, the installation will fail, and the server will nag you to run the Add/Remove Programs applet to install applications on a terminal server. You cannot install an application for a single user if you've set up the server to be an application server.

NOTE Some applications allow you to bypass Add/Remove Programs because the Setup program isn't named Setup.exe. For these applications, you'll need to make sure that you put the server into Install Mode manually, either by running Add/Remove Programs or by using the change user command (discussed below).

When the application's Setup program finishes running, you'll go back to the wizard, which will prompt you to click the Next button. Finally, you'll see a dire-looking dialog box telling you to click the Finish or Cancel buttons when the installation process is complete but warning you in capital letters not to do so *until* the installation is complete. Clicking Finish or Cancel returns the session to Execute mode.

Install mode's usefulness isn't limited to the installation process. Using application compatibility scripts or hand tuning, you can use Install mode to configure an application with general settings to apply to all users. Outside of Add/Remove Programs, you can put a session into Install mode with the change user command-line utility. change user has three options:

◆ /execute, the default, in which applications install in single-user mode

◆ /install, used to put the session into Install mode so that applications will be available to all users

◆ /query, which reports the mode that the session is in, like this:

```
Application EXECUTE mode is enabled.
```

So, before running a setup program, open a command prompt and type **change user /install**. This will cause the server to shadow new Registry entries, as I described earlier, so that they'll be copied to each user's personal Registry settings as the user runs the application for the first time. Just bear in mind that *any* changes you make to an application while in Install mode will be copied to that Registry key and therefore apply to all users using the application for the first time.

USING APPLICATION COMPATIBILITY SCRIPTS

Given that just about all of the applications the terminal server users will be running were originally designed for a single-user environment, many applications require a little manipulation to get them optimized for a multiuser system. Server 2003 includes application compatibility scripts for some applications. You can find the scripts for the applications in %systemroot%\Application CompatibilityScripts\Install.

These scripts are designed to customize the application's setup to be appropriate for terminal server users, first setting up the command environment, then making sure that the session is in Install mode, checking the Registry for evidence of the application to be configured, and finally editing the Registry as needed. The contents of the scripts vary based on the application, but generally speaking, they do things like turn off processor-intensive features, add multiuser support to the application, or set user-specific application directories for applications that need them.

To use the scripts, just run them right after you install the application they customize, before anyone has had a chance to use the application. For example, when you run the script for Outlook 2003, Notepad will open and display the RootDrv2.cmd file, prompting you to pick a drive letter for the customized installation to use. Provide a drive letter, save the file, and close Notepad, and the script will run. Log out and log back in, and the new settings will be applied.

TIP   To make sure that no one tries to use the application before you've run the compatibility script, disable the RDP connection while finalizing the application setup.

You're not limited to using the default settings included in these scripts. To edit one of them, right-click the script's icon and choose Edit from the context menu to open the file in Notepad. You'll need to be familiar with the command-line tools to do this.

What if your application doesn't have a script made for it? The Templates folder in the Install directory includes KEY files (you can open these in Notepad as well) that show you where each Registry entry for application settings is located and what the values should be. Based on this information and using an existing CMD file for a template, you can use the Windows scripting language to create a new script. Alternatively, you can manually edit the user settings from the application interface while the session is in Install mode, as described in the later section "Hand-Tuning Applications."

INSTALLING MULTIUSER-ENABLED APPLICATIONS

As Terminal Services becomes more widespread, it's probable that more applications will come with multiuser installation packages. Microsoft Office XP is one that presently does. If you try to run the normal installation program on a terminal server, you'll see a nag screen telling you that you can't do that and prompting you to use the installation files provided with the Office 2000 Resource Kit:

1. First, get the terminal server transform file, TermSrvr.mst, and place it in an accessible location for the installation. You can obtain the transform file from the \ORK\PFiles\ORKTools\ Toolbox\Tools\TermSrvr folder of the Office 2000 Resource Kit CD, or in \Program Files\ ORKtools\Toolbox\Terminal Server Tools if you installed the Resource Kit.

2. Install Office Disc 1 on the Terminal Server computer.

3. In the Control Panel, double-click Add/Remove Programs, click Add New Programs, and then click CD or Floppy. Click Next, then click Browse, and then move to the root folder of the installation CD and select `Setup.exe`. Click Open to add `Setup.exe` to the Run Installation Program box.

4. Don't run it yet. On the command line, append the following command after `Setup.exe`, separated by a space: **TRANSFORMS=**_path__TermSrvr.mst_, where _path_ is the location where you copied `TermSrvr.mst`.

5. From here, all goes as expected. In successive windows of the installation wizard, provide your customer information and accept the EULA, then choose Install Now. When you see a message telling you that the installation completed successfully, click OK, click Next, and then click Finish.

HAND-TUNING APPLICATIONS

If you don't need to edit many per-application settings, it might be simpler to make the changes from the user interface while in Install mode, rather than trying to create a new compatibility script. You can also manually edit applications that _have_ compatibility scripts but don't include some settings that you need to configure.

Turn Off Processor- and Bandwidth-Stressing Features

Terminal servers are designed to squeeze every last bit of juice out of system resources so that nothing is wasted. Therefore, they're often stressed—they're _supposed_ to be stressed. Given that, don't waste processor cycles on producing effects that don't necessarily add any real content to the end product, and don't waste network bandwidth on sending those useless effects to the client.

Provide Path Information

Many applications have settings for file locations—places to save files to, places to open files from, template locations, and so forth. However, those locations will often be different for different users. To make sure that file locations for each user are correct, enter a drive letter—and then map that drive letter to different locations for each user. For example, the Save As location for all Word users could be H:, but H: would direct each user to their private home directory.

USING THE REGISTRY TO TUNE APPLICATIONS

Of course, if an application doesn't have a setting in its interface, you can't use Install mode to tune that setting. However, all is not necessarily lost. You can edit some application settings directly within the Registry, in `HKLM\Software\Microsoft\Windows NT\CurrentVersion\Terminal Server\Compatibility\Applications`. (Obligatory warning follows.)

WARNING   Be careful when editing the Registry. The Registry Editor has no Undo feature and will not tell you if you give a meaningless value to an entry. Back up the Registry before you edit it, and remember that a mistyped entry in the wrong place can wipe out needed information or render the server unbootable.

More specifically, keep the following in mind:

◆ When editing value data, notice whether the values are shown in hex, decimal, or binary. When you're editing string values, you can choose to display them in any of those formats. Just be sure that you're entering the data in the chosen format. 15 decimal is F hex, but 15 hex is 21 decimal. Mixing up hex and decimal could get very ugly very quickly.

◆ If you're replacing a key (and, if you try out these hacks, you will be), be sure that the key that's selected is the one you want to replace. Restoring a key deletes all the present information in the key and replaces it with what's in the restored key. For example, say that you want to replace the contents of the MSOFFICE key that's a subkey of Applications. If you have Applications selected when you restore the saved REG file, you will wipe out every subkey of Applications and replace it with the information that should have gone into MSOFFICE.

◆ Never run a REG file unless you know exactly what it contains and what it will do. Executing a REG file imports the contents of that file into the Registry—permanently. There is no Undo feature.

Now that you're thoroughly intimidated, read on to see how to make your applications play well with others and call you by your name.

Bad! Bad Application! Go to Sleep! Reducing Demands of Windows Applications

Even if you turn off processor-hogging effects, some applications are just more cycle-hungry than others. In a terminal server environment, this is a Bad Thing. Not only do processor-sucking applications themselves under perform in a multiuser environment because they're contending with other applications, but they hurt other applications' performance by denying them cycles. You can edit the Registry to make the server keep a closer eye on Windows application management, denying processor cycles to applications that use too many, known internally as Bad Applications. Doing so will give more cycles to the other applications that the processor-sucker was starving, but will also make the errant application less responsive itself.

To make the edit, open the Registry Editor and turn to the key HKLM\Software\Microsoft\ Windows NT\CurrentVersion\Terminal Server\Compatibility\Applications. As you can see in Figure 10.37, within the Applications key, you'll see a long list of keys for available applications.

FIGURE 10.37

The contents of the Applications subkey

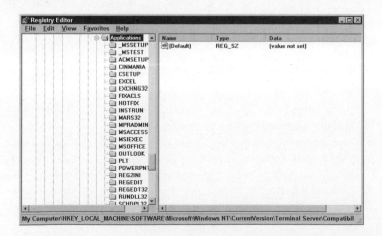

First, check to see whether the application you want to configure is already listed; if it is, then a key with the name of the application will be present. If the key exists, then open it and look at the values within it, which are described in Table 10.5.

To make your edits in the dialog box shown in Figure 10.38, double-click the value data to edit the values, bearing in mind the information I gave you about what those edits will do. Make sure you've set the flags properly according to whether the application you're editing is a 16-bit or 32-bit application, and don't forget to notice whether you're making changes in hex or decimal.

The settings will take effect when you next open the application. Because you edited a key in HKLM, the changes will apply to all instances of the application running on this terminal server.

TABLE 10.5:   Bad Application Registry Values

VALUE NAME	DESCRIPTION	DEFAULT VALUE
FirstCountMsgQPeeks-SleepBadApp	Number of times that the application will query the message queue before the server decides the application is a Bad Application. The lower this value, the sooner the server will decide that the application is bad, and the more quickly the other two values will apply.	0xf (15 decimal)
MsgQBadAppSleepTime InMillisec	The number of milliseconds that a suspended application will be denied processor cycles. The higher this value is, the longer the application will sleep.	0
NthCountMsgQPeeks-SleepBadApp	The number of times that a Bad Application can query the message queue before the server will put it to sleep again. The lower this number, the more often the misbehaving application will go to sleep.	0x5 (5 decimal)
Flags	The type of application to which these settings apply. Your options are 0x4 for Win16 applications, 0x8 for Win32 applications, or 0xc for both types.	0x8 (Win32 only)

FIGURE 10.38
Edit string values to set the Bad Application parameters you want.

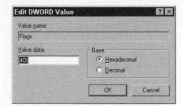

Making Applications Reference User names

Windows Terminal Server, and terminal sessions running on early betas of Win2K Server, had a little problem when it came to running WinChat, the graphical chat application that came with Windows. Because WinChat referenced computers, not users, you couldn't use it from a terminal server session to talk to someone running another terminal session. Try to connect to someone, and you'd see a list of computers to choose from. Chat sessions with yourself get dull, so that made Win-Chat pretty well useless from terminal sessions.

The intrepid user of Terminal Services is not foiled by such petty machinations, however. You can edit the Registry to make the application reference user names instead of computer names. In `HKLM\Software\Microsoft\Windows NT\CurrentVersion\Terminal Server\Compatibility\ Applications`, where you just edited the Bad Application settings, there's a value for Flags, which in the previous section was 8 or c, signifying that the settings applied either to a Win32 application or to both Win16 and Win32 applications.

TIP To apply more than one flag to an application, add together the value of all the flags you want to use and make that the value of the Flags entry.

You can apply several other compatibility flags to Flags with varying results. One flag tells the server to make the application return the version number; another tells it to make the application use the system root directory instead of the user's system directory. For our purposes, the important value is 0x10 (that is, 10 hex), which tells an application to look for users by their user names, not their computer names. So, you could edit the value of Flags for the `WINCHAT` key to 18, telling the server, "Not only is this a Win32 application, but it should reference user names, not computer names." No reboot would be necessary; you'd just restart WinChat. It wouldn't display user names—that would have been handy, but no dice—but if you plugged a user name into the browse function, it would find that user and place the call.

You're probably thinking that I'm going to tell you that Microsoft fixed this problem. In a way, you would be correct: You will no longer have problems running WinChat in a terminal server session and only being able to reference computers. This is because Microsoft decided there was no point in having a messaging application that "didn't work" from terminal server sessions available to those sessions. Now, if you attempt to run WinChat from a terminal session on a terminal server, you get an error message telling you that that application can't be used from a terminal server remote session. Well, that's *one* way to cut down on support calls, I suppose.

The good news is that this hack will still work if you have any other applications that reference computer names instead of user names—just edit that application's key as I described here. You just can't use it any longer to fix WinChat.

Managing Terminal Sessions

Thus far, you've configured client settings and set up applications. Everyone's happily typing away in their sessions. But what if they're not so happy? Terminal Services management capabilities allow you to keep tabs on what's happening on the terminal server. These capabilities work both from the GUI and from the command line.

Introducing Command-Line Tools

Terminal Services has some excellent GUI tools that make it easy to quickly get used to working with the service. That GUI can't do everything, however, and what it can do it can't always do *quickly*. Thus, the command-line tools that allow you to manage terminal sessions come in handy when it's time to make batch files—or just to do something quickly without taking the time to hunt down the right tool or part of the MMC.

There are far too many options to go into complete detail about every one of the command-line tools listed in Table 10.6, but the following sections should help you get an idea of how you can manipulate Terminal Services from the command line and the graphical administration tool.

TIP To see a complete list of all options for a command, type its name and */?* at the command line.

Those who went straight from TSE to Server 2003 will notice that their tools are here, but many of the command names have changed. The utilities still provide the same functions as the commands in TSE, but you'll have to learn new names for most of them.

TABLE 10.6: Supported Terminal Services Utilities

COMMAND	FUNCTION
change logon	Temporarily disables logons to a terminal server.
change port	Changes or displays COM port mappings for MS-DOS program compatibility. For example, you could use this utility to map one port to another one so that data sent to the first would actually go to the second.
change user	Flips between Execute mode and Install mode.
cprofile	Removes unnecessary files from a user profile. You can only run this tool on profiles not currently being used.
dbgtrace	Enables or disables debug tracing.
flattemp	Enables or disables redirected temporary directories, which you can use to send TMP files to a location other than the default.
logoff	Ends a client session specified by session name or Session ID, either on the local terminal server or on one specified.
msg	Sends a message to one or more clients.
query process	Displays information about processes.
query session	Displays information about a terminal server session.
query termserver	Lists the available application terminal servers on the network.
query user	Displays information about users logged on to the system.
register	Registers applications to execute in a system or user global context on the computer.
reset	Resets (ends) the specified terminal session.
shadow	Monitors another user's session. Cannot be executed from the console and cannot shadow the console. Equivalent to the graphical remote control tools.
tscon	Connects to another existing terminal server session.
tsdiscon	Disconnects from a terminal server session.
tskill	Terminates a process, identified by name or by Process ID.
tsprof	Copies the user configuration and changes the profile path.
tsshutdn	Shuts down a terminal server.

Using the Terminal Services Manager

To help you keep track of who's using the terminal server, what processes they're running, and the status of their connections, you'll use the Terminal Services Manager, found in the Administrative Tools program group and shown in Figure 10.39.

The left pane shows all domains in the network and all terminal servers within those domains. (You can use this tool to manage any terminal server that's listed; you don't need to be physically at that console.) The right pane's content depends on what's selected: If it's the domain or the entire network, then all current connections to that server (active or disconnected) and the name of the server hosting them are displayed; if it's a terminal server, then all current connections to that server are displayed; if it's a user name, then all the processes running in that user's context, or information about the user session, are displayed. Notice also that the right pane is tabbed, with the contents of the tabs depending on whether you've got a domain, server, or user selected on the left. Broadly speaking, you use the administration tool to get information about:

◆ Users, including what their Session IDs are, what applications they're running, and what server they're using

◆ Sessions, including what the ID of that session is, what's running in that session, what the status of the session is, how long the client has been logged in, and information about the computer the client is logged in from (IP address, RDP version, and so forth)

◆ Processes, including the Process IDs and the executable files (*images*) with which these processes are associated

NOTE It's not hard to figure out what information you're looking at—a short period of poking around will teach you where everything is. More important is the question of what you can do with this tool. In the following example, I'll show you how to use the management tools to see what's running on the server, send messages to people on the server, terminate remote processes, and close user sessions. For this example, I'll refer to a fictional game called TSQUAKE, a Terminal Services–compliant version of Quake. (Yes, it's fictional. Sorry.)

FIGURE 10.39
The Terminal Services Manager tool

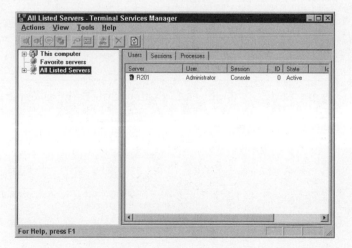

GATHERING INFORMATION

Who's playing TSQUAKE again?

To find out, you'll need to know who's logged in to the server or servers and what processes are running in their sessions. You can use both the Terminal Services Manager and the command line to get this data.

From the GUI, select the terminal server or domain for which you want information. In the right pane, three tabs will become visible: one listing users currently logged in to the terminal server, one showing the current active and disconnected sessions, and one showing the processes currently running on the terminal server.

Flip to the Processes tab associated with the domain (see Figure 10.40) to see a complete list of all processes running in the domain, the server they're running on, the session they're in, and the name of the user who owns that session. This screen will also show the Process ID (PID), which will come in handy when it comes time to terminate processes.

You can get more than just process information from this screen. Select a terminal server in the left pane. From the tabs that appear on the right, you can find the information described in Table 10.7.

FIGURE 10.40

Viewing processes running on a terminal server

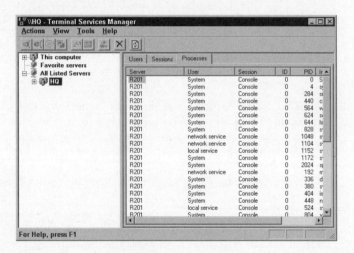

TABLE 10.7:   Finding Information in the Terminal Services Manager

DATA TYPE	TAB
Client computer name or IP address	Sessions
Image names for processes	Processes
Process IDs	Processes
Protocol used for each session	Sessions
Session idle time	Users

TABLE 10.7: Finding Information in the Terminal Services Manager *(CONTINUED)*

DATA TYPE	TAB
Session IDs associated with processes	Processes
Session status	Users, Sessions
User logon time	Users, Sessions
User name associated with processes	Processes
User Session IDs	Users, Sessions

Everything you need to find out—which user and which PID is associated with which session, and how busy that session is—is here. If you use the command-line `query` utility, you can get much the same information that you can from the Terminal Services Manager tool, but you have to do it a piece at a time. From the command line, there's no way to retrieve a list of all processes running in a domain or across all domains, so first you'll have to isolate the terminal server. For example, to see a complete list of all terminal servers in the current domain, type **query termserv**. The server will return a complete list of all terminal servers in the domain, like this:

```
Known Terminal servers
-----------
BETANET
GAMMA
TERMSERV
-----------
```

Need the list from another domain? Add the domain name you're retrieving the list from to the command, like this:

```
query termserv /domain:domainname
```

You'll get the same output, customized for the domain you specified.

Once you've got the name of the server you need to check out, look for TSQUAKE by querying for processes, like this:

```
query process
```

The server will return a list of all user-launched processes running in the current session (even if that session is the console), as shown:

```
USERNAME        SESSIONNAME  ID   PID IMAGE
>administrator  console       0  1152 explorer.exe
>administrator  console       0  1348 osa.exe
>administrator  console       0  1360 findfast.exe
>administrator  console       0   532 infoview.exe
>administrator  console       0  2052 depends.exe
>administrator  console       0  2172 cmd.exe
>administrator  console       0   764 taskmgr.exe
```

```
>administrator      console       0  1256 tsadmin.exe
>administrator      console       0  1636 mmc.exe
>administrator      console       0  1500 winword.exe
>administrator      console       0  2092 regedit.exe
>administrator      console       0  1776 query.exe
>administrator      console       0  1652 qprocess.exe
```

To query the process list for a different user, add that person's user name to the command, like this:

query process gertrude

TIP You can also list processes associated with a particular session name or Session ID, although for most purposes I find it easier to reference user names. You'll use the Session ID to determine if a user has more than one session open.

Okay, but what you really want is a list of everyone who's goofing off and using up processor cycles. Although you can't get a list of all processes running in a single domain or across domains, you can retrieve a list of all users with a particular process running in their sessions, like this:

```
C:\>query process winword.exe
  USERNAME          SESSIONNAME    ID   PID IMAGE
>administrator      console         0  1500 winword.exe
 christa            rdp-tcp#1       1  1400 winword.exe
```

Use this command to track down those TSQUAKE users.

SENDING MESSAGES

Once you've got your list of people running TSQUAKE, you can let them know that they're caught. From both the GUI and the command line, you can send messages to a single person, to multiple people, and even across domains.

From the left pane of the Terminal Services Manager tool, select the terminal server the people are using. In the right, select the people to whom you want to send a message (Ctrl+click to select multiple user names). From the Actions menu, choose Send Message to open the dialog box. Click OK, and the message will instantly pop up on the screen of everyone you included on the recipient list.

You can also send messages from the command line with the msg utility. This works much like msg did in single-user Windows, with one exception: messages sent to a user name will be sent to all instances of that name, not just one. This is so that a person running multiple sessions will be sure to get their message.

msg has lots of options. Its basic syntax looks like this:

msg {*identifier*}[/SERVER:*servername*] [/TIME:*sec*] [/v] [/w] [*message*]

The *identifier* can be a user name, Session ID, session name, or filename containing an ASCII list of all users to whom the message should go. The /TIME parameter doesn't delay the message; rather, it's a time-out period that cooperates with the /w switch that waits for user response before giving control of the command prompt back to the message's sender.

NOTE Like the other command-line utilities, msg operates on the server you're connected to unless you specify otherwise.

To send a message to a single user, run `msg` like this:

```
msg gertrude Gertrude, please close TSQUAKE. You're wasting processor time.
```

If you want some kind of record that Gertrude saw the message—or at least clicked OK—use the /v (for "verbose") switch as follows:

```
msg gertrude /v Gertrude, I mean it. Close the game.
```

You'll see output like the following:

```
Sending message to session RDP-Tcp#1, display time 60
Timeout on message to session RDP-Tcp#1 before user response
```

To send a message to everyone logged in to that terminal server, use an asterisk, like so:

```
msg * Hey, everyone-Gertrude's got enough free time to play TSQUAKE. Anyone got
anything for her to do?
```

Alternatively, send a message to a preset group by typing all recipient names into a Notepad file and saving it, then referencing the file like this:

```
msg @users Hey, everyone-Gertrude has enough free time to play TSQUAKE. Anyone
got anything for her to do?
```

The only catch to sending messages to multiple users is that if you add the /w option, `msg` works sequentially. That is, it will send the message to the first person in the list (going in order of Session ID) and wait for either a response or a time-out before sending the message to the second person in the list.

TERMINATING APPLICATIONS

Gertrude and the other TSQUAKE players aren't paying attention to your pleas. Time to get tough and terminate the application. Every instance of TSQUAKE that you close will exit immediately, with no warning to the user and no chance to save data.

NOTE Before I get into this, let me distinguish again between terminating and resetting. Both options close applications with no warning, but single processes are terminated and entire sessions are reset.

To kill a single application from the GUI, select the server or domain in the left pane and turn to the Processes tab in the right. All running processes will appear here, identified by the name of the server they're running on, who's got them open, the PIDs of the processes, and other relevant information. As elsewhere, you can Ctrl+click to select multiple processes. When every process to be terminated is selected, right-click and choose End Process from the context menu (it's the only option). The selected applications will close instantly.

You can also terminate applications from the command line. Just be careful. This procedure is open to error, and you will not make people happy if you accidentally close the wrong process and lose all their data.

The command to kill terminal server applications is `tskill`, related to the `kill` command that appeared for the first time in NT 3.5's Resource Kit and which stops an application by killing its process. Like the Terminate menu command, `tskill` will stop an application as soon as it's executed, with no time allowed for saving data or other tasks. It's very intrusive, so you should only use it when there's simply no other way of getting an application to stop.

The syntax of `tskill` is as follows:

```
tskill processid | processname [/SERVER:servername] [/ID:sessionid | /a] [/v]
```

Notice that you can reference a process either by its name or its Process ID. The former is easier and necessary if you're using the /a switch to close all instances of an application on the terminal server. The latter is necessary if you're only trying to close specific instances of the application, perhaps leaving untouched the instance of TSQUAKE that your boss has open.

So, to kill all instances of TSQUAKE running on the currently selected server, you type:

```
tskill tsquake.exe /a
```

To kill only selected instances, get the PID by running `query process` or `query user` and plug it in, like this:

```
tskill 1875
```

Sadly, you can't list several PIDs at once to kill, so if you need to pick and choose processes without killing all instances, you'll need to terminate instances of a process one at a time.

TIP Although you need to supply the executable extension with `query process`, the command won't work if you supply the extension with `tskill`. So, it's **query process tsquake.exe**, but **tskill tsquake**.

TAKING CONTROL OF USER SESSIONS

Sometimes, the best plan isn't to just shut down applications from the terminal server. Instead, you can take control of a user session and see what they're doing (as opposed to listing processes, which just tells you what processes are active in the context of a given session). This can be especially helpful for troubleshooting purposes, such as if Gertrude says she didn't mean to run TSQUAKE but couldn't figure out how to shut it down once she had it running. Taking remote control of the session gives you the same degree of control that you'd have if logged on as that user.

You can remotely control a user's session in one of two ways: from the Terminal Services Manager or from the command line.

TIP You can only take remote control of a terminal server session from another terminal server session, not from the console. The remote control option in the Terminal Services Manager and the `shadow` command-line utility won't work from the console.

To use the GUI, start a terminal server session, logging in with an account with Administrator privileges. From within the session, start the Terminal Services Manager. Select a terminal server in the left pane and switch to the Users tab so that user sessions are showing. Find the session you want to shadow, and choose Remote Control from the Actions menu. A dialog box will prompt you for the hotkey combination you want to use to end remote control of your own session (so you can get back to the original session).

If the user session is configured to require user permission for control, then a dialog box will appear on the screen, letting the user know that someone has requested permission to control their session. If they permit the control, then you're in charge of their session without further ado. If they don't permit the control, then you'll see an error message telling you that you couldn't get permission to control the session. The degree of control you have over a user's session that you're remotely controlling depends on the settings in the user's account settings.

The command-line utility for taking remote control of a user session is called `shadow`, after the WinFrame and MetaFrame name for remote control. Its syntax is as follows:

```
shadow {sessionname | sessionid} [/SERVER:servername] [/v]
```

To use it, start a terminal services session with administrative privileges. Open the command prompt and run **query user *username*** or **query session *username*** to find the Session ID or session name of the user whose session you want to shadow. You can't shadow based on *username*, so you'll need this information even if you know the account name of the person whose session you're shadowing.

If shadowing a session on the same terminal server that you're logged in to, the command syntax for shadowing Session ID 1 is as follows:

```
shadow 1
```

If that session requires user permission to be remotely controlled, then you'll see the following message while your session waits for permission to take over the remote one:

```
Your session may appear frozen while the remote control approval is being
negotiated.
Please wait...
```

Once you have permission, you're in, just as you would be when using the GUI remote control option. The session must have someone logged in at the time—you cannot shadow a disconnected session.

The only tricky part to shadowing from the command prompt is that you had best do it at least once from the GUI before trying the command-line utility. The `shadow` command does not prompt you for a hotkey combination to end remote control and return to your session. It will use the one defined for the GUI, so if you know what that hotkey combination is, you can use it. Just make sure you know how to return to your own session from the remote control.

Ending—or Preventing—User Sessions

That's it—Gertrude's kicked off the server until she can learn to stop using it incorrectly.

If you want to stop an entire terminal session, not just a single process within it, you can either disconnect or reset the connection. Disconnecting, you recall, cuts the user off from the session (although there's normally nothing to keep a user from reconnecting), but leaves all applications running and data in memory. When the user reconnects to a session they were disconnected from, then they're right back where they left off. A reset connection, in contrast, closes all applications the person had open and ends the session without saving any changes to the user profile. Disconnected sessions still use some system resources, albeit not much because their data will eventually be paged to disk and they won't have new user input to process. Reset sessions use no resources.

To disconnect or reset a session from the Terminal Services Manager tool, select it in the left pane and choose Reset or Disconnect from the Action menu. You'll see a dialog box warning you that the session will be disconnected or reset; click OK, and the selected session or sessions will be ended.

You can also end user sessions from the command line with the `tsdiscon` and `reset session` commands. The syntax for `tsdiscon` is as follows:

```
tsdiscon [sessionid | sessionname] [/SERVER:servername] [/v]
```

Once again, you can choose to identify sessions to close by session name or Session ID. To find out both, run `query session` to get output like the following:

```
SESSIONNAME    USERNAME        ID  STATE   TYPE   DEVICE
>console       Administrator   0   active  wdcon
 rdp-tcp       65537               listen  rdpwd
 rdp-tcp#2     Christa         2   active  rdpwd
                               1   idle
                               3   idle
```

Find the session name or ID you want, and plug it into the `tsdiscon` command like this: **tsdiscon 2**. Once you've pressed the Enter key, the user of the selected session sees a message, "Terminal Server has ended the connection," and is given a Close button to click.

TIP   I find it easiest to reference Session IDs. You always have to use a number—you can't choose to disconnect a session attached to a particular user name—so you might as well choose the shortest identifier you can get away with.

The syntax for resetting a session is similar to that used for disconnecting it:

```
reset session {sessionname | sessionid} [/SERVER:servername] [/v]
```

Once again, the user will see a dialog box telling them that Terminal Server ended the connection and prompting them to close.

What if you'd like to keep people off the terminal server altogether, perhaps while you're installing new applications on it? If no one's yet connected, you can disable the RDP protocol from the Terminal Services Configuration tool located in the Administrative Tools program group. Right-click the RDP protocol, and from the pop-up menu that appears, choose All Tasks/Disable Connection.

WARNING   If you disable the connection from the Terminal Services Configuration tool, you'll reset any existing sessions.

If you've reset all connections in preparation for shutting down the server, you can also shut down the server without going to the console. `tsshutdn`'s syntax is as follows:

```
tsshutdn [wait_time] [/SERVER:servername] [/REBOOT] [/POWERDOWN] [/
DELAY:logoffdelay] [/v]
```

Most of these options are what they appear to be. *wait_time* specifies the amount of time (in seconds) until the server is shut down, and *servername* specifies a server if you don't want to shut down the one you're currently logged in to. /REBOOT reboots the server, and /POWERDOWN shuts it down if the server has Advanced Power Management drivers (if not, the server shuts down all server processes and displays the Click to Restart message).

TIP   Use `tsshutdn` to circumvent the nag screen asking you why you want to shut down a perfectly good server. This works on any Server 2003, not just terminal servers.

So, for example, you could combine `tsshutdn` and `msg` to tell everyone that the server's going to be rebooted in five minutes. First, send the following message:

```
Msg * The server will go down in 5 minutes for maintenance. Please log out.
```

Second, run the `tshutdn` command with the following parameters:

```
tshutdn 300 /reboot
```

NOTE Any dialog boxes that require user response (for example, one asking you if you want to save changes to a MMC snap-in that you edited) will want your response—they won't just go away without a response. Therefore, if using `tsshutdn`, you must respond to those dialog boxes before the `tshutdn` timeout period. Otherwise, `tsshutdn` will respond that the shutdown operation completed successfully, but the server will still be running.

Say, however, that you don't want to shut down the server. You just want to keep any new sessions from starting. To disable the protocol for new sessions without disturbing the ones already in place, you'll need to use the `change logon` command utility. Its syntax is as follows:

```
change logon {/QUERY | /ENABLE | /DISABLE}
   /QUERY    Query current terminal session login mode.
   /ENABLE   Enable user login from terminal sessions.
   /DISABLE  Disable user login from terminal sessions.
```

Typing **change logon /disable** prevents any further connections from being made until you re-enable the protocol. Anyone who tries to connect will see an error message telling them that remote logins are currently disabled. Disabling RDP does not, obviously, affect the console session as it's not dependent on RDP. As I mentioned earlier, you'll need to disable logins if you want to keep people off the terminal server, as the service itself does not shut off.

Troubleshooting Connection Problems

When you set up a connection properly, it should work—but *should* is a nice word that doesn't always apply to reality. Windows Server 2003 added a lot of error messages attempting to explain precisely what the problem is when a user cannot connect. Microsoft documented these error messages here: `http://technet2.microsoft.com/WindowsServer/en/Library/159e6ff8-4edb-43fd-8767-3d9858897e2c1033.mspx?mfr=true`. Generally, though, the errors fall into a few large categories: licensing problems, network problems, and permission problems.

Licensing Problems

Licensing problems account for most of the most serious login problems. There are a few exceptions such as the license on the client computer having been corrupted, but most often, the terminal server hasn't been able to find licenses of the kind it needs. That means that either the terminal server can't find a license server at all, or the available license servers haven't got the right kind of licenses. SP1 introduced many new pop-up error messages that warn the user that their license is temporary and about to expire or warning administrators that the terminal server can't find a license server. Don't disregard them, since an expired license will lead to a user who can't log onto the terminal server.

A terminal server can give out temporary licenses during its grace period, a period of up to 120 days during which it does not need a license server. These temporary licenses are just that—temporary. If the error messages state that the temporary license is about to run out, then the odds are good that one of two things is wrong. Either the terminal server has not been able to discover a license server, or the terminal server's mode doesn't match the license server.

Terminal Server Configuration can help you solve both of these problems. To circumvent automatic discovery, go to the Server settings. Double-click License Server Discovery mode to open the dialog box shown in Figure 10.41. Previously discovered license servers will appear as well.

TIP Always check names when manually typing IP addresses or server names.

You can do the same thing with group policy. Go to Computer Configuration\Administrative Templates\Windows Components\Terminal Services and open the properties for Use the Specified Terminal Server License Servers to show the dialog box in Figure 10.42.

You'll also define the right license mode from Terminal Services Configuration. The problem here is that per-user licensing became available with Windows Server 2003, but the default license mode on a terminal server is per-device. People who installed per-user licenses but didn't change the license mode weren't able to get permanent licenses installed on the client devices.

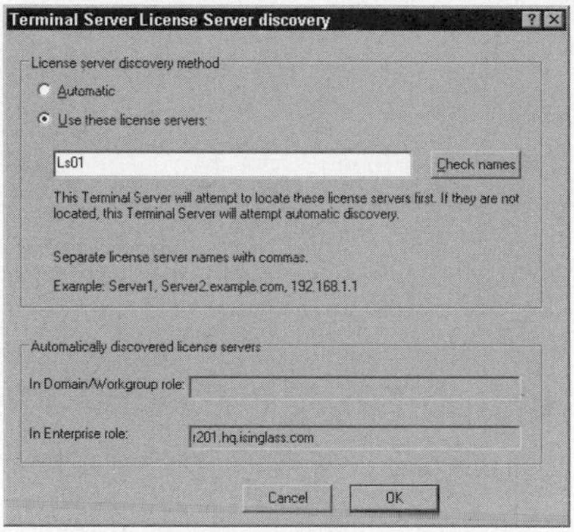

FIGURE 10.41
Point to a specific license server from Terminal Services Configuration.

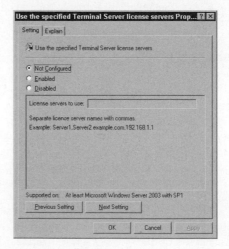

FIGURE 10.42
To define specific license servers for multiple terminal servers, use group policy.

One way to avoid the whole mess is to change the licensing mode to per-user. You should definitely do this if using per-user licensing, and possibly even if you have per-device licenses or a mixture. Per-user licenses aren't tracked, or even issued—turning the license mode to per-user effectively turns off the logic in the operating system that requests a license at user logon. It is not legal to under-license. It is, however, legal to have per-device licenses but to use per-user licensing mode.

To change the license mode from Terminal Services Configuration, go to the Server Settings section and double-click the licensing mode to open the dialog box in Figure 10.43.

You can also use Group Policy to configure the license mode. Go to Computer Configuration\Administrative Templates\Windows Components\Terminal Services and open the policy Set the Terminal Server Licensing Mode to open the dialog box in Figure 10.44.

Permission Problems

Another problem keeping people from connecting to the terminal server is that they don't have permission to do so. Make sure that anyone you want to use the terminal server is in the Remote Desktop Users group.

Network Problems

Finally, network problems can show up. These problems may appear through users getting error messages when they try to log in now, only to be able to log in with no problems when they attempt to reproduce the problem for their administrator. If this is happening frequently, you may be having latency problems, and it's worth checking out the network.

FIGURE 10.43
Configure the license mode according to the kind of licenses you've installed.

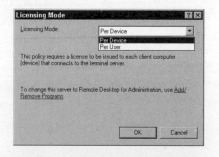

FIGURE 10.44
In SP1 and later, a group policy can control the license mode.

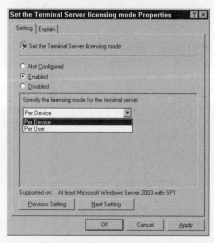

Using Remote Administration Mode

This chapter is generally about how to use Terminal Services to create application servers, but as I've said, Terminal Services gives you a handy way of accessing *any* server that can accept incoming RDP connections. If you've never used Terminal Services for remote management and you've just read this chapter about how to set up an application server, you may have some questions about how Remote Administration mode works and what you can do with it, so let's address those now.

Enabling Remote Administration

Although Terminal Services is installed by default, for security reasons the server will not accept incoming connections by default. To enable them, open the Control Panel and turn to the Remote tab of the System applet (see Figure 10.45).

Once you've done that and ensured that the RDP port is open for the network connection, the server can accept incoming connections.

FIGURE 10.45

You must enable Remote Desktop to permit incoming connections.

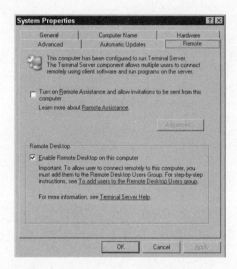

Connecting to Remote Servers Using the Remote Desktops Tool

The Remote Desktop Connection client comes preinstalled on Server 2003, but this isn't the best tool for server administration unless you normally only interact with one server at a time. Instead, try the Remote Desktops tool in the Administrative Tools section of the Start menu. Using this tool, you can connect to multiple servers and flip back and forth between them without having to maximize and minimize session windows. This tool works for both Windows 2000 and Server 2003 servers—the servers just have to have Terminal Services installed and be accepting incoming connections.

When you first open Remote Desktops, it won't have any servers in it—just a Remote Desktops icon. To create a connection, right-click this icon and choose Add New Connection from the context menu. You'll open the dialog box in Figure 10.46.

There's an annoying bug here (or feature—I suppose it depends on your outlook). See that Browse button in Figure 10.46? It looks like you can browse for servers to connect to, doesn't it? Well, you can but the only servers that it will return are application servers (and Windows 2000 servers in remote administration mode, if you have any). Server 2003 computers using Remote Administration will not appear. However, you can connect to them by typing their names or IP addresses—you just can't browse for them.

FIGURE 10.46
Adding a new Remote
Desktops connection

Notice that you can connect to the console of the server, both for Server 2003 computers and Windows 2000 computers. This is helpful if you're doing something that requires interacting with the console directly—for example, running software that sends messages to the console, not to sessions. If you connect to a server's console session, you'll lock the local console session so that two people aren't interacting with it at once.

Finally, notice that you can provide a name and password to use when connecting to the remote computer. When you're finished setting up the connection, click OK to save the connection. The new connection will appear in Remote Desktops. To launch the connection, right-click a server's icon in the left pane and choose Connect. To toggle between multiple open sessions, just click the appropriate server's icon in the left pane.

To end a session, either disconnect or log out as you would if using Remote Desktop Connection, or right-click a server's icon and choose Disconnect. Disconnecting, once again, does not completely close a terminal session. Disconnected sessions count toward the two concurrent administrative logins permitted.

Questions about Using Remote Administration

You've connected, but how does this work? Read on.

HOW MUCH WILL REMOTE ADMINISTRATION MODE AFFECT SERVER PERFORMANCE?

You're probably aware that a terminal server requires a lot of horsepower to support all those clients and may be wondering whether Remote Administration mode is going to require you to seriously beef up your ordinary servers. Nope. Application servers require so much memory because many people are using them at once, not because the service itself is particularly power-hungry. The total memory requirements for running Terminal Services in Remote Administration mode are a little less than 2.5MB of RAM. That server probably should have about 2GB or more of RAM installed. In other words, if the server can do what it's supposed to do, unless it's very stressed, remote administration shouldn't faze it.

HOW MANY PEOPLE CAN LOG IN TO THE SERVER?

When you install Terminal Services into this mode, you're permitting up to two simultaneous administrative connections to the terminal server. (Anyone whose account does not have administrative privileges on the domain will be denied access to the server, so you don't have to worry about Joe User logging into the web server if he doesn't have an administrative account.) The licenses for these connections are built in, so you don't need additional licenses for server management—or a Terminal Services license manager—if you're only using Terminal Services for this purpose.

CAN I RUN ANY MANAGEMENT TOOL FROM A TERMINAL SESSION?

Sort of. Microsoft notes several tools that won't work in a terminal session and that you must operate from the console. Microsoft SQL Server 6.5 and 7 PerfMon counters cannot be accessed from a remote session (this is fine; you really don't want to be running System Monitor from an RDP session anyway—too many graphical updates) and must be viewed from the console. Also, Pervasive SQL v7 has a namespace problem that prevents the tool from installing properly from a terminal session. Otherwise, though, most tools will work in a remote session. With the faster RDP connections available today, even fairly graphically intense management tools are working pretty well.

Summary

Server-based computing is one of those overnight successes that takes ten years to come to fruition, and as part of the new virtualization craze it appears to have gotten there. In this chapter, you've learned some of the ways you can use server-based computing and how to use Terminal Services to accomplish this. I've also explained some of what's going on under the hood and the source of some common problems to help you keep accomplishing without interruption.

Each time that Microsoft comes out with a new version of the OS, Terminal Services becomes more capable. Why is this overnight success still struggling? Part of the reason has to do with Terminal Services itself. Although Microsoft's capabilities now meet the basic criteria for users— mapped printers and drives, full color depth, more secure connections—using applications run from a server still, in most cases, requires some changes for end users. There are improvements on this front coming in the next version of Windows Server. For example, in the next version (due out in late 2007 or 2008) Microsoft has included support for application publishing both to the desktop and through a Web portal, so that users can truly use only a single application and not an entire desktop. Internet-access security is also vastly improved, and device redirection expanded. Although Microsoft realizes that most people don't replace the desktop with Terminal Services, the new features make it much easier to really integrate the remote applications with the local ones. Although Microsoft's native server-based computing isn't really truly enterprise-ready, Microsoft is targeting the small and medium enterprise with Longhorn Terminal Services. For smaller organizations, Terminal Services is already fine. With the next release, it will be ready for larger ones.

The larger difficulty has nothing to do with the feature set, but with the complexity of server-based computing itself. Installing a desktop with an application set is a trivial task. Installing an application server farm of fifty servers (or even five) and keeping all those servers both in working order and consistent with each other is not a trivial task at all. We're still working on this front (and it's been the basis of many software companies building tools to support flaws in server-based computing). The nirvana point would be automating the installation and maintenance of server farms more easily.

In the meantime, everything you learn here about how Terminal Services really works will help you keep those server farms running. Keep your application set XP-capable, use per-user licensing if possible, and use the security features added in Service Pack 1—you'll be glad you did.

## Chapter 11

Tightening Security with the Security Configuration Wizard

2003 SP1's features almost perfectly mirror those of XP SP2's, with one very significant difference: the Security Configuration Wizard (SCW). Microsoft has long recommended server *hardening*, a process whereby you examine a long list of potential Registry changes, group policy settings, NTFS permission adjustments, and firewall tweaks to see which, if any, can work in your organization. They've released a number of white papers of significant sizes, all with the same goal: to show you all of the places where you can shore up your server's security.

But many people don't do it for two reasons. First, it's a nontrivial job to read and understand all of the things that the hardening guides recommend, and second, there's the problem that tightened security always presents: will making this change cause something on my server to stop working?

The SCW makes hardening a bit easier in a few ways. First, it saves you a lot of research, as its wizard-driven user interface walks you through the hardening process and actually does quite a nice job of explaining to you what it's about to do and in some cases even why. Then the SCW generates an XML file with all of its recommended changes, and you can use SCW to execute those changes. SCW also has a command-line interface that lets you convert the SCW changes into a group policy object or lets you simply apply a set of changes to a list of machines or an organization unit in Active Directory. But perhaps best of all, SCW has a "rollback" feature that lets you undo most—but not all—of its changes. That's really nice because you're more likely to try out easily reversed change, and anything that makes you more open to a bit of security tweaking is a good thing.

In this chapter, I'll show you how to install it, I'll walk you through a run-through of the SCW, and then you'll use its command-line interface to expand SCW's power.

Warning: Using SCW May Void Your Warranty!

Well, not really. But understand that while SCW makes it easier for you to examine and adjust dozens of security settings, "easier" doesn't mean "safer and more compatible." As I've already said, and as you may have discovered if you've ever played with locking down services, when you force digital signing on communications, restricting anonymous access and the other kinds of things that SCW does (and if any of that sounded unfamiliar then don't worry, I'll explain the concepts as we go along), it is possible to make your server so secure that it doesn't do what it used to do.

Furthermore, SCW does indeed have a rollback feature that can roll back any adjustment of services, opening or closing of ports on the firewall, and many other security settings, but it *cannot* roll back changes to your system's NTFS permissions or your system's Registry permissions. So please, please, please listen to this advice:

WARNING SCW makes hardening your system easier, *not* safer. As with all hardening exercises, please try any SCW-created templates out on test servers before rolling them out to a production server. Again, this is important: blindly running SCW on a production server may cause that server to stop working. And while that may not void your warranty, it *can* be a CLM (career-limiting move).

Building a Test System

Like many of the concepts we've examined so far in this book, SCW is best understood with a mixture of conceptual background and a solid example. If you'd like to follow along, then try this: my test system was a 2003 SP1 system with SMTP, POP3, IIS, and DNS on it. All I had to do was install those modules in Add/Remove Programs and then give the POP3 server a domain to support; I gave it "bigfirm.com." You have to put a `default.htm` file in `c:\inetpub\wwwroot` to get the web server to wake up completely. A quick `netstat -ano` then demonstrated that it was listening on ports TCP 25 (SMTP), TCP 110 (POP3), both TCP and UDP 53 (DNS), and the Web (TCP 80). Then I set up a DNS zone for bigfirm.com, pointed the server to itself for DNS name resolution and created a domain called bigfirm.com. I did not have Windows Firewall enabled. (If you're not sure how to install SMTP, POP, DNS, or IIS or how to create a domain, please review Chapters 7, 8, and 17 in *Mastering Windows Server 2003*.)

Installing Security Configuration Wizard

SCW comes with SP1 but does not install itself automatically. To install it, follow these steps:

1. Click Start ➤ All Programs ➤ Control Panel ➤ Add or Remove Programs.

2. Click Add/Remove Windows Components.

3. In the Windows Components Wizard, scroll down to Security Configuration Wizard and check the box next to it. Click Next.

4. The Windows Components Wizard may need your 2003 Server install disk.

5. When it's done, just click Finish and then close Add/Remove Programs and the Control Panel.

Once you've done that, you'll find SCW on the Administrative Tools menu.

SCW's Scope

As you run SCW, you will see a *lot* of pages to its wizard—more, in fact, than you've probably ever seen on another wizard. In fact, after I'd run it on a few systems, it seemed to me that it's less of a "wizard" and more of an "expert system." SCW works in several phases:

Welcome and Overview Which machine to work on, is this a new, old, or rollback setup?

Role-based Security Configuration The wizard guesses what server roles you use the system for and asks in effect, "I think this is a file server, DNS server, and DHCP server; is that right or do you do other things with this?" It then analyzes what *client* roles the system must be able to fulfill. Once it's got those questions asked, it reviews the services that you have running on your system and suggests ones that could be disabled. You review that information and, if necessary, adjust its suggestions and move on to the next phase.

Network Security   Using what it knows about your system, SCW suggests blocking all ports save for a list that it shows you. As before, you can tweak its suggestions.

Registry Settings   Windows Server 2003 has a bunch of settings that can significantly secure your network but *only* if all of your client and server systems are XP and 2003, or even 2000 in some cases. By asking some questions, SCW enables or disables things called SMB signing, LAN Manager hashes, LM and NTLM authentication methods, LDAP signing, and the "named pipe firewall." (We'll cover what all of those are later in this chapter.)

IIS Security   If SCW detects that you've got IIS running, it asks a few questions and tightens up some common IIS vulnerabilities.

Audit Policy   Based on a few questions, SCW suggests turning on different levels of security auditing.

Once past all of that, SCW comes up with a pile of settings and stores them in an XML file called a *Security Configuration Wizard policy* (*template* always seems a better word in my opinion) that you can then apply to a server or a bunch of servers either immediately, or whenever you'd like.

Running the Security Configuration Wizard

You start SCW from the Administrative Tools menu. Its first page looks like Figure 11.1.

Phase One: SCW Reads Its Database and Your System

Unlike most wizards, this one's not cluttered with a lot of pages that feature text so obvious that they make you shake your head and say, "Why don't they just remind me to keep breathing?" In contrast, this first SCW page makes a couple of good points. First, it's got to figure out what server software you're running, and it can't do that unless the server software is active, and, second, that this isn't the Manage Your Server component, and so SCW won't install new software for you. You might say that Manage Your Server *adds* software and open doors to your server…and this one nails unnecessary doors closed. Click Next to see the next page, as you see in Figure 11.2.

FIGURE 11.1
Opening SCW page

This asks whether you're going to create a new SCW policy (which is stored as an XML file), edit an already-existing one, apply a policy to some computer, or roll back the last applied policy. You're creating a new policy, and as that's the default, you can just click Next to see Figure 11.3.

It wasn't initially obvious to me, but you needn't run SCW on every system that you'd like to create a security policy for. Here the text field was automatically populated with SP1TESTER, the name of the machine that I ran SCW on, but you can punch in the name of *any* system that you have administrator-level permissions on. SCW can work remotely, assuming that you've got the right ports open on the target system. Recall also that the previous screen offered the option to apply an existing SCW policy with the wizard, meaning that you can also use the Security Configuration Wizard to apply an SCW policy to a remote system. Actually, you'll see later that there's an accompanying command-line tool, scwcmd, that lets you apply policies both locally and remotely; with a one-line command, scwcmd can apply a policy to an entire organization unit's worth of systems.

FIGURE 11.2
What will this
SCW run do?

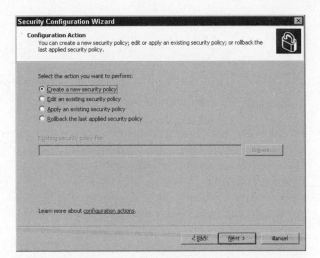

FIGURE 11.3
SCW works remotely.

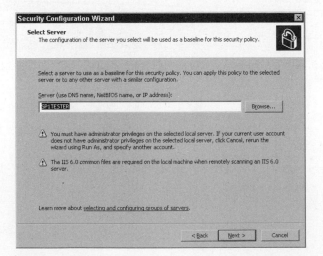

Click Next and SCW will go out and read a number of XML files that basically tell it, "If your server runs X server software, then it needs Y ports open, and Z system services running." Those are XML files in \windows\security\msscw\kbs, and you can add your own if you'd like to add some extra non-Microsoft service to the SCW's analysis. (Just look at the XML files in that directory for examples.) It'll take a minute or two for SCW to find, read, and analyze those files, and then you'll see a screen like Figure 11.4.

I point this page out because of the View Configuration Database button. Click it and you see the database that SCW's about to work from, as you see in Figure 11.5.

NOTE But before I discuss this, let me make an important point. SCW is a useful and very flexible wizard that does a large variety of things based on what it sees in your computer. I've tried in this chapter to show you everything that you might see from SCW, and as a result I may show you a page or two that you don't get, or you may come across a page that I don't have. In that case, don't worry; it's just that your system's different from my deliberately-overloaded-demo system.

FIGURE 11.4
Database read and viewable

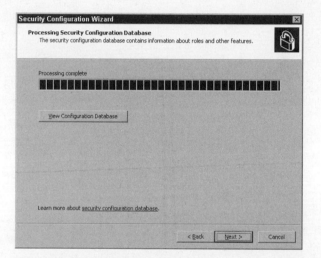

FIGURE 11.5
SCW Viewer showing DNS server and DC requirements

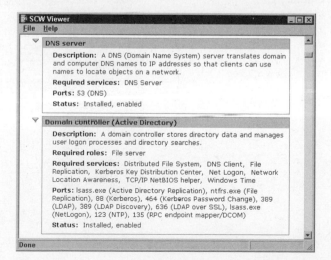

Here, I've opened the DNS server and domain controller roles. The DNS server's pretty simple to read. It first says that if you're to run DNS, then you need the server software called DNS server running, and you also need port 53 open. Then it reports that a scan of this system shows that the server software is both installed and started. The DC entry is more interesting; notice the sheer volume of information about services needed to make a DC role work. Scroll further down and you'll see a section with more specific port information, as you see in Figure 11.6.

FIGURE 11.6
Service and port-specific details for DNS

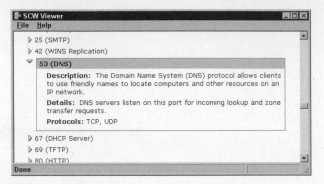

In the earlier entry about DNS, you might have noticed that it referred to port 53 for DNS, but not whether it was 53 on TCP, UDP, or both. The "port" section of the SCW database covers that, showing that DNS needs both TCP and UDP.

That's something that I really like about SCW: its relative transparency. I'm normally skeptical about wizards for two reasons. First, they don't explain what they're doing or why they're doing it and, second, once they've done whatever they've done, you're stuck with it; wizards tend to be irreversible. SCW meets both of those objections in that you can see the database that it works from, you could modify its XML files if you really wanted to, and it is largely reversible.

Phase Two: Which Services Can Go?

Close the SCW Viewer and click Next in the SCW to see a screen like Figure 11.7.

FIGURE 11.7
Starting the Role-Based Service Configuration

As I've said before, SCW works in several phases. First, it found out what you wanted to do (create a new security policy, edit an existing one, apply an existing one, or rollback an already-applied one), then it read its database and scanned your system to figure out what you used it for. Now it's going to take that information and try to compile a list of unnecessary services and, if you allow it, to turn off those unnecessary services. Click Next and you'll see a screen like Figure 11.8.

Based on what SCW's seen on your system, it thinks that your system functions as a server in one or more ways. Then, as SCW knows which services each server program requires, it can then compile a list of the minimum set of services required to support those server programs. But, again, SCW's designed to be a good wizard, not a bad wizard, and so it doesn't just make pronouncements; nope, instead SCW says, "These are the server functions that I *think* I detected on your system; did I miss anything, or would you like to add any?"

The Select Server Roles page by default shows you only the server applications installed on your system, with check boxes next to the ones that are enabled. For example, notice that the box next to Print Server is unchecked. That's because SCW saw that while I had print sharing enabled—it's on by default on every Windows system—I'd not actually created any print shares, and so SCW deduced correctly that I didn't really have any interest in sharing a printer with this system. But if I wanted SCW to leave things copacetic for print serving, then I'd just check the box. I could even tell SCW that I intended in the near future to put Exchange on the box and to leave untouched services and ports that weren't necessary now, but would be soon. I'd just click the drop-down list box next to the View text, where I'd see that I have four choices. I could ask SCW to show all possible roles—that is, everything in the SCW's XML files, which include things like SQL Server, Exchange, and ISA Server as well as more obscure things like Commerce Server, Biztalk Server, and Host Integration Server. Or I could tell it to just show the checked services or all of the services installed on the system, whether used or not (that's the default). Finally, I could tell it just to show the *uninstalled* roles.

FIGURE 11.8

SCW shows you the "server" things that it thinks this system does.

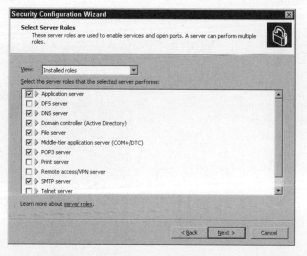

Once you're finished working with Select Server Roles, click Next and you'll see a couple of similar-looking screens, so I hope it's okay if I skip a few screen shots. SCW's intended for servers (which is kind of unfortunate, because I wish they'd built a version for XP), but there's no such thing as a system that acts only as a server, so SCW then compiles a list of the *client* programs that the system needs. For example, as I've mentioned before, the "workstation" service is an ancient service whose primary purpose is to act as a client for the file server, but in truth it's impossible to run any Windows system without it. Similarly, every system needs the DHCP client (it handles dynamic DNS registration, counterintuitive as that sounds) and the DNS client. Client programs often need at least one system service, and so SCW adds those services to that list of necessary services. You get the same set of choices in the wizard page: disable one, enable one, add one that's not on the list. Click Next to advance to the next page.

Then SCW adds to this the list of types of administrative tools that you expect to need on the server. Now, technically, any software that allows for remote control is, as you've seen in the Windows Firewall chapter, server software, so I'm not really sure why "administrative tools" gets a separate section. But again, you can examine SCW's best guesses of what remote admin tools you'll need and adjust it before moving along to the next phase.

TIP SCW disables the browser option, which keeps you from being able to do a number of remote admin commands with the net commands. I'd re-enable it.

After clicking Next, you'll see a screen showing you the services that it *doesn't* recognize. For example, my test system showed the "VMWare Tools Service," as I was working with a VMWare virtual machine. By default SCW checks all of these unrecognized services on the assumption that if it's not a standard Microsoft thing and you're running it, then you must want it. Click Next, and you get to a most important question, as you see in Figure 11.9.

It's an easy enough question, but the answer can have a major impact. Now that you've identified the *necessary* services, what do you do with the remainder, the *un*necessary services? By default, SCW just leaves them as they are. But…if you dare…if you trust the SCW…then heck, choose to disable them. I mean, this *is* a test machine you're running this on, right? Then click Next to see something like Figure 11.10.

Here, SCW shows you everything that it's about to change. Give it a close, long look for any things that make you uncomfortable; if anything does, then flip back to the server roles, client roles, or administrative pages and make whatever changes are needed to restore the service in question.

FIGURE 11.9
What to do with the decommissioned services?

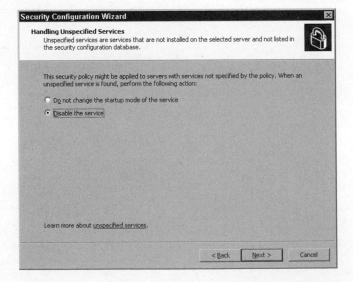

FIGURE 11.10
SCW checks
in with you.

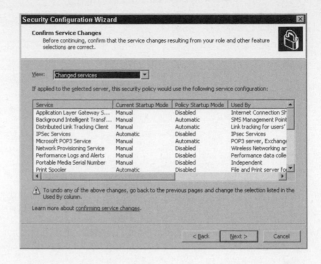

Phase 3: Port Lockdown with WF and IPsec

When you're happy with what SCW's going to do, click Next to see something like Figure 11.11.

In the previous phase, SCW discovered what services could be safely disabled on this system. In the next phase, Network Security, it raises Windows Firewall and determines which ports should be opened based on what it knows of the services that you're running.

Click Next to see the Open Ports and Approve Applications page, as you see in Figure 11.12.

By default, SCW first figures out what server and client apps you run and then looks up the ports that they use in its database. You can see which ports SCW thinks your system needs in the Open Ports and Approve Applications page from Figure 11.12. SCW will, if you don't object, then raise Windows Firewall and block all ports except for the ones that it's seen that you need. The ones that it opens, it opens to the whole world. But that's not all SCW can do port-wise.

FIGURE 11.11
Next phase:
port lockdown

FIGURE 11.12
The ports SCW
thinks you need

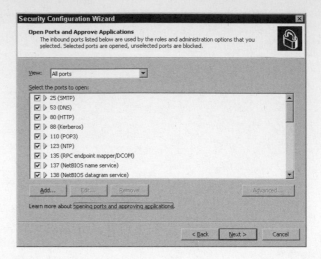

SCW AND IPSEC: REVIEW

Simply opening or closing ports to the entire world may be fine for many situations, but if you'd instead like a bit more fine-tuned control of access to your ports, then SCW lets you take things a bit further. You could open a port just to a set of subnets, as you may recall that Windows Firewall allows. Or, even better, SCW will create IPsec rules for you, so that you might say, "Port 25's open, but only to clients who maintain an established IPsec security association," or "25's open, but only to systems doing encrypted communication with me."

Most folks' eyes glaze over when I say IPsec, so permit me to digress a bit and quickly review what you may already have read in Chapter 6 in *Mastering Windows Server 2003* or from the Windows Firewall chapter in this book.

- IPsec changes how IP communications works from IP's pre-IPsec days. When TCP/IP was first invented, IP's job was to just route packets from system to system without concern for security. IPsec lets systems get more choosy about which packets they accept or reject.

- IPsec makes the IP stack more selective by letting you define IPsec *rules*. Rules have at least two pieces to them: a *filter list*, which says when to activate the rule, and a *filter action*, which says what to do with the packet if the conditions of the filter are met.

- Filter lists can be specific to the point of describing source address, destination address, port, and protocol. For example, a filter list might say, "Activate this rule only if there's data coming from any port at address 192.168.1.4 to my TCP port 25."

- Filter actions let a rule specify what to do when the criteria of the filter list have been met. There are four possible filter actions. First, IPsec can simply let the data pass unfettered, as did all IP software before the advent of IPsec. Second, IPsec can block the data, discarding it and refusing to retransmit it to its intended destination. Third, IPsec can send the data, but only if the data's digitally signed and, fourth, IPsec can send the data, but only if the data's encrypted.

- The last two filter actions—digital signing and encryption—require a third part of a rule in addition to a filter list and a filter action: some form of authentication. IPsec supports three kinds—a shared text password, an exchange of X.509 certificates, or Kerberos authentication—but most people working in a domain environment will use Kerberos, as it's easiest.

IPSEC AND SCW

How does SCW help in building IPsec rules? It's got a fairly simple ("simple" compared to most IPsec tools) GUI that'll build and install IPsec rules. To see it in action, click any port (I'll use 110 for this example, but any one works) and you'll see an Advanced button that's visible but grayed out in Figure 11.12; once you click a port, the button will become enabled. Click that button and you'll see a dialog like Figure 11.13.

Here, I've clicked the Restrict Remote Access to This Port to Only the Following Remote Addresses option, which enables the Add button. Click that, and you get several options, as you see in Figure 11.14.

Microsoft's been trying to make the GUI for IPsec easier to understand since its first inception in February 2000 in Windows 2000, but they've got a tough job, as IPsec is, well, complex. (You've got to cut them some slack here; how easy can it be to build a simple UI for a tool built atop a dozen RFCs?) But, as you'll see from Figures 11.14 through 11.16, this dialog box tries to fill the bill as one-stop-shopping for those two main ingredients to any IPsec rule: an IPsec filter list and an IP filter action. The top of the dialog box is the IPsec filter list part; below that is the IPsec filter action part.

FIGURE 11.13
Starting out
IPsec on SCW

FIGURE 11.14
The IPsec filter action

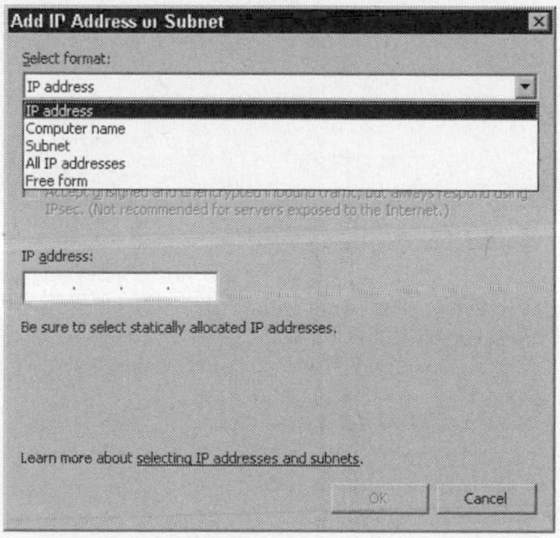

An IPsec filter list needs to know about two things: the source and the destination. More specifically, it needs to know

◆ About the destination: IP address or range of addresses, TCP or UDP protocol, and port number.

◆ About the source: IP address or range of addresses and port number.

Sounds like a lot to ask for, but SCW manages to simplify these questions because recall that SCW's attempting to create rules concerning packets arriving at *this* system, and on port TCP 110. *That* means that I already know that the destination IP address is "me," the protocol is "TCP," and the port number is "110." Half the work's already done; all you've got to do is to specify the source information. SCW makes things even simpler in that it assumes that you don't care what the *source* port is. That's because you typically wouldn't care in an application like this, because we're talking about securing server applications here (the destination), and clients (the source) speak from any random port. You only care about the destination port, which, again, you already know—110.

Because much of that hard work's done, all you've got to do in the Select Format dialog is to define the source IP address or addresses. You may choose whether you want this rule to apply to all systems on the Internet (All IP Addresses), a particular IP address (IP Address), a subnet (Subnet), a particular computer name (usually not a good idea, as IPsec doesn't really resolve DNS names—it just resolves the name once, now, and never again, so better to use IP addresses), or a free-form list of IP addresses and/or subnets. Depending on which of those options you choose, the IP Address field changes to let you punch in a computer name or specify a subnet, or just becomes a free-form field where you can specify a list of IP addresses and/or ranges, separated by semicolons. You specify a free-form list of addresses as one or more *IP address/subnet mask*, and/or just IP address. Separate the items in the list with semicolons. Again, express a range of IP addresses by typing the first address in the range, then a forward slash, then the subnet mask, as in 192.168.1.1/255.255.255.0. So, for example,

192.168.1.1/255.255.255.0;10.0.0.0/255.0.0.0;100.100.100.1

Would mean, "Make this rule apply to any incoming transmissions from the 256-host group starting at 192.168.1.1, the 16-million-host group staring at 10.0.0.0, and the single IP address 100.100.100.1."

But what about filter actions? The same Add IP Address or Subnet dialog box has a drop-down list named How to Allow Traffic (Signing and Encryption Options Require IPsec), and you can see the options that it offers in Figure 11.15.

FIGURE 11.15
Filter actions
supported by SCW

The dialog's five options are actually *three* different IPsec filter actions—permit, require, and encrypt—with caveats. Signing has the Require Signing and Request Signing options. There are two because Microsoft is offering here a more-strict rule ("require") versus a less-strict rule ("request") in reference to digital signing. The dialog offers the same more or less strict options for encrypting. But what about Block, the fourth IPsec action? Why is there no "block" offer? That'll become clear as you go further in this wizard, but basically "block" is the default here; you're just specifying exceptions. Here, I've chosen Require Signing as a filter action. Once I select that, or any other signing or encrypting option, I'll get a new check box in the existing dialog; clicking Require Signing brings it up, as you see in Figure 11.16.

That new box says Accept Unsigned and Unencrypted Inbound Traffic, but Always Respond Using IPsec. (Not Recommended for Servers Exposed to the Internet.). Choosing that check box does the same sort of thing that choosing Request Signing rather than Require Signing does: it weakens your choice in security settings. These requested-rather-than-required settings in SCW have corresponding settings in all of the other Microsoft UIs to IPsec, because there are still many old, pre-2000 clients in Microsoft networks, and those systems can't understand IPsec. The idea is, "Hey, let's be more secure by using IPsec but, um, if someone doesn't want to do IPsec then let's not press the matter." I personally think that if you're going to do IPsec, then you need to realize that you're burning a lot of CPU time to handle IPsec's computational overhead. But choosing Request Signing or checking the Accept Unsigned box defeats the whole purpose. The point of doing IPsec and wasting those CPU cycles is not that there are tons and tons of bad guys in your network; no, rather you're assuming that there are a very small number of bad guys, and you want to thwart them. Well, if the 99 percent of the network that is operated by good guys must use CPU power to do IPsec, but the 1 percent of bad guys can opt out without anyone refusing to communicate with them, then you're worse off than if you didn't bother with IPsec at all. In *both* cases, you're insecure. In the former case, you're still insecure, but your computers are slow. So I'd recommend unchecking the thing. But, again, test this on a test network before you roll it out to your production network and find the next day that the CEO's grandkids can't log in any more from their Windows Me systems. (It's one of those potential CLMs.)

Once you make the call whether or not to require rather than allow IPsec, click OK, and you'll return to a dialog like the one in 11.13. Click OK to clear that and return to the wizard and the Open Ports and Approve Applications page, and then click Next to show a wizard page like the one in Figure 11.17.

FIGURE 11.16
Choose sign or encrypt, and this appears.

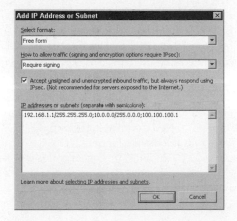

FIGURE 11.17
Choose an IPsec
authentication
method.

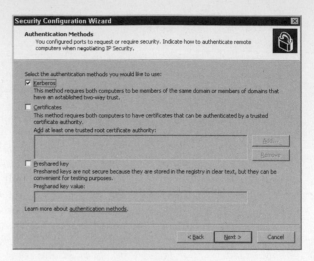

You only see this wizard page if you've previously specified an Advanced port rule that requires or requests signing or encrypting. That's because, again, you need some way to exchange a key for signing or encrypting, and authentication's the only way to do it. IPsec supports shared secrets, certificates, and Kerberos authentication, and this dialog offers three of them. If you're working with clients and servers all in the same AD forest, then it's a no-brainer: use Kerberos.

The end result is that SCW has built for you a complete of IPsec rules. Now, remember, these are just *server* rules; if you want your clients to play along, then be sure to either craft an IPsec rule on your clients, or at least enable the default Client (Respond Only) rule built into every Windows system since 2000.

And if you create an SCW policy that builds an IPsec policy, then take a look in `gpedit.msc` at your list of IPsec policies. In addition to the standard three policies, you'll have one named SCW Policy, and it'll be assigned.

IPSEC LITE: PERMITTING A SUBSET OF THE INTERNET

Look back at Figure 11.15 and you'll be reminded that it offers five filter actions. Four involve signing and encrypting and so *must* involve IPsec. But simple Permit All?" Heck, you don't need IPsec for that. Recall that Windows Firewall (that 60-page journey we took a while back) supports the idea of specific port blockages rather than all-or-nothing ones. So if you were to specify that free-form list of 192.168.1.1/255.255.255.0;10.0.0.0/255.0.0.0;100.100.100.1 and an action of Permit All, then you'll end up with a properly configured Windows firewall, but no IPsec to worry about.

SUMMARIZING THE JOB

Whether you followed along the Advanced/IPsec discussion or not, you should be at the SCW Wizard page labeled Confirm Port Configuration. (If you can't see it, click Next—it's probably the next screen.) It'll look like Figure 11.18.

This is SCW's second "are you sure, this is what I'm gonna do" screen. As with Figure 11.10, it's just SCW's professional and informative way of keeping you in the loop. Click Next to move to the next phase.

FIGURE 11.18

SCW's "progress update" report

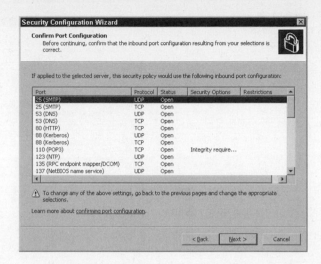

Tightening Security with Registry Settings

When you clicked Next from Confirm Port Configuration, you saw a screen like Figure 11.19.

This part of the wizard takes some educated guesses about those "windows hardening" settings that you may have read about in the various security hardening guides that Microsoft's posted on their website in the past few years. But SCW needs you to help it out a bit, so click Next to see the first set of questions as in Figure 11.20.

SMB signing refers to a feature that first appeared in Windows in NT 4.0 SP3. It's possible for a bad guy to intercept and modify the communications between a file server and its clients, an attack called a *man-in-the-middle* attack. SMB signing adds a digital signature to both server and client communications so that any packet modified en route will be detected. It's still possible for someone to launch a man-in-the-middle attack, but the bad guy won't be able to digitally sign the changes that he makes to the SMB packets, so the client and server will be able to tell that their communications have been tampered with, and they'll just reject the unsigned packets.

FIGURE 11.19

Next phase: Registry security tweaks

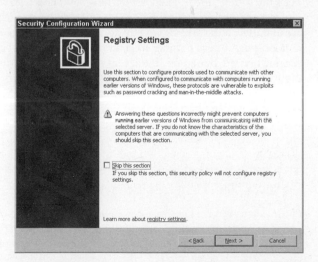

FIGURE 11.20
Can we require
SMB signatures?

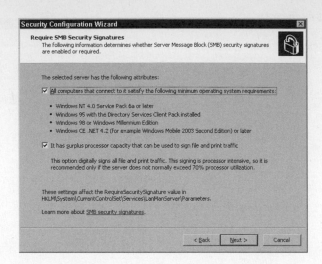

NOTE You can read more about SMB signing by visiting my website, www.minasi.com, and reading my Newsletter #46.

Enabling SMB signing's a good idea, but like many security tweaks, it can present some compatibility problems. Some operating systems, like Windows 95, need an add-on program in order to be able to do SMB signing. Others, like Windows for Workgroups or DOS, can never do SMB signing. The more modern ones, like Windows 2000, XP, and 2003, can do SMB signing but need you to hack the Registry either with Regedit or via group policies in order to get SMB signing to work. This wizard page is asking about operating system versions because if you have older OSes that cannot do SMB signing at all, then the wizard can't configure your server to *require* SMB signing, as requiring it would render those old clients completely unable to communicate with your newly-locked-down server.

SMB signing's good, but it comes at a price: processor power. Signing involves cryptographic functions like hashing and encryption and that can chew up your CPU, leading to slower response from the server. That's the point of the second check box.

Most modern Windows server systems (2000 after SP2, XP after SP1, all copies of 2003, and R2) are already doing SMB signing by default but only on a voluntary basis. If a client talks to a server and includes a digital signature, then the server will check the signature and will reject any messages with bad signatures. But if that client stops sending signatures, then the server doesn't complain and just accepts any messages. I've always thought that was a bad idea. After all, if you're going to slow down your server a bit in order to protect it from man-in-the-middle attacks, then be *sure* that you can't be attacked, and *require* SMB signing. That's what this page is trying to determine: will it be safe for it to enable the Require SMB Signing setting on your server? If you uncheck either of those check boxes, then SCW will not change the Require SMB Signing setting. (Notice also that SCW tells you in the bottom of the page exactly which Registry value that it's thinking of changing; a nice touch.) Once you've made your choices here, click Next to consider the next security hardening possibility, as you see in Figure 11.21.

Just as SMB signing hardened SMB against man-in-the-middle attacks, this page offers to add signatures to all Active Directory communications, which consist mostly of LDAP queries. LDAP signing appeared first in Windows 2000 SP3, and so the wizard asks if all systems on the domain are at least up to 2000 SP3. The check box is unchecked by default, but I've checked it here, and if you can check it, then I recommend it. Click Next to see the next set of questions, as you see in Figure 11.22.

FIGURE 11.21
Can we sign
Active Directory
communications?

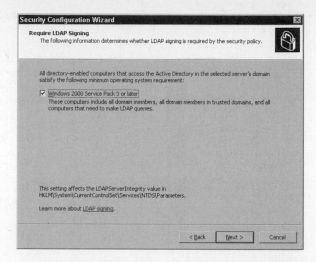

FIGURE 11.22
Can we give LAN
Man the gate?

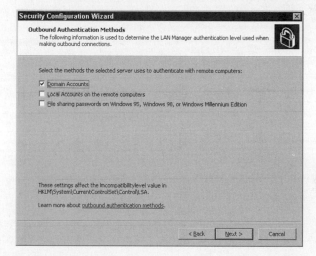

Sometimes it seems to me that Microsoft's biggest competitor and biggest source of trouble is itself. You see, as time goes on, they secure their OS more and more…but that creates compatibility problems with earlier systems. In this particular case, we're talking about two things: LAN Manager hashes and the LM compatibility level.

LM hashes refer to how Windows stores your passwords. Like most other operating systems, Windows never actually saves your passwords to your computer's hard disk. Instead, it runs the passwords through a *hash* function, a mathematical formula used in cryptography to boil down long sequences of data into a short and nearly unique 128-bit number. In theory, hashes are one-way in that while it's easy to convert a password into a hash, it should be nearly impossible to reverse the process. For example, if hashing a password of "swordfish" yielded a hash of 47, then there wouldn't be any easy way to look at that hash of 47 and say, "Aha, the password that led to a hash of 47 was 'swordfish!'"

Hash functions *shouldn't* be reversible, but unfortunately the hash function that Microsoft devised for its circa-1989 network OS, LAN Manager, had a hash function that isn't that hard to reverse-engineer, given the speed of today's computers. When NT appeared in 1993, Microsoft improved how it hashed passwords and started creating a second hash called the *NT hash* via a cryptographic hash function named MD4. It wasn't a bad choice, and in fact MD4 provides adequate security even in 2006, 13 years after NT's inception. But by default every Windows system continues to *also* create the older, more easily reversed LM hashes, and that offers a serious vulnerability. You can tell a system not to create LM hashes via a Registry entry/group policy setting, and I tend to think that it's a good idea, but, again, you may find that you've got something on your network that needs LM hashes, and so getting rid of them would break your network. SCW would like to configure your computer to stop creating LM hashes but doesn't want to bring your network to a halt, and so it asks the questions on Figure 11.22 and the following two wizard pages, which you'll see in Figures 11.23 and 11.24 in a moment.

Similarly, both LAN Manager and the NT family need a cryptographic procedure for transferring information across a network during logon attempts. When you sit down at your workstation, press Ctrl-Alt-Del, and punch in a user name and password, you're asking your workstation to let you access that workstation. The workstation then wants to say to a domain controller, "Hey, I've got a guy here who says his name is Mark and has a password of 'swordfish;' is that a valid account on the domain?" But there's no way that you can actually ask the DC directly if a given name/password pair is valid, as anyone listening on the network would then have my user name and password. So instead, Windows clients do a series of cryptographic calculations at both the workstation and the domain controller that let the domain controller validate the username/password combination for the workstation without actually having to hear the password over the network. These methods are called *challenge/response* authentication methods. LAN Manager had one, and then NT got one of its own with NT 3.1, and Microsoft improved it further with NT 4.0 SP4. The LAN Manager challenge/response procedure is usually just called LM authentication, the original NT challenge/response procedure is called NT LAN Manager or NTLM authentication—and no, that name *doesn't* really make much sense, in case you were wondering. The SP4 improvement is called NTLMv2.

Active Directory in general doesn't use LM, NTLM, *or* NTLMv2, and instead uses a procedure called Kerberos to handle authentications. But even the most modern Active Directory regularly falls back to the LMs, and NTLMv2 is far more secure than either LM or NTLM. (And bad guys can take advantage of Windows' good nature and ask it to fall back to LM, NTLM, or NTLMv2 so as to launch a kind of attack. As NTLMv2's harder to hack, telling your system never to accept LM or NTLM protects you from attacks of this nature.) You can configure your network to never use NTLM or LM, and only use NTLMv2 when Kerberos won't work. But, as before, tightening the screws security-wise might break things in your network, and so SCW's asking questions to divine whether or not it can transform your network into an LM-free, NTLM-free network.

NOTE You can learn more about LM, NTLM, NTLMv2, and choosing compatibility levels by visiting my website at www.minasi.com and reading my Newsletter #33.

Armed with that information, we can take a look at what exactly SCW's getting at with its questions. The three check boxes on the page you saw in Figure 11.22 ask if your server ever tries to talk to other systems on the domain or logs onto other servers using local accounts, or tries to connect to Windows 9*x* systems. I'm not really certain why it asks about connecting to other domain members or local accounts on other Windows NT systems, as you can do that with all three of the LMs, but it's asking about Windows 9*x* because when attaching to them vile file sharing passwords, then they use the LM protocol only. Thus, if you'd checked the box next to the Windows 9*x* question, then SCW wouldn't ask any more questions, as it'd know that it had no choice but to enable LM hashes and authentication. But assuming that you don't check that box and check either the domain or local account box, click Next to see Figure 11.23.

This screen shows that SCW's on the trail of configuring the system to require NTLMv2. By default, Windows systems only offer the LM and NTLM authentication systems. The more secure NTLMv2 exacts a price in that all systems on a network must have their clocks fairly well synchronized. Any system whose clock is more than 30 minutes different from a server's can't connect to that server. And, of course, you need a fairly up-to-date version of NT 4.0, and that's reflected by the check box asking if you've got SP 6a on your NT 4.0 systems. (Although to be honest, I can't see why it requires 6a—NTLMv2 arrived in SP4 for NT 4.0.)

If you checked the Local Accounts on the Remote Computers box back in the Outbound Authentication Methods page, then you'll see another page very much like Figure 11.23 asking about those remote servers; handle it as you handled the page in Figure 11.23. You're almost done with the NTLMv2 interrogation; click Next to see the last page of questions, as you see in Figure 11.24.

FIGURE 11.23
Can everything talk NTLMv2?

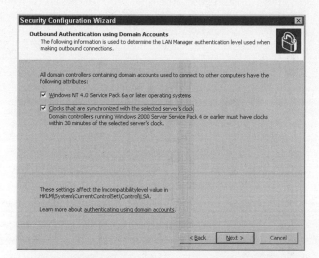

FIGURE 11.24
Checking for client compatibility

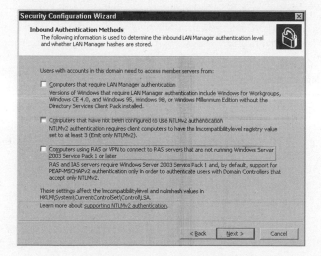

The first two screens asked you about how the server that you're running SCW on acts as a *client*—how does it expect to talk to other servers? This last page in this section asks what sort of client systems expect to be able to access this server. All three check boxes are checked by default; if you can uncheck them all, then SCW will not only tell your system to try talking NTLMv2 to other servers, it'll also tell it to *require* NTLMv2 of its clients. Once you've checked or, better, unchecked the boxes, then click Next to see Figure 11.25.

This shows you the five Registry security tweaks that SCW proposes to do. The first one, Activate Named Pipe Firewall, is a bit of a surprise because none of the wizard pages so far have referred to it. XP SP2 and 2003 SP1 offered a new security option in the venerable file server service, a *named pipe firewall*. Named pipes are an old method for programmers to allow two programs to pass data between themselves. (You might know the one called IPC$, as it can be used to connect an administrator to a remote server.) They're built atop the file server service and are seen by some folks to be a possible avenue of entry for bad guys. So Microsoft created a pair of new Registry settings in HKEY_LOCAL_MACHINE\SYSTEM\CurrentControlSet\Services\Lanmanserver\parameters. The first is a REG_DWORD value called pipefirewallactive. When set to 1, it activates the new named pipe firewall. This blocks any incoming communications to this server on any named pipes except for those named in a REG_MULTI_SZ entry AllowedPipes.

NOTE You won't find either of these entries already created in the Registry; you've got to create them to set their values. If you decide to turn on the named pipe firewall, then you should enter the names of the named pipes that you want accessible over the network into AllowedPipes, pressing Enter after each pipe name. But I'd caution you that it's not trivial figuring out what named pipes are on your system and which you can block to network traffic.

Anyway, SCW enables the named pipe firewall in some situations, and so it's in this summary page on the off-chance that it enabled the firewall. It will enable the firewall if you've chosen either a print server or file server role for this system, and if it knows with certainty which named pipes you'll need. That means that SCW will *not* enable the named pipes firewall if you have either

◆ Enabled some other server role that relies upon the file server service (SCW can't be sure if that role isn't opening some named pipe that SCW can't predict, and so doesn't want to end up breaking that other server role), or

◆ SCW notices a named pipe that it doesn't recognize. For example, in my case I'm running VMWare, and VMWare opens a few named pipes. SCW doesn't recognize them, and so has not enabled my named pipe firewall.

FIGURE 11.25
Summarizing the
Registry changes

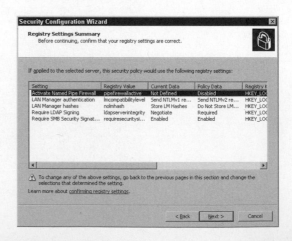

TIP Wondering what named pipes your system runs? Visit www.sysinternals.com and search for their pipelist utility.

The rest of this summary page should be easy to understand from our earlier discussion of SCW's options. The first shows that our system will now offer NTLMv2 responses rather than the NTLMv1 responses that it previously offered, that the system will no longer store LM hashes, that AD communications will require LDAP signing, and that SMB communications must all be signed.

If all of the proposed Registry settings are to your liking, press Next to move to the next section.

Change Audit Settings? Perhaps Not

The next section opens with a page like Figure 11.26.

WARNING It is *very* important that you read this section before clicking any further in the SCW. In my opinion, you may be best off simply checking the box labeled Skip This Section, so you'll *really* want to pay attention to the next few paragraphs and make your own mind up before giving the mouse any more exercise.

Again, SCW offers an opening page that's not just the same old blah-blah, warning you that this section will recommend changing the audit permissions on a bunch of system folders and Registry keys. As I've already mentioned, and as you learned in the *Mastering Windows Server 2003* book, you can roll back just about any kind of security template option except for NTFS and Registry permissions.

It's nice that the SCW warns you about the change in permissions, but there's something that I think is a bigger concern about which SCW's mum. You see, this section of the SCW offers you three options vis-à-vis security auditing. You see them in the next wizard page. If you were to click Next—and I don't recommend that you do yet!—then you'd see a page like Figure 11.27.

This first page seems kind of innocuous, particularly if you've ever messed with audits before. (Which you've done if you read *Mastering 2003* or the chapter in this book about per-user auditing, right?) I looked at it and figured, "Okay, so it'll add a few new things to whatever audit settings I've already got in place." The page then offers three settings: don't audit, just audit successes, and audit successes and failures.

FIGURE 11.26
Starting the Audit Policy section with a warning

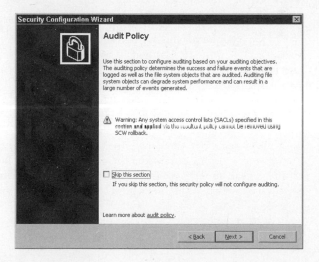

FIGURE 11.27
How much
auditing to do?

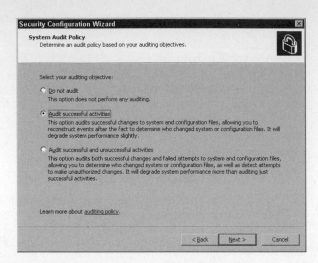

If you choose either Audit Successful Activities or Audit Successful and Unsuccessful Activities, then SCW sets up auditing on your system so that it does some combination of successes and/or failures on all of the nine categories of auditable things, except privilege use. You'd think that the Audit Successful radio button would cause you to audit only successes in the eight audited categories, but that's not the case, actually: the radio button also leads you to audit failures of both kinds of logons and of system events. Choosing Audit Successful and Unsuccessful causes you to audit successes and failures of everything except, again, privilege use.

So what's wrong with this? I noticed that when I chose the Do Not Audit radio button, finished building the SCW policy, and applied it, my system stopped doing auditing of any kind, *despite the fact that I had already been auditing a number of things.*

In other words, I'd been expecting SCW to suggest some audit changes and to then *merge* them with whatever existing settings I was using. But my surmise was wrong: choosing any of the three radio buttons in Figure 11.27 causes your system to lose its existing auditing settings.

WARNING The only way to retain your existing audit settings is to skip the Audit Policy section altogether.

On the other hand, you may not mind what SCW's trying to do, so let's look a bit more closely into what it's trying to accomplish. Mainly, it causes your system to audit just about everything except the use of user rights (and I'm not sure why it skips that one), and to tell your system to track any changes to a set of important system areas. Your system then audits any file or folder creation, file or folder deletion, changes in NTFS permissions, or any ownership changes on the entirety of whatever hard disk contains your operating system, as well as some more specific tracking in various folders in the Windows folder.

You can see the exact changes by looking at scwaudit.inf, a text file that you can find in \windows\security\msscw\kbs. (While you're in that folder, notice another template, defaultsacls.inf. You can apply that template to your system to undo the changes wrought by scwaudit.inf, should you ever need to.) Boiled down, however, these auditing settings make your system watch and record changes to pretty much everything related to system integrity. If someone messes with your system, whether it's applying a legitimate patch or an attempt to install a rootkit, then you'll have the details in the Security log. (Oddly enough, though, SCW seems not to increase the size of the Security log, and given all of the things that SCW wants you to track, you're almost certainly going to need to expand the Security log.)

If you're comfortable with having any of your existing settings wiped out, then click Next to get to the page that looks like Figure 11.27. Choose from the three radio buttons the options that you want—I went with the default setting of Audit Successful Activities—and click next to see a summary screen, as you see in Figure 11.28.

Notice the check box allowing SCW to load the `scwaudit.inf` file that we've already discussed. As the page says, the SCW rollback function can't undo the audit permissions, but again, the `defaultsacls.inf` template *can* roll back your security permissions. Click Next, and you're on to the next section.

FIGURE 11.28
Confirming your
choices in auditing

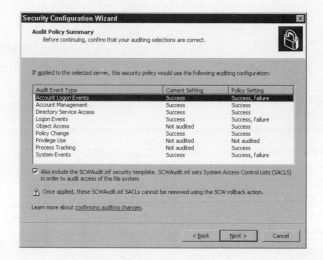

Securing Internet Information Services (IIS)

If you're running SCW on a system with Windows' web server—Internet Information Services, or IIS—installed, then you'll next see another section opening page, as you see in Figure 11.29.

IIS has a bad name because of the Code Red and Nimda worms that successfully targeted and attacked IIS 5.0 back in 2001. Since then, no successful exploits have occurred to my knowledge, and none at all against Server 2003's IIS 6.0. Nevertheless, the memory of Code Red and Nimda keeps every webmaster on her toes when configuring a web server, and of course one way to make a server less vulnerable is to shut off the things that it's not using. IIS hosts a variety of platforms, and so offers a wide set of opportunities for disabling things. That's why it's best to have your website up and running before running SCW. Click Next and you'll see a screen like Figure 11.30.

Sometimes it's hard to figure out if you actually use any of these things, and of course turning something off that a website relies upon will cause trouble with that website's users. Here are a few ways to figure out what your website needs.

First, of course, you could consult the documentation that your webmaster created about your website…

FIGURE 11.29
IIS section opening

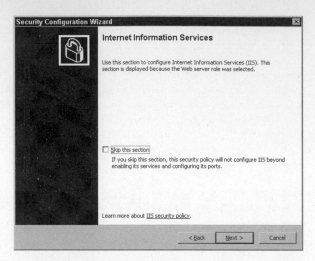

FIGURE 11.30
IIS extensions that
you can disable

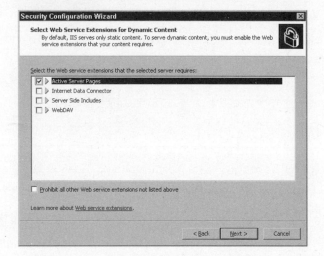

Well, now that we've had a little laugh, you could just corner that webmaster guy and ask him if any of the things in Figure 11.30 ring a bell. If none of that helps, then here are some clues that you might look for on your website that'll help you guess what your website requires.

Active Server Pages This one's dead easy. Look in the wwwroot folder for any files with the extension .asp rather than the more common .htm or .html. If there are any, then be sure that the Active Server Pages box is checked. One other clue is to look in the Web Service Extensions page on the Internet Information Services Manager. If Active Server Pages are enabled, then you probably need that box checked.

Internet Data Connector Another easy one. It's an old way to build web pages that dynamically update themselves based on some database source; my guess is that any websites built after 2001 wouldn't use this. If any files in your website have the extensions .idc or .idx, then you need the Internet Data Connector. It's also enabled or disabled in the IIS manager in the Web Service Extensions page.

Server Side Includes   These are a little harder to find. It's a neat facility that lets you stuff one HTML file inside another file, and you can expect to see it in both ancient and modern websites. Server-side includes (SSIs) offer a couple of hints as to their existence. First of all, they can only occur *inside* files with an .asp extension. Second, they'll have a line in them that starts with <!--# followed by some command. If you see one of these in a file on your website, and that file has the extension .asp, then you'll need to include SSIs. Server-side includes also need to be enabled in the IIS manager; if you find that SSIs are not enabled already and no one's complained, then you don't need that box checked.

WebDAV   This is the generic name for a standardized way to share files over HTTP. In the Microsoft world, it's called WebFolders. As with the other three settings, it doesn't work unless it's enabled in Web Service Extensions in IIS Manager.

Once you're happy with those settings, click Next to see Figure 11.31.

I'm actually sort of puzzled about why they bothered with this page. IIS 4.0 and 5.0 both loaded by default with all kinds of unnecessary and, in retrospect, junk files. The usual ones include the following: example code exploitable by hackers, a Help system that included a search engine that bad guys used to peek into your hidden areas, a remote administration system that lacked a lot of the basics of security, and the notion that you should put server-side script programs all in a standard directory called "scripts," making life easier for attackers.

But then came IIS 6.0. The Microsoft guys got smart and, well, that stuff's gone. So this page comes along and SCW says, "Should I turn this junk off?" Seems like a good question, except for two things:

◆   First, IIS 6.0 doesn't load this junk, and

◆   *Second*, SCW only works on IIS 6.0.

Perhaps it's intended to be of help to people who've *upgraded* a 2000 system. If you even *try* to check any of these boxes on a freshly installed IIS 6.0 system then SCW will tell you that "this virtual directory does not exist on the selected server," which I guess is SCW-ese for "duh." Anyway, on the off-chance that you've got an IIS 6.0 configuration in need of tightening, there are these guys. Click Next to move along to the last IIS question, as you see in Figure 11.32.

FIGURE 11.31
Prompting to remove the default unnecessary stuff

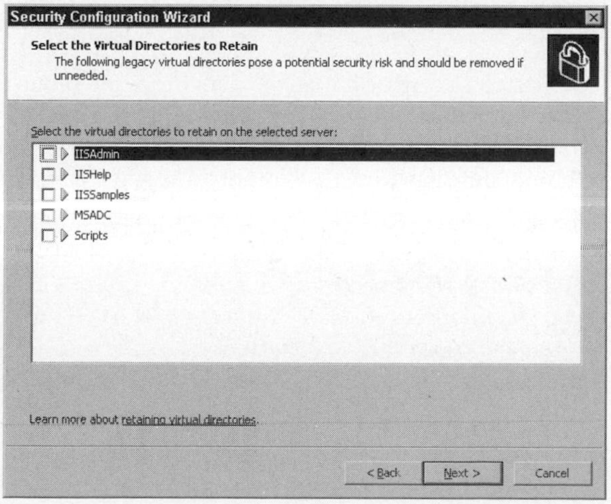

FIGURE 11.32
Shall we make it
harder for dirtbags?

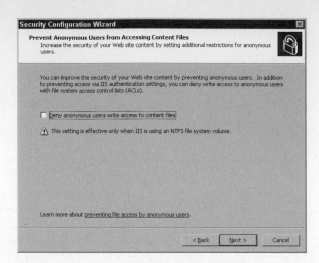

When people visit your website as anonymous visitors, they're not entirely anonymous; they look to your system like the local IUSR account that IIS creates when installed. One way to nail down Internet security just a bit would be to explicitly deny IUSR write access to any folder that contained a web page. I've used this to good advantage for years, and it's good to see that SCW offers to do that.

Now, some websites will break if you do this…but most won't. And honestly, any website built after 2001 should run fine with this extra tweak, but some might not, so sadly again I've got to repeat my old refrain: try it before you roll it out to production servers.

TIP But the fact is that if your website can't tolerate this tweak, then I strongly suggest that you have a chat with the webmaster. A nice polite one, to be sure, but a chat nonetheless.

That was a useful tip, but in all honesty it needs an accompanying warning:

WARNING Remember the part in the beginning of SCW about how a few things couldn't be reversed easily with the "rollback" feature of SCW? This is one of those things that SCW can't roll back, as it's an NTFS permission setting.

Once you've made the call on denying anonymous users write access to content files, click Next for the summary screen, as you see in Figure 11.33.

All of the things that you see here mostly reflect the changes mentioned in the wizard and, although they look drastic, most of them show up in the IIS metabase which is, thankfully, simple to roll back.

Finishing Up SCW

Click Next, and you'll see a simple page that just tells you that you're about done with SCW and that you can now save your SCW policy and, if you like, apply it to this system right now. Click Next to see a page like Figure 11.34.

FIGURE 11.33
IIS "Are you sure?"
screen

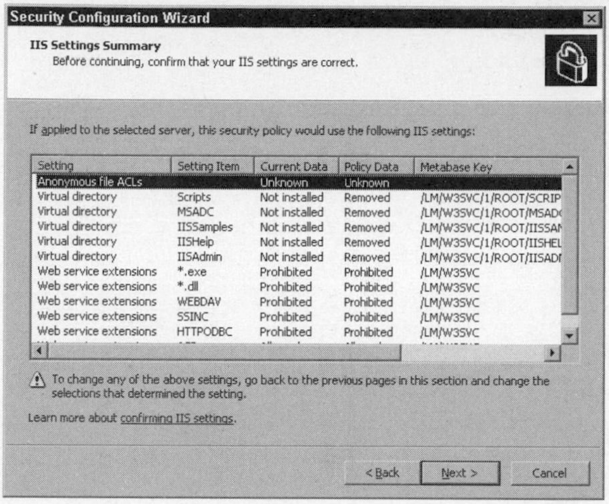

FIGURE 11.34
Saving the
SCW profile

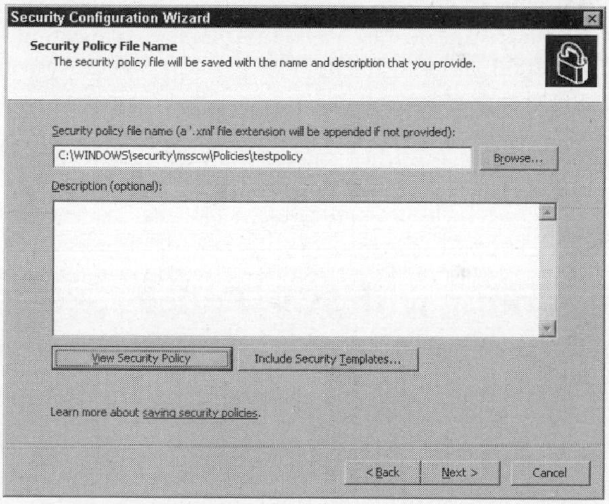

This screen lets you do three important things. First, you can click View Security Policy to see a nice all-in-one-place report describing everything that will change when you apply this policy. Second, you can add security templates of the type that we discussed in *Mastering Windows Server 2003* to this SCW security policy. This might be useful if you already have a security template that you apply to new servers. Having an SCW policy that included templates would simplify securing future servers, as you could build those future servers in just two steps: install the operating system, and then apply the SCW policy, which would include the security template or templates.

Most important, you can use this page to finally save your security policy. They go into \windows\security\msscw\policies and are stored as XML files so you could, I suppose, hack one directly with Notepad. (I'd avoid doing that.) Type in a name for your policy and click Next. You might get a dialog box warning you that if you apply the policy that you'll have to reboot the server; if so, just click OK to clear the dialog box and you'll see a page like Figure 11.35.

FIGURE 11.35
Ready to pull
the trigger?

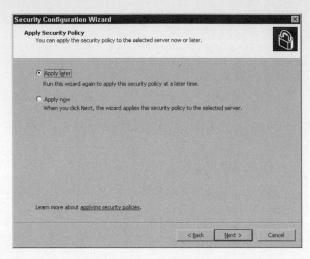

"Ya gotta ask yourself, punk…do you feel lucky today?" Heck, sure I do—this is a test system, so let's test! If *you* do indeed feel lucky, then click Apply Now, and SCW will apply the template, and then you can click Next and then Finish to complete SCW. Or just click Apply Later and then click Next and Finish. Either way, congratulations, you've completed what must be the world's record-length wizard!

NOTE   If SCW warned you that it'd need a reboot, then you won't be prompted to do that reboot. To see the changes, reboot now, or if you can't, then reboot sometime soon, or you won't see all of the changes that SCW has wrought.

Working with SCW Policies, Post-Wizard

Once you've got that policy made, what can you do with it? Several things:

◆ You can view a report summarizing any SCW policy, using the command-line tool scwcmd, which I'll cover soon.

◆ You can create a group policy object on your domain that implements all of the aspects of a given SCW policy, using scwcmd.

◆ You can modify the policy by returning to SCW, as you may remember from Figure 11.2.

◆ You can apply the policy to a single machine either with the wizard as, again, Figure 11.2 showed, or with scwcmd.

◆ You can apply the policy to either a list of machines or to every 2003 Server/R2 Server in a given organizational unit, using scwcmd.

◆ You can compare a machine's (or a list of machines, or an OU full of machines) current state to the state that it would be in if you applied a given security template, using scwcmd.

◆ You can roll back the last 100 applied policies.

Let's finish this chapter with a look at these capabilities.

Looking at an SCW Policy

How do you know what an SCW policy would do? You can, of course, load it into SCW and page through its options. But the easier way is to just open the SCW viewer, the program that let you see the summary of your just-created policy back in Figure 11.34. Do that with this command line (be sure to include the path as part of the *nameoftemplate*):

```
scwcmd view /x:nameoftemplate
```

Try it once, and I think you'll understand why it's so important to include a description when you save an SCW policy!

Creating a GPO from an SCW Policy

The real power in policies and security templates is in distributing them to large numbers of machines automatically, and one of the most powerful tools for propagating them is a group policy object (GPO). Sure, you could sit down by hand and create a GPO that did everything that an SCW policy does, but it'd be blasted tedious. Instead, you can just open up a command line and type

```
scwcmd transform /p:filenameoftemplate /g:"name of new group policy object"
```

For example, if I'd just created an SCW template called "test" and I wanted scwcmd to create a corresponding group policy object named "Cool SCW stuff to do to the domain," I'd type

```
scwcmd transform /p:"c:\windows\security\msscw\policies\test.xml" /g:"Cool SCW
stuff to do to the domain"
```

Even though that broke on the page, be sure to type it as all one line at the command prompt. You'll then see that your domain does indeed have this new group policy object—if you're not logged onto a domain as someone with the power to create group policy objects on the domain then the operation will fail—but that it's not linked to anything yet. Link it to an OU, a domain, or site as you like. (We covered linking GPOs to OUs in Chapters 8 and 9 of *Mastering Windows Server 2003*.)

But suppose you apply this group policy object to an OU that contains systems that *aren't* running Server 2003 SP1 or Server 2003 R2? I was surprised to discover that many of the settings applied just fine to 2000, XP, or pre-SP1 copies of Server 2003. Actually this was pretty good news, as I've always wanted to build an SCW policy for XP systems and apply it to them, but SCW foils any attempt to run it against an XP system. Being able to create a policy on a 2003 system, but with XP in mind, and then to make that policy a GPO, which can then apply to XP systems, is pretty neat.

WARNING   It can, however, be something of a mixed blessing. After all, the things you do to harden a Server 2003 system might not be the same things that you'd want done to a desktop operating system. So be careful how you apply an SCW policy that you created for a *server* on an XP system; you may not get the results that you expected. (Perhaps the better answer would be to create a completely separate SCW policy built with XP boxes in mind, even though you've got to build the policy on a 2003 system.)

Applying an SCW Policy Remotely

You've already seen how to use SCW to apply an existing security policy to a remote system; just start it up and when you get to the page you saw in Figure 11.2, choose Apply an Existing Security Policy. But you can apply a policy remotely with scwcmd, and doing that offers more options.

APPLYING A POLICY TO ONE SYSTEM

The basic scwcmd command to apply a policy is the `scwcmd configure /p:`*`policyname`* command. You add different options to it to apply a policy to one system, an OU, or a list of machines. To apply to just one system, add `/m:`, followed by either the IP address or the name of the machine to apply the policy to. For example, to apply a policy `test.xml` to a system named server1.bigfirm.com, you'd type

```
scwcmd configure /p:c:\windows\security\msscw\policies\test.xml /
m:server1.bigfirm.com
```

Again, that should be all on one line; don't press Enter in the middle of the command even though it's broken on the page. (This is true for all of the scwcmd commands that you'll see in the remainder of this chapter.)

APPLYING A POLICY TO AN OU

Installing a template to a single system remotely is nice, but it's a lot cooler to be able to apply a template to a whole pile of systems. Like, say, an organization unit. You *could* transform the policy into a GPO and then apply that GPO to the OU, but applying something as big as an SCW policy could slow down logons, so you might want to just apply the policy once and for all, rather than wait for the next logon. To do that, use scwcmd but replace the `/m:` option with a `/ou:` option. Then follow the `/ou:` with the LDAP path describing the OU. For example, to apply `test.xml` to an OU inside bigfirm.com called servers, you'd type

```
scwcmd configure /p:c:\windows\security\msscw\policies\test.xml /
ou:ou=servers,dc=bigfirm,dc=com
```

If that LDAP notation stuff looks a bit unfamiliar, please review Chapter 8 in *Mastering Windows Server 2003* for more LDAP examples.

APPLYING A POLICY TO A LIST OF PCS

Being able to apply an SCW policy to an entire OU is good but can sometimes be a mite too scattershot. So it's nice that SCW lets you alternatively create a file listing the systems that you'd like a policy applied to. The list can even specify that a given machine gets a particular policy. You can then hand that list to scwcmd, and it'll apply the right policy to the right machine.

That file must have a particular XML format; it looks like this:

```
<?xml version="1.0" encoding="UTF-16"?>
<MachinePolicyMap>
<Machine Name="firstmachinename" Policy="name of policy test file"/>
<Machine Name="secondmachinename" Policy="name of second policy test file"/>
…
</MachinePolicyMap>
```

Note that because that's XML, case matters! For example, if I wanted a machine named sv1 to get a template file named `m1template.xml` and if I wanted a machine named SV2 to get a template file called `websvr.XML`, the XML file would look like

```
<?xml version="1.0" encoding="UTF-16"?>
<MachinePolicyMap>
<Machine Name="sv1" Policy="m1template.xml"/>
```

```
<Machine Name="SV2" Policy="websvr.XML"/>
</MachinePolicyMap>
```

Typing `<machinepolicymap>` wouldn't work. So, presuming that I'd gotten the case right, I'd then save that file with a name like, say, `mylist.xml`. Any name will do. Then I invoke scwcmd like this:

```
scwcmd configure /i:mylist.xml
```

(Notice that there aren't any folder structures in the file names in my example. I'm assuming that I'm working from the directory where they all exist. Otherwise, I'd have to specify not just `mltemplate.xml` but the entire file and directory path to that file.)

CHECKING ON A SYSTEM: ANALYZE

Rolling out an SCW security policy does great things to lock down a system. So long, that is, that those lockdowns don't inconvenience someone.

Anyone who's a local administrator on a server can, with a little work, override any configuration change caused by SCW. After all, most of the changes are stored in the Registry, and any local admin can hack the Registry. Domain-level admins might, then, want a nice method to compare a given server's *current* configuration to the configuration created when those domain-level admins applied the SCW policy. The scwcmd analyze command does that. It looks like

```
scwcmd  analyze /p:policyfilename [/l] [/e] machine specifications
```

scwcmd analyze creates reports (in the current directory; add the `/o:foldername` option to put them elsewhere), but you can take that further by creating logs of the analysis process; that's what `/l` does. Specify it and you'll get log files of each analysis in addition to the analysis report. `/e` says to log any anomalies in the machine's Application event log.

`machine specifications` refers to the fact that you can tell scwcmd to do an analysis on one machine, a list of machines, or an OU, with the same syntax as with the `scwcmd configure` option. So, for example, to log anomalies to a local Applications event log and to do analysis reports for every system in the webservers OU of bigfirm.com, and to create those analyses by comparing the system's configuration against a policy file named webs.xml, type

```
scwcmd analyze /p:webs.xml /e /ou:ou=webservers,dc=bigfirm,dc=com
```

ROLLING BACK A TEMPLATE: ROLLBACK

Finally, if you didn't like the outcome of an SCW policy, you can roll that policy back save, of course, for any ACL changes in NTFS or the Registry. This magic becomes possible because every time you apply an SCW policy, SCW or scwcmd writes a file named `policyn.xml` into a directory `\windows\security\msscw\rollbackfiles`, where *n* can range from 1 to 100. These files are just SCW policies that undo the effect of their originating policies. The rollback function just picks the `policyn.xml` file with the largest number and applies it to the server, returning it to a pre-policy state.

Roll back from a command line with scwcmd rollback. It looks like

```
scwcmd rollback /m:machine
```

Where, as before, `/m:` lets you specify a machine name or IP address.

Summary

As I've already said, SCW is a great lockdown tool and has to be seen not as a simpleminded wizard but a rich and pretty flexible expert system. It's something well worth your time if you've given it a miss so far. Its only pitfall is, in my opinion, the way that it handles audit settings, and so I recommend that you either take a good, long look at what it intends to do audit-wise before running it, or just skip the audit settings section altogether until you *do* have the time to examine it.

Part 2

New to R2

In this part:

Chapter 12

Setting Up Windows Server 2003 R2

Windows Server 2003 R2—"R2" for the rest of this chapter—installs in a manner very much like Server 2003. You've already learned from Chapter 5 of *Mastering Windows Server 2003* how to install Server 2003, so this chapter focuses on how installing R2 is different than installing 2003, both as a fresh install or an upgrade. The big points of difference between 2003 and R2 are

Two CDs   R2 ships on two CDs and no, there's no single-DVD option unfortunately. Unlike many multi-CD operating systems, however, you needn't have the second one on hand immediately when installing, as you can do a basic install from just the first CD and end up with a fully working operating system; you just lose out on the new R2 features. You can, further, decide to install the items on the second CD at any time in the future, at which point you'll have a fully functioning copy of R2. (You can even use just Disc 2 to convert an existing 2003 SP1 system to an R2 system, as you'll learn in this chapter.)

Schema Changes   If you plan on installing an R2 server in an existing Active Directory, you'll have to modify your AD's schema if you want to add an R2 domain controller, use any of the Unix/Windows integration features, employ the Print Management Console, or set up a DFS namespace with the new DFS-R replication engine. If, on the other hand, you intend only to set up a file server, DHCP, DNS, WINS, or the like, then you won't need a schema upgrade.

Client Access Licenses   As noted in an earlier chapter, your Server 2003 CALs are fine for a R2-using network. You needn't upgrade or rebuy any CALs. (That'll happen with Windows Server 2007/8.)

In brief, here's how an R2 install goes. As I've already said, if you're comfortable installing Server 2003—and please consider looking over Chapter 5 in *Mastering Windows Server 2003* if you're not—then an R2 setup is a snap. Basically you use Disc 1 to install 2003 SP1. The system boots for the first time, you log in, then you're prompted to run a program called `setup2.exe` on the second disc to get the Control Panel's Add/Remove Programs applet ready to install the R2-specific features. At that point, R2 setup is done and you can add any R2 features using the normal Add/Remove Programs process. You can also, as you'll see, convert an existing 2003 SP1 system into an R2 system using only Disc 2 and the `setup2.exe` program.

Two CDs, Four Names

Space forced Microsoft to move R2 to two CDs and while that sounds like a pain, the two-disc arrangement actually has a few benefits, as you'll see. The first CD is nearly identical to the "Server 2003 with SP1 preinstalled" CDs that you could buy from Microsoft between SP1's release and R2's release. I say "nearly identical" because while I don't know every single byte's difference between R2's Disc 1 and an installation CD for 2003 with SP1 preinstalled, the main differences seem to be that the Setup program labels itself an R2 setup program, and the first disc adds commands to the

Registry that cause the newly installed 2003 SP1 system to prompt you for the second disc when it first boots up.

R2's Disc 2 contains the "new to R2" things like DFS Namespaces and Active Directory Federation Services and "downloadable but now included" stuff like SharePoint and the Unix interoperability tools. That means that some of the files for Add/Remove Windows Components are on Disc 1, and some are on Disc 2, so that for example if you were to add SharePoint to a system, you'd be prompted for some files from Disc 1 to install Internet Information Services and some files from Disc 2 for SharePoint.

That doesn't sound particularly difficult, except for one confusing thing: parts of R2 refer to Disc 1 and Disc 2 by names other than "Disc 1 and Disc 2." When asking for Disc 1, the Add/Remove Programs dialogs say "Please insert the Compact Disc labeled 'Service Pack 1 CD-ROM' into your CD-ROM drive and then click OK." Service Pack 1 CD-ROM? Yup, that's Server R2 Disc 1's other name. When it needs Disc 2, it asks for "Windows Server 2003 R2 Disc 2." So just remember:

◆ Disc 1 = "Service Pack 1 CD-ROM"

◆ Disc 2 = "Windows Server 2003 R2 Disc 2"

You'd think those Microsoft guys would have better editors. On the other hand, perhaps it's *my* fault; after all, I noticed the goofy labels during beta and should have filed a bug report.

Upgrade Your AD Schema

Before installing an R2 server that meets the criteria just mentioned—one that will become a DC, uses Print Management Console (PMC), employs the Unix interop stuff or DFS Namespaces—then first modify your AD's schema. Using an account with permissions to modify the schema—an Enterprise Admin or Schema Admin will do it —log onto whichever domain controller holds the Schema Master role and pop Disc 2 into that system's CD drive. Then open a command prompt and navigate to Cmpnents\R2\Adprep. Then run adprep.exe from the command prompt like so:

```
adprep /forestprep
```

Unlike 2003, you needn't do an adprep /domainprep command. You'll get a response like

```
D:\CMPNENTS\R2\ADPREP>adprep /forestprep

ADPREP WARNING:

Before running adprep, all Windows 2000 domain controllers in the forest should
be upgraded to Windows 2000 Service Pack 1 (SP1) with QFE 265089, or to Windows
2000 SP2 (or later).

QFE 265089 (included in Windows 2000 SP2 and later) is required to prevent
potential domain controller corruption.

For more information about preparing your forest and domain see KB article
Q331161 at http://support.microsoft.com.

[User Action]
```

```
If ALL your existing Windows 2000 domain controllers meet this requirement, type
C and then press ENTER to continue. Otherwise, type any other key and press ENTER
to quit.
```

Presuming all's well, type **C** and press Enter, and you'll see something like

```
Opened Connection to DC1
SSPI Bind succeeded
Current Schema Version is 30
Upgrading schema to version 31
Connecting to "DC1"
Logging in as current user using SSPI
Importing directory from file "C:\WINDOWS\system32\sch31.ldf"
Loading
entries......................................................................
............................................................
139 entries modified successfully.

The command has completed successfully
Adprep successfully updated the forest-wide information.
```

Now you're ready to go set up your first R2 server. (Don't forget to grab Disc 2 from the CD drive of the DC that you just used to upgrade your AD schema; you'll need that disc to install R2 on the new system!)

R2 Installation Options

You can, of course, just install R2 from scratch on a freshly formatted hard disk, but that's not the only option. There are four ways to put R2 on a system:

- Hand-installed clean build: install "from scratch" using Discs 1 and 2, wiping out anything that previously existed on the server's hard disk

- Upgrade of an SP1 system: if you have a system already running Server 2003 with SP1 installed and you want to upgrade it to R2, then this is gonna be the easiest upgrade you've ever done. As R2 Disc 1 is almost identical to 2003 with SP1 installed, all you've got to do is run a program called `setup2.exe` on R2 Disc 2.

- Unattended upgrade of a 2003 SP1 system to R2 via a command-line invocation of `setup2.exe` on Disc 2.

- Unattended install of the entire operating system: start from a clean hard disk and install the OS with either `winnt.sif`, Remote Installation Services (RIS), or from a network share with minimal setup interaction needed.

We'll consider each of those options in order.

Hand-Installed Clean Builds of R2

First let's see how to take the two CDs and a system with nothing on its hard disk and get an R2 system from it.

Installing R2, Part 1

The first part of an R2 install looks exactly like a Server 2003 install, as it basically *is* one. We covered that in ugly detail back in Chapter 5 of *Mastering Windows Server 2003*, so I won't recapitulate that here. Once Disc 1 has done its work, it'll reboot the computer and you'll see a logon screen identical to a Server 2003 logon screen. Log in, and you'll see the usual blue Windows background but with a dialog box taking center stage telling you that

> *"Windows Setup is not complete. We recommend that you continue Setup so that you can install the additional components that are available in this version of the Windows Server operating system. For more information about the new components, see the documentation on Windows Server CD 2. To continue Setup, insert Windows Server CD 2, or specify the location where the Windows Server CD 2 files are stored, and then click OK."*

It then prompts you for the location of Disc 2. To continue, just pop Disc 2 into your CD drive and click OK. But before you do, let's ask: what happens if you don't use the second disc? Then you essentially don't have a copy of R2 running; you're running Server 2003 with SP1. For example, a trip to Control Panel's Add/Remove Windows Components will show that you don't have the option to install SharePoint, ADFS, or the like. (And as far as I can see, it's the easiest way to visually verify that you've installed R2 instead of just 2003 SP1.) Making the new Disc-1-only-installed server into an extra DC on an existing 2003-based AD will not require a schema upgrade if you do not let R2's extra Setup program run (but it would if you decided to install Disc 2 later).

Installing R2, Part 2

But what's the fun of running a new operating system without getting all the new goodies? So pop Disc 2 into the CD drive, click OK, and you'll see a wizard panel like the one in Figure 12.1.

TIP   If you told Setup to skip Disk 2 previously, you can start it up later either by popping Disk 2 into your CD drive—the Autorun feature will start it up, assuming that you've not disabled it— or navigate on Disk 2 to \CMPNENTS\R2 and run the file setup2.exe.

Click Next, and R2 Setup will tell you that it's copied files and is ready to continue. Click Next, and it'll copy files for a while. When it's done, you'll see a wizard pane like Figure 12.2.

Once you close that wizard, the Windows Server Post-Setup Security Updates page comes up, as you see in Figure 12.3.

FIGURE 12.1
R2 Setup Part 2

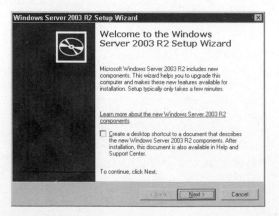

FIGURE 12.2
R2's basically set up.

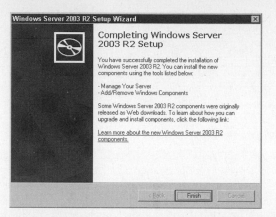

FIGURE 12.3
Windows Server
Post-Setup Security
Updates page

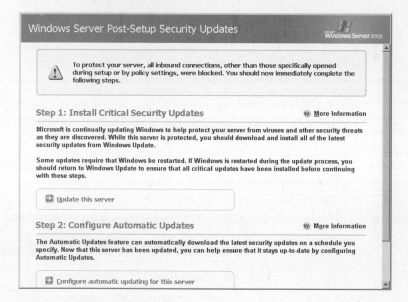

This page first appeared in 2003 SP1, but you only see it if you install 2003 with SP1 preinstalled; you wouldn't have seen this page if you merely added SP1 to an existing 2003 installation. Basically, it's a big page that does two things: it bugs you to get the latest updates and configure automatic updates for the server—both good things to do but things that you've done before, so I won't go through them in detail. One nice thing about this page is that Windows Firewall is enabled without any exceptions and stays that way until you're properly patched. That way, if some worm's running around the Internet (and perhaps your intranet), then you can complete installing the server without fear of your system getting infected before you've even finished installing it.

Clicking the first link on the Post-Setup Security Updates page takes you to Windows Update, where as always you've got to tell Internet Explorer that it's okay to install Windows Update. Then you'll be prompted to click a button allowing IE to install Windows Update on your system. Once Windows Update is installed, you click the Express button to get a list of available updates. Click Install Now to get them all, accept the license agreement, and you'll soon be completely up to date patch-wise.

Once you're done with that—you'll have to reboot—the Windows Server Post-Setup Security Updates page will return, and you can then schedule regular Windows Updates. (Don't bother doing this if you're running Windows Server Update Services or some other patching solution). Then just click the Finish button. You'll get a nagging dialog box warning you that clicking Finish will cause the page to drop the firewall. You've already loaded all of the up-to-date security settings, so there's nothing to fear; to the question "Do you want to close this page?" click Yes. Should you ever want to bring up this page again, just click Start ⮞ Run, fill in oobechk.exe, and click OK.

Manage Your Server

But Setup's not done with you yet. Once you've closed the Post-Setup Security Updates page, Windows presents you another page, as you see in Figure 12.4.

You'll recognize this Manage Your Server page if you've worked with Server 2003. We didn't cover this in the *Mastering Windows Server 2003* book because to be truthful it didn't do all that much, and that hasn't changed much in R2/SP1. Basically, it's a wizard that provides a pretty interface for adding server functions. You can use this to make this server a web server, a SharePoint server, a DNS server, or the like. So why don't I like it much? Because as far as I can see, it doesn't do anything that going into the Control Panel, choosing the Add or Remove Programs applet and then the Add/Remove Windows components button doesn't do, and the Control Panel applet can add a bunch of things that the Manage Your Server (MYS) page can't, so why bother learning two tools when one does the job?

When SP1 was in development, there were claims that MYS would become a must-use feature because the information that MYS stores—that is, your "server roles"—was to be read by the Security Configuration Wizard. SCW wasn't out at the time, so we didn't know what that meant. It turns out, however, that Manage Your Server and the Security Configuration Wizard don't appear to interact, and that's a shame. It'd be neat if installing the DHCP server automatically told Windows Firewall, if active, to open port 67, the one that DHCP uses. Rumor has it that Server 2007/8 will incorporate something like that; we'll see.

FIGURE 12.4
The Manage Your
Server page

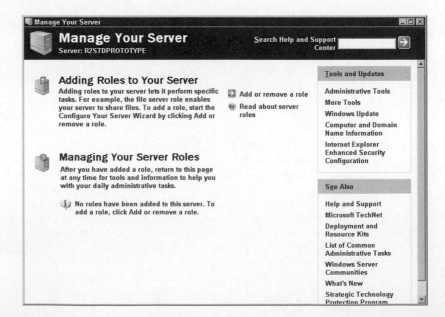

Using or not using MYS is a matter of taste, so you'll read some of the other authors in this book using it. There's *nothing* wrong with it *per se* as far as I'm concerned; I just don't find it useful. You can get rid of MYS by checking the box at the lower left-hand corner of the page labeled Do Not Display This Page at Logon. Then close the window and it's gone for good. If you want to run it at some point, just click Start ➢ All Programs ➢ Administrative Tools ➢ Manage Your Server.

At this point, you've got an R2 server installed. Configure its TCP/IP settings, install whatever ancillary programs you wish, decide whether or not to set up Windows Firewall, and you're ready to start offering network services. (Or you're ready, assuming that you've read the rest of this book and its precursor or their equivalents.)

Upgrading a 2003 SP1 System With Setup2.exe

Recall that Disc 1 of R2 contains almost exactly the same files as does an installation disc for 2003 with SP1 preinstalled. If you have a Server 2003 system with SP1 installed and want to upgrade it to R2, then, it's quite easy. First, run `adprep /forestprep` if you haven't done that yet. Then leave the R2 Disc 1 in its box, and pop R2 Disc 2 into your 2003 SP1 system's CD drive. The Autorun routine on Disc 2 will pop up a familiar-looking screen with a few choices, as you see in Figure 12.5.

Click Continue Windows Server 2003 R2 Setup, or, if the screen never appeared because Autorun was disabled, just navigate to the `cmpnents\r2` folder on Disc 2 and run `setup2.exe`. You'll see the same thing you saw in Figure 12.1. If you like, check the box offering a shortcut to information on R2. Click Next to reveal Figure 12.6.

What's with the product key? I mean, this is an already-running system, right? Yes, but Microsoft wants to see that you paid for your copy of R2 before you get to add it to your current 2003 SP1 server. Punch in your 25 characters and click Next to see Figure 12.7.

FIGURE 12.5
Main Disk 2
menu screen

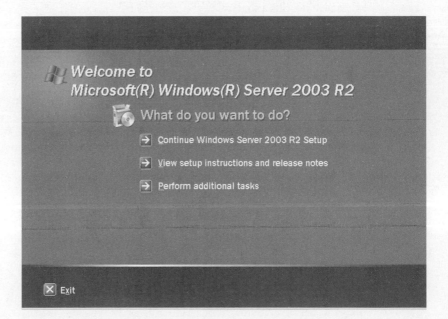

FIGURE 12.6
A product key?

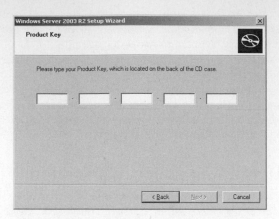

FIGURE 12.7
A wishy-washy
warning

What this is trying to say is that in most cases you've got to activate the copy of Windows Server a second time because, again, Microsoft wants to see that you've paid for your copy of R2, even if you did pay for your copy of 2003 Server. Click Yes and you'll see that aspect of software that has become as inevitable as death and taxes, the End User License Agreement, or EULA. Agree to the terms and click Next, and you'll see a screen saying that `setup2.exe`'s got all that it needs, and you need only click Next. Do that and `setup2.exe` will copy some files for a bit. Once it's done, you'll see the same wizard pane that you saw in Figure 12.2…and R2's installed. Just do whatever you like with the Manage Your Server page and add whatever R2 components you need.

Where This Falls Down: Mixed Build Types

Just going straight to Disc 2 to upgrade a 2003 SP1 system to an R2 system is a neat option, but it does have an annoying drawback: the type of R2 discs must match the type of disc used to create the original 2003 SP1 system. Microsoft releases Standard Server (and Enterprise Server as well) in four flavors or "builds:" OEM, retail, evaluation, and volume licensing. The four are nearly identical except in one way: they all contain one or two slightly different files and use different kinds of 25-character product keys.

While all product keys may *look* alike—they're all 25 characters long—there are four different mathematical functions that check an OEM key versus a retail key versus a volume licensing key: one to recognize OEM product keys, one to recognize retail keys, one for evaluation keys, and one for volume license keys.

Microsoft doesn't want you upgrading one kind of build with another—I have no idea why—and so if you had, for example, a Server 2003 SP1 system that you'd purchased with your computer (in other words, an OEM copy), then you wouldn't be able to go buy a retail copy of R2 and upgrade, because your current server is an OEM type and the copy of R2 is a retail type.

That doesn't mean that you can't put that copy of R2 that you paid for on the server hardware, not at all. It just means that you've got to start the upgrade from Disc 1, which involves more baby-sitting and time.

What happens if you try to run `setup2.exe` from one kind of build atop another kind of 2003 SP1 build? When `setup2.exe` asks for a product key and you punch in your product key, `setup2.exe` will tell you that it's invalid.

If this has got you curious about exactly which build you have on an existing server, then take a look at Microsoft's Knowledge Base article 889713. It claims that if you right-click My Computer and choose Properties, and then look at the General tab, you'll see Registered To and your name (or whatever you punched in when you ran Setup and it asked for a name) and, below that, a Product ID (*not* a Product Key) that might look like 69712-270-7773322-97632. The first part is the Microsoft Product Code and identifies the product. For example, 69712 is Windows Server 2003, Standard Edition in either retail, volume, or OEM builds. (69713 supposedly means it's an evaluation copy, which is odd because I didn't know that there *was* an evaluation copy available for Standard Edition.) The second part is called the *channel ID* and tells more about the specific build. For example, in Standard Server, 270 means that it's a volume license copy. If the three characters are "OEM" instead of a number, then it's an OEM build. 335 means that it's a retail version, and anything in the 308–347 range means that it came from a Microsoft Action Pack subscription. (There are other values, but apparently Microsoft doesn't document all of them.)

Anyway, the bottom line is that your R2 software must be of the same build type as the 2003 SP1 build was, or you'll have to upgrade starting with Disc 1.

Running *Setup2.exe* Unattended

Being able to upgrade to R2 with just Disc 2 (sometimes) can be pretty useful, but you can make it even easier if you've got a bunch of systems to upgrade by partially or completely automating the process. Disc 2 isn't bootable, so you can just put it on a network share and then connect to the network share and run `setup2.exe`. But while that's convenient, it still requires you to baby-sit `setup2.exe`, punching in a product key and so on...boring. That's why it's nice that `setup2.exe` can be run from the command line with parameters answering all of its questions. The syntax looks like

```
setup2 /quiet [/p:productkey] /accepteula [/createshortcut] [/suppressrestart]
```

Those parameters work like so:

- ◆ `/quiet` tells setup2 that you don't want it to pop up wizards and ask you questions. In fact, it's mandatory: if you specify any of the other command-line parameters and do *not* specify `/quiet` then you'll get an error and `setup2.exe` will refuse to run. (I know, so why force us to type **/quiet**? It's one of those mysteries of the universe.)

- ◆ `/p:` or `/productkey` lets you punch in the product key. Just type **/p:** and immediately follow it with the product key, with a dash between each five-character group. No need to surround it with double quotes.

- ◆ `/accepteula` means that you've agreed to the software license. Also mandatory.

- ◆ `/createshortcut` creates the shortcut on the desktop to the document with information about R2's new features. This is optional.

- ◆ `/suppressrestart` tells `setup2.exe` not to reboot your system once `setup2.exe`'s finished. I'm honestly not sure why this is here, inasmuch as the Disc 2 part of R2 Setup doesn't reboot automatically, nor does it need to.

To tell `setup2.exe` to install on a system with product key XPQJK-PY2CT-VK6P2-PNNNR-A8B8B without any further questions to us carbon-based units, then, you could navigate to `cmpnents\r2` on Disc 2 or a network share containing the Disc 2 files, and type

```
setup2 /p:OFCOU-RSEIW-ONTTE-LLYOU-MYKEY /accepteula /createshortcut /quiet
```

(And no, that's not a real product key. That I know of, anyway.)

Performing a Complete Unattended R2 Install

But what about the best possible world, a complete from-the-ground-up installation, hands off and unattended? Well, if you already know (from Chapter 5 of *Mastering Windows Server 2003* or a similar resource) how to build an unattended install of Server 2003, then you're most of the way there. All you've got to do is to put the pieces together.

First, get the OS on the system. You can do that by following the approaches and procedures explained in detail in Chapter 5 of *Mastering Windows Server 2003*. RIS, `winnt.sif`, or the `winnt.exe/winnt32.exe` approaches work identically for R2 as they did for 2003.

Then get `setup2.exe` to run. But how? Simple: as you read in Chapter 5, either use the `cmdlines.txt` batch file to kick off `setup2.exe`, or use the GUIRunOnce scripted feature to start `setup2.exe`. In both cases, just build the command as one long `setup2.exe` command with parameters, as you just read in the last section.

Installing the R2 Admin Pack on XP

Once upon a time—back in the days of NT 3.1 through 4.0—all of us server admin types needed to administer our servers from our desktops, and so we just used Server as our desktop OS. (Anyway, I know *I* did, and I can offer as supporting evidence that I'm not the only one that one of the members of the original team that built NT. A very nice fellow named Lou Perazzoli commented in 1998 in response to a question about the then-upcoming Windows 2000 Professional desktop system, "I'm really sorry, but I don't even know how to install NT 4 Workstation. I'm a Server guy." Perazzoli's also the guy who, when I once interviewed him about Windows 2000 in the late '90s, said "Mark, I know your first question." I played along and said, "Okay, Lou, what's my first question?" He replied, "You want to know when will NT 5 [the name at the time of what eventually became Windows 2000] ship?" I said, "Okay, when *will* it ship?" He smiled and replied, "Late!")

But those days are gone forever. IT's become a more regular, well-managed outfit and we don't run Server on our desktops any more. (That's my story, and I'm sticking to it.) But how to control a server from a workstation operating system? Ever since 2000, Microsoft's shipped their server OSes with an "admin pack," a set of MMC snap-ins that lets you administer your servers from your desktop. R2 is no exception, so no self-respecting R2 rollout would lack a desktop component, and Microsoft's provided that component or, rather, components. It's all simple once you know where to go and what to install, so here's a quick look at what your system needs to do server administration.

First of all, inasmuch as most of R2 is just 2003, then you'll want to install the 2003 Admin Tools pack, as you've probably already done if you have 2003 servers in your enterprise. Nothing changes there. (If you don't have the download, search `www.microsoft.com/downloads` for "2003 admin pack.")

Next, pop R2 Disc 2 into your CD-ROM drive. It contains a folder with four files:

WINDOWSXP-MMC30-KB907265-X86.EXE   An update for XP that allows XP to run MMC 3.0. That's necessary, as most of the R2 snap-ins require MMC 3.0. (In case you've never heard of MMC 3.0, it's just a minor update to MMC. We'll cover it in the next chapter and trust me, it'll be a brief one.) Oddly enough, this update only works on XP; you can't get it to work on any pre-R2 Server 2003 systems.

FSRMGMT.EXE   A snap-in that lets you administer the various pieces of R2 that Microsoft took from Microsoft Storage Server. But don't try to install this without first downloading and installing the Microsoft .NET Framework 2.0 runtime. (It's another download from www.microsoft.com/downloads.) Once .NET 2.0's in place install these Administration Tool for File Server Management.

PMCMGMT.EXE   An XP-ready copy of the Print Management Console (covered in Chapter 14). It's a neat tool that offers one-stop-shopping for all of your print servers and queues, and with this file you can extend that power to your XP workstation. (Vista's got it built in.)

IDMU.EXE   Another client-side tool for controlling the tools that Microsoft took from Services for Unix and incorporated into R2.

All of these files install in the same way. Start up the EXE, you get a Welcome wizard pane, then you have to agree to the End User License Agreement, and you've got the tool. Once you've equipped your XP desktop with these, you can truly be the master of your domain!

WARNING   For some reason, you can't install these new tools on a pre-R2 copy of Server 2003.

Summary

You've seen in this chapter that R2 setup is actually a fairly small change over 2003 setup, thankfully. Setup2.exe is fairly easy to use or even to automate, and the included XP tools in the Admin folder are quite welcome. Time to move on to R2's slightly modified interface…MMC 3.0.

## Chapter 13

Using MMC 3.0, R2's New Interface

What would a new version of Windows be without a bit of fiddling with the user interface? Well, despite its "minor upgrade" nature, R2 wasn't left out, with a minor—*very* minor—change to the Server 2003 UI. That change comes in the form of a revision to the Microsoft Management Console, the framework for holding and organizing programs called "snap-ins" that first appeared in Windows 2000 and that we covered in *Mastering Windows Server 2003* in Chapter 3. MMC gets a version bump from 2.0 to 3.0 and a couple of cosmetic changes, one of which you won't see in R2 without a Registry hack.

"Huh?" you may be saying. "Why'd they bother going to 3.0 if all they did was a couple of visual changes?" As I tracked the progress of R2 through its betas, I got a number of briefings kindly provided by our friends at Microsoft. Every briefing trumpeted—usually early in the presentation—about the imminent release of MMC 3.0, and it never made sense to me why anyone gave a hoot. But eventually I got it when I remembered: Microsoft is driven by developers, not administrators. MMC 3.0 is, as you'll see, a relatively minor change for us keep-things-running types, but constitutes a big "woo-hoo!" for developers because Microsoft changed things so that building MMC 3.0 snap-ins is, um, a snap. The big difference is apparently that developers can now build MMCs using the .NET programming framework, and for those who don't know what the .NET framework does, well, it simplifies programming many kinds of jobs. You know how figuring out how to do something from the command line can be powerful and flexible, but using a wizard's easier? Think of .NET as The Big Wizard for the programming community. So being able to make your own MMC 3.0 snap-in with .NET is apparently a big win.

MMC Feature 1: The Actions Pane

That said, let's take a look at the new stuff. Take a look at a typical MMC snap-in, like the File Server Resource Manager, as you see in Figure 13.1.

You're probably used to this sort of layout: a two-pane window. The pane on the left is the *console tree*, and the one on the right is the *details pane*. What you may not have noticed, however, is a new icon across the top toolbar. I've circled it in Figure 13.1, and it's called the Hide/Show Action Pane icon. If I click it, then MMC acquires a whole new pane, as you see in Figure 13.2.

FIGURE 13.1
Example MMC
snap-in

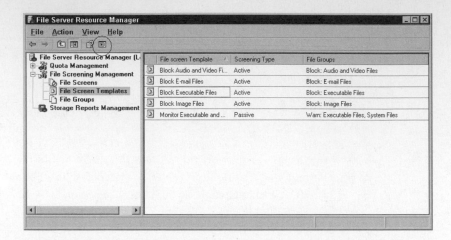

FIGURE 13.2
MMC snap-in with
actions pane opened

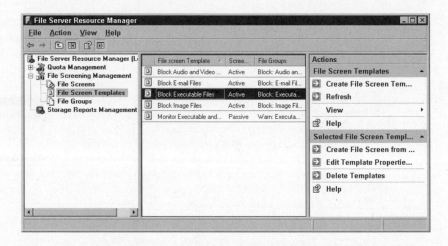

That rightmost pane is called the *actions pane*, and its job is basically to save you right-clicking. In either the console tree pane or the details pane, I can usually right-click any object and get a context menu. For example, notice that in the console tree pane (the leftmost pane), I've selected File Screen Templates, and in the details pane (the middle one), I've selected Block Executable Files. (Chapter 18 explains what this MMC is doing; for now, let's just look over the layout of an MMC 3.0 snap-in, as this tool is.) If I were to right-click File Screens Template in the console tree pane, I'd get a context menu that included Create File Screen Template and Refresh, and you see both of those options in the actions pane (the rightmost one). Similarly, right-clicking Block Executable Files in the details pane would offer a drop-down context menu that included Create File Screen from Template and Edit Template Properties, and you see those options in the actions pane.

In sum, then, this first feature of MMC 3.0, the actions pane, basically copies the context menu items from objects in the console tree pane and the details pane and offers them as one-click-style options in the actions pane.

MMC Feature 2: Add/Remove Snap-ins

Many MMC 3.0-aware applications do some interesting things with the actions pane. But that's not the only thing new in MMC 3.0. There's also a new dialog box controlling which snap-ins you've loaded.

You have probably started up an empty MMC dozens of times to load some occasionally used snap-in that lacked its own entry on the Windows menu. Click File ➢ Add ➢ Remote Snap-in and then you get to click Add, which brings up a dialog box showing you snap-ins, which you choose and click yet another Add dialog box. Not too efficient, and by default R2's MMC behaves the same way. But with a Registry change, you get to see a smarter Add/Remove Snap-in dialog.

Just open Regedit and navigate to HKEY_LOCAL_MACHINE\SOFTWARE\Microsoft\MMC, and then create a new key—yes, that's a *key*, not an entry—named UseNewUI. Close Regedit, start up a new MMC (no reboots necessary), click File ➢ Add/Remove Snap-ins and you'll see something like Figure 13.3.

Nice, clean, and self-explanatory. Gotta like it.

Summary

Well, that's the new MMC 3.0. Turn on the actions pane and give it a try, you might like it better than right-clicking, and definitely add the UseNewUI key. No, on second thought, *definitely* do it, because, well, guess what MMC looks like under Vista and Server 2007/8?

FIGURE 13.3
MMC 3.0's new way to add snap-ins

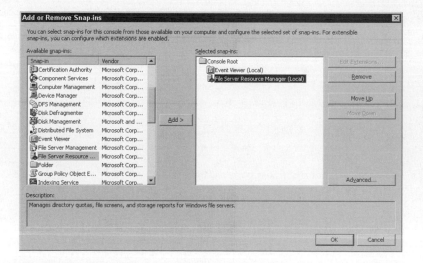

Chapter 14

Print Management Gets Easier: Print Management Console

One of the headaches of printer management on Windows Servers has always been all the running around you had to do. Want to add a printer? Go one place. Want to configure port timeouts? Go another place. Add a printer to Active Directory? Go somewhere else. The same goes for printer server settings (separate from printer settings) and printer permissions—both are in different places. One of the key tools in Chapter 13 of *Mastering Windows Server 2003* is a section telling you where to configure various settings. The short version, if you don't care to look right now, is that your mouse hand will get a big workout opening tools and you'll spend a bit of time searching for the tool containing the setting that you need.

To add insult to injury, the tools more or less assume that every organization has only a single print server. Without connecting remotely to another computer using Remote Desktop, it's not possible to manage printers and printer server settings on a remote print server.

In Windows Server 2003 R2, this has changed with the introduction of the Print Management Console (PMC). This is a great addition to the operating system interface, finally allowing you to do *everything* printer-related from a single console. Go take a victory lap around the office and when you return I'll tell you how to use the PMC, including:

◆   Installing the Print Management tool

◆   Adding new printers

◆   Assigning printers

◆   Managing printer settings and drivers

◆   Monitoring printer status and configuring alerts

◆   Connecting to remote print servers so you can do all this for your entire enterprise

The Print Management Console: An Overview

Back from that victory lap? Great. Let's take a look at this thing.

The Print Management Console (PMC) is available in R2 (when you add the Printer Server role) as well as for download on the Microsoft website. You can use it in a limited way to work with any modern Windows-based print server, but you'll get the most use from it on printer servers running R2. When it's installed, it's in Administrative Tools and it looks like Figure 14.1.

FIGURE 14.1
The PMC gives you centralized management to all printers and print server settings.

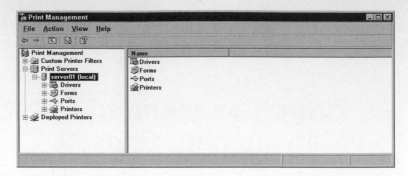

The tool is divided into three main sections:

- Custom Printer Filters gives you a look at *all* the printers managed from this console, regardless of which printer server they're connected to. As we'll discuss, the tool comes with both a complete view and a couple of default filters; we'll also look at how to create your own.

- Print Servers lists all the print servers managed from the Print Management Console. These servers are listed individually here, with folders for the printers, drivers, forms, and ports on each one.

- Deployed Printers lists the printers that you have deployed using Group Policy.

The catch? The PMC is not installed by default. It's installed as part of assigning the Print Server role to a server.

Installing the Print Management Console

The PMC isn't installed by default because it has no purpose on any server except a print server. To install it, you'll need to install the Print Management Role, as in Figure 14.2.

FIGURE 14.2
Add the printer role to the member server.

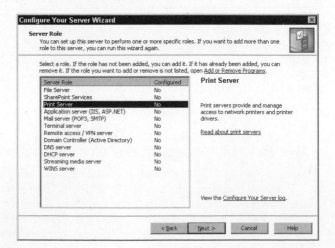

When you've picked this option, the next step is to install Print Management, which the wizard will do for you automatically. You'll need access to the R2 installation files to install the PMC. Once you do, it will be added to Administrative Tools.

Adding New Printers

One of the pieces of good news about the PMC is that you can use it to do something you couldn't before: automatically detect printers. This will only work with network printers on the local subnet, but it can sometimes save you a step. For those times when you can't, there's still the Add Printer Wizard, which you can launch from the Print Management Console.

Whichever method you use, once you've added a new printer you can configure its properties from the PMC exactly as you would by choosing it in Printers and Faxes and configuring its properties there. The PMC has a UI you can use to manage the Web interface of network printers.

Automatically Detecting Network Printers

To automatically detect network and locally connected printers on the local subnet, open the PMC and select the local print server from the Print Servers section. Right-click it and choose Automatically Add Network Printers. This will begin a broadcast on the subnet (see Figure 14.3).

This will return all available local network printers so you can manage them from the console, stored in the Printers section. The catch is that this will work only for the local subnet. To add a network printer located elsewhere, you'll either need to run this tool from a PMC in that subnet or add the network printer using the Add Printer Wizard as described in "Connecting to a Network-Enabled Printer" in Chapter 13 of *Mastering Windows Server 2003*.

Manually Installing New Printers

This procedure hasn't really changed much from previous versions of Windows Server, except that the Add Printer Wizard is now available from the PMC. Right-click the server you're managing (in the Print Servers section) and choose Add Printer to open the familiar wizard that walks you through the steps of choosing a printer type, installing its drivers, and setting its properties so that it's accessible to users on the network. For details, see Chapter 13 of *Mastering Windows Server 2003*—the process of manually installing a new printer has not changed in R2.

FIGURE 14.3
Broadcasting
for printers

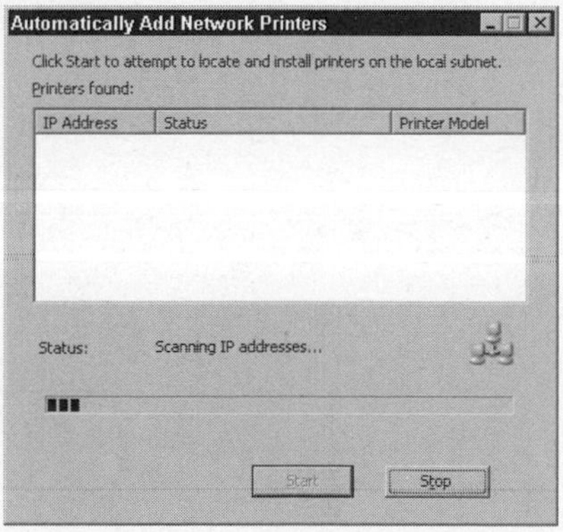

Deploying Printers to the Masses

Deploying printers to the masses *has* changed in R2, however. The PMC now includes an easy way to not only install shared printers on a printer server, but to get those printers available to the people who need them. You can list a printer in Active Directory to make it easily findable, assign it through group policy, or both.

Listing a printer in Active Directory is very simple. To publish a printer in Active Directory, open the PMC. From the Printers folder on a server (again, in the Print Servers section) or from the All Printers custom filter, right-click the printer to publish and choose List In Director. This is *not* the same thing as assigning a printer through Group Policy; it just gets the printer out there and findable. You can tell whether a printer is listed or not by looking at the List in the Directory check box in its Sharing tab, as in Figure 14.4.

If this doesn't work, check the connection to the domain controller.

Assigning printers through group policy makes life much easier for users, since they won't need to search for an appropriate printer—it's already given to them. To assign a printer, first set up the appropriate GPO Next, right-click the printer in Print Management, and choose Deploy with Group Policy to open the dialog box shown in Figure 14.5.

From here, you can assign printers to users (assigned when they log on) or to computers. Click Browse to choose the right policy, check the boxes according to whether you want to assign the printers to users or computers in that policy, and click Add. You can add printers to as many group policy objects as you like, just keep browsing for them and clicking the Add button.

> **TIP** You can also deploy printers from the Group Policy snap-in. Go to the Deployed Printers section in Administrative Templates and right-click its folder. From the context menu, choose Deploy Printer to browse for the print server in question.

The assigned printers will appear in the user's Printers and Faxes according to the group policy you set. If you remove the printers from their GPO, they will disappear from those client machines.

FIGURE 14.4
A printer published in
Active Directory may
be searched for.

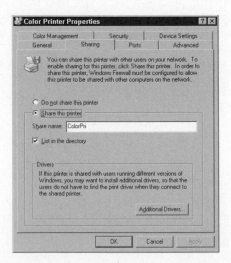

FIGURE 14.5
Deploying a printer
through Group Policy

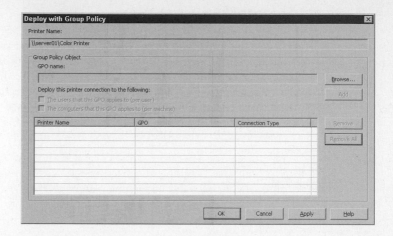

Configuring and Viewing Settings and Resources

Installing a printer is the first step, but just installing the printer does not guarantee that it'll have the right drivers or the right forms available to users. In this section, I'll show you how the PMC organizes these settings to help you review and configure print server settings for drivers, ports, and available forms.

Managing Printer Drivers

To set up a printer, you'll need drivers for it that are compatible with the print server's OS. For any-one *else* to use the shared printers you set up, they'll also need drivers for it since modern Windows clients assume that they can get their printer drivers from the print server. The drivers your print server needs may be identical with those your print clients need…or they may not. 32-bit operating systems and 64-bit operating systems can't use the same drivers. (For that matter, Itanium and x64 don't use the same drivers, either, even though they're both 64-bit Windows operating systems.) NT 4 workstations can't use the XP drivers, and should you be supporting Windows 98 or Windows ME clients, you'll need different drivers for them, too. Not sure which printer drivers are installed on a particular server? You can find out by choosing that server from the list and browsing to its Drivers folder, as in Figure 14.6.

FIGURE 14.6
All the drivers
installed on a print
server are listed in
this folder.

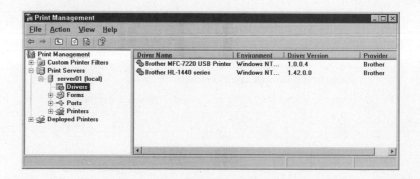

INSTALLING NEW PRINTER DRIVERS

You can begin adding new printer drivers from the PMC by right-clicking the Drivers icon for the print server and choosing Add Driver to open the Add Printer Driver Wizard. Again, this hasn't really changed from previous versions of Windows Server 2003. Choose the platform you want to support (if you choose more than one platform and one isn't supported, no drivers will appear) and then choose the make and model of the printer you need to install. If the driver doesn't come with Windows, you'll need to download it from the manufacturer's website and browse to it with the Have Disk button.

TIP The manufacturer's website will allow you to select the right driver for the operating system that you need to support.

If the driver has passed Windows Logo testing then you're done. If it hasn't, then you'll see a nag screen warning of you of the fact and telling you not to install it. The manufacturer may not have a driver that is certified, so if you need this printer you may *have* to install it. Just test the driver before distributing it widely.

CHANGING PRINTER DRIVER VIEWS

By default, the printer driver views show you the printer's name, its driver type, the name of the server it's attached to, and the driver provider. Some additional information might be useful for troubleshooting information or for creating a more complete inventory, as in the following section. For example, I want to add the URL for the driver's manufacturer so I can easily go get updates.

NOTE For drivers for older printers, not all information may be available. You can still choose the columns, but the columns will remain empty.

To add more columns to the driver view, right-click the Drivers icon for a print server and choose View ➤ Add/Remove Columns to open the dialog box in Figure 14.7.
When you click OK, the dialog box will close and the new column will be visible.

FIGURE 14.7
You can add more columns to the Drivers inventory.

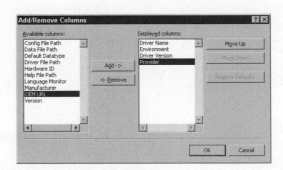

ARCHIVING DRIVER INFORMATION

You can export the driver list to a comma-separated file or tab-delimited file for inventory purposes. Right-click the Drivers icon for a print server and choose Export List from the context menu, then choose the location to save the file to and its type. You'll end up with output like the following:

```
Driver NameEnvironmentDriver VersionProvider
Brother HL-1440 seriesWindows NT x861.42.0.0Brother
Brother MFC-7220 USB PrinterWindows NT x861.0.0.4Brother
```

While this output contains no information different from what's currently displayed in the PMC (that is, there is no way to show an abbreviated set of columns in the PMC and an extended view in the exported list, not without manually changing the available columns first), it allows you to create a general inventory and stick in it an Excel file or the like.

TIP   Use this inventory to help you return to a working state if a new version of a printer driver causes problems, because you'll have a record of a working version.

Viewing and Editing Port Settings

Each printer server's ports are listed in its Ports folder, as in Figure 14.8.

Most of what you can do from this screen is tell which printers are connected to which port. For example, here you can see that one printer is connected to a USB virtual port and one to a LPT. The configuration you can do from here is limited; it's possible to configure the timeouts for a parallel port and the bit flow on a COM port (if you still have any printers using COM ports), but there's nothing to be done beyond that.

FIGURE 14.8
Available printer ports

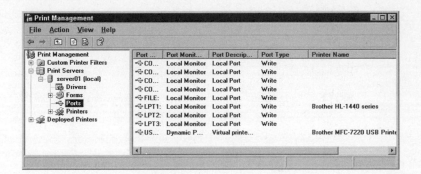

Viewing Forms

The forms on a server show the various print layouts the installed printers can support (see Figure 14.9). The forms are shown on a per-server basis, not a per-printer basis.

If you right-click the Forms folder and choose Manage Folders, you'll open the printer server properties to the Forms tab that's part of server properties, where you can create custom forms.

FIGURE 14.9
Form settings are shown on a per-server basis.

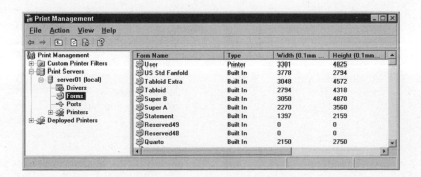

Monitoring Print Job Status and Creating Alerts

The meat of printer management isn't just about installing and configuring printers and viewing their settings but about being proactive about problems. The new PMC makes it easier to catch potential problems such as offline printers, paper jams, or very long print queues *before* someone's calling the Help Desk.

Monitoring Printers and Job Status

If you've got only one printer—or even only one print server—then keeping tabs on its status is pretty straightforward. Right-click the print server's icon and choose Extended View to open the Jobs area in the bottom half of the PMC's right-hand pane. In the top part of the pane, you can see the number of jobs in the queue for a particular printer, its queue status, and its server name. To get more information about the printers attached to a print server, you can add more views. For example, I want to know a printer's share name and its location so it's easier for me to go add more toner and troubleshoot printer-related Help Desk calls.

Right-click the Printers icon and choose View ➤ Add/Remove Columns just as you did for editing the view of the Driver folder. This time, the options will be slightly different from the ones for Drivers (see Figure 14.10).

Again, when you click the OK button the view will change to reflect the columns you added or deleted. You can always revert to the defaults with the Restore Defaults button visible in Figure 14.10 Editing this view will also set the view for the Custom Filters, and vice versa.

NOTE You can also edit the visible columns for ports and forms but only to streamline the view. Only Printers has much in the way of additional information.

You can send email from this console to let the intern in charge of adding more paper to a printer know that they need to hotfoot it to the printer on the third floor, or a "try again" message to the user whose huge print job you cancelled so the CEO could print a one-page memo. To do so, right-click the icon for the print server hosting the printer in question and choose Set Notifications to open the dialog box in Figure 14.11.

Using Custom Filters

Keeping tabs on a single printer or print server is fairly simple. Where problem notification *really* shines is in the Custom Filters section, where you can use that Notifications feature to email people or run scripts in response to events. In this section, we'll talk about how to use the existing filters and edit them to meet your requirements, as well as how to create new filters and make sure they work.

FIGURE 14.10
You can add more details to the list of printers for a print server.

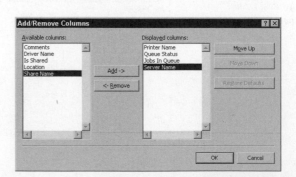

FIGURE 14.11
Email the office intern to add more paper to the printer.

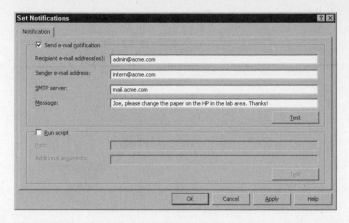

Open the Custom Filters folder, and you'll see three built-in options: All Printers, Printers Not Ready, and Printers with Jobs. (The contents of each of these filters is left as an exercise for the reader.) All three options normally display the printer name, the queue status, the number of jobs in its queue, and the server name. Again—you can add more columns here as you can for the printers listed for each print server managed from the PMC, and the settings here will apply also to printers listed on a per-server basis in the rest of the PMC.

EDITING EXISTING FILTERS

As it stands, the default filters just list the printers, not taking any action if a printer appears on a filter. You may want to edit this to run a script to record the usage when a user starts a print job, or to email a printer administrator if the printer shows up on the Not Ready List. To do so, right-click an existing filter and open its properties and turn to Notifications to open the dialog box in Figure 14.12.

You can also edit the filter's name and view the command-line filter description from the General tab or the contents of the filter from the Filter Criteria tab. We'll look at the latter in more detail in the next section on making your own filters.

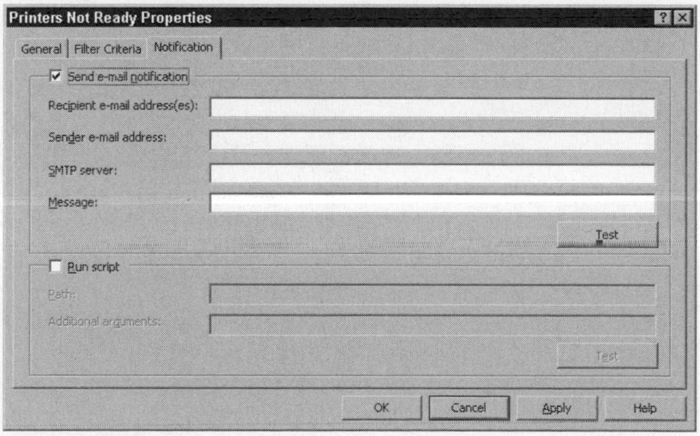

FIGURE 14.12
You can send email or run a script when a printer shows up in a new filter.

MAKING NEW FILTERS

The process of making a new filter is very simple in terms of what you need to accomplish: name the filter, select the criteria to apply to it, and you're off. That's just clicking. Getting the criteria right and ensuring that the filter works as expected may be slightly less easy.

To create a new filter, right-click the Custom Printer Filters icon and choose Add New Printer Filter from the context menu to open the dialog box in Figure 14.13.

First, choose a new name and description for the printer filter that reflects the filter's role, such as Paper Out to reflect that condition. Click Next to move to the screen in Figure 14.14, where you can create queries against printer name and condition for the filter. You can specify up to three fields and conditions to test for, described with possible applications in Table 14.1. Where a condition is either/or (such as Is Exactly versus Is Not Exactly), I put the (not) parentheses to indicate that there are two opposing options.

NOTE Is Not Exactly translates to "Is Exactly Not," not "May or May Not Be." For example, if the filter is Queue Status Is Exactly Not Paper Jam, then only printers without a paper jam will show up in that filter, not all printers that may have a printer jam or may not. (For the Venn Diagram-minded, it's a NOT statement, not an OR statement.)

FIGURE 14.13
Creating a new printer filter

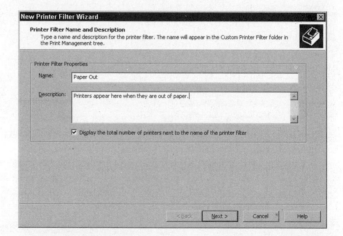

FIGURE 14.14
Defining the criteria for the filter

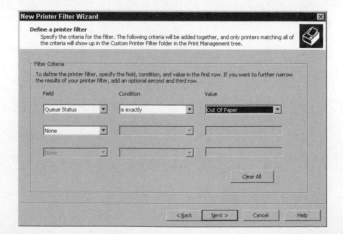

TABLE 14.1:   Available Filter Criteria

FIELD	CONDITIONS	SAMPLE VALUES	FUNCTION
Printer Name	Is (not) exactly; (not) begins with; (not) ends with; (not) contains	Printer name	Filters to a specific printer. Would likely be combined with other filter criteria to apply them only to a single printer.
Queue Status	Is (not) exactly	Ready; paused; error; deleting; paper jam; out of paper; not available; waiting; processing; initializing; warming up; toner low; processing; no toner; page punt; user intervention required; out of memory; door open	Check the queue status for a specific error condition or generally whether there are any errors at all.
Jobs in Queue	Is (not) exactly; is less than (or equal to); is greater than (or equal to).	Any numeric value that makes sense to you	Report when the queue has too many jobs in it to function well. What that number is depends on your experience in your office, but too many jobs can slow down user productivity.
Server Name	Is (not) exactly; (not) begins with; (not) ends with; (not) contains	The name of the print server	Filters to a specific server. Would likely be combined with other filter criteria to apply them only to a single server's printers.
Comments	Is (not) exactly; (not) begins with; (not) ends with; (not) contains	The comments applied to the printer	Further information about the printer, such as whether it's a multi-function device, to help you identify it.
Driver Name	Is (not) exactly; (not) begins with; (not) ends with; (not) contains	The name of the driver	Offhand, I don't see much purpose in filtering for drivers unless you are testing to see whether a new driver is apt to lead to other problems. This criterion would likely be combined with others.

TABLE 14.1: Available Filter Criteria *(CONTINUED)*

FIELD	CONDITIONS	SAMPLE VALUES	FUNCTION
Is Shared	Is (not) exactly	Yes or no	Filter would display only shared printers so you didn't have to concern yourself with printers used only locally.
Location	Is (not) exactly; (not) begins with; (not) ends with; (not) contains	The location of the printer	Like the comments, this filter would help you narrow down which printer you were talking about. This filter would also enable multiple administrators to divide responsibilities by physical location.
Share Name	Is (not) exactly; (not) begins with; (not) ends with; (not) contains	The share name of the printer	Filters to a specific printer. Would likely be combined with other filter criteria to apply them only to a single printer.

The last stage of creating a new filter is to (optionally) add notifications when the conditions of the filter are met. Here's where you can run a script to send messages to all printer users that a printer's queue has exceeded five jobs—"please try another printer"—or email that hapless intern that three new printers have joined the Paper Out list. When you've configured these settings, click OK, and the filter will begin working immediately.

Wait a minute! I created a filter and the printer doesn't show up even when it meets the stated criteria! Why not?

Not all printers will support reporting specific errors. To test, you can connect to a printer with a known error condition (a printer out of paper is easy to reproduce) and create a filter that addresses that error condition. Click the Apply button and see if the printer shows up in the filter. If it doesn't, then try Queue Status ➤ Is Exactly ➤ Error to see if the printer shows up then. If it does, then your printer is capable of saying that something is wrong, even if not specifically what.

Managing Printer Queues from the PMC

One of the built-in custom filters in the PMC (yes, that's a bit of an oxymoron; we'll let it slide) is Printers with Jobs. As you would expect, this filter displays all printers that currently have jobs, the number of jobs, and (if you've enabled Extended View) the jobs themselves when you select the printer in question. See Figure 14.15 for one example.

FIGURE 14.15

A printer's queue

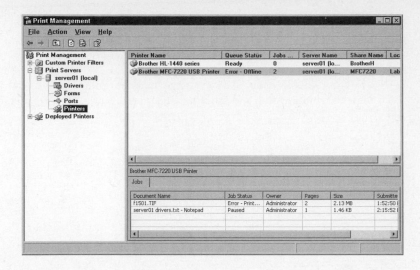

NOTE If you're not using Extended View, you can right-click a printer's name and choose to open its print queue.

From here, you can pause, resume, delete, or view the properties for a print job as you would from the printer's properties in Printers and Faxes.

Adding Remote Print Servers to the PMC

Everything we've described so far works not only on the local print server but on remote print servers as well (although you don't get the complete experience on print servers not running R2). To add a new print server to the console, right-click the Print Servers icon and choose Add/Remove Print Server from the context menu to open the dialog box in Figure 14.16.

The Browse button allows you to browse the network but unfortunately doesn't do anything nifty like include a filter to display only servers with the Print Server role installed. When you've connected to the new print server, it will show up in the Print Servers section of the PMC.

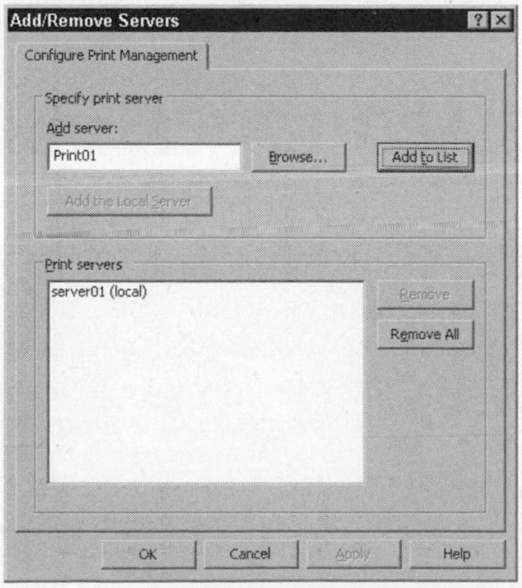

FIGURE 14.16

Adding a new
print server

Summary

Some of the tools that the PMC exposes aren't new—they're just a more convenient way to get to the printer server properties or to the Add Printer Wizard without having to bounce back and forth between tools. Generally, though, the PMC makes Windows print serving more enterprise-ready by consolidating tools, allowing you to manage multiple print servers from a single location, and enabling notification and scripting when certain conditions are met for a printer.

Chapter 15

Watching Your Disks with Storage Reports Management

You recently installed a new file server with four 500GB (2TB) hard drives to find that 4 months later you only have 300MB left. How could that be possible? Maybe the better question is, who or what is using all of the hard drive space? Have you ever had to determine which user is storing hundreds of gigs of data, only to find that the data being stored is not work related at all? Well, help's on the way: Windows Server 2003 R2 has a new suite of tools designed to help administrators monitor and control the amount and types of data that their users store.

That new suite of tools is called File Server Resource Manager (FSRM). In this chapter, we will begin our exploration of FSRM with the Storage Reports Manager (SRM) tool. SRM lets you create eight different kinds of reports that can gather a plethora of information based on exactly what you are looking for.

Installing File Server Resource Manager

Before we can look at the Storage Reports Manager, you need to first install FSRM.

WARNING   By the way, before we get started let me warn you—you will have to reboot the server to install FSRM. If rebooting your server is an issue in your environment, you may need to plan a time to install FSRM when it won't affect your users.

You will need your Windows Server 2003 R2 Operating System CD (disc 2), so make sure you have it handy.

To install FSRM, open Control Panel ➤ Add or Remove Programs ➤ Windows Components. Click Management and Monitoring Tools and then click the Details button, and you'll see the dialog box shown in Figure 15.1.

Check the box next to File Server Resource Manager and click OK.

NOTE   The component above File Server Resource Manager, File Server Management, also installs FSRM, but in addition to FSRM you get the Shared Folder Management and Disk and Volume Management snap-ins. In order to keep things simple, we will focus on installing only FSRM.

FIGURE 15.1
Details view of
Management and
Monitoring Tools

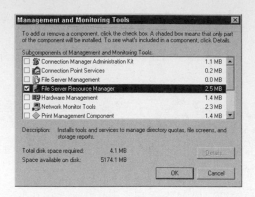

If you are prompted to insert the Windows Server 2003 R2 disc 2, insert it. Now, FSRM needs the .NET Framework 2.0 to run, so if you don't have it installed yet, FSRM will install the .NET Framework 2.0 for you. Unfortunately, that will add about 15 minutes or so to the installation process. The .NET Framework 2.0 took so long for me to install, I kept thinking my system was hung, but it wasn't; so be patient, go get that cup of coffee and relax.

TIP In fact, make it a *big* cup of coffee, because here is that reboot I warned you about earlier.

The installation of FSRM actually installs four new services, two of which are kernel-mode-minifilter file system drivers and must be placed in the correct location in the I/O stack. In fact, the placement of these two services in the I/O stack is the reason you have to reboot. The two kernel-mode-minifilter file system drivers are the DataScrn.sys and Quota.sys. The DataScrn.sys is responsible for implementing file screening checks in real time, and Quota.sys, as you've probably guessed, allows you to implement quota checks in real time. The other two services can be seen in the services applet in Computer Management. The File Server Resource Manager Service is Srmsvc.dll and runs as svchost.exe. The File Server Storage Reports Manager Service is srmhost.exe.

NOTE If you would like to manage FSRM from an XP SP2 workstation, you may install the FSRM snap-in by installing the Windows Server 2003 R2 AdminPak.

You will also have a new snap-in called File Server Resource Manager (fsrm.msc) under your Administrative Tools. To open FSRM, click Start ➤Administrative Tools ➤File Server Resource Manager, and you will see a screen similar to Figure 15.2.

We will be working with the Storage Reports Management item. If you highlight Storage Reports Management, you will notice the Actions menu in the Action Pane (far right). There are three actions you can perform:

◆ Schedule a New Report Task

◆ Add or Remove Reports for a Report Task

◆ Generate Reports Now

TIP There is also a Refresh option, but that simply refreshes the screen.

FIGURE 15.2

File Server Resource Manager Opening Screen

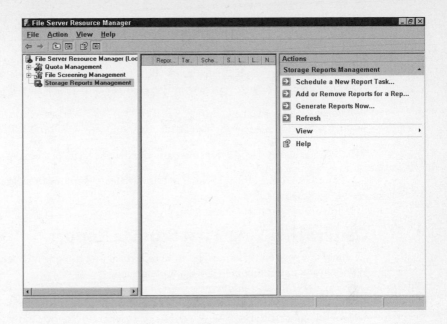

Configuring File Server Resource Manager to Email Reports

Before we get started with the reports, let's see how to configure the File Server Resource Manager to email reports to you. This comes in handy when you schedule reports to run and would like to have them emailed to you and whomever else you choose.

To introduce FSRM to your SMTP server, right-click File Server Resource Manager and select Configure Options; you will see a dialog box similar to Figure 15.3.

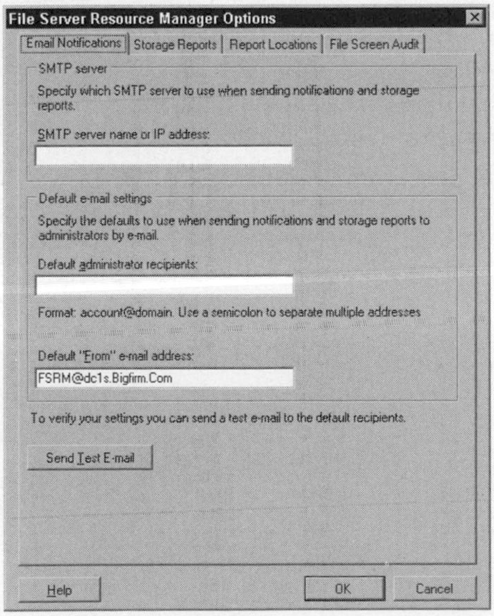

FIGURE 15.3

Configuring FSRM's SMTP server

The Email Notifications tab is where you input the SMTP's server name or IP address. The email address you would like to send the reports to goes in the default administrator Recipients box.

TIP If you would like to send reports to multiple administrators, separate the email addresses with a semicolon. For example, both Christa and Darren have email addresses at Bigfirm.Com and need reports emailed to them, so you would type **Christa@Bigfirm.Com;Darren@Bigfirm.com**.

The Default From email address is FSRM@*machineDNSname*. From a machine named dc1s in the Bigfirm.Com domain, the default From email address would be FSRM@dc1s.Bigfirm.Com

TIP This is nice! To send a test email, simply click the Send Test email button.

We will get to the other tabs later in this chapter, except for the File Screen Audit tab…that's covered in the next chapter.

Generating Your First Storage Report

At this point, you could look at the eight reports or just run one and see what you get. Let's run one! We will look at the others in just a couple of pages.

You can create an on-demand report manually by either right-clicking Storage Reports Management in the console pane (make sure SRM is highlighted first or you will just get Help) and then selecting Generate Reports Now, or selecting Generate Reports Now from the Actions menu. This will open a Storage Reports Task Properties dialog box that resembles Figure 15.4.

Notice there are two tabs, Settings and Delivery. On the Settings tab there are three distinct areas of the dialog box: Scope, Report data, and Report formats. The first step is to tell the report where to start reporting from by setting the Scope. Scope is the answer to the question, "Which storage area should I run this report on—a volume or a particular folder?" To set the scope, click the Add button and you will see a familiar Browse for Folder dialog box; from here you can select a volume or browse to a specific folder.

FIGURE 15.4
Storage Reports Task
Properties dialog box

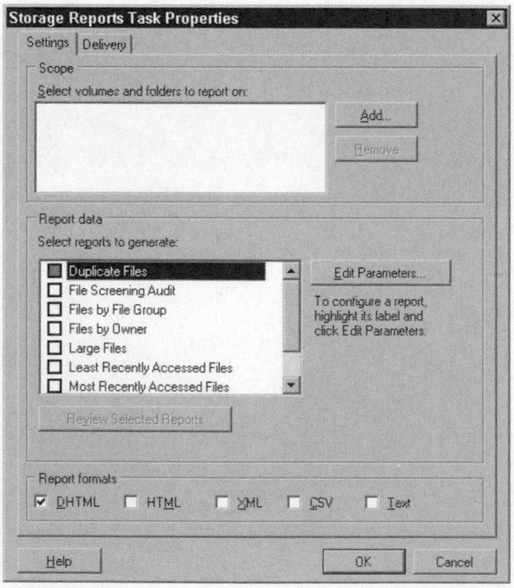

TIP   If you choose to browse to a specific folder, all of its subfolders will be included in the report.

The second step is to select one or more reports to run (remember, we will go into detail on the data gathered for each report later in this chapter). You are going to choose to run the Duplicate Files report, which will show you all files that have the same name, size, and last modified date/time stamp.

If you choose multiple reports, it is sometimes helpful to review the data to be gathered for each report by clicking the Review Selected Reports button. The third and final step is to choose the format you would like the report to be displayed or saved in. Your choices are DHTML, HTML, XML, CSV, or Text (and yes, you can choose more than one, but you still only get just one report...more on this later). In an effort to help keep things simple, leave your format set to the default DHTML. DHTML stands for dynamic HTML, which means display output as a web page.

Once you have set your scope, chosen the report data to be gathered, and selected the format, you can click OK. You will be prompted to choose how you would like to proceed—either Wait for reports to be generated and then display them (which is the default and the one we will choose), or Generate Reports in the Background. If you choose to generate reports in the background, they will be saved, or you can email the report output.

TIP   Remember, you can only email reports if you have previously configured File Server Resource Manager with an SMTP Server.

The Storage Reports Management console is easy to get around in, but what if you would like to script the same reports to be generated on multiple servers and do not want to go through the GUI on each server? `StorRept.exe` is the command line utility that will allow you to generate scheduled or on-demand storage reports, as well as list, add, modify, delete, and cancel existing reports from the command-line interface (cli).

To generate an on-demand duplicate files report with a scope beginning on your HF folder, which is on the E:\ volume (this is the folder where all your user's home folders reside), type the following:

```
StorRept Reports Generate /OnDemand /Report:DuplicateFiles /Scope:E:\HF
```

You should receive a "Storage reports run successfully" message. The StorRept help file is really very helpful; to find a listing of what the `StorRept.exe` is capable of type, **StorRept /?** at a command prompt. To find a list of available switches you can use when generating a storage report, simply type **Storrept Reports Generate /?**. The switches available at this level of the command are displayed and explained, including what data each switch will give you, and there are even some great examples. The help file reveals that you can actually set multiple scopes by separating them with the pipe (|) symbol, so if you want to run the previous duplicate files report and include the C:\ volume, you would type

```
StorRept Reports Generate /OnDemand /Report:DuplicateFiles /Scope:E:\HF|C:\
```

To create the same report to run nightly at midnight, you need to create a scheduled task from the Control Panel's Scheduled Tasks. Choose Add Scheduled Task to launch the Scheduled Task Wizard. Give the task a name such as DupRpt and, on the page that lists the programs you want Windows to run, browse to `C:\Windows\System32` and select `StorRept.exe`, then choose Daily and 12:00 A.M. and type in the username and password of the user account for which you would like this task to be run. On the Finish page, select Open the Advanced Properties for This Task

When I Click Finish. When the Advanced properties open, the Task tab is displayed. In the Run box, you will see C:\Windows\System32\StorRept.exe; type in the exact same command as before so the run box looks like this:

```
C:\Windows\System32\StorRept.exe Reports Generate /OnDemand /Report:
DuplicateFiles /Scope:E:\HF|C:\. Click OK.
```

Your task will now generate a duplicate files report every night at midnight. To run this report outside of the scheduled time, type the following:

```
Storrept Reports Generate /Scheduled /Task:DupRpt
```

(Remember, DupRpt is what you named the scheduled task.)

Report Output

Once you have generated a report, you'll have a good bit of data that has been gathered. I would love to show you an entire report, but most of these are too large to get on one piece of paper, so we will break the report into four sections: the Report Totals (which is a summary), Size By Owner, Size By File Group, and Report Details. Wait a second, what's a file group?

File groups are defined by the filename extensions so files can be grouped together by their type. Some examples are the Audio and Video Files file group, which contains 37 different file extensions, some of which are .avi, .mp3, and .wma. The Office Files file group contains .doc, .xml, and .dba extensions, among others. FSRM contains some default file groups. If you find the predefined file groups do not meet your needs, please refer to the "Customizing Your Reports" section later in this chapter.

Remember, you are going to run a report to show you all the duplicate files. What better place to run this report than on the storage location that contains your administrative tools for your network administrators? Most organizations have more than one network administrator. As network admins, we all need some pretty basic tools, but what happens if you have five network admins and each has their own copy of the same tools? Some tools are very small when it comes to storage space, but some are not so small (remember XP's Service Pack 2). Storage reports help you quickly determine how many copies there are of the same file.

Figure 15.5 shows the Report Totals section for the duplicate files report. The report identifies two duplicate groups. A "group" is made up of each of the duplicate files—that is, all the files with the same name form one group. In this report, two files have duplicates, forming two groups; there is a total of 10 files (including the original and duplicate files) within the two duplicate groups . The Total size on Disk is 344MB for all 10 files. The Wasted Space is 275MB for the duplicate files alone. Granted, this is not a huge amount of hard disk space, but you see how quickly this could become an issue.

FIGURE 15.5
Report Totals summary

Report Totals						
Files shown in the report			All files matching report criteria			
Duplicate Groups	Files	Total size on Disk	Duplicate Groups	Files	Total size on Disk	Wasted Space
2	10	344 MB	2	10	344 MB	275 MB

The second section, Size By Owner, displays each user and the amount of disk space they have used due to duplicate files. The data will be displayed in both a pie chart and a corresponding table, beginning with the users who have consumed the most space, as shown in Figure 15.6.

NOTE The size by owner calculation is based on users *only*, not groups. This is due to the fact that groups still cannot own files, except for the Administrators group.

The third section is Size By File Group and represents the amount of space utilized by particular file groups. This could help you quickly see if someone is storing a large number of audio and video files or Microsoft Office files. This data is also shown as both a pie chart and corresponding table displaying which file group has used the most amount of storage space due to duplicate files, as shown in Figure 15.7.

These reports are great for managers to take to meetings to request money for new hard drives or, in more extreme examples, new servers. Just don't tell them how easy it was to get them!

The last section is easily the largest for most reports: the detail section. You saw in the first section that you have two files that each have at least one duplicate. The detail section will show information on each of these files, listing the locations of all the duplicates for each group. To help keep things simple, we will only discuss one of the groups of duplicates, those files named XPSp2.cab.

FIGURE 15.6
Size By Owner

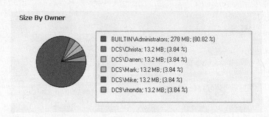

Size By Owner

- BUILTIN\Administrators; 278 MB; (80.82 %)
- DCS\Christa; 13.2 MB; (3.84 %)
- DCS\Darren; 13.2 MB; (3.84 %)
- DCS\Mark; 13.2 MB; (3.84 %)
- DCS\Mike; 13.2 MB; (3.84 %)
- DCS\rhonda; 13.2 MB; (3.84 %)

Size by Owner		
Owner	Total size on Disk	Files
BUILTIN\Administrators	278 MB	5
DCS\Christa	13.2 MB	1
DCS\Darren	13.2 MB	1
DCS\Mark	13.2 MB	1
DCS\Mike	13.2 MB	1
DCS\rhonda	13.2 MB	1

FIGURE 15.7
Size By File Group

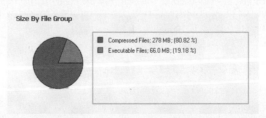

Size By File Group

- Compressed Files; 278 MB; (80.82 %)
- Executable Files; 66.0 MB; (19.18 %)

Size by File Group		
File Group	Total size on Disk	Files
Compressed Files	278 MB	5
Executable Files	66.0 MB	5

The File Count represents the number of duplicates and how much space is being used and wasted for each. If the File Count number is greater than 10, you will only get expanded information on the first 10 found, so don't be surprised if you get a larger number in the File Count box but still only see detailed information for 10 files. Probably the most useful piece of information here is when the files were last accessed; if it's been a while you may want to delete or archive the files. Figure 15.8 shows that there are five copies of XPSp2s.cab with a total of 278MB of space being used and that 223MB of the 278MB is considered wasted space. The individual file size of each is 55.6MB, so if you stored only one copy you would be using 55.6MB of space instead of 278MB.

FIGURE 15.8
File details

Duplicate Group				
File Count	Total size on Disk	Wasted Space	Single file size on disk	Last modified
5	278 MB	223 MB	55.6 MB	11/30/2005 8:00:00 AM

File name	Folder	Owner
	Last accessed	
XPSp2.cab	e:\Home folders\Christa	
	4/26/2006 8:43:47 AM	BUILTIN\Administrators
XPSp2.cab	e:\Home folders\Mark	
	4/26/2006 8:44:20 AM	BUILTIN\Administrators
XPSp2.cab	e:\Home folders\Darren	
	4/26/2006 8:44:07 AM	BUILTIN\Administrators
XPSp2.cab	e:\Home folders\Mike	
	4/26/2006 8:44:46 AM	BUILTIN\Administrators
XPSp2.cab	e:\Home folders\Rhonda	
	4/26/2006 8:44:30 AM	BUILTIN\Administrators

Report Formats

You also may have noticed the report format choices. Whenever you run an on-demand report, the default format is to display the results in DHTML. As mentioned previously, there are four other formats you can choose in which to have your data displayed: HTML, XML, CSV, or Text. While you might think you could have the same report data displayed in all five formats, that's not true when you create *on-demand* reports. Whichever report type from the furthest left is selected is the format your *one* report will be displayed in. So, if I selected all five report formats and ran an on-demand report, I would get one report in the DHTML format. If I choose XML and Text, I would get one report in the XML format, and there would be no Text report generated. This occurs only when you run on-demand reports, *not* scheduled reports (more on this in the section "Scheduling Reports to Run").

Let's Meet the Other Reports

There are eight different reports that can be run once or scheduled to run at defined intervals (you as the administrator define these intervals—more on that later). Most of these reports tell you what type of data they gather based on the report name. There is one, however, that may need a little explanation, and that is the File Screening Audit report.

For the File Screening Audit report, there are two steps. First, you must create a file screen (creating a file screen is covered in detail in Chapter 16). A file screen can be either active or passive, which means the file screen can either block users from storing data or allow storage but track which users are violating company policy.

The following table lists the eight reports available and the type of data gathered for each:

Report Name	Data Gathered
Duplicate Files	Files with the same name, size, and last modified date/time stamp
File Screening Audit	Users who violate file screens
Files by File Group	Which file groups are using the most disk space
Files by Owner	Which owner is using the most disk space
Large Files	Which files are over a specific size
Least Recently Accessed Files	Files that have not been used in the last 90 (or whatever number you choose) days, so you may archive or delete them to reclaim used disk space
Most Recently Accessed Files	Files that are accessed most often so you can determine the best method to make them available to your users
Quota Usage	Which users are getting close to exceeding their quota limits (which you have set—everything you would ever want to know about quotas is in the next chapter) so you may take the appropriate action

Scheduling Reports to Run

Up to this point, we have discussed running reports interactively. Wouldn't it be nice to run reports every Sunday night and email the report data to yourself (and whomever else you choose), so when you come in on Monday you can glance through the data and know if there are issues that need to be addressed?

You can schedule one or several reports to run at a time. In fact, it is a good idea to schedule multiple reports to run at a time to help minimize the impact of report processing on the server while SRM gathers the data.

To schedule a report task to run, select Schedule a New Report Task, either under the Actions menu or by right-clicking the Storage Reports Management node. You will see the Storage Reports Tasks Properties dialog similar to Figure 15.9.

Notice there are three tabs. The first tab is the Settings tab. On the Settings tab you will need to set the Scope and select the reports to be generated and the formats you would like the data saved as.

NOTE Report formats are different for scheduled report tasks than for on-demand reports. If you choose more than one format, you will get a report generated for each format chosen.

On the Delivery tab, you can input email addresses to have the reports emailed to you or multiple email addresses by separating them with a semicolon.

FIGURE 15.9
Storage Reports
Task Properties

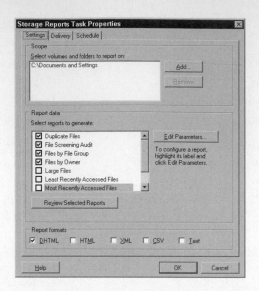

TIP You must have previously configured FSRM with an SMTP server before any emails may
be sent.

The third and final tab allows you to create the schedule you would like this task to run on. Click
the Create Schedule button to begin, then select the New button. You will notice the default schedule is to run the task daily at 9:00 a.m. You can schedule your reports to run pretty much whenever
you would like. Your options for scheduling a task to run are

◆ Daily

◆ Weekly

◆ Monthly

◆ Once

◆ At System Startup

◆ At Logon

◆ When Idle

Select the start time, and you have a newly scheduled task. If these settings are not flexible
enough for you, there are advanced settings you may set by clicking the Advanced button, shown
in Figure 15.10.

Now that you have created a scheduled report task, you may view the current status of the
report (queued, running, or completed), the last time the report ran, and the next scheduled run
time by highlighting your scheduled report in the middle pane of Storage Reports Management.

If you would like to quickly add or remove a report to or from a scheduled report task, highlight
the scheduled report task and select Add or Remove Reports for a Report Task by right-clicking
Storage Reports Management on the console pane or from the Actions menu.

Figure 15.10
Advanced Schedule
Options

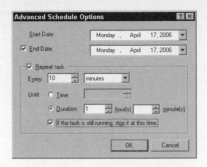

NOTE You will not be able to change the scope or the schedule through the Add or Remove Reports for a Report Task. You will only be allowed to add or remove reports from the scheduled report task.

If you would like to add or remove reports and edit the scope or the schedule, select View/Modify Report Tasks Properties either by right-clicking the scheduled report task itself (in the middle pane) or choosing the same on the Action menu under Selected Storage reports.

Finding Saved Reports

You have been working with reports that are generated and displayed immediately, but there is an additional option to schedule the report and save it to be viewed later. Okay, so you have saved a report and would like to view it. Where did Windows put it?

Based on the type of report, there are three default storage locations, and all are subfolders to `%systemdrive%\StorageReports`. The incident reports are stored in the `Incident` folder (that makes sense). An incident report is generated when a specific incident occurs, such as a user exceeding their disk quota or violating a file screen.The scheduled reports are stored in the `Scheduled` folder (wow, that makes sense, too), and the reports run on-demand are stored in the `Interactive` folder (and we were doing so well).

To edit the default locations, right-click File Server Resource Management, choose Configure Options, and go to the Report Locations tab. Here you will see the three default paths. If you choose to edit the default storage location, all new reports generated will be stored in the new location. The existing reports must be moved manually.

NOTE Before you edit the default Report Locations, you must first create the folder path to store the reports in.

You know where they are, but how do you open one? If you saved the report in DHTML or HTML, there will be a new folder in the `StorageReports` folder. This new folder will be named by the type of report run and the date/time it was run. For example, if you ran a duplicate files report on 4/29/2006 at 2:30 p.m., the folder name would be `DuplicateFiles##_2006-04-29_14-30-00_files`. There will also be a corresponding HTML file for DHTML, or an HTM file for an HTML report named `DuplicateFiles##_2006_04_29_14-30-00_html` (notice the only difference in the folder/file name is the extension). The folder contains the images to be displayed for the report. The file contains the instructions to display the report, calling for the images.

Once you have a large number of reports stored, all the folders will be displayed first, so you may have to *scroll down* to the HTM or HTML file to display the entire report.

NOTE   Be cautious when scheduling reports to run because storing the reports takes space, right? If you scheduled reports to run but no longer need the data gathered by the report, delete the scheduled task to prevent eating up all your hard drive space.

Customizing Your Reports

Now that you know what information the default reports can give you, let us look at what you can customize about each report. The following table shows just that.

Name of Report	Configurable Parameters
Duplicate Files	No configurable parameters
File Screening Audit	Minimum days since file screening event occurred
	All users or a specific set of users
Files by File Group	Which file extensions belong to which file group, or create new file groups
File by Owner	All users or a specific set of users
Large Files	Size and type of file by extension
Least Recently Accessed	The number of days since the file was last accessed
Most Recently Accessed	The number of days since the file was last accessed
Quota Usage	Administratively defined percentage of disk space used based on the quota set

Problems Customizing Reports

Editing the default report parameters can be tricky…*please proceed with caution*. The report parameters may be edited by either right-clicking File Server Resource Manager and selecting Configure Options ➢ Storage Reports tab, or when selecting the reports to run, highlight the report and click the Edit Parameters button. Please keep in mind when you edit a report parameter that the report parameter is changed for *all* reports, not just the one you are currently working on.

Let's look at editing a file group. You have scheduled a Duplicate Files report to run every Sunday evening. You now know the report gives you a totals summary, files by owner, and files by file group, as well as the details of the report. Two months after you have created the schedule, you edit the Audio and Video Files file group by removing the .mp3 extension. From this point forward, any report (even the scheduled report created two months ago) that reports on duplicate files by file group will no longer consider files with the .mp3 extension to be in the Audio and Video Files file group.

So if you need a specific file group, it's probably a good idea to create a new custom file group.

Deleting Scheduled Report Tasks

To delete a scheduled report task, you may highlight the report and press the Delete key or select Delete Report Tasks from the Actions menu. If the scheduled report task is currently running when you attempt to delete the task, the report task will complete before it is deleted.

Summary

Of course, no one likes rebooting production servers, but I think the benefits of installing and using FSRM far outweigh the time consuming task you will endure when one of your servers runs out of hard drive space and it is up to you to determine why. Anyone who has ever taken on this daunting task knows of what I speak.

Storage reports can help you stay one step ahead of your users by allowing you to keep an eye on the type and amount of data being stored on your servers. This gives you time to address storage space issues before your users are affected—you can order that new hard drive *before* your server runs out of storage space! Also, knowing that 45 of your users are storing the 100MB company policy and procedure manual in their home folder may prompt you to place a copy of the company policy and procedure manual in a shared folder accessible to your users. What about those files that have not been opened in the last 90, 120, or 180 days? It may be safe to archive these files to help free up some storage space.

We have covered how to create reports to help you monitor your storage space, but what if you would like to *control* what is actually stored on your servers? In the next chapter, we will continue discussing FSRM and address in detail Quota Management and File Screening Management.

Chapter 16

Controlling Folder Usage: Quotas and File Screens

In the last chapter you learned how to install File Server Resource Manager (FSRM). FSRM is a suite of tools that allows administrators to have much more control over how much data your users store and the type of data being stored on your servers. In this chapter, we are going to continue our journey through FSRM; more specifically, we will take a look at the new Quota Management and File Screen tools.

Quota Management empowers administrators by letting them control the *amount* of data their users store on a volume or in a folder. Sound familiar? It might, if you have ever used NTFS volume quotas. NTFS volume quotas have been around since Windows Server 2000, but as you will soon see, FSRM's Quota Management feature set is much more flexible and robust.

File Screens allow administrators to control the *type* of files that your users store, and takes it one step further by allowing you to block certain types of files from being stored on your servers. You may choose not to actually block the file types from being stored, but would like to track which users are storing data that your company has deemed unacceptable (according to the company's "Acceptable Use Policy" or AUP). For example, if you're not in the music industry, MP3s may not be considered by the company to be work related. File Screens would permit you to track users who violate the company's AUP and ultimately consume much more storage space than necessary.

Quota Management

Quotas in FSRM allow you to control and monitor the amount of storage space on a volume or folder. There are two types of quotas that can be set, hard or soft. A hard quota prevents users from saving files after the quota limit is reached. A soft quota allows the user to continue storing data even after the quota limit has been reached but can be configured to perform an action such as sending an email to the user and possibly the administrator, notifying them that the quota limit has been exceeded. With a soft quota, the user can continue to work but be aware of the fact that she has exceeded her allotted disk space. Now, most users would stop what they are doing immediately and delete their old files, being cognizant of their coworkers and the fact that they need storage space as well. Are you done laughing? Okay, maybe you should also send an email to the administrator to let them know Meghan (for the twelfth time this month) has exceeded her quota limit. Whether you set hard or soft quotas, you can configure one or more actions to be performed by FSRM. Dirquota.exe is the command-line equivalent to FSRM and can be run on the local machine or remotely. In fact, I think it is safe to say, "Anything FSRM can do, Dirquota.exe can do better." Okay, maybe not better, but just as well. There are even some things Dirquota.exe can do that FSRM cannot, and these are covered at the end of this section.

Let's take a small, 50-user company called Bigfirm. You, as the network administrator, are responsible for ensuring that each user gets 200MB of storage space in their home folder on Server1, and no more. The users should receive an email notifying them when they have reached 85% of the 200MB limit (170MB), another email notifying them when they have reach 95% of the 200MB limit (190MB), and to help the administrators keep track of storage space, you would also like an event generated in the Application event log on Server1 at the 95% usage level. When the users reach their 100% limit of 200MB, an email should be sent to the user who has exceeded their quota, as well as the administrator, and an event should be generated in the Application event log on Server1.

NOTE   Vocabulary: In the preceding scenario, 200MB is the *space limit* (the space limit is calculated on the files physical file size, if a file is compressed—the compressed size is reflected, this is different that NTFS volume quotas which do not take compression sizes into account—with NTFS volume quotas all file sizes are based on their logical or uncompressed size even when compressed), and 85%, 95% and 100% are *Notification thresholds* (the storage level at which you want FSRM to notify users that they are running low on space). Generating emails or an event in the Application Log are the *actions* that should be taken when a Notification threshold has been reached.

So you decide to set the quotas via NTFS volume quotas (if you need a refresher on how to set the NTFS volume quotas, please refer to the *Mastering Windows Server 2003* book), but the first problem you run into is that whoever installed the OS onto Server1 left the C drive (which is the only drive) as one great big volume. You set the quota to allow each user to have 200MB of storage space on C—but where on C? Okay, you set the security permissions so that the only folders the users have access to are their own home folders. That is one way to do it, but what if you want to allow users to store data in more than one folder on that server? NTFS volume quotas only allowed you to control the amount of storage space a user received on an entire volume only, not a folder. And how do you set up email notifications? The answer to these questions are just a couple of the nice new features of File Server Resource Manager–Quota Management, and there is much more. You decide to disable the old NTFS volume quota and use FSRM–Quotas instead. Good decision!

WARNING   Be careful if you are using both NTFS and FSRM quotas: whichever one is more limiting is the one that will win!

Creating a Quota

Currently at Bigfirm Corporation, your users' home folders are on Server1 in a shared folder called Home Folders on the E volume, which is formatted as NTFS (Quotas are only available on NTFS volumes). There are no storage limits set, and you keep running out of storage space. With the new File Server Resource Manager (FSRM), you have the ability to set a quota limiting the amount of storage space each user receives. The new company policy states the amount of storage space each user should have is 200MB in their home folder, and any new users in the future should receive the same 200MB quota limit automatically. So let's dive right in and create a quota.

To launch FSRM, click the Start button, highlight Administrative Tools, and select File Server Resource Manager. Within the FSRM Snap-in, expand Quota Management and you will see two nodes, Quotas and Quota Templates, as shown in Figure 16.1.

To create a quota, highlight Quotas, then, right-click Quotas in the console tree (if you do not highlight Quotas prior to right-clicking Quotas "Help" will be your only option on the menu), and select Create Quota, or select Create Quota from the Actions menu (on the left). Either way you choose to get there, you will see the Create Quota dialog box in Figure 16.2.

FIGURE 16.1
FSRM–Quota
Management

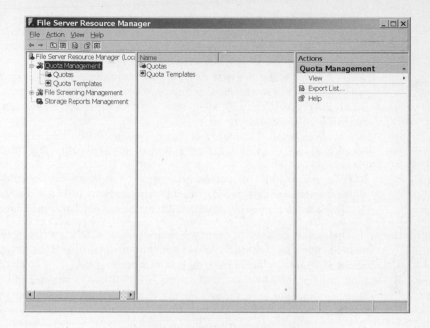

FIGURE 16.2
Create Quota
dialog box

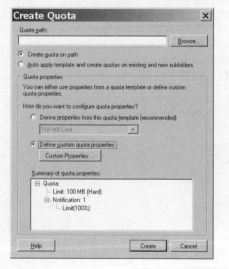

The Quota path defines *where* the quota will be applied. You can apply quotas to a volume or folder. Browse to the volume/folder (my favorite—less rooooom for error), or type the *complete* path E:\Home folders (which contains Bigfirms 50 users' home folders—to keep things simple we will focus on only two, Meghan and Wendy). Next, notice the two settings beneath Quota Path: Create Quota on Path and Auto Apply Template and Create Quotas on Existing and New Sub-folders. If you choose Create Quota on Path and set your Space limit to 200MB, the result might not be what you expected—it certainly was not what I expected. I assumed that every user's home folder beneath the E:\Home Folders folder would be allocated 200MB of storage space, but I was wrong. The 200MB quota limit is applied to the entire subtree, not each individual subfolder. The amount of data stored in the Home Folders folder and all subfolders *combined* can only be 200MB, and did you notice we never typed in a user's name right? That is because the quota limit pertains to all users, or anyone who has write access to the folder.

Wait a second, so you're saying that if Wendy stores 150MB of data in her subfolder, Meghan only gets 50MB of storage space? Yep, that's what I am saying. Hmm, not exactly what I wanted. So, how do I give Wendy 200MB of storage space in her home folder and Meghan 200MB of storage space in her home folder?

The Auto Apply Template and Create Quotas on Existing and New Subfolders option, that's how. Go ahead, you can look back at Figure 16.2 again, I'll wait). Okay, ready?

NOTE   A *template* is a set of predefined properties for a quota, including the space limit, type of quota (hard or soft), and the type of notification you want given when a user reaches a particular threshold— Templates are covered in greater detail in the Quota Template section later in this chapter.

This option applies the template settings individually to existing subfolders and any newly created subfolders within the quota path automatically but does not apply a quota to the top level folder E:\Home Folders. Hey, that sounds pretty good. So, if you had chosen Auto Apply Template and Create Quotas on Existing and New Subfolders, and selected the 200MB Limit Reports to User template (for now, please take my word for it, this is the template you want) from the drop-down list, when you click Create and apply your quota to the E:\Home Folders folder, both Wendy and Meghan's home folders receive a 200MB quota set individually on their home folder. Now, *that's* what we wanted. Better yet, when a new user is hired, their home folder will automatically receive a 200MB quota applied directly, no muss, no fuss, no administrative overhead. Come on now, that's pretty cool!

Let's create a custom quota , so we can walk through all the properties. Within the FSRM snap-in highlight Quotas, right-click Quotas and choose Create Quota. For the Quota path I am choosing E:\Home Folders. Where you see the question, "How do you want to configure quota properties?" select Define Custom Quota Properties and click the Custom Properties button. You will see the Quota Properties of E:\Home Folders dialog box, as shown in Figure 16.3.

FIGURE 16.3
Quota Properties
dialog box

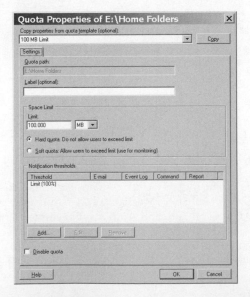

In the middle of the Quota Properties dialog box, under Space Limit, set the limit to 200MB and select Hard Quota. At the bottom of the dialog box, there is a section called Notification thresholds; by default there aren't any configured. What exactly is a Notification threshold, and what can you do with them? Well, really, quite a bit—notification thresholds are one of the reasons FSRM quotas are so much more flexible than NTFS volume quotas. In fact, there is so much you can do with them, they really deserve their own section.

NOTIFICATION THRESHOLDS AND ACTIONS

To find out what you can do with notification thresholds, on the Quota Properties dialog box (Figure 16.3), under Notification thresholds click the Add button. Figure 16.4 shows the Add Threshold dialog box. The first parameter is Generate Notifications When Usage Reaches (%). This is the threshold, and the threshold defines what *percentage* of the quota limit has been used. You could set one threshold at 70% of a quota limit, one at 85%, and another at 100%, with each threshold configured for a different set of actions to occur . There are four different actions you can configure using the four tabs in the Add Threshold dialog box: email to be sent, a warning event generated in the Application event log on the local server, a command or script to be run, or a storage report to be generated (Chapter 15 covers storage reports in detail). So, at 70%, you may choose to send an email to the user, notifying them that they have used 70% of their allocated storage space; at 85%, you may choose to send an email to the user and generate an event in the Application event log; at 100%, you could send an email to the user and the network administrator and generate an event in the Application event log. Let's look at each type of notification and how you configure them.

TIP Remember, before you can set the email options, you must first configure FSRM with the name or IP address of your SMTP server (please see Chapter 15 for details).

FIGURE 16.4
Add Threshold
dialog box

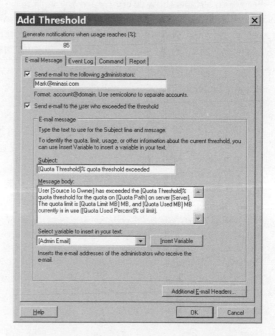

Placing a check mark in the Send email to the Following Administrators check box allows you to input the email address of an administrator or a list of administrators (separate the email addresses by a semicolon) that you would like to notify when a threshold has been exceeded. The second box, Send email to the User Who Exceeded the Threshold, will do exactly what it says: send an email to the user who performed the last I/O call that exceeded the threshold set by the administrator. Okay, but how does FSRM know the email address of the user who exceeded the threshold?

NOTE FSRM performs an LDAP query to a domain controller (DC) requesting the email address from Active Directory (AD) for the Security Identifier (SID) of the user who exceeded the quota limit. The email field in the AD properties of the user must be populated for this feature to work properly, and the server running FSRM must be able to send and receive LDAP queries to and from a DC, even if it entails traversing a firewall.

The email a user or administrator receives will be similar to the following:

```
Subject: Quota limit exceeded
User BIGFIRM\Wendy has reached the quota limit for quota on E:\Home Folders on
server Server1. The quota limit is 100.00MB and the current usage is 91.23MB (91%
of limit).
```

Or you could customize the subject line and Message body for the email that is sent. In fact this is really nice, you could compose a subject line and message that is different for each notification threshold that is exceeded. For example, you could configure an email to be sent to a user when they have exceeded 85% of their allotted storage space simply notifying them that they are about to run out of space, and a more explicit email when they reach 100% of their storage allocation, explaining the steps to clean out their folder.

Figure 16.5 shows how to configure an event to be generated in the Application event log on the local server. Place a check mark in the box next to Send Warning to Event Log. If you would like to customize the text that is generated in the event, you may do so in this dialog box under Log entry.

The event that is generated will look something like this:

```
Event Type:Warning
Event Source:SRMSVC
Event Category:None
Event ID:12325
Date:5/21/2006
Time:5:22:11 PM
User:N/A
Computer:Server1
Description:
User Server1\Wendy has exceeded the 85% quota threshold for the quota on
E:\Wendys folder on server Server1. The quota limit is 100.00MB, and 86.46MB
currently is in use (86% of limit).
```

Figure 16.6 shows the Command tab, where you can input a command or script to run when a threshold is reached, along with any command line arguments, the working directory you would like the command to be run in, and the security context the command should run as Local Service, Network Service, or Local System.

FIGURE 16.5
Add Threshold–
Event Log tab

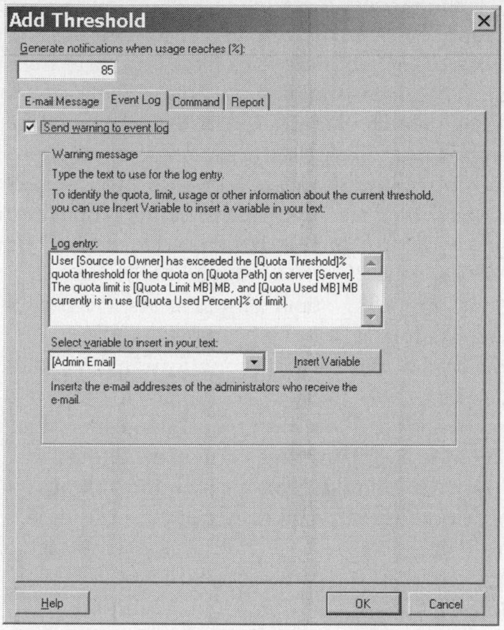

FIGURE 16.6
Add Threshold–
Command tab

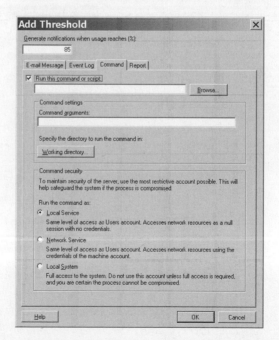

Figure 16.7 shows the Report tab. Chapter 15 covers in detail the eight storage reports and the information gathered by each. You can choose which storage reports to generate and which threshold will generate them. If you choose to generate storage reports, the storage report (by default) can

be found in the `%systemdrive%\Storage Reports\Incident` folder; you can also email the storage reports to the user who exceeded their threshold, an administrator, or both by placing a check mark in the appropriate box on the bottom of the Report tab. If you would like to send the reports to more than one administrator, use a semicolon to separate the administrators' email addresses.

On all notification thresholds there is a built-in 60-minute timing interval designed to prevent users and administrators from being overwhelmed with emails, events in the application log, commands being run repeatedly, or reports being generated unnecessarily. Each time a threshold is reached, whichever form of notification you have chosen will occur once in a 60-minute period. The only way I could find to edit this was to create a quota template, export the new template to an XML file, change the RunLimitInterval (here's the scary part), delete the quota, and re-import it. Exporting and importing quota templates are covered in the section titled "Exporting and Importing Quota Templates."

Once you have set which notification thresholds you would like to occur, on the Add Threshold dialog box, click OK, and you are back to the Quota Properties dialog box. Click OK again, and you are now back to the Create Quota dialog box; when you click Create, you are given the option to create a quota template based on the new quota properties you have just set, as shown in Figure 16.8. If you would like to create a new quota template simply give it a name and click OK, or you may choose not to create a quota template at this time. In fact, if you find this dialog box annoying, you can select Do Not Ask Me to Save as a Template Again (this will get rid of the dialog box for good). You may be asking yourself, "Why would I want to create a quota template?" The next section, Quota Templates, will answer this question.

FIGURE 16.7
Add Threshold–
Report tab

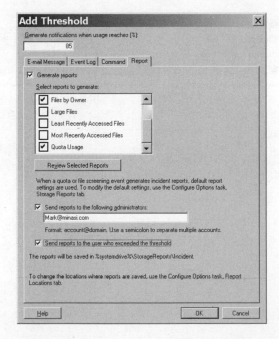

FIGURE 16.8
Save Custom Properties as a Template dialog box

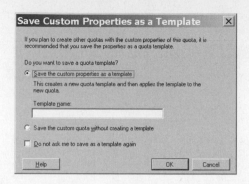

DISABLING AND ENABLING QUOTAS

If you are not quite ready to implement your new quota, you may choose to disable the quota by placing a check mark in the Disable quota box on the Quota Properties dialog box (bottom left corner of Figure 16.3), or right-click the quota and choose Disable Quota from the menu or highlight the quota and click Disable Quotas from the Actions menu. When you are ready to implement the quota, enable the quota by using one of the three methods used to disable the quota; remove the check mark from the quota properties, or right-click the quota and choose *Enable Quota,* or select it from the Actions menu.

Quota Templates

Creating quota templates allows you to create a quota that defines the quota limit, type, and notification thresholds once and apply them via the template to as many folders and servers as you choose. But wait, it gets better: after you have applied a template to multiple folders and you decide to edit the template settings, you can have all quotas based on this template updated automatically (this is optional). How cool is that? Not only do you have the ability to create your own templates, Microsoft has conveniently created six prebuilt templates that you can use or copy to create custom templates.

These prebuilt templates are a great place to start when building your own templates. Table 16.1 lists the six built-in templates, their limits, type, and threshold notification limits and actions. In an effort to keep this table simple, I have created some abbreviations:

W-1 = first warning (I'll bet you can guess what W-2, W-3, and W-4 are)

Limit = folder has reached 100% of the quota limit

Event = an event is generated in the Application event log

E-U = email user

E-A = email administrator

CMD = run a command

TABLE 16.1:   Prebuilt Quota Templates

TEMPLATE NAME	LIMIT	TYPE	W-1	W-2	W-3	LIMIT	W-4
100MB Limit	100MB	Hard	85% E-U	95% E-U Event		E-U E-A Event	
200MB Limit Reports to User	200MB	Hard	85% E-U	95% E-U Event		E-U E-A Event	
Monitor 200 GB Volume Usage	200GB	Soft	70% E-A	80% E-A	90% E-A Event	E-A Event	
Monitor 500MB Share	500MB	Soft	80% E-A	E-A 80%		E-A Event	120% E-A Event
200MB Limit with 50MB Extension	200MB	Hard	85% E-U	95% E-U Event		E-U E-A *CMD	
250MB Extended Limit	250MB	Hard	85% E-U	95% E-U Event		E-U E-A Event	

*CMD—runs a command that applies the 250MB Extended Limit quota template, extending the limit from 200MB to 250MB.

USING AND CREATING QUOTA TEMPLATES

I recommend using quota templates when creating quotas to help centralize the management of your quotas. There are two ways to create a quota based on a template. The first is to highlight Quotas under Quota Management in FSRM and then right-click Quotas and select Create Quota (you did this earlier), set your Quota path and then under "How Do You Want to Configure Quota Properties?" select Derive Quota Properties from This Quota Template, and choose the template you would like from the drop-down list. The second way is to find the template you would like to use from the Quota Templates node under Quota Management, right-click the template, and select Create Quota from Template. However you choose to create your quota based on a template, the template will fill in the quota limit, type, and notification thresholds for you.

Creating your own templates couldn't be easier, but there are a number of ways to create them. Under Quota Management, you can highlight the Quota Template node and then right-click Quota Template, or select Create Quota Template. Most of the fields should look familiar to you; just give the template a name, set the Space Limit, type, and notification thresholds you would like, click OK and you have a new quota template.

Another way to create a template is to copy an existing template's settings and edit them to produce your own custom quota template. To copy another template's settings into your new quota template, you begin as you did above, by highlighting then right-clicking Quota Template and selecting Create Quota Template, but this time in the Create Quota Template dialog box under Copy Properties from Quota Template select the template whose properties you would like to copy from the drop-down list and click the Copy button (this will fill in the space limit, type, and notification thresholds based on the template you have chosen). Give the new template a name, and click OK.

The last way to create your own quota template is my favorite. You already have a quota that you have created and would now like to create a quota template from that quota: right-click your quota and choose Create Template from Quota, name the new template, and when you click OK, voila—new template (how easy is that?).

TIP   When creating new templates, I find it helpful to leave the built-in templates in their original state; this way, whenever you create a new template you are starting from the same settings.

Linking Templates Together

You can also link templates together, it's as easy as 1-2-3. In fact, you already have one set of built-in, linked templates to cheat with…oops, I meant to learn from. In Table 16.1, where you saw the configuration parameters of the built-in templates, there was one template that ran a command when it reached 100 percent of its limit. Do you remember which one? You're right, it is the 200MB Limit with 50MB Extension template. This template will automatically load the "250MB Extended Limit" template. When the 200MB limit has been reached, a command is run to change the template currently set on the folder to apply the 250MB extended limit template to the folder, thereby increasing the limit on the quota from 200MB to 250MB. How exactly does this happen, what command is run, and, how can you link a couple of your own custom templates together? To answer these questions, let's look at the command that is run. Dirquota.exe is the command (don't forget to type in the path to Dirquota: **%windir%\system32\dirquota.exe**), and the command line arguments are

```
quota modify /path:[Quota Path] /sourcetemplate:"250MB Extended Limit"
```

The previous command will modify the current quota settings by replacing the 200MB quota limit with a 250MB quota limit via the "250MB Extended Limit" template.

So, let's create a couple of new templates, one that is identical to the 200MB Limit with 50MB Extension template, except you would like yours to have a 300MB limit instead of a 200MB limit. The second template will act as your extended template, once the 300MB limit has been reached, this template will allow an additional 100MB of storage space, for a whopping 400MB limit. The easiest way I can think of to do this would be to use what you already have and copy the built-in templates, then make a couple of small changes and create new custom templates. Follow these steps:

1. Right-click Quota Templates and choose Create Quota Template.

2. In the Copy Properties from Quota Template drop-down list, choose the 250MB Extended Limit template, and click the Copy button.

3. Name the template **400MB Extended Limit**.

4. Change the Space limit to 400MB, and click OK.

You have just created the template that will extend your 300MB template to 400MB (you needed to do this one first because you are going to use it when you create the 300MB template).

1. Right-click Quota Templates and choose Create Quota Template.

2. In the Copy Properties from Quota Template drop-down list, choose the 200MB Limit with 50MB Extension template, and click the Copy button.

3. Name the template `300MB Limit with 100MB Extension`.

4. Change the Space Limit to 300MB.

5. Under Notification Thresholds, highlight Limit (100%) and click the Edit button, go to the Command tab, and edit the /sourcetemplate: setting from /sourcetemplate:"250MB Extended Limit" to /sourcetemplate:"400MB Extended Limit" (the quotation marks are only necessary if your template name contains spaces, ours did so I used them but if you create template names that do not contain spaces there is no need to use the quotation marks).

6. Click OK twice and you are done.

That was pretty simple, right? With these basic steps, there is no end to the custom quotas you can produce. Enjoy!

UPDATING QUOTA TEMPLATES

Once you start setting quotas based on quota templates, you might have a need to edit one of the settings in a template—maybe you need to increase the storage space limit or add another notification threshold. How can you get the new quota template settings to apply to the existing quotas that are already in use, and are you sure you want them to? When you edit a Quota template either by right-clicking and choosing Edit Template Properties, or double-clicking the template and choosing OK to save the changes for the new template, you will receive the dialog box in Figure 16.9.

TIP The term *derived* means the quotas were created (derived) from the quota template you are editing.

What do those three settings actually do? Let's create a scenario and see what the different settings can do to you...oops I meant *for* you, of course. You have applied a quota template to your user's home folders which set a 500MB hard quota limit. In FSRM, you will now see that each user's home folder has a quota applied to it, and this quota is based on the template settings, so they are all the same. You receive a call from the HR manager: she is out of storage space on her home folder. You realize this one user needs 1GB of storage space, so you edit her quota directly by right-clicking her home folder quota (not the quota template), increasing the quota limit to 1GB. You realize later that each user needs their home folder limit increased to 700MB, and you edit the original template (the one that allocated 500MB of storage space) to allow 700MB of storage space. If you choose the first setting Apply Template Only to Derived Quotas That Match the Original Template as shown in Figure 16.9, the HR manager's folder with the 1 GB quota limit would not be overwritten because her quota no longer *matches* the original quota applied by the template (remember, the original template allocated 500MB of storage space). Given the same scenario, the second choice, Apply Template to All Derived Quotas would change all quotas created from the template, including the quota you had increased to 1GB for the HR Manager. The last setting, Do Not Apply Templates To Derived Quotas, would *not* update any of the existing quotas that were created from the template; only new quotas from that point forward would receive the new settings.

FIGURE 16.9
Update Quotas
Derived from
Template

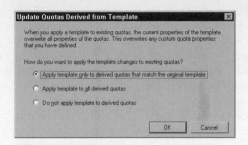

Exporting and Importing Quota Templates

You have seen how to create custom quota templates, link them together, and edit existing quotas that were based on templates. But you still have not seen how to export quota templates from one server to another. This is done with the `Dirquota.exe` *command-line* tool (I could not find any way to export or import from within the FSRM UI). In this scenario you need to export a custom template you have created named 500MB Limit from Server1 and import it to Server2 so you can apply the same template settings to folders on Server2. The first step is to export the template settings to an XML file on Server1. Once you have the XML file, you can import it to Server2.

To export the 500MB Limit template from Server1 to an XML file named 500MB.xml, type the following at a command prompt:

```
Dirquota template export /file:C:\500MB.xml /Template:"500MB Limit"
```

You should receive the message, *Templates exported successfully*, and you should also have a file named `500MB.xml` in the root of C on Server1.

There are a couple of ways to import the 500MB Limit template to Server2. The first is to copy the `500MB.xml` file to the root of C on Server2 and run the following command:

```
Dirquota template import /file:C:\500MB.xml
```

TIP   You may copy the `500MB.xml` file to any folder you choose, just be sure you type in the complete path to the folder where you put the `500MB.xml` file, in the Dirquota command. For example, if you copied the `500MB.xml` file to a folder called `C:\temporary`, then the Dirquota command would look like this: `Dirquota template import /file:C:\temporary\500MB.XML`

OR

Leave the `500MB.xml` file on Server1 and run this command from Server1:

```
Dirquota template import /file:C:\500MB.xml /Remote:Server2
```

NOTE   You may have to close and re-open FSRM to see the newly imported quota template.

Viewing Quota Details

After you have created your quota, you might like to check it every once in a while to see how much space is being used and how much is available. To view the details of a quota, launch FSRM and highlight the quota whose details you would like to view. In the bottom center of the screen you will see the quota details, including the path, limit, type of quota, how much space has been used as well as the amount of space that is still available, and (I thought this was cool), the peak usage as shown in Figure 16.10. The Peak Usage displays the date and time that the Peak Usage was reached. You can reset the Peak Usage by right-clicking the quota and choosing Reset Peak Usage).

The quota details give a 10,000 foot view for the entire path. This is fine if you are looking at a folder that only one user is allowed to store data in, but what if you have a folder that many users store data in? For example, you have a shared folder named Project Upgrade that several users store data for collaboration in, and you have set a quota on this folder. When the thresholds are reached, how do you know which user has used the most space in the folder? Remember the Report tab on the Notification thresholds (it was the last type of notification we could do)? There is a report named Files by Owner that will show you how much data each individual user has stored in the shared folder (for detailed information on the Files by Owner report and others please see chapter 15).

File Server Resource Managers–Quota Management has come a long way from the NTFS volume quotas. Being able to place limits on the amount of data that can be stored in a folder vs on a volume is a big step in itself, but being able to notify users that they are approaching the limits of storage space prior to actually running out is a real plus. I also like the fact that administrators have such control over the notification methods; busy administrators will probably enjoy the email notifications they receive when a user has exceeded a limit moreso than having to search through Application event logs on multiple servers to determine which user has exceeded a limit.

With this information I hope that you are now well equipped to dive in and create your very own quotas based on your company's needs and I hope you have enjoyed learning about the new FSRM quotas as much as I did. I can tell you one improvement I would still like to see, and that is quotas on folders being specifically applied to users, so Wendy could have 300MB of space and Meghan could have 200MB of space on the same folder…maybe the next release.

FIGURE 16.10
Viewing the
quota details

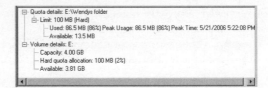

File Screens

As you saw in the last section, quotas allow administrators to define the amount of storage space users may have, but users could store anything…couldn't they? Fill up their home folders with their favorite Peter Frampton MP3 collection (granted this wouldn't be that big—okay, how about a Beatles collection)? or, worse yet, image files, maybe even images that don't belong at work. Well, that's where file screens save the day. When file screens are implemented in tandem with quotas, not only can you restrict the amount of space your users get, but also the type of data they are allowed to store in that space.

In this section, I will show you how easy it is to set file screens that complement the quotas you set previously. File screens (FS) provide two *screening types*, Active and Passive. An Active file screen will block users from storing unauthorized (you as the administrator define what is authorized and what is not) data on your server; if a user attempts to store an unauthorized file, they will receive an "Access Denied" error message. A Passive file screen may be used to monitor (instead of block) the types of files users are storing, giving the user the freedom to store any type of data but, at the same time allowing administrators a tracking mechanism to ensure that the users are not violating their company's "Acceptable Use Policy."

Most FS are performed in real-time, but not to worry; the benchmarks I have seen so far about implementing file screens on production servers do not appear to cause significant performance degradation. You may also choose to store the file screen data in a database and use the File Screen Audit feature to create storage reports at a later date.

When it comes to File Screens, FSRM provides a rich and crisp user interface where you can perform *almost* everything you need. There are a couple of features that you will see later that can only be done from the command-line tool `Filescrn.exe` (`Filescrn.exe` can do anything the UI can, and some the UI can't).

Let's explore File Screens by expanding the File Screening Management tool in FSRM where you will see the three nodes File Screens, File Screen Templates, and File Groups, as shown in Figure 16.11.

The third node "File Groups" is where we will begin. File screens are based on file groups, so before we get started creating file screens, let's understand file groups better. File groups are defined by the file's extension, so files can be grouped together by their type. For example, the *Audio and Video Files* file group includes 37 different file extensions, some of which are .avi, .mp3, and .wma. The *Office Files* file group includes .doc, .xml, and .dba extensions, among others. Microsoft has already defined some File Groups for us, but if the predefined file groups do not meet your needs, you may edit the existing file groups or create your own.

WARNING Please see the "Creating and Editing File Groups" section later in this chapter before you edit the predefined file groups, or you may regret it.

FIGURE 16.11
FSRM—File Screening
Management nodes

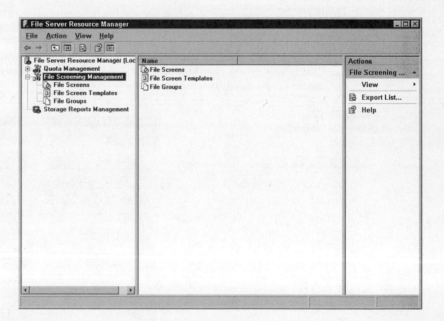

Creating a File Screen

Creating file screens can be quick and easy. In the last section you set a 200MB hard quota on your users' home folders; In this section we will create a file screen that prevents users from storing files from the Audio and Video Files file group, in their home folders. Each user has a home folder based on their username under the `E:\Home Folders` folder.

To create a file screen, under File Screening Management, you can highlight File Screens and then right-click File Screens, select Create File Screen; go through the Actions menu; or find the template under the File Screen Templates node (file screen templates serve the same purpose as quota templates did earlier, and are covered under the section titled Creating, Editing, and Updating File Screen Templates later in this chapter) that you would like your file screen based on, right-click the template, and select Create File Screen from Template. However you choose to open the Create File Screen dialog box, you will see Figure 16.12.

The File Screen Path is similar to the Quota Path: this is the volume or folder to which your file screen will apply. Browse to the E:\Home Folders folder for your File screen path.

TIP   The file screen by default will apply to all subfolders of E:\Home Folders folder. To change this behavior, see the Creating File Screen Exclusions section later in this chapter.

Under File Screen Properties, there are two answers to the question How Do You Want to Configure the File Screen Properties? They are:

Derive Properties from This File Screen Template (Recommended)

OR

Define Custom File Screen Properties

You are creating a custom file screen, so choose the second option, Define Custom File Screen Properties, and click the Custom Properties button. You will see the File Screen Properties on E:\Home Folders dialog box, as in Figure 16.13.

In the File Screen Properties dialog box, on the Settings tab, ensure the Screening Type is set to Active Screening. Under the File Ggroups section, select the Audio and Video Files file group to block, click OK, and then click the Create button. This will not only create a new file screen, but also give you the option to create a template based on the new file screen (you might want to use the same settings somewhere else without having to recreate them each time). Figure 16.14 shows the Save Custom Properties as a Template dialog box.

FIGURE 16.12
Create File Screen
dialog box

FIGURE 16.13
FIGURE 16.13
File Screen Proper-
ties on E:\Home
Folders dialog box
(Settings tab)

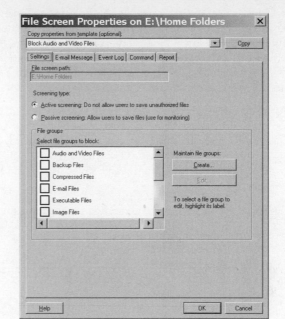

FIGURE 16.14
Save Custom Proper-
ties as a Template
dialog box

To create a template based on your new file screen, you would choose the first option, Save the Custom Properties as a Template, give the template a name, click OK, and you'd have a new template. The second option, Save the Custom File Screen without Creating a Template, will create your file screen, but will not create a template. If you want this dialog box to go away for good, put a check mark in the box next to Do Not Ask Me to Save as a Template Again. In this case, select the second setting, Save the Custom File Screen without Creating a Template, for your file screen.

You now have a new custom file screen that is designed to prevent users from storing audio and video files in their home folders. But how will you know which users continue to *attempt* to store these unauthorized files? You have to edit the properties of the file screen, either by double-clicking or right-clicking the file screen and selecting Edit File Screen Properties. Look closely: there are four additional tabs to the Settings tab, do they look familiar? They should, because they are the same actions you could configure in Quotas. You can choose to send emails to the user and administrator, generate an event in the Application event log, run a command or script, and generate reports to be run and emailed directly to the user or administrator. These actions are configured identically to the actions you saw in Quotas, but as you probably guessed, the text in the email will pertain to file screens, and the text in the event generated in the Application event log will also pertain to file screens. Following is a sample email of a user (Wendy) attempting to store an MP3 file after you have set your file screen:

```
Subject: Unauthorized file matching "Audio and Video Files" file group detected

The system detected that user BIGFIRM\Wendy attempted to save E:\Home
Folders\Wendy\DoyoufeellikeIdo.mp3 on E:\Home Folders on server Server1. This
file matches the "Audio and Video Files" file group which is not permitted on the
system.
```

The event that would be generated in the Application event log will be similar to the following:

```
Event Type:Warning
Event Source:SRMSVC
Event Category:None
Event ID:8215
Date:5/24/2006
Time:5:41:46 PM
User:N/A
Computer:Server1
Description:
The system detected that user BIGFIRM\Wendy attempted to save E:\Home
Folders\Wendy\ DoyoufeellikeIdo.mp3 on E:\Home Folders on server Server1. This
file matches the "Audio and Video Files" file group which is not permitted on the
system.
```

TIP   The text generated in both email and the event is configurable through the properties of the specific file screen. The text can be different for each file screen, email, or event generated.

So, from this point forward, your file screens are in place and will perform whatever actions we have configured…but what about all those MP3s that already exist in the user's home folder? Well, nothing—unless they try to rename one. The files that existed prior to the file screen being implemented are not included in the new file screen, unless a user attempts to rename one. In this case, any actions you have configured (notifying you of the unauthorized file) will occur, the user will receive an "Access Denied" error message, and the file will remain unchanged (it will not be deleted).

The one action that has not yet been addressed, and I promised in Chapter 15 it would be, is the File Screening Audit Report. This report gathers information regarding users and applications that have violated, or attempted to violate, your file screening policies.

There is one step that must be performed prior to any information being gathered by this report, and that is first enabling Record File Screening Activity in Auditing Database. To enable this setting, in the FSRM snap-in, right-click File Server Resource Manager, choose Configure Options, go to the File Screen Audit tab, and put a check mark in the only box on the screen.

You can now choose to generate a File Screening Audit report, from the Report tab of your file screen properties (you could have selected this setting before you enabled Record File Screening Activity in Auditing Database, but your reports would have been empty, because no data had been gathered yet). From this point forward whenever a user or application attempts to store (or rename) an unauthorized file, a report named "FileScreenAudit##_date_time.html" will be generated and stored in the default storage location C:\StorageReports\Incident folder. For example, `FileScreenAudit61_2006-07-21_13-31-26.html` is the name of one of my reports; this report was the 61st report generated on July 21st 2006 at 1:31:26 PM. To view this report, I double-clicked the report name; you may have to scroll down past the folders to find the actual report name. The folders you scroll past contain the information used to display the report in a nice graphical representation and will be named similarly to the report name. The folder name for the above mentioned report is FileScreenAudit61_2006-07-21_13-31-26_files (notice the *file* name ended in .html and the *folder* name ends in files).

When I viewed the report I got a lot more information than I anticipated. With our previous file screen on the E:\Home Folders folder configured to block Audio and Video files, I expected a report that would simply tell me that Wendy attempted to store `DoyoufeellikeIdo.mp3` in her home folder. Imagine my surprise when I received a fully comprehensive report beginning from the E:\Home Folders folder listing every file that any user had attempted to store in their home folder that violated the file screen policies from the time I enabled Record File Screening Activity in Auditing Database. So be prepared, this report may be rather large, and every time a violation occurs a new *full* report is generated.

TIP   You may need to keep an eye on the amount of storage space your reports are consuming so you do not run out of disk space.

Exactly how does this report gather information? Once you enable Record File Screening Activity in Auditing Database, all unauthorized activity will be stored in .XML logs. These .XML log files reside in the *System Volume Information*\SRM\DSAuditLog folder. The *System Volume Information* folder is a *hidden/system* folder found in the root of the volume you have set your file screen path to, so ours would be E:\System Volume Information\SRM\DSAuditLog. The first log created will be named `log00000001.xml`; once this log is full (10MB is the largest I have seen) or the server is rebooted a new log will be created named `log00000002.xml` and so on. As you can see, over a period of time, there could be many logs created and much data stored.

NOTE   To view the System Volume Information folder launch Windows Explorer, highlight the root of the volume you have implemented file screens on and click the "Tools" menu, select "Folder Options", and go to the "View" tab. Under *Advanced Settings* scroll to "Hidden files and folders", and select "Show hidden files and folders". You will also need to remove the checkmark from "Hide protected operating system files" and click yes to the warning message explaining that it is now possible to delete critical operating system files that could render your computer inoperable.

When a user or application attempts to store an unauthorized file, an entry is added to the latest .XML log file. The entry contains the name and complete path of the unauthorized file along with the date and time the attempt occurred and the Security Identifier (SID) of the user who tried to store the file. When the File Screening Audit report data is gathered as an action triggered by a file screen, all the .XML log files are read to create the report.

You can choose to generate a File Screening Audit report that contains data at least XX number of days old (you determine the number). For example, to cleanup disk space it might be nice to create a report that would inform you of all unauthorized files that have been stored for more than 30 days. Here are the steps:

1. In the FSRM snap-in highlight Storage Reports Management (SRM)

2. Right-click SRM and choose Generate Reports Now

3. Set your scope on the folder you would like the report to begin gathering data from (ours was E:\Home folders)

4. Select the *File Screening Audit* report to be generated and you will see the Storage Reports Task Properties dialog box as shown in Figure 16.15

5. Click the Edit Parameters button

6. In the Minimum days since file screening event occurred; input 30 as shown in Figure 16.16

After you implement your new file screen, your manager receives a phone call from the manager of the Marketing Department. His team (which consists of Joni and Tony) can no longer store certain file types. When asked what type of files they are attempting to store, you learn they are MP3, MP4, and WAV files. Due to corporate policy, all users' home folders must reside within the E:\Home Folders share, where you have created your file screen to block all audio and video files from being stored (also as a measure to enforce corporate policy). What you need the end result to be is the file screen blocking audio and video files applied to the E:\Home Folders folder and all subfolders *except* Joni and Tony's right? That is where file screen exceptions come in.

Do you ever feel like a law degree might come in handy when attempting to understand some of Microsoft's dialog boxes? Whew—I sure have and this is one of those times. It seems fairly simple to be able to create an exception to the preceding file screen, but in creating the exception would I include or exclude the needed files in my file screen exception? Well, if you're not confused, you're doing better than I did, because this totally confused me the first time I looked at it. Let's create a file screen exception to fully understand them.

FIGURE 16.15
Storage Reports Task
Properties dialog box

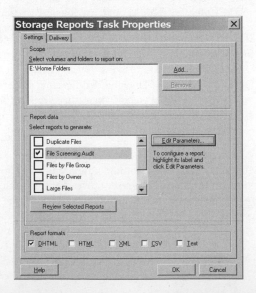

FIGURE 16.16
Report Parameters

Creating File Screen Exceptions

Based on the preceding scenario, you need to create a file screen exception that will allow Joni and Tony to store MP3, MP4, and WAV files (which are all members of the audio and video files file group) in their home folders. To create a file screen exception, within the FSRM snap-in expand File Screening Managementand highlight File Screens, then right-click File Screens (remember what happens if you right-click File Screens before you highlight it? Right: you get only Help, and isn't that helpful?) and select Create File Screen Exception. You will see a dialog box similar to Figure 16.17.

FIGURE 16.17
Create File Screen
Exception dialog box

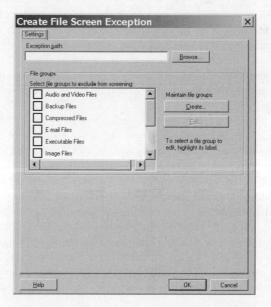

Browse to Joni's home folder for the Exception Path. Under the File groups section, choose Audio and Video Files to exclude from screening and click OK. Perform the same steps for Tony's folder (as far as I can see, there is no way to create a file screen exception template). If you have a large number of folders you would like to create a file screen exception on, I recommend creating a top level folder, moving the other folders to be subfolders, and applying the file screen exception to the top level folder, allowing the file screen exception to be inherited to all subfolders.

Do not attempt to create a file screen exception directly on a folder that you have previously configured a file screen on. When I attempted to create a file screen exception on the E:\Home Folders folder instead of a subfolder I received the error message shown in Figure 16.18.

You can get more granular on your file screen exceptions by creating a new file group. For example, in the preceding scenario, Joni and Tony only needed to be able to store MP3, MP4, and WAV files, not all 37 file types contained in the audio and video files file group. There is no existing File group that *only* contains these three file types, so you will need to create a custom File Group, which is exactly what we are going to do in the next section.

FIGURE 16.18
FSRM screen
exception error

You can get more granular on your file screen exceptions by creating a new file group. For example,

Creating and Editing File Groups

In Chapter 15, I mentioned editing the existing file groups, and it's an issue I believe is worth mentioning again. File groups belong to FSRM as a whole—not only do file screens use them, but so do storage reports. Why is that a big deal, you ask? Because if you edit an existing file group, all file screens, templates, and reports configured to use the file group will be affected. For example, in the preceding scenario Joni and Tony needed to be able to store MP3, MP4, and WAV files in their home folder. If you had removed those three file types from the Audio and Video Files file group, that scheduled report you configured to run every Sunday night on your users home folders (you remember the one, it lets you know how much storage space is being used based on your file groups), well, that report would no longer consider MP3, MP4, and WAV files to be in the Audio and Video Files file group.

You need to create a file group that includes only the three file types that Joni and Tony want to store. To create a File group, within the FSRM snap-in, expand File Screening Management, highlight File Groups, then right-click File Groups, and choose Create File Group, or go through the Actions menu, by highlighting File Groups and choosing Create File Group. Give the new file group a name of "Joni &Tony Exclusion", under Files to include add *.MP3, *.MP4, and *.WAV file extensions as shown in Figure 16.19. Click OK, and you have a file group that contains only the three file types you needed to exclude from your file screen.

If you are like me, I am always looking for shortcuts when it comes to getting the job done quickly and efficiently. I mean, why type in *.MP3 and *.MP4 when creating the file screen exception? Wouldn't adding *.MP* under Files to include allow MP3 and MP4 files to be stored? Yes it would, but it would also allow .MPP (Microsoft Project), along with .MPG, .MPD, .MPE, .MPA, etc., to be stored, and you may not want that. If you did not want to allow Microsoft Project files to be stored in the users' home folders (corporate policy dictates all .MPP's must be stored in a central location) but had previously added *.MP* as the Files to include in your File Screen Exception, you would need to add *.MPP under Files to Exclude *from this file group* as shown in Figure 16.20, therefore Microsoft Project files would not be affected by this File Screen Exception.

TIP File screen exceptions are placed on subfolders whose parent folder has a file screen applied to it. The exception list is *usually* more specific than the file screen applied to the parent folder; therefore, file screen exceptions override file screens.

FIGURE 16.19
Create File Group
Properties dialog box

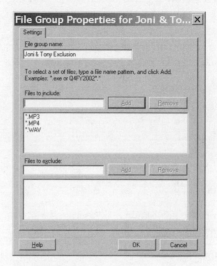

FIGURE 16.20
File Group Properties

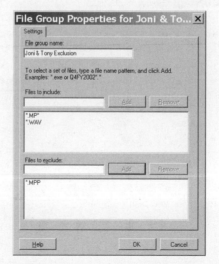

File Screen Templates

Templates work exactly the same way with file screens as they did with quotas. Microsoft has conveniently created five prebuilt templates that you can use or copy to create custom templates.

TIP To keep things simple, copy the original template when you are creating your own custom templates. This way it is easy to know what settings you are starting from each time.

Table 16.2 describes the five built-in templates; the file group name denotes the type of files that the file screen will perform actions on and the last three columns show the actions taken when a user attempts to store that type of file.

TABLE 16.2: Prebuilt File Screen Templates

FILE GROUP NAME	SCREENING TYPE	EMAIL USER	EMAIL ADMIN	EVENT
Block Audio and Video Files	Active	X		X
Block Email Files	Active	X		X
Block Executable Files	Active	X		X
Block Image Files	Active	X		X
Monitor Executable and System Files	Passive	X	X	

Using, Creating, and Updating File ScreenTemplates

There are two methods you can use to create a file screen based on a template. The first is within the FSRM snap-in expand File Screening Management, highlight File Screens and then right-click File Screens, select Create File Screen. You should see a dialog box similar to Figure 16.21.

FIGURE 16.21
Create File Screen
dialog box

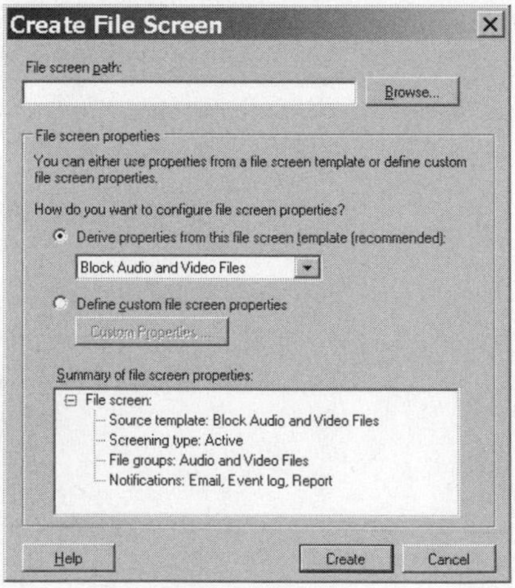

Browse to the folder you would like to set your File screen path on, then under How Do You Want to Configure File Screen Properties select Derive Properties from This File Screen Template, choose the template you would like from the drop-down list, and click the Create button. The second method is to expand the File Screening Mangaement node within the FSRM snap-in, highlight File Screen Templates, in the detail pane right-click the template you would like to use, select Create File Screen from Template, once again Browse to the folder you would like to set for your File screen path, click the Create button and you're done. The template will fill in the screening type, the file groups to block, and the actions to take when a user or application attempts to store an unauthorized file.

Creating your own templates is a snap, but as always, there are a number of ways to create them. One is to highlight the File Screen Templates node under File Screening Management, then right-click File Screen Templates , and select Create File Screen Template. Give the new template a name and choose your Screening type, File groups to block, and actions you would like taken when a user attempts to store an unauthorized file as shown in Figure 16.22.

My favorite way to create a FS template is to copy another FS template's settings. To copy another template's settings, begin as you did previously by highlighting File Screen Templates, right-click the File Screen Templates node, and select Create File Screen Template (you should see the same dialog box as you did in Figure 16.22). In the Copy Properties from Template (Optional) select the template whose properties you would like to copy from the drop-down list, click the Copy button (this will fill in all the properties from the template you have chosen), name the new template, and you're done. The last method is probably the quickest: you have already created a custom file screen and would like to create a FS template from your file screen settings. Right-click your custom file screen and choose Create a Template from File Screen, name the new template, and click OK.

FIGURE 16.22
Create File Screen
Template dialog box

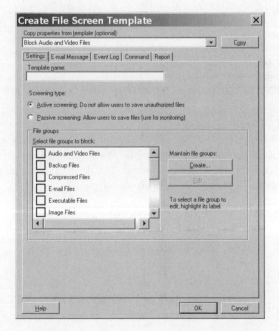

TIP When creating new templates, I find it easier to always start from familiar settings, by leaving the built-in templates intact and simply copying and editing the new template; whenever you create a template you are starting from the same settings.

When you start applying file screens based on templates, you will have the same file screens settings on various folders—isn't that the reason we use templates? Yes, it is, but there may be a need to edit one of the file screens so that it no longer matches the original template settings that it was created from. What happens then? Well, if you are not careful, bad things could happen. When you edit a file screen template either by right-clicking the template and choosing Edit Template Properties, or double-clicking the template, making your changes, and clicking OK, you will receive the dialog box in Figure 16.23.

The first option, Apply Template Only to Derived File Screens That Match the Original Template, will update all existing file screens based on this template only if the file screen has not been modified. The second setting, Apply Template to All Derived File Screens, will update all file screens based on this template, regardless of whether you have individually edited them or not. The last setting, Do Not Apply Template to Derived File Screens, will not edit your current file screens; only new file screens created from this template will inherit the new template settings.

TIP I recommend using File Screen templates to help centralize management of your file screens.

FIGURE 16.23
Update File
Screens Derived
from Template

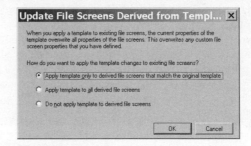

Exporting and Importing File Screen Templates and File Groups

Up to this point, everything you have done in this chapter can be performed in the FSRM snap-in. To export or import file screen templates or file groups, you must use the command line utility, Filescrn.exe (you cannot export or import from within the FSRM UI). For example, say you created a file group that contains all authorized file types that are documented in your company's Acceptable Use Policy, named "AUP," and you would like to export the new file group from Server1 to Server2. Here are the steps:

1. Export the File Group "AUP" to an .XML file on Server1, called Server1AUP.xml, by typing the following at a command prompt:

```
Filescrn filegroup export /file:C:\Server1AUP.xml /filegroup:AUP
```

You should receive the message, "File groups exported successfully," and there will be an XML file in the root of C named Server1AUP.xml.

2. There are a couple of ways you can import this XML file to Server2. The first is to copy the `Server1AUP.xml` file to the root of C on Server2 and run the following command:

```
Filescrn filegroup import /file:C:\Server1AUP.xml
```

OR

Leave the Server1AUP.xml file on Server1 and run this command:

```
Filescrn filegroup import /file:C:\Server1AUP.xml /Remote:Server2
```

NOTE As you did with quotas, you may have to close and re-open FSRM to see the newly imported file group or file screen templates.

Summary

Well, I hope you agree that Microsoft is on the right track when it comes to Quota Management and File Screens. The old NTFS Volume Quotas were a far cry from being useful, the new Quota Management feature really gives administrators a much higher level of control when it comes to storage space on their servers, and I love not only the reporting capabilities, but how easy they are to implement.

File Screens are the icing on the cake; sure, in the past we could have fumbled around with various methods to prevent users from storing a specific file thru GPO's software restrictions, but that was a lot of work and seems like a lot of trouble to go through to prevent one file from being stored. So now, why bother? We can prevent our users from storing many types of files instantaneously or simply monitor the users and applications that store unauthorized files, because remember, someone is always watching on corporate networks today—aren't you glad you're one of the Administrators?

Chapter 17

R2's New Distributed File System Namespace (DFSN) and Distributed File System Replication (DFSR)

R2's new Distributed File System Namespace (DFSN) is an enhanced version of Windows Server 2000/2003's Distributed File System (DFS). DFS was covered in the *Mastering Windows Server 2003* book; this chapter is intended for readers who would like to understand Microsoft's new DFSN product, not for readers in search of DFS information.

Distributed File System Replication (DFSR) is a complete rewrite of the product previously known as the File Replication Service (FRS). You may have heard of FRS—it's the service responsible for replicating DFS and SYSVOL in Windows Server 2000/2003. The bad news is R2 still uses FRS for replicating SYSVOL (you cannot use DFSR for replicating SYSVOL in R2, that is coming in Windows Server 2007/2008); the good news is you can use DFSR to replicate the new DFS Namespaces. Both tools, DFSN and DFSR, come with some pretty cool enhancements, starting with the new user interface. The DFS Management snap-in allows you to create and manage DFS Namespaces and, for the first time ever, provides a front end in which to manage DFS Replication (the Windows 2000/2003 version of FRS was practically hidden from administrators and was a real learning experience to troubleshoot). In this chapter, you will create a DFS Namespace, add some fault tolerance, then use DFSR to replicate your DFSN (even though the two tools are exclusive, they can be used in tandem to provide multi-master replication).

The purpose of DFSN is to present a *virtual* tree of folders to users for data access. With no more UNC paths in their logon script, administrators can easily migrate data from one server to another without disturbing the users at all. The data can be made available on multiple servers, providing the end user with fault tolerant access, offering load sharing across the servers to prevent any one server from being overwhelmed with connections, and allowing users to connect to the server closest to them via least cost routing.

First Things First—Installing the DFS Management Snap-in

Before you begin, you will need to install the DFS Management snap-in. There are two methods you can choose from to perform the installation: Manage Your Server or Add/Remove Programs. Let's look at each installation method because they are very different. Both methods require the Server Installation CD Disc 2, and one method requires a reboot due to features other than DFSN and DFSR being installed.

Installing DFSN and DFSR by adding the File Server Role through the Manage Your Server snap-in also installs File Server Resource Manager (FSRM), and File Server Management. FSRM requires a reboot of the server (two kernel-mode minifilter file system drivers are installed and need to be placed in the correct location in the I/O stack). I prefer to install using the second method: Control Panel's Add/Remove Programs applet, which gives you more control as to exactly what you are installing. To install the DFS Management snap-in via Add/Remove Programs, open Control Panel ➤ Add or Remove Programs ➤ Add/Remove Windows Components. Highlight Distributed File System and click the Details button, and you will see a dialog box similar to Figure 17.1.

FIGURE 17.1
Distributed File
System details

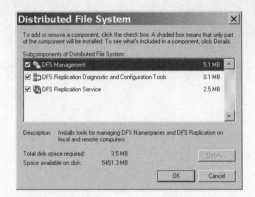

You may choose to install only the DFS Management snap-in or the DFS Replication Service (the DFS Replication Diagnostic and Configuration Tools are selected automatically whether you choose to install the DFS Management snap-in or the DFS Replication Service) or both by putting a check mark in the box to the left of your selections, and clicking OK.

NOTE   If you have not already installed the .NET Framework 2.0, it will be installed when you click OK. You will not be prompted to install the .NET Framework 2.0, but the DFS Management snap-in requires .NET Framework 2.0 to run.

Not only does installing via the Add or Remove Programs applet give administrators more control as to what applications are running on their servers, it also gives them the flexibility to load only the DFS Management snap-in or the DFS Replication Service. You do not need to install both, but you will probably want to after you read the "DFS Replication" section later in this chapter; I know I would (go ahead and install all three if you are following the step-by-steps in this chapter).

In order to manage DFSN or DFSR remotely the DFS Management snap-in must be installed on either a member server running Server 2003 R2, or a computer running XP SP2 which must also be a member of the domain where DFSN or DFSR is being implemented. When an administrator opens the DFS Management snap-in, if the snap-in connects to a server that is not running 2003 SP1 or 2003 R2, some of the new features will be unavailable. Exactly which features will be unavailable depends on the operating system of the server the DFS Management snap-in connected to (for details please see the "Mixing OSes" section later in this chapter). To open the DFS Management snap-in, click Start ➤ Administrative Tools ➤ DFS Management. Alternatively, click Start ➤ Run and type **Dfsmgmt.msc**. The first thing you may notice is that the new snap-in uses MMC 3.0 technology, which adds an actions pane (on the right side of the screen) and some fantastic links that provide step-by-step instructions on DFS Management Tasks. Figure 17.2 shows the DFS Management snap-in.

FIGURE 17.2
DFS Management
snap-in

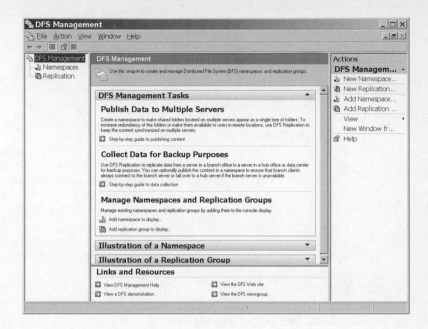

Terminology

Before you get started creating your DFS Namespace, it may be helpful (especially for administrators who managed a Windows Server 2000 DFS environment) to take a historical look and compare the new DFSN terminology to the 2000 DFS terminology. Table 17.1 shows the correlation between the DFS and DFSN terms and their definitions.

TABLE 17.1: Comparison of 2000 DFS and 2003 R2 DFSN Terminology

2000 DFS TERM	NEW R2 DFSN TERM	DEFINITION
Root	DFS Namespace (DFSN)	A virtual tree of folders, beginning with server or domain name*rootname* (*rootname* being the name of your namespace)
Root server	Namespace server	A server that hosts a namespace
N/A	Namespace root	Top-level folder in the namespace
Link	Folder	A folder that appears in the namespace and contains data users connect to
Link target	Folder target	A copy of a folder that appears in the namespace

Creating DFS Namespace and Folders

There are also some requirements you should be aware of before you begin creating your namespace. Administrators must create namespaces on NTFS volumes, and to get the most robust and consistent DFSN environment, all of your Domain Controllers (DCs) and namespace servers must run either Server 2003 SP1 or Server 2003 R2. If your environment has servers running Windows Server 2000 or Windows Server 2003 *without* SP1 acting as DCs or namespace servers, there are some features that will not be available. For a complete listing of features that may not be available, please see the "Mixing OSes" section later in this chapter.

You know which operating system your servers need to be running—what about which clients? The client list is quiet extensive and includes the Windows Server 2003 family, Windows XP Professional, the Windows Server 2000 family, Windows 2000 Professional, NT 4.0 Server (SP6a), NT 4.0 Workstation (SP6a), and Windows 98 with the Active Directory Client Extension (for additional information on the AD client extension, please see KB323455).

Now, for your very first DFS Namespace, the Marketing Department at Bigfirm has requested that their users have access to the data stored on two servers. Server1 contains the shared Budget folder and Server2 contains the shared Projects folder. The name of the domain is Bigfirm, and the name of our domain controller is DCS. DCS is running Windows Server 2003 R2 Standard Edition as its operating system.

Creating the DFS Namespace

To create a new DFS Namespace, within the DFS Management snap-in, right-click Namespaces in the console tree and choose New Namespace, which starts the New Namespace Wizard. Type in the name of the server you would like to host the namespace (this server may be a DC or a member server). This server will be your namespace server, as shown in Figure 17.3.

FIGURE 17.3
Namespace Server

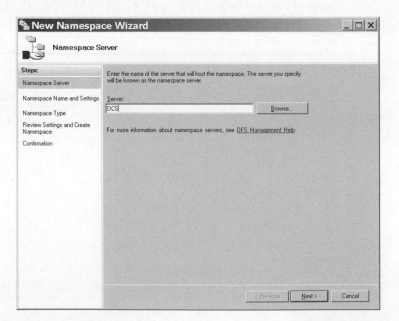

Clicking Next takes you to the Namespace Name and Settings page. This is where you type in the name of the Namespace, which will be appended to the domain or server name which is determined by the type of namespace (domain-based or server-based) you are creating—but we're getting ahead of ourselves, or at least ahead of the wizard. To create a namespace named Marketing, type in the name `Marketing`, as shown in Figure 17.4.

Notice on the Namespace Name and Settings dialog box there is an Edit Settings button. Click the Edit Settings button to see a screen similar to Figure 17.5.

FIGURE 17.4
Namespace Name and Settings

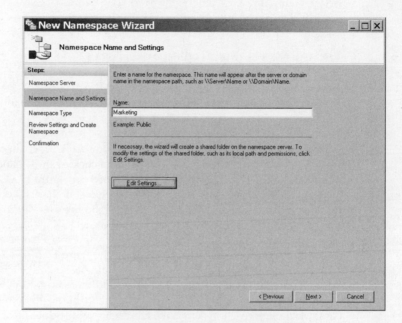

FIGURE 17.5
Edit Settings

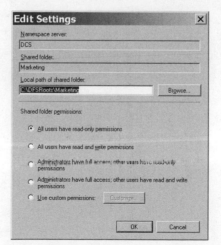

The Edit Settings dialog box displays the name of the server you would like to store the namespace on (which you cannot change from here) and the shared folder in which you would like to store the namespace root. The namespace root is the top-level folder of your namespace. The Local path of shared folder box is where you type the name of the shared folder in which you want the DFS Namespace stored. Accept the defaults of C:\DFSRoots\Marketing, and DFSN creates the shared folder Marketing in the C:\DFSRoots folder. If you would like to place the root in another folder, you can edit the defaults by browsing to or typing the name of the folder you would like to use for your namespace root on the Marketing namespace.

At the bottom of the Edit Settings dialog box is where you set the permissions. The default permission is All users have read-only permissions. There are four others you may choose from:

◆ All users have read and write permissions

◆ Administrators have full access; other users have read-only permissions

◆ Administrators have full access; other users have read and write permissions

◆ Use custom permissions

If the first four permissions do not meet your needs, you can configure more granular permissions by selecting Use Custom Permissions and clicking the Customize button, which will take you to the Permissions for Share dialog box as shown in Figure 17.6.

Does the Permissions for Share dialog box look familiar? If you have ever set shared folder permissions it should, because that is what it is. Add the user or group, choose which level of access they require (full control, change, or read), and click OK, you are now back to the Edit Settings dialog box, click OK again. Clicking Next on the Namespace Name and Settings dialog box will lead you to the Namespace Type page, as shown in Figure 17.7.

The two namespace type choices are Domain-based and Stand-alone. Domain-based namespaces are stored in Active Directory, and there is no limit to the number of domain-based DFS Namespaces you may have. Notice the name of the domain-based namespace \\Bigfirm .com\Marketing (Bigfirm.com is the DNS name of the domain and Marketing is the name of the namespace).

FIGURE 17.6
Permissions for Share

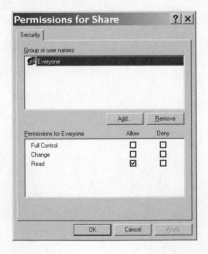

Stand-alone namespaces are stored on the local server in the Registry. For a fault tolerant solution with stand-alone namespaces, you will need to create the namespace on a cluster. Notice the name of the Stand-alone namespace, \\DCS\Marketing (DCS is the name of the server). If you do not have Active Directory, your only option for DFSN will be a stand-alone namespace. After choosing the type of namespace you would like (you are creating a domain-based namespace, so leave the Domain-based namespace radio button selected), click Next to go to the Review Settings and Create Namespace page, as shown in Figure 17.8.

FIGURE 17.7

Namespace Type

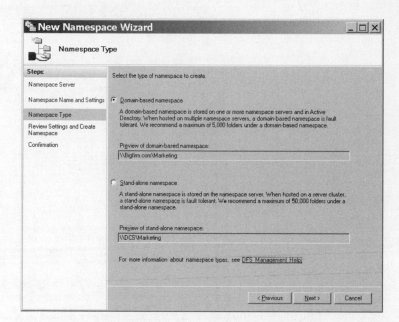

FIGURE 17.8

Review Settings and
Create Namespace

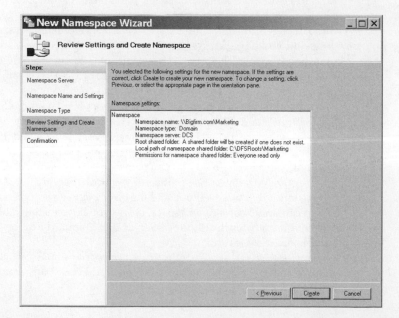

The Review Settings and Create Namespace page allows you to review the choices you have made prior to creating the namespace. If the settings are correct, click the Create button; if not, click the Previous button to find the page you would like to change, or select the page you would like to change from the Orientation Pane (Orientation Pane is on the left side of the page under Steps, where you see a listing of the previous pages we have covered). Take the time to review your settings: if they look good, click Create. Next, you will see the Confirmation page, as shown in Figure 17.9.

FIGURE 17.9
Confirmation
Tasks tab

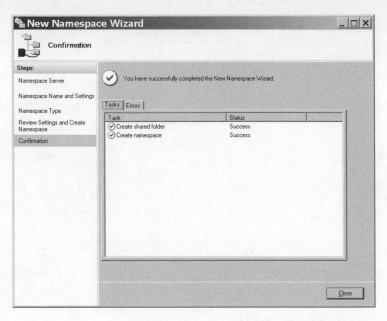

Now this is really nice. You know immediately if your new namespace was created or not. As you can see on the Confirmation page Tasks tab in Figure 17.9, you have successfully created a namespace and stored the namespace in a newly created shared folder. Click the Errors tab and you will see a page similar to Figure 17.10. "No Errors Occurred" is exactly what you want to see. Click Close, and you have just created your very first DFS Namespace. You successfully created a namespace root, which you must now add some folders to. These folders are what the users connect to when accessing the data they need. But, before you create the folders, what would happen if your Confirmation Errors page had contained errors?

Microsoft has done a great job with the errors displayed on this page, and I found them very easy to understand. For example, after I created the Marketing namespace, I attempted to create another namespace named HR on the same server and received the following error message on the Confirmation Screen Errors tab: "\\bigfirm.com\HR: The namespace server \\DCS\HR cannot be added. The server already hosts a namespace. You can host multiple namespaces only on Windows Server 2003, Enterprise Edition or Windows Server 2003, Datacenter Edition." Now, you have to admit that was well put, and the error message is correct, Windows Server 2003 Standard Edition can only host *one* namespace, unless you have installed hotfix 903651 (a reboot is required to install the hotfix on the Windows Server 2003 Standard Edition server that you would like to host multiple namespaces on).

Okay, back to our successfully created *empty* namespace. You now have a shared folder, Marketing, in the C:\DFSRoots folder. It is time to add your Budget and Projects folders so the users can access the data.

FIGURE 17.10
Confirmation
Errors tab

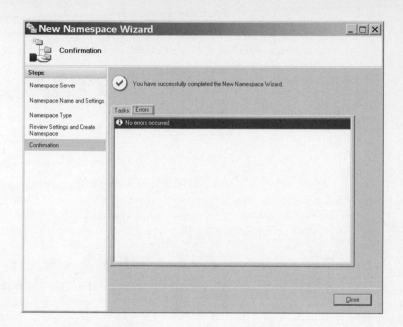

Adding Folders to the DFS Namespace

The Marketing Department currently accesses data from \\Server1\Budget and \\Server2\Projects through drive mappings (yuck, this can be quite a mess for the users), and you want them to access these shared folders via a DFSN. Let's begin with the Budget folder on Server1. Within the DFS Management snap-in, right-click your new namespace and select New Folder, then give the new folder a name. This is the name that will be displayed to your users in the virtual folder tree, and it does not *have* to be the name of the actual share or folder. You want your users to see Budget, so Budget is what you type in for Name, as shown in Figure 17.11.

FIGURE 17.11
New Folder dialog box

In the New Folder dialog box (Figure 17.11) under Folder targets, click the Add button and browse to or type the path of the folder target (where the data actually resides). In the example, the Path to the folder target is \\Server1\Budget as shown in Figure 17.12.

FIGURE 17.12
Add Folder Target
dialog box

I prefer to browse (less chance of mistyping) to find my server name in AD. Once I have selected my server, I can expand the server name to display a list of shares on that server. In fact, if the share does not already exist, I can create a new share easily by clicking the New Shared Folder button at the bottom left corner of the Browse for Shared Folders dialog box as shown in Figure 17.13.

FIGURE 17.13
Browse for Shared
Folders dialog box

If you currently have a shared folder and would like to use the existing shared folder but with a different DFSN folder name, don't worry, you can (this is one of the really cool features of DFSN). For example, if you have a folder on Server1 shared as Bud that contains the marketing budget data users are currently accessing, and would like to use that share as the new *Budget* folder in your Marketing namespace, you would type Budget as the Name in the New Folder dialog box (as you did before in Figure 17.11) and click the Add button. In the Add Folder Target dialog box (Figure 17.12), the Path to folder target would be \\Server1\Bud which is the name of the actual shared folder.

The same steps are followed to create the Projects folder, except the folder name will be Projects and the folder target will be \\Server2\Projects. Go ahead and create the Projects folder.

Done with the Projects folder? Great, you now have a DFS Namespace named Bigfirm\Marketing with two virtual folders, Budget and Projects. In the DFS Management snap-in, highlight the new namespace; you should see a screen similar to Figure 17.14.

There are three tabs in the details pane. The Namespace tab lists the contents of the namespace, which is your two folders, Budget and Projects. The Namespace Servers tab lists the Namespace Servers that host the namespace ("host" is just a fancy way of saying they keep a copy of the namespace). The last tab is the Delegation tab, which displays the permissions associated with your namespace (more on Delegations later in this chapter).

FIGURE 17.14
Bigfirm.com\
Marketing
Namespace

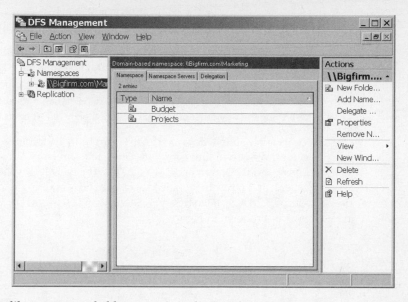

If you're curious like me, you probably want to see what's in the C:\DFSRoot\Marketing folder in Windows Explorer. I expanded the folder and saw two subfolders: Budget and Projects. When I attempted to expand the Budget folder, I received the following error message: "C:\DFSRoots\ Marketing\Budget is not accessible." Any management you would like to perform on the new DFS folders will need to be done in the DFS Management snap-in. What is physically stored in the Budget or Projects folders are called reparse points. Reparse points contain the UNC (universal naming convention, anything that begins with "\\") path information needed for a user to connect to a folder target. In the Budget folder, the reparse point contains \\Server1\Budget, and in the Projects folder, the reparse point contains \\Server2\Projects. Well, if you as the administrator cannot access the reparse points, how do you suppose the clients get the Marketing namespace and ultimately connect to the reparse points?

Clients Accessing the DFS Namespace

How do the clients connect to the namespace? There are a couple of different ways, of course. You could map a drive to the DFS Namespace in a login script with a simple net use statement (net use M: \\Bigfirm\Marketing) for your users, which would automatically connect them to the namespace upon logging in. Or, a user could browse to \\Domainname\DFS Namespace through IE—in this example, \\Bigfirm\Marketing (remember, you chose to create a domain-based DFSN). The users could then access the data they have permissions to access.

But what really just happened? When it comes to troubleshooting a user's failed connection to one of the DFS Namespace folders, wouldn't it be nice to know step by step how the client finds a namespace server and then connects to one of the folder targets? Let's examine a client accessing one of the folder targets a little more closely. A user browses to \\Bigfirm\Marketing in Internet Explorer and:

1. A request is sent to a DNS server for a list of DCs.

2. From the list of DCs the client requests a list of namespace servers who have a copy of the \\Bigfirm\Marketing namespace. In this example, there is only one namespace server, and that is DCS.

3. The client requests the \\Bigfirm\Marketing namespace from DCS. The Marketing namespace will be displayed containing the Budget and Projects folders.

4. When a user clicks the Budget folder, they are connected to \\Server1\Budget; if the user were to click the Projects folder they would be connected to \\Server2\Projects.

TIP Notice the steps include DNS, DCs, Namespace Servers, and folder target servers—failure anywhere along the way causes the user to fail in their attempt to access the namespace.

That seems fairly simple doesn't it? Let's complicate it a bit more. One thing I didn't tell you is that you actually have two sites configured in Active Directory Sites and Services (ADSS): the New Jersey (NJ) site and the New York (NY) site. The The New Jersey site contains a DC (DC2), a DNS Server, Server2, and 50 users who need access to the Marketing namespace. The New York (NY) site contains a DC (DCS), a DNS Server, Server1, and 50 users who also need access to the Marketing namespace, as shown in Figure 17.15.

FIGURE 17.15
Site configuration

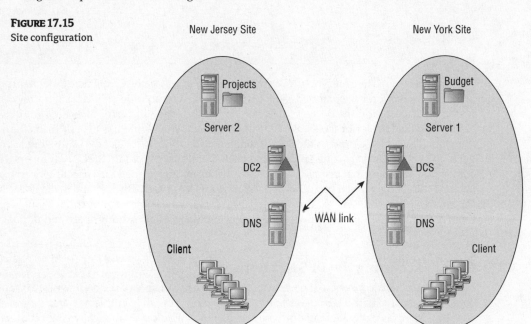

The two sites are connected by a WAN link that at times is unreliable. Recently, users from the New Jersey site were not able to access the \\Server1\Budget folder through the newly created DFS Namespace. How can you ensure that the users from the NJ site have access to the Budget folder data regardless of WAN link availability? Well, if you put a copy of the \\Server1\Budget folder on Server2, then your users in the NJ site could access the Budget data locally from Server2 first, connecting to Server1 only if Server2 were unavailable, thus providing fault tolerance and high data availability for the users in the NJ site. Does this help the users in the NY site in any way? You bet it does. The NY users will continue to access Server1 for the Budget folder first but, in the event that Server1 becomes unavailable, the NY users will be redirected to Server2 in the NJ site. Placing a copy of the \\Server1\Budget folder on Server2 is only the first step; the Marketing Namespace doesn't know about the new Budget folder on Server2, and if the namespace doesn't know about the new folder, how will your clients ever find out about it? The process of adding a copy of a folder is referred to as a folder target. What you need is a folder target for the Budget folder on Server2 but, before you create a folder target, let's delve a little deeper into what a target is and the different types of targets you can create.

What Is a *Target*?

Think of the word *target* as simply meaning a *copy*. In the preceding scenario you decided that you needed a copy of the \\Server1\Budget folder on Server2 for the users in the NJ site to access locally first, and that they'd only connect to the \\Server1\Budget folder in the New York site if Server2 were not available. This copy of a folder is referred to as a *folder target*. Creating a folder target on Server2 for the Budget folder would take care of fault tolerance for the Budget folder, but what about building in a little fault tolerance for the \\Bigfirm\Marketing namespace itself? DCS is currently the only namespace server you have, and it resides in the New York site, so on those occasions when the WAN link is down, how do users from the NJ site get the \\Bigfirm\Marketing namespace? The answer is they don't. But if you look at Figure 17.15 again, you'll notice you have a DC in the NJ site named DC2. Let's store a copy of the \\Bigfirm\Marketing namespace root (remember, it can also be stored on Server2 which is a member server) on DC2. This copy of the namespace root is called a *root target*.

Creating a Root Target

Storing the namespace on more than one server not only provides fault tolerance in the event that a local server becomes unavailable, but also assists in load balancing, so one server doesn't get over-burdened with requests. You as the administrator have full control over which server your users connect to first. I will cover how to control these settings in just a bit, but first let's create a root target.

To create a root target, right-click the \\Bigfirm\Marketing namespace and choose Add Namespace Server. You will see a screen similar to Figure 17.16.

Browse to the server you would like to store a copy of the namespace on (the new root server must reside in the same domain as the namespace); put yours on the server named DC2. Notice the share name of the DFSRoot will be the same on the new namespace server (in the example, Marketing), and click OK. If DFS is not currently running on DC2, you will be prompted, "This Server does not have the Distributed File System service running. Do you want to set the service start state to automatic and start it?" Answering yes will do just that; of course, you must have DFSN installed on DC2 also.

FIGURE 17.16
Add Namespace
Server dialog box

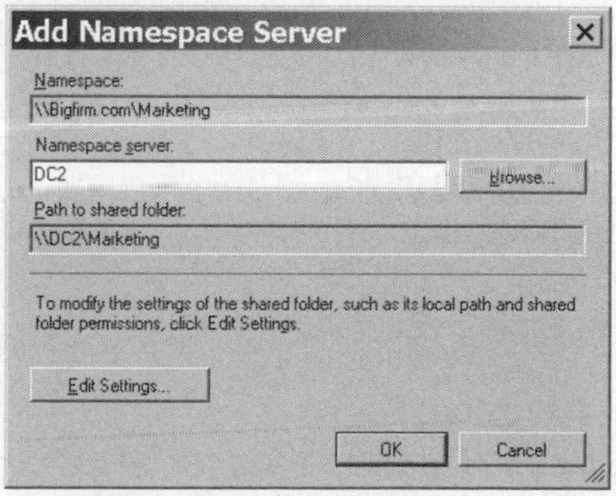

When you add namespace servers, it can take a few minutes for the new namespace server to get a copy of the namespace root. The reason is because domain-based namespaces are stored in the Active Directory DFS object and the new namespace servers request the namespace root from the PDC Emulator. The request for the namespace root is called *polling* and the initial polling request is always sent to the PDC Emulator to ensure the namespace root is consistent among all namespace servers. Subsequent polling intervals used to refresh namespace information may be optimally configured by the administrator for either consistency, where all namespace servers *always* poll the PDC Emulator or scalability that allows all namespace servers to poll the DC closest to them based on Active Directory Sites and Services (ADSS).

To configure your *polling optimization* in the DFS Management snap-in, right-click the namespace name and choose properties. Then, on the Advanced tab choose either consistency or scalability.

NOTE Microsoft recommends no more than 16 root targets when your polling optimization is configured for consistency, to prevent overwhelming the PDC Emulator.

CREATE A FOLDER TARGET

To create a folder target for the Budget folder, in the DFS Management snap-in, expand your namespace (\\Bigfirm\Marketing) in the console pane. Beneath your namespace right-click the Budget folder and select Add Folder Target, as shown in Figure 17.17.

The next screen should look familiar to you; simply browse to the \\server\share you would like to create the Budget folder target on. For this example, browse to \\Server2\Bud. Notice the shared folder name on Server2 is not the same as the shared folder name on Server1 (the point is, they don't have to be). After clicking OK, you are prompted to create a replication group for the Budget folder. Replication groups allow you to use DFS Replication to automatically keep the data in the Budget folder on Server1 and Server2 in sync. Replication groups are covered in the DFS Replication section later in this chapter.

FIGURE 17.17
Add Folder Target

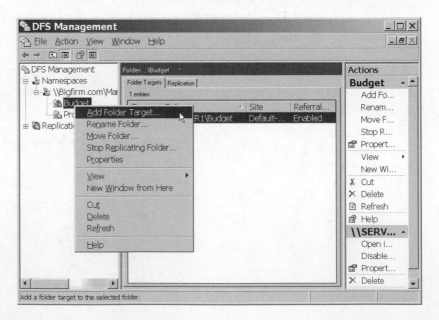

NOTE Microsoft recommends having no more than 5,000 folder targets in a domain-based namespace and limits a stand-alone namespace to 50,000 folder targets. If you exceed these limits, performance for the namespace may degrade and it may take an exceedingly long time for the namespace to initialize.

If you would like to view the data in the Budget folder target (to verify data consistency), expand your namespace \\Bigfirm.com\Marketing, the Budget folder will be listed, highlight the Budget folder. In the details pane (center window) you will see two folder targets, \\Server1\Budget and \\Server2\Bud; right-click the folder target whose data you would like to view and choose Open in Explorer. You could open both folder targets for the Budget folder and compare the data in each for troubleshooting purposes.

Clients Accessing the DFS Namespace Now

Now that you have fault tolerance consisting of two namespace servers (DCS in the NY site and DC2 in the NJ site) and two folder targets for the Budget folder (\\Server1\Budget and \\Server2\Bud), let's re-explore the process of a client accessing the data in the Budget folder. Once again, the user browses to \\Bigfirm\Marketing in Internet Explorer. Here we go:

1. A client sends a request to a DNS server asking for a list of DCs and receives:

NJ Site client	NY Site client
DC2	DCS
DCS	DC2

2. The client requests a list of namespace servers who host (have a copy of) the \\Bigfirm\Marketing namespace from a DC (a NJ client would query DC2, and a NY client would query DCS first). The client receives a *Root Target Referral* list:

Root Target Referral

NJ Site client	NY Site client
DC2	DCS
DCS	DC2

3. The client requests the \\Bigfirm\Marketing namespace from the first server in their list (which will become their *preferred namespace server*); a client in the NJ site will request the namespace from DC2, and a client in the NY site would request the namespace from DCS. The user receives a *Folder Target Referral* list:

Folder Target Referral

NJ Site	NY Site
\\Server2\Bud	\\Server1\Budget
\\Server1\Budget	\\Server2\Bud
\\Server2\Projects	\\Server2\Projects

4. When a user in the NJ site clicks the Budget folder, a connection is attempted to \\Server2\ Bud. If \\Server2\Bud is not available, they will then attempt to connect (*failover*) to \\Server1\Budget. When a user in the NY site clicks the Budget folder, they will attempt to connect to \\Server1\Budget first and—yes, you guessed it—if \\Server1\Budget is not available, they will attempt to connect (*failover*) to \\Server2\Bud.

NOTE Failover simply means the server the user was previously connected to is no longer available, therefore they will be connected to the next server in their Folder Target Referral list.

What you have just seen is the default *referral ordering method*, which attempts to keep DFSN traffic local within a site, yet provide a fault tolerant solution in the event of a server becoming unavailable. But wait, there's more to the referral ordering method than meets the eye—okay, well, more than you have seen so far. Let's dig a little deeper.

REFERRAL ORDERING METHOD

The referral ordering method dictates which server becomes the preferred namespace server by the order in which the servers are listed in the root target referral and the folder target referral. You have three choices for the referral ordering method: Lowest Cost (default), Random Order, and Exclude Targets Outside of the Client's Site.

The Lowest Cost referral ordering method is also known as "least expensive target" and is determined by Active Directory Sites and Services (ADSS) site link costs (for a detailed explanation of ADSS site link costs, see *Mastering Windows Server 2003*). Random Order lists the namespace servers in the same site as the client in random order and lists targets outside of a client's site in lowest cost to highest cost order. If you select the last choice, Exclude targets outside of the client's site, the list of referrals offered to the clients will only contain targets within the client's local site, so be careful with this one. From our previous scenario, if you select Exclude Targets Outside of the Client's Site for the \\Bigfirm\Marketing namespace, clients in the NY site will only receive DCS in their Root Target Referral list, and clients in the NJ site will only receive DC2 in their Root Target Referral list. So if DCS in the NY site becomes unavailable, your users in the NY site will not connect to DC2 in the NJ site to request the \\Bigfirm\Marketing namespace. The same is true for users in the NJ site; they would only connect to DC2.

To configure the referral ordering method for the namespace root, right-click the namespace in the DFS Management snap-in and select Properties, click the Referrals tab, and you will see a screen similar to Figure 17.18.

Under the Ordering Method drop-down box in the middle of the dialog box (Figure 17.18), click the down arrow and select one of the three referral ordering methods.

Once the client has received the Root Target Referral list for the \\Bigfirm.com\Marketing namespace, how often does this list get refreshed? As seen in Figure 17.18, at the top of the dialog box is the Cache Duration of 300 seconds (five minutes). The Cache Duration defines how often your clients will refresh their Root Target Referral list containing a list of namespace servers. The cache is always cleared when a client reboots, or you can choose to clear the cache with the command line utility Dfsutil.exe by typing **Dfsutil /pktflush** or **Dfsutil /spcflush** at the command prompt.

TIP Keep in mind, clients receive their Root Target Referral list from the Domain Controller closest to them. If you have recently added or removed a namespace server from the root target referral list, this information is stored in AD and may take some time to replicate to all of your DCs.

FIGURE 17.18

Namespace Properties Referrals tab

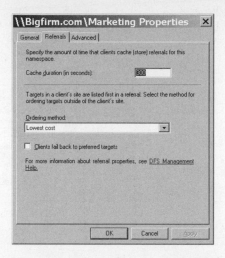

The last configuration parameter on this screen allows you to enable the Clients Fail Back to Preferred Targets setting. Why would a client want or need to failback? How did it failover in the first place? Let's look at a typical work day for a user named Bubba, whose workstation is in the NJ site and who has DC2 as his preferred namespace server. If the DFSN client on Bubba's workstation attempted to refresh the \\Bigfirm\Marketing namespace and the preferred server (DC2) was not available, the DFSN client would failover to DCS in the NY site (assuming your referral ordering method allowed this) and request the namespace information from DCS. When DC2 is available again and failback is enabled, the DFSN client on Bubba's workstation would again choose DC2 as the preferred namespace server.

TIP   The client failback feature is only available for XP SP2 and Server 2003 SP1 systems that have installed Microsoft's hotfix 898900, which requires a reboot.

The referral ordering method configured on the root of your DFSN is inherited by the folder targets within that namespace. You may choose to edit the folder target referral ordering method to be different on just one folder target that will override the referral ordering method of the root target. To configure the referral ordering method for a folder, expand your namespace in DFS Management, right-click the folder in the console pane, and choose Properties. Figure 17.19 shows the Referrals tab of the Budget folders properties.

The first configuration parameter is the Cache Duration of the folder. The default value is 1800 seconds, or 30 minutes. The cache duration for the folder defines how often the client refreshes the list of folder targets for this particular folder, and adding or deleting a folder target is discovered when the cache is refreshed. A client's cache is refreshed when a client reboots or a user runs `Dfsutil /pktflush` from a command prompt (`Dfsutil /spcflush` works also).

Notice the Effective Referral Ordering method is inherited from the root of the namespace (Lowest Cost, in this example). The only choice you have on the folder is to enable Exclude Targets Outside of the Client's Site, which will override the Lowest Cost setting received from the root of the namespace.

FIGURE 17.19
Budget Properties
Referrals tab

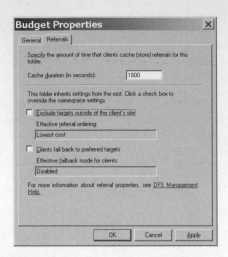

WARNING   Please use caution when enabling the Exclude Targets Outside of the Client's Site setting. If you enable this setting and you would like to provide fault tolerance for your users, you will need at least two servers in the client's local site that hosts the folder target.

A client's ability to *failback to preferred targets* can be configured per folder, and just as Exclude Targets Outside of the Client's Site folder settings will override settings inherited from the root namespace, so does the failback setting.

Once a client selects a root target or folder target from the referral list, the client will continue to access that target until one of the following actions occur: the computer is restarted, the user clears the cache (Dfsutil /pktflush, Dfsutil /spcflush), or the Time To Live value for the root or folder expires. The next time the client attempts to access the target a new referral is obtained. If the user currently has a document open on a server they have failed over to, everything is fine as long as the folder the document resides in is set to be available offline; otherwise, there could be data loss.

What if you wanted all users to access data from the \\Server1\Budget folder and only connect to \\Server2\Bud as a last resort? This can be achieved by setting the target priority.

TARGET PRIORITY

The target priority may be configured to always direct clients to a specific folder target first, or ensure a folder target is always last on the Folder Target Referral list, by setting the target priority directly on the folder target.

To illustrate target priority, you need to modify your scenario slightly. You still have two namespace servers (DCS and DC2) and two servers hosting our folder targets (Server1 and Server2) in your Bigfirm.com\Marketing namespace. But now there is only one site with 100 users. You would like for all users to connect to Server1 to access the Budget data and to only connect to Server2 if Server1 becomes unavailable.

Expand your namespace in DFS Management and highlight the Budget folder in the console pane. You should see the folder targets \\Server1\Budget and \\Server2\Bud in the detail pane as shown in Figure 17.20.

In the details pane, right-click \\Server1\Budget, select Properties, the General tab allows you to disable/enable referrals for that specific folder target (if you remove the checkmark from the

"Enable referrals for this folder target box", you are disabling this *folder target* from being included in the *Folder Target Referral list*). The Advanced tab allows you to override the referral ordering method that was inherited from the namespace root. Figure 17.21 shows the Advanced tab settings; by placing a check mark in the Override Referral Ordering box, four Target priority options are available for you to choose from: First Among All Targets, Last Among All Targets, First Among Targets of Equal Cost, and Last Among Targets of Equal Cost. For this scenario, choose First Among All Targets so that all users will connect to \\Server1\Budget first and only connect to \\Server2\Bud if Server1 becomes unavailable. But what do the other three settings do? Well, the second setting, Last Among All Targets, would place this folder target at the end of the Folder Target Referral list. The last two, First/Last Among Targets of Equal Cost, refer to the cost links assigned in Active Directory Sites and Services Site links. For a full explanation of ADSS site links, please refer to *Mastering Windows Server 2003*.

FIGURE 17.20
Budget's folder targets

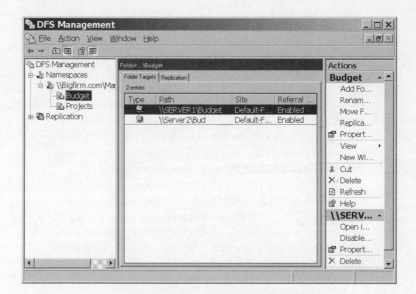

FIGURE 17.21
\\Server1\Budget Properties Advanced tab

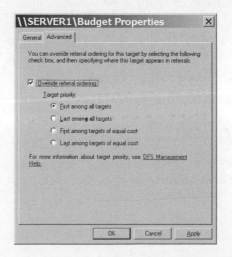

NOTE To find which target the client is currently connected to, from the client, right-click the folder (Budget) and choose Properties. The DFS tab lists who the current folder target is. From this dialog box, you can also clear the cache for this folder target referral and check the status (to ensure connectivity).

Let's return to the original scenario with the New York and New Jersey sites, where everything is working great. Your boss just let you know that you have to come in this weekend and decommission Server1. Not to worry, everyone can failover to Server2 if they need to access the Budget or Projects folders.

Everything goes smoothly decommissioning Server1. On your way to work Monday morning you stop for the usual non-fat latte at Starbucks, you get to work and find a parking place right up front (this almost never happens), you are feeling like it's going to be a great day when you open the door and hear "Hey, the Bigfirm.com\Marketing DFS Namespace is down." Your first thought is: thank goodness I stopped for my Starbucks this morning," and then you are catapulted into the throes of troubleshooting. Ahhh Monday mornings, so peaceful!

This one wasn't so bad, once you realized that the DFS Namespace wasn't down for everyone. In fact it seemed like only the users in the New York site were having difficulty accessing the namespace. You start poking around in the configuration of the namespace and—wait, what is that? Who enabled Exclude Targets Outside of the Client's Site for the Budget folder? Yep, that was the problem, but you still don't know who enabled that. You decide it is time to lock down permissions as to who exactly is allowed to create and manage your namespaces through delegations. Oh yeah, delegations are not just for Active Directory anymore.

Delegating Management Permissions

Domain Administrators are, by default, delegated the ability to create and manage domain-based namespaces in the domain where the namespace is created. In large environments there may be a need to grant a user or group the ability to create or manage namespaces but making them members of the Domain Admins group would be granting a much higher level of administration than necessary. DFS management offers its own delegations.

You can delegate the ability to create and manage domain-based namespaces in just a few simple steps:

1. Open the DFS management snap-in.

2. Right-click the Namespaces node in the console pane (not a namespace, the actual Namespaces node, the one that just says "Namespaces"), and choose Delegate Management Permissions.

3. Add the user/group and click OK.

4. Add the user/group to the local administrators group on the namespace server.

To grant the ability to create a stand-alone namespace, adding the user/group to the local administrators group on the namespace server is all that is necessary.

WARNING On a domain-based DFSN, ensure that the user/group is a member of the local administrators group on each server they need to manage, or their ability to manage the namespace may be inconsistent.

To delegate the ability to add a server or edit the configuration of a specific namespace (domain-based or stand-alone), right-click the namespace in the DFS Management snap-in, then select Delegate Management Permissions, add the user/group (just like you did before), and click OK. On a domain-based namespace the user/group name will be listed on the Delegations tab of the Namespace. Once again, the user/group needs to be added to the local administrators group.

To delegate the ability to *create* a stand-alone namespace, the user/group simply needs to be added to the local administrators group on the server hosting the stand-alone namespace.

Maintenance of Folder Targets

In addition to delegating permissions for a namespace, there may be other routine tasks involved in the maintenance of a DFSN folder target. Renaming a DFSN folder target or restructuring the namespace tree to display the Projects folder first and then the Budget folder are a couple of common maintenance tasks you may be asked to perform.

For example, imagine your boss has asked you to rename your Budget folder target to the more descriptive moniker of Marketing Budget. Renaming a DFSN folder target is as easy as renaming a directory folder using Windows Explorer. Simply right-click the folder, choose Rename Folder, and you will see the Rename Folder dialog box as shown in Figure 17.22. Type the new name **Marketing Budget**, and click OK.

After renaming the Budget folder to Marketing Budget, the Marketing Department requests that you move the Marketing Budget Folder to be under the Projects folder. To move a folder to a different location within the same namespace, you can click and drag the folder to the new location or right-click the folder and choose Move Folder, then browse to the new location and click OK.

If that new location is also in a new site, all namespace servers should receive this updated information automatically, unless the namespace server is a Windows 2000 Server. Windows Server 2000 would never discover the new site information. Please see the section titled "Mixing OSes" for a full explanation.

To remove a folder target from a DFSN folder, expand the namespace in the DFS Management snap-in and highlight the folder containing the folder target. On the Folder Targets tab in the detail pane, right-click the folder target and choose Delete. You will be prompted with a "Confirm Remove Folder Target" warning message, letting you know if this is the last folder target, then the folder will also be deleted. This will remove the folder target from the DFSN but does not physically delete the folder from the server. However, it does allow you to perform a simple deletion on the folder through Windows Explorer.

FIGURE 17.22
Rename Folder
dialog box

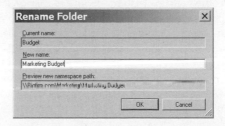

DECOMMISSIONING A ROOT NAMESPACE SERVER

There may come a day when you purchase new hardware and decide to move the entire DFSN to the new server and decommission the current DFSN server. You have already seen the steps to adding a DFSN root target which will take care of adding the new server. After the new server has received the DFS Namespace, you are ready to decommission the old root namespace server by removing the DFSN root server entry from the DFS AD object in the System/Dfs-Configuration container in Active Directory Users and Computers (you may need to enable the advanced view in ADUC to see the system container) and cleaning the DFSN off the old namespace server.

1. Highlight your namespace in the DFS Management snap-in and click the Namespace Servers tab in the details pane.

2. From the list of servers hosting the namespace, right-click the namespace server to be decommissioned and choose Delete or, from a command prompt on the namespace server you would like to remove, use the Dfsutil command-line utility `Dfsutil /UnmapFtRoot /Root:<DFSName> /Server:RootTargetServer /Share:<Share>`. For example, to remove DC2 as a root target from the \\Bigfirm\Marketing Namespace, which you stored in the Marketing share, you would type: `Dfsutil /UnmapFtRoot /Root:\\Bigfirm\ Marketing /Server:DC2 /Share: Marketing`.

3. To clean unwanted Registry settings from the decommissioned server type: `Dfsutil / Clean /Server:RootTargetServer /Share:<RootName>`, for example (still decommissioning the Marketing namespace from DC2): `Dfsutil /Clean /Server:DC2 / Share:Marketing`.

4. The last step is to delete the Marketing folder from the DFSRoots folder in Windows Explorer. The Marketing folder will no longer be a shared folder; right-click the Marketing folder and choose Delete.

After you decommission a root target, it may take a few minutes for all domain controllers to receive the update to the DFS Active Directory object. The amount of time it will take depends on your Active Directory replication schedules.

Mixing OSes

Do you still have Windows 2000 or Windows 2003 Servers as domain controllers or namespace servers? In a perfect DFSN world, all of your DCs and namespace servers would be running Windows Server 2003 SP1 or Windows Server 2003 R2. Why, what happens if you have not yet achieved this DFSN utopian environment yet? The answer is maybe not so much what *will* happen as what *won't* happen. Microsoft has improved the feature set of DFSN by taking advantage of new functionality in the latest Server operating systems. While this new functionality provides us with a more robust and consistent DFSN experience, some of the older Server OSes simply cannot take advantage of the new features because they do not understand them. If you have Windows 2000/ 2003 *without* SP1 servers acting as DCs or namespace servers and a couple of new DCs or namespace servers running Windows Server 2003 SP1 or Windows Server R2, you, my friend, have what is called a *mixed environment*, because there is a mix of server operating systems. In a mixed environment some of the new features are unavailable and some are available rather inconsistently. The next two sections cover common issues when you are running Windows Server 2000 or Windows Server 2003 (without SP1) as a DC or namespace server.

WINDOWS SERVER 2000 AS DCS OR NAMESPACE SERVERS

If you have a DC or namespace server running Windows Server 2000, there are three DFSN features that will not be available: target priority, client failback, and ordering targets by lower cost.

A Windows Server 2000 DC or namespace server may unexpectedly direct clients to namespace servers or folder targets outside the client's local site, even when there are folder targets within the client's site. To fully understand how this can occur, you need to explore how site membership is discovered and updated.

When an administrator creates a DFS Namespace, site membership information is retrieved from Active Directory Sites and Services. Windows Server 2000 places a copy of the site membership information in the DFS object in AD and *never* refreshes the information. So, if a namespace server or server hosting a folder target is moved from one site to another, Windows Server 2000 will never update the new site membership information.

To force the Windows Server 2000 to update the site membership information in the DFS object in AD, on a 2003 Server from a command prompt type **Dfsutil /UpdateWin2KStaticSiteTable**. The information will be updated this one time. Keep in mind that any time a namespace server or server hosting a folder target is moved from one site to another site, this Dfsutil command will need to be run again.

The DFS object in AD contains all of your DFSN information (namespace servers and all servers who host folder targets). Windows Server 2000 is the only client that accesses the site information from this object, and the maximum recommended size of the DFS object in AD is 5MB. For this reason, once all of your DCs and namespace servers are running Windows 2003 Server, you should clean out the DFS object of the site information by running the following at a command prompt:

```
Dfsutil /PurgeWin2KStaticTable
```

Due to the way Windows Server 2000 discovers site information, in a mixed environment, you should always use the 2000 tools that shipped with the Windows Server 2000 Resource Kit (Distributed File System snap-in or the 2000 version of Dfsutil) to create and modify namespace servers and folder targets. Using the Server 2000 tools will copy the site information to the DFS object in AD.

Inconsistent results can occur when running the DFS Management snap-in on a Windows 2003 SP1 or XP SP2 machine and the snap-in connects to a 2000/2003 (Non-SP1) Server. Some features such as client failback, target priority, renaming or moving folders, and delegations will not be available.

WINDOWS SERVER 2003 WITHOUT SP1 AS DCs OR NAMESPACE SERVERS

If you have a DC or a namespace server running Windows Server 2003 *without* SP1, target priority and client failback functionality is lost.

TROUBLESHOOTING COMMON DFS CLIENT PROBLEMS

Why would a client unexpectedly be directed to a DFS resource (namespace server or folder target) outside the client's site when there is a DFS resource in the client's local site? Actually there are a few reasons this may occur; here are some of the more common reasons:

Same-site target is temporarily unavailable.   DFSN uses ADSS to determine the IP address-to-site mappings. If a target's (root or folder) IP address is not mapped to the correct site, the order of the targets in the referral list could be incorrect. An incorrect ordering of the targets in a referral list may occur if a subnet is not configured for the correct site or when a DC or server's IP address is not correctly configured for the site the server physically resides in (you may have moved the server to a new site physically but left the old IP address—oops). Always check to make sure the server object was not left in the Default-First-Site-Name site, where all servers originally belonged.

Ensure your site link Cost settings are correct; if not, a client could unexpectedly choose a high-cost target.

The DFS object in AD may not have replicated to all DCs yet.   Replication latency could cause new information in the DFS object to take longer to replicate to one server than another.

DFSN requires the *Bridge all site links* option to be enabled in ADSS.   The Intersite Topology Generator (ISTG) relies on site links to be bridged in order for the least cost and high cost values to be calculated correctly.

TIP   To find the Bridge All Site Links setting, open Active Directory Sites and Services, expand Sites, and expand Inter-Site-Transports; IP and SMTP will be listed. Right-click IP, choose Properties, and on the General tab, you will see the box that should contain a check mark for the Bridge All Site Links setting (perform the same steps for the SMTP Inter-Site-Transports properties).

If you have checked everything up to this point and your clients are still being referred to DFS resource outside the client's site, it is possible that site awareness itself is not working properly. DCs and namespace servers running Windows 2000/2003 may have had their RestrictAnonymous Registry setting enabled. This setting may be enabled in a number of ways—maybe you attempted to make your DCs more secure by applying the Hisecdc security template on them. If this security template has been implemented on your DFSN root namespace servers running Windows Server 2000/2003, they will not be able to accurately sort targets in a referral list. This is due to the Registry setting HKLM/SYSTEM/CurrentControlSet/Control/Lsa, RestrictAnonymous value being enabled (Value Data:2), so set this value back to 0 (KB 246261).

DNS lookup issues for the DFS root could fail if a root server has multiple IP addresses and not all of the IP addresses are mapped to AD sites in ADSS.

Up to this point, you have been manually keeping the data in sync between the folder targets \\Server1\Budget and \\Server2\Bud, but wouldn't it be nice if the data could automatically be kept in sync? DFS Replication (DFSR) is the tool that allows us to do this.

DFS Replication

In the past, the File Replication Service (FRS) was responsible for replicating both the data in your DFS folders and the SYSVOL folder between domain controllers (SYSVOL contained login scripts and GPO settings among other things). While DFSN is an updated version of DFS (you could call it DFS version 2), DFSR is a completely new product from FRS. DFSR replicates data more reliably and efficiently than its predecessor by implementing a number of new technologies: Remote Differential Compression (RDC), state-based replication, bandwidth throttling, and automatic recovery to name just a few. RDC allows DFSR to replicate only what has changed in a file and not the entire file, as FRS would have done. State-based replication allows DFSR to replicate the latest information; if a file were modified more than once in a replication cycle, only the last modification would be replicated. For example, if Budget.XLS were changed three times within a replication period, DFSR would replicate only the most recent version of the file (FRS would have replicated the entire file three times). Bandwidth throttling ensures line of business applications have the amount of bandwidth needed and is fully configurable. Scheduling is more granular (every 15 minutes, instead of once per hour). DFSR even knows how to repair itself in the event of a journal wrap or database failure. Data conflicts are handled better so there are no more morphed files/folders. You can also delegate control of replication groups, which gives you much more flexibility with administration.

In this section, I will cover how to create a replication group and explain step-by-step how replication occurs so you may understand better how to configure DFSR optimally for your environments. Don't be concerned if I just threw a bunch of new terms at you, if you are not familiar with journal wraps, data conflicts and bandwidth throttling, I promise…you will be an expert in each by the end of this chapter!

While DFSR can be used to keep our DFSN folder targets in sync, it can also replicate *any* NTFS folder's data between two or more servers—the folder doesn't even have to be shared!

For those of you who currently have a 2000/2003 DFS structure replicating via FRS and would like to look at the new features of DFSN replicating with DFSR, you will be happy to hear that both may co-exist on the same member server or domain controller, so relax and take your time to learn all the new features.

NOTE   DFS Replication is not supported for SYSVOL replication in Windows Server 2003 R2 (that's coming in Windows Server 2007).

Before we get started, there is some terminology it will be helpful to understand. With DFSR being a new technology, there is no "old terminology" to correlate the new terms with as I did with DFSN. Table 17.2 lists the new DFSR terms.

TABLE 17.2:   DFSR Terminology

TERM	DEFINITION
Replication group	A set of servers, called members, that participate in replicating one or more folders. The replication group name will be the same as the namespace.
Replicated folder	A folder whose data is replicated between servers.
Connection topology	Which members replicate with other members.
Schedule	When replication is available.
Upstream partner	The partner who sends the notification that it has changes for a replicating partner.
Downstream partner	The partner who received the notification from an upstream partner to initiate replication.

When you left the DFSN scenario, you were manually copying data between \\Server1\Budget and \\Server2\Bud. Let's set up DFSR to automatically replicate this for you by creating a replication group for the Budget folder in the \\Bigfirm.com\Marketing namespace.

Before you can create a replication group for the Budget folder, you must ensure that the DFS Replication service and the DFS Replication Diagnostic and Configuration Tools are installed on all servers participating in the replication group (that would be Server1 and Server2 for this example). The DFS Management snap-in needs to be installed only on the machines you would like to configure and manage DFSR from. In fact, if you would like to use the command-line utility DFSRAdmin.exe, you don't need to install the DFS Management snap-in at all.

There are a couple of ways to install DFSR and its tools; I recommend installing the DFS Replication service and the DFS Replication Diagnostic and Configuration Tools from Control Panel ➢ Add or Remove Programs ➢ Windows Components. Highlight Distributed File System and click the Details button, select DFS Replication service (DFS Replication Diagnostic and Configuration Tools will be selected also). To review other methods of installing DFSR, please see the beginning of this chapter. Now that you have DFSR and its tools installed on Server1 and Server2, you are ready to create a replication group for the Budget folder in your \\Bigfirm.com\Marketing namespace.

Creating a Replication Group

To create a replication group, open the DFS Management snap-in, right-click the Replication node in the console pane, and choose New Replication Group. This will launch the New Replication Group Wizard. On the first page you need to select the type of replication group to create. You have two options, multipurpose or data collection, as shown in Figure 17.23.

FIGURE 17.23
Replication Group
Type page

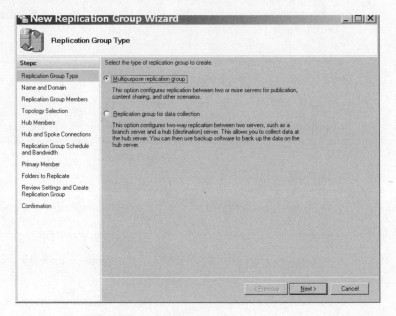

The Multipurpose replication group option is for shared data that your users will access. The Replication group for data collection option is used for collecting data from branch offices to ease the task of backing up data to a central location. The central office collects data from the branch offices and performs backups on the data, therefore alleviating the need to perform backups at an office that may not have administrative personnel capable of performing the backups. For your replication group type, choose Multipurpose replication group.

Clicking Next will take you to the Name and Domain page. As shown in Figure 17.24, you type the name of the replication group as Budget; in the description box, you can type a short description if you choose; and the domain name is already input for you (or you could choose to input a different domain name, but be sure in a multidomain environment that the trust relationships and permissions are set correctly).

Click Next and you are on the Replication Group Members page. Click the Add button and type the name of the servers you would like to participate in the replication group (separate the names with a semicolon) or choose Advanced and find the server names in AD. Input **Server1** and **Server2**, as shown in Figure 17.25.

FIGURE 17.24
Name and
Domain page

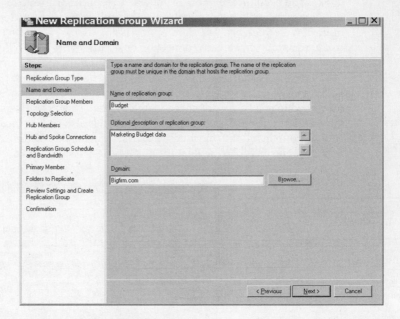

FIGURE 17.25
Replication Group
Members page

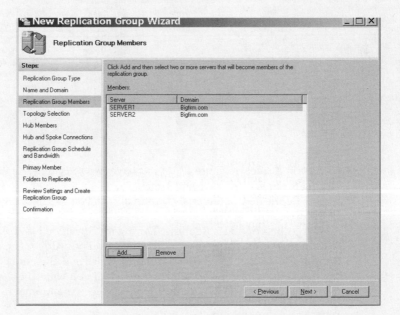

After adding your servers, click Next, and you advance to the Topology Selection page, where you have three options, as shown in Figure 17.26.

The topology is defined by the replication group members and who they are supposed to replicate to, based on the connections created between them. The first of the three options are Hub and spoke. You need three or more members in a replication group for this selection. The second option is Full mesh and allows all members in the replication group to replicate with each other providing built-in fault tolerance. The third option is No Topology, which allows the administrator full control to manually create each connection object, therefore controlling which member replicates with other members. DFSR's topology is independent from Active Directories replication topology. FRS used Active Directories connections and site schedules from Active Directory Sites and Services. DFSR's topology is stored in the DFS object in AD found in the System/Dfsr-GlobalSettings (you may need to enable the advanced view in Active Directory Users and Computers) and replicated via AD Replication. The topology information is also cached locally on each member of the replication group in an XML file in case a DC is not available. Choose the default topology of Full mesh and click Next to go to the Replication Group Schedule and Bandwidth page.

FIGURE 17.26
Topology
Selection page

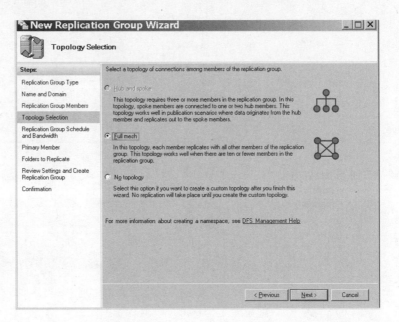

As you can see in Figure 17.27, you have two selections, Replicate Continuously or Replicate During the Specified Dates and Times.

The Replicate Continuously option allows you to select the amount of bandwidth DFSR uses.

The second option is Replicate During the Specified Days and Times, which allows the Administrator to create custom schedules, and boy, do I mean custom—check this out: select Replicate During the Specified Days and Times and click the Edit Schedule button. As you can see from Figure 17.28, you must first decide if you want the schedule to be based on Universal Coordinated Time (UTC) or Local Time of Receiving Member.

NOTE   Universal Coordinated Time (UTC) is the same as Greenwich Mean Time, or GMT.

FIGURE 17.27
Replication Group
Schedule and Band-
width page

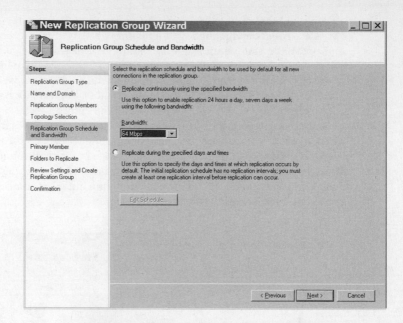

FIGURE 17.28
Edit Schedule page

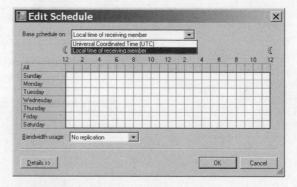

The daily and hourly grid probably looks familiar; this grid allows you to get extremely granular.
Set the following replication schedule:

◆ Every night from 12:00 a.m.–4:00 a.m. allow replication at full bandwidth

◆ Monday–Friday:

   ◆ 8:00 a.m.–9:00 a.m. no replication allowed

   ◆ 9:00 a.m. to 12:00 p.m. allow replication at 256Kbps bandwidth

   ◆ Noon–2:00 p.m. no replication allowed

   ◆ 2:00 p.m.–5:00 p.m. allow replication at 256Kbps bandwidth

   ◆ 5:00 p.m.–7:00 p.m. allow replication at 128Mbps bandwidth

   ◆ 7:00 p.m.–12:00 a.m. allow replication at 256Mbps bandwidth

Highlight midnight to 4:00 a.m. for Sunday through Saturday, and in the Bandwidth usage box select Full. Then highlight 9:00 a.m. through 12:00 p.m. on Monday through Friday and select 256Kbps in the Bandwidth usage box. I think you get the picture. Speaking of pictures, after you have set your schedule your screen should look something like Figure 17.29.

From looking at Figure 17.29, can you tell which timeframe is supposed to replicate using only 128Mbps' worth of bandwidth? I certainly couldn't, but wait—what is that Details button? Clicking the Details button shows you a screen similar to Figure 17.30.

You can now see that on Sunday at 12:00 a.m. through 4:00 a.m., Full bandwidth is available for replication. Monday is a little more interesting: 12:00 a.m. through 4:00 a.m. Full bandwidth is available, 9:00 a.m. through 12:00 p.m. 256Kbps, 2:00 p.m. through 5:00 p.m. 256Mbps, 5:00 p.m. through 7:00 p.m. 128Mbps, and 7:00 p.m. through 12:00 p.m. 256Mbps. I think you get the idea. I don't know how many times I have had to figure out what someone else configured and failed to document. This Details button is invaluable.

FIGURE 17.29
Configured schedule

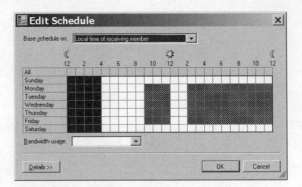

FIGURE 17.30
Edit Schedule,
Details button

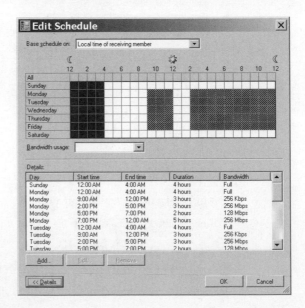

The replication schedule is stored in Active Directory and can be viewed using `ADSIEdit.msc`. Open `ADSIEdit.msc` and expand your Domain, System, DFSR-Global-Settings, and right-click your replication group name. The attribute ms-DFSR-Schedule contains the schedule.

NOTE   The schedules may be set differently on each connection object. If the schedule is not set at the connection object level, the connection schedule will be inherited from the replication groups schedule.

Once you have configured the schedule for replication, click Next, and you are on the Primary Member (Primary Server) page. This page is very important! Whichever server you choose as the primary member is the one that will be authoritative for the entire replication group. Okay, what I mean by that is the server that you deem the primary member will have the most correct and up-to-date data—or should I say it *should*, because the primary member's data will be written to all other members of the replication group upon initial replication. Choose your member from the Primary Member drop-down box (all servers who are members of the replication group will be listed), as shown in Figure 17.31.

FIGURE 17.31
Primary Member

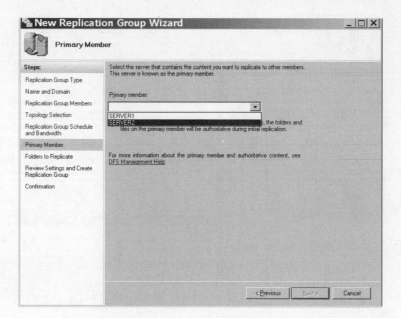

Choose Server1 as your primary member, click Next, and you are taken to the Folders to Replicate page. Click the Add button and you will see a screen similar to Figure 17.32.

The first box is already filled in for you. The member is the primary member you selected in the last page (you can't change that within this window, but you can use the Previous button to go back later and change it). The second box is the local path of the folder to replicate. I like browsing to the folder, so click Browse, expand the drive the shared folder resides on (C$), and choose the Budget folder, as shown in Figure 17.33.

After selecting the Budget folder, click OK, and you are back to the Add Folder to Replicate dialog box. On the bottom of that screen, you can choose to leave the name the same as the folder (which is the default) or to create a custom name. You may also set your NTFS permissions by clicking the Permissions button in the bottom left corner. The two options for permissions are to leave the existing permissions intact or customize them to be whatever you choose. Click OK and you should see a completed Folders to Replicate page, similar to Figure 17.34.

FIGURE 17.32
Add Folder to
Replicate dialog box

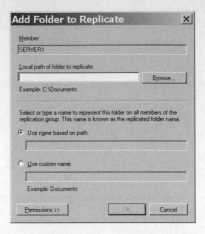

FIGURE 17.33
Browse For Folder
dialog box

FIGURE 17.34
Folders to
Replicate page

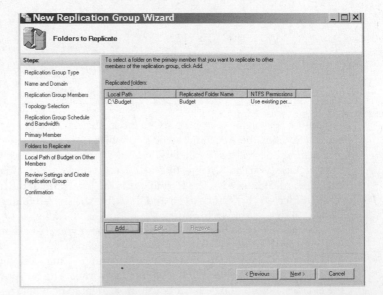

Clicking Next will take you to the Local Path of Budget on Other Members page. Server1 is your primary member; Server2 is the other member that you would like to receive a copy of Server1's Budget folder. But where on Server2 do you want to put it? Notice Server2 is listed under the Member details in Figure 17.35.

Highlight Server2 and click the Edit... button. This will take you to the Edit Local Path dialog box, as shown in Figure 17.36. Select the Enabled radio button, and browse to Server2's Bud folder (remember, your folder names were not the same on Server1 and Server2).

Click OK in the Edit Local Path dialog box and click Next on the Local Path of Budget on Other Members page. The Review Settings and Create Replication Group page will be displayed, as shown in Figure 17.37. On this page you may review your settings and choose to change them at this time either by clicking the Previous button until you arrive at the page you would like to change, or choosing the page you would like to edit by clicking on it from the Orientation pane (on the left sidebar of the page under Steps).

FIGURE 17.35
Local Path of
Budget on Other
Members page

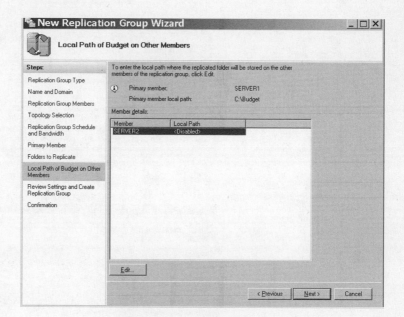

FIGURE 17.36
Edit Local Path
dialog box

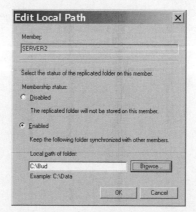

After you have reviewed your settings and found them to be correct, click the Create button. You are almost done. This is the cool part: once you click Create, the Confirmation Page will list each task as it is completed. Upon successfully completing each task there will be a green check mark to the left side, and the status of each task will be Success, as shown in Figure 17.38.

FIGURE 17.37
Review Settings and Create Replication Group

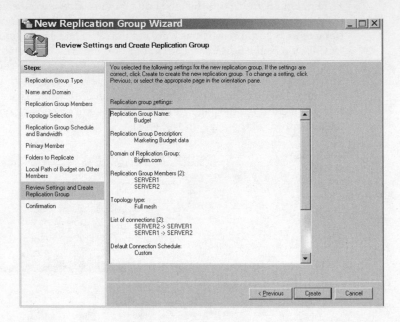

FIGURE 17.38
Confirmation page Tasks tab

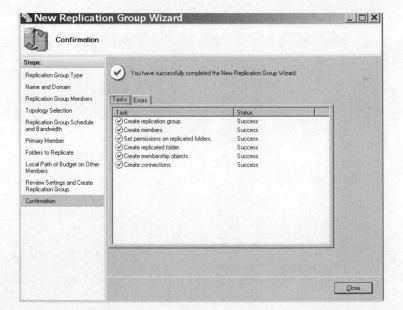

The Error tab on the Confirmation page should display "No Errors Occurred", as shown in Figure 17.39.

The last thing you will see is an informational message, letting you know that there may be a delay in replication because all members of the replication group must get the new replication group settings from Active Directory; you only have two servers, so it shouldn't take long for your replication group information to be replicated. But what if you had 40 servers across the nation? That could take some time due to replication schedules being taken into account. Once the new replication group configuration has replicated to all DCs and the namespace servers receive the replication group configuration information, each namespace server will cache a copy of the configuration in an XML file locally. If a namespace server could not contact a DC for an extended period of time, DFS Replication will not be affected. The informational message you will see is displayed in Figure 17.40.

Wow, that was quite a wizard wasn't it? Now, I can tell you there are a couple of other methods to creating replication groups. There is an easier, and a more complicated way; let's look at the easier way first.

You already have a Budget folder in your DFS Namespace created earlier in this chapter. Expand your namespace in DFS Management and right-click the Budget folder (not the folder targets) in the Console pane and select Replicate Folder. The Replicate Folder Wizard is launched. I am not going to show you this wizard page by page because they are the same pages we just walked through, but the nice thing about this method is that a lot of the information is already filled in for you.

FIGURE 17.39
Confirmation page
Errors tab

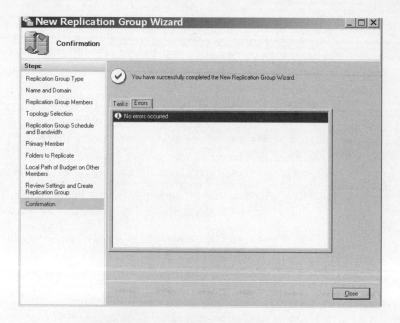

FIGURE 17.40
Replication Delay
message

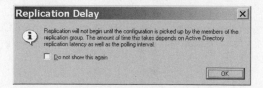

On the Replication Group and Replication Folder name page, your Replication group name is Bigfirm.com\Marketing\Budget and the Replicated Folder name is Budget; you simply click Next. The Replication Eligibility page lists Server1\Budget and Server2\Bud for you—remember you previously created these two folder targets for the Budget folder—once again, just click Next. Choose your primary member, topology, scheduling, and bandwidth throttling settings. Review your settings, click the Create button, and confirm that all tasks completed successfully.

Now for the slightly more complicated method to create a replication group: from the command line.

DON'T LIKE GUIS? MEET DFSRADMIN.EXE

DFSRAdmin allows you to create and edit replication groups, replication folders, and connection objects and to set configuration parameters on members of a replication group. Anything you can do in the DFS Management snap-in may also be performed by the DFSRAdmin command-line tool. This tool allows you scripting capabilities for your DFSR environment. You can also force replication, even outside the replication schedule, and it actually works this time (unlike forcing replication in FRS)!

Let's start by reviewing each task that must be performed:

1. Create a replication group named Budget.

2. Add Server1 and Server2 as members to the Budget replication group.

3. Create a replicated folder named Budget.

4. Set Server1 as the primary server.

5. Set Server2's local replication folder.

6. Create connections.

7. Set the topology for replication.

8. Set the schedule.

After each task is successfully completed you should receive "Command completed successfully and in most cases, you may verify the completed tasks in the DFS Management snap-in."

1. Create a replication group named Budget in the Bigfirm domain and base the schedule on UTC time, not the local time of the server; from a command prompt type the following:

```
DFSRAdmin RG new /RGName:Budget /IsScheduleInLocalTime:False /Domain:Bigfirm
```

2. To see your new replication group in the DFS Management snap-in you must first right-click the Replication node (the one that says Replication) and choose Add Replication Groups to Display. Select your Scope, domain, or Server for a stand-alone replication group (you created a domain-based replication group, so select Domain and you should see your domain name in the box beneath Domain, if not you may have to browse to your domain name). Choose the Budget replication group from the list; if your new replication group is not listed, click the Show Replication Groups button. Click OK and the Budget replication group should appear beneath the Replication node.

3. Make Server1 and Server2 members of the Budget replication group by typing the following from a command prompt:

```
Dfsradmin mem new /RGName:Budget /MemName:Server1
Dfsradmin mem new /RGName:Budget /MemName:Server2
```

4. You cannot verify that Server1 and Server2 are members of the replication group until you have performed step five (creating the replication folder).

5. Create a replication folder named Budget by typing the following at a command prompt:

```
Dfsradmin rf new /rgname:budget /rfname:Budget
```

6. To verify the creation of the new replication folder via the DFS Management snap-in, expand Replication and highlight the Budget replication group in the console pane; the Replicated Folders tab in the details pane shows the Budget folder. Now you can verify that Server1 and Server2 are members of the replication group by looking at the Memberships tab. Server1 and Server2 will be listed.

7. Define Server1's local path to replicate from Server1's C:\Budget folder, and set Server1 as the primary server by typing the following at a command prompt:

```
Dfsradmin membership set /RGName:Budget /RFName:Budget /
MemName:Bigfirm\Server1 /LocalPath:C:\Budget /MembershipEnabled:True /
IsPrimary:True
```

8. Define Server2's local path to receive the replicated folder from Server1 into Server2's C:\Bud folder by typing the following at a command prompt:

```
Dfsradmin Membership Set /RGName:Budget /RFName:Budget /MemName:Server2 /
LocalPath:C:\Bud /MembershipEnabled:True /IsPrimary:False
```

9. To verify the local paths on each server via the DFS Management snap-in, expand Replication and highlight the Budget replication folder in the console pane; the "Memberships" tab will list the Local Path of the folders (you may have to refresh the snap-in by pressing F5).

10. Create the replication connection objects between Server1 and Server2 (you will need to create connection objects for both directions). These connection objects are the vehicles through which replication will occur. You need to create a replication connection from Server1 to Server2, and another from Server2 to Server1 by typing the following from a command prompt:

Connection from Server1 to Server2:

```
Dfsradmin Conn New /RGName:Budget /SendMem:Server1 /RecvMem:Server2 /
ConnEnabled:true
```

Connection from Server2 to Server1:

```
Dfsradmin Conn New /RGName:Budget /SendMem:Server2 /RecvMem:Server1 /
ConnEnabled:true
```

11. To verify creation of the connection objects in the DFS Management snap-in, expand Replication and highlight the Budget replication folder in the console pane. The Connections tab will list the newly created connections. If you receive a yellow triangle containing an exclamation point along with the following text:"The topology is not fully connected. For details, click here," refresh the screen by pressing F5 or choosing "Refresh" from the Action menu. You should see a green checkmark and the following text, "The topology is fully connected. Data can replicate throughout the topology."

12. Define the topology to full mesh by typing the following at a command prompt:

```
Dfsradmin mem set /rgname:Budget /memname:Server1 /memberkeywords:mesh
```

Don't forget Server2:

```
Dfsradmin mem set /rgname:Budget /memname:Server2 /memberkeywords:mesh
```

13. I could not find any way to confirm this setting in the DFS Management snap-in, but from the command prompt you can confirm by typing:

```
Dfsradmin mem list /rgname:Budget /attr:all
```

14. Set the schedule for when you would like replication to occur. I strongly recommend that if you are setting a customized schedule, it is much easier to create the schedule in the DFS Management snap-in; in fact, I would create a mock replication group for the sole purpose of exporting the schedule to a file, then you could use the exported schedule file to import the schedule for your new replication group. If you are not creating a customized schedule, there are three options to choose from: Default, Full, and Empty. The Default and Full settings appear to be identical; they both allow replication 24 hours a day, 7 days a week, which is displayed as 168 hours a week. The Empty setting turns off replication. Remember that our connections are bidirectional so you will have to set both the sending and receiving connections, by typing the following from a command prompt:

15. To use the Full switch:

```
Dfsradmin Conn Set Schedule Full /RGName:Budget /SendMem:Bigfirm\Server1 /
RecvMem:Bigfirm\Server2
```

```
Dfsradmin Conn Set Schedule Full /RGName:Budget /SendMem:Bigfirm\Server2 /
RecvMem:Bigfirm\Server1
```

16. To use the Default switch:

```
Dfsradmin Conn Set Schedule Default /RGName:Budget /SendMem:Bigfirm\Server1 /
RecvMem:Bigfirm\Server2
```

```
Dfsradmin Conn Set Schedule Default /RGName:Budget /SendMem:Bigfirm\Server2 /
RecvMem:Bigfirm\Server1
```

17. To use the Empty switch to disable replication:

```
Dfsradmin Conn Set Schedule Empty /RGName:Budget /SendMem:Bigfirm\Server1 /
RecvMem:Bigfirm\Server2

Dfsradmin Conn Set Schedule Empty /RGName:Budget /SendMem:Bigfirm\Server2 /
RecvMem:Bigfirm\Server1
```

Now, the one you have all been waiting for: setting custom connection specific schedules can be a little more fun from the command line. Let's set the same custom schedule you set previously for your replication folder for our new connections using the New Replication Group Wizard. Do you remember the schedule? For review, the schedule was:

- Every night from 12:00 a.m.–4:00 a.m. allow replication at full bandwidth

- Monday–Friday

  - 8:00 a.m.–9:00 a.m. no replication is allowed

  - 9:00 a.m.–12:00 p.m. allow replication, at 256Kbps bandwidth

  - Noon–2:00 p.m. no replication allowed

  - 2:00 p.m.–5:00 p.m. allow replication at 256Kbps bandwidth

  - 5:00 p.m.–7:00 p.m. allow replication at 128Mbps bandwidth

  - 7:00 p.m.–12:00 a.m. allow replication at 256Mbps bandwidth

Okay, I could not find any easy way to do this: I attempted to type in the schedule for all seven days at once, but the buffer did not allow this much data at one time. So I had to create seven individual commands: Let's take a look at Monday's schedule:

```
Dfsradmin Conn Set Schedule Custom /RGName:Budget /SendMem:Bigfirm\Server1 /
RecvMem:Bigfirm\Server2 /Day:Monday /Schedule:
ffff,ffff,ffff,ffff,0000,0000,0000,0000,0000,4444,4444,4444,0000,0000,4444,4444,4444,dddd,
dddd,eeee,eeee,eeee,eeee,eeee
```

"What are all those 0000, 4444, eeee, ffff's?" I hear you cry. When you count the sets of characters separated by commas, you count 24 sets. There is one set of characters for each hour of the day. Each hourly set consists of four characters, which represents 15-minute increments. For example, a set of 0000 would define the following:

0000	12:00 a.m.–12:15 a.m. No replication
0000	12:15 a.m.–12:30 a.m. No replication
0000	12:30 a.m.–12:45 a.m. No replication
0000	12:45 a.m.–1:00 a.m. No replication

So, if 0 means no replication is available, what does a 1 or a 9 or an f depict? Table 17.3 shows the values you can choose from and the amount of bandwidth each value is allowed to consume for that replication connection.

TABLE 17.3: Allowable Values for Bandwidth Utilization

VALUE	AMOUNT OF BANDWIDTH UTILIZED
0	No replication
1	16Kbps
2	64Kbps
3	128Kbps
4	256Kbps
5	512Kbps
6	1Mbps
7	2Mbps
8	4Mbps
9	8Mbps
a	16Mbps
b	32Mbps
c	64Mbps
d	128Mbps
e	256Mbps
f	Full

I stated earlier that there were 24 sets of characters one set for each hour of the day—so where does the day begin? The very first set of characters (on the far left) represents 12:00 a.m.–1:00 a.m., so what would 1234,0f0f represent in the first two sets?

1234   12:00 a.m.–12:14 a.m. Replicate using 16Kbps of bandwidth

1234   12:15 a.m.–12:29 a.m. Replicate using 64Kbps of bandwidth

1234   12:30 a.m.–12:44 a.m. Replicate using 128Kbps of bandwidth

1234   12:45 a.m.–12:59 a.m. Replicate using 256Kbps of bandwidth

0f0f   1:00 a.m.–1:14 a.m. No replication

0f0f   1:15 a.m.–1:29 a.m. Full replication

0f0f   1:30 a.m.–1:44 a.m. No Replication

0f0f   1:45 a.m.–1:59 a.m. Full Replication

Can you see why I saved the custom schedule for last? Don't forget the schedule must be set in both directions, you have set the replication schedule from Server1 to replicate with Server2. Now you need to set the replication schedule from Server2 to Server1:

```
Dfsradmin Conn Set Schedule Custom /RGName:Budget /SendMem:Bigfirm\Server2 /
RecvMem:Bigfirm\Server1 /Day:Monday /Schedule: ffff,ffff,ffff,ffff,0000,0000,
0000,0000,0000,4444,4444,4444,0000,0000,4444,4444,4444,dddd,dddd,eeee,eeee,
eeee,eeee,eeee
```

TIP Remember, each connection will inherit the schedule settings of the replication folder. To view the replication folder's schedule in the DFS Management snap-in, right-click the replication folder Budget, and choose "Edit Replication Group Schedule". To view a specific connections replication schedule—highlight the replication folder Budget, go to the Connections tab, right-click the connection, choose Properties; on the Schedule tab there will be two options to choose from. View the Replication group schedule and Edit Custom connection schedule. I think this is worth mentioning again. It is easier to create a mock replication group schedule in DFS Management, export the schedule to a text file, and then import the schedule into the replication group you would like the schedule to affect.

First you will have to create a mock replication group (name it whatever you choose, for this example let's use the name Mock), set the schedule to be what you want thru the DFS Management snap-in UI, and then export the schedule to a text file named Sched.txt stored in the root of C: by typing the following at a command prompt:

```
Dfsradmin Conn Export Sched  /RGName:Mock /SendMem:Bigfirm\Server1 /
RecvMem:Bigfirm\Server2 /File:C:\Sched.txt
```

To import the Sched.txt to the new replication group (Budget) schedule type the following at a command prompt:

```
Dfsradmin Conn Import Sched  /RGName:Budget /SendMem:Bigfirm\Server1 /
RecvMem:Bigfirm\Server2 /File:C:\Sched.txt
```

Remember to export/import the connection specific schedule in the opposite direction, with Server2 as the /SendMem and Server1 as the /RecvMem. To verify the connection specific replication schedule, in the DFS Management snap-in expand the Replication Node, highlight Budget, go to the Connections tab, right-click the connection object for Server1 (under Sending member), and choose properties. The Schedule tab should already have "Custom connection schedule:" selected; to view the schedule click the Edit Schedule button. To verify the connection specific replication schedule from a command prompt type: Dfsradmin conn list /rgname:Budget

What's New on the Namespace Servers Now?

What changes on the namespace servers after creating a replication group? Well, once a replication group containing a replication folder is created, the information is stored in the DFS AD object and must replicate to all DCs. The namespace servers will poll the DCs for the replication group information and store the configuration information locally. Each namespace server will have the following folder structure created:

C:\System Volume Information\DFSR

Config

DfsrMachineConfig.XML

Replica_GUID.XML

Volume_GUID.XML

Database_ID

FileIDTable_#

SimilarityTable_#

Replicated Folder\

DfsrPrivate

ConflictAndDeleted

Deleted

Installing

PreExisting

Staging

PreExistingManifest.XML

DfsrMachineConfig.XML　This file contains information pertaining to the last time a change occurred to a file/folder on that namespace server, as well as the last time the namespace server polled AD to find any updates that may have occurred to the namespace or replication settings.

Replica_GUID.XML　This file contains the last change number, scheduling and connection information, the replicated folder GUID (which you may need later for some command line maintenance), and the member GUID.

Volume_GUID.XML　This file contains the DFSR database path, the NTFS change journal size, the replication group GUID, and which server is set as the primary server.

These three .XML files are cached locally on each namespace server to ensure that, in the event a DC cannot be located to retrieve this information, the namespace server will continue to replicate according to the information cached locally in these files. Of course, there is more information than what I just listed but to understand that information you need to look at the entire DFSR process. What really happens during replication?

The DFSR Process

The very first time a server replicates, the replication folder is referred to as initial replication. During the initial replication all members participating in the replication group will copy all folders and files for the replication folder (Budget was your replication folder) from the designated primary server. After the initial replication has occurred with *every* member of the replication group, the designation of "primary server" is removed and replication will continue based on your topology connection settings and schedule.

The steps to replicate a file from one server to another might seem fairly simple. In the example scenario you have a replication folder named Budget and a replication group that contains two servers, Server1 and Server2. It makes sense to say that any files created on Server1 should be replicated to Server2, and vice versa. At the same time, any files modified on either server should be replicated to the other as well. The 10,000 foot view would show three steps to replicating a newly created file named File1.doc in the \\Server1\Budget folder.

1. \\Server1\Budget\File1.Doc is created.

2. File1.Doc is replicated from \\Server1\Budget to \\Server2\Bud.

3. Any files that have changed on \\Server2\Bud are replicated to \\Server1\Budget.

Well, let's start at the beginning, where DFS Replication uses RPC connectivity and DNS as well as NetBIOS name resolution. For reporting capabilities to assist Administrators in monitoring the health of DFSR, Windows Management Instrumentation (WMI) is used along with the Distributed Computing Object Management (DCOM), and Performance Counters. Now let's explore step by step how file1.doc is replicated from \\Server1\Budget to \\Server2\Bud.

Step 1: \\Server1\Budget\File1.Doc Is Created

File1.doc is created in the Budget folder on Server1. The USNC thread (Update Sequence Number Consumer) creates a new file entry in the NTFS change journal named $USNJRNL (Update Sequence Number Journal). To view this new entry for File1.doc, you will use a command-line utility for NTFS called FSUtil. From a command prompt, type the following: **FSUtil USN ReadData** *path of file*. For the example of File1.doc, that would be **FSUtil USN ReadData C:\Budget\ File1.doc**. The output should resemble the following:

```
Major Version:      0x2
Minor Version:      0x0
FileRef#:           0x0003000000002f8c
Parent FileRef#:    0x0008000000001d35
Usn:                0x0000000000089e00
Time Stamp:         0x0000000000000000 12:00:00 AM 1/1/1601
Reason:             0x0
Source Info:        0x0
Security Id:        0x192
File Attributes:    0x20
File Name Length:   0x10
File Name Offset:   0x3c
FileName:           file1.doc
```

Please note the FileRef# of 0x0003000000002f8c and the USN of 0x0000000000089e00—I am going to expand on these later.

Before DFSR begins to process a file for replication, the file must be sent through something called a *filter*. Filters are used to determine if a folder or file is to be replicated or filtered out of the replication process. There are two types of filters, file and folder filters. By default, your file filters include files whose filename begins with a tilde (~) or that have an extension of .bak or .tmp, or are encrypted via EFS (EFS files will be filtered out of the replication process). So if any files meeting those criteria exist in our Budget folder on Server1, they would be filtered out of the DFSR process and would not be replicated. By default, there are no folder filters.

Filters are set individually on replicated folders, so you could exclude Microsoft Project (.mpp) files from being replicated from the Budget folder but allow .mpp to replicate from the Projects folder. To edit/create a filter, in the DFS Management snap-in, expand Replication, highlight your replication folder (Budget in the example) and, in the details pane, click the Replicated Folders tab, right-click your folder name (Budget), and select Properties. You should see a screen similar to Figure 17.41.

To set a file filter simply type in the extensions of the file types you would like excluded from replication in the File Filter box (remember to separate them with commas). For this example, leave the defaults and add ***.mpp** to the list (to set a folder filter, add any subfolder names you would like to exclude, being sure to separate them with commas also) and click OK.

From this point forward, no .mpp files will be replicated from the Budget folder—but what happens to the existing .mpps in the Budget folder that were happily replicating in the past? On the next replication cycle, the filter will be read and applied, the existing .mpp's in the Budget folder will be tombstoned in the DFSR FileIDTable (you will see the FileIDTable next) and flagged as Filtered to prevent the files from replicating in the future.

NOTE In the past, FRS only applied filters when a file was created and never again. If there is currently a file that is being filtered out of the replication process and it is renamed to a file type that should be replicated, FRS would not begin replicating the file. The same is true if a file is currently being replicated and is renamed to a file type that should not be replicated; since the filter is never read again FRS would continue to replicate the file as before. DFSR's handling of filters far surpasses its predecessor FRS!

FIGURE 17.41
Budget Properties

Well, that takes care of the requirement for the Budgets folder, but say that upon reviewing the file filter on the Projects folder, you find that someone has also added the .mpp extension to exclude replicating the .mpp's for the Projects folder. That is easy enough to fix: you remove the .mpp extension from the Projects folder filter list. So now what happens to files that were not previously replicated due to this filter? By removing the .mpp extension from the Project folders file filter list, the filters will be read on the next replication cycle and all the .mpp files in the Projects folder will get a new File ID (FID) in the FileIDTable in the DFSR database, and the files replicate.

Once the entry is placed in the NTFS change journal by the USNC thread and has made it through the filter, the Load Byte Index (LDBX) thread updates DFSR's FileIDTable_# (found in the %Systemroot%\System Volume Information\DFSR folder), and the Version Vector (VV) tables in the DFSR database.

Let's look at the FileIDTable_# record information for File1.doc first by using another command-line tool. This tool is called WMIC and allows you to get information from a Windows Management Instrumentation (WMI) provider. The WMIC command-line interface will pass the request to the correct DFSR process; all you have to do is type in the following at a command prompt: **wmic / namespace:\\root\microsoftdfs path dfsridrecordinfo** where filename="File1.doc". The output will be similar to the following:

```
Attributes    32
Clock         20060613001719.383754-000
CreateTime    20060612205142.699156-000
Fence         3
Fid           844424930144140
FileHash      ed29f6280e62f501 f6989f9e7f0c8e01
FileName      file1.doc
Flags         5
GVsn          {E8D0AE56-1D79-4735-8736-C41D1F5E965F}-v30
Index         6
ParentUid     {DB0C5C34-556D-4FA5-A349-D1245A10809D}-v1
Replicated
FolderGuid    DB0C5C34-556D-4FA5-A349-D1245A10809D
Uid           {E8D0AE56-1D79-4735-8736-C41D1F5E965F}-v24
UpdateTime    20060613001719.415050-000
Usn           564736
Volume        \\.\C:
```

Now, remember the two values you noted from the NTFS change journal? The FileRef#: 0x0003000000002f8c, and the USN: 0x0000000000089e00. Convert those hexadecimal numbers to decimal (yes, I am going to cheat and use the scientific view on the calculator, choose Hex, copy and paste the number into the calculator, and select decimal). The FileRef#: 0x0003000000002f8c converts to 844424930144140 and the USN: 0x0000000000089e00 converts to 564736. Do you see those decimal values in the information from the FileIDTable_#? Yep, you got it, the FileRef# in the NTFS change journal maps to the FID in the FileIDTable_#, and the USNs map also. This is how the NTFS change journal and the FileIDTable_# stay in sync. Stay in sync? What would happen if they didn't for some reason? The NTFS change journal is a circular log with a fixed size; if the log were to overwrite the last entry that the DFSR database was aware of, an error condition called a journal wrap would occur. Not to worry—DFSR can now automatically recover from a journal wrap error condition. For a detailed look at journal wraps please see the section titled "Trouble-shooting Conflicts, Morphs, and Journal Wraps, Oh No!" at the end of this chapter.

The file File1.doc is now placed in the staging area on Server1. The staging area is used for DFSR to have a storage location where DFSR has complete control of the files and does not have to concern itself with things like write-locks, which would indicate the file is being used by another process, or ensuring there are no file permissions that may restrict DFSR from replicating the document properly. The staging area, by default, is 4GB in size, and there is good reason for it to be this big (bigger is better for RDC and CFR, as you will see in just a few seconds). You will find you have a staging area for every replicated folder. "So, wait a minute, if I have four replicated folders all on the same physical volume of a server, I would have 16GB reserved for the staging area?" No, not really; the 4GB size is a maximum size restriction; when I looked at mine it was only 12MB in size.

The staging area resides in the Replicated Folder\DfsrPrivate\Staging\ Staging\ContentSet{ Replica Set ID}\. For example your Budget folder's staging area would be C:\Budget\DfsrPrivate\ Staging\ContentSet{Replica Set ID}. So, if your staging area has a maximum size of 4GB, what happens when it hits the 4GBGB limit? DFSR is smart enough to start a self-cleaning process prior to the maximum staging area size being encountered. The cleanup process is triggered if the staging area consumes 90% of the allowed storage space (applied via a quota). Cleanup is handled by deleting the least recently used files, allowing space for new files to be placed in the staging area. This cleanup process will continue until the staging area is at or below 60% of the maximum staging area size. Whenever the cleanup process is initiated, there will be events generated in the Application event log. If the 90% quota limit is never reached in the staging area, old files are not removed from the staging area unless a newer version of the same file replaces it. Small files (less than 64 K) are not staged.

After the file is placed in the staging area an entry is created in the Version Vector (VV) tables. All members in the replication group will contain a version vector table which contains Global Version sequence numbers (GVsns) that determine if a member has the most current replication information from each replication partner. Let's say that when Server1 replicated File1.doc to Server2, the VV on Server2 was 3. Someone modifies File1.doc on Server2, and Server2 increments its VV table to 4. When the VVs are compared at the next replication cycle, Server1 knows something has changed on Server2 because the last time Server1 replicated from Server2 , Server2's VV was 3 and it is now 4, therefore Server1 requests the changes from Server2.

I wish it were really that simple.

To find the GVsns from the version vector tables, you first need to find the Globally Unique ID (GUID) for the Budget Folder. For this we use the Dfsradmin command-line utility and, to help keep things simple, you create a text file named Guid.txt in the root of C:\ that contains the output of the command by typing the following:

```
dfsradmin rf list /rgname:Budget /attr:rfname,rfguid >C:\Guid.txt
```

When you open your C:\Guid.txt in Wordpad, you should see the replicated folder name (RfName) budget and the replicated folder Guid (RfGuid):

RfName	RfGuid
budget	81cce24e-ea2b-470d-aef3-a4ea874a3fa1

Now, you have your replicated folder Guid in a form you can copy and paste. Believe me, you won't want to try to type that GUID into the next command; there is enough to type without worrying about that as well. The next command is a wmic command to retrieve the version vector numbers of the budget folder's GUID and should be typed as one line of text (with spaces after the word path and the replicatedfolderguid):

```
wmic /namespace:\\root\microsoftdfs path
dfsrreplicatedfolderinfo.replicatedfolderguid='81cce24e-ea2b-470d-aef3-
a4ea874a3fa1' call GetVersionVector
```

The output will look similar to the following:

```
VersionVector =
{2ABDCA1C-4ABE-4B51-8E72-BD7740D84090} |-> (11, 18]
{956C46E4-EA7D-4E75-BC05-3D698E02C9C3} |-> (9, 11]
```

Wow, okay, let's break this down so we can understand it a bit better. These are actually the GVsn's "Global Version sequence number":

```
2ABDCA1C-4ABE-4B51-8E72-BD7740D84090 represents Server1
956C46E4-EA7D-4E75-BC05-3D698E02C9C3 represents Server2
```

So you could replace those long ugly strings of characters with Version Vector tables on Server1 and Server2:

Server1	Server2
VV=11,18	VV=9,11

In reality, they both have each other's VV tables more like this:

Server1	Server2
VV=11,18	VV=9,11
Server2 VV=9,11	Server1 VV=11,18

If someone were to edit File1.doc on Server2 and once again dump the Version Vector tables, the output would look similar to:

```
VersionVector =
{2ABDCA1C-4ABE-4B51-8E72-BD7740D84090} |-> (11, 18]
{956C46E4-EA7D-4E75-BC05-3D698E02C9C3} |-> (9, 13]
```

or,

Server1	Server2
VV=11,18	VV=9,13
Server2 VV=9,11	Server1 VV=11,18

Notice the only change is the VV table on Server2; on the next replication cycle Server1 will compare the known VV=9,11 (for Server2), with the current VV=9,13 sent from Server2. This is how Server1 knows changes have occurred on Server2 and will replicate the changes.

Step 2: File Is Replicated from Server1 to Server2

When it is determined that data exists that needs to be replicated, do the partners replicate the entire contents of the files? Wow, on large files with small changes that could cause a lot of unnecessary replication traffic. The answer to this question is "No"—or well, "Maybe not" is a better answer. The more correct answer is not if you use the Remote Differential Compression (RDC) algorithm along with Cross-File Replication (CFR).

RDC allows you to replicate only what has changed for a file—better known as the deltas—not the entire file. This is a welcome change from the way FRS replicated data: FRS could only replicate entire files. The way RDC works is this: a file is broken up into byte-sized bits...okay, the data is broken into 128-bit chunks, or 16 bytes. Then each 16-byte chunk is hashed, producing a hashed result called a message digest (to produce this message digest, MD4 is used).

NOTE Hashing is a way of keeping track of whether something has changed or not. For a full explanation of hashing, please see *Mastering Windows Server 2003*.

So, let's look at a small example of how RDC works once replication has occurred between Server1 and Server2. They both contain the file GettysAddress.doc, with matching hashed results:

Server1 GettysAddress.doc		**Server2 GettysAddress.doc**	
Text	MD4 hash	Text	MD4 hash
Four score and eight	25	Four score and eight	25
years ago our fathers	42	years ago our fathers	42
brought forth on this	62	brought forth on this	62
continent, a new nation	38	continent, a new nation	38
conceived in Liberty,	58	conceived in Liberty,	58

If you updated the `GettysAddress.doc` on Server1 by changing the "Four score and eight" to "Four score and seven," the hashed result for that chunk of data becomes 35. Thus, on the next replication cycle, an RDC comparison (shown below) of the hashed results on each chunk would indicate that only one 16-byte chunk of data needs to be replicated, and not the entire file.

Server1 GettysAddress.doc		**Server2 GettysAddress.doc**	
Text	MD4 hash	Text	MD4 hash
Four score and seven	35	**Four score and eight**	25
years ago our fathers	42	years ago our fathers	42
brought forth on this	62	brought forth on this	62
continent , a new nation	38	continent , a new nation	38
conceived in Liberty,	58	conceived in Liberty,	58

RDC rocks doesn't it? Saving that precious bandwidth. But what if replication did not have to occur at all; what if the file that needed to be replicated from Server1 to Server2 could be completely built from files that already existed on Server2? Building files locally to produce the same effect of replication is the purpose of Cross File Replication (CFR). CFR can use up to five locally stored files to create the one file that needs to be replicated. This makes replication even more interesting: Server1 sends in the VV update to Server2 that File5 needs to be created and then sends the MD4 hashes called traits. CFR will then look at the files in its local staging area for files containing these traits and build the file locally.

Monitoring DFSR

Generating health reports with the command-line utility DFSRAdmin.exe is a great way to find out which servers in the replication group are currently having issues. There are three types of reports you can run. You can run a report that generates information from all members in the replication group, or you can choose to gather report information on just one member, or you could choose to gather report information from as many servers as you like. Table 17.4 explains some terminology that will be used for the generation of reports.

TABLE 17.4: Terminology for DFSRAdmin Utility

ATTRIBUTE	ATTRIBUTE EXPANDED	DEFINITION
RgName	Replication group name	Name of the Replication Group
RefMemName	Reference member name	Contains the most up-to-date files. Files on the ref member will be used to compare files on other members.
RepName	Report name	Report name and Path
FsCount	File System count true/false	Determines whether the number of files in each replicated folder should be counted or not.
MemName	Member name	Member to compare to the Reference Member (RefMemName)

The following DFSRAdmin commands are being run on the DCS DC. They could be run on any server that has the DFSRAdmin.exe installed. The point is, the report that is generated will be stored on the server that the DFSRAdmin command-line utility is run on.

The following example will generate a health report that will gather information from *all* members of a replication group. First, you must first define the reference member (yours will be Server1), which contains the data that will be compared to all other servers in the Budget Replication Group to ensure that they are consistent with the data on Server1. The report will be stored in the C:\Reports folder and named HealthReport.html. Using the FsCount:true switch will count the number of files in each replicated folder to verify that the same number of files exist in each server's Budget replication folder:

```
DfsrAdmin Health New /RgName:Budget /RefMemName:Bigfirm\Server1 /
RepName:C:\Reports\HealthReport.html /FsCount:true
```

After you receive the message "Command completed successfully" at the command prompt, you can browse to the C:\Reports folder and double-click the report named HealthReport.html. The report you receive should be similar to Figure 17.42:

Did you notice in the report that you had some errors? Figure 17.43 shows the expanded view of the Errors section of that report.

The following example will generate a health report that gathers information *only* fromServer2, using Server1 as the Reference Member for the Budget replication folder. The report will be stored in the C:\Reports folder and named Server2Health.html. Once again, you are also counting the files in each server's Budget Replication Folder:

```
DfsrAdmin Health New /RgName:Budget /MemName:Bigfirm\Server2 /RefMemName:Server1
/RepName:C:\Reports\Server2Health.html /FsCount:true
```

The third type of report you can generate is a report that feeds a text file into the DFSRAdmin command listing the servers you would like to gather data from. The /MemberListFile attribute allows you to create a text file that contains a list of your servers. These are the servers we will gather health data from.

TIP   The Servers.txt file looks like the following:
Server1
Server2

FIGURE 17.42
DFS Replication
Health Report

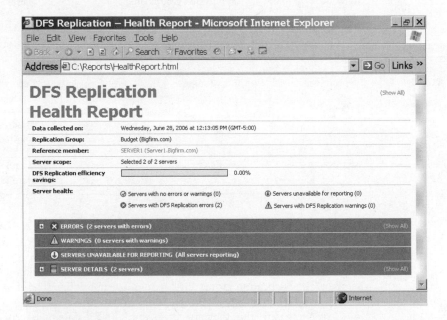

FIGURE 17.43
DFS Replication
Health Report
"Errors"

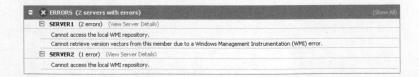

The following command will gather report data from Server1 and Server2, using Server1 as the Reference member and creating a report in the C:\Reports folder named ServersHealth.html:

```
DfsrAdmin Health New /RgName:Budget /MemberListFile:C:\Servers.txt /
RefMemName:Server1 /RepName:C:\Reports\ServersHealth.html /FsCount:true
```

You can also get similar health reports from within the DFS Management snap-in by expanding the Replication node, right-clicking your replication group, and choosing Create Diagnostic Report.

Troubleshooting Conflicts, Morphs, and Journal Wraps, Oh No!

Conflict Resolution And Morphed Conflicts can occur for a few reasons. When two (or more) servers have a copy of the same file but it has been edited on two different servers within one replication cycle or, two different files are created on two different servers within the replication group with the same name and in the same folder of the replication tree. Let's look at the two most common reasons conflicts occur:

Scenario 1

File1.doc is created on Server1 and is assigned a Unique ID (UID)

File1.doc is replicated from Server1 to Server2, maintaining the same UID

File1.doc is modified on Server1

Before Replication occurs

File1.doc is also modified on Server2

or

Scenario 2

File1.doc is created on Server1 and is assigned a UID

BEFORE replication occurs

File1.doc is created in the same folder on Server2 and is assigned a different UID

The dilemma is which file wins (and is therefore replicated) when it comes to the replication process? In the past with FRS you would have received a morphed file, which was a real mess to clean up. In scenario one when Server1 attempted to replicate with Server2 by giving Server2 its File1.doc, Server2 would have renamed the incoming file to "_NTFRS_xxxxxxxxFile1.doc (the xxxxxxxx are 8 random hex numbers, pretty huh?). The same would happen on Server1 when Server2 attempts to send its File1.doc. To clean a morphed file/folder, you had to rename both files (the good and the morhphed) and wait for that to replicate to all DCs. After full replication has occurred (and you better be certain it has or you just created even more problems), you can choose the version of the file you would like to keep, rename it back to the original and delete the other file/folder (kb328492).

You will be happy to hear that the new R2 conflict resolution is much more automated than the FRS morphing business, but is that good or bad? Lets first look at the rules applied to conflicts and then address which file would win in our previous two scenarios. In the table below four of the conflict conditions and their results are shown:

File vs Folder	Same Name	Same UID	Different UID	Result
File	X	X		Last writer wins
File	X		X	First created wins
Folder	X	X		First created wins
Folder	X		X	Contents is consolidated

There is one more conflict you should be aware, if a file and folder have the same name, the folder will always win, so what happens to the file/folder that loses in the conflict resolution process? The file/folder that loses in the conflict resolution process will be moved to the ConflictAndDeleted folder which resides in the replication folder\DfsrPrivate folder (from our Budget example earlier, on Server1 it would be `C:\Budget\DfsrPrivate\ConflictAndDeleted`). This folder has a maximum size limit of 660MB and also performs cleanup automatically, similar to the staging folder.

From our previous two scenarios which file would win?

Scenario 1 = The file that has the latest modification date/time stamp

Scenario 2 = The file that has the earliest creation date/time stamp

Journal Wraps

The NTFS change journal is a circular log (named $USNJRNL), and has a default size of 512MB. The size can be seen in the System Volume Information\DFSR\Config\`Volume_GUID.XML file`—Min NTFSJournalSizeInMB attribute. When the max size is reached, the oldest information is discarded to allow more data to be stored. It is possible that the NTFS change journal could get out of sync with the DFSR database; when the NTFS change journal and the DFSR database become out of sync it is called a journal wrap error.

History of the NTFS change journal's size:

Windows Server 2000, SP2 $USNJRNL was 32MB

Windows 2000 SP3 increased the $USNJRNL to 512MB

Windows 2003 pre-SP1 reduced the $USNJRNL to 128MB

But, Hotfix 823230 or installing SP1 increased it again to 512MB

The maximum size was 2TB, and to change the log size you had to hack the Registry: HKLM\ System\CCS\Services\ntfrs\Parameters\`Journal Size in MB (REG_DWORD)`. Microsoft recommended increasing the change journal size by 128MB for every 100,000 files/folders.

TIP Increasing the change journal size is easy, but decreasing the size means you have to reformat the volume.

In Windows 2003 R2 to change the size of the $USNJRNL, you use a `wmic` command. To increase the size to 1024MB, type the following:

```
wmic /namespace:\\root\microsoftdfs path dfsrvolumeconfig set
minntfsjournalsizeinmb=1024
```

Okay, back to journal wrap errors: they can occur for a few reasons: turning off DFSR for an extended period of time, deleting the $USNJRNL file, or data corruption in the log. Whatever causes the journal wrap, the end result is that DFSR processes no longer know if they have all the information from the NTFS change journal. In a sense, DFSR is lost and does not know where in the NTFS change journal to begin reading from because it cannot find the point at which it previously left off.

What happens when a journal wrap occurs? Windows Server 2003 R2 can automatically repair itself, which is called *self-healing*. When a jounal wrap error condition is encountered the following steps occur:

1. DFSR Processes stop attempting to process changes from the NTFS change journal.

2. Replication is stopped.

3. All entries in the DFSR File ID table are flagged as JWED (Journal Wrapped).

4. Update Sequence Numbers (USNs) for all replicated files are compared between the NTFS change journal and the DFSR File ID table by the Directory Walker thread (DIRW).

TIP All files have a USN in the NTFS change journal and a corresponding USN in the DFSR File ID table for all replicated files. The USN's job is to keep the NTFS change journal and the DFSR File ID table in sync. When a file is created the USN will be the same in the NTFS change journal and the DFSR File ID table, as we saw earlier the NTFS change journal's USN is in hexadecimal format and DFSR's File ID table's USN is in decimal—yet when converted, they are the same number. When a file is modified, the USN in the NTFS change journal is incremented and the next time DFSR processes the NTFS change journal, DFSR recognizes that a file's USN has changed therefore notifying DFSR that a file has been modified and the changes need to be replicated.

Upon comparison of the USN's three conditions may be found: the USN's are the same, the USN's are not the same, and there is no USN found at all for a file in the DFSR File ID table. Let's look at each of these conditions in more detail:

1. If the USNs in the NTFS change journal and the DFSR File ID table are identical, DFSR knows it has the latest changes for a file, and the JWED flag is cleared.

2. If the USNs are different, the USN in the NTFS change journal is increased, the JWED flag is cleared, and the file (or its changes) will be replicated on the next replication cycle.

3. Once all files in the DFSR File ID table have been compared to the NTFS change journal and their JWED flags are cleared, the file ID table is scanned for any files still flagged JWED. This occurs if a file is deleted from the NTFS volume (which will delete the file from the NTFS change journal), but still has an entry in the DFSR File ID table. Those files are tombstoned and eventually deleted from the replication process.

Once this self-healing process completes, replication begins again as normal. DFSR will process changes from the NTFS change journal, replication will occur as before, and all's well! At least until the next time a journal wrap occurs. If you are having an excessive amount of journal wraps, increasing the size of the NTFS change journal might help reduce the amount of journal wraps. If this doesn't help you may need to address the exact files that are causing journal wraps and why; the event viewer on the server encountering the journal wraps is a good place to start.

Summary

Well, I think that about covers DFSN and DFSR, okay most of it anyway. I hope I have helped you to feel more confident in creating your own Distributed File System Namespace, either from the user interface, or by scripting or just enjoying the command line options. Most of what is under the hood for DFSN really has not changed much, apart from the new terminology used. One thing I found interesting while researching DFSN is that even the Microsoft documents explaining DFSN still used the old terminology. I had to keep going back to the title of many documents to be sure I was actually reading DFSN information and not DFS.

The big newcomer is of course DFSR. Now here, some great strides have been made. Anyone who has ever been unfortunate enough to be put in a position where they had to troubleshoot FRS can attest to this. The new DFS Management snap-in sure makes configuration and management of replication groups much easier. Some of the new technologies like bandwidth throttling, RDC, and CFR are just a few of the features that I think make DFSR by far superior to FRS. I am really looking forward to Windows Server 2007, where SYSVOL will be replicated via DFSR.

If you are new to both of these technologies, I highly recommend creating a test environment (make it a virtual environment—you can do that for free) and playing with these two new features before you implement them. Make sure you have a true test environment, for example, if you have some Windows Server 2000 servers acting as DCs you should also have one in your test environment, and so on. I hope you enjoy these new technologies as much as I have and the knowledge will help you to implement, manage, and when necessary, even troubleshoot both DFSN and DFSR.

Chapter 18

Communicating and Collaborating with Windows SharePoint Services

So, your boss wants you to whip up a collaborative website in your spare time. It needs to be cost effective (meaning free), of course, your responsibility, even though you told you him you are not a web developer, and ready by next week (because that's what he told *his* boss). He's heard about something that lets information workers upload their shared documents to a website where it can be checked out and edited by others, then checked back in for review, complete with versioning. Oh, and he'd like to keep some lists of contacts and maybe have some Discussion Group functionality if that's okay. Of course, the product he'd heard of costs about $5000 a server and $70 a client access license. But he's sure you can come up with the equivalent with what you already have, you're clever like that…

…And, thanks to Windows SharePoint Services, you can.

Yeah, you *are* clever like that.

Windows SharePoint Services (which I generally refer to as SharePoint) create a powerful collaborative tool by themselves and are the free underpinnings, the foundational features and functions if you will, that make SharePoint Portal Server possible. You first install SharePoint Services, then you install SharePoint Portal Server, which is what costs thousands of dollars per server and about $70 per client license, to add additional functions to SharePoint Services. That's right, the free services come first, then you install SharePoint Portal Server over them. So I think, for thriftiness' sake, you should first learn what SharePoint Services can do for you for free, before investing in the Portal Server add on. Don't you?

To start with, what can Windows SharePoint Services do out of the box? A lot. There's a reason it's not called Windows SharePoint *Service*. Here's a brief list of SharePoint's most popular features:

Share Documents   Meant to replace shared folder as the tool to share documents, SharePoint uses *document libraries* to store and organize shared documents.

Check in and Check out Documents   Shared documents can be checked in and checked out by users. This means a user can check out a document they intend to edit, locking it as read only until they check it back in. Helps keep editorial conflicts to a minimum.

Document Versioning   SharePoint can also track shared document changes in case of editorial error, making it easy to restore an earlier version of the document.

Share Contacts   There is a contacts list created by default when SharePoint installs. This contact list can be shared between all users of the site.

Share Calendars   It is easy to create lists with calendar views in order to share project dates and deadlines.

Surveys   Surveys and polls can easily be created. Track user interest and opinions anonymously, with the ability to disallow multiple entries or the right to edit an entry.

Discussion boards   Encourage collaborative communications with threaded discussions lists.

Announcements   Conveniently displayed by default on the SharePoint site home page, easily communicate congratulations, awards, and activities. Announcements can be set to expire, so they can be removed from the home page after the event passes.

List Moderation   Content approval can be required on any list or shared document library.

Dynamic Web Modules   Display compact, self-updating, summary views of data on the SharePoint site home page. Customizable without requiring any programming.

Custom Subsites   Encourage additional collaboration by letting users create their own workspaces to collaborate on projects. Use subsites to organize and record meeting attendees, agenda, and objectives.

Role-based Permissions   Easy to use and apply permissions for the site based on user roles. As the SharePoint site grows, users can have unique roles and permissions for particular lists or subsites, in addition to those of the primary team site.

Tight Integration with Office 2003   Seamlessly integrates with the Office 2003 system to encourage user collaboration with tools they already know.

Member Availability Notification   Increases smoother user communications by displaying when members are logged in and active on the SharePoint site.

Custom Reports   Lists can be displayed in customized report views. Group data by field content; use lookup fields; do calculations on numerical data, running totals; and more.

Alerts   Allows users to be notified if changes have occurred to a particular list, library, or item. Lets them avoid having to waste time regularly going to multiple lists just to see what's happening.

So obviously (see Figure 18.1), SharePoint is more than a document collaboration tool. It is an idea-generating, decision-making, productivity tool that allows users to discuss, experiment, and build consensus; as well as access, add, and manipulate data. All within a consistent web-based environment. And, of course, you can share documents too.

All for free.

It takes some planning, it's true. But that's why you're here. Not only to learn what SharePoint Services are, but how to use them. By the end of this chapter, you will be able to install, use, configure, and administer a standard SharePoint Services site collection and even learn how to make more if you need them.

Speaking of planning, what I'd like to do with this chapter is first give you a glance at SharePoint under the hood, then go on to the install with some details as to what happens when SharePoint is actually on a server. Then I'll give you an overview of what everything is and how to use SharePoint, move on to administration, permissions, and, finally, finish with a little disaster recovery. The idea is to get you up and running in a test environment, get a feel for everything and how SharePoint might apply to you. Then, once you get through this chapter, you will better understand how you want to install it, configure it, and use it in your business. Mind you, this is not a SharePoint book, it's a SharePoint chapter. So in addition to what I will be covering, to give you a taste of its collaborative powers, I will also be pointing to other free resources to give you more in-depth information about details that might be outside of a single chapter's limits.

FIGURE 18.1
SharePoint
site home page

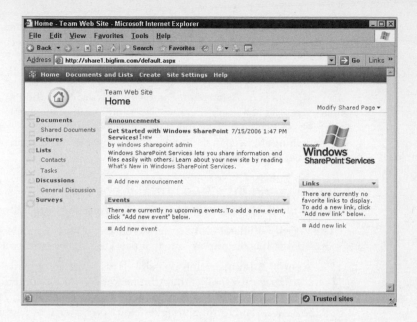

TIP Speaking of free resources, there is an excellent SharePoint Services reference called "Windows SharePoint Services 2.0 Administrator's Guide" available both online and as a downloadable compiled HTML help file. It gives you step-by-step information about how to do just about anything you can think of with and/or to SharePoint, and probably a few things that never occurred to you. Look it up online and check it out.

SharePoint Services: The Wizard Behind the Curtain

SharePoint, lest we forget, is free. Because of this, it depends on several free features of Windows Server 2003 R2 to function. Those features are

IIS 6.0 The Windows Server family already has IIS built in, making it a perfect choice for supporting SharePoint's web interface. It is scalable and relatively easy to manage. IIS defines all things that relate to accessing SharePoint's website, such as authentication (Windows Integrated and/or Anonymous) and the port number.

WMSDE SharePoint is deeply dependent on some sort of back-end database. That's where all of the data about the SharePoint sites and their content is stored. Unless you prefer to use your existing SQL 2000 or 2005, SharePoint will install a free copy of WMSDE (Windows Microsoft SQL Database Engine 2000), the less throttled cousin of MSDE. Although it does have its limitations, it is convenient for small to medium businesses and test environments.

ASP .NET 1.1 (or 2.0, or Both) This makes it possible to have "web parts" that create a consistent look, feel, and functionality on the SharePoint home pages, while working with nothing more than a web browser. Web Parts are little ASP .NET web applications, used to display items on SharePoint pages that are meant to hold Web Parts (most SharePoint pages display lists, list items, or settings). Web Parts can be very useful to prepopulate a SharePoint site home page with quick summary views of various lists or libraries. They can also be used to display practically anything you can view in a window. Pretty convenient, that ASP .NET stuff.

TIP I'd like to remind you that Windows SharePoint Services version 2 is included in Server 2003 R2 as a server role. You know that, otherwise this chapter wouldn't be here. However, it has been available as a free download for Server 2003 for quite a while. So, if you need to, you can easily install and run SharePoint on Server 2003 as well. It's just easier on Server 2003 R2.

So now you know what SharePoint's underlying components are (and the other reason it's called Windows SharePoint *Services*. The plural form of the name has as much to do with the fact that it is based on several components as it does the fact it offers many services). Of course, there are some things to keep in mind when installing and running SharePoint. The following sections cover a brief list of consideration highlights.

About SharePoint's Two Initial Websites

Windows SharePoint Services creates two websites (or *Virtual Servers* in SharePoint parlance):

The Windows SharePoint Services Website This is what people think of when they think of SharePoint. It is the primary site that users access. It manages site data and content.

The Central Administration Website This manages overall SharePoint configuration data. For added security, the Central Administration site is bound to a port randomly selected by SharePoint between 1023 and 32767 at time of installation. It was not meant to be accessible by the masses, and I strongly suggest you don't open that port in your firewall (or, if it is open, close it).

NOTE When Windows SharePoint Services takes over an IIS Web Site , it's called "extending a virtual server." That means if you want to (and there can be some good reasons for this) have Windows SharePoint Services manage a different Web Site on the same server (with its own port, directory, application pools, authentication method and the like), you create a new Web Site in IIS, then "extend" SharePoint into that Virtual Server (remember that "virtual server" is Windows SharePoint Services' way of referring to what IIS calls "Web Sites." Ah, Microsoft). You'll see the administrative setting for it later, or you can read all about it in the Windows SharePoint Services 2.0 Administrator's Guide.

About SharePoint's Two, Coinciding, Initial Databases

Windows SharePoint Services creates two databases when it is installed, the configuration database and the content database. They coincide with the two websites created at install.

- The configuration database is created during the configuration of Windows SharePoint Services (makes sense when you think about it) and will control the configuration data of all of SharePoint websites. There are certain configuration settings (like user account modes) that cannot be changed after configuration. That's why putting thought into your Windows SharePoint Services install before you do it will save you a lot of grief later on. Keep in mind there can be only one configuration database per SharePoint server or server farm.

NOTE No matter how many virtual (or physical) servers you extend SharePoint to, they can all share the same configuration database. This can become an issue if you want to have more than one physical server hosting SharePoint and you are using WMSDE for your databases. WMSDE cannot be used in a "server farm" configuration. Sorry about that. If you want to go further than single server, you have to upgrade to SQL 2000 or 2005.

◆ The content database will hold all the content in the site (including all files stored in libraries). Due to the fact that a single SharePoint Virtual Server can hold many sites, which in turn can hold a lot of content, it is not unusual to have multiple content databases on one SharePoint server. You can even set alerts and quotas on a content database to warn you when it gets too big, so you can create another one if necessary. This means that SharePoint can have multiple content databases.

About WMSDE

WMSDE, despite not being as limited as plain old MSDE, can really only support ten active Web Sites (or Virtual Servers). If you are going to have more than ten active IIS websites, you should seriously consider upgrading to SQL 2000 or 2005 for your configuration and content databases. Hey, Microsoft has to have a reason for SQL to be worth the money, right?

Also, because Windows SharePoint Services is using an SQL database (be it WMSDE or straight-up SQL 2000 or 2005), you will have to think about things like authentication for the database itself. WMSDE is set up to use Windows Integrated authentication by default.

About User Account Modes

There are two different ways to manage the user accounts that will be given permissions to use Windows SharePoint Services:

Domain Account Mode   Is used inside organizations to let users with existing Microsoft Windows domain accounts access Windows SharePoint Services. That means you have to create the user account in AD first, then you can assign them rights within Windows SharePoint Services second.

NOTE   Windows SharePoint Services assumes you are in a domain, but you do not necessarily have to install SharePoint on a domain server. You can install it on a stand-alone server, and then accounts will be managed locally. Initially, only members of the Administrators group will have access to the default website until the site is configured to allow other users/user groups access.

Active Directory Account Creation Mode   Allows the Windows SharePoint Services administrators to create unique user accounts for users in an organizational unit in Active Directory. These accounts can then be assigned to groups in Windows SharePoint Services to grant customers the appropriate access.

Domain account mode is the default if you install Windows SharePoint Services typically. If you want to use Active Directory account creation mode, you have to use the server farm install method.

WARNING   Account mode is one of those things that cannot be changed after SharePoint has been configured (heck, it can't be configured if you wanted to during a typical install). In addition, choosing to use Active Directory account creation mode isn't for the faint of heart. It's actually considered a separate kind of Windows SharePoint Services server deployment. Read the Windows SharePoint Services 2.0 Administrator's Guide, "Separate Active Directory Directory Service Organization Unit Deployment", for the complete lowdown on this mode before trying it.

About SharePoint's Dependence on Email

SharePoint has a lot of features that are email dependent. As a matter of fact, it really prefers that all users have an email address to send alerts and notifications to. Despite that, you can run Windows SharePoint Services on a server in an environment with no available email server to relay messages. Just realize that all features requiring email will have to be handled some other way.

About FrontPage Extensions (Just Say No)

Strangely, despite Windows SharePoint Services' past close association with FrontPage; it does not want FrontPage extensions enabled on its website, especially if they are listening on port 80. Due to this fact, if the default website in IIS has FrontPage 2002 server extensions enabled, Windows SharePoint Services won't install into that Web Site. You must disable and even uninstall FrontPage extensions.

About SharePoint Services Hardware Requirements

Windows SharePoint Services does have minimum hardware requirements, but there is no real hard-and-fast rule as to what hardware requirements to suggest for your environment.

Realistically, you need to run a test version of your SharePoint setup to see what your environment requires. Just keep in mind that you will need to know how many people will be using the site, how often, in what way, and how much data will be stored there. That will give you a hint as to what kind of processor(s) you will need, as well as the amount of RAM and storage space you might require (more storage is almost always better). Also, keep in mind when thinking about hardware that you will need to have some sort of backup and recovery available for SharePoint just as you would any other server. In this case, remember that RAID is your friend. Back up often, restore occasionally to make sure it works, and remember that SharePoint is practically infinitely expandable if you should need more resources to grow.

TIP   For more insight concerning hardware requirements for your SharePoint server, check out the Capacity Planning section of the Windows SharePoint Services 2.0 Administrator's Guide (hey, I told you that guide is useful).

On to the Installation

Windows SharePoint Services has two different modes of installation, typical and server farm.

Typical   The typical install assumes you are starting with a blank slate, that you have one server to install SharePoint on, and that you have no database software (namely SQL) installed to be used for SharePoint's databases. That means you'll need WMSDE installed and set up for you during the SharePoint install. This is the easiest way to install SharePoint, as most of the process is automated without any interaction from the human at the keyboard (except to maybe swap discs). Absolutely perfect for setting up SharePoint in a learning environment. This, of course, is the installation you will be using for this chapter (with a few caveats of course).

Server Farm   The server farm installation is more advanced. Because SharePoint is so useful, it's built to be extremely scaleable. Basically, Microsoft assumes that you are going to, or already have, outgrown a single server configuration. You're going to need more storage space, more juice, a more robust set of databases than what WMSDE can give you. So the server farm installation initially assumes that you are at least going to install SharePoint on a server that will *not* be using the free but limited WMSDE to handle data management, and instead are going to use

SQL 2000 or 2005 to do the job. Second, it also assumes that the installation will be a part of one of several web servers hosting IIS and SharePoint, with at least one database server on the back-end hosting SQL. This means that the installer doesn't use the IIS default website (so you have to configure the Virtual Server the SharePoint site will extend into), and you will have to manually configure your configuration and content databases.

TIP You will be using the typical installation for this chapter. However, if after getting the hang of SharePoint, you want to use your SQL server to manage SharePoint's databases, you easily can (especially since Microsoft prefers you do that). Just refer to the Windows SharePoint Services 2.0 Administrator's Guide for more information.

If you are going to do a typical install, keep in mind that Windows SharePoint Services works as simply as possible and can be surprisingly inflexible in that fact. The typical install will take over the default Web Site in IIS, regardless of whether or not something is already there. So if you already have IIS 6.0 up, let's hope you aren't using the default website.

If you don't have IIS with ASP.NET installed, they can be installed if the Configure Your Server Wizard is used during the typical Windows SharePoint Services installation process (kind of convenient, that). If you've already got them installed, then you are a step ahead of the game.

NOTE The installation file for Windows SharePoint Services is named `setupsts.exe` (see, there's that reference to SharePoint Team Services) and is located on the second install disc for Windows Server 2003 R2 in the `cmpnents\R2` folder. This is why, no matter what method you use to install Windows SharePoint Services, the `setupsts.exe` file will be required. So, have that disc handy.

Keep in mind that you can install Windows SharePoint Services four different ways:

◆ Use Manage Your Server ➤ Add or Remove a Role ➤ SharePoint Services. That calls up the Configure Your Server Wizard and installs SharePoint in the typical configuration only.

◆ Use the Configure Your Server Wizard directly and choose SharePoint Services. That understandably installs SharePoint in the typical configuration only.

◆ Manually run the install by going to the command prompt and navigating to the *CD drive letter*:\CMPNENTS\R2, and typing **setupsts.exe**. Lets you choose whether or not you want to install typically or as part of a server farm. Does not use the Configure Your Server Wizard and therefore does not helpfully install IIS 6.0 with ASP .NET during install. You are just going to have to install it on your own before you run the command.

TIP By the way, the downloadable version of Windows SharePoint Services version 2 `stsv2.exe`, when extracted, uses `setupsts.exe` to install. The Windows Server 2003 R2 version simply is pre-extracted because it's stored on a CD. So if you want to do this `/datadir` trick on a pre-R2 2003 server, extract `stsv2.exe` to a folder first (**stsv2.exe /c /t:"path"**), then, from that folder run `setupsts.exe` with the `/datadir` switch. The switch doesn't work with `stsv2.exe`.

◆ Choose Add/Remove Programs ➤ Windows Components ➤ SharePoint Services. This method also lets you choose whether or not you want your install to be typical or server farm.

TELLING SHAREPOINT WHERE TO STICK ITS DATABASES

You can also choose to specify where the WMSDE databases will be installed (like a larger drive or partition other than the one the operating system is on) when running the Windows SharePoint Services install from the command prompt by using the /datadir switch, as in

```
setupsts.exe /datadir=e:\databases\\
```

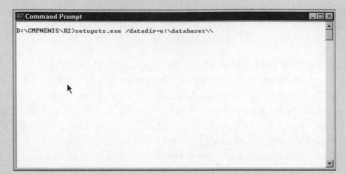

This is a good idea, because the typical install puts the WMSDE databases in a Microsoft SQL Server folder on the operating system partition of your server. This is obviously not the best place for healthy, busy, growing databases. Once you get the hang of SharePoint, you will want to explore this installation option.

Typical Install

Because you are going to do the typical install, it's fine (and easier) to use the configuration wizard, so go to Start ➢ Administrative tools ➢ Configure Your Server Wizard.

NOTE   You cannot install Windows SharePoint Services without administrative rights. So before trying to install SharePoint on your server, be sure you are logged in as an administrator, either of your local server or domain. Of course, you already knew that. I am using a domain admin account I created specifically for SharePoint administration creatively called wssadmin with the full name (in case you weren't sure) of "windows sharepoint admin." SharePoint uses an account's full name to indicate the creator of item entries, so you'll see that account name several times in this chapter.

Once the wizard opens, feel free to read the welcome screen, then click Next, and Next again at the preliminary steps.

When you get to the Server Role page, choose SharePoint Services. Note that the information along the right-hand side of the page states that the install will be a typical one and reminds you how to install with more options should you forget (see Figure 18.2). Click Next.

You'll get to a summary page. Make sure that you are installing SharePoint Services (and IIS 6 and ASP .NET if they are not already installed), and click Next.

At this point, it's a good idea to have the Windows Server 2003 R2 installation disks handy. Initially, the Windows Components Wizard will need the setup file for SharePoint (setupsts.exe), which is available on the Windows Server 2003 R2 installation Disc 2 (in the R2 folder under CMP-NENTS). If you haven't already installed IIS 6.0, then you will need the first Windows Server 2003 R2 installation disk—and don't be surprised if you are prompted for the SP1 disc too, which is on the first Windows Server 2003 R2 disc as well (see "Please Insert Service Pack 1 Disc?!" sidebar for more).

FIGURE 18.2
Server Role, Share-
Point Services

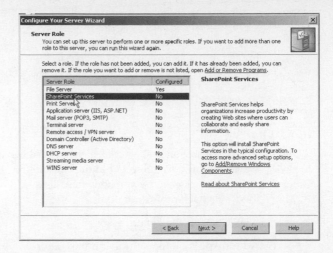

When IIS 6.0 and ASP .NET 1.1 are done installing, the Windows Components Wizard will ask for the second Windows Server 2003 R2 installation disc. In order to install ASP .NET 2 (mentioned in the next note) and WMSDE, the wizard requires files from the CMPNENTS\R2 folder on the second Windows Server 2003 R2 installation disk. Unless these installation files are cached locally or you installed the server from a network share, be prepared to swap discs.

NOTE If you installed IIS 6.0 with ASP .NET 1.1 extensions prior to installing Windows SharePoint Services, then only ASP .NET 1.1 will be enabled. But if you don't preinstall IIS 6.0 and ASP .NET and install them as part of the Windows SharePoint Services installation, then ASP .NET 2 gets installed as well as ASP .NET 1.1. They are both enabled in IIS 6.0 after install. For me, installing ASP .NET 2.0 actually slows down the installation process quite a bit. However, one of the selling points for upgrading Windows SharePoint Services to Service Pack 2 was support for ASP .NET 2.0, although Windows SharePoint Services does not require 2.0 at this point. I guess, as an added bonus, you get ASP .NET 2.0 for installing Windows SharePoint Services in Server 2003 R2. Consider it another convenient thing about SharePoint.

When the installation wizard has completed its tasks, the Configure Your Server Wizard page will appear with the notice that "This server is now a SharePoint Services server." Click the Finish button. The Manage Your Server window will open, and you can see that SharePoint Services is now listed as a role on your server. Congratulations.

That's it for the typical install. A very hands-off experience. Which is why you need to know what's going to happen before you use it. So *before* we get down to actually messing with Share-Point, I'd like to show you what happened behind the scenes that makes Windows SharePoint Services possible.

First, let's see what happened with IIS 6.0.

IIS 6.0 Changes

Open the IIS 6.0 console and take a look at what has been added (see Figure 18.3). You may need to click the plus sign next to the server in the console tree, then click the plus signs next to Application Pools and Web Sites to see the new items lists.

There should be two application pools:

♦ StsAppPool1, for the default website

♦ StsAdminAppPool, for central administration

And two web sites:

♦ Default Web Site

NOTE The default Web Site holds all of the pages that will ever be made within this virtual server/Web Site. However, most pages in Windows SharePoint Services are ASPX pages. For example, a single page called listedit.aspx is called up every time any list is ever edited and propagates the page with the correct fields and data based on the list you are modifying. This means that most of SharePoint is made up of dynamic pages, so there is usually no static page for a home page or list. The only pages that are standard static pages are ones edited or created in FrontPage.

♦ SharePoint Central Administration site

Each site should have permissions set to Integrated Windows authentication and be using the correct application pool.

To check, start by right-clicking the default website and go to Properties (to open the Properties dialog box, go to the Directory Security tab and click the Authentication and access control Edit button).

Under Authenticated access (as you can see in Figure 18.4), Integrated Windows authentication should be checked.

FIGURE 18.3
IIS changes

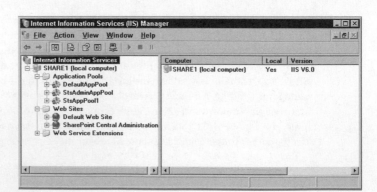

FIGURE 18.4
Authentication
Methods

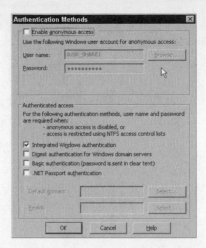

Click Cancel if the authentication method is correct (if it isn't, correct it, of course, and click OK).

Back on the Default Website Properties, go to the Home Directory tab, and check the application pool name (at the bottom of the dialog box). It should be StsAppPool1 (see Figure 18.5).

Close out of the Default Website Properties dialog box.

To check the properties of the SharePoint Central Administration site, repeat the steps you used to see the properties of the Default Website. The SharePoint Central Administration site should have the same permissions as the default site, with the application pool name StsAdminAppPool, but more importantly, you need to know what *port* your Central Administration site is using. Remember, that site is going to give itself a random port number between 1023 and 32767. In order to access it from the browser on your workstation (as opposed to the server itself), you will need to know what that port is. So on the Web Site tab in the SharePoint Central Administration site properties, see what port it gave itself. As you can see in Figure 18.6, mine is using port 8552.

Finally, to make sure that ASP .NET is installed and allowed in IIS, select Web Service Extensions in the IIS console tree. In the contents pane, as you can see in Figure 18.7, both ASP .NET 1.1 (or v1.1.4322) and ASP .NET 2.0 (v2.0.50727) are installed and allowed.

Next, let's make sure that the WMSDE databases were created, where they are actually located, and how big they are.

FIGURE 18.5
Default Web Site
application pool

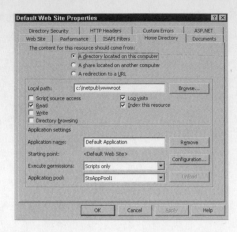

FIGURE 18.6
Central Administra-
tion port

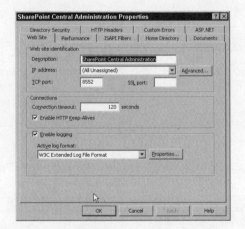

FIGURE 18.7
IIS Manager

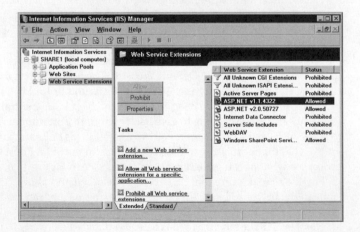

WMSDE

Navigate to wherever you keep your program files (mine are in the usual place, `C:\Program Files`) and note that there is now a Microsoft SQL Server folder containing two subfolders, 80 and MSSQL$SHAREPOINT. The folder with the longer name is obviously the one containing the new WMSDE databases for SharePoint (the folder called 80 actually stands for 8.0, as in version 8.0. It holds tools and utilities for WMSDE).

NOTE WMSDE also starts three services: MSSQL$SHAREPOINT, SQLServerADHelper, and SQLAgent$SHAREPOINT. MSSQL$SHAREPOINT must be running, but don't be surprised if the other two services turn themselves on and off at will.

To actually see the two databases that SharePoint built—configuration and content—browse to the Data folder beneath MSSQL$SHAREPOINT and take a look at STS_Config.mdf and STS_SHARE1_1.mdf (SHARE1 is the name of my server, and the additional "1" indicates it's the first content database. Remember that SharePoint allows you to add content database as your content grows, so each is identified (nonsequentially) with its own unique number). Note their size. Right now mine are 1280KB and 4544KB, respectively. Although there are several monitoring tools built into SharePoint for monitoring the content database, it is never a bad thing to know where and how big your databases are (see Figure 18.8).

FIGURE 18.8
SharePoint databases

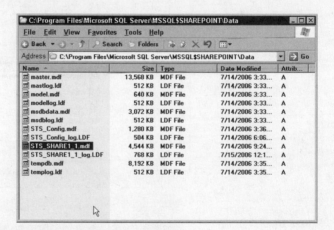

CONGRATULATIONS, YOU ARE NOW A DATABASE ADMINISTRATOR!

Because Windows SharePoint Services uses databases for organization and data storage, when you install Windows SharePoint Services, you also have WMSDE (if you don't already have SQL). This means that you do have yet another thing to support, but don't be too concerned. WMSDE is pretty robust and built to do what it is doing with Windows SharePoint Services. For more information about managing and maintaining your WMSDE databases, check out KB325003, "How to Manage the SQL Server Desktop Engine (MSDE 2000) or SQL Server 2005 Express Edition by Using the osql Utility" and Mark's excellent newsletter, issue #48. It is all about administering MSDE. Very useful stuff.

SharePoint also created a security group called STS_WPG during install. This account is used by SharePoint to access server resources (like its own log files). Keep STS_WPG in mind if you ever move the log files, because it will need access to them at some point.

I'd like to confirm the STS_WPG group got created correctly, so open the Active Directory Users and Computers Console, select the Users container, and then scroll through the list of Users and Groups in the content pane until you find STS_WPG (see Figure 18.9, if it isn't there, then, Houston, we have a problem because, at least eventually, SharePoint will not work properly without it).

Finally, I'd like to insure that the critical SharePoint Timer Service is actually installed and running.

SHAREPOINT TIMER SERVICE

Go to Start ➤ Administrative Tools ➤ Services console, and scroll down the list of services until you find SharePoint Timer Service. It should already be running and the Startup type should be set to Automatic (see Figure 18.10).

Now that you've seen what happens when SharePoint installed, let's see what it actually looks like.

FIGURE 18.9
SharePoint's STS_
WPG Security Group

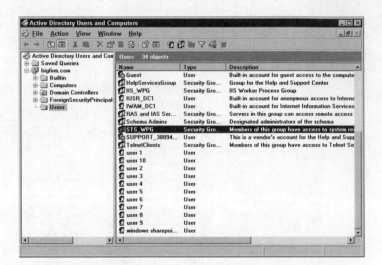

FIGURE 18.10
SharePoint
Timer Service

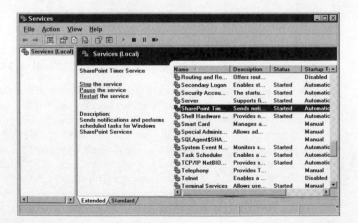

Windows SharePoint Services—Using SharePoint Out of the Box

When you install SharePoint, all you appear to get is a web page. It's an innocuous looking home page, with a few Web Parts, a navigation bar, and something called a Quick Launch bar down the left side.

That's it. But keep in mind that that is supposed to be a convenient access point, the top of the collection of pages that make up the SharePoint site. It looks simple to use on purpose.

You see, when SharePoint installs, it creates the first team website from the team site template. The site has, already built in, some convenient lists, a library, and so on, so you can just get started. The home page is where the links to the other pages are located.

Now, because SharePoint is extended into the default web site in IIS and that site is listening to all traffic on port 80 of the server, all HTTP requests made to the server address are captured and directed to the SharePoint Team Web Site home page. Which is why all you have to do to access SharePoint's site is type the address of the server in the address bar of Internet Explorer and hit Enter (or the Go button, or whatever). I specify Internet Explorer because, and I know that you'll be shocked by this, SharePoint has been "optimized" to best function in IE.

So, to bring up your SharePoint site, open IE, and type your SharePoint server's address in the address bar, and hit Enter (I'm using **http://share1.bigfirm.com** as my SharePoint server).

That will trigger a prompt for a Windows username and password. This is because the site is set to Integrated Windows authentication in IIS (as you may recall). So use the administrative account that you used to install SharePoint. You may also be prompted to add the site address to your Trusted Sites list in IE. I feel confident that, at this point, it is safe to do so if you wish).

And voila—your SharePoint Team Web Site home page comes up (see Figure 18.11).

Now this page, as I mentioned earlier, uses the default "Team" template, default layout, default Web Parts, and default theme. And still it's very serviceable. Many of these things can be changed without using any special HTML editor, as you will see later.

FIGURE 18.11

SharePoint Home Team Web Site

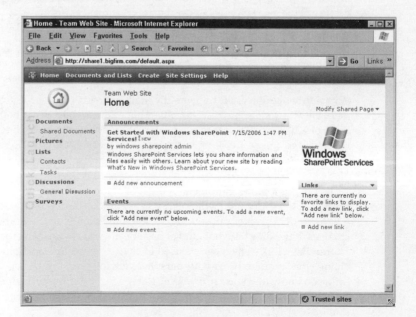

Let's check out the home page in a bit of detail. Across the top is a standard navigation bar. It contains links for:

Home   Brings you back to the Home Team Web Site page. A "take me up to the top page of this site" link.

Documents and Lists   Takes you to a page used to both find all the kinds of lists available in this site and create all kinds of lists and document libraries. A one-stop shop for list creation and discovery.

Create   Used to create anything new. Almost identical in content with Documents and Lists, this link focuses not on lists of all kinds, but anything that can be created in the SharePoint site, including web pages and subsites of any kind, as well as libraries and lists. The Create link on the Documents and Lists page inevitably comes to this page (yes, they chose to be redundant for the sake of being convenient).

Site Settings   The administrative page for managing this site and its settings.

Help   Links to the general Windows SharePoint Services help files. I would like to give you fair warning that Help may not be that helpful. Also not all pages, settings, or drop-down menus will have help listed. That is another reason I suggest using the Administrator's Guide.

Along the left side is another navigation sort of bar called the Quick Launch bar, which lists, well, the lists that your site has (you can choose what goes there, except for the general, list type headings. They weren't meant to be removed).

CAN'T FIND SEARCH?

You may have noticed in your perusal of the Team Web Site Home page that there is no search bar. You are right. One of the limitations that Microsoft has given WMSDE is that it cannot be searched. This is probably my single biggest pet peeve about Windows SharePoint Services, but I will endeavor not to dwell on it too much throughout the chapter. The service is just too useful otherwise to give in to despair.

In order to enable searching, full text or otherwise in Windows SharePoint Services 2.0, you must be using the full version of SQL 2000 or 2005 to run your databases. Since we are not, I am not going to be including anything in the chapter about setting up SQL to be searched in Windows SharePoint Services. There is information about it the built-in help and in the Administrator's Guide.

With that being said, you can apparently enable searching on a per-list basis by field (including the body field, but still not documents). It requires building a Web Part in FrontPage, but it can be done. So for those of you who really need it but aren't willing to shell out the big bucks for SQL Server, this could be the way to go. Check out the www.wssdemo.com website for the details.

Below the top navigation bar is the title of the page (useful if, because all the pages are so uniform, you have forgotten what page you are on). To the left of the title is a medallion-like circle with a house in it. This is supposed to indicate that you are on the home page of a site. This medallion changes depending on what kind of page or site you are on. Next to the title, on the right, is a Modify Shared Page link (which can be used to change Web Parts and can even be set to personal view to change the layout only for your personal viewing pleasure. When you see the Modify Shared Page link, you know that you are on a Web Part page. The home page of the Team Web Site and the home page of most workspaces or subsites you make from here are practically the only pages by default that have Web Parts.

NOTE   If you were not at the top-level SharePoint website, then above the Modify Shared Page link would be a link to go up to this site's parent site.

That leaves the center of the page, which was meant to contain Web Parts. There are actually two "zones" on the Team Web Site Home page for Web Parts—left and right (right is kind of skinny). You can see that Announcements has a pregenerated entry authored by your account name (hey, did you write that?). During the install of Windows SharePoint Services, a stock entry is created under your account context for that list. Think of it as a welcome present. In addition to the Announcement Web Part, Events and Links are also part of the Web Part zone of the home page, and what do you know, they're lists too.

Web Parts

A List View Web Part has a title area (light blue in this template), and if you move your mouse over the name of the Web Part it will highlight, indicating that if you were to click on it, you would go directly to that list's page to see what else is in there. Also on the right side of the title area is a down arrow, which drops a menu to let you:

Minimize   Rolls the Web Part up into the title area like a window shade.

Close   Gets rid of the Web Part altogether.

Modify Shared Web Part   Goes into edit Web Part mode, opening the tool pane under Modify Shared Page for that particular Web Part and going into design view.

Help   Context sensitive, opens a separate window.

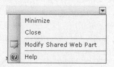

To see what this Web Part stuff is about, click on the Modify Shared Page link on the top right of the Team Web Site Home page. Mind you, there are two ways to see the Team Web Site Home page: with the Web Parts arranged as they would be for any user visiting the site (the shared view), or you can create your own personal view (which causes the Modify Shared Page link to politely change to Modify My Page. Isn't that nice?).

You can see in the Modify Shared Page drop-down list:

Add Web Parts   By browsing, searching, or importing, you can find existing Web Parts (there are a bunch available by default) and add them to the Web Part zones.

Design this Page   To add, move around, and delete Web Parts that are already there. Puts the page into Design view.

Modify Shared Web Parts   Pops out a list of the Web Parts already on the page (basically takes you to Design this Page, with the Web Part properties already open. Convenient, really).

Shared View   The Web Part Page that is usually set up to be seen by anyone who can access the site.

Personal View   Depending on a user's permissions, they can be given the right to have a personal view of the Web Part Page. This means they can access Add Web Parts and choose to put whatever Web Parts are available on the page for their viewing alone. Remember that choosing one or the other view will close out the drop-down list and change how the Modify link is displayed, to either Modify Shared Page or Modify My Page.

TIP   If you are designing a page like mad but it only seems to change for you: you're Modifying My Page, not the shared page. If that happens, click the Modify My Page link, and choose Shared View in the drop-down menu. It will set you back to the shared page view, which you can now modify to your heart's content. It happens more often than you might think.

Since we're administrators, we can change the shared view (which only administrators and web designers can do by default). That's the view that everyone else will be seeing when they visit the site, so let's do that.

I'd like to show you what it's like to be in design view, move some Web Parts around, see what Web Parts you can add, and then maybe add one of the built-in Web Parts, just to give you an idea of some of the powerful things you can do with Web Parts without opening FrontPage or being an ASP .NET developer.

MOVE A WEB PART

1. Before you move any Web Parts around, make sure that the link to the right of the page title says Modify Shared Page and click it (if you aren't already in the drop-down menu).

2. In the drop-down menu, pick Design this Page (see previous graphic for reference).

   The page displays with borders around the two Web Part zone areas, which are now titled left and right. You can see that, for that added designer touch, the left column is a little larger. It's the left column that gets bigger and smaller if you resize the browser window; the right side remains pretty fixed in size, and always skinnier than the left side. That can be useful to know as you are arranging your Web Parts.

   Each Web Part has a down arrow and a close button on the title bar. Also, if you hover your mouse over a Web Part title bar, it will change to a four-headed arrow, indicating that if you grab the title bar at that time, you will be able to move the Web Part around. There are a limited number of places you can put it. Namely, above, between, or below the existing Web Parts in the two columns.

3. Grab the title bar of the Site Image and drag it over Announcements. When you left click to drag the Site Image, you will notice a blue bar shows up just above the title bar (see Figure 18.12 to see what I mean).

TIP   The Site Image Web Part, when not in design view, does not have a title bar. There is a Web Part setting called Frame Style that allows a Web Part to have no title bar or borders. In design view, the Web Part must have a title bar so you have something to drag around and it indicates the actual name of the Web Part in the gallery.

That's a sort of location marker as to where the item is. SharePoint is very picky about where you put a Web Part. Do not drop it until you drag the Site Image to just above the title bar for the Announcements Web Part (you'll see the blue bar). If you drop it approximately in the area, nothing will happen, so be sure you see the blue bar. When I finished moving the Site Image, the Web Parts rearranged themselves like so (see Figure 18.13). It takes a little practice.

FIGURE 18.12
Blue moving bar

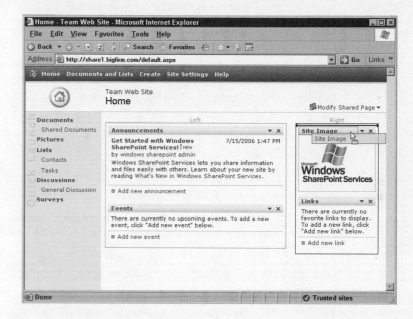

FIGURE 18.13
New Web Part layout

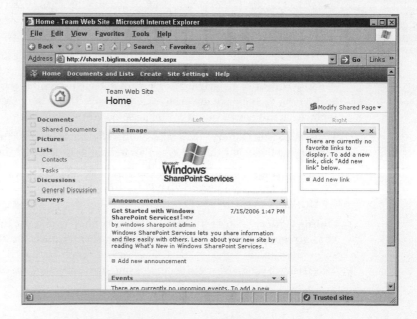

ADD A WEB PART TO THE TEAM WEB SITE HOME PAGE

Moving existing Web Parts around can get boring after a while. There are numerous Web Parts available in SharePoint without having to build new ones. SharePoint stores all of its known Web Parts in galleries. You can easily import Web Parts that you download from the Internet or build yourself, and when you do, you'll be prompted to add them to a gallery.

To see the quick and easy way to work with Web Parts, go to the Modify Shared Page drop-down menu and choose Add Web Parts. This should pop out a menu containing:

Browse   Opens a list of galleries already prepopulated with some default Web Parts.

Search   Lets you do a text search through the galleries in case you remember the name of the Web Part but can't remember which gallery it's in.

Import   Lets you first browse to where you have downloaded or saved a new Web Part, then lets you upload it to the Virtual Server Web Part gallery.

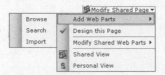

To get a good idea what Web Parts are available out of the box for SharePoint, just browse amongst the existing Web Parts and find something to add to the home page.

TIP   The pop-out menu actually controls the "state" of the Add Web Parts tool pane. The contents of the pane changes to reflect if you are browsing for Web Parts, importing them, or searching for them.

To do this, from the Add Web Parts pop-out menu, select Browse.

The Add Web Parts tool pane opens, obscuring the right Web Part zone (as you can see in Figure 18.14). You will have to use the scroll bars that come up if you want to get to the right Web Parts zone directly. The Add Web Parts tool pane displays the Web Part galleries that are available.

Web Part Page Gallery   The Recycle Bin of Web Parts, this lists all the Web Parts that were once on the page that have been closed from view on the page but not deleted. Useful if you accidentally close a Web Part and don't want to have to scroll through its original gallery to put it back. If the Web Parts were customized, they also keep their settings (a good reason to always replace default names on the Web Parts you edit).

Team Web Site Gallery   Contains all the Web Parts for this site, including the List View Web Parts, as well as some default Web Part templates called Built-in Web Parts.

Virtual Server Gallery   Contains the Web Parts you create or download and import. Web Parts imported from the Add Web Parts drop-down are made available to all sites contained in a virtual server.

Online Gallery   Holds the Web Parts that connect to and use Internet resources. Microsoft has kindly prepopulated this gallery with some MSNBC parts.

WARNING   If your server does not have an Internet connection, the Online Gallery will be empty.

FIGURE 18.14
New Web Part
tool pane

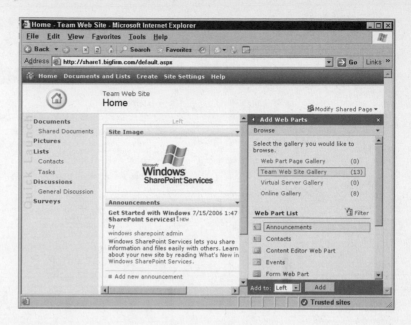

By default, when you browse for a Web Part, the default site (or whatever your site's name is) gallery is selected. At the bottom of the Add Web Parts tool pane is the list of the default site's gallery; feel free to scroll through it. Every list that is made on the site, such as those displayed in the Quick Launch bar, has a List View Web Part.

In addition, there are some built-in Web Parts in there that are a kind of template or bare structure of some standard Web Parts. You see, most Web Parts do nothing but display something from somewhere else. Sometimes it's lists, sometimes it's hockey scores. Because of that, developers found themselves building Web Part after Web Part that all were basically the same—only their content varied. That's what the built-in Web Parts are: the basic structure of some standard Web Parts that you can customize yourself. No ASP .NET programming required (thank goodness).

To get an idea as to how to use a built-in Web Part, I am going to briefly demonstrate how to use the Content Editor Web Part. Scroll down the list of Web Parts until you find the Content Editor Web Part. Select it.

There are two ways to add a Web Part: drag and drop it, like you moved the image Web Part across the home page earlier, or scroll down to the bottom of the Add Web Parts area to the Add to bar at the bottom. It has a drop-down field that lists the Web Part zones available. Since you might want some space to add an image and text to the Content Editor Web Part, I think it would be a good idea to add it to the left, and larger, zone.

So click the down arrow in the drop-down menu next to Add to at the bottom of the Add Web Parts area in the tool pane. Make certain that Left is selected. Click Add (see Figure 18.15).

If you are following along, you will also see that the Content Editor Web Part was added to the *top* of the left zone. A good thing to know. Now if you ever need to put a Web Part at the top of an area, you have an easier way of getting it there than dragging it.

FIGURE 18.15
Add Content Editor
Web Part

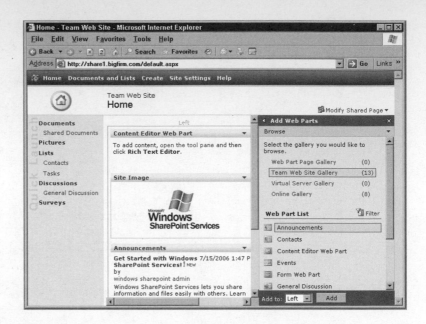

THE BUILT-IN WEB PARTS THAT COME BY DEFAULT WITH WINDOWS SHAREPOINT SERVICES:

Content Editor Web Part   Lets you add content to a web page using a rich text editor, using an HTML editor, or by specifying a file or URL to link to as content (we'll be test driving this one).

Form Web Part   A simple and small (useful if your Web Part zone is getting too busy) Web Part. It's just one data entry field and a Go button. It uses a Web Part Connection (a built-in feature of Web Parts, since most are just tables anyway) to build a single-field relationship with a different Web Part's list.

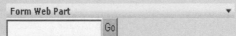

Then, when data is typed into the Form Web Part's field and the Go button is clicked, it sends that data to the other Web Part, telling it to bring up only the record(s) that match the data sent. Very useful if you have a contacts Web Part on your home page and you want users to be able to filter by last name or something. Unfortunately, it's so simple that there isn't an "I'm done, put the other Web Part back to all items view" feature to the Form Web Part. Once it's filtered the list of that other Web Part, that's it until you refresh the page, such as when you select Home in the navigation bar.

Page View Web Part   Creates a frame element, which means that it can display anything a window can—any file, folder, or web page. Seriously. For example, you can specify the UNC for a shared folder on a server and it will show the contents exactly like it was an Explorer window (complete with that "common tasks" view if that's how the client has it set). Because of this, it's a bad idea to put this Web Part in a narrow Web Part zone (like the one on the right on our home page).

Image Web Part   Has to be one of the simplest of the built-in Web Parts. It simply holds and displays an image. That's it. It can be connected (like the form Web Part) to another Web Part that has a field that contains a picture.

XML Web Part   Displays XML (extensible Markup Language) files in a Web Part. Like the Page View Web Part (which can display, among other things, HTML pages), this Web Part can be very powerful because you can essentially program it to display or do anything XML can do.

MODIFYING A BUILT-IN WEB PART

Of course, built-in Web Parts can't just be dropped on a page and forgotten. You need to give them content. That means you need to modify the one we just added.

Oh, and another thing: with the Add Web Parts tool pane open, the right Web Parts zone can be obscured. So how do you modify a Web Part if it is under the tool pane (hey, there's only so much screen space!)?

I'll show you a trick. Go to the Modify Shared Page link still above the tool pane and select it. In the drop-down menu, select Modify Shared Web Parts, and then click on the Web Part you wish to modify from the pop-out menu. (Of course, the scroll bars do come up when you are modifying a Web Part, so you can scroll over to a Web Part under the tool pane if you want to. But frankly, it is a little more difficult that way.)

WARNING   If you are in personal view you can still see a Web Part added in shared view. You can try to edit it, but all you will be able to do is change the way it looks on the page in your personal view. In order to actually edit the custom properties of a Web Part, you actually need to be in the view in which it was added.

From the list of shared Web Parts in the Modify Shared Web Parts pop-out, select Content Editor Web Part (see Figure 18.16).

FIGURE 18.16
Modify Shared Web
Parts pop-out menu

The Add Web Parts tool pane will change from a list of galleries to browse to a tool pane for the Web Part you have selected to modify. At this point that should be the Content Editor Web Part.

Of course, before you modify this Web Part, you do need to know what you are going to do with it. In this case, just as an example, I decided to use the rich text editor control to make an eye-catching reminder to users to turn in their vacation requests. First, I pull up a nice wallpaper from the %windir%\Web\Wallpaper folder (Azul.jpg should do the trick). Shrink it a little, add some text under it, and see what happens.

TIP You can also modify a Web Part at any time by clicking the down arrow in the Web Part's title bar and selecting Modify Shared Web Part from the drop-down menu (if you are in personal view it will say Modify My Web Part). This will add a yellow dotted line around the Web Part you are modifying (should you forget) and open the tool pane to the correct set of tools to edit that Web Part. Like most things Microsoft, there is more than one way to modify a Web Part.

The tool pane contents do vary depending on what Web Part you are modifying. However there are three sections that remain the same for most Web Parts:

Appearance   In charge of how the Web Part will appear on the page. Has settings for adjusting the height and width of a Web Part or letting it simply fit the Web Part zone. You can choose to have the Web Part display rolled up with only the title bar showing or for it to appear normally (frame state minimized or normal), or you can select the frame style itself.

Layout   Relates to where and how the Web Part will show up on the page. Sets whether or not a Web Part will be visible, in what zone, and where in the order of the Web Parts for that zone it will be.

Advanced   Specifies controls of the Web Part, whether or not it can be closed, minimized, or moved. It also offers additional fields to specify the link the Web Part actually goes to, its Help file, if the Web Part has an icon. You can even specify its missing assembly error.

Notice in Figure 18.17 at the top of the tool pane there are three ways to add content this particular Web Part: by a button that opens a Rich Text Editor, a button that opens an HTML editor (Source Editor), or a field in which you can put the path or URL to a file (Content Link). I'd like to show you how to use the really convenient (if a bit limited) Rich Text Editor, so click that button.

To activate the Rich Text Editor control, click in the window or hit the spacebar. The Content Editor isn't fancy; it pretty much looks like a pared down WordPad, only without, strangely enough, a menu bar. It does have some interesting abilities, such as inserting images and tables.

To get a feel for it, just move your mouse over the tool buttons slowly enough to get the pop-up tool tips. That will let you know what tools are available in this editor (see Figure 18.18). It might surprise you. I am rather impressed with what tools they chose to make available in the small space they have.

In this case, I'd like to insert an image of something vacation-like. You, of course, can choose whatever image you have handy. To do that, click the Insert Image button (it should be the standard image icon, one that looks a little like a landscape picture).

Browse to an image of your choice. Mine is a wallpaper of a beach scene (%windir%\Web\Wallpaper\Azul.jpg as you may recall), so it is huge and will have to be shrunk considerably. Once you have chosen your image and clicked the Open button in the Picture dialog box, click the OK button in the Content Editor Picture dialog box. The Content Editor control doesn't have much in the way of image editing, but if you think your image is too big for the left Web Part zone, you can click the image, grab its edges, and resize it.

FIGURE 18.17
Tool pane for Content Editor Web Part

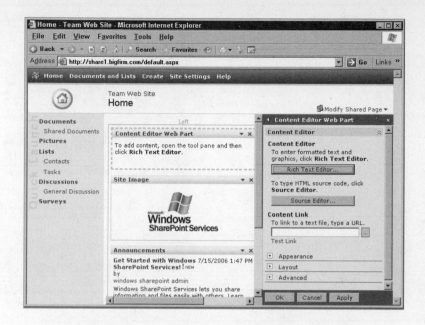

FIGURE 18.18
Rich Text Editor control

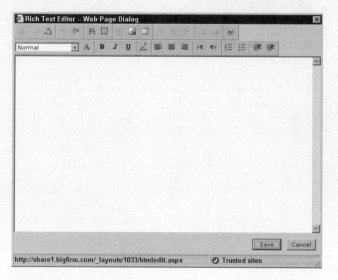

In addition to inserting an image, you can do text editing (the teeny tiny inserting point should be blinking just at the bottom right of your inserted image, so click in the editor, away from the image, and hit Enter). I am going to add some text and format it. I am not going to limit your creative freedom here (or insult your intelligence by telling you how to use a simple text editor). Feel free to add whatever text seems appropriate. See Figure 18.19 for my snazzy reminder.

FIGURE 18.19
Editing Content
Editor Web Part

Once you are finished, click Save. You are in no way prompted to name the file or specify location. This document is part of the Web Part and is saved as such.

TIP   If you ever have a problem modifying a Content Editor Web Part, try editing from the server upon which the Web Part resides.

That creates the content, but the Web Part itself still needs a name. Back in the tool pane you might remember the three headings: Appearance, Layout, and Advanced. To change the title of the Web Part, go to the Appearance heading in the tool pane and click the plus sign next to it.

You'll see the settings pertaining to the Web Part's appearance on the web page are now available. The first item in the Appearance settings area is the field for the title of the Web Part (see Figure 18.20). I don't know about you, but Content Editor Web Part just doesn't scream "vacation request" to me. Remember, it is always a good idea to give Web Parts relevant names in order to be able to find them again in the Web Parts gallery if you accidentally close them. I am going to change the title to Vacation Request Reminder.

TIP   You may have noticed the Visible on Page setting under Layouts and thought that that was odd. Why put a Web Part on a page and not make it visible? Good question. The reason is that there are Web Parts that do tasks that need to be added to a web page in order to be configured and run. Otherwise, they are not meant to be viewed by the general public. So you add them, modify them, then uncheck Visible on Page.

Since we're not going to be changing any other settings at this point, it's okay to finally finish modifying this Web Part and see what it looks like. Click OK at the bottom of the tool pane.

And that's it. Notice how the Web Part zone adjusted to the size of the picture in Figure 18.21? Keep that in mind as you add images to your Web Parts. The Adjust the Width to Fit Zone setting also seems to adjust the zone to fit the Web Part. Notice how the right zone has gotten a bit skinnier? If this doesn't work for you, then either mess with the absolute width of the new Web Part until it fits the way you like it, or get a smaller picture.

TIP   Now that you've experienced Web Part zones on the Team Web Site Home page, it's time to let you in on a secret. There are all kinds of different templates for Web Part pages. The Home page template is set with only two zones because the Quick Launch bar is there. However, if you'd like to try a different layout, there are several different templates for Web Parts pages. Just check them out under Web Pages on the Create page.

FIGURE 18.20
Changing title of Content Editor Web Part

FIGURE 18.21
Completed Vacation Reminder Web Part

CONNECTIONS AND MODIFYING EXISTING WEB PARTS

If you'd like to modify a Web Part that is already in a Web Part zone, just click the down arrow in the title bar and select Modify Shared Web Part. That will put you into design view of the page; then open the tool pane for that Web Part and put a dotted border around the Web Part you are currently modifying.

While you are modifying the Web Part, you may notice, if you click the drop-down menu on its title bar, a new item shows up. Under Modify Shared Web Part is now Connections. You might've seen it. Sometimes it's grayed out, sometimes it has a pop-out menu.

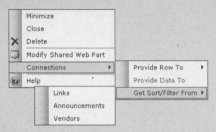

Connections is an interesting feature of a Web Part that has to do with the fact that most Web Parts are based on underlying tables. It makes it possible to create a temporary relationship between one List View's Web Part and another. The catch? The two Web Parts must be displayed on the page, and can only connect by fields that are visible. That is, that are in the View being displayed by the List View Web Part.

If that List View Web Part displays only a portion of the fields available in the list, and you want to connect by a field not showing, you need to create a custom view that includes the fields you want (you'll learn about creating list views later in the chapter), then select that view for the Web Part when you modify it.

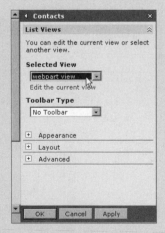

(And by the way, you can add a basic toolbar (otherwise known as an action bar) to any List View Web Part from the tool pane as well. So many nifty things, so little time...)

Any Web Part that is based on a list (or, strangely enough, the image Web Part) can create a connection with any other Web Part as long as they have a common field. One of the common uses for Web Part connections is filtering one List View Web Part based on a common field in another Web Part. For example, say you had a Contacts List View Web Part that had several contacts per company, and you had all those same companies listed in the Vendors List View Web Part, one company per vendor, of course. This makes it possible to connect the two Web Parts by company name. Then you could select (a radio button will appear) an item from the Vendors List View Web Part to filter only the items in the Contacts List View Web Part that match that Vendors company name.

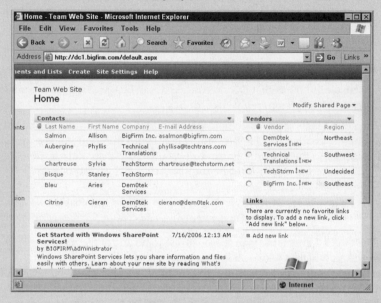

Just yet another nifty thing you can do with Web Parts. Check out the built-in help file, About Connecting a List View Web Part, for more detailed information because this is just the beginning of what connections can do.

And that's about as far as I am going to go with modifying Web Parts in this chapter. I hope that you see the potential Web Parts have, and that I've given you some ideas. What I did here is really only the tip of the iceberg. Realize that with a little ingenuity they can be more than useful.

TIP   Not only can you create really powerful web parts from the built-in tools, and you can develop your own in ASP. NET, but you can also download prebuilt web parts as well.

Admittedly, the Team Web Site home page is great, with convenient Web Parts and nice navigation bars, but let's face it, most of the work happens elsewhere. Namely, in the lists. That's where the data actually is. The home page is important because it is the page everyone comes to first to go somewhere else. So, make your Web Parts useful, convenient, and well-organized, and pay attention to how the users get from the Team Web Site Home page to the lists they need.

Quick Launch Bar (and Other Navigational Goodies)

Web Parts are good for conveniently using the lists that are displayed on the Team Web Site Web Parts Home page. But what about all of the other lists? I doubt it would be convenient to stack Web Parts on the Team Web Site Home page for every single list your company needs. That brings me to the Quick Launch bar. The Quick Launch bar is a way to give users access to all the lists that you want them to use in a space saving, efficient way. The links are basically organized by what the lists do, or contain, under the general headings:

Documents   Document libraries are listed here. Document libraries are lists that have a Type field, a sort of attachment field that contains the document object and lists the document's filename.

Pictures   Picture libraries are listed here. Like document libraries, only for pictures.

Lists   The general heading for miscellaneous lists that are not libraries.

Discussions   Lists that have records that can be spawned from another record, causing a threaded, discussion/reply structure.

Surveys   Lists where each field (or column if you are thinking of a list in terms of a table) is manually created (no default sample here) with different kinds of questions. The permissions can be set so the item author can be obscured, or set so that only one item can be entered by an author. There is a nifty built-in graphic view for this kind of list.

NOTE   Surveys are a list we aren't going to go into for this chapter. However, they are cool. So when you are comfortable using, modifying, and creating lists, check the surveys out.

The Quick Launch bar is probably going to be one of the most used components on your site's home page, which is why deciding on titles of lists (since that's what is going to show up here for everyone to use) is important. Also important is whether or not you want a list to be displayed here at all. If you want to obscure a list (maybe some users have limited permissions to it) to make it not quite so easy for average users to access it, start by not having it on the Quick Launch bar. That could deter most users from even realizing the list exists.

However, if you have created a list and set it not to show up on the Quick Launch bar (you'll see how to do this shortly), you (and the users) can still get to it, it's just a little harder.

There are two ways to get to lists. The first is to go to the navigation bar at the top of the page and click on Documents and Lists, then scroll down the page of document libraries and lists (hence the name "Documents and Lists," I guess) until you find the list you are looking for. The other is to use the Quick Launch bar. To see a list that is not displayed directly on the Quick Launch bar, just select a general heading for the type of list you are looking for (such as a discussion or survey). Both methods take you to the Documents and Lists page, but the Quick Launch just takes you directly to the part of the Documents and Lists page displaying the type of list you chose.

USING QUICK LAUNCH BAR GENERAL HEADINGS

To see what I'm talking about, click on the Lists general heading on the Quick Launch bar on the Team Web Site Home page.

You'll see in Figure 18.22 that, according to the page title (and the medallion that looks like a simple table), you are in the Documents and Lists page, but you are actually only seeing a subset of all the Team Web Site's list types. That's because the page view is set to Lists over in the blue bar on the left (the action pane), under Select a View. Feel free to check out the other views if you'd like.

FIGURE 18.22
Lists view in Documents and Lists

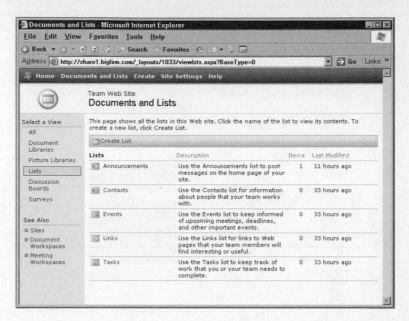

This page gives you a chance to see all existing lists, even filter the view to see lists of a particular type (Document Library, List, Discussion, and so on), even if they are not displayed in the Quick Launch Bar.

By the way, Documents and Lists does double duty of both displaying all existing lists as well as giving you an environment from which to create a new list of some type if you so choose.

Of course, that brings up a bit of a navigational question. If you can create lists in Documents and Lists, then what is the Create link in the navigation bar for? Well, it's there because the Create List link on the action bar in Documents and Lists *takes* you to the Create page in the navigation bar. Create actually focuses on creating just about anything in the SharePoint sites (we will be using the Create page to build a workspace later, so you'll see what I mean). The Create page contains all the templates that can be used in SharePoint. And I mean all of them: lists, libraries, subsites, even individual web pages, as well as blank templates to custom build them all. Who needs FrontPage?

Documents and Lists displays all details concerning existing lists and those that can be made. This distinction can make navigation a little confusing to those who don't see the difference (the pages do look very similar), but there is a method to SharePoint's madness.

WHY CAN YOU MAKE A SITE FROM THE DOCUMENTS AND LISTS PAGE?

So you might've noticed that there are some links to Sites, Document Workspaces, and Meeting Workspaces on the left side of what should be a page about lists. And you might be wondering why they did that.

Here's my take on it.

Because they had to. If the Create page only gives you the tools to create things but does not display what has been created, and you created a subsite, how would you find it? If it is not on the Quick Launch bar, you forgot the link (and didn't add it to the Links List View Web Part), and the Create page where you made it can't display it, where would it be displayed?

Despite the fact that the Documents and Lists page should, conceptually speaking, only be concerned with lists and document libraries, it is the page in charge of collecting and centrally displaying all existing parts and objects of this website.

Of course, including the means to create and display sites and workspaces (which are the same thing as subsites under the Team Web Site, only with different templates) in the Documents and Lists page is a bit, um, problematic from a design point of view. The page says it only shows libraries and lists, so you can't just add Sites and Workspaces to the list of lists. It would break the whole metaphor.

But there is that action pane on the left side of the Documents and Lists page with a lot of space on the bottom. So they just stuck a couple of quick links under Select a View in that action pane, and grouped them together under See Also. It makes it (almost) look like they meant to do that, and it does take you to the page that lists existing subsites, organizing them based on their templates. So you can still create sites, document workspaces, or meeting workspaces (remember, all are basically the same thing, only with slightly different templates) and find them in a list after you have created them. You just have to remember to view Documents and Lists and click a link under See Also.

Lists

You know that SharePoint built several lists by default when Windows SharePoint Services installed. Each list has a unique trait or two that makes it particularly useful:

Announcements   Items can expire so they don't clutter up the List View Web Part. This is obviously a priority for this list, because its Web Part is placed prominently on the Team Web Site Home page by default.

Contacts   Links to Outlook 2003 and so has fields that match those of the contact list in Outlook. You can customize this list with no problems, and the Outlook equivalent fields are a convenience.

Events   Has a calendar view as one of the default views. Can be linked to Outlook as well. Has the ability to create a workspace from any event entry (in case you need one to organize attendees, agenda, documents, minutes, and other details).

Links   An interesting and very simple list that is specifically designed for its List View Web Part. The action bar actually has a link to change the order of how the link items are displayed in the Web Part. You can simply look at the links in the list instead of the Web Part, and you can sort by the URL column.

Tasks   Has a calendar view and has a lookup field (for those of you that work with Access or SQL), Assign to, that pulls account names from the user information of the site. You can't "assign" a task to anyone who doesn't have a user account. Has a convenient list of different ways to view tasks.

Other default lists are, of course, the Shared Documents (which is the default document library) and a general discussion (which is the default Discussion Group). Mind you, you can build your own lists as well. The default lists and their templates are just there for your convenience.

Now that you've seen the lists available by default, it's time to get to work on one. I actually have devious plans for the Contacts list, so let's get started.

Conveniently enough, we are already in the Documents and Lists page, so you can just click the Contacts lists link.

ADDITIONAL THINGS CREATE MAKES

Something that is listed under Create but that isn't listed conveniently in Documents and Lists is Web Pages. It is here you can use some default templates for some standard SharePoint Web Part pages. However, they are not actually added to the site. They are treated like documents and are saved into a document library of your choice (which makes me think that they should have been listed under Documents and Lists in addition to Create, but they didn't ask me). When you open the web page back up, you'll see that it has had the site template and theme applied, it's the right color, and the navigation bar is on the top. It works, it's just in a document library.

The other item not listed under Documents and Lists that exists on the Create page is something called a form library. Meant to be used specifically by InfoPath 2003, a form library is supposed to be full of forms created from forms uploaded or "published" from InfoPath. The forms can only be opened with InfoPath 2003 on the client side.

So, this is the Contacts list (see Figure 18.23). It's your standard list page, which is an ASPX page generated to display the records of a table in a particular view. The default view for most lists is the All items list view, which is basically a report generated to display all the records in the list's table with the most likely fields you might want to see, in the order you'd most likely want to see them. The list can display only the fields that exist for an item but does not necessarily have to display all of them (sometimes there isn't really room). Just like any report, you can control how it's viewed. The default All Contacts view for the Contacts list displays Last Name, First Name, Company, Business Phone, Home Phone, and Email Address for its entries. If this doesn't suit you, don't worry, you can create your own view, in which you can chose what fields you wish to display in whatever order you'd like.

FIGURE 18.23

Contacts list

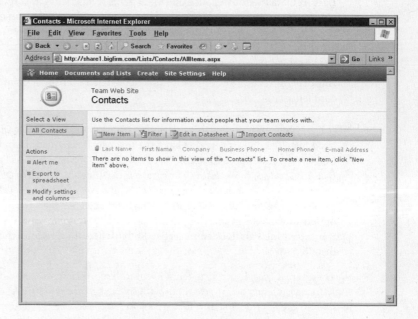

On the left of the page is the action pane (it replaces the Quick Launch Bar, because we are not on the home page of a site and helps indicate that we are "in" a list) that holds the views and actions for a list. It can change from list to list, depending on which one you're in. Currently the Contacts list has one view (All Contacts) and the Actions are:

Alert me   Any list can send email (if SharePoint is set up to use email) if an item is added, changed, or deleted. You can choose what triggers the alert and if it is sent immediately or in a daily or weekly summary.

Export to spreadsheet   An integration bit between Excel 2003 and SharePoint. Not only can you export a list to Excel, but you can actually use Excel (2003, of course) to synchronize its list with SharePoint, so if someone adds data to either list, they can both be updated to reflect the change (complete with conflict checking, which is nice).

Modify settings and columns   This is how you both manage the properties and add fields (referred to here as "Columns" to give you that reassuring datasheet feeling) to the list.

On the Contacts list page, you still have the navigation bar. The page title's there (with its medallion of a contact record) and a bar with links on it above the area where the list items will be. These bar items are links for a reason. In order to work on anything regarding a list, it opens into its own web page. If you edit an item, it opens a form page of that item's record so you can change the text in its fields. IIS and WMSDE in action. Now, these links are sort of laid out like buttons based on the actions you can take with the list and its items, so I tend to call this bar an "action bar" for convenience' sake. It has a consistent look and feel for all list objects, with four links in the action bar:

New Item   Takes you to the page in which you can create a new item for the list.

Filter   Standard list filter, useful in case the list of items is long and you'd like to filter the view to find something you are looking for in particular.

Edit in Datasheet   Because a list is a table, it has fields and records (otherwise known as columns and rows), and it can be used as a datasheet. Of course, you need to have Excel 2003 installed to even see the datasheet (see the "About Microsoft Office 2003 Integration" sidebar for more on that), but the option is there. We'll come back to the usefulness of both filters and Edit in Datasheet in a moment.

Import Contacts   Requires Outlook 2003, used to import Contacts from an Outlook 2003 contact list.

NOTE   If you are accessing this site and list from a workstation with Office 2003 (particularly Outlook) installed on it, the action bar has a few new links. In addition to New Item, Filter, Edit in Datasheet, and Import Contacts, there is a Link to Outlook link. As I mentioned earlier, the contacts list is one of those that can integrate with Office 2003. Link to Outlook literally creates a link that synchronizes your local contact list in Outlook and the Contacts list in SharePoint. For some reason, I imagine a hundred users linking here, and I feel fear. I don't know why. Regardless, the option is available. In addition, as the name indicates, the Import Contacts link imports contacts from someone's Outlook contacts list. Both of these links require the user to have Outlook 2003 installed.

There are a couple of things that I would like to show you how to do with lists. Common tasks that, once you learn how to do them with one list, you can do them on all lists. So, I am going to add an item to the Contact list and take a look at it in the current All Items view of the list (since you are in the Contacts list, the all items view is called All Contacts). After that, I'd like to propagate some more contacts with the datasheet view, add a review date field to the Contacts list, check out alerts, and then introduce you to views in general (which are essentially report templates you can customize to display the list data in different and useful ways), especially to point out how you can do totals, grouping, and more. Then I'll show you how to create a new view for the Contacts list so you can see a calendar of everyone's review date. And, while we're messing with the Contacts list settings themselves, you'll get an idea of how to manage lists so you can go mess with the other lists as you'd like.

ABOUT MICROSOFT OFFICE 2003 INTEGRATION

SharePoint is practically married to Office, and to do most of the more nifty information worker tasks, you will need to have Office 2003 installed (earlier versions of Office can do some, but not all of, the integration that 2003 can). To edit a list in datasheet view, you must have Microsoft Excel installed (preferably Office 2003, of course) because Office 2003 installs a datasheet component so datasheets can be managed within IE. As a matter of fact, Office 2003 installs components for most of the Office products to integrate with SharePoint. I am going to try to avoid most of the Office system because I can't guarantee everyone has it, and I want to show you what SharePoint can do with minimal interference from anything else you'd need to buy. That being said, I am going to have to use Word 2003 to demonstrate how users can add documents to a document library and use Excel 2003 to use datasheet view.

Although I am not going any further with Office, I thought you should know what integrates with what really briefly, in case it is something you need to work with more extensively.

A QUICK LIST OF THE THINGS YOU CAN DO WITH AND TO SHAREPOINT WITH OFFICE 2003

Just about any Office 2003 product that offers the task pane has the capability of displaying shared workspace information for whatever shared document or file they are in and encourages them to make a new workspace if they are on a new, unshared document.

The Shared Workspace task pane can allow a user to create a workspace from whatever document they are working on (if they have the rights to), check the status of a document, update the copy of the document they have locally from a document library, check tasks, set alerts about tasks and new documents, see documents in a document library…heck, it even tells you if other members of the site are online and displays the links from the Links List. There will be more about the Shared Workspace pane later in the chapter.

More specifically, here is a quick list of what the Office 2003 products can do with SharePoint:

Word 2003   Uploads, checks out/in, edits, versions, saves files to a document library.

Excel 2003   Imports/exports lists, links lists, and edits lists.

Access 2003   Like Excel, imports/exports, links, and edits lists.

Outlook 2003   Exports Contacts lists, imports individual contacts or events, links to a Contacts list or Events, views SharePoint calendars side by side with personal calendars, manages alerts, creates meeting workspaces, sends shared documents.

PowerPoint 2003   Essentially treated like Word 2003: uploads, edits, checks out/in, versions, saves files to a document library, and even creates a document workspace for the PowerPoint file.

FrontPage 2003   Customizes and edits SharePoint websites and pages. (Will be renamed SharePoint Designer in Office 2007.)

InfoPath 2003 Has its own library called the form library (since InfoPath is all about forms). Like the document library, each form library has an underlying template to use to create the items it contains. Unlike the document library, you can customize that template using InfoPath 2003. Each InfoPath form template needs its own library. Really, really customized forms.

Any new form library you make is listed in the Documents and Lists page under Document Libraries, because there is no Form Library heading. Which is a little counter-intuitive for me. That's why I suggest you add links to your form libraries to the Quick Launch bar, so users can easily get to it if they need it.

The Picture Manager that comes with Office 2003 can be used to do bulk uploads of pictures to the picture library.

Even the less mundane, more specific Office products, such as Visio, Project, or Publisher have the capacity to work with SharePoint.

Check out Microsoft's "Integration Guide for Microsoft Office 2003 and SharePoint Services" online for more detailed info.

In SharePoint the words "item" and "record" are used interchangeably and refer to a list entry. Similarly, "column" or "field" are synonymous and basically refer to a field in a list entry. Remember, a list is a table in the underlying content database of the site. A table is like a spreadsheet and made up of rows and columns. So, in trying to have a comfortable paradigm for users, a table of contacts is called a Contacts list, and the records in that list are referred to (but not consistently so) as items. But (I guess because those users should not be adding fields to lists, and therefore don't need to be comforted) fields in the items are actually often referred to as columns, because of the nature of the underlying database.

Speaking of lists and underlying data, in my case the Contacts list (and probably yours) is empty because I haven't put anything in it yet. Which is why I'd like to add some data now.

WARNING SharePoint was designed to be best viewed in 1024x768 (or higher) and relies heavily on long lists and your ability to scroll. Unfortunately, screen shots can't scroll and that resolution makes teeny-tiny, unreadable pictures in a book. Because of this, sometimes a page or list of settings may not all show up in the figures I refer to. They will require some scrolling to get to even on a full screen. I would like to apologize for the inconvenience beforehand.

ADD A NEW ITEM

Adding a new item to a list is as easy as clicking on the New Item link in the action bar in the Contacts list page.

As you can see in Figure 18.24, the action bar, while in the New Item page, has links that are relevant to what can be done while creating a new item. Namely, Save and Close, which works like a Save and Go Back to List button; Attach File (because the Contacts list does allow attachments, so if there is a resume, report, or something, you can add it to a Contacts item); and Go Back to List, which should take you back to the Contacts list.

NOTE Go Back to List is an interesting item because it indicates a bit of a weakness in the navigation bar. It's not dynamic. In other words, it doesn't actually change depending on where you are. So if you are in an item in a list, you need the action bar (unless you want to hit the back button in your browser) to get you back up one level to wherever you came from. In our case, we came from the Team Web Site Home page, so that's where we'll go back to, regardless of what the link in the action bar says it does.

You might notice that you are going to have to enter more data in more fields here than there were field titles out in the list view. Remember, that's because the All Contacts view does show all items but not all of the fields in the item records. It only displays what the SharePoint creators thought you would find useful to look at in a list of contacts. They assumed that if you wanted more details, you'd click the item in question and view it.

Just to demonstrate, I am going to create a fictitious contact record; you can check out Figure 18.25 to see what data I entered. Once you've filled in all of the fields you feel are necessary, click Save and Close in the action bar. It should take you back to the Contacts list, All Items view. And you should see the new contact item listed.

FIGURE 18.24

Contacts: New Item

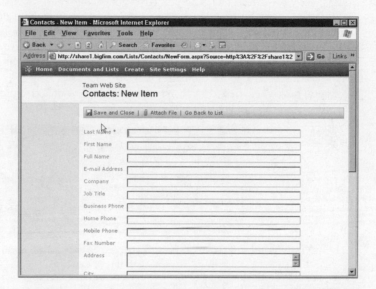

FIGURE 18.25

New contact data in Contacts list

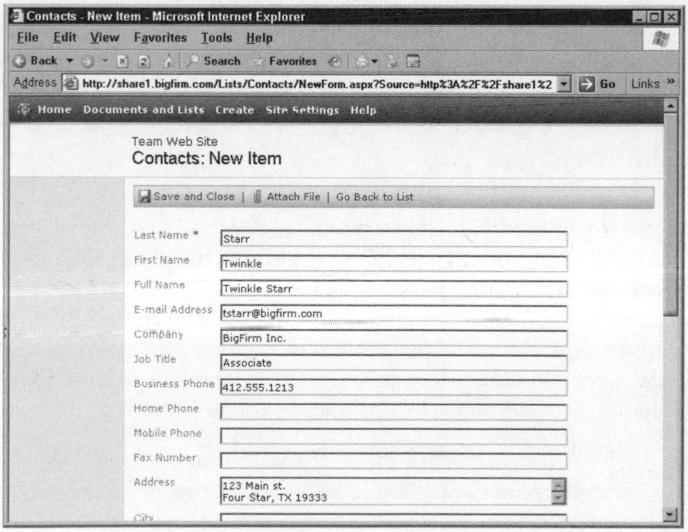

We added a single item, and that was nice as a one shot. But what if you had to add several, even many, items to the Contacts list? It could be kind of tedious having to click New Item, tab through every field (even those you don't fill in), click Save and Close, wait for the page to display the All Items view of the Contacts list, click New Item for the next entry, and so forth until all the entries are made. That is why there are several ways to enter data into a list in SharePoint.

If you already have all the contacts that you intend to put in the SharePoint site's Contacts list in a contact list in Outlook 2003, then you can import the contacts from Outlook to SharePoint. Or, if you have a spreadsheet with the contacts already created in Excel 2003, you can import the records from there. But, just in case you don't have the contacts conveniently premade, then datasheet view is for you (I told you we'd get back to that).

If you have to enter a lot of data into a list, you can just choose Edit in Datasheet, which will cause the list to be displayed in a little spreadsheet, allowing you to zip through the fields, just as you would in Excel, typing as you go and tabbing down to create the next item. As a matter of fact, as I've mentioned before, you must have Excel 2003 installed on the computer you are accessing the SharePoint site with to use datasheet view.

If you have ever tried to edit a list in datasheet view on a computer that doesn't have Excel 2003 installed, chances are you got this error:

And, now you know why (although you might've had an inkling earlier in the chapter).

TIP   At this point I am going to move over from working on the server where I installed Windows SharePoint Services to working on a domain workstation in the local network. The reason for this is that in order to demonstrate some of the integration features of Word and Excel 2003, I need to be on a machine that has them installed. I do not intend to install Office on my server. Having said that, you are likely to be working from the server where you installed SharePoint. If you don't have Office 2003 installed on any convenient machines, no sweat—that's what screenshots are for. Just read along. About 85 to 90 percent of the chapter is not Office 2003–related.

EDIT IN DATASHEET, BULK ITEM ENTRY

Remember that this requires Excel (preferably 2003). Since I am working on a workstation with Excel 2003 installed, I am going to go ahead and click Edit in Datasheet on the action bar in the Contacts list.

As you can see in Figure 18.26, there is a little spreadsheet (just exactly like one in Excel because it is using Excel to do this) where the fields would be if I were editing an item. The items are now rows, the fields are columns (notice that there is a column for attachments). The action bar has changed considerably. In addition to Link to Outlook and Import Contacts, there are now links for:

New Row   Creates a new row at the bottom of the datasheet.

Show in Standard View   Takes you out of datasheet view and back to the selected view of the list.

FIGURE 18.26
Edit Contacts list in datasheet

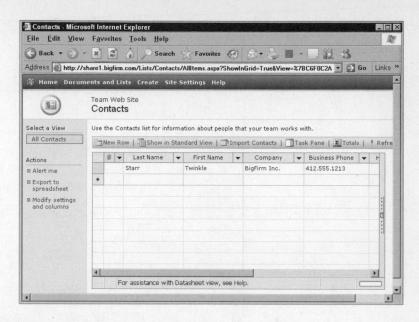

Task Pane A scaled down Excel 2003 task pane.

Totals Takes lists to a whole new place. It creates a row in datasheet view that allows you, once created, to select the column you want to total and see the total. In standard list view, the total row actually is displayed above the other items listed. Remember, because datasheet view makes your otherwise static list (which, in case you have forgotten, is a table in the content database on this server) into a spreadsheet, it can do formulas like a spreadsheet. You can use a column to do calculations as well.

Refresh Data Refreshes the data between the list you are working on and whatever Office product is linked to it. (At least, supposedly; in complicated, multiple products using a Share-Point table environment, synchronizing and refreshing can get tricky. There are extensive tips and tricks online. Read them over for best results.)

While we're here, let's enter some data in the fields. See Figure 18.27 to see some idea of what I entered. Basically, I'm just filling fields so we can use the records to do other things. Once you get to the end of a row and move to the next, the previous row gets written to the underlying table in the content database.

Once the data entry's done, take a look at the list in standard view by clicking Show in Standard View in the action bar. You can see the data that has been entered in Figure 18.28.

One thing that you might notice right away is that !NEW icon next to every item. This icon lasts for 24 hours after the item's creation. And now you can see why people want to just get rid of it.

TIP KB825510 tells you how to disable !NEW in all lists in a website by setting its days-to-show-new-icon to zero. But if you want to instead extend the duration of the new icon, try adding the number of days you want it to last. See the KB article for full details as to the command and syntax.

FIGURE 18.27
Datasheet data entry

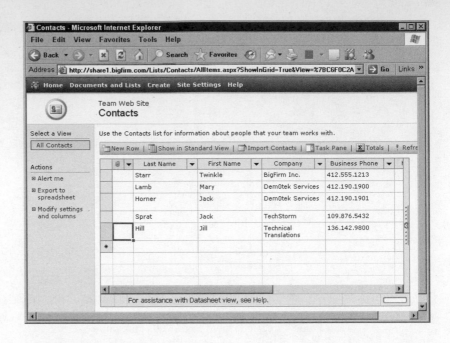

FIGURE 18.28
Data from
datasheet in list

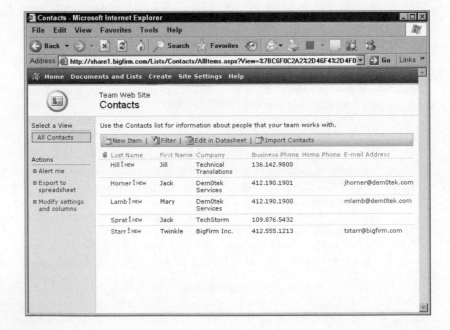

TOTALS

If you'd like, take a look at the Total row, click the Totals link in the action bar (and to turn it off, click it again). Notice that it creates a row at the bottom of the table. If you click in a field, it will become active, allowing a drop-down containing the kinds of totals you can use for that row. We don't really have any number fields in the Contacts lists to calculate, but you can count entries if you'd like.

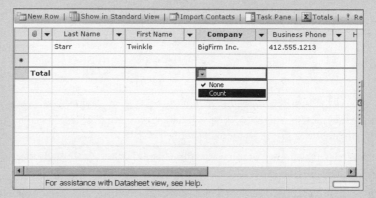

In the All Contacts standard view, Totals are handled in a way that is a little unusual. Instead of being displayed on the bottom of the view, they are at the top.

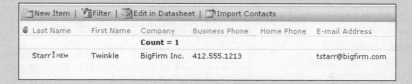

DID YOU NOTICE THE DATASHEET HAD FEWER FIELDS PER RECORD THAN ENTERING DATA THE STANDARD WAY?

The datasheet view gives you a datasheet to enter data into that does not contain every single field that the New Item form does. In other words, datasheet view is good for adding data quickly to a list, but it does it based on the *view* you've selected. If the view only displays some of the fields (and remember, the default view for Contacts only shows the name, company, business, home phone, and email), then that's all you get to put data into a datasheet.

Just something to keep in mind. If you are going to be doing a lot of data entry into a datasheet on your SharePoint server (rather than doing it elsewhere and then importing it), I suggest you create a view that contains all of the fields you need (if not every single one) and set it to be a personal view. That way you can see it when you go to that list, but no one else can.

THERE'S FILTERING AND THERE'S *FILTERING*

Now that you've seen datasheet view, I'd like to let you in on a secret: there are several ways to filter data in SharePoint. But, most people don't use all of them.

For example, in standard list view, you can filter the list items by field content.

But that is a bit limited. If you need to filter your data by more than exact match, then you need custom filtering. Custom filtering allows you to enter an argument like "less than but equal to" or "contains" to better isolate the items you want than simply listing field values.

So, there has to be another, better way to filter lists. And there is. Actually there are two ways to filter list data using custom filters.

The first is using datasheet view. In datasheet view, the column titles have a drop-down arrow next to them.

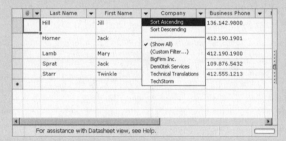

If you click a column title drop-down arrow, you can select (Custom Filter) and enter the criteria and argument (or arguments, if you'd like to get complicated) you need to filter the column by.

Much more useful than the filter link in the action bar. Of course it does require Excel 2003.

But, if you don't have Excel 2003, don't despair. The second way is to create or customize a list's standard view. Views are basically reports about the list data, and therefore they have settings for filtering built in. We'll be checking out how to customize standard views later in this chapter while looking a creating new list view, and in the "Filtering by Keyword Using a Standard View" sidebar in the Document Libraries section of the chapter.

A QUICK GLANCE AT ALERTS

You've seen how easy it is to create items in a list. But what if you wanted to know if an item were changed or if there was a change to the list overall without actually visiting the list every day? Then you'd set up an alert.

Alerts are automated email responses that can be set to track a change on a single item in a list, or to indicate a change in a list overall. Of course, because alerts are email based, they do require email to be set up for this site at the Virtual Server level and that the user who is setting the alert have an email account to send it to. See "If You Don't Have Sharepoint's Email Configured Yet" sidebar for a quick look at what I'm talking about.

Let's take a look at how to set an alert for a particular list item. Click the last name of one of the items you just created. This allows you to view all the fields of a particular contact.

On the Contacts page, the action bar now has an Alert me link. This is because there is no action pane when you are viewing a contact directly. It's actually pretty slick and keeps the users focused on using the action bar while they're there.

So to take a look at how to create an Alert, on the Contacts page that comes up to view an item, click the Alert Me link in the action bar (see 18.29).

This will bring you to the New Alert page (see Figure 18.31). The layout and design of this page is very much like most configuration pages throughout Windows SharePoint Services. The settings for a New Alert are pretty straightforward:

Send Alerts To   Normally displays the email address of the person who is logged in, but if you want to send the alert to a different email address, you can set it here. Right now we don't have email set up, but you can see why it would be worth doing.

Change Type   Because we are setting up an alert on an item, there is really only one action that can be taken. Therefore Change Item (which alerts you if the item is edited or deleted) is the only option to trigger an alert for this item.

Alert Frequency   When you want the alert to be sent. You can be alerted immediately, or if you know you are not going to act on it immediately (or if it is possible the item will be changed often), you can choose to be sent a summary of alerts for this item either daily or weekly.

FIGURE 18.29
Alert Me link

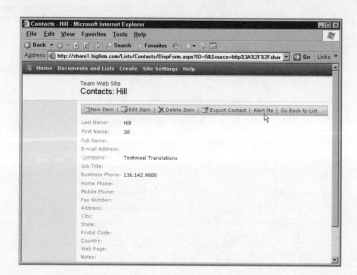

It's in the Alert Frequency section that the link View My Existing Alerts on this Site is located. This link will take the user to a list of all of the alerts they have created, regardless of which list or item they were created for (see Figure 18.30). Because site administrators tend to set limits on how many active alerts a person can have at one time, it is good to keep track of your alerts by using this link.

Once you've familiarized yourself with this page, you can click Cancel.

That should put you back on the Contact item. From there click Go Back to List in the action bar.

Now you know what the Alert me link over in the action pane on the left does. This alert is exactly like the item alert except there are more ways a list itself can change—items can be added, changed, or deleted. There are alerts on all lists, libraries, and items as a way of being able to keep track of changes remotely or quickly check the number of active alerts you have currently.

IF YOU DON'T HAVE SHAREPOINT'S EMAIL CONFIGURED YET (OR DON'T PLAN TO EVER CONFIGURE IT)

Mind you, if you are following along with me, we have not configured email for this SharePoint server yet. That's fine. It demonstrates what doesn't work without configuration, it shows you something the users might come across on an under-configured SharePoint server, and demonstrates the need for email. Alerts are not rocket science. I think you get the idea.

As a matter of fact, if you don't have an email server in your environment for some reason, you can disable Alerts for your site altogether. It saves resources on the server and saves space on the hard drive. Later, when you see the setting under Administration that lets you enable or disable Alerts, keep this in mind. However, the Alert Me link in the action pane is hard coded, so it will show up regardless of whether or not the user's rights to Alerts have been disabled.

FIGURE 18.30
New Alert

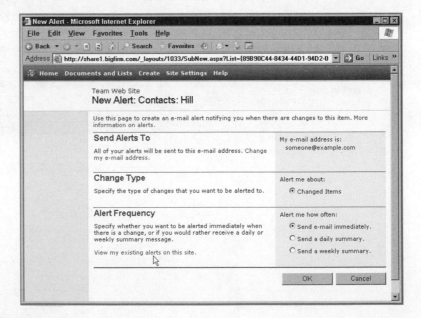

FIGURE 18.31

My Alerts on this Site

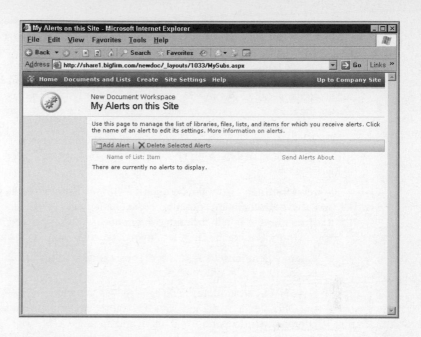

MANAGING ALERTS

There are two lists that are rather unique in SharePoint, and one of them is the Alerts list. It's basically an administrative-level item for users. Just like their user information, users can and should manage their own alerts. The problem is there is no easy link from the Quick Launch bar to get to them. The user needs to know to go to the nearest Alert Me and then View My Existing Alerts for this Site. Otherwise, they can go to Site Settings in the navigation bar and scroll down to the My Alerts for this Site.

Of course, since the Site Settings page has a lot of site settings (as the title suggests), it may be best to train the users to manage their alerts from Alert Me in the action pane of any convenient list rather than encourage them to give Team Web Site management a try.

A Windows SharePoint Services administrator configures alerts at the top-level site for all subsites, for all users, and may have created user limits or disabled alerts altogether. They can also manage alerts for an individual user who gets overly optimistic about how in touch with SharePoint they really need to be.

MODIFYING A LIST

The default lists that come with Windows SharePoint Services are great, but there is always room for improvement. All lists can be modified: you can add or remove fields, decide what fields are going to be viewed, even add or remove views of the list itself. There is one central page for modifying a list and you get to it from the Modify settings and columns link (columns meaning fields, as you may recall, since a list is actually a table in the content database).

To start modifying a list, I am going to show you a neat, built-in list feature called Content Approval. Then I'll add a field to the existing Contacts list. Then I will add a new view to the Contacts list that takes advantage of the new field.

In this case, I've decided to use this Contacts list for all of the employees of my fictitious company. I plan to eventually have several people who are going to be able to add contacts to the list, so, to ensure that all information is accurate, I am going to require Content Approval before all users can see an item. All of my employees have review dates coming up, and getting reviews scheduled on time is always a problem. So in an attempt to fix this, I am going to create a new field for all contacts called Review, format it for dates only, and then create a new calendar view that shows the review dates so I can more easily see whose reviews are coming up.

To begin, I click on Modify settings and columns in the action pane.

There are three general areas of the Customize Contacts page (not all of them are visible in Figure 18.32 unfortunately, so don't be surprised if you have to scroll down to see all the settings listed below):

General Settings   Contain the details about the list page itself, like its title, description, actual web address, whether or not it is on the Quick Launch bar, whether or not the items can have attachments, and whether or not content needs to be approved before it is displayed to normal users. Under General Settings are links that actually contain the settings:

Change general settings   All of the general settings just mentioned and then some. We'll be spending a lot of time here.

Save list as a template   You can create a list, set the views, general settings, fields, and so on. Once you are satisfied, save it as a template with no content, just the framework, or with content included, and use it again and again.

Change permissions for this list   This is where you can set permissions for this list that override the permissions that control the site. More on that later. It is also where, if anonymous access is set on the Virtual Server containing this site, you can set whether or not this list allows anonymous access. And if email is configured on the server, you can enable access requests.

Delete this list   Just what it sounds like, deletes this list. They are not kidding.

FIGURE 18.32
Customize Contacts

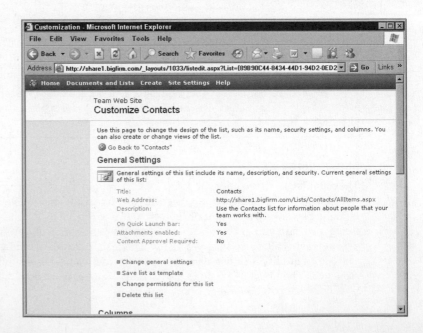

Columns   Because columns and fields are synonymous in SharePoint, it contains the list of fields in the list. You can edit an existing field's properties by clicking the field title listed below, add a new column, and change the order of the columns from here.

Views   Contains the current views so you can edit them, and you can create a new view from here. There are three styles to choose from, standard, datasheet, and calendar.

To take a look at and even change some general settings, click on the Change general settings link.

You'll see in Figure 18.33 the list settings for Contacts.

Name and Description   Useful for changing the names of lists created by default to make them more personalized for your company. Also important to note is the name here of this list is what shows up in the Quick Launch bar. So make sure it is spelled correctly, is descriptive, and is something you want displayed on the home page of the site.

Navigation   This is the all-important yet simple setting as to whether or not you want a list to display on the Quick Launch bar.

Content Approval   Requires extra administration, but a list can have a moderator (usually someone with the right to manage lists and/or an administrator) who can see all new items and can choose to approve or deny an item. While it is pending, the user who created the item can see that it is pending approval, and the moderator who needs to approve it can see it, but none of the other users can see the item until it is approved. It creates two new uneditable fields in the list called Approval Status and Approver Comments.

WARNING   If you apply Content Approval to a list, it may render datasheet view read-only because the Approval Status and Approver Comments are uneditable. If you decide to disable Content Approval after it has been applied to a list, all pending or rejected items are simply absorbed into the approved list for all to see until deleted by the moderator.

FIGURE 18.33
General settings
for Contacts

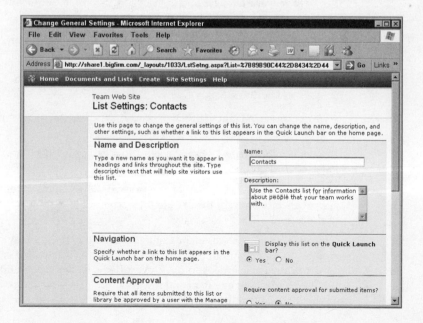

Attachments   Particularly useful for Discussion Groups, this option allows you to decide whether or not to allow users to attach files to items in this list. It tends to be on by default.

Item Level Permissions   Although limited, this is where you can easily enforce item-specific permissions for a list:

Read Access   Whether or not a user can read all items or only their own. Great for personal entries, like assistance requests, or applications that no one but the moderator or creator of the item should see.

Edit Access   Whether or not a user can edit all of the items (almost never a good idea), their own item, or none.

Content Approval

Most of the default settings are fine, but as I mentioned, I am going to set the Content Approval to Yes because I want to check whatever contacts the users add to the Contacts list before they go public. I also don't want anyone editing the records I add to the list, so I am going to allow the users to edit only the items they create.

NOTE   Even if no one else has contributed to the list at this point, you can still test out this feature. So follow along. It, of course, is more fun with more people, but there will be plenty of time for that later. I want to present this to you straight from the install because it is the least complicated way to introduce you to these features.

1. Click the Yes radio button in the Content Approval section.

2. And to make sure users can't edit anyone else's item but their own, click the Only Their Own radio button under Edit Access in the Item Level Permissions section near the bottom of the page.

3. To save these changes and go back to Customize Contacts, click OK at the bottom of the page.

4. Now, back on the Customize Contacts page, you can see under General Settings that Content Approval is Yes. But let's see what change that has made to the list itself.

5. To get back to the Contacts list, oddly enough, you click the Go Back to Contacts link above General Settings.

As you can see in Figure 18.34, on the Contacts page there are now two new views in the action pane under Select a View:

Approve/reject Items   Displays items in a list grouped by approval status: Approved, Rejected, or Pending.

My submissions   Very similar to Approve/Reject Items in that items will be grouped by approval status, except the list should be filtered to display only the currently logged in user's items.

Of course, all of the items in the Contacts list should be automatically approved, since they were created by an administrator. But to see that the items we created earlier are actually all grouped under Approved, click the Approve/Reject Items view in the Action pane (Figure 18.35).

If a user had created an item and it was waiting for your approval, it would be listed under a group heading of Pending. But in my case, all of my items are preapproved.

FIGURE 18.34
Contacts list with
content approval

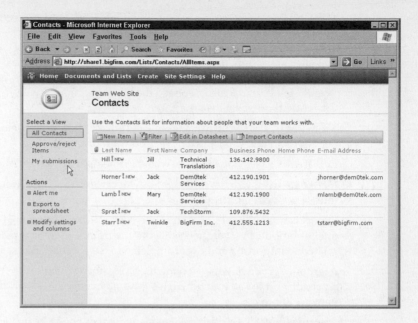

FIGURE 18.35
Approve/Reject
Items view

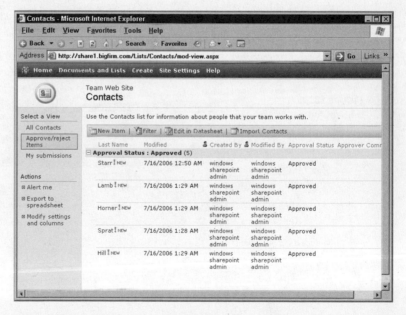

Even if yours are the only entries so far into the list, you can still see how to approve or reject an item. It's not a one-time thing. You can still reject an item or set it to Pending with a comment after it has been approved (and vice versa). Then the user can see the item's status in the My Submissions view and make a change based on that comment. At that point you can review it and change its status from Pending to Rejected or Approved.

Move your mouse over the title of one of the items until a selection box with a down arrow appears (it doesn't matter what view you are in, this option simply exists for the item, regardless).

That selection box and down arrow compensate for the lack of context menu in a web interface, so consider it the equivalent of right-clicking. The contents of the drop-down menu do change depending on what can be done to an item in a list. They basically give you the same functionality you would get if you actually opened the item to edit or view it, from the list, which is useful.

Currently for this list item they are:

View Item   Takes you to a page to view what is in all of the fields for this list, for this particular item (record, entry, post, whatever you want to call it).

Edit Item   Takes you to a page where the fields are editable. Allows you to change or add data.

Delete Item   If you have the right to, you can delete an item from here rather than having to go into view or edit an item.

Export Contact   Saves the contact item as a VCard. You don't have to have Outlook installed on the computer you are accessing the site from, either. Surprising really, since most things related to importing and exporting seem to have Office 2003 strings attached.

Alert me   If you have been following along, then you know that this option is the way to set up an email alert for an individual. It's the equivalent of the Alert me link in the action bar when viewing an item.

Approve/reject   This drop-down menu item only occurs in a list that has Content Approval enabled. It takes you to an Approve/reject submissions page where you can set the approval status. It has two sections: Approval Status with radio buttons for Approve, Reject, and Pending; and Comment, which is a text box to type comments in.

In order to change the automatically approved status of an item, click the drop-down arrow, and select Approve/Reject (see Figure 18.36).

FIGURE 18.36
Item drop-down menu to approve/reject

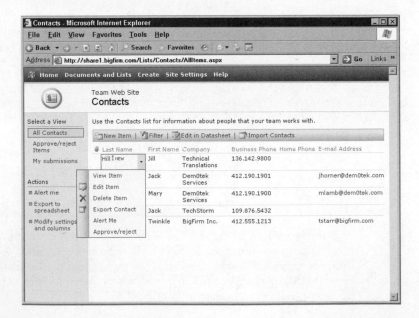

We are going to set this item to Pending, with a comment of how to change it to get approved, so select Pending in the Approval Status section, and type in a comment in the Comment section for the user to comply with. Then click OK.

There should now be two group by headings in the list, with the item you set to Pending in the Approval Status: Pending group (see Figure 18.37).

Click the last name of the pending item.

You'll be in the Contacts page of that item. Notice that the action bar has all of the options that the drop-down menu for the item did (including Approve/Reject Item). There is also a Go Back to List link that is the equivalent of a back button. Something else to notice about this page is, as you would expect, the fields are simply text on the page and not editable.

If you scroll down to the bottom of the item (the content approval fields are added to the end of the item record, so the fields are at the bottom), you can see the approval status and comment. If you wanted to you could edit the item and save it (leaving it still pending), but it is actually fine as is, so you can approve it from here (and you should approve or reject items after you have read them, right?).

Click on the Approve/Reject Item link in the action bar. It will take you back to the approve or reject submissions page. Approve the submission and delete the comment. Then click OK.

The list should look like it did from the start. All items approved.

FIGURE 18.37
Approval pending in Contacts list

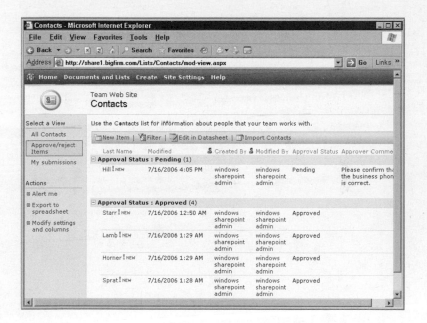

Add a Field

In SharePoint, fields are considered columns, and in the help files and other literature the words field and column are interchangeable. Adding a field is rather easy, but there are a few settings to consider. If a field is required, it means that if the user has opened a New Item page; they cannot save it if the required field does not have data in. Fields can exist in list and not show up in the default All Contacts view. Generally, web pages are longer than they are wide, so being conservative with the number of fields displayed in a view is not unexpected. The first field in a list is usually

Title and is by default both required and the unique field for that list. SharePoint isn't really super interested in complicated, multifield unique keys to keep lists organized.

Now that you are comfortable working with the list, first in All Contacts view, then with the two new Content Approval views, it's time to create a new Review Date field for this Contacts list and then create a new view to make use of it.

1. To add a field to a list, click on Modify settings and columns in the action pane.

   In the Customize Contacts page, go to the Columns section (you may need to scroll down). Notice that all of the fields that can be edited are listed here to be clicked (that means that, although they exist, Approval Status and Approver Comments are not listed).

2. Click the Add a new column link.

In the Add Column page (Figure 18.38), you have to create a column name and choose the type of format the data needs for that column; all other settings are optional. I am going to take a second here to mention the different types of data formats available for a column.

Single line of text   As simple as it gets. A single line, single field of text. Can be explicitly limited to a certain number of characters (which makes sense, you wouldn't want an epic in a single, seemingly endless line); 255 is the default.

Multiple lines of text   Like the single line of text field except that it displays in several lines, and like the single line of text field it has a character limit. 255 is the default.

Choice (menu to choose from)   Offers the user a choice among options that you create. You type in the different choices in a text box, then choose how the choices will be offered—radio button, drop-down list, or check boxes (allows more than one to be selected). You can also allow fill-in choices if necessary.

FIGURE 18.38
Add a new column

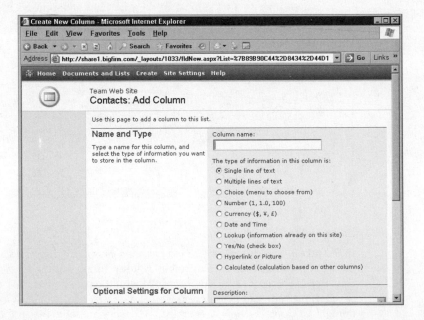

Number (1, 1.0, 100) Particularly useful if you are going to use this field for calculations or totals, this field type requires numeric values only. Can be displayed as a percentage, have a specific number of decimal places, and have minimum/maximum values.

Currency ($, ¥, £) Like the numeric field, but the value will be displayed as currency. The currency type is specified during configuration.

Date and Time Field used for calendar view, can be configured to use date and time or just date. The date can be formatted and have a default value. The calculated value for Date and Time default value can be used to specify =[Today]+30.

Lookup (information already on this site) Very useful field. Because all of the lists on a site are contained in the same database, you can actually pull a field from a different list and use it as the value of a lookup field.

Yes/No (check box) Literally displays a description and two radio buttons. You can decide the default.

Hyperlink or Picture A field formatted for hyperlinks. The picture should actually be in a picture library and therefore have a hyperlink to point to it.

Calculated (calculation based on other columns) Very cool field that shows that the whole list is a table and not just a static bunch of data. Can be used to do any calculations you could reasonably do in a single spreadsheet based on the data in the table. Really comes in handy when used with lookup fields.

The Add Column page is dynamic and the optional section changes depending on what format you choose:

1. Let's name the column Review Date, and give it a Date and Time format.

2. Scroll down to the Optional Settings for Columns section. This section contains options like:

   Require that this column contains information A yes or no question. If the answer is yes, then if someone is creating or editing an item in this list, they cannot save the item until there is a date in this field.

   Date and Time Format Allows you to specify if the field takes date only or date and time.

   Default value You can set a default value for the field, like a set date, today's date, or a calculated value (I can't think of a reason I would need to do that for a date, but the option's there if you need it).

   Add to default view Checked by default, you can decide whether a column is hidden by default or shows up in the default All items view.

3. The field does not need to be required, so Require That This Column Contains Information can be set to No.

4. It does need to be date only, no need for exact times when scheduling yearly reviews. So leave the default setting for the date and time format.

5. The default date could be today's date after all records are in and correct. Going forward, in an ideal world, the contact record would be created the day someone was hired…okay, leave no default value.

6. I don't want this to be part of the default view of All Items. So uncheck Add to default view. This means that Review Date will be a field in the contact records, but it will not show up if you use the All Contacts of the list.

7. And that's it. Click OK to create the new column. It will take you back to the Customize Contacts page.

Back on Customize Contacts, scroll down to the Columns section and see that Review Date is listed (see Figure 18.39). If ever you need to edit its settings, just click its link on this page and you will end up in the Change Column page for that field.

NOTE   The Add to Default View check box is available at the creation of a column but not when you edit it in the Change Column page. To change whether or not a column displays in a view, you must edit that view and check or uncheck the column's Display box in the Columns section.

Now let's go back out to the list and add a review date to some of the records.

FIGURE 18.39
Review Date column

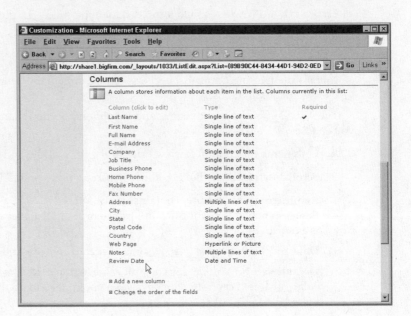

EDIT AN ITEM

Of course, in order to add a date to an item you need to edit it.

1. To do that you need to get back to the list, so scroll back to the top of the Customize Contacts page and click the Go Back to Contacts link.

   Back on the Contacts list, notice that the Review Date field is not listed in the All Contacts view (or any other view there, for that matter) because it was not added to the default view.

2. To see if the Review Date field is there, view an item (either by clicking its title or clicking the down arrow in the box around the title, and choosing View Item). Notice that there is a Review Date field listed way at the bottom (just above the approval status).

3. To enter a date into the new Review Date field, click Edit Item in the action bar.

4. Scroll all the way down to the Review Date field at the bottom the page (see Figure 18.40).

5. Notice that there is a convenient calendar button next to the date field. You can either choose a date sometime next month, or type one in M/D/YYYY format (by the way, that is their formatting, not mine because I think there are several months and days in the year that require two digits. But hey, what do I know?).

6. Click Save and Close to get back to the Contacts list.

7. Move your mouse over the title of a different item in the list, click the down arrow, and choose Edit Item from the drop-down list.

8. Feel free to add a date to the Review Date field that is about a week after the review date of the previous item you edited.

9. Click Save and Close to go back to the Contacts List.

FIGURE 18.40
Review Date
data entry

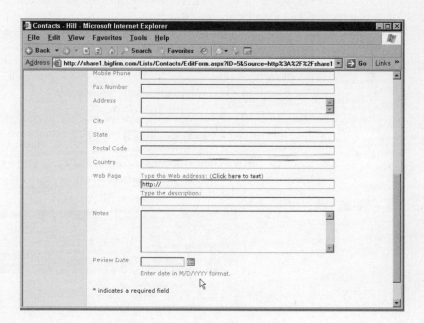

CREATE A NEW VIEW

So, two records have had their review dates entered (can you see how convenient editing items in a datasheet is?). Now it's time to create a calendar view.

For those of you following along, you have already worked with views, in the Documents and Lists page, the All Contacts view of the Contacts, and then with the two new Content Approval views. I am going to go over two of the views, the standard view generally, and a step-by-step set up of calendar view.

1. Click Modify Settings and Columns in the action pane.

2. Scroll down the Customize Contacts page to the Views section.

3. In the Views section, click Create a New View.

This takes you to the Create View page, which lists the three different default ways to view list items (see Figure 18.41).

Standard View Creates your standard list report on a web page. However, there is more to it than that.

Datasheet View You've seen this briefly. You can create datasheet views for users rather than a report layout, as long as the list does not have fields the user is not allowed to edit (like the Approval Status field). Because the view is like a spreadsheet, the users can manipulate the data like a spreadsheet, doing things like right-clicking a column heading to go to add a column (which takes you to the Add Column page for that list), or autofilling fields.

Calendar View Just what it says it is. Very useful view and one that can be underused by those who are creating these lists. Remember, if there is a date, or a range of dates (such as start and due date for Tasks) in a list, you can create a calendar for it.

I want to spend just a moment showing something about standard view. For those of you following along, we are not going to actually really go in and set up this view for a reason, but I encourage you to click on Standard View and take a look at what it offers. So far, most of the lists we have seen use this view, so you might take it for granted. It has some features that people familiar with Crystal Reports might recognize (see Figure 18.42), but you'd be amazed how few of these options people actually use.

Click the Standard View link in the Create View page.

NOTE Keep in mind that the Create View pages have some setting sections that expand or collapse to hide or display their content, like folders do in the folders view in Windows Explorer. So to see some settings, you may need to expand them. Also keep in mind that in most cases you will need to scroll down (way down) on a lot of these settings pages in SharePoint, so if you don't see something in a screen shot, it means the setting is further down the page than I could capture.

FIGURE 18.41
Create View page

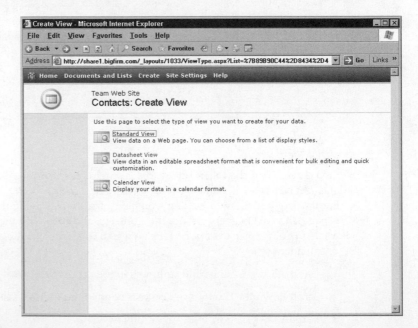

FIGURE 18.42
Standard view
settings

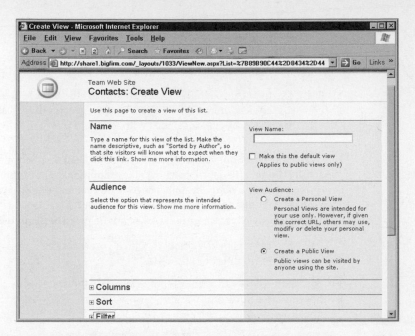

The standard view is very much like the standard report you would generate from a table or database. You can use it to choose what fields you display in the view and in what order. But (as the Approve/Reject view demonstrates) you can also group items, have several levels of sorting, filter by as many columns as you wish, create totals by columns that will be displayed (the calculations available by data type are displayed in a drop-down box next to the field name), choose from a short list of styles, and even decide what kind of limit there might be on how many records get listed in this view. Up to this point you haven't really seen the capability of this kind of view to its fullest extent, so I thought you should know. This is not just a list view, but a pretty useful reporting tool as well.

Here are some of the setting sections:

Name The name of the View is essentially the title that will be displayed in the action pane of the list. However, SharePoint helpfully generates a web page for each view, directly using the name you give the view as the web page name. This could be a problem; see the "SharePoint Gotcha— Keep Hyperlinks Short" sidebar for more.

Audience Sets whether this view is going to be a public view for all users or a personal view for you to see alone. Can be useful if you are an administrator or manager and you want a quick overall view of something that doesn't need to be a convenient view for everyone to see. No need to clutter the action pane with views only you will use. However, a personal view is only personal by virtue of not showing up on the action pane. If an enterprising user knows the web address for your view, they can both see it and change it. Just thought you should know. Like many things these days, personal is not as personal as you would think.

Columns This is the meat and potatoes of the list. This is where you decide what columns will show in the view and what order they'll be displayed in.

Sort Limited to two columns, you can sort items in a view by one column's contents first, then the second column's content. For example, you can sort a contact first by state, then by city.

Filter Uses criteria to filter the view of a list by field content, limiting the items displayed to a subset of the whole list. The section contains three fields that control what items show in a filtered view:

◆ The field you use to select the column you are applying the filter to (such as State).

◆ The field that contains the argument that the filter will use against the criteria you enter (the choices are is equal to, not equal to, greater than, less than, greater than or equal to, less than or equal to, begins with, contains).

TIP Very, very useful if you are filtering for more than an exact match with your criteria. For example, if your users type in whatever they think are keywords for a document in a field, they might use the same words (or similar ones) in different orders. So if you want all documents that are concerning "lifestyle", you can use the argument "contains" and therefore any record that has the word "lifestyle" anywhere in the keywords field will be displayed.

◆ The criteria field, or field in which you enter the criteria you are filtering for, such as "Pennsylvania" or "lifestyle."

If you want to filter by multiple columns to really isolate only the items you want, you can choose to filter by as many arguments on the same column, or as many columns as you wish, connecting the filters by "and" or "or."

Of particular usefulness, you can filter by variables such as [Today] or [Me], even though they are not actually fields in the current list. You can use these built-in variables to limit a view to something by today's date, such as created, modified, or, even Review Rate The [Me] variable could be used to match the contents in a Created By column to filter a list to display only items the user you are logged in as created. Of course, these are only simple suggestions; you can get really creative with this stuff.

Group by One of the more visually effective way of changing the layout of a View, Group by is like Sort on steroids. And, like Sort, it limits you to two levels of groups to work with. But if you check out a list with Content Approval on, you can see what Group by can do.

Totals You may've seen what Totals can do if you messed with the Totals link in datasheet view. You can total by column based on the data type of the column. Totals show up at the top of a list.

Style If you are getting complicated with how you are grouping and sorting your view and you want the groups to stand out, choose one of the predefined styles. Fill a Contacts list with records, then come in here and go to town. See what the styles do to change the look and feel of the view. You'll be surprised (and eventually disappointed because you wish there were more).

Item Limit This sets a limit on either all the records that will show up when a view is applied to a list, or how many per batch. It simply helps facilitate a speedy display of items from what could be a huge list. Of course, ours isn't, but someday this might become a necessity for you.

Now, I've stepped back to mention standard view, but you can see that only extensive messing with that view would do it justice. So back to walking through the creation of a calendar view.

1. If you are following along, you will need to click Cancel to go back to the Create View page.

2. Click on Calendar View in the Create View page.

   In the Create Calendar View page (see Figure 18.43) you should recognize a few things like Name and Audience. Here are what the calendar-specific settings are and what they are about.

FIGURE 18.43
Create Calendar
View settings

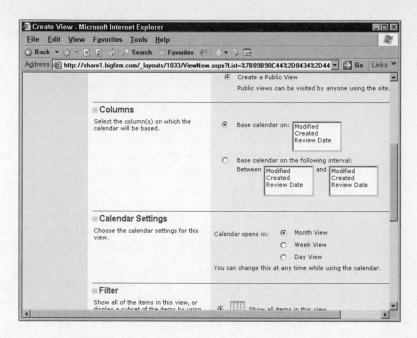

Columns   Keep in mind that this view is going to be a calendar, so really you are just trying to establish by what field the items are being organized across the dates displayed. Will it be by the modify date of the item? How about created date? Any field that has the Date and Time format in the list will show up in the Columns section. You can base the calendar on a single date or a range of dates (called an interval). This can be duration of an event, or the start and due date of a task.

Calendar Settings   Lets you set whether the view opens in month, day, or week view. If you choose one and want to see another real quick, that's fine. When you are looking at a list in calendar view the action bar changes, showing links for Week, Month, or Day view to go to at will. This just sets the default.

1. The first thing we need to do, of course, is name our view in the View Name field. I am going to call it Reviews. Short, to the point, works for me. Remember, even though there is no field here for it, SharePoint is going to create a web page out of your title. Also in the Name section is a check box to make this view the default view instead of the All Contacts default that exists now. I don't want to change the default.

NOTE   The Add View page for a list does not offer a field to edit the View's hyperlink, it assumes that the name you give the View is good enough. In order to have a web address for the view that is different from the view name you gave it, you must go back and edit the view after you have created it by going back to Modify Settings and Columns and clicking the view name. Also note, calendar view is the only view that cannot have its web address changed. So remember to keep the name short.

2. The next setting is whether or not you want the audience of this view to be public or personal. Creating a personal view of a list is very much like the Web Parts personal view; if you make it, only you will be able to see it. Because I don't intend to make it too easy for everyone

to see each other's review dates (at this point they need to actually view an item and scroll down to the Review Date field to see it), I am going to make this view personal. That way I am the only person who can see this calendar view. It will show up in the action pane for me, but not for anyone else who happens to use the list.

3. Under View Audience click the Create a Personal View radio button to make the view personal.

4. In the Columns section, because I only have one date that I want to track in this view, I am going to choose to base the calendar on Review Date. Notice that Modify and Created are date fields that all items have by default. If you have more than one date in a list, you can create a date range rather one date. The Tasks list really makes use of this fact.

5. In Calendar Settings, I am going to leave the default, Month View.

6. I'm not interested in filtering this View to any one criteria or more, so leaving the radio button selected next to Show all items in this view in the Filter section works for me. And that's it, so click OK to create the Reviews Calendar View for the Contacts list.

7. You should be back on the Customize Contacts page. Feel free to scroll down to the Views section. Reviews should be there (see Figure 18.44). To see if Reviews is in the action pane of the Contacts list, click Go Back to Contacts in the Customize Contacts page.

8. Voila. It's there. (Go ahead, check out Figure 18.45.)

FIGURE 18.44
Reviews view

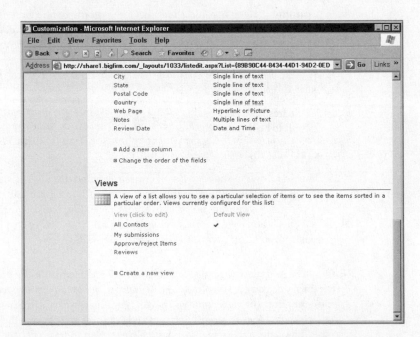

FIGURE 18.45
Reviews view in
action pane

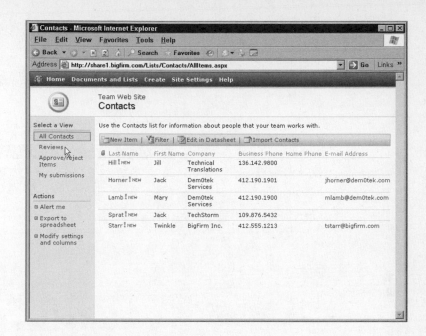

SHAREPOINT GOTCHA—KEEP HYPERLINKS SHORT

SharePoint can only support web addresses that are 255 characters long or less. This means that if you use a view name that is several words long with spaces, you will get something like A%20Long%20Web%20Page%20Name for the web address of that view, complete with "%20" as a holder in the web address for spaces. You can see how huge a web page name can get if you are not careful. If there is a limit to how long a hyperlink can be in terms of characters, then it's a good idea to be conservative about page names throughout your site(s). Keep this in mind as a general naming convention whenever you are creating a new list, library, page, site, workspace, and so on.

To see if the two review dates we entered into those Contacts list items show up in the reviews view, click on Reviews in the action pane.

There it is, a calendar in month view. The action bar contains links for linking and importing to Outlook (as expected—this is the Contacts list, regardless of how you are viewing it), and, of course, the New Item link. In addition, there are the calendar view links for Today, View by Day, View by Month, and View by Week views.

In the title bar of the calendar itself there is an arrow on either side. These indicate that you can scroll back and forth, past or future, in whatever way you are viewing the calendar. We added our reviews to next month or later, so scroll with the right arrow in the calendar title bar to get to next month (whatever month that is for you).

Once there, you should be able to scroll to see the entries for the two items that have review dates, about a week apart (see Figure 18.46).

FIGURE 18.46
Reviews
calendar view

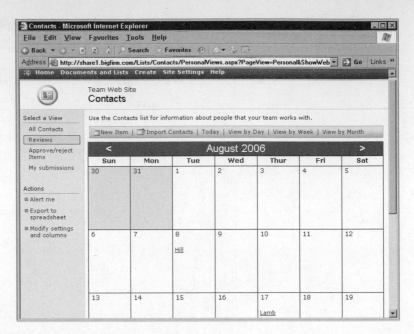

To view the item, just click on the link for it on the day it is listed. You should immediately end up in the page for that Contacts item, able to see all of its fields, including Review Date.

And there you go—who knew you could have a calendar view of a contact list?

So far we've worked on an existing list, adding items, creating a column, and creating a view. Now it's time to create a new list altogether (which will be a cake walk) and then move on to document libraries.

CREATE A CUSTOM LIST

In order to create a new list, you can go to one of three places:

- The general heading of Lists on the Quick Launch bar, which will bring you to the lists view in the Documents and Lists page, in which there is a Create link at the top of the page.

- The Documents and Lists link in the navigation bar, which will bring you to the Documents and Lists page, where you can click the Create link at the top of the page.

- The Create link in the navigation bar.

All ways take you, eventually, to the Create page. So that's where I am simply going to go.

Click Create in the navigation bar. Then, once on the Create page, click Lists in the action pane under Select a View (see Figure 18.47). This view filters the page's contents down to just list items, just like Documents and Lists except that all you can see are lists you can create, not ones that have already been created.

As you can see, you can use the templates for the default lists to create a new page. Very useful if you want to create a copy of an existing default list's columns, views, and settings. Also note that there is a built-in list template that didn't get used to make a default list when Windows SharePoint Services was installed, Issues. This list is very much like a Tasks list, with priority, assign to, and progress fields. I am not sure why it isn't part of the preinstalled lists. Maybe having the word "issues" in the Quick Launch bar from the start might give a bad impression?

FIGURE 18.47
List view on
Create Page

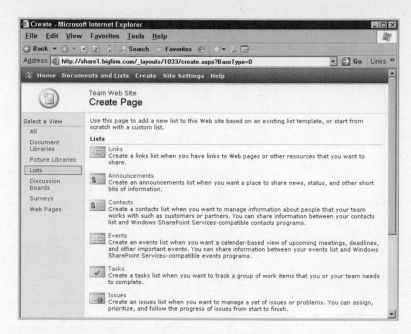

We are not going to mess with preexisting templates for lists (although if you ever wanted to, they're there); what we're going to do is create a custom list. So scroll down to the aptly named Custom Lists section of the page. Take a look at your options (Figure 18.48). You can see that there are several, including the option of creating a custom list by importing a spreadsheet. I highly recommend this for those times you have huge lists of content and you simply need to make them into lists in SharePoint. It requires Excel 2003 of course. We don't have a premade spreadsheet of data, so we'll just have to create a custom list the old-fashioned way—in standard view, one field at a time. Well, actually we could use the Edit in Datasheet button, but that's not the point…

1. Click on Custom List at the top of the Custom Lists section.

   The first two required settings are the name and description of the list and whether or not it is going to appear on the Quick Launch navigation bar.

2. I am going to name the list Vendors. It's descriptive and short. Be sure that the Yes radio button is selected in the Navigation section so this list will show up on the Quick Launch bar. Then, of course, click the Create button.

And that's it, you go back to a list that is empty called Vendors. Notice that there is a field called Title already there. You didn't get the chance to create that field, so why is it there? As you may remember, like any good table, the list requires a unique key field. In lieu of one you might've created, it had to make one, and Title is always a safe bet as far as fields go. Just about everything needs a title.

Let's reuse the Title field, add a field, and make some changes to this list. Click Modify settings and columns in the action pane.

Notice in Figure 18.49 that the title of the list is Vendors, and the web address is `http://share1.bigfirm.com/Lists/Vendors/AllItems.aspx`. The name of the list is in the URL, and the page being displayed is the default view, All Items. This demonstrates a few things:

◆ Both the name of the list and its views need to be kept short because they both contribute to the length of their URL.

◆ There is no field to change the URL for the list. In other words, if I had misspelled Vendors as Vendor, I could go in and change the name in the name field, but it would not change the URL for the list. As you can see, that is static.

FIGURE 18.48

Create custom list

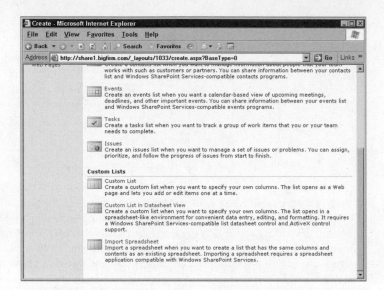

FIGURE 18.49

List URL

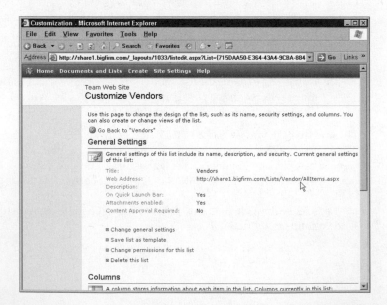

So be careful typing in the name of lists if the URL matters to you.

If you are following along you may also notice that On Quick Launch Bar is Yes, Content Approval Required is No, and Attachments enabled is Yes. Although you did not enable attachments, it is set by default (a lot of people find it useful to add attachments to items for this or that). It can be changed by modifying general settings.

If you scroll down to the Columns area you'll see that the Title field is required. That means that if you try to create a new item (or a new row in datasheet view), you will not be able to save the entry unless the title field contains data.

Since there is already a default field called Title, we'll keep it and just rename it Vendor. A title is unnecessary for our purposes, but because it was the first default, required field, it is difficult to delete. Because we need Vendor to be the unique field for this list and required for each item anyway it's a perfect candidate for a little recycling:

1. Click Title to edit the Title field.

2. Change Column Name from Title to Vendor.

3. Scroll down to the Optional Settings section and make sure Yes under Require That This Column Contains Information is selected. You can also specify the maximum number of characters in the Vendor field (the default of 255 is more than enough), and I don't want a default value for the field, so that field is going to remain blank.

4. Make sure that the check box is checked to add to default view so we can see it when we view the list in All Items view, and click OK.

This will take you back out to the Customize Vendors page. While we're here, let's make a field from scratch:

1. Scroll back down to the Columns section and click Add a new column.

2. For this column, let's name it Region.

3. For the type, choose Choice.

4. Scroll down to the Optional Settings section (you'll see that it has changed due to your type selection).

   This section changes depending on what field format you chose. The major difference is that there is a text box to type your choices in, an option as to whether or not you will allow users to type in an answer rather than have to choose from your selection, and a requirement that one of the choices to be the default value.

5. Select Yes under Require That This Column Contains Information so this field cannot be left empty if a user tries to save and close out of a New Item.

   You may have noticed the Type Each Choice on a Separate Line box. You need to replace each line with text that will display as choices. You do not have to be limited to three, they are just examples (see Figure 18.50).

FIGURE 18.50
Add choices to field

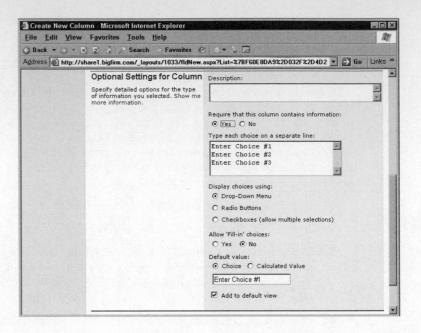

6. Replace the sample text that is already there and type in the Type Each Choice on a Separate Line box:

   Undecided

   Northeast

   Northwest

   Southeast

   Southwest

7. For the display choices you can have a drop-down menu, radio buttons, or check boxes (if you need to be able to have multiple choices selected). Let's select Drop-Down Menu.

8. Make certain that No is selected for Allow 'Fill-In' Choices. There is no need for anyone to make up a region.

   Because a drop-down menu or radio button set requires a default selected value, the first one on the list, Undecided, is the default value by, well, default. You can type in a value in the default value field if the first field does not work for you (or change the order of your choices).

9. Make sure the default value is a choice (not a calculated value), and you can either leave "Enter Choice #1," because it will become Undecided, or you can manually fill the default value field with your default option from the choices if you wish.

10. Make sure that there is a check in the check box for Add To Default View and click OK.

    So that gives us a new field called Region.

NOTE   When you go in to change an existing field most of them can be deleted. But if you look, the default Title field has no Delete button, only OK and Cancel.

Now we could continue in this vein, filling the Vendors list with fields, but I think you get the point, so I am going to stop at two. What I'd like to do now is create a new Vendors item and see how the Region field is going to work.

1. Go to the Vendors list page by selecting the convenient Go Back to Vendors link in the Customize Vendors page.

2. On the Vendors list page, click New Item in the action bar.

   Notice in Figure 18.51 that the Vendor field is blank but ready to receive text and that the Region field has Undecided as the default value.

3. Enter a vendor name in the Vendor field, and select a region. Click Save and Close. This will bring you to the Vendors List.

TIP   To create a list you can go to Create or Documents and Lists, but you can only delete a list by going into its customization page and choosing to delete there.

At the Vendors list level you should see your new Vendor item displayed in the All Items view. Congratulations.

FIGURE 18.51
Using the Vendor field
to enter data

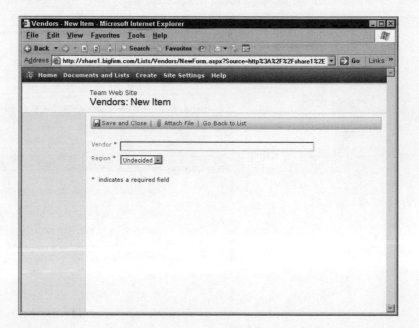

USING A LIST VIEW WEB PART

So far in this chapter you've seen lists, created lists, added items, and changed views. You've messed with Web Parts, learned how to move them around, add them, and even made your own Web Part using the Content Editor, but we've never actually *used* one of the List View Web Parts.

So, I am going to briefly cover using a Web Part to access a list. I would also like to, incidentally, show you a unique feature of the Announcements List, and a unique use for a date field.

To get to the Web Parts, you need to be on the Team Web Site Home page. So if you are not on already on that page, click Home in the navigation bar.

Scroll down to the Announcements Web Part if you need to. Notice that it has that Get Started with Windows SharePoint Services! entry. (If it doesn't, that's okay, announcements are set to expire so old ones don't linger on the home page—just read along, you'll see why and catch up by the end of this section.)

NOTE There are at least two active links in all List View Web Parts, the title of the entry (which takes you to the entry's web page so you can read its contents) and the add new whatever-the-title-of-the-list-is (which takes you to an add item page for that list, so you can add a new entry). In the Announcements Web Part, the entry author's name is also a link that will take you to that user's information page.

To view an item displayed in a List View Web Part like Announcements, just move your mouse over the item's title. It will highlight, indicating, if you click on it, you will be taken to that entry.

Go ahead, click on the Get Started with Windows SharePoint Services! title for the new Announcements entry.

Unsurprisingly, you are on the Get Started with Windows SharePoint Services! view item page. (For those of you who have had this entry expire, you aren't missing much, check out Figure 18.52).

I'd like to remind you about the Go Back to List link in the action bar of this view item page. It lies. It functions as a back button and doesn't necessarily take you back to the list. In this circumstance, you got to view this item from being out on the Team Web Site Home page. If you click the Go Back to List link, it will take you, not to the Announcements list, but back to the Team Web Site Home page.

To prove a point, click the Go Back to List link in the action bar. And sure enough, it should take you back to the Team Web Site Home page.

FIGURE 18.52
Announcements
entry

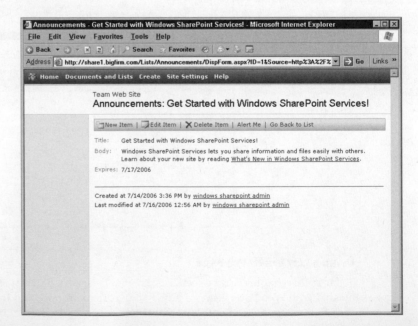

Add a New Item from a List View Web Part

Now, you know that List View Web Parts give you a convenient way to populate the home page of a site with small glimpses of the contents of a list or two (or more), but you can create a New Item for a list from the Web Part as well.

I'd like to show you two things here, one is pretty straightforward, adding a new item to the Announcements list from the List View Web Part, the other is to show you how the Expires field works with Announcements.

Go ahead and click on the Add new announcement link in the Announcements List View Web Part.

As you can guess, the fields available for an Announcement item are Title, Body, and the unique Expires field, which allows you to set a time that an announcement expires from being displayed on the List View Web Part.

Feel free to enter some data in the Title and Body fields (see Figure 18.53) and set the Expires date to two days from now. Then click the Save and Close link in the action bar.

You should be back on the Team Web Site Home page because Save and Close does the same thing as Save and Go Back. Scroll down to the Announcements List View Web Part and see that there is a new item (Figure 18.54).

Notice the little green !NEW to the right of the new entry? Remember that it will last for 24 hours after the item's creation, regardless of whether or not it has been read.

Now that you've created the new item, let's see what you can do with it. Which brings me to the Expires field. I mentioned earlier that this field decides whether or not an Announcement shows up in the List View Web Part or not. We set the new item to expire two days from now, and we went out to the Announcements Web Part and saw it there. But let's see what expiring an Announcement actually does.

If you are following along, we have viewed an item from the Announcements List View Web Part. We've added an item. The last thing to do with the Web Part is access the underlying list of a List View Web Part.

To access the Announcements list from the Web Part, click the Announcements Web Part's title.

FIGURE 18.53
Entering data into an Announcement item

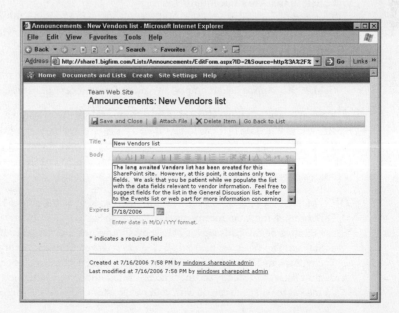

FIGURE 18.54

New Entry in Announcements Web Part

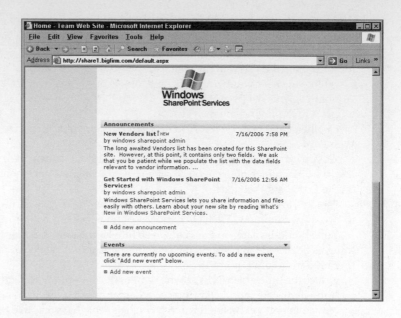

Edit a List Item Revisited

To cause an Announcement item to expire, you first need to be able to edit the item. Make sure you are in the Announcements list. Move your mouse over the item's title. Click its selection box down arrow, and select Edit Item (I am going to use the Get Started with Windows SharePoint entry).

The Announcement item should have a date in the Expires field; mine is set for two days from now.

Set the Expires date to yesterday, and click Save and Close in the action bar. That should take you back to the Announcements List.

To see if the announcement actually expired, click Home in the navigation bar and scroll down to the Announcements List View Web Part. The announcement that we set to expire should not be displayed (see Figure 18.55).

TIP By the way, if you want an Announcement to never expire, remove the date from the Expires field. If the Expires field is empty, an Announcement cannot expire.

Keep in mind that you did not, at any time, delete the missing announcement. You only set the Expires field to a date prior to today. If you were to go back to the Announcements list, it would still be there. That's a good thing to know if you are worried about your Announcements list filling up with old news, or if you need to find an old announcement item—it will still be on the list until it is deleted, regardless of when it expired.

TIP Most of the default lists have useful traits based on being able to filter the static data by view. For example, the Announcements List View Web Part uses a summary view that filters the items by the Expires field. That's why it only shows items not expired, even if those items are still in the actual list. The Tasks List has several views that let you filter and/or organize the task items by Due Today, Assigned To, and so on. These are just views. Feel free to check out the view settings of these default lists (go to Modify settings and columns and then click the view you are interested in) to get an idea as to what you can do with your own custom list views. Get more out of your data.

FIGURE 18.55
Announcements list

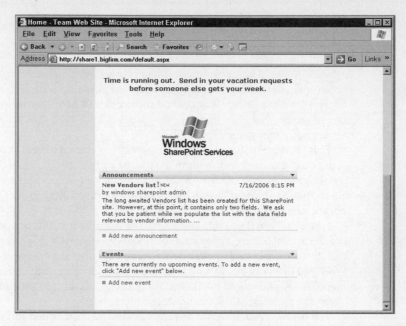

That's about it for simple lists. I hope this section of the chapter has given you the skills, terminology, and concepts that you need to create your own custom list or experiment with the other premade lists, as well as the other premade list templates. Don't be afraid to explore. A list you don't want can always be deleted (on the list's customization settings page under Modify settings and columns) when you are done.

Now it's time to check out libraries, primarily document libraries.

Document Libraries

A library is an interesting kind of list. Instead of opening a form in which you enter data when creating a new item, they open a file from a template that will (when saved or uploaded) be attached to an item in the library's list.

For example, the default Shared Documents library that got created upon the installation of Windows SharePoint Services has a blank Word template as its template file. That's why, if someone doesn't have Word 2003 installed on their computer, they can't use the use the New Document link on the action bar.

TIP   What about form libraries? They're the same thing, only their type of template is not a document file but a form you create in InfoPath 2003. That being said, picture libraries just have to be different. There's no template for a picture library. They assume you are going to just upload existing photos. However, in the Add Picture page there is a link for Uploading Multiple Files which, if you click it, will open Microsoft Office Picture Manager. From there you can select multiple files and upload them. If you don't have the Picture Manager installed, you are out of luck unless you use Explorer view to drag and drop multiple files.

Don't get me wrong, you can upload any kind of file you'd like to the document library without Word 2003 (as long as the file extension has not been blocked—you, as an administrator can set that), but the library gets its individual identity from the template it uses for the New Document link in the action bar. So keep that in the back of your mind when designing your SharePoint site for business or private use. Yes, usually people create document libraries specifically for what they already have or are going to create on their workstations, and then upload those files to the libraries. But, because this is Windows SharePoint Services, the real reasons for the libraries are more obscure. You can create (or have already) special document templates for publications, manuals, brochures, contracts, presentations, whatever, and have one of *those* define a document library. In other words, the library is supposed to specifically hold the documents made with the New Document button that pulls from the template you specify in the general settings under the document library's Customization page.

This is also why document libraries really need and expect Word 2003 or some other Office product. If you can create a template file for a product, like PowerPoint, FrontPage, Excel, or even web pages, then you can have a library about it. You simply choose the template type when you create the new document library. So you use an Office 2003 product to create a new file from the library's template and edit it.

However, you don't actually need to be using Word 2003 to open, edit, or *upload* an existing file in a document library. A person can click and open a DOC file from a document library with Word-Pad, available practically everywhere. The user just cannot *save* it to a document library, because WordPad does not know how to save a file to a content database. But, the user can go to the document library and *upload* the file edited in WordPad, keeping the filename and checking the box to overwrite the original file being stored there.

The result? Well, if that Word 2003 document they edited in WordPad had had a lot of fancy Word formatting, the formatting will be all gone after having been saved and uploaded as a Word-Pad document. Otherwise, hey, the user's content changes are all there. In brief, if a file can be opened, edited, and saved in a equivalent program of the Office 2003 product expected, the file can be saved and uploaded (edited, saved over, and be part of the version history of a file) to a document library. This is why Microsoft can say that SharePoint will work with Office-*equivalent* products. But Office 2003 still reigns supreme with all of the fancy things it can do regarding SharePoint.

Now that you know what a document library is about, let's see one in action. What we're going to do is use the default Shared Documents library (but remember, you can easily create your own document libraries from the Create page should you need to), then check out its settings under Modify Settings and Columns, change its name, add a field, and make sure versioning is enabled. Then we'll add a document from a workstation that has Office 2003 installed (take a look at the SharePoint Workspace task pane), check it out, edit it, save the change, check it back in, and see what versioning does.

Delving into everything we could possibly do with a document library (especially with Office 2003 integration) would be a book unto itself. What I'd like to do is give you a look at the tools, practice doing some standard tasks, and give you ideas as to what else can be done.

To get to the default document library called Shared Documents the easy way, click Home in the navigation bar. Then click Shared Documents in the Quick Launch bar.

NOTE   For those of you who created the custom Vendors list from the Lists section of the chapter, you might notice that Vendors is displayed on the Quick Launch bar under the Lists general heading.

To get acquainted with a document library, here is a quick rundown of what's new here compared to some of the other lists (see Figure 18.56).

To start, there is an Explorer View under Select a View in the action pane. Also there is a New Folder link in the action bar for creating folders in the Documents list (should you be so inclined). Explorer view actually changes the list view to a Windows Explorer window (complete with that Common Tasks bar if the user has that set on the computer). Mind you, that is a bit of magic, because the documents library is just a table in the content database. The documents you upload or add to a library get added to a list item like an attachment. List items have fields just like any other record in the table (although in this context they are considered "metadata"), such as title, modify date, created by, or whatever field you feel you need. So if the documents are not actually saved separately in a folder in the file system, it turns out to be kind of nifty that you can use an Explorer window to see the documents in a document library as if they were files in a folder. In Explorer View (see Figure 18.57), the only SharePoint tasks you can do are Upload Document or create a New Document.

FIGURE 18.56

Shared Documents list

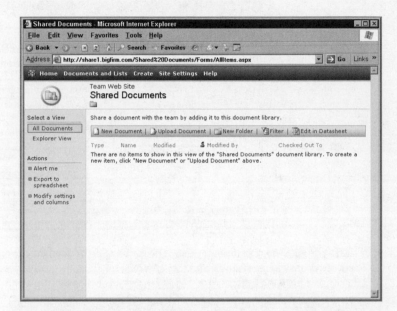

FIGURE 18.57

Explorer View

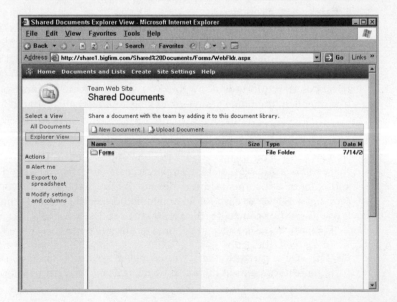

WEBCLIENT

Explorer View requires the machine that is viewing it to be running the WebClient service. Servers usually aren't.

Check in the Services console. You can start the WebClient by going into the properties of WebClient and setting it to automatic and starting it (you can make it manual if you'd like and start it only when you wish).

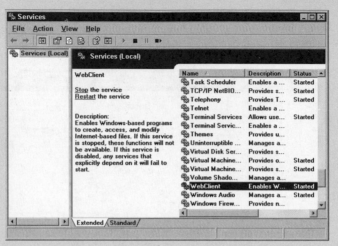

If that doesn't work (and sometimes it doesn't on Server 2003 R2), check to see if it is an IE-enhanced security configuration problem. Access your SharePoint site locally (if you are on the SharePoint server, as we are) by using http://localhost in the address bar.

If that works, then it's an IE problem. Try adding your SharePoint site address to the Local Intranet sites zone.

The need for Explorer View has always baffled me (except as a convenient web folder). It draws a direct corollary between an old shared folder and the new document library (of course, if you look at the medallion icon next to the title of the page, you can see that it is a folder with some pages. I should have known folders would appear somewhere). You can not only view the document library as an Explorer window, but you can also create folders from the action bar and organize documents in them like you were making subfolders in a shared folder.

TIP As an administrator, you can delete the Explorer View from a document library if you'd like.

You've seen how you can group, filter, and sort a list. It's a useful feature, particularly in lists that can't be full-text searched. However, I am sure there is a good reason to store documents in a subfolder of a documents library despite the fact that they can't conveniently be found by filtering (you have to go into each folder and look there until you find what you are looking for). Because it has its use (for someone), the capability to add a folder to a list and then put files and subfolders in it is there. I am not going to go into it, but it is there if you need it.

NOTE There is a rumor that if you use folders to store documents in a document library, you can fit more documents in there that way. But if you need a single library to be that big, you have other issues.

USING EXPLORER VIEW AS A CONVENIENT DROP-OFF ZONE FOR BULK UPLOADS

Having said that I wasn't a big fan of Explorer View, it is good for something. Say you did have a bunch of documents that you did want to store in a document library (ignoring the fact that libraries are supposed to store documents based on the library's template). You can open a Windows Explorer window on your desktop. Browse to the folder containing the documents you want to add to the document library. Then in Internet Explorer, go to the document library you want to use, and select Explorer View. Select all of the documents that you want to copy from the folder in Windows Explorer to the document library in SharePoint. Drag selected documents into the Explorer view area of the document library's page, and voila. You have bulk uploaded a bunch of documents to the document library of your choice.

In addition to the Explorer view and the New Folder link in the action bar, the New Item link has become New Document (which makes sense), there is no Edit Item link—that's in the drop-down menu for each individual item—and there is an Upload Documents link in order to upload an existing document or file to the library. Upload Documents is how someone who either has a pre-existing document or does not have Word 2003 installed on their machine can add a file to a library.

CUSTOMIZING A DOCUMENT LIBRARY

Before adding a document to a document library it is good to set it up properly and know how it works. So I am going to show you the library's settings before I show you how to add and edit documents.

Click Modify settings and columns in the action pane of the Shared Documents library.

As you can see by the customization page, a document library is just another kind of list (see Figure 18.58) except that, in the Customize Shared Documents page, there is a Document Template listing in the General Settings section (as you know, lists don't need a template, only libraries). The template in this case is a Word document template, and you can edit it.

FIGURE 18.58
Customize Shared Documents General Settings

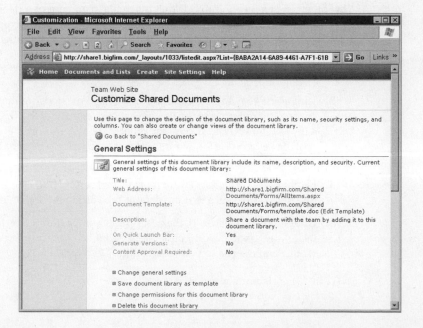

If you did click the link Edit Template it would open Word 2003 and display that template's settings. As is usual with a template, I don't suggest you save changes to the original file. But you can use Edit Template and then save the changes to the new name. It will save the file in the same location as the default template. This becomes handy later when you want to use that new template to replace the default one.

If you already have a template for a library, you can add it to the forms folder where the document library keeps its template (again another use for explorer view). Then specify the filename in the Document Template section of the General Settings for that library. Either way, you are not limited to just using the blank template that the library offers you by default.

To be sure there are no other big changes on the Customize Shared Document page, scroll down to the Columns section. You'll note the ubiquitous Title field. The reason there are no other fields here, although there are several others listed back on the Shared Documents page, is that those other fields are automated. They cannot be edited and therefore are not displayed here for modification.

TIP As with any list, you can always add more columns to a document library, which is good. Since you can't search through the text of the documents without upgrading your WMSDE to SQL, it's a good idea to consider creating some fields that encourage the users to enter key words about the document that can be filtered for later (which, oddly enough, is what we're doing next).

Add a New Field

Document libraries are like any other list in that they have fields, and those fields can be required. This can come in handy if you need to search for documents by keyword but you don't have SQL so you can't do full text searching.

What I'd like to show you is how to add a required field to items in a document library and what happens when you do. Logically, I am going to call it Keywords in the hope that the users will add keywords to it about the document. This will make it possible to sort or filter by the keywords field to find a document.

Something to keep in mind is that the fields in an item of a document library are considered *metadata*, data about the properties of the item. If you add a keyword field, it will actually contain data about the contents of the document *in* the item, so it all works out.

1. To add the Keywords field, go to the Columns section of the Customize Shared Documents page, and click Add a New Column.

2. I am going to name the column Keywords. I'm choosing the plural form because, although sorting and filtering in the list view occurs essentially by first letter, if you filter by creating a new view, you can choose the criteria "contains" and therefore isolate items that have a specific keyword or keywords. So I want the users to be specific as possible as to the contents of their documents.

3. Having said that, I don't want them to write an epic, so I am going to keep the field as a single line field. Make sure that the default type as Single line of text is selected.

4. Under Optional Settings, the description is important. In order for this Keywords field to be useful, the users need to understand what it is for. To that end, type in a description that would make sense to your users in the Description box.

5. I am going to require that this field contain information before the item can be added to the library. This may need to be optional in your environment. Select Yes under Require That This Column Contains Information.

   You might also want to either limit or extend the number of characters a user can put in the field. I feel comfortable at this point with the maximum number of characters of 255, so I am going to keep that default setting.

   I also definitely do not want to have a default value for this field. If all keyword fields for all documents had the same value, it would defeat the purpose of having the field at all.

6. In order to filter by a field in a list, I need to be able to see it. Because we have no other view built, I definitely want this field in the default view. Make certain that the Add to Default View is checked and click OK.

WARNING   Doing it this way might bloat the list if users write an epic. If that is the case, by all means, remove this field from the default view and create your own list view. Then put the fields you would find useful and the Keywords field in there instead, so the All Documents view won't be cluttered.

That should put you be back on the Customize Shared Documents page. The library now has a Keywords field.

Modify Document Library Settings

One of the biggest selling points of a document library is the fact that it will store different versions of a document. That feature is not on by default. You must enable it. While we are changing General Settings for the library, I would like to change its name. Like changing the name of a field in a list, there is no reason to keep a default name if you don't want to.

1. To enable Version History and change a library's name, click Change general settings in the General Settings section. This is where you can change the name and description of this library. In the time-honored tradition of "waste not, want not," there is no reason why you can't take this perfectly good premade library and personalize it with a new title.

2. In the Name field, change the name of this document library from Shared Documents to something more appropriate (see Figure 18.59 for inspiration). I am going to use Internal Documents.

3. It is good to have a document library easily accessible to users, especially initially. So in the Navigation section, I think it is a good idea to keep the current setting of Yes to Display This Document Library on the Quick Launch Bar?

We don't require Content Approval for this library, but you can if you want to.

If you are going in order (as I am) down the different sections of the General Settings page, you should be looking at the Document Versions setting, or Create a Version Each Time You Edit a File in This Document Library. This is obviously the other setting that simple lists don't have.

FIGURE 18.59
Internal Documents
settings

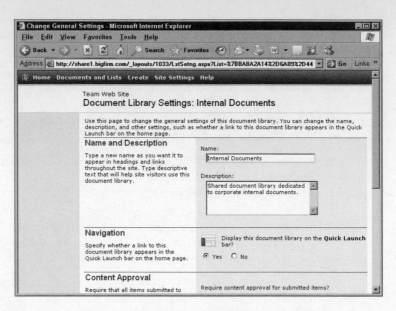

Here's the scoop. When versioning is on, it works like magic. There are no intermediate settings that let you control it. Versioning keeps a version history, essentially an old copy, of every document in the library. Versions are saved if:

◆ A user uploads a copy of an existing file in the library (with the overwrite the existing file check box checked). It is considered the new version, and the previous one is considered an older version.

◆ A user checks out a file, makes changes, and checks it back in. That is considered the newest version of a file.

◆ A user opens a file, makes a change once, then saves. After that no other changes get saved as a new version, even if you hit Save several times while you have the document open. That is because those changes are considered changes made in one version session.

◆ A user restores an older version of the file, and it is saved as the newest version. (That is the point of restore. To restore from a previous version if the changes made since then were a bad thing.)

4. To enable Document Versions, make sure that Yes is selected under Create a Version Each Time You Edit a File in This Document Library?

And finally, the last section, Document Template. It is singular; there can be only one. If you've edited a default template and saved the changes to the default location where the original template was but with a different filename (an easy cheat for creating a template for a library after you've made the library), you can specify that new template name here. That replaces the original template that the New Document link calls on in the document library, from the old template to the new one. Of course, if there were documents in the library based on the old template, they will not be changing.

At this point using the default template (essentially `Normal.dot`) for my purposes is fine, but I thought you should know.

Those are the settings for a document library. We've made a few changes, and in particular enabled Version History. So click OK.

ANOTHER QUICK TRICK TO CHANGING THE TEMPLATE FILE ASSOCIATED WITH A DOCUMENT LIBRARY

Say you had a document template for contracts one of the departments of your business uses. You created a document library for them, *then* they told you what template they wanted. No sweat. Make sure you are logged in as an administrator, open the document library, and select Explorer View. The forms folder for this library is available there and is the default location where libraries save their base template. (Keep in mind that Forms is used to store templates and the active server pages used for creating views and edit pages. Use caution here when messing about.) Just drag and drop the department's template into that forms folder. Then it's easy to just change the file name in the URL in the General Settings' Document Template section.

Do you remember me mentioning that you need to be careful about naming things that have a web address? If the name of that thing was to be misspelled or something, and you went back to change it, then the web address would, unfortunately not change.

Take a look at Figure 18.60. Note that now the document library is called Internal Documents but the web address is still `http://share1.bigfirm.com/Shared Documents/Forms/AllItems.aspx`.

What this means to the user is that they will click the link in the Quick Launch bar that says Internal Documents, but if they bother to look at the URL when they get there, Internal Documents will not be in the address, Shared Documents will be. If you have ever messed with Windows SharePoint Services and been confused when a list or library was called one thing in the title area and another in the URL, well, now you know why. Either someone made a mistake when they originally built the list, or they are just recycling. No big deal, but it's good to know.

To see the modifications that have been made to the document library, click Go Back to Internal Documents.

The page title should now be whatever you named it (mine is Internal Documents) and your description should be listed above the action bar.

FIGURE 18.60
Original URL cannot change if library is renamed.

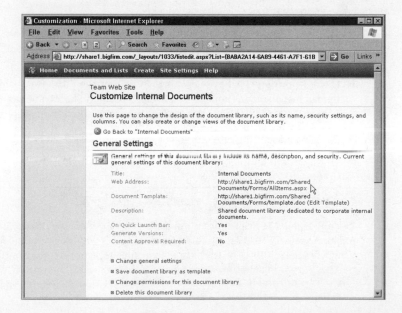

Because the library has versioning set and a Keywords field, it's time to actually use this document library.

> **NOTE** For these exercises I am going to be logged in as my wssadmin account from a workstation with Office 2003 installed. Something I have not been dwelling on is that you cannot contribute files to a library (or items to a list) without the permission to do so. Up to this point I have been working on getting you familiar and comfortable with SharePoint logged in as the administrator who made the site, both for convenience (a "let's learn one thing at a time" approach) and because you will spend most of your time as an administrator or someone with equivalent rights. Nonetheless, we are going to be saving actual files from a workstation to a database on the server. It should not be assumed that being allowed to do that is a given. Rights must be set. More on that a little later, or you can skip to the Working with Permissions section of the chapter.

UPLOAD A DOCUMENT

Document libraries, as you may recall, can use the template to create a new document, or they can accept uploads of preexisting files.

I am going to show you how to upload a document first, then how to create a new document (which requires Word 2003) using the Word template, then how to save it, edit it, and check its version history.

1. To upload a document to the Internal Documents library, just click the Upload Document link in the action bar.

   Notice in Figure 18.61 that there are very few things in the Upload Document page, just two required fields, a link, and a check box. The Name field is your standard upload attachment field, complete with a Browse button. The keywords field should look familiar, since that's the one we added, complete with the description.

   And finally, the Overwrite Existing File(s)? check box. If you want to overwrite the file in this library with the same filename (which is what you would want to do if you were updating an existing file in the library with the changes you have saved from your local version), make sure that that check box is checked.

2. I am going to click the Browse button next to the Name field and go to the file saved in the My Documents folder called, aptly enough, uploadme.doc.

> **NOTE** If you don't have a pre-existing Word file but you'd like to try this uploading thing, you can upload just about any nonexecutable file. By default SharePoint has many executable file types, such as EXE or MSI, blocked. There is an administrative setting page that lets you modify that.

3. Add something relevant to the Keywords field. (see Figure 18.63 to see what I used for keywords).

FOR YOUR MULTIPLE FILE UPLOADING CONVENIENCE

The link Upload Multiple Files is interesting. If you select it you will come to a page that contains an Explorer view (complete with folder pane) that lets you browse to the folder containing the files you want from the folder list on the left and then put check marks next to multiple files on the right to select the files you want to upload. Convenient for those mass uploads you need to do (see Figure 18.63).

FIGURE 18.61
Upload Document

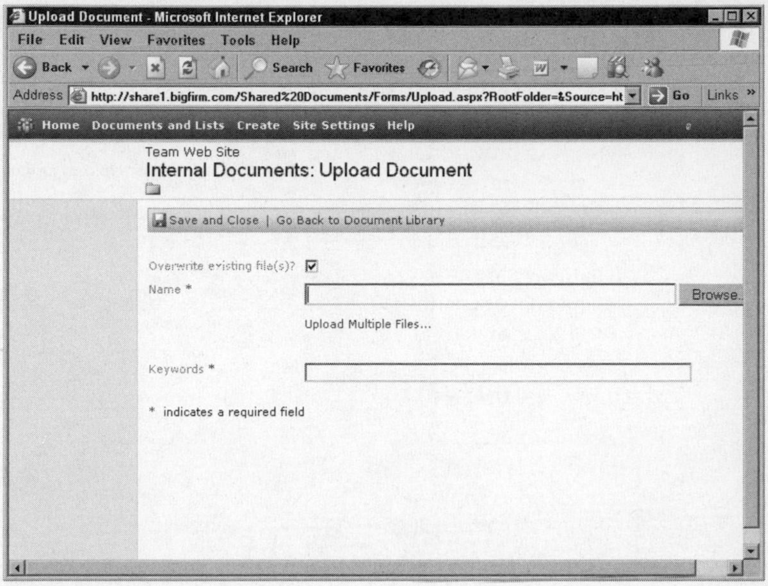

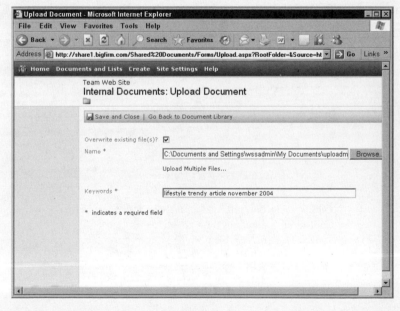

FIGURE 18.62
Adding keywords
to Upload

And that's all it takes to upload a document to a document library. I don't really have to worry about overwriting an existing file, but I'll leave the check box checked anyway, no harm done. Click Save and Close.

The file is now listed in the document library. There are obviously things that can be done to documents in a document library that can't be done in a normal list.

The best way to get a quick idea as to what those actions are is to move your mouse over the file-name of a document, and click the down arrow in the selection box (see Figure 18.64).

FIGURE 18.63
Upload multiple files

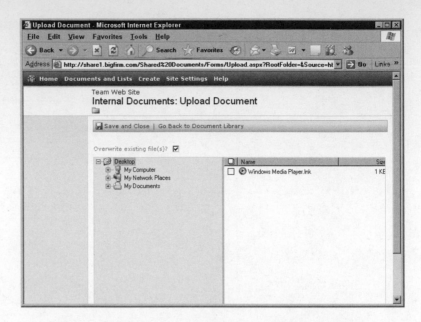

FIGURE 18.64
Document library
item drop-down
menu

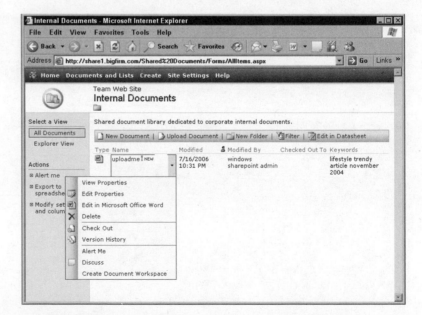

In the drop-down menu are the following options:

View Properties   Lets you view the item that the document is attached to and therefore its metadata.

Edit Properties   Lets you edit the fields in the item the document is attached to (otherwise known as editing the metadata). This would be useful in our case if we needed to change some of the words in our Keywords field.

Edit in Microsoft Office Word   What actually happens if you click the name of the document. It simply opens in Word 2003 locally, presumably so you can edit the document. If the document was a spreadsheet, it would say Excel instead of Word.

Delete   Allows you to delete the item and its associated document from the library. No, really, no Recycle Bin here.

Check Out   This will lock the library copy of this document until you check it back in. Other users will only get to open a read-only copy. Remember, Check Out is voluntary, *not* mandatory. This means that a person can open a file and edit it without checking it out. That means that it will not be locked as read-only for anyone else who uses it in the meantime. This is one of the reasons that versioning is so wonderful.

NOTE   Because Check Out locks a document until the document is checked back in, administrators and other users can be granted special permission to cancel Check Out on a document.

Version History   Version History really works. It simply takes each file and treats each Save as a copy of that file and stores those copies in chronological order. The most recent version is displayed in the library. The others can be accessed by selecting Version History in the drop-down menu associated with that document.

So if a user completely messes up a document, you can identify that user's changes and recover a previous version. Of course, if two people have a document open at the same time and make changes, the two different versions do not merge. They are both saved as different versions, the most recent being the one listed in the library. This should indicate why users should be strongly encouraged to use the Check Out feature.

Alert Me   Standard alert settings. Useful to let you know when a checked out document is checked back in.

Discuss   A Word 2003 integration feature that can embed a discussion into a document. However, that document does have to be formatted for HTML.

Create Document Workspace   Something we haven't gone into that much yet. Because SharePoint is so document-centric, not only can you have document libraries about documents, discussion lists about those documents, surveys about those documents, but you can also actually spawn off a subsite from the site that houses this document library to be all about this document. The catch? The user who selects this menu option must have the right to create a subsite in order to create a workspace.

IF YOU ABSOLUTELY, POSITIVELY NEED TO VIEW AN OFFICE 2003 DOCUMENT

If you have users that must be able to read a document, spreadsheet, or PowerPoint presentation, but they only have Internet Explorer (no Office 2003 and can't install the individual product viewers), you can enable the HTML Viewer in SharePoint. The HTML Viewer will use a HTML Viewer server (usually a dedicated workstation with Office 2003 loaded, because transforming Office .xls, .doc, .ppt, or .pps files to HTML is very processor intensive—don't do this on your SharePoint server unless you have many processes to spare) to do the heavy lifting and make a passable WYSIWYG HTML version of the file for the user. It is to read, not edit, and it is clunky, but available to you if necessary. The native help files are kind of sketchy on the HTML viewer; for more info check out the Windows SharePoint Services 2.0 Administrator's Guide.

While in the drop-down menu, I would like to see what the properties of this document are. Select View Properties in the drop-down menu.

As Figure 18.65 shows, this is the metadata for the uploadme document (or whatever you named your document). Notice the action bar contains the same actions as the item drop-down did.

Click the Go back to Document Library link in the action bar.

FIGURE 18.65

Uploaded file metadata

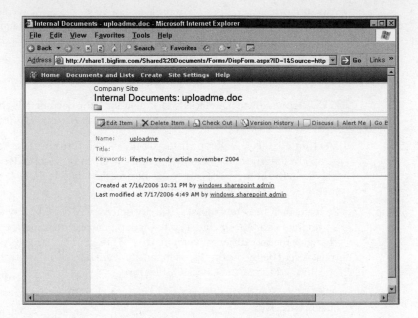

SO ALL OF YOUR USERS WANT TO CREATE A SEPARATE WORKSPACE FOR EVERY ONE OF THEIR DOCUMENTS...

The interesting thing about creating a document workspace from the innocuous looking drop-down menu is that SharePoint is smart enough to take a copy of the document and use it in the new workspace's document library with a link to publish the document *back* to the original library when it's complete.

However, despite its niftiness, this menu item alone could really bloat your server with lots of little baby sites. If you must allow users to create workspaces, and you dread the idea of babysitting those workspaces and deleting them at the end of each project, then there is another way to go.

It is possible, but scary, to allow users to create top-level websites (like the Team Web Site we have now). That is really pretty powerful as far as what they can do with owner rights to a top-level site (as you are learning in this chapter), but only top-level sites can be automatically managed and deleted based on use. Keep Confirmation and Automatic Deletion Settings in mind when we get to the Administration section of this chapter. It could be a dangerous trade-off, but it might be worth considering in your environment.

MICROSOFT OFFICE SHAREPOINT WORKSPACE TASK PANE

Whenever you open a document from a SharePoint library, Word (and several other Office products) will open that space-consuming task pane on the right side of the window (see graphic). The task pane can change content depending on context. In this case, because you are connected to a SharePoint site, Word would love to take advantage of that. So, it opens the task pane with SharePoint Workspace paraphernalia in it. This feature of Word 2003 could fill an entire chapter of its own and doesn't belong in a book about Server 2003 R2. So here's a quick overview of some of the things you should expect.

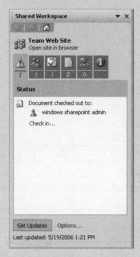

The SharePoint Workspace task pane is divided by tabs that display SharePoint site related information with related links on the bottom:

 Status Lets you know the status of the document itself: if it is checked out, and if so, who has it checked out. If you are the one that has it checked out, you can check it back in from this tab.

 Members This tab changes depending on what's going on. If you are on a new document with this pane open, the Members tab tries to get you to create a workspace for this document. If you are editing a document that was opened from a document library, then it will display the users that have permission to the library and indicate if they are logged in or not (online). If you move your mouse over on of the members listed and click the down arrow that shows up, a long list of things you could do with Office products to or with that member will display.

 Tasks Links to the Tasks list on the SharePoint site that contains the document library that holds this document.

 Documents Displays a list of the documents that are in the same library that the open document is in. Contains convenient links at the bottom to add a new document or folder to the library or create an alert for changes made to the library.

 Links Shows the links that are in the Links list on the SharePoint site, with a convenient link at the bottom of the tab to add a new link.

 Document information Displays who created and modified the document when. If there are required fields for items in this library, they will be here for entry or editing.

CREATE A NEW DOCUMENT

Now let's actually create a new document, type something, and save it. Because it was opened from here, it will save to this library. Convenient, that.

1. To create a new document, click the New Document link in the action bar. (You may get an Internet Explorer warning that opening files from the Internet is harmful. Although this is true, this file is safe; you may click OK.)

WARNING   You may be prompted to provide your authentication information for the site when you open or create a document in a document library. That isn't really a SharePoint thing, it's because Word 2003 wants to be able to use the task pane to show information about the Share-Point site. Because of that, even though you logged in to the site and went directly to the document (so your authentication information did not time out), you may still be prompted so Word can find out what your rights are and what you can or cannot do from the task pane.

You should be in Word 2003 on a blank document created from the Template.doc file in the Internal Documents library.

2. We will be editing this document, so feel free to type in some text, format it, get as fancy as you'd like.

3. When you're done, save the document in whatever way you usually do.

You'll get the standard Save As dialog box, but because you created the file from the document library, Word assumes you want to save it there as well (see Figure 18.66). Welcome to the beginning of integration. It actually will display a limited version of the page formatting, complete with a limited list view, just to make you comfortable.

TIP   A user can save a document to (or open a document from) a document library without leaving Word 2003. Word is smart enough that if you go to either the Open or Save dialog box and type the HTTP address of the SharePoint site in the Filename field, it will realize that you are trying to access that site's document libraries (because there can be more than one) and will display a list of those libraries for the choosing (complete with a bit of color in the background to match the site's theme).

4. I am going to name this document mynewdoc. Name yours whatever you'd like. Then click the Save button.

5. Ah, ha. What's this? Before you save, a dialog box pops up with the fields that you required for the document library items (see Figure 18.67). Remember the Keywords field? I bet you wondered how exactly the users were going to be required to fill in a field in SharePoint while they were working in Word 2003. Well, here it is, in a nice big dialog box. If you try to blow this Web File Properties dialog box off by canceling, then you can't save the file. Feel free to type in some keywords appropriate for your file, and click OK.

FIGURE 18.66
Saving a document
to a library

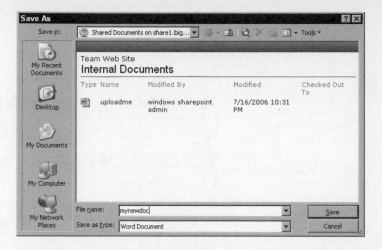

FIGURE 18.67
Required
Keywords field

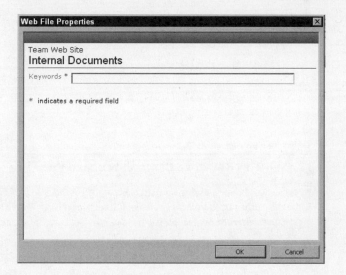

TIP When you open a document from a SharePoint library, the fields in the item associated with this document become part of the documents properties. There is a reason for this. While in the document in Word 2003, if you go to Properties on the File menu, you will get the Web File Properties dialog box with a button on the bottom left to add additional file properties. If you save a document created from a document library, it will try to extrapolate a title from the first line of the document and fill that default Title field listed in View Properties (sometimes with hilarious results).

6. Close out of Word 2003 and go back to the browser window you have been using to work with the Internal Documents library.

The new document is now listed (if it's not, refresh the page) in the Internal Documents library list, as shown in Figure 18.68.

FIGURE 18.68
New document in Internal Documents library

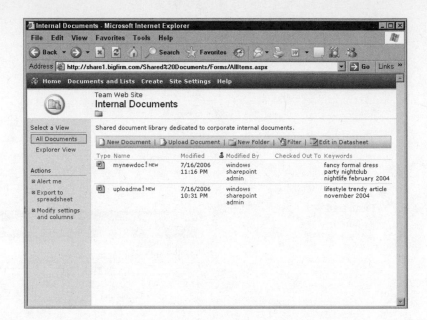

(see the sidebar "There's Filtering and There's *Filtering*" in the Lists section of the chapter for more details).

FILTERING BY KEYWORD USING A STANDARD VIEW

By the way, I keep insisting on using keywords to find a document in the library because I expect you to filter the library by keywords in lieu of full text searching. I have mentioned filtering, as well as standard views, before, but now I think it's time to pull the concepts together.

For the users, if they have Office 2003 installed (and they probably will to get the most out of a document library), remember to make sure they know how to use datasheet view, so they can take advantage of the custom filter function there to search the library for documents that contain keywords they are looking for (see the sidebar "There's Filtering and There's *Filtering*" in the Lists section of the chapter for more details).

Administrators (who may not be somewhere Excel 2003 is installed) can use a standard view to filter a document library by keywords. In other words, create a new view in that document library and use it to display only the items in the library that contain the keyword in the keywords field that you are looking for.

For example, go to Modify settings and columns on the library you want to filter, then scroll down to Create a new view.

Choose a standard view template, name it, choose an audience (I usually make it personal and edit it every time I need to filter the library) and the columns you want to display. Then configure the filter settings to limit the items listed in the view by the keywords field that "contains" the keyword criteria you are looking for. Remember, it's got its limits, but you can make it pretty complicated if you'd like.

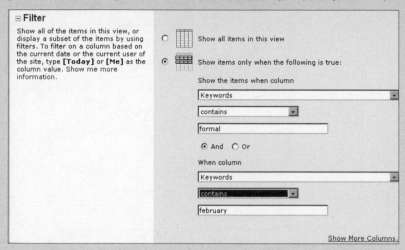

It's that easy. Now, you just need to know what document library you put a file in, in order to filter for it.

CHECK OUT AND EDIT A DOCUMENT

We've uploaded a document and created one. Those are two out of the three things information workers do in a document library. The third is to edit a document and save the changes back to the library.

It is during the editing process of a document that you might hear about the Check Out feature. Although checking a document out is voluntary, it's a good thing to teach users to do. It really ruins the process of one person editing at a time if they don't comply with checking documents in and out.

1. To check out a document in order to edit it, move your mouse over the file you'd like to edit. I am going to add text to mynewdoc and do some formatting.

2. When the selection box shows up around the document name, click the down arrow, and choose Check Out to check the item out and lock it so everyone else will know it is being edited.

3. You should now be listed in the Checked Out To column in the Internal Documents library list (see Figure 18.69).

   There are two ways to open a document to edit it. You can actually just click the document name (almost too easy), or you can get the drop-down menu and choose Edit in Microsoft in Microsoft Office Word. Choose whichever you'd like, just open the document you checked out.

FIGURE 18.69
Checked out item

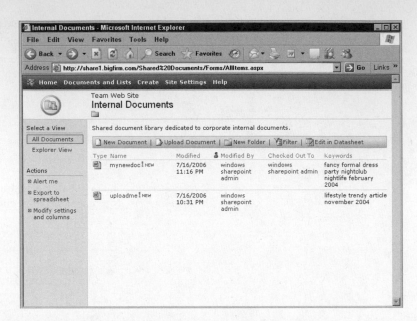

Once Word 2003 is open, you should be in your document, ready to do some editing. The task pane may have opened on the right side of the window, displaying that you have the document checked out. You can close the task pane if you'd like, we're just editing a document here.

Feel free to make some changes to the document and click Save and close out of Word. Closing Word should trigger a dialog box giving you some options concerning the checked out state of the document:

Check in file Lets you check the document in from here rather than going back to the document library and choosing Check In from the drop-down menu. Should prompt you for comments before letting you move on.

Keep checked out Takes the changes you saved and makes a new version out of them. However, you will still have the document checked out. Useful if you want to make changes, save, and close the document, then open it to edit later before checking it in for someone else to work with.

Discard changes and undo check out Essentially cancels the check out. It will delete the saved version history and place the document in a ready to check out state.

Feel free to check the file back in (that's what I am going to do) by making sure Check In File is selected and clicking OK.

NOTE If the Check In dialog box does *not* come up when you close out of Word, then you can manually check in the document by moving your mouse over its filename, then clicking Check In in the drop-down menu.

Check in gives you the option to make comments; when the Check In Comments dialog box pops up, type in some comments about editing the document and click OK.

Go back to the Browser window that contains the Internal Documents library. If you checked the document back in, your account name should be no longer listed in the Checked Out To column next to the document you edited.

CHECKING VERSION HISTORY

To check if the document version setting we made when we customized this list actually took, move your mouse over the document you just finished editing, click the down arrow, and select Version History.

If you enabled Document Versions in your document library general settings, there should be two versions of this document (see Figure 18.70). The active one (most recent) should be on top and have a larger number. That is the one linked to the document name in the library. The bottom one should be older and have a lower number. That's the first version.

1. To see what you can do with a document version, move your mouse over the date and time of the older version of the document. Click the down arrow and see that you can View, Restore, or Delete this version.

2. To see what happens if the older version of the document is restored, choose Restore.

FIGURE 18.70
Version History

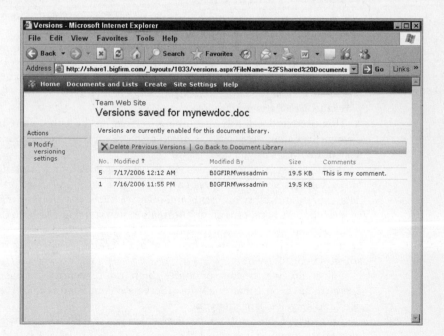

3. You will be warned that you will be replacing the current version with the selected version. To restore means that the edits and the check-in comment we made when we edited the document will no longer exist in the restored version.

4. Click OK. Now there should be *three* versions of the document. In other words, as far as anyone at the document library level knows, the restored version is the best and only version. Version History does not *remove* the most recent version it is replacing, it just puts a copy of the version you chose to restore as the most recent copy.

5. To check to see if the document listed in the document library is the restored version, click the link for Go Back to Document Library in the action bar.

6. Click the name of the document you edited and restored an earlier version of. The document that opens in Word 2003 should be in the state it was when you first saved your document to the Internal Documents library, before you edited it. In other words, the restore was a success. But don't worry, if you really wanted the newer version of the document, it is still stored in Version History. Version History doesn't delete versions itself, you have to do that manually. It simply changes their order if you require it.

7. I am done with Word 2003, so I am going to close out and return to the Internal Documents library in the browser.

That's the whirlwind tour of document libraries. Remember that there are other kinds of libraries as well. Feel free to take them for a test drive with the skills you learned with Internal Documents.

Workspaces and Subsites

At several points as we explored our SharePoint Team Web Site we've come across references or links about Sites and Workspaces.

It's time to go over them. First, we need to think about SharePoint and website design.

Because SharePoint is an open-ended collaboration tool, it can be as basic or advanced as anyone would like. That means that it needs to start somewhere, so it starts with a simple single Team Web Site, that has about five premade lists, a bunch of Web Parts, and a home page that holds and displays the Web Parts for the site.

This, of course, is only the beginning. You can just keep that site. Change its title and description. Change the names of the lists to something more appropriate for your environment. Then add more lists and libraries as you need them.

But if your environment needs you to have, essentially, a portal site (without paying for the full-blown big brother of Windows SharePoint Services, SharePoint Portal Server) that holds general lists, events, and announcements and otherwise acts as a jumping off point for subsites you create for each department, project, or information worker, you could do that too.

You could also, because of politics or security or prestige, rename the Team Web Site something appropriate and then create several sites at that same top level, equal to the Team Web Site, with subsites beneath them.

You could even, because of politics, high traffic, security settings, or authentication methods, decide to have more than one Virtual Server on your SharePoint server with many, many top-level sites and subsites beneath them.

And each of these options can happen on just one physical server. I think you might be seeing why SharePoint is a deceptively large product—not in its use, but in its design (which defines its administration).

NOTE IIS and most web servers focus on Web Sites in terms of them containing multiple web pages. But SharePoint doesn't focus on containing multiple web pages (because it has few to no static web pages), it focuses on containing multiple websites. That is why they have the term *site collection*: a top-level site and its subsites are called, all together, a site collection. This is particularly relevant because there are settings made at the first top-level site of a collection that affect all sub-sites that are created below it. You will see this in the "Administration" section of the chapter.

Despite that, it is incredibly easy to use. Take, for example, if you did want to create a website for a team of people to work on just one document. You could go to the document library where the document is stored, click the down arrow that shows up when you move your mouse over the document name, select Create Workspace in the drop-down menu, and then give those users rights to that workspace. Then you just let them know where the site is, and they can start working on it. Of course, it would be good if you knew what that actually means in terms of administration before you did that. Or better yet, before you let your users do it.

To start with, a workspace is a kind of minisite. It's a fully functional subsite beneath the team site that simply has the lists and Web Parts Microsoft assumes a workspace might need, conveniently premade and applied from the workspace default template.

And, even though a workspace is a fully functioning website, it is especially intended to be impermanent. It is intended to be user driven, created when a user needs it, and deleted by you or some administrative mechanism when they don't need it anymore. You, as the administrator, are going to have to manage deleting the workspace at some point because it is not supposed to last. That being said, it is a website, no question. Just like the team site (only maybe with fewer lists), it can last forever, cluttering up your server with no activity for eons if you don't keep track of it. Or, because it can last forever, you could use a document workspace as a permanent subsite if you wanted to. Either way, while they exist, workspaces and other subsites add to the site collection and take up space (however small) on the server that someone has to administer.

There are two different ways to create a document workspace (and a third way if you include creating a site with Office 2003, another integration innovation). One is very user driven, using the drop-down menu for a document name (you may remember seeing that). The other way is more impersonal: from the Create or Documents and Lists links on the navigation bar. What I mean by impersonal is that it doesn't realize automatically what document you want to focus the workspace on, and there is a chance that you might want to specify what template it should use (because there are meeting workspaces, too) and what permissions it should have.

Creating a document workspace straight from a selected document in a document library is more user friendly and more in the personal interest of the users for three reasons:

♦ It automatically *does not* inherit the permissions from its parent, meaning no one has rights to the workspace by default except the creator and the administrator(s). This was intended to give users control over their workspace and choose who gets access. The workspace literally does not exist for anyone not given permission to use it. The permissions page and settings have the same look and feel as those on the top-level site. I feel that this actually gives them a mini-lesson on how permissions work overall, which is potentially a problem for those more clever users. Otherwise, it does give the workspace owner the ability to secure their data.

♦ It uses the default document workspace template (instead of getting to choose from all eight) automatically. No choice also means no confusion.

♦ Because it knows the specific document that the workspace is being created for, the new document workspace automatically adds the document to the workspace's own document library with a link in the document's drop-down menu to publish it back to the original document library when it's finished.

When you create a workspace manually from Create or Documents and Lists in the navigation bar, you will be asked to give the workspace a title, explicitly be given an opportunity to specify the website address (to insure it will be short, even if the title is several words long), and decide whether or not the site requires unique permissions or should inherit permissions from the parent site above.

TIP If you change your mind about what permissions should be applied to a workspace, they can always be changed.

Then SharePoint offers up a choice among eight standard templates. These are the same templates that are offered whether you selected to create a document workspace, a site, or meeting workspace (that's what I meant by them being all the same thing). There are only eight default templates (actually they are based on site definitions) for any subsite you want to make off of the main, top-level website (which our Team site is by virtue of being the only site we have), but you can add many more.

NOTE Since SharePoint has come out, Microsoft has created many new site templates that they call *applications*. They should be located at Microsoft's Windows SharePoint Services site under Applications. They are pretty nifty and offer good jump off points for customization that you may need to do. They include templates for help desk, publication management, time sheets, expense reports, and more. Before you reinvent the wheel, go check them out.

In order to see the difference between workspaces, I plan on walking through creating a document-focused document workspace, then creating a manual, nondocument-centric document workspace, then finishing up with a meeting workspace (another kind of impermanent site) nested beneath a document workspace (to manage a meeting about the document), showing that a workspace can have subsites below it.

A BIT OF TECHNICAL DETAIL ABOUT SITE TEMPLATES AND DEFINITIONS

A site definition is sort of an uber-template, containing every single detail of what the site is and can do, including the set of basic pages and schema from which all SharePoint sites and lists are derived. They are usually stored on the file system of the server (Program Files\Common Files\Microsoft Shared\web server extensions\60\TEMPLATE\1033) and are called onet.xml.

The two main onet.xml files are located under subfolders called STS and MPS. Those folders hold the specific files required by their site definitions, and in the XML folder for each, there is an onet.xml file that specifies the definitions for each type of site, STS for SharePoint Team site and document workspaces, and MPS for Meeting Workspace sites.

A real template, according to SharePoint parlance, is just a record of the changes made to a particular site definition.

This helps explain why all the sites and document workspaces have a very common look and feel and why any site template (or application) you might download also has the same look and feel. No matter how tricked out they are, they are still based on the one of the original definitions. On the other hand, it also explains why meeting workspaces are just a little bit different. Remember that they have their own onet.xml file in the MPS folder.

You can create your own definitions and custom templates. Check out the Windows SharePoint Services Software Development Kit for more info.

CREATING A DOCUMENT WORKSPACE BASED ON A DOCUMENT

1. To create a Workspace from a document, be sure you are in the Internal Documents library (if that is what you named the default document library).

2. Click the down arrow that shows up when you move your mouse over the document that you added and edited (mine is called mynewdoc).

3. From the drop-down menu, click Create Document Workspace (see Figure 18.71).

4. This will promptly bring you to a window asking if you are sure you want to create a document workspace, because it was so easy to do that you could do so by accident. Notice that this window says that a copy of the document will be stored on the new site and be able to be published back to the original location. Another more subtle point is that the document workspace's web address will be the filename of the document. Another reason to have a single word, no spaces naming policy in place for documents if they are going to be spawning workspaces (see Figure 18.72). We, in fact, are not doing this by accident, so click OK.

Welcome to your new document workspace. No fuss, no muss, no effort. Let's look around.

Although there are a lot of elements that are reasonably identical to the Team Web Site, such as the navigation bar and Quick Launch bar, there are some differences. To start, the little medallion icon in the top left corner is of three people around a piece of paper, indicating that this is not the home page of an ordinary site, which is useful if you have to tell at a glance if a page is a document workspace or not.

Next, of course, is the title of the site, mynewdoc Home. Also new is the link at the far right on the navigation bar. The Up to link is another indicator that the site you are on is not at the top of the hierarchy. However, it does not indicate how far down this site might be buried. For that you need to look at the address bar for to see where you are in relation to the top site. In this case we are just beneath the default Team Web Site for the server, so our address is the `server address/mynewdoc/default.aspx` (the home page for mynewdoc). That shows that we are only one step down from the top-level site (see Figure 18.73).

FIGURE 18.71
Document drop-down menu

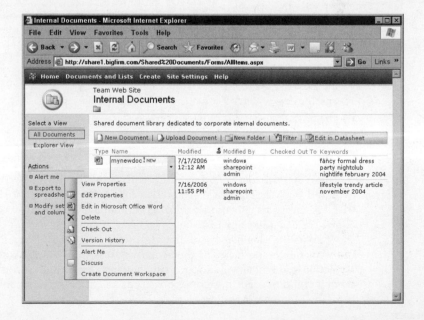

FIGURE 18.72
Create Document
Workspace page

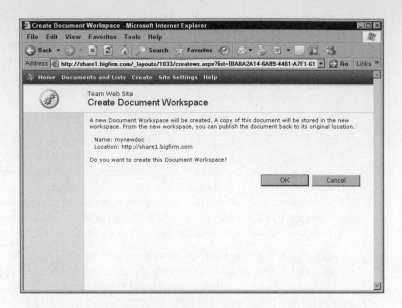

FIGURE 18.73
New workspace
address in browser

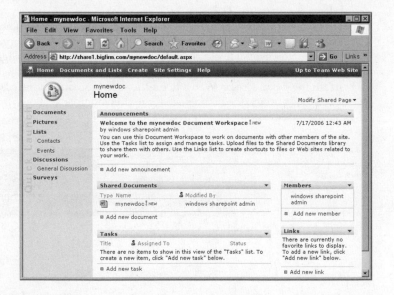

The Web Part zone is laid out differently as well, with a new Web Part that we haven't explored yet. Members is a Web Part that connects to the user information for this website (notice that it is empty except your account).The Members Web Part can be added to the Team Web Site Home page just like any List View Web Part. As you add people to a SharePoint site, they will show up on the Members list of that site. Better yet, because SharePoint is aware of who is logged in and using the site (based on their email address and instant messenger), the Members list items are active and will let you know if site members are online so you can email or instant message them if you'd like. Furthermore, you can, as an administrator, conveniently add users to the site from the Members Web Part.

PERSON NAME SMART TAGS AND OTHER INTERESTING THINGS ABOUT THE MEMBERS WEB PART

In the Members Web Part, if you move your mouse pointer over a user name, a little Instant Messenger icon called a "Person Name Smart Tag" (I'm not making that up) pops up. If you click on it, it gives you a menu that offers different ways to contact that user, like email or instant messenger (Windows or MSN of course).

If you are accessing the site from a machine that has MSN or Windows instant messenging running, then it will also indicate that person's online presence (grouping them by red or green balls next to the user name) based on whether or not that person is logged in and active in instant messenger (using the email account that SharePoint associates with that user of course).

If you don't want your users to be distracted by who is logged on and available to chat, then disable "Person Name Smart Tags and Presence Settings" in the Virtual Server general settings (you'll learn more about them in the Administration section of this chapter).

In addition, some of the standard List View Web Parts are here in a slightly different configuration. The Announcements List View Web Part is basically the header Web Part, with Shared Documents as a Web Part underneath (notice that the mynewdoc file is already there). Tasks and Links are also working the Web Part zone, with Contacts, Events, and the default General Discussion lists on the Quick Launch bar. In addition, on the Quick Launch bar is a general heading Pictures that links to the Documents and Lists' picture library view so you can easily add and manage any picture libraries that are appropriate for the site's focal document. This is particularly useful if the document is large, like a book, and the pictures for the figures referred to in text need to be stored somewhere outside of the document for anyone to use, edit, or manipulate.

So there you go, a default document workspace. One of the things you may have noticed is it is a bit redundant. It has lists with the same purpose and name as those on the Team Web Site above it. This is one of the inherent dangers of the kind of conformity that SharePoint offers. Your users remember saving a document to a document library, the question is, which one? This is one of the reasons that you have to be clear about how SharePoint works, so you can create naming conventions and consistent practices to help avoid confusion. I tend to avoid default names as often as I can and try to be sure that all lists, libraries, and subsites are uniquely and correctly named.

The document that this workspace centers on is located in the Shared Documents library for this site. It is a copy of the one up in the original Internal Documents library. This is a different library, and therefore the metadata has been stripped, particularly the Keywords field.

REMEMBER TO LOCK THE DOCUMENT BEHIND YOU

That brings me to an interesting point. The document stored in this document workspace is a copy of the original that still exists in the Internal Documents document workspace. That original copy of the document can continue to be edited while the copy is being edited in its dedicated workspace. Meaning that there could be two, unsynchronized sets of edits on the same document going on.

My suggestion? Make certain that the creator of the document workspace for a document goes back up to the originating document library and *checks out* the original document. That will make it read-only and therefore lock it down in that library and allow edits only from its own workspace. The workspace owner can even post an entry that doesn't expire in Announcements so that other interested parties know what's going on.

To check it out, move your mouse over the document (in my case mynewdoc), click the down arrow, and select View Properties. You will see (in Figure 18.74) that there is no Keywords field.

NOTE This walkthrough is going to require Word 2003, so if you are not working from a workstation with Word 2003 installed, opening and editing the document in Word will be tough. This is the last time the workstation will be required.

FIGURE 18.74
View properties
of mynewdoc

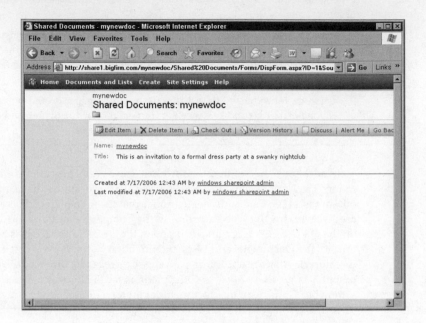

Using the New Document Workspace

I'd like to make sure that the document in this workspace is the correct version from the original document library and I'd like to practice publishing a document back up to its origins. To do this we need to edit this document in Word 2003, make some changes, save them and close (and see that the Keywords field doesn't exist here because it does not force a web properties dialog box). That way we know the document is different from here. Then we'll publish this copy back up to the original library and see if it changes up there.

1. To open and edit the document in Word 2003, click the name of the document in the Shared Documents List View Web Part to open it in Word 2003.

2. It should open the correct version of the document in Word 2003 (you can go back to the Internal Documents Library and check if you aren't sure). Feel free to type some text in that will make it obvious that a change has been made since you last edited this document. I typed something along the lines of "These changes are being made from this document's own document workspace."

3. Once you have changed your document to your liking, save and close out of Word 2003.

Publishing a Document to Source Location

Having established that the document is the correct version and then changing it a little, we can now publish the change back up to the original Internal Documents library.

1. To do that, move your mouse over the name of the document you just edited, click the down arrow, select Publish to Source Location.

NOTE In case you were wondering, we didn't enable Version History on the document library in this workspace. I didn't see the need.

2. You'll get a warning that this document will replace the source document with your latest changes (see Figure 18.75). That is actually supposed to be the idea, right? So click OK.

3. You will get a terse confirmation page in response, but the real test is back in the source location. Click Home on the navigation bar of the confirmation page (notice that you don't have much choice, there's either Home or Help).

4. On the home page for your document workspace, click the Up to Team Web Site link on the far right of the navigation bar because that's where the Internal Documents library is.

5. Once on your Team Web Site's home page, click the Internal Documents link in the Quick Launch bar.

First we'll see if the version of the document we just published back to the Internal Documents library is the version we changed, then I'll show you something a little odd in the version history.

1. Click the name of the document we just published up to source location.

FIGURE 18.75

Publish to Source Location page

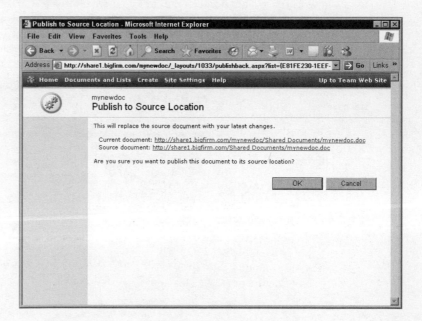

2. It should open in Word 2003 with, in fact, the changes we did make back on the document workspace. You don't really need to change the document at this time, so don't save and simply close out of Word 2003.

3. Back on the Internal Documents library page, let's check the version history of the document we just looked at: move your mouse over the document's name, click the down arrow, and select Version History.

You'll notice that the most recent version of the document is the time and date that you published it to the Internal Documents library. In fact there may be two copies with that date and time, one indicating changes made and the other being the replacement, displayed model.

So, we've tested the whole point of the document-centric, user driven document workspace. Now let's check out the less personal way of building a document workspace.

CREATING A DOCUMENT WORKSPACE FROM THE CREATE PAGE

To create a standard workspace or subsite, you go to the page of all creation, otherwise known as the Create page.

1. Make sure you are on the Team Web Site Home page (so you are at the top of the collection). Click Create on the navigation bar at the top of the page.

2. On the Create page, scroll down to the Web Pages section and click Sites and Workspaces.

The page that opens (see Figure 18.76), New SharePoint Site, requires a title, a web address, and permissions for the new site.

3. I am going to title the site New Document Workspace with the brief description "A test workspace," but don't let me curb your creativity—call it whatever you'd like. Just remember that in this chapter I will refer to it by the unimaginative name New Document Workspace. For the web address, I am going to use newdoc, and I am going to have this workspace inherit permissions from the parent site (notice that, at least here, you get a choice).

FIGURE 18.76
New SharePoint
Site page

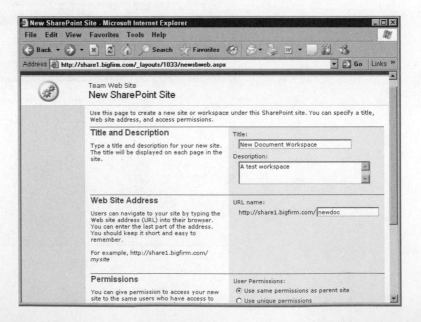

TIP   There is an interesting note in the Permissions section of the New SharePoint Site page that you should keep in mind. If you give a user the right to create a workspace (the Create Subsite right), they don't need to be administrators or otherwise managers of the parent site. This means that a user can freely create workspaces (and therefore the official creator/owner of the new site) without actually being allowed to administer permissions of the new workspace. How does this happen? If the user selects Use Same Permissions as Parent Site during the creation of the workspace, one set of user permissions is shared by both parent and subsites. Consequently, if they do not have the right to change user permissions on the parent site, they cannot change user permissions on the new site. Their new workspace would need to have unique permissions in order for them to break away from this restriction (and therefore have to manually add all users they want to use their workspace). We, of course, are currently an administrator, with essentially full control permissions (because we are an administrator in Active Directory) so we can do it all. However, it is an indication that rights and permissions in SharePoint might be a little more complicated than one might think.

4. If you are done setting the title, description, web address, and permissions for this new site, click the Create button at the bottom of the page.

   The next page to open in the process of creating a new document workspace is the Template Selection page (see Figure 18.77). This page gives you a box of eight different choices, depending on your intentions for your new workspace. Selecting one in the list might change the graphic and will display a brief description of the template's contents and intentions.

   Team Site   You could actually have intended to make a document workspace, but if you chose this template you would end up with a website laid out and designed exactly like our existing Team Web Site was when we first saw it. Keep this in mind if you'd like to create a team subsite beneath the parent site.

   Blank Site   Just what it says it is, a single blank home page. Expects you to use FrontPage to build it to do what you want it to do.

FIGURE 18.77
Template
Selection page

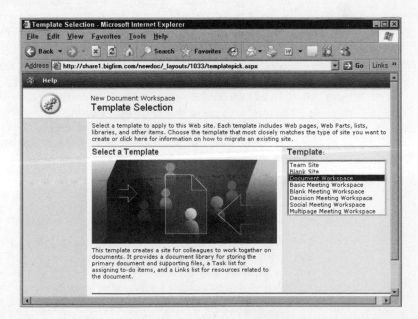

Document Workspace This is what we are going to choose inevitably. We've already seen one. Notice that it there is only one kind of document workspace.

Basic Meeting Workspace Actually built from a fundamentally different site definition than a document workspace, very List View Web Part-centric. Does not have the Site Settings navigation bar link and uses a tabbed interface for additional navigation instead of a Quick Launch bar. Obviously meant to be very limited in use and scope but doesn't actually have to be. The Basic Meeting Workspace just has Objectives, Attendees, Agenda lists, and a document library. Each page is basically a Web Parts page. The tabs bring up a page that holds just one Web Part (but more can be added). There appears to be no way to easily create a subsite beneath a meeting, but it is possible to do so.

Blank Meeting Workspace A meeting page that doesn't have any Web Parts on it. Not really a blank page, it requires FrontPage to design.

Decision Meeting Workspace Has more List View Web Parts (and therefore more lists), including a Decisions list that lets you add decision items.

Social Meeting Workspace Has an additional Image Web Part with a party theme. Has Things to Bring and Directions lists.

Multipage Meeting Workspace Has a home page with List View Web Parts for Objectives, Attendee, and Agenda, and two additional Web Part pages on which you can put other lists, such as a discussion or survey.

5. To see how a document workspace works without a document to associate with looks, select Document Workspace from the list of templates and click OK.

That's it, the New Document Workspace gets generated. As expected, it looks like the other document workspace we made, minus a document automatically added to the Shared Documents document library. If you click the Add new document link in the Shared Documents List View Web Part, it will let you upload an existing document (assuming you have a pre-existing document to base this workspace on). If you click the title of the Shared Documents List View Web Part, it will take you to the New Document's Shared document library, where you can create a New Document if you'd like.

CREATING A MEETING WORKSPACE

To prove a point about how workspaces can get away from you (and get some practice creating a different kind of workspace), let's say that this new document workspace has an important document in it that a lot of people are working on. They've had some problems and need an emergency meeting. Therefore, it's a good idea to create a meeting workspace to work through their issues, rather than argue on the conveniently located General Discussions discussion list on the document workspace. So, we are going to build a meeting workspace from here. A meeting workspace made under a workspace uses the same templates as one built at any level.

1. Click Documents and Lists in the Navigation bar on the top of the New Document Workspace Home page.

2. In the action pane, under See Also, click the link for Meeting Workspaces.

It will take you to a Sites and Workspaces page that looks a lot like the Documents and Sites page, with different views focusing on sites and workspaces as opposed to lists. This Sites and Workspaces page will show all the sites and workspaces that are under this site. Notice the different views available here and the fact that we are simply on the Meeting Workspaces view. If you need to see all of the sites, document, and meeting workspaces, just select the All view. There is also a Create link on the action bar which takes you to the Create page.

Right now there should be nothing here. This workspace doesn't have any sites or workspaces beneath it. Let's create one.

3. Click Create in the action bar.

4. For the title, I am going to use Emergency Meeting.

5. For the Web Address I am going to use the word emergency (you might notice in Figure 18.79 that the web address is going to be `servername/newdoc/emergency`, an obvious sign that this workspace is beneath the document workspace New Document).

FIGURE 18.78
New Meeting Workspace settings

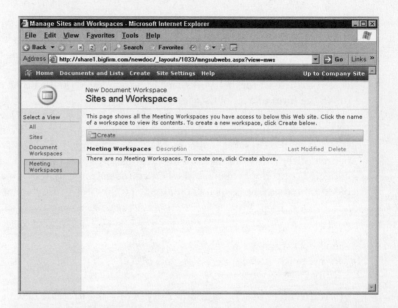

FIGURE 18.79
New Meeting Workspace settings

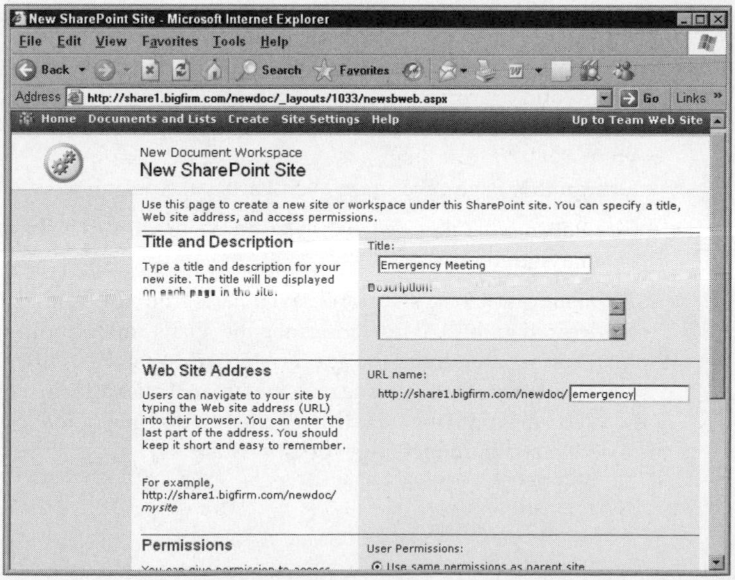

6. I am going to allow this site to inherit its permissions from its parent. Mind you, the parent site of this workspace is *not* directly the Team Web Site. If the parent site (our New Document document workspace) had special permissions, then those are what would be inherited. At this point, I am fine with this workspace using the same permissions as its parent.

7. Click the Create button if all the settings are complete.

8. You should be on the Template Selection page. Choose Decision Meeting Workspace (the more complicated of the Meeting Workspaces).

9. Click OK.

The Emergency Meeting Decision Meeting Workspace should open. Notice in Figure 18.80 that the Navigation bar on the top of the page does not have Documents and Lists, Create, or Site Settings links. They're buried elsewhere. There is a tab named Home to indicate you are on the home page, and there is no Quick Launch bar. The lack of a Quick Launch causes all of the lists that were meant to be used for this workspace to be displayed on the home page somehow, and in this case it's in the form of a lot of list view Web Parts.

Notice that, in the navigation bar, far right, there is a Up to New Document Workspace link to give you a way to navigate up to this workspace's parent site (or in this case, parent workspace).

Beneath the Up to New document workspace link is the Modify This Workspace link. This link bears notice. Tidily hiding all of the administrative and creative tasks of the workspace, it has the expected drop-down menu, but when you select an item, it opens a unique tool pane for each item listed. The drop-down menu contains the following:

Add Web Parts   Does double duty of offering to create new lists based on the template of lists available for a meeting workspace, allows for the creation of custom lists, and also works as a normal Add Web Parts gallery.

Add Pages   Creates another Web Part page for this workspace and gives it a tab of its own to allow users to get to it.

Manage Pages   Lets you change the order that the page tabs are displayed. Doesn't work if you have no additional pages.

Design this Page   Standard Web Parts page design view.

Site Settings   Takes you to the standard site settings management page for this site. It just isn't on a navigation bar.

To take a quick look, select Add Web Parts from the Modify This Workspace drop-down menu. Notice in Figure 18.81 how the tool pane opens and the home page goes into design view. At the top of the tool pane, under the darker blue Add Web Parts title, is the lighter blue bar Create Lists. This indicates that the tool pane is in the Create Lists state. In this state, if you drag one of these List View Web Parts onto the page, it will create a new list of that type. It looks like you are stuck with the existing standard meeting workspace lists.

FIGURE 18.80
Emergency Meeting
Workspace

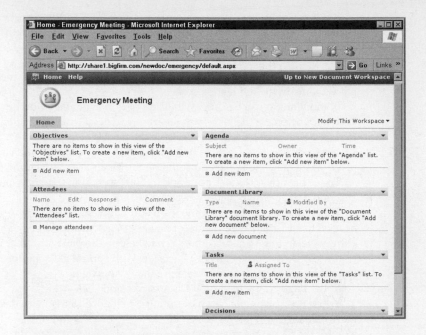

FIGURE 18.81
Add Web Parts
tool pane

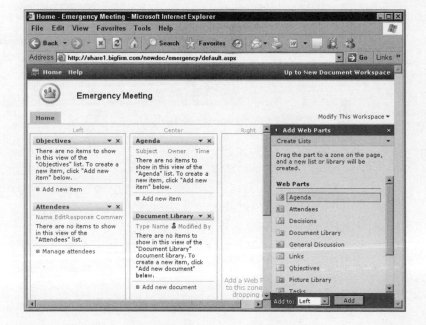

But if you want to create a custom list of your own, scroll to the very bottom of the tool pane and click the unintuitive Show all Lists link. It doesn't show you all existing lists; instead it brings you to this workspace's Create page (see Figure 18.82). Here you can choose to create your own custom lists or lists of any kind.

If you checked out the Create page, go back to the Emergency meeting workspace's home page (click Home in the navigation bar).

If you want to use the Add Web Parts option to actually add new Web Parts, create a custom Web Part, or access the Web Part galleries, you need to toggle the tool pane to its other state. Click the Create Lists bar. Click Browse from the drop-down menu.

Now you should be able to browse the Web Part galleries and choose a Web Part from them to place on the page, just like you could on the Team Web Site Home page.

To see how to add a web page and its corresponding tab, click the Modify This Workspace link, and in the drop-down menu, select Add Pages.

This will change the tool pane to an add pages state (see Figure 18.83). Now the tool pane can be used to add, rearrange, delete, or manage page settings (if there are any) by clicking the Add bar. Otherwise, in the Add state, there is one field in the pane, and that is Page Name.

Since this site does not have a List View Web Part for a discussion, I'd like to create a Discussions (plural in case you want to have more than one) page.

In the Page Name field type Discussions, and click Add.

You'll now be on the Discussions tab (see Figure 18.84), with design view open, and the tool pane ready for you to drag a list into the web zones. Scroll through the tool pane until you see the icon for the General Discussion List View Web Part. Click and drag it to the first web zone on the left and drop it there. Now that's all we want on that tab/page for now.

FIGURE 18.82

Emergency Meeting's Create page

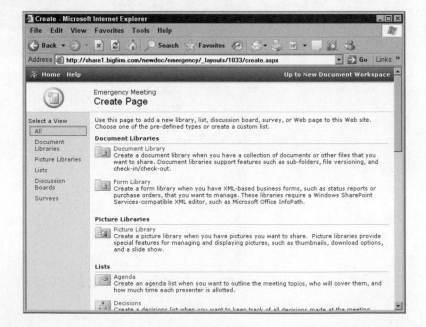

FIGURE 18.83
Add Page tool pane

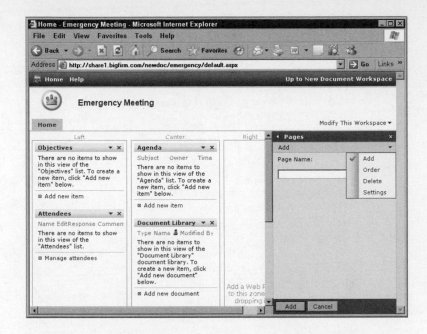

FIGURE 18.84
New Discussions page

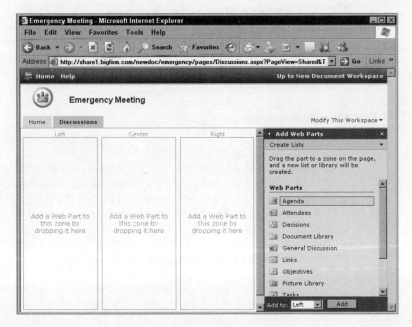

Click the X in the blue Add Web Parts bar in the tool pane. That will take the page out of design view. Notice in Figure 18.85 how the General Discussion List View Web Part has stretched to take up to whole top of the page. Web Parts do that. They will shrink to accommodate each other in each column or across columns. But, lacking competition for space, a Web Part will take up the whole page if it can. So now you know.

FIGURE 18.85
New Discussions Page
with Web Part

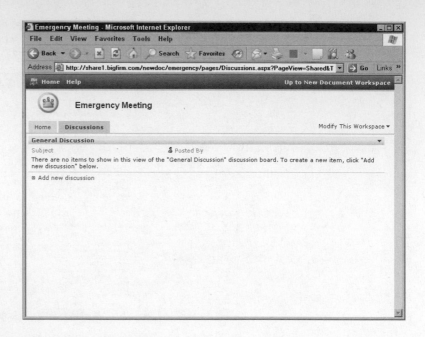

TIP To create a site from a meeting workspace, use the Site Settings link, then click the Manage sites and workspaces link on the Site Settings page. In this case, you can see that you could practically bury workspaces beneath each other infinitely. You might want to refrain from going that far. But it can take some serious planning and discipline not to end up with, instead of the simple, orderly site collection you intended, a huge site collection with nested workspaces several (even many) subsites deep.

Navigating Subsites

There is one more thing I feel is important to cover about workspaces and subsites in general, and that is navigation. Going up from a subsite (or a sub-sub-subsite) is relatively easy. But how do you find a nested subsite or workspace from the top-level site to begin with?

We finished the last set of instructions on the Discussions page of the Emergency Meeting Workspace under the New Document Workspace beneath the Team Web Site (try saying that ten times fast). To get back to the Team Web Site Home page, click the Up to New Document Workspace link in the navigation bar.

That should put you on the New Document Workspace Home page. If you click the Up to Team Web Site link in that page's navigation bar, it will take you to the now familiar Team Web Site Home page.

Notice that there is no further Up to… you can go. You are at the first and topmost site in the site collection. From here, how do you get back to the Emergency Meeting Workspace?

Over in the Quick Launch bar you have the familiar lists, Internal Documents, Contacts, Vendors, but there is no way to add a workspace's link to the Quick Launch bar, so the new workspaces aren't listed here. The Quick Launch bar is for that site's lists only (a little bit of inflexibility there).

So there are basically two ways you can get to a subsite—go to Documents and Lists and navigate down through the subsites that way (our only option at this point), or add a link for the buried site to the Links List View Web Part on the Team Web Site Home page. If you want a lot of users to easily get to your workspace, then Links is a great idea.

In order to show you how a user would navigate to a nested subsite, I am going to try to get back to the Emergency Meeting Workspace.

It will be a bit tedious. But rest assured, by giving the users a direct link to the page (or at least its parent page), it will get easier. I'll show you how to do that, by copying the web address of the New Documents Workspace and using it to make an entry in the Links List View Web Part on the Team Web Site Home page (finally a use for that Web Part):

1. From the Team Web Site Home page, click the Documents and Lists link in the navigation bar.

2. Once on that page, click the Document Workspaces link in the action pane under See Also.

   In the Sites and Workspaces page is the New Document Workspace. Notice that there are two document workspaces listed, New Document Workspace, and the one we made earlier that was spawned off of a document in the Internal Documents library (mine was called mynewdoc and therefore the workspace is named that). I can see both because I am the creator and site owner of both.

3. To see if you can see the Emergency Meeting Workspace from here, click the Meeting Workspaces View in the action pane.

   Nope. You cannot see the Emergency Meeting Workspace from the Team Web Site because it is too far removed (see Figure 18.86). You can only see the subsites and workspaces from a site if they are directly below that site. We are going to have to navigate to the New Document Workspace first, then go from there to the Emergency Meeting Workspace.

FIGURE 18.86
No meeting workspace listed at top-level site

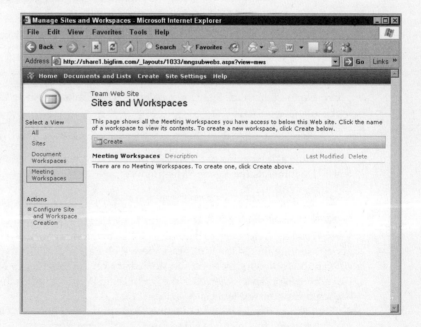

NOTE I hope you are getting an idea of how complicated a site collection can get. If this gets you down, there is hope. From the top-level site, there is a link on the Site Administration page that lets you view the whole site collection hierarchy. Remember though, only administrators are allowed to see the site hierarchy, so from the users' perspective it is still difficult to get around.

4. To get to the Emergency Meeting Workspace's parent site, click the Document Workspaces view in the action pane again.

5. Then click the New Document Workspace item in the Sites and Workspaces list (the parent of the Emergency Meeting workspace).

   Now you should be on the New Document Workspace Home page. Click the Documents and Lists link in the navigation bar.

6. In the New document workspace page, click Meeting Workspaces in the action pane.

7. There's Emergency Meeting. Click it to confirm that it's the right one.

   You should be on the Emergency Meeting Workspace Home page. So that's it. If a user can get to the New Document Workspace site they can get to the Emergency Meeting page for that site. To round this out, I am going to add a link to the Emergency Meeting Workspace to the Links List View Web Part because it is one of the easiest way to point users, from the Team Web Site Home page to a subsite of whatever depth (if the user has permissions to the subsite).

8. Notice the web address of the Emergency Meeting page in the browser address bar. We need to get the address of this page to put in the Lists List View Web Part back on the Team Web Site, so select the whole address and copy it.

9. To get to the Emergency Meeting Workspace's parent site, New Document Workspace, click the Up to New Document Workspace link.

10. Click the Up to Team Web Site link in the navigation bar.

11. On the Team Web Site Home page, find the Links List View Web Part. Click Add a New Link.

12. On the New Item page for the Links list, click in the URL field, remove the text that is already there, and paste the Emergency Meeting Workspace's web address.

13. Type a description of the link (which will be posted as the link itself). I am going to use New Document's Emergency Meeting.

14. Click Save and Close on the action bar.

Now there should be a link that says New Document's Emergency Meeting in the Links List View Web Part (refer back to Figure 18.87). To make sure it works, click the New Document's Emergency Meeting link in the Links List View Web Part.

Yup. It worked for me. You should be back on the Emergency Meeting page. Click Up to New Document Workspace, then click the Up to Team Web Site link in the navigation bar to return to the home page of the top-level site.

That was our quick tour of meeting workspaces and how to deal with sub-subsites. And now you have seen how to create a document workspace from a particular document, how to create a document workspace without a particular document in mind, how to create and modify a meeting workspace, and that workspaces are just like any site, they can be nested under each other.

FIGURE 18.87
No meeting work-space listed at top-level site

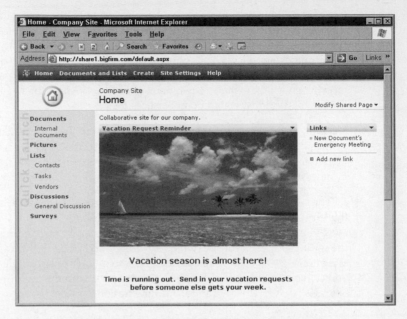

You also now know, even though we didn't go that route, that you could easily just use a team site template instead of a meeting or document workspace template, and create a team site as a subsite. It is an option from a design perspective of using the Team Web Site as the top portal and creating a bunch of subsite team sites for all of your projects or departments or something.

We have explored the default Team Web Site that was created when we installed Windows SharePoint Services. We looked at the Team Web Site Home page. Used the navigation bars. Got acquainted with the Web Parts; used, modified, and created lists and libraries; created some work-spaces, and looked at the default site templates available for SharePoint out of the box.

But at no time did we actually do any administration. You may have noticed this. That is because SharePoint is amazingly versatile in its scope of function, with all the workspaces, lists, libraries, fields, settings (and settings, and settings...), Web Parts, and Office 2003 integration, that administration can get a little complicated. Okay, actually it's not that bad, but it does take some explaining to really understand. So I chose to have you use the product before we began administration. My intent was to teach you what you have so you can better understand how to administer it.

Administration

One of the nice things about SharePoint administration is that, no matter how madly changeable the content can be, depending on user inclination and rights, administration never changes. Administration works in layers. Settings often trickle down from the Virtual Server, to the top site, to the lowliest of workspaces, to the smallest of lists. Partially because administrative access might trickle down as well. There could be a overall administrator of the server, someone who adminis-ters all the site collections in a Virtual Server, someone in charge of one site collection, someone in charge of a subsite or workspace, then there could be managers of lists. All have to be able to have settings they can access at their level, with bigger, general things set further above.

Each list has permissions and settings. Each subsite or workspace has permissions and settings. Each Top-Level Site at the top of a site collection has permissions and settings. Each Virtual Server that contains site collections has settings. And finally, the configuration database's Central Administration page has overall settings for the actual physical server (or servers in the case of server farms) and whatever Virtual Servers that contain SharePoint sites in IIS.

Administration is a bit simplified in our case, because we have only one server. On this server we have one Virtual Server (the Default Web Site in IIS that was used by Windows SharePoint Services when it first installed), and one top-level web site, which is the Team Web Site also created during the Windows SharePoint Services install.

NOTE There was a second Virtual Server created during the Windows SharePoint Services install, but it is dedicated to the Central Administration web site is associated with the configuration database and configuring the server, server farm, and Virtual Servers. You cannot use it (or at least you shouldn't) for anything else.

The settings we need to be concerned with are ones that impact the SharePoint server overall, the Virtual Server that holds our Team Web Site, and the Team Web Site itself because it is a top-level Site (Parent sites can affect the permissions and other settings of children sites). In addition, the settings for each subsite (which includes workspaces in this case) and each list on the top-level Site and all subsites (not that we are going to modify every single list's settings, but you could if you'd like). To get started, we are going to work from the top down, beginning with managing SharePoint overall with Central Administration.

Central Administration

In order to manage the configuration of the SharePoint server, you need to use the Central Administration page. It is at the same address as the Team Web Site, just on a different port. You may remember me mentioning that it chooses a random port number between 1023 and 32767. As you also may recall, my SharePoint Central Administration Virtual Server is on port 8552 (see Figure 18.88).

If you are on the server where Windows SharePoint Services is installed, you can go to the Central Administration site by opening Manage Your Server and clicking the Manage SharePoint Services link or simply going to Start ➤ Administrative Tools ➤ SharePoint Central Administration. Or you can just open Internet Explorer and use the web address `http://localhost:8552` (or whatever the port is for your Central Administration Virtual Server is on).

FIGURE 18.88

Central Administration's Virtual Server's port setting

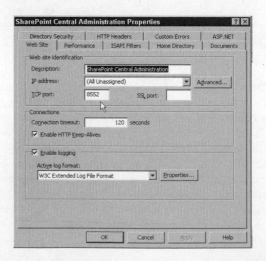

If you are not on the server, you can still access the site by IE, specifying the servername and port number; in my case that's `http://share1.bigfirm.com:8552` (which you may see in the title bar of the Central Administration in a few screen shots).

However you want to do it, open the Central Administration web page in Internet Explorer.

The page obviously has a different theme (as you can tell if you compare it to Figure 18.89) than the Team Web Site, with the navigation bar empty except for a wrench and hammer icon. Below that is the administration medallion (two cogs in blue—I'm telling you, SharePoint is sticking with that little medallion icon to the bitter end) and page title. This theme is consistent throughout the Central, Virtual Server, and Site Administration and Settings pages.

The Central Administration page is laid out in general sections. Each link in the list takes you to a page where you can apply settings. Many of the settings for Central Administration are configuration defaults for convenience later when you create new Virtual Servers or top-level websites. The nice thing about all of the settings is there is always a brief explanation as to what each is and does, sometimes with useful warnings and details. There are also links in several of the sections that take you to yet another administration page. There is a pattern to it though, as you'll discover. In addition, there are settings here that are not relevant to what we are doing, because they involve creating or managing additional servers, databases, extending Virtual Servers, and creating additional top-level sites. Because we are keeping it simple and sticking with what we have (so you can see the power of a simple, typical installation alone). However, I will be explaining each one of these settings. And, if you are interested in any of the more advanced, high traffic, large environment settings, by all means, check out the help files and the Windows SharePoint Services 2.0 Administrator's Guide. This chapter is to get you started, but once you see the value of Windows SharePoint Services, I expect you to want to go further.

The following sections cover the Central Administration pages and their contents.

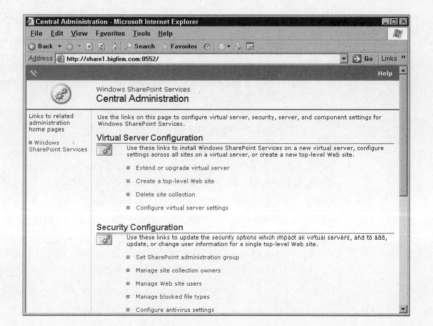

VIRTUAL SERVER CONFIGURATION

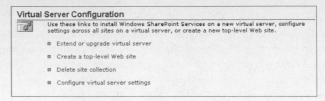

This page is meant to manage Virtual Server things like installing Windows SharePoint Services on a new Virtual Server you've created in IIS, create new top-level sites (like the Team Web Site), or even delete site collections (a very powerful setting for a disgruntled administrator and a good reason for keeping backups). There is also the link for configuring Virtual Server settings. An innocent looking link, it actually takes you to a page listing all Virtual Servers that belong to SharePoint. It's the only way to configure the rather powerful settings that control the site collections a Virtual Server contains.

Extend or upgrade virtual server At this point we have one Virtual Server with one top-level website. We could, based on our collaborative needs, create more top-level sites in the same virtual server. However, there are three reasons I can think of to have more than one Virtual Server host your SharePoint sites (there may be more):

◆ A lot of settings that affect a site collection are done at the Virtual Server level. If you have sites that you need to have dissimilar settings, you may want to put them in their own virtual server.

◆ If your websites get so much traffic that you need to create new Virtual Servers, offload some of the sites onto a different port or IP address.

◆ You can make anonymous access available as an authentication method at the Virtual Server (in IIS), allowing the top-level site, lists, libraries, and workspaces to choose to be accessed anonymously. If you have sites (or site administrators) that cannot possibly be allowed to have that as an option, you might want to place them on their own Virtual Server and ensure that Anonymous access is disabled. Then otherwise, on other Virtual Servers, allow anonymous access so administrators could choose to allow anonymous access per site or list.

Create a top-level Website This setting allows you to choose a Virtual Server in which to create another top-level site. This is basically a convenience, because you can also go directly to the settings of a particular Virtual Server and create a top-level site there.

Delete site collection Deceptively easy to use. Just give it a URL of the top-level site, and it will be deleted along with all of its subsites.

Configure Virtual Server settings The last item in this section (which is often the case with links that go deeper to another administration page), this link takes you to a Virtual Servers List page where you can pick the Virtual Server you want to configure (we have only one).

We will get back to this configuration page setting when we've finished the others on this page.

SECURITY CONFIGURATION

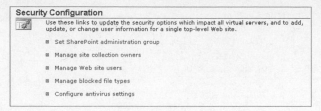

This section contains links to update the security options for all Virtual Servers and to add, update, or change user information for a single top-level website.

Set SharePoint administration group   At this point the local administrators (and those at the domain level) are SharePoint administrators by default. This setting was meant to be used with a group you create in Active Directory especially for administering SharePoint (and actually expects the syntax Domain\Group). If you want to add a group to control SharePoint that are not actually administrators otherwise, then this is where to do it. Be very careful, as they will have godlike control over SharePoint from here.

Manage site collection owners   Site collections start at a top-level site and contain all subsites and their contents. By default, the site collection owner is the person who created the site. But if you have created a site for someone else (maybe that is the SharePoint policy for your business) and need to transfer ownership of it now that it is up and functional, this is where you do it. You specify the URL of the top of the site, specify the account name of the owner (domain\ username or on a stand-alone server servername\username), and even a backup owner if the first one is unavailable.

A site collection owner is someone who has site collection administrator privileges and is the one who receives the emails from the SharePoint server about quotas and auto-deletion (we'll get to those).

Manage Website users   Another way to access adding or changing users on a particular site, this simply offers a different way to manage users for the busy administrator who happens to be on the Central Administration page when asked to quickly add another user to a site. You specify the URL for the site (or subsite even, they are all listed in the configuration database), add the user account name, the display name for the user, their email address , and their permissions. Permissions are based on something called Site Groups. We haven't gone there yet, but they are permission sets based on roles. The defaults are Reader, Contributor, Web Designer, and Administrator (more on this later). You can also, instead of adding a user, change a user's information or delete him from the site (listed in the URL at the top of the page).

Manage blocked file types   If a file type is blocked, a user cannot use that type of file as an attachment for an item in a list or upload it to a library. There is a large group of standard dangerous file types here already. Displayed in a simple text box, this is the way to see what file types are blocked, add a new file type to block, or delete a file type you want to allow.

Configure antivirus settings   Requires a third-party, SharePoint-aware antivirus program. From here you can manage how files are scanned.

SERVER CONFIGURATION

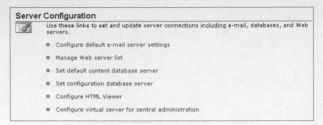

This section is a bit of a catch-all for server tasks.

You can administer different web servers in your farm by choosing them from a list, as well as configure the default email used by all Virtual Servers (if you want them all to use the same email address; otherwise specify it per virtual server), set the default content database for all Virtual Servers being managed by this Central Administrations configuration database, set up the configuration database for SharePoint, and specify the application pool for the Virtual Server running Central Administration. Several of the settings here are what you manually configure if you are installing SharePoint as part of a server farm.

Configure default email server settings A trickle-down setting that lets you set up email for all of your Virtual Servers (and any site collections they may contain) in one shot. It requires an email server that can relay outbound mail, a From and Reply email address, and the character code (I use the default). SharePoint uses email to send out alerts, invitations, access requests, and warnings.

Manage Web server list Central Administration administers the server it's actually installed on by default, but if you want to administer a different physical server, its Virtual Servers, and site collections, this is the link to click. Displays a list of servers that have Windows SharePoint Services installed on them in the server farm. If you select a server from the list, it takes you to the Central Administration page for that server.

Set default content database server Allows you to define a default, single content database for any additional Virtual Servers you create to connect to. There are pros and cons to having a single database used by all Virtual Servers in SharePoint. This is also a nice confirmation that the database we saw at the beginning of the chapter is the one SharePoint thinks we're using.

Set configuration database server When you install Windows SharePoint Services with the Server Farm setting chosen instead of Typical, you will have to set your configuration database. This is supposed to give you the option of what version of SQL server to use, the database name, and database authentication type.

Configure HTML Viewer The HTML Viewer allows for on–the-fly conversion so users who need to view spreadsheets, documents, or PowerPoint presentations can. This is where you set up your HTML Viewer. Requires that you download and install the viewer software (currently `htmlview.exe`) onto a computer that can be dedicated to the task of transforming documents into HTML views for SharePoint clients.

Configure Virtual Server for central administration This is where you specify the application pool and its security account that the Central Administration Virtual Server uses to connect to the configuration database. Another required setting for a server farm install.

COMPONENT CONFIGURATION

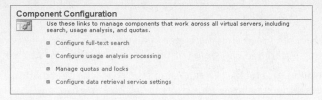

Component Configuration

Use these links to manage components that work across all virtual servers, including search, usage analysis, and quotas.

☐ Configure full-text search

☐ Configure usage analysis processing

☐ Manage quotas and locks

☐ Configure data retrieval service settings

This section has links to manage searches, usage reports, and quotas.

Configure full-text search   This is where you set up your SharePoint server to use SQL to do full text searches. Unfortunately, SharePoint is well aware that the content database is in WMSDE and therefore will not even allow any settings to be displayed until we get SQL. Very, very useful feature and almost worth the price of SQL.

Configure usage analysis processing   I really rather love this setting. It gives me usage information in terms of number of hits per page and unique users, browser and OS used to access the sites, and referring domains or URLs. Great to see how your server is doing and if it is being overwhelmed. Lets you know what pages are most popular, and therefore which aren't. I am going to stop a moment and really delve into the settings of this one.

Usage analysis is not enabled by default for a reason, it is resource heavy because it is storing logs and then analyzing them.

There are only really two sections:

Logging Settings   Where you enable logging and specify the log location and how many logs will be created in a 24-hour period of time.

Processing Settings   When the logs will be processed. It does take server resources to process Usage data. Schedule processing at the least busy time of the day.

The log files are stored by default in the %windir%\system32\LogFiles\STS folder. Each Virtual Server gets its own log folder, with folders in it for each day. If you choose to move the log to a different location (maybe a separate drive from the operating system of the server, for example), you need to give the user group STS_WPG (that SharePoint creates on install) the same permissions on the directory where the logs will go as there are on the default STS folder.

It takes about 200 bytes to record a hit on a web page (give or take). So if you are having a million hits a day, your log could be 200MB for a day.

Usage Analysis does not delete logs when it is done using them; you will need to manage deleting older ones (Usage Analysis statistics stay in the content database for about 31 days for daily info, 31 months for monthly statistics).

Processing the logs for data to be displayed in the usage analysis list is memory intensive, because a whole log is loaded into RAM at one time. So if the log is 400MB for that day, then 400MB of RAM could be taken up processing that Usage log. Which is why you can specify the number of logs to use in a day. The default is one, which means it holds all the usage information for a 24-hour period and could be pretty large on a busy SharePoint server. To break the usage information down into less bulky reports, you can increase the number of logs used in a day. For example, if you set it to four logs, then in a 24-hour period you'll get four smaller, six-hour reports. If you don't get that many hits to your site, then one log should be fine. You know where they will be so you can keep an eye on it. If it gets too big, you know what to do.

Also, because processing the Usage analysis logs is RAM intensive, you might want to schedule a start and end time within which to do it that is not a busy time for your server.

Manage quotas and locks Usage Analysis also tracks information about disk space which is useful in tracking how large your content database is growing. That is why this is another setting that bears closer review.

Not surprisingly, one of the weak points of SharePoint is it can store a lot of data in one content database for all of the sites connected to it. It can grow to be huge if not managed properly. To that end you can create individual quotas on top-level sites (and thus their site collection) or create quota templates at the Central Administration level and apply them to top-level sites (a good idea if you have several top-level sites and had a standard quota per purpose or something).

There are two ways you can apply quotas to site collections; by either applying quotas to each individual collection, or by creating a quota template, a sort of persistent set of settings, that can be used to be applied again and again to site collections. The Manage quotas and locks link gives you the option to either Manage (which also includes create) Quota Templates or Manage site collection Quotas and Locks directly. Quotas are applied to the top-level site and restrict the combined storage size of that site and all sites below it in the collection.

Quota Templates contains two sections (see Figure 18.90):

Template Name Where you can choose a pre-existing template that you'd like to change (maybe you created it and applied it and found it lacking), or you can create a new template. New templates can actually be based on previously created templates. But, if you have none to start, there is a blank default template to work with. You also, of course, name your new template here.

Storage Limit Values There are two values in this section, Limit Site Storage to a Maximum Of, which is the absolute largest this quota will go in megabytes. It will lock the site collection at that point until you unlock it. The other value is Send Warning Email When Site Storage Reaches, which will trigger an email sent from SharePoint to the site owner concerning the quota.

Of course, if you are going to create a mechanism that locks site collections, then there has to be a mechanism for unlocking it as well.

Manage Site Collection Quotas and Locks starts out with one section requiring the servername of the top-level website collection you want to manage. Once you enter that correctly, then click the button View Data. The page then contains considerably more settings (see Figure 18.91 for an idea of what I am talking about. Remember that you would need to scroll down to see all the settings).

Top-Level Web Site The section where you entered the server name and address of the top-level website you want to manage.

Site Lock Information The section where you can actually see the lock state of your top-level site. It is here that you would set whether it is completely locked to all access, allows viewing but no contribution, or is not locked at all.

Site Quota Information Where you can set the current quota, either individually for this site collection or by a quota template you made earlier. You can set the maximum storage in megabytes, and if a warning email is sent and at what storage total should trigger it. It also displays the current storage amount for that site collection.

WARNING   Just keep in mind that you can use Manage Site Quotas and locks to forcibly lock a site if you need to. Locking denies all access. And you can unlock a site here if needed.

   Configure data retrieval service settings   The last setting on the Central Administration page is either enabled or disabled. Enabled by default, this setting refers to a short set of data retrieval services, with sections for limiting response time, update support, and data source timeout.

FIGURE 18.90

Manage Quota
Templates

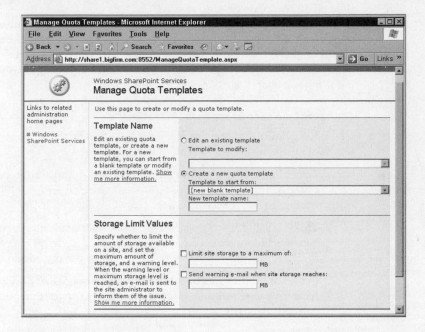

FIGURE 18.91

Manage Site Collec-
tion Quotas and Locks

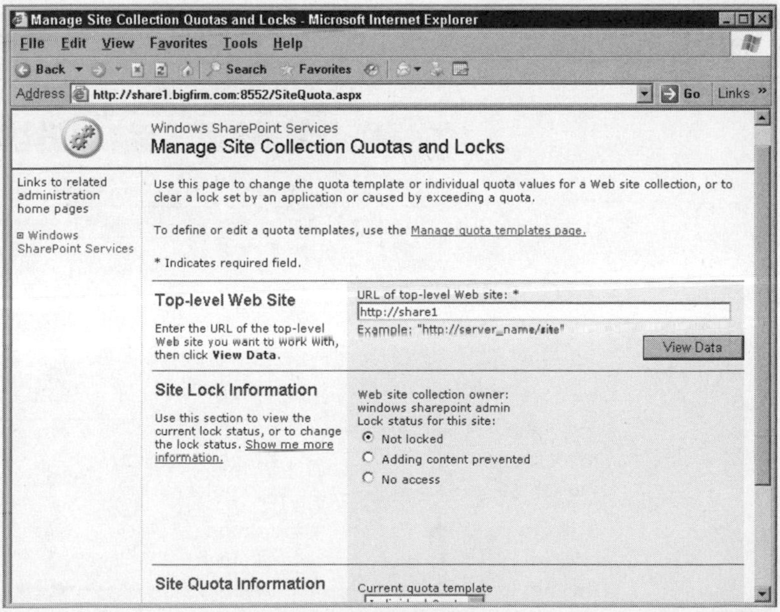

CONFIGURING SETTINGS AT THE CENTRAL ADMINISTRATION LEVEL

That's our brief overview of the main Central Administration page and its goodies. Before we head over to configure Virtual Server settings, let's configure some settings for our SharePoint server here. Although we only have one virtual server, I am going to make it easy on myself (should I have to quickly create more) by specifying the default email set up here at the Central Administration level to get it done. That means, if I create any other Virtual Servers they will automatically have their email set up, no fuss, no muss.

I would also like to set up usage analysis processing and create and apply a quota template on our Team Web Site and subsites (altogether making one site collection). We won't get instant results on them (it takes about a day to generate usage logs and it's unlikely that I will max out the quota on my Team Site right now), but they would be settings I would use if I were quickly installing Windows SharePoint Services to get it up and running.

Configure Email Server Settings

First up, configuring the SharePoint's default email settings. Remember that because email is set up, I can finally do alerts and send other notifications.

1. To configure email settings on the Central Administration page, go to the Server Configuration section, and click Configure default email server settings. That will bring us to the Configure Email Server Settings page (see Figure 18.92).

   This email address is the one that will be that sends alerts, warnings, and so on to users on behalf of SharePoint. You will probably want to create an email account or two specifically for SharePoint administration. I am going to use my administrative email at this point.

2. In the Mail Settings section, type in the Outbound SMTP server address (I am assuming you have Exchange running or some other email service that allows outbound mail) for your network.

3. In the From and Reply fields, enter the appropriate email addresses.

FIGURE 18.92
Configure Mail
Settings

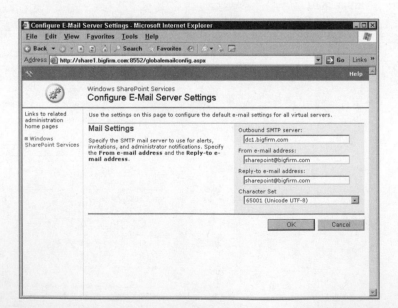

4. Choose your character set; UTF-8 is fine for me.

5. If all of your settings are complete, click OK.

Configuring Usage Analysis Processing

Back on Central Administration, the next setting I'd like to walk through is configuring Usage Analysis Processing. So scroll down to the Component Configuration and click the Configure Usage Analysis Processing link.

1. In the Logging Settings section, enable Logging by checking the check box.

2. You can leave the logs in the current location under the system32 folder if you'd like, at least for now (see Figure 18.93).

3. I am going to set the number of logs to two. That means that every 12 hours a new log will be created.

4. In the Processing Settings section, check the Enable usage analysis processing box. I am going to set the processing run time to start at 1:00 a.m. and end at 3:00 a.m. daily. That should be a relatively inactive time in most businesses.

5. If your settings for configuring usage analysis processing are complete, click OK.

WARNING   It takes 24 hours to generate the usage analysis, which is understandable, so don't expect immediate results.

I only have one top-level site on this server, and therefore one site collection, so I don't really need to create a quota template per se (since templates were meant to be used over and over). However, they are very handy if you grow to have more site collections, so I would like to walk you through it, because templates are convenient for reuse and it's always a good idea to get a warning before a site collection gets too large and have a means to stop it from growing past a certain boundary.

FIGURE 18.93

Configure Usage Analysis Processing

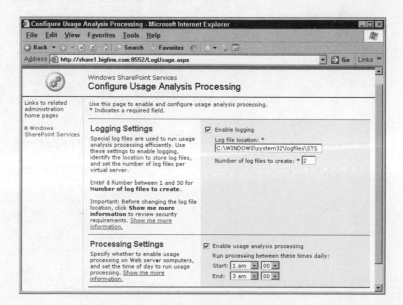

Managing Quotas Templates

Because we are going to build a template first, applying a quota to our site collection is going to be a two-step process. First you'll create the template, then you'll go to Manage Quotas and Locks and apply it.

1. To create and manage our site collection quotas and their templates, click Manage Quotas and Locks in the Component Configuration section.

2. There will be two links to two different settings pages on the Manage Quotas and Locks page, Manage Quota Templates and Manage site collection quotas and locks. Click Manage Quota Templates.

3. In the Manage Quota Templates page shown in Figure 18.94, in the Template Name section, you'll see two radio buttons. The first is Edit an Existing Template, which won't work for us, because we don't have any. So make certain that the Create a New Quota Template radio button is selected.

4. In the Template to start from field, the [new blank template] is the default and the only option. In the New template name field, type in a good site collection quota template name. I decided to call mine Standard Quota.

5. In the Storage Limit section, check the check box in front of Limit Site Storage to a Maximum of and set that maximum to 700. If I have a 10GB drive to dedicate to the content database, and I am supposed to have no more than 10 active top-level sites on one server using WMSDE, then I can safely use 700MB per site before maxing out. Also note that my site collection is currently using 2MB of storage space. Smokin.'

FIGURE 18.94

Creating Quota Template

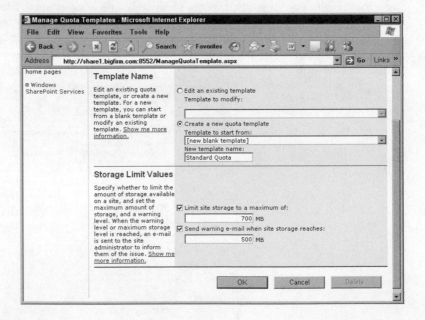

6. Check the check box in front of Send Warning Email When Site Storage Reaches and set that value to 500.

NOTE You cannot set Send Warning Email When Site Storage Reaches without also having Limit Site Storage to a Maximum Of configured as well. In other words, you cannot just be warned about reaching a certain storage level without also having a limit that will lock the site collection to any other additions.

7. When you've finished configuring your site collection quotas, click OK.

This is one of the few configuration pages that does not go back to the previous page when closed. That's because you might want to create more quota templates before leaving this page. You will need to click the Windows SharePoint Services link on the left side, top, of the page when you are done to go back to Central Administration.

Now that we've created a quota template, we need to apply it to a site collection.

1. Go back to Manage Quotas and Locks in the Component Configuration section of the Central Administration page.

2. On the Manage Quotas and Locks page, click the Manage the Site Collection Quotas and Locks link.

3. In the Manage Site Collection Quotas and Locks page, there'll be only one section containing only one field. In the Top-level Web Site section, enter **http://***servername* for your SharePoint server (we don't have any other sites but the default, so that's as long as the address gets, mine is Http://share1) in the URL of top-level Website field.

4. Click the View Data button. As expected, the page generated two new sections now that it knows what site collection we want to manage.

In the Site Lock Information section, notice that our site is Not locked. This is where you would go to lock a site (if you wanted to) or unlock a site if necessary. Notice that locking comes in two flavors, Adding Content Prevented (allows access but no new data) and No Access (access completely denied, and no new data).

5. Now down to the last section, Site Quota Information, to apply our quota template to our site collection. In the Current quota template it says, by default Individual Quota. That makes it possible to apply quota settings on an individual basis here. But we want to apply our template, so click the field and select the quota template we made (mine is Standard Quota).

6. That will cause the page to refresh, so you may have to scroll down to the bottom of the page to get back to the Site Quota Information section. Please do so in order to see that the settings of the quota template we applied are now displayed. Also note that current storage use is pretty tiny (as you can see in Figure 18.95).

Now that we have finished messing with the settings at the Central Administration level, let's look at the next level of administration down, the Virtual Server settings.

FIGURE 18.95

Applying quota to site collection

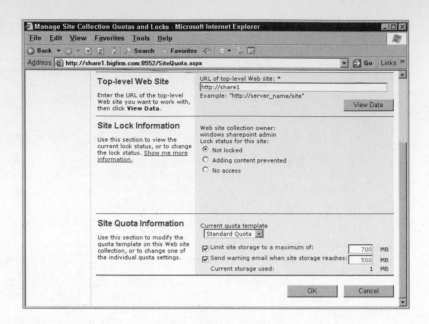

Virtual Server Settings

Virtual servers are what contain top-level sites and their collections. You can have as many site collections as you'd like in a virtual server, but they cannot exist outside of a virtual server. Because of that, there are a lot of general settings under Virtual Server Settings that are meant to affect all of the top-level sites and subsites in the Virtual Server at one time. You also will find that there are some settings that could have been configured from Central Administration. Just as we did with Central Administration, I am going to list and describe everything (some things will need a deeper looking into, some are far beyond what we are going to be doing). And then I will be configuring a few settings after the list after I am done explaining.

To get to the Virtual Server Settings from the Central Administration page, click the Configure Virtual Server Settings in the Virtual Server Configuration section.

This will bring you to the Virtual Server List page. It lists all the Virtual Servers on this server. From here you choose the Virtual Server you would like to administer.

We only have one Virtual Server, called Default Web Site. (Remember when we checked IIS after the install? Well, the solid proof is here that what SharePoint calls a virtual server, IIS calls a Web Site.)

To manage our only virtual server, click the link for Default Web Site in the Virtual Server List page.

This will take you to the Virtual Server Settings page (Figure 18.96).

There are five sections of settings here, so let's take a moment to go over them before making any changes.

FIGURE 18.96
Virtual Server
Settings page

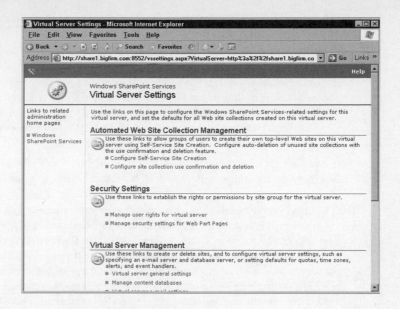

AUTOMATED WEBSITE COLLECTION MANAGEMENT

This is a potentially scary section that can blur the line between a workspace and a top-level site. SharePoint, in an attempt to please everyone, allows administrators to give the right to create top-level sites to groups of users. This right, which is enabled on a Virtual Server basis, is called Self-Service Site Creation.

Also in this section, as if to balance good with evil, is the Configure site collection use confirmation and deletion setting. This is the setting to manage those top-level sites and all their subsites, complete with emails requiring confirmation that the site is still active, to actual auto-deletion of inactive sites.

Configure Self-Service Site Creation

This setting has two sections and a lot of things to think about. To start, it makes certain you know what Virtual Server you are on because this setting can have a profound effect on the contents of a virtual server. The second section is deceptively small and easy to set (as you can see in Figure 18.97). It has two settings:

Self-Service Site Creation   An innocent set of radio buttons, this setting is either on or off. If it is on then a few things happen.

By default all site groups (such as Reader, Contributor, and Web Designer, but not guest) get the right to create a top-level site. You need to remove that right from the groups who shouldn't have it as soon as you can. Otherwise, everyone's got it. You'll be messing with permissions soon, and you'll see that all default site groups have the Self-Service Site Creation right by default. Just for your convenience.

When Self-Service Site Creation is enabled, an Announcement item is created with a blank Expires field so it will remain in the Announcements List View Web Part indefinitely. This item announces that Self-Service Site Creation has been enabled and offers a link to a form for users to sign up and create their own site.

Because the top-level sites the users will be creating are going to be in the Virtual Server selected above, all existing quotas and other global settings you created at the Central Administration level, as well as all Virtual Server settings created to affect top-level sites, will be applied. Now you know why those settings are there. Not all top-level site owner/creators will be qualified administrators. Sigh.

If users are given the right to create a top-level site, they can create as many as they want. Nowhere on this page is there a limit. It's either on or off, your choice.

NOTE   If a user creates their own top-level site (otherwise known as a site collection since it controls the subsites below it), the web address or path to their site will be, by default, *http://servername/sites/theirsitename*. That is because, when you first install Windows SharePoint Services there are two URL managed paths, or default paths, that you can put SharePoint managed sites in: the root (which is where our Team Web Site is) and one called sites. If you are feeling generous, there is a setting coming up with which you can create more managed paths so that your users can, during signup, use something other than sites to indicate where their new top-level site is.

Require secondary contact   This setting basically requires a second person to sign up to be responsible for the site should the primary contact be on vacation or neglecting their duties. If this check box is checked, then during signup, the user will be prompted to enter a second contact for the site. Then if the site owner gets any email concerning the fact that they are over quota or that the site is going to be deleted, the second contact will get those emails as well.

FIGURE 18.97
Configure Self-Service
Site Creation

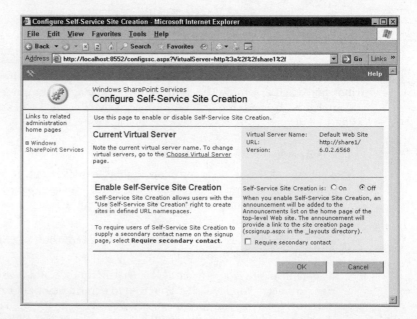

Configure site collection use confirmation and deletion

This has two settings as well (see Figure 18.98). The first confirms the Virtual Server you are going to apply this setting to. The second section, Confirmation and Automatic Deletion Settings, has the following settings:

Send email notifications to owners of unused site collections This setting is absolutely required before you can configure automatic deletion of site collections. Although you can just simply send automated emails asking for confirmation about site activities, you cannot set automatic deletion of a site collection without setting the notification emails. SharePoint just won't let you automate deletion without warning.

The email that is sent to the site owner has links that they select to confirm that the site is still active or is inactive.

If the setting to automatically delete site collections is not on and the user clicks the link to indicate that the site is inactive, they will be given information as to how to delete their site themselves (great training for those clever users).

Once the check box next to this setting is checked, the other options stop being grayed out.

WARNING At no time does SharePoint actually check to see if the site is unused. It considers "unconfirmed" to be unused. So if you or your users think they can ignore a notice because their site is obviously being used, think again. If they get a notice, they need to respond.

Start sending notifications This total can be no less than 30 days and no more than a year. This is how long after site creation that SharePoint waits to start sending notices to the site owners confirming whether or not the site is active.

Check for unused site collections, and send notices Schedule how often sites are checked for activity and at what time of day (because this can take up some processor resources).

FIGURE 18.98
Use Confirmation
and Auto-Deletion
settings

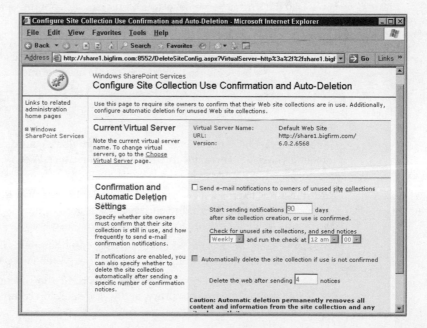

Automatically delete the site collection if use is not confirmed This check box makes it possible to set the number of confirmation notices the Virtual Server sends without user response before the site is deemed inactive and simply auto-deleted.

Delete the web after sending *X* notices Sets the number of email notifications that are ignored by the site owner before their site collection gets deleted.

This is why it is a good idea to insure that all self-created sites have a secondary contact. If the site owner is out due to an injury or on vacation, their secondary contact (who receives these emails as well) can respond and give the site collection a reprieve until the next wave of notifications.

SECURITY SETTINGS

There are two somewhat mismatched settings in this section. Manage user rights begins us down the path of permissions in SharePoint. Manage security settings for Web Parts pages specifies whether users will be able to create connections between Web Parts and whether they can use online gallery Web Parts.

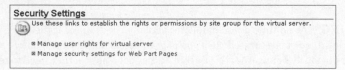

Manage user rights for virtual server

This is a biggy. Rights are basically the tasks that can be performed on something, and it is here that you get to see all the rights that can be given to (or taken away from) all users of any of the site collections in this virtual server. If a right is checked, it is enabled. If it is unchecked, then it is disabled, which means that that right will not be available for use in any of the site collections on this virtual server. It is at the Virtual Server level (per virtual server), not the Central Administration level, that these rights are set.

List Rights are as follows:

Manage List Permissions This right allows the user to manage permissions on the Configuration page of a list. Can grant, deny, or change user permissions.

Manage Lists This lets the user do approvals and rejections on content in lists, as well as add or remove columns in a list and add or remove public views of a list—the list manager's typical tasks.

Cancel Check-Out The manager of a document library needs this right. It lets them cancel someone's check-out on a document so others can use it. When Check-Out is canceled, it checks in a document without saving the current changes.

Add Items Standard list contributor's right. It allows a user to add items to lists, add documents to document libraries, and add web discussion comments (if enabled on the site, and if the documents in the library are formatted to do web discussions—lots of ifs).

Edit Items Allows users to edit items in lists, edit documents in document libraries, edit web discussion comments in documents, and customize Web Part pages in document libraries.

Delete Items Delete is always a concern. This right allows a user to delete items from a list, documents from a document library, and web discussion comments in documents.

View Items   Standard Reader right. It lets a user view items in lists, documents in document libraries, and Web discussion comments and set up email alerts for lists. Notice that someone who is otherwise only a viewer can create an alert with this right and nothing else.

Site Rights are as follows:

Manage Site Groups   Site Groups are basically a set of rights that you put together and name as a set. They are normally named after a role that those tasks would be appropriate for. Then, when you add users, you apply that particular Site Group to them, and they will have the rights of that set. Site Groups are obviously made at the site level, but what rights they can possibly use are set here. If a right is not selected here, it doesn't show up to use in a Site Group on the site.

View Usage Data   Allows the user to view reports on website usage. If a user does not have this right, they can't get to the usage analysis data.

Create Subsites   Ah ha. The long-awaited right that decides who gets to create a subsite or workspace. If you don't give this to the users, no matter how tempting it is to try, they cannot create subsites such as team sites, meeting workspace sites, and document workspace sites. You can give this right to a user without the Manage Website right. Then the user could create subsites but would not be allowed to manage them. It's funny to watch their faces when you do that.

Manage Website   Allows the user to perform all administration tasks for the website as well as manage content and permissions.

Add and Customize Pages   This right refers to a user who is adding, changing, or deleting HTML or Web Part pages on the site, not in a document library. Is the right that lets you Modify Shared Page; otherwise your Web Part page view always defaults to your personal view. Also allows the user to edit the website using a Windows SharePoint Services–compatible editor (FrontPage 2003). Potentially dangerous because the user can actually edit pages one by one, even if they are not allowed to change themes, borders, or style sheets.

Apply Themes and Borders   This right allows a user to change the theme of a site. Is a nice right to have if you have a new workspace and would like to personalize it a little (luckily, site owners are site administrators and have all rights to the site by default). Also useful if you are doing real web design work on a site and want to change themes and border used throughout a site. Potentially dangerous (or at least humorous) in the wrong hands.

Apply Style Sheets   Standard web designer's right. Lets a user apply a style sheet (CSS file) to the Web Site. Dangerous setting as well.

Browse Directories   Useful for web designers and administrators. Browse directories in a website.

View Pages   Everyone who is going to use the site needs to be able to view pages in the website. This right, plus View Items, are the basis of a Reader Site Group.

Personal Rights are as follows:

Manage Personal Views   Allows the users to create personal views in lists.

Add/Remove Private Web Parts   Lets a user add or remove private Web Parts on a Web Part page. Basically allows a user the ability to add Web Parts of their own to their personal view. Any Web Part they create (like a vacation request Content Editor Web Part) or import while in personal view is a private Web Part and not available for anyone else. Depends on the Update Personal Web Parts right.

Update Personal Web Parts   Lets users edit their Web Parts to display personalized information. Without the preceding right, the user will be able to use whatever Web Parts are available already on the page. They cannot create, import, or configure new ones.

Create Cross-site Groups   A Cross-site Group has nothing to do with the Site Group defined above. A Cross-site Group is just a group of users that may or may not already be members of a site. You can create as many different Cross-site Groups as you'd like. Cross-site Groups were intended to work like a normal user group, brigning together user accounts that you can add to sites in one go, applying permissions to them altogether.

Manage security settings for Web Part Pages

Lets you set two controls on Web Parts:

Web Part Connections   Specifies whether users will be given the option of connecting Web Parts on a Web Parts page.

Online Web Part Gallery   Specifies whether users will get access to the Online Web Part Gallery.

VIRTUAL SERVER MANAGEMENT

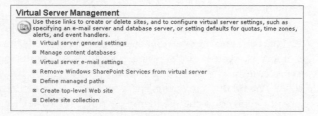

This section manages the Virtual Server itself, letting you manage its content databases (if there is more than one), create top-level sites, and more.

Virtual server general settings

These are useful, general settings that apply to the Virtual Server's site collections overall. It's a good idea to know what the settings are on this page because they can have quite an effect over the look and feel of the site and the user's experience:

Default Time Zone   Sets the time zone for all of the site collections in the virtual server.

Default Quota Template   Since we created a default quota template at the Central Administration page, it would be available in the drop-down box in this section. If you set it here, that quota will be applied to all site collections created in this virtual server. Pretty slick, huh? Also in this section is the actual storage limit and number of invited users. Inviting users is only possible if you are using Active Directory Account Creation Mode, so it doesn't apply to us.

Person Name Smart Tag and Presence Settings   Nifty, easy little setting that lets a user know if other users are online. The Members List View Web Part makes use of this feature. It is on by default.

Maximum Upload Size   Set by default to 50MB, it is the limit to how large a file a user can upload to a document library. You can make it smaller if you wish. It definitely impacts users who upload large files.

NOTE   By the way, Maximum Upload Size is per session, not per file. So if you are uploading multiple files, make certain that they don't all add up to 50MB, or upload in smaller batches.

Alerts   Set to On by default, this section can be used to disable alerts altogether for all site collections in the virtual server. The link will still be on the pages, but users will not be able to use it. Notice also that you can set a limit to how many alerts a person can have. Alerts, like everything else, takes up storage space and processor resources to keep track of. If that isn't an issue, you can set alerts per user to unlimited here.

Web Page Security Validation   This is also On by default. This is what causes a page to time-out if you take too long to enter data and submit it. If a user takes longer than 30 minutes to finish entering data on a page, they will have to refresh the page to continue. You can set the expiration time in minutes, or never. You can also turn this setting off if you'd like.

Send User Name and Password in Email   Set to On by default, this setting only matters if you are using Active Directory Account Creation Mode. Which we aren't. Otherwise, SharePoint creates a user account for a new user and puts it in an Organizational Unit in AD, and then sends an email to let the user know what the password is.

Email Enabled Document Libraries   Also something we aren't going to use. This setting is if you need to send email attachments from public folders.

Event Handlers   An interesting setting. It allows you to use custom code for handling events in document libraries to trigger addition actions or notifications. It is Off by default, so if you want to try your hand at this sort of thing, you need to remember to enable this setting.

Manage content databases

This is an important settings page. It is here so that you can set the capacity of the content database, create new content databases if the first one gets too full, set their capacities, and more. It is also a good page to take a quick glance at the status of your existing content database. Well worth a moment to dwell on it further.

TIP   When you create a server farm, you can connect the Virtual Server to an existing content database in the Manage Content Databases page. This page is also useful for recovering a Virtual Server's sites by connecting it to a restored copy of a content database. Check the Windows Share-Point Services 2.0 Administrator's Guide for more info on content databases.

As you can see in Figure 18.99, in this page the Current Virtual Server section confirms what Virtual Server you are on. The Content Databases section confirms what content database you are using by server and database name. It is here that you can check the status of the database. If it is Ready, then it can take more data. But if it is Offline, then it can't. It goes offline because it reaches a maximum allowed capacity (which you can set). Also on this page you can either manage the current settings of a content database, or add a new content database.

To view and change the settings of an existing content database, you can click the link for it in the Manage Content Databases page (see Figure 18.100). In my case, the content database is called STS_SHARE1_1.

You can see the database information, and change its status (ready or offline) here in the Database Information section. In the Database Capacity Settings section, the capacity of the content database by site can be set (content database capacity is measured by how many sites it can contain). There can be a maximum number of sites a content database can hold before it sends a warning to the administrative email for the Virtual Server (by default 9000—that's sites, not lists or pages.) There can also be a maximum number of sites set before the content database simply goes offline (15,000 sites by default—and that's one content database).

FIGURE 18.99
Manage Content
Database Page

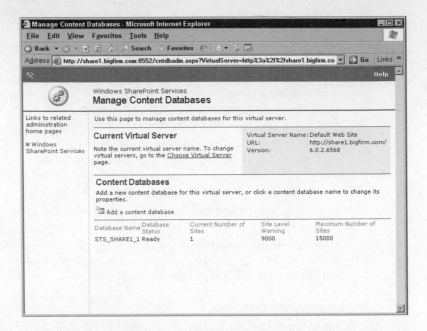

FIGURE 18.100
Manage a selected
Content Database
Settings

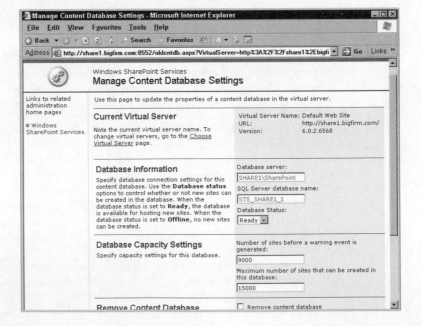

And finally, the Remove Content Database section is where you can remove a content database from SharePoint altogether if you need to. If you do that, all sites that are listed and active are gone, but the database has not actually been deleted, so if necessary it can be restored by adding it back.

Also on the Manage Content Databases page, if you wanted to (or needed to) add a new content database, you could click on the Add a content database link.

In the Add Content Database page (see Figure 18.101) there is a section to confirm the Virtual Server you are using, a section where you can specify the database server where you would like your new content database (or use the default one), and the name the new database. The next section is where you set the content database's capacity, with the maximum number of sites before sending a warning and the maximum total number of sites before the database goes offline.

FIGURE 18.101

Add a Content Database

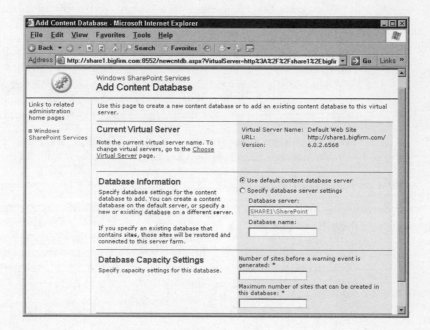

Virtual server email settings

This setting page should simply contain what you set on the Central Administration page for email. Feel free to check it and confirm that it is the same. If for any reason you need to change the email addresses or SMTP server for this virtual server, it can be done here. You don't set the administrative email on separate sites or even site collections. All sites and site collections in a Virtual Server get their administrative email account from either here, or from the Central Administration site above.

Remove Windows SharePoint Services from virtual server

There may be a time when you need to decommission a Virtual Server (or the physical server if it is in a server farm) and therefore you need to remove SharePoint from it. This is also useful if you installed Windows SharePoint Services on a whim, made a mess of it, and need to remove it. It has two settings: Remove without deleting the content database (lets you disconnect the database from the Virtual Server without actually deleting the database), and Remove and delete content databases (which actually gets rid of the databases).

WARNING   Do not click OK in Remove Windows SharePoint Services from Virtual Server if you are just looking around. The default setting is to remove Windows SharePoint Services and not delete databases. It would be a shame to undo all the work you've done so far by clicking OK here. It should warn you, but why take that chance? Of course, if you do accidentally disconnect the content database, you can always add it back in the Add a Content Database under Manage Contact Databases in This Section.

Define managed paths

Managed paths come in two varieties, included and excluded.

An excluded path is a file system or URL path for which SharePoint will not try to intercept any HTTP requests. Sometimes there are additional web applications that you would like to run in the same Virtual Server as SharePoint. In order to work together, you need to tell SharePoint what virtual directories, websites, and so on, it should disregard. Otherwise, it intercepts all incoming data on port 80, even if it is a particular virtual directory in the IIS Web Site that was there before SharePoint. If it is set to exclude a particular path, it will ignore all port 80 traffic to that path.

An included path is a URL that SharePoint manages. That means that it is a path that you can add top-level sites to. This setting is very useful if you have to manage multiple top-level sites and need the option to have some control of the path, so I will go into it a little further later on.

TIP   Sometimes you need to edit the Web.config file to get exclusions to completely work. Refer to the Windows SharePoint Services 2.0 Administrator's Guide for more complete details.

Create top-level Web site

This is the page that the Central Administration link of the same name goes to eventually: it's the page of settings to create a new top-level site. It contains sections for specifying the site address (with a drop-down list of included managed paths), the site collection owner and secondary owner (the users who will be the Administrators of the site and receive all notifications), the quota template (if one was made at Central Administration), and site language (if you have the language pack installed). It's pretty self-explanatory.

Delete site collection

And of course, if you can create a site collection in this section, it seems only fitting that you can also delete site collections from here. This setting takes you to a page where you simply type in the URL for the site collection's top-level site and click OK. Not for the faint of heart.

VIRTUAL SERVER LIST

This section only contains one link, which lets you choose a different Virtual Server to manage if you are done with the one you are on.

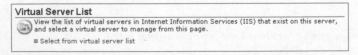

Select from Virtual Server list

The Virtual Server List page that contains the list of Virtual Servers available.

COMPONENT CONFIGURATION

This section contains only one link, which offers you a chance to specify if this Virtual Server wants to inherit the configuration data retrieval service settings from the Central Configuration page.

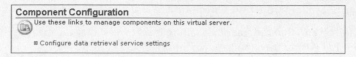

Configure data retrieval service settings

Identical to the settings from Central Administration, except that there is a Customize Virtual Server setting where you can disable inheriting the global settings from Central Administration. Otherwise, the page is filled with the Central Administration settings.

CONFIGURING A FEW VIRTUAL SERVER SETTINGS

Phew! That's it for the Virtual Server Settings. Now that you've seen them, let's make some changes.

First, we'll change some of the general settings.

General Settings

On the Virtual Server Settings page, go to the Virtual Server Management section and click the Virtual server general settings link. This is a really long page, so expect to scroll (the screenshot for this one can't capture more than a couple of the settings).

1. In the Default Time Zone section, select your time zon (see Figure 18.102).

FIGURE 18.102
Virtual Server
General Settings

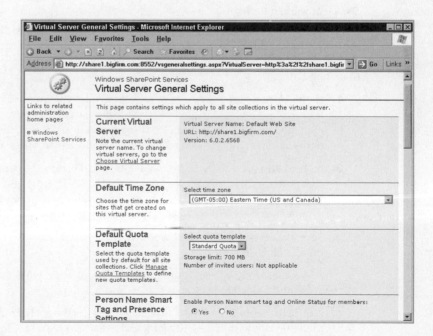

2. Because we created a quota template earlier in order to make our lives easier, it would be good to select it in the Default Quota Template section. That means that it will apply by default to all other site collections from now on. Notice that when you do this, it displays the warning and maximum limits. The number of invited users is only relevant if you are running SharePoint in Active Directory Account Creation Mode.

3. Make certain that the smart tag setting is set to Yes, that the maximum upload size is 50MB, and that Alerts are on with a maximum of 50.

4. For the Web Page Security Validation section, set the Security validation expires time to at least 60 minutes. I find the validation setting to be one of the more frustrating defaults in SharePoint.

   The Send User Name and Password in Email is not a relevant setting in this situation, since the users use their Active Directory account to log in and don't need to be sent their password. You can turn this off if you'd like.

   You can leave the Email Enabled Document Libraries setting to Off because we don't have any Exchange public folders to accept attachments from.

   And, because we don't have any need to handle document library customized code events, I think you can leave the Event Handler setting at Off for now.

5. If you've completed the settings, click OK.

Although we are not going to create any top-level sites, I wanted to show you how easy it is to create a new managed path. If you do ever have to create and manage more than one top-level site, then you probably are going to want a little control over what the path will look like in the web address.

Define Managed Paths

At this point, if you were to create another top-level site, its path (to differentiate it from the original top-level site) would be *servername/sites/newtoplevelsitename*. To create a new path (that's more relevant than `sites`) for SharePoint to listen for and manage, you need to create an Included Managed Path:

1. In the Virtual Server Management section, click the link to Define managed paths. The sections in the Define Managed Paths page list the current virtual server, the current included managed paths (with a means to delete them if you wish), the current excluded managed paths, and a section within which you can add new managed paths.

2. In the Add a New Path section (see Figure 18.103), notice where it says, "Note: To indicate the root path for this virtual server, type a slash (/)." This means that if you want a web address that goes from the root to a folder called helpdesk to the site name, you would use the URL syntax /helpdesk. Go ahead and try it. In the Path field type **/helpdesk** or whatever you'd like.

3. To make certain that the URL does what you want it to and is not already in existence, click the Check URL button.

   A browser window (see Figure 18.104) will open trying to get to the site helpdesk. There isn't a site at that location yet, so it fails to find a web page.

4. Notice the address bar, the actual site address, is the root or path for the Virtual Server in IIS, then the path within the URL namespace that you created. Close out of the browser window you opened to check the URL, and go back to the Define Managed Paths page.

FIGURE 18.103
Add a New Path

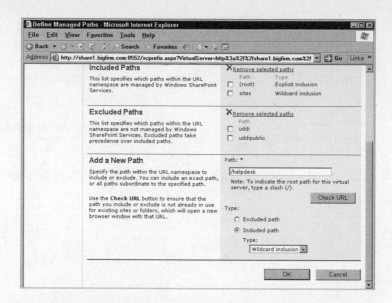

FIGURE 18.104
Testing URL

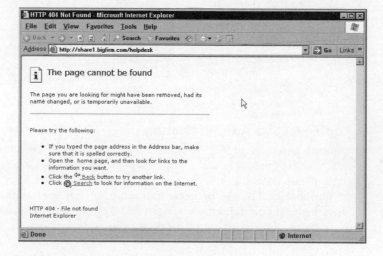

5. To make sure that this path is allowed to be used when you create a top-level site, it must not be excluded. Make certain that the Included path is selected.

6. Also, there is a drop-down menu below the Included path selection, and from here you can choose to wildcard the inclusion, which is the default. That means that SharePoint will manage any subfolders below helpdesk as well. Explicitly stating your path is the only option if you are excluding something, although you can be explicit with the included path if you'd like (maybe you don't want SharePoint automatically managing subfolders beneath a specific included path).

7. If you've finished configuring your included managed path, click OK.

Because you may want to add more managed paths, clicking OK does not take you out of this page. Notice while you're here that helpdesk is now on the list of included paths (see Figure 18.105).

Click Cancel, which is the fastest way back to the Virtual Server Settings page.

That's it. You got an overview of what the settings are for Virtual Servers, and you even set a few. Now it is time to manage the administrative settings for the next level down: the top-level Team Web Site.

FIGURE 18.105
New managed path

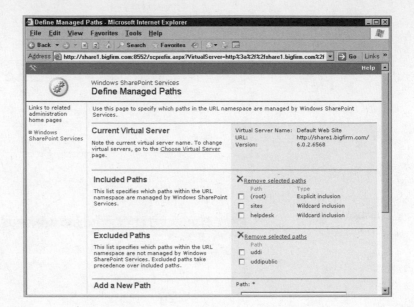

Top-Level Site Administration

You may have noticed that there has been no option yet to actually create user accounts for Share-Point. Access things, like users, Site Groups, and Cross-site Groups, are all the job of the top-level site and each of its subsites.

Now that you know all of the rights that can possibly be applied to a user of a site collection, adding users and applying permissions should be pretty easy. Many of the settings at the site level are much more immediately useful for a site collection administrator. It is in the next few administrative pages that you will be spending most of your time.

There are two different pages to manage every site (and I mean every, from workspace to top-level): Site Administration and Site Settings. I think they put the settings for the site on two pages because the Site Settings page is accessible directly off of the navigation bar of the site. This means those settings may be accessible to nonadministrators, so some standard settings can be viewed if not changed. Therefore, the more far-reaching settings were put on the Administration page to allow only those who have the Manage Website right to access.

To add to the confusion, in the unique situation of a top-level site, the Site Administration page is called the Top-Level Site Administration page to indicate that this top-level site has to manage the whole site collection as well as itself, and the page has several settings that lower level sites don't require.

You may have begun to notice a fair bit of redundancy in the settings from one level to another. That has been a major point of confusion for a lot of people. Don't be confused. A lot of settings at the top are meant to be used for convenience. But, to allow for a Virtual Server or top-level site to differ from the default, the same settings have to be available at their level as well. In addition, there may be administrators who do work at different levels, and therefore some settings need to be available both at the top (like managing users) and at the site level (like, you guessed it, managing users). Also, at this level, working with certain settings seems more hands-on. Working with alerts means actually looking at user alerts instead of the overall big picture of allowing or denying them. By the time you get to the sites, allowing or denying should have been taken care of.

So let's take a look at what available at the Top-Level site level of Administration.

To get to the top-level site administration page for our Team Web Site, you need to start at the Team Web Site Home page.

Once there, click Site Settings in the navigation bar. You will find yourself on the Site Settings page for the Team Web Site. The settings layout and sections may seem eerily familiar, but don't click around just yet, we'll come back to this page when we are done with administration.

To get to the Top-Level Administration page, click the Go to Site Administration link in the Administration section. This page (see Figure 18.106) is all about administrative tasks for both this site's management and the site collection as a whole.

FIGURE 18.106

Top-level Site Admin-
istration page

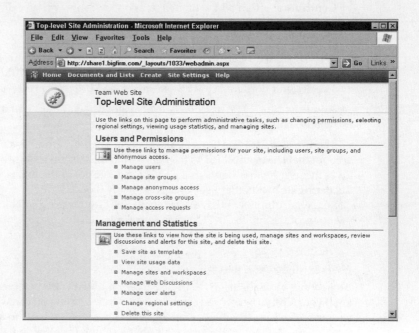

USERS AND PERMISSIONS

Use these links to manage permissions for your site, including users, Site Groups, and anonymous access.

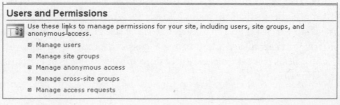

Manage users

This is where you actually add users. Remember, SharePoint expects you to add each user one at a time. There are ways around it, some of which you will see later. Once you have added users, you can apply permissions to them by using Site Groups.

NOTE I tend to consider Site Groups to be permission sets. As a matter of fact, SharePoint version 3 will probably do away with the name Site Group and use something like permission level instead.

Manage site groups

As I mentioned earlier, a Site Group is not actually a group of users. It is instead a group or set of rights that you lump together to apply to users (or more accurately, add users to). Generally, administrators create Site Groups based on user roles within SharePoint. That is why they are usually named something that indicates what the users will be doing. There are several default Site Groups already defined when SharePoint is installed:

Reader Can view items and view web pages.

Contributor Can add, edit, delete, and view items; browse directories; view pages; manage personal views; work with personal Web Parts; and, for some reason, create their own Cross-site Groups, which I find rather worrisome.

Web Designer Can do everything a Contributor can do, plus manage lists and even cancel check-out. Also included in Web Designer permissions are Add and Customize Pages, Apply Themes and Borders, Apply Style Sheets, and Browse Directories.

Administrator Has absolutely every right listed at the Virtual Server level. There is, by default, nothing an administrator can't do.

There is also fifth Site Group called Guest. This site-group is an automatic listing for a user account that has been added to the permissions of a list on the site but not the site itself. It basically gives the user Reader rights to the site in order to get to the list. However, that also gives the user Reader rights to all other lists, unless explicitly blocked.

For some administrators, these default Site Groups are good enough for what they need the members of the site to do. However, for people like me, creating new Site Groups to have permission sets that do exactly what I want them to do is more realistic.

Manage anonymous access

This setting requires that the Virtual Server's authentication method include anonymous access in IIS. If your Virtual Server can do anonymous access, then you can work with these settings. If anonymous access isn't what you want, but you don't want to have to add users to SharePoint, then don't overlook this link because it also has a setting for allowing all authenticated users a default level of access. For this reason, I'd like to look at this setting a little closer.

There are two sections for managing anonymous access on the Change Anonymous Access Settings page:

Anonymous Access The settings in this section are not even available if the Virtual Server in IIS doesn't have authentication set to allow anonymous access. If anonymous access is allowed at the virtual server, then you can choose to have the entire site allow anonymous access to read all content, or you can allow anonymous access only on lists and libraries. With that setting enabled, it still does not take effect until anonymous access is specifically enabled in the permissions per list or library.

All Authenticated Users This setting is something of a hidden gem. If you need all the users in your active directory domain to be able to access your SharePoint site collection, then just enable this setting and decide whether or not they will all have Contributor or Reader rights. Then the users will be able to access the site without you having to enter their accounts individually. When the user uses the site for the first time, SharePoint will recognize their domain account as a user account and add them to the user information list. However, they may not have an email address associated with their account until they set it up themselves (an easy way is when they try to set their first alert, it prompts for an email address if a user does not have one in their user information for the site).

NOTE You may be wondering why I am not going to use at least All Authenticated Users and save myself some time when adding users to the site. The reason is this chapter's site is for information workers. Not all authenticated users are information workers. The sales staff, HR, and administration do not need access to the site. It also gives me considerably more control over who sees what.

Manage Cross-site groups

Cross-site Groups are used to group users together that tend to need the same access to the same subsites, lists, and libraries. It is convenient because otherwise SharePoint has no other easy way to create user groups to add to sites and lists or apply specific permissions to.

Because SharePoint is so dependent on being able to send users email, it was created with the idea that each user would be added individually rather than by Active Directory group to ensure that each individual user will have an email address (SharePoint prefers it if you add a user by email address). This is a pain in the butt though, especially if you have to do this sort of thing with each and every user you want to give special permissions to at certain lists, libraries, and subsites.

So to make it easier, you can create a Cross-site Group, then add users to that, then add that Cross-site Group of users to the site, subsite, or list. Of course, you are supposed to add each user to a top-level site individually, then create Cross-site Groups of those users so that they can easily be added to subsites and workspaces from that point. However, you can create a Cross-site Group and add users to it that are not members of the top-level site with the intention of only allowing those people access to a subsite or even single list only. Cross-site Groups can be very useful in certain conditions. But, despite the name, Cross-site Groups only cross subsites, not site collections, meaning site collections cannot easily share users. Not that helpful if you have multiple top-level sites or multiple Virtual Servers.

Manage access requests

This is a great setting that requires the Virtual Server's email to be configured. It exists under the premise that users tend to try to access something they need more often than something they shouldn't. Oh yes, they will poke around at first, trying to see what they can do, but after a while, they generally just want to get things done. To that end, you can enable access requests for the users. When access requests are enabled, a user is presented with a Request Access page whenever they try to access something for which they do not have sufficient rights. It displays who they are logged in as (very convenient) and has a field in which they can make their request for access (and a Send Request button to send it, of course).

To configure access requests on the Manage Request Access page, all you have to do is check the Allow Requests for Access check box and supply an email address. Bear in mind, someone needs to monitor that address and respond to the requests. Otherwise it is just teasing, and that's not fair.

MANAGEMENT AND STATISTICS

This section lets you view how the site is being used, manage sites and workspaces, review discussions and alerts for this site, and delete this site.

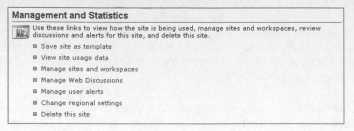

Save site as template

A means to make a template out of a site that you have set up exactly as you want it. You can also choose to have content already in lists and libraries saved in the template as well. Can be used to back up small sites and workspaces.

View site usage data

This setting depends on the Usage Analysis Processing settings at the Central Administration level. It takes about 24 hours for data to be processed after usage analysis is enabled. You can sort the data by page, user, OS, browser, or referrer URL (see Figure 18.107). Really a nice little reporting feature.

Manage sites and workspaces

Takes you to the Sites and Workspaces page that you can get to from Documents and Lists.

Manage Web Discussions

Lets you enable or disable web discussions. On by default, it requires the documents being discussed to have HTML formatting enabled (that's why it is called "web discussions," apparently—essentially, the discussions appear embedded in the documents themselves. It's an Office 2003 integration thing).

FIGURE 18.107
View site usage data

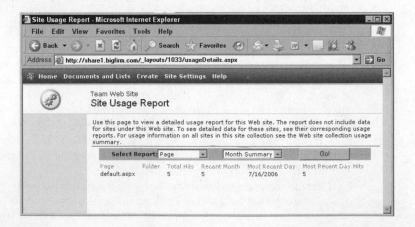

Manage user alerts

This setting is not about enabling or disabling alerts; that's already been done. This actually lists the alerts on your site (you can sort by user) to see who has how many and let you delete some if need be.

Change regional settings

I know that time zone and language were set elsewhere, but these regional settings are more detailed. They let you specify locale, sort order, time zone, and time format.

Delete this site

This setting will simply delete this site. It just specifies this site's address, warns about the dangers of deletion, and offers Delete and Cancel buttons. This setting is standard for the administration of any site. The only problem here is that this is the top-level site. Which means if it is deleted, all sub-sites and their contents are deleted too.

SITE COLLECTION GALLERIES

This section manages galleries, Web Parts, list templates, and site templates available to this site and all sites underneath it. It is here that you can upload new templates you might have created, purchased, or downloaded from the Internet.

Manage Web Part gallery

This is the list of existing Web Parts for this top-level site. It is here that you can upload a Web Part to be used by all sites in the collection.

NOTE   Don't confuse this with where the Web Parts go if you choose to import in the Add Web Parts tool pane on a Web Part page like the Team Web Site Home page. In that case, the Web Part you import is stored in the Virtual Server Gallery. That means that if you import a Web Part in the Add Web Parts tool pane, it is made available to the entire Virtual Server's site collections. Not all users are allowed to do this (generally only administrators can), obviously. In IIS, check under wpresources or wpcatalog to see the Web Part files. Strangely, there is no Virtual Server setting for managing the Virtual Server Web Part gallery.

Manage list template gallery

If you acquire or create any list templates, and you'd like to make them available to the whole site collection, then this is where'd you'd upload them. Displays existing list templates if you have any.

Manage site template gallery

Like the other two galleries, this is where you upload the site templates that you have created or acquired that you would like to make available to the whole site collection.

SITE COLLECTION ADMINISTRATION

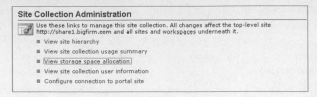

This is a profoundly useful section. These links are used to view the site collection overall, from this top-level site down. In this section is also the link to connect this SharePoint top-level site to a SharePoint Portal.

View site hierarchy

This is where you can easily find "lost" workspaces and subsites. It lists all sites that exist in the collection by their titles and URLs, with a convenient Manage link next to each one that takes you to the Site Administration page for that subsite (see Figure 18.108).

View site collection usage summary

This setting summarizes three of the reports that are available from this page: Site Usage Report, Manage Web Discussions, and Storage Space Allocation, with links to each report for more information.

FIGURE 18.108

View Site Hierarchy

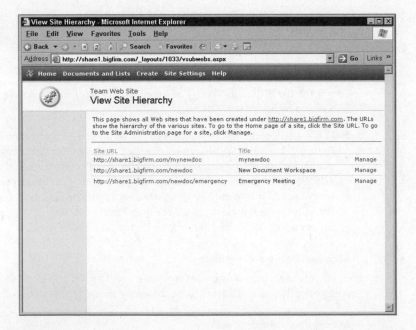

View storage space allocation

Summarized in the previous setting, this is a great way to get an idea of what is taking up all the space in your site collection—one of those pages you'll frequently visit to see how much space everything is using on your server. It's well worth a moment to delve into deeper.

The Storage Space Allocation page displays a bar that shows how much storage space this site collection is using—every list, document, and library. Do you remember the quota that you set for this top-level site back on the Central Administration, Manage Quotas and Locks page? That is the limit displayed at the right side of the bar. It all comes together eventually.

As you can see in Figure 18.109, beneath the bar is the key for space used, estimated new space (sometimes SharePoint estimates how much space an empty new site might take), and space remaining. Below the keys is a convenient sort bar for displaying the things your site collection is storing. And beneath that is the list of what is actually in your site collection and how much storage space each thing is consuming. In the action pane on the left, you can select to view document libraries, documents, or lists. Depending on the view, you can see the pertinent information about each item, such as type, number of items, last modified, and path. This page does show everything that is stored for the site collection, including galleries, list view ASPX pages, document library templates, and every single list from every single workspace and subsite. If an item is taking up more storage space than you'd like, you can click its name and go to whatever page manages it to start paring down its storage size.

Also for your convenience in the Storage Space Allocation page are check boxes next to each item, so you can simply delete documents, libraries, or lists from here to recover storage space. Then, when all is checked, you can click the Delete button and recover the storage space those items were consuming.

FIGURE 18.109

Storage Space Allocation

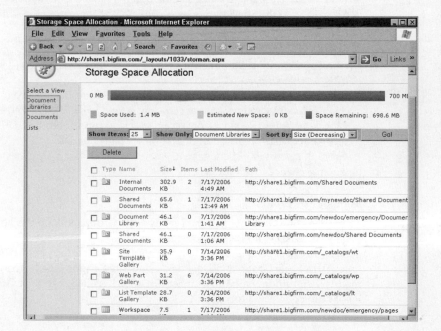

View site collection user information

As the name implies, this setting displays all users for the whole site collection. It displays a narrow list of the user's name, account name, and their Site Group. If you need to see more details about a user's information, you can just click the user's name and it will take you to that user's information page.

Also on the Manage Site Collection Users page is an action bar link to view the Cross-site Groups for the site collection, as well as a link to delete selected users (there are check boxes next to each user for this purpose).

Configure connection to portal site

This setting allows you to connect this site collection to a SharePoint Portal Server and use its resources. We don't have a SharePoint Portal Server to connect to, so this setting is not really relevant to us at this point.

And that's it for the Top-Level Site Administration page. Now you can see what the settings the higher levels wrought at the lower levels of administration.

CONFIGURE A FEW TOP-LEVEL SITE ADMINISTRATION SETTINGS

At this point I would like to configure a few things before moving on to Site Settings.

First, I'd like to enable Access Requests and create a Site Group to be able to give users the permissions that someone who manages lists would need. You will see that the Site Group we create here can affect the way we use permissions all the way down to the list level.

You might be wondering why I don't just add users while I am here. We can do that several different ways later. Manage users is a link that is available both at this level of administration for convenience and at the Site Settings level. They both take you to the same add user ASPX page.

Manage Access Requests

On the Top-Level Site Administration page, click the Manage Access Requests link in the Users and Permissions section.

As you can see in Figure 18.110, the Manage Request Access page has just two settings in it: a check box to allow requests for access, and a field to send email requests.

Check the Allow Requests for Access check box and enter the email address that you would like to receive requests on behalf of SharePoint. Then click OK.

From this point on, whenever a user tries to access something they don't have rights to, they will be given a chance to ask for access.

Manage Site Groups

To manage Site Groups, click the Manage Site Groups link on the Top-Level Site Administration page in the Users and Permissions section.

As you can see in Figure 18.111, the Manage Site Groups page has an action bar with only two links, Add a Site Group and Delete Selected Site Groups. The list contains the default Site Groups made when Windows SharePoint Services was installed. Each Site Group has the check box next to it so it can be selected for deletion.

FIGURE 18.110
Manage Request
Access

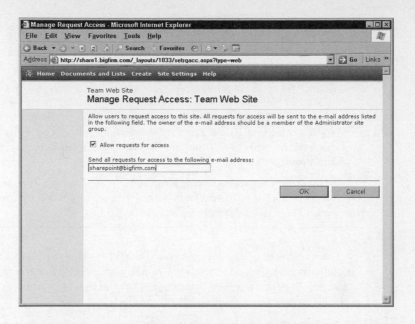

FIGURE 18.111
Manage Site Groups

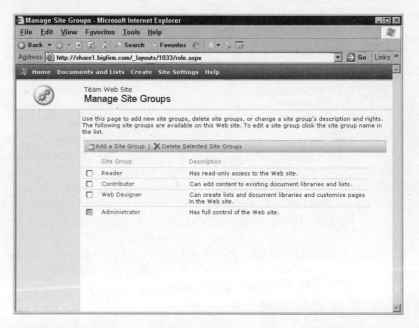

NOTE It's hard to find an explicit reference in the SharePoint interface that connects the word role and the concept of Site Groups. But if you've ever wondered if there is one, look at the address bar of the Manage Site Groups page.

ABOUT THAT ACCESS REQUEST EMAIL

Just a heads up: the Access Request email that is sent on behalf of the user is formatted in HTML and has two links:

Grant user access to the site Takes you to the add user page with the user already selected. Mind you, the user already has access to the site or they wouldn't be there, but the Add User page has a list of Site Groups that you can easily add the user to. The problem with the Access Request email is it doesn't specify what access the user was denied that they require. It is really important that you teach the users to clearly supply a detailed request in the request access text box, or else you won't know what they want.

Manage request access setting for the site Takes you to the Manage Request Access page we were just in off the Top-Level Site Administration page. Basically, this link is included in the access request email so the administrator can turn Request Access off.

I realize that this page doesn't do anything to manage existing Site Groups except to delete them. To actually manage one of the Site Groups, you need to click the name of it in the list. When you do, you will come to a page that does not say "Manage" but instead "Members of *name of the Site Group you clicked on*." Yeah, members.

1. To see what this is about, click the Site Group name Contributor in the list of Site Groups.

   This brings you to the Members of "Contributor" page (see Figure 18.112). If there were users that had been added to this Site Group, then they would be here. The action bar has some new links:

   Add Members Goes to an Add Users page. It is not a unique Add a Member to a Site Group page. It just adds a user as if you were doing so from the Manage users link on the "Top-Level Site Administration page. It is a convenient way, after creating a Site Group, to add users and apply the new Site Group to them.

   Delete Selected Members If there were members listed here, they would have check boxes that could be selected so they could be deleted. The users are not deleted from accessing the site, just from this Site Group. However, if the permissions from that Site Group were the only ones the user had and they were deleted from this Site Group, they would not be able to even access the site until at least Reader permissions were applied.

   Edit Site Group Permissions This is the link that allows you to truly manage the Site Group. It takes you to a list of rights (which should look familiar—if you had disabled any rights at the Virtual Server level, they would be conspicuous in their absence at this level). The ones that are checked are the ones being applied by this Site Group.

   Go Back to Manage Site Groups Acts like a Back button, taking you (let's hope) back to the Manage Site Groups page.

2. To see what permissions the Contributor Site Group has, click the Edit Site Group Permissions link in the action bar.

   The Edit Site Group "Contributor" page (see Figure 18.113) lists the description field and the rights selected to apply for this Site Group. It is here that you get to see exactly which rights are used by this Site Group (and, indirectly, which rights are enabled at the virtual server).

FIGURE 18.112
Members of
Contributor

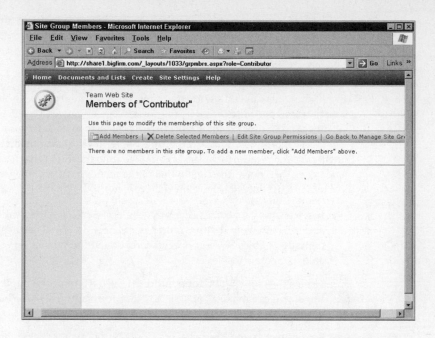

FIGURE 18.113
Edit Site Group Contributor permissions

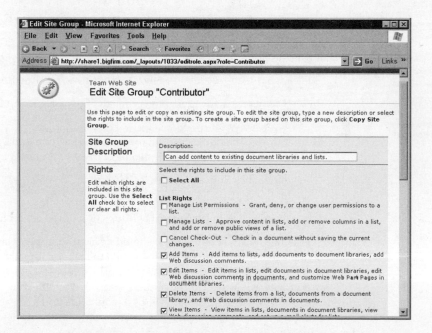

3. Scroll through the rights and notice that Contributors can basically do everything with items in a list, browse directories (so they can add Web Parts, which are located in directories outside of the site's URL), and view pages (which even Readers need). They also have all of the Personal Rights, which allow Contributors to modify their personal view of Web Part pages. Also listed under Personal Rights is the right to create Cross-site Groups.

I don't know why that is a right the Contributors have by default. (More on Cross-site Groups in a moment.) Another right I haven't mentioned is the Use Self-Service Site Creation, which is selected by default in all Site Groups, in case an administrator enables that feature at the Virtual Server level.

TIP If you want to only allow a certain group of nonadministrative users to be able to create top-level sites, create a Site Group for those users. Then remove Use Self-Service Site Creation from all other Site Groups except the Site Group applied to those select users. Then enable Configure Self-Service Site Creation at the Virtual Server level and immediately go to the Announcements list and remove (or at least expire) the announcement that has the link to sign up to create a site. Then email the signup link to the members of the Site Group (or maybe copy and paste it to a list only they have the right to view).

4. Just for safety's sake, uncheck the Use Self-Service Site Creation right (you can come back and select it again if you would like to later). This just insures that, if an administrator accidentally enables Self-Service Site Creation at the virtual server, this Site Group will not be able to create a top-level site.

 Notice the Copy Site Group button at the bottom of the page. If you like most of these settings, you can make a copy of this Site Group and use it as a base for a different one. Just for your convenience.

5. To get back to the Members of "Contributor" page, click Submit.

6. Click the Go Back to Manage Site Groups link in the action bar on the Members of "Contributor" page.

That was the Contributor's rights. Now let's look at the Reader default Site Group permissions:

1. To see what read-only access actually looks like, click the Reader Site Group name.

2. In the Members of "Reader" page, click the Edit Site Group Permissions link in the action bar.

3. Scroll through the rights. See that readers can view items and view pages. Also note that Use Self-Service Site Creation is selected. Feel free to deselect it if you'd like.

4. Then either click Submit or Cancel (if you made no changes), to get back to the Members of "Reader" page.

5. Click the Go Back to Manage Site Groups link in the action bar.

At the Manage Site Groups page, it should be clear that the default Site Groups have names based on their roles in the site collection and that the Site Groups are simply a collection of common rights that let their members perform certain tasks.

Now that we have looked at the settings that are available to users and seen how they are configured for some of the default Site Groups, I would like you to create a Site Group called List Managers and select rights that a list manager might need, like the right to delete items in a list, approve items, cancel check out, modify lists, and create/remove public views:

1. Click the Add a Site Group link in the action bar.

 The Add a Site Group page should look almost identical to the Edit Site Group page except there is an additional name field, as well as a description.

2. Name the Site Group List Manager, and describe it as "Users who manage lists; or something more descriptive.

3. Then select the following rights:

   ◆ Manage List Permissions

   ◆ Manage Lists

NOTE Notice that to allow someone the right to approve items, you also have to allow them to modify the list and the list public views. This is another of the inflexible bits of SharePoint. This is as granular as the permissions get; sometimes it's all or nothing. You can't allow someone to add columns to a list without also allowing them to approve items. Many rights have dependencies, like View Item cannot work without the View Pages right as well. If you want to see what dependency affects what, try enabling each right one at a time, and see what other rights also end up enabled. Be forewarned that dependencies might mean that you accidentally give a user more rights than you expected because some rights, like manage lists, are actually a combination of rights that cannot be made any more specific. For more information concerning the unexpected dangers of some of the permissions, check out the Windows SharePoint Services 2.0 Administrator's Guide.

   ◆ Cancel Check-Out

   ◆ Add Items

   ◆ Edit Items

   ◆ Delete Items

   ◆ View Items

View Pages and Manage Personal Views should also be selected (they will automatically be checked).

The settings you have not selected mean this Site Group will not let a user mess with shared Web Parts on the Team Web Site Home page (or any other Web Part page in the site collection, because that requires the Add and Customize Pages right, which also allows users to actually change the underlying HTML of site pages if they wish, which we don't). It also cannot create subsites, Cross-site Groups, top-level sites, or manage any sites. It is almost solely for giving someone the right to manage lists.

4. If you have the correct rights selected, click Create Site Group at the bottom of the page.

Back on the Manage Site Groups page, there is now a new Site Group listed, complete with the brief description (see Figure 18.114).

You've enabled access requests and created a Site Group, as well as learned about the default Site Groups and their settings. Now it is time to move on to Site Settings, where we will be adding users (applying Site Groups to the users), working with permissions, changing the theme of our site, and changing the site title, finally, to something more appropriate than Team Web Site. This is the home stretch, where the settings become more immediate and more relevant for a single site.

Figure 18.114

Manage Site Groups

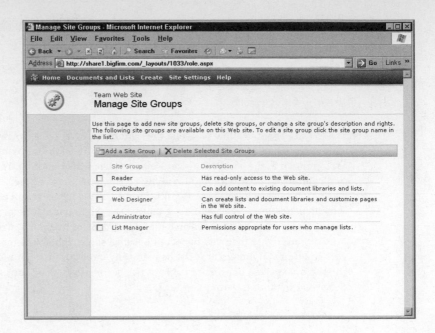

Site Settings

To get to the Site Settings for the Team Web Site, click Site Settings in the navigation bar.

Site Settings contains sections that pertain to adding and removing users, managing the Site Settings, and user information (see Figure 18.115). This page is most likely to be accessible to nonadministrators because they can make use of the Manage My Information section.

ADMINISTRATION

This brief section is literally about managing users, subsites, workspaces, subsite creation (interestingly), and getting to the Administration page.

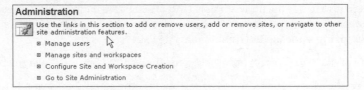

Manage users

It is here that you can add, remove, or modify the Site Group of users. The Manage Users link on the top-level site Administration page links to this setting.

Manage sites and workspaces

This link conveniently takes you to the Sites and Workspaces page from the Documents and Lists action pane. From there you can see the sites and workspaces beneath this site (and this site only), or create new ones.

FIGURE 18.115

Site Settings page

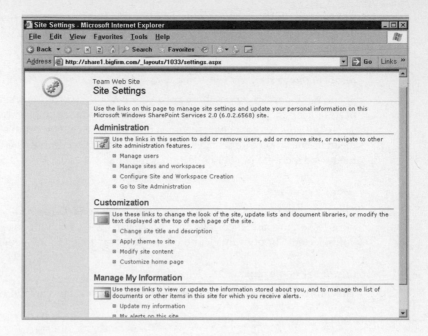

Configure Site and Workspace Creation

This is an interesting setting that should appeal to the "keep it simple, keep the defaults" kind of administrator.

Like a younger cousin of Self-Service Site Creation, this link brings you to the Modify Site and Workspace Creation page. All you can do here is give the Contributor and/or Web Designer default Site Groups the right to create subsites. All it does, literally, is just check the check box next to Create a subsite in the Site Group permissions for Contributors or Web Designers when you select to give them this permission. That's it. It does not even realize you have created other Site Groups. It just offers to change those two.

But, if you had never seen the rights beneath the default Site Groups, you would probably like this setting. And if you are in a hurry and are willing to let anyone who can contribute to a list be capable of creating workspaces and subsites, then this is the setting for you.

Go to Site Administration

We have used this link already. It is, other than typing in the web address or bookmarking it, the only way to get to this site's Administration page.

CUSTOMIZATION

Use these links to change the look of the site, update lists and document libraries, or modify the text displayed at the top of each page of the site.

Change site title and description

This is the link to use to change the site title and description that will show up in the title area for this site. Finally, we can start personalizing the site.

Apply theme to site

Speaking of personalizing, there are a long list of different themes for SharePoint sites. You don't need to keep the default. The consistent layout, the medallions, and Web Parts will remain the same, but you can change (sometimes radically) the color scheme of a site. And when I say site, I mean it. The whole site changes, but not the subsites beneath it. It is a good idea to have a different theme for each site in your collection. It will make it easier to tell them apart.

Modify site content

This link takes you to a Modify Site Content page which essentially summarizes the lists (and libraries) on this site. If you click one of the list names, you will go to the Customize page of the list you selected. Simply a quick and convenient way to get to the general settings of a list or library.

Customize home page

This link takes you right to the site's home page in design view with the Add Web Parts tool pane open.

MANAGE MY INFORMATION

This section is rather user-oriented for the most part. Two of the links will show the user or alerts information for the person who is looking at it (based on the account they are logged in with). The third link is for the list of all users who have ever used the site, even if someone is just a guest or part of a group that was added to the site.

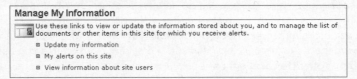

NOTE Although it is discouraged because SharePoint can't capture everyone's email that way, you can add users by domain group. Then, when the individuals use Integrated Windows authentication to log in to the site, SharePoint resolves their username, but unless the user has an email address associated with their Active Directory account, that user will have no email listed for alerts and notification. The users will show up individually in the User Information page but not in the Manage User page, because they were added there only as part of a group.

Update my information

Takes you to the user information page for the account you are logged in with; an excellent way to add or change the email address for the account.

My alerts on this site

This is the page that you can only reach by going into a list or library, clicking Alert me, then using the New Alert page to see all of your alerts for this site. As you can see, this way is often easier.

And this setting is not just a list of your alerts. You can select Add Alerts from here that takes you to a page that is hard to get to otherwise. It displays all of the lists that are available on this site. Each list has its own icon indicating its type, and a radio button. You can just select a radio button next to the list you want to be alerted about, and click Next. It will take you to the New Alert page for that list. If that's not enough, say you can't remember the list you want to be alerted about by name and icon alone. Well, next to each list name is the description and a link that will take you to that list (so you can look around and see if you recognize anything).

View information about site users

Takes you to the User Information page. Displays all of the users that ever logged into the site. It is from this list that you get the Members List View Web Part. It is also the list that smart person tags use. If you move your mouse over a user name in the list, a little MSN person icon will show up if you are on a workstation with MSN Messenger and/or Outlook installed.

Also on the User Information page are links to either Add Users or Manage Users. Each list item displays the display name, username, and email address. If you click a user, it will take you to their User Information page, which contains fields for, you guessed it, display name, username, email address, and a notes field (I guess you can use that for personal advertisements or something).

That's it for Site Settings. Now you know all of the Administrative settings and configuration. We've cleared up why the same settings show up on several administrative pages, why there are two pages to manage and administer a site, and just what Central Administration is for anyway.

CONFIGURING SITE SETTINGS

Now that we've finished learning about what the site settings are, it's time to configure some. In this section we'll finally personalize the Team Web Site as well as explore the site settings of one of our subsites.

Change the Site Title and Description

I feel that it's about time to make the Team Web Site our own by giving it a less generic title (but in my case only slightly less).

1. To change the site title and description of the Team Web Site, go to the Customization section of the Sites Settings page and click the Change site title and description link.

2. In the Change Title and Description page, change the title from Team Web Site to Company Site (okay, not that unique, but better than Team Web), or whatever you'd like.

3. Add a description of some sort. I am going to use Collaborative site for our company. Then click OK. That should take you back out on to the Site Settings page. Notice that the title is now Company Site Site settings.

Now for the coup de grace, changing the site color scheme.

Apply a Theme to the Site

1. In the Customization section of the Site Settings page, click the Apply Theme to Web Site link.

   This should put you on a page (see Figure 18.116) with a preview of the themes and a list box of theme names. If you select a theme in the box, it previews it nearby.

FIGURE 18.116
Apply Theme
to Web Site

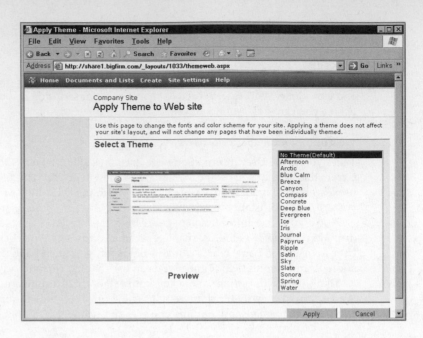

2. Pick a theme. I am going to choose Spring. It shows up well in screen shots but is not just a different shade of blue. Click Apply.

The color scheme for the Site Settings page should have gone from blue and light orange, to gold, black, and reddish orange.

3. Click Home on the navigation bar.

Notice the new site name Company Site and description (see Figure 18.117).

1. Click Contacts in the Quick Launch bar.

2. Notice that the scheme extends to the lists. Select the Reviews view in the Action pane. It should be gold and black too, no more default theme here.

3. Go back to the Company Site Home page by clicking Home in the navigation bar.

It's obvious that's the theme for the site, but did it change the subsites?

4. On the Company Site Home page, click Documents and Lists in the navigation bar. Once there, click Document Workspaces in the action pane, then select New Document Workspace.

The New Document Workspace still has the default theme. That's because themes affect sites, not site collections. It is a good thing to have different themes for each site. It makes them easier to tell apart.

Figure 18.117

Home with
new theme

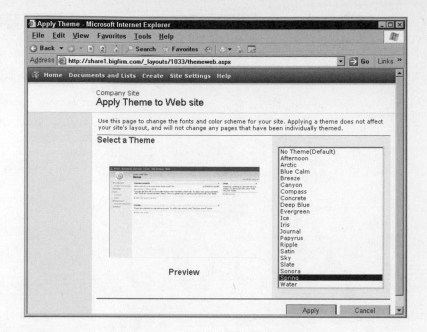

Explore Subsite Site Settings

The new document workspace is a site in its own right. To see the New Document Workspace's settings, starting at that site's home page, click Site Settings in the navigation bar.

The settings are almost identical to the settings available at the top-level site, except that you can't seem to manage users from here. That is because this site, if you remember, was set to inherit permissions from the site above it. Because of that, user management happens at the parent site and trickles down here.

If you wanted to change that (we don't, but we can go look), you would need to go to the Administration page for this site. Click the Go to Site Administration link in the Administration section.

In the Users and Permissions section, the first link is Manage Permission Inheritance. Click it.

It is here (see Figure 18.118) that you can change the permission inheritance of a site at any time. Click Cancel to return to the Site Administration page.

You'll notice that most of the settings are exactly like those of the top-level site, except for those that relate to managing a site collection overall. You can still view usage of this site, change regional settings, and so on.

Speaking of site collections, as a convenience while you are administering this site, if you want to pop straight up to administering the top-level site, you can just scroll down to the Site Collection Administration section and click the Go to Top-Level Site Administration link. It will take you to the Company Site's top-level site administration page. Go on, click it.

At this point the site collection is pretty much set up the way we want it for now. And, usually, once the site is ready for a user, it becomes time to add users and set permissions.

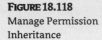

FIGURE 18.118
Manage Permission
Inheritance

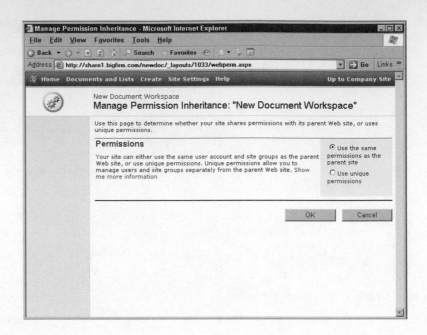

Working with Permissions

SharePoint has an interesting take on permissions. NTFS permissions don't quite cut it when you are working in a collaborative environment. In SharePoint, rights are focused on collaborative roles (unintuitively called Site Groups), such as Readers, Contributors, maybe some editors, a moderator of lists or libraries, and Administrators. Their permissions (which are just combinations of rights) are task focused and can be a bit limited in that way. Just remember that you cannot add a user to a site without also applying some sort of permissions to them (although you can add them to a Cross-site Group without permissions, as you'll see later in this chapter). Don't get me wrong, there are a lot of task-oriented permissions that can be set, but you might want to brace yourself for the way SharePoint approaches them.

We know that the Manage Users link on the top-level site Administration page takes you to the same place as Manage Users on the Site Settings page; it doesn't really matter which one you use to add users. So, since we should be looking at the top-level site administration page if you've been following along, I'd like to simply add a user, apply Reader rights, and then log into the Company Site with that user account. I'd like to see what a normal Reader can actually see on the site. From there, we can add more users in several different ways, with several different permissions, and see what happens to each.

NOTE In order to do these steps, I created ten domain users (if you are on a stand-alone server, create them in the Computer Management console) with names like user1, user2, user3, and so forth. I am not sure what your Active Directory structure is like. You can use whatever accounts you wish. These are just accounts I know no one else will be using, so I can delete them after I am done without harming anyone.

ADD A USER

To add a user, click the Manage Users link in the Users and Permissions section of the top-level site Administration page (or you can go to the Site Settings page and click Manage Users there. Your choice).

In the Manage Users page there is an action bar with links for Add Users, Remove Selected Users, and Edit Site Groups of Selected Users. In the user list there should be only one user, the one you created the site with and have been using all along (see Figure 18.119).

Before we create a new user, I'd like to check on what Edit Site Groups of Selected Users does. Put a check in the check box next to the administrative account you have been using and click Edit Site Groups of Selected Users in the action bar.

You will see in Figure 18.120 that you cannot change the user name from here, and that the Site Group Membership is Administrator. That is a good thing. However, notice also that our new Site Group is also listed as an option.

There has to be at least one Administrator for a SharePoint site, so we don't want to change this user's Site Group settings. Click Cancel to get back to the Manage Users page.

1. Click the Add Users link in the action bar.

2. There are two steps on the first Add Users page (see Figure 18.121). You can use several formats to add a user. SharePoint would like it if you added a user by email address, which I could do because all of my accounts have email addresses. Or you can use a DOMAIN\username. I am going to use a domain name format, so to add my user, in the Users field, I type bigfirm\user1.

3. Now, for step 2. For user1's Site Group, I choose Reader. That is the most limited of Site Groups and I want to see what a Reader can and cannot do in comparison to the administrative account I have been using all this time. Select the Reader Site Group and click Next.

FIGURE 18.119

Manage Users page

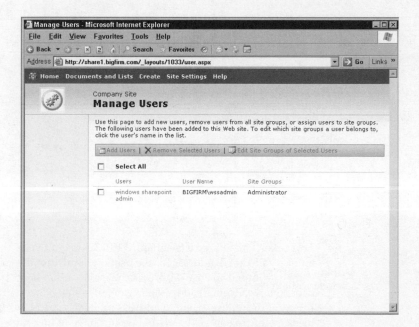

FIGURE 18.120
Edit Site Group
Membership

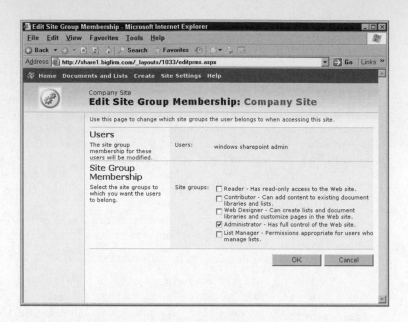

FIGURE 18.121
Add Users, page one

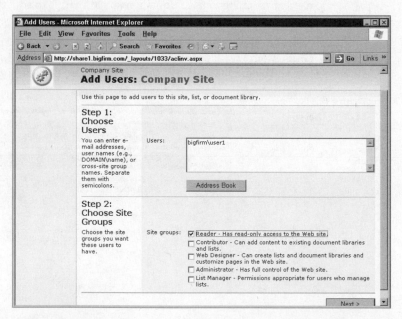

4. This takes you to Step 3 (see Figure 18.122), page two of the Add User process. You can enter a valid email address for the user on in the Email address field in Step 3 (this is a necessary prompt if an email address is not specified in step 1 because SharePoint wants every user to have an email address). My email is integrated with Active Directory, so even though I didn't use an email address in Step 1, Add User picked up the email address of user1@bigfirm.com. Otherwise, I would have to enter the address manually.

FIGURE 18.122
Add Users, page two

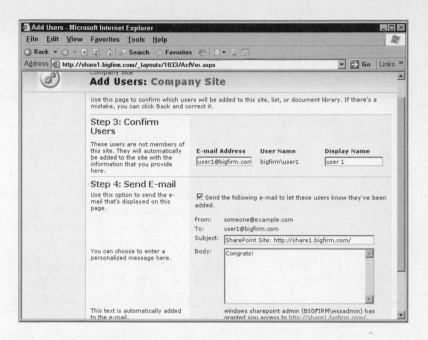

5. If there is an email address in Step 3, then the check box in Step 4 becomes available to send an email to the user to invite them to check out the SharePoint Site. I am going to check the box next to Send the Following Email to Let The User Know They've Been Added. I am also going to type Congrats! in the body of the message. At the bottom of the page the text is added to the message body, telling the user who gave them access to the site, the user's Site Group, and website address.

6. Click Finish when you are done composing your message.

Tada! There is your new user. Time to take him for a test drive.

Testing the New User Account with Reader Permissions

At this point you are going to notice that we do a lot of closing out of Internet Explorer, opening it back up, and logging back in. This could be problematic on an XP workstation, because it tries to be helpful and authenticates you with the user account you are logged onto it with to access the SharePoint site. If you have problems with that, it may be easier to work on the server for this part (or change the IE security settings to prompt for username and password).

1. To see what Reader Site Group permissions actually look like from a user's perspective, close out of Internet Explorer altogether. Reopen Internet Explorer, and type in the Share-Point site's address in the address bar (mine is good old share1.bigfirm.com).

2. You should be prompted for a username and password. Use the user account you added with Reader rights. Mine is bigfirm\user1.

3. You should end up on the Company Site Home page. Notice that you cannot modify the page. That is because that requires the right to add and update personal Web Parts.

A Reader has the right only to view things, not add, or edit, modify, or approve. To test this, I'd like to try to edit the properties of a file in the Internal Documents document library.

4. To attempt to edit the properties of a file in a document library, click Internal Documents in the Quick Launch bar.

5. Move your mouse over the name of one of the documents, and click the down arrow.

6. In the drop-down menu, select Edit Properties.

7. You will be able to open the Edit Properties page because you are allowed to view items and view pages. However, add a word to the Keywords field and click Save and Close in the action bar.

   You should be prompted for a username and password. To add insult to injury, the page already seems to know what your username and password are—they are already in the prompt dialog box. You're obviously expected to supply some other username and password.

8. Feel free to click OK in the dialog box. It will pop back up with the same request for a user-name and password. Obviously the one it has isn't working.

You can try logging in with this username and password or you can hit Cancel. Either way, you will be denied access to a right you didn't have (to edit an item). If you try to enter a valid username and password three times or Cancel, it will bring you to a Request Access page (see Figure 18.123) because we enabled it at the top-level site.

This request will trigger an email to the address you configured for Request Access.

If you can, send the request to see what it does. Type something relevant in the request text box and click the Send Request button.

FIGURE 18.123
Request Access

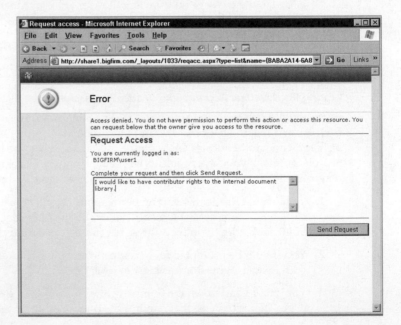

If you receive the email (see Figure 18.124) for the request and click the link to grant the user access, it will take you right back to the Add User page to add them with different, better, stronger, faster permissions. You have already seen the Add Users page, so I am not going to do this part. However, Request Access works. If you enable this on your SharePoint site and get a lot of Requests for Access, consider this: it means the users are exploring your site. Like wild animals you want to lure into a sanctuary, it is good that they use the site that your boss told you to set up for them. Just don't completely ignore their requests if they make them.

FIGURE 18.124
Request for access email

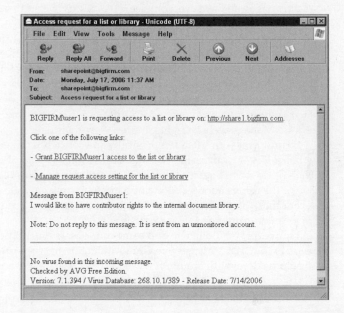

From the user end, after you send the request for access, you'll find yourself on a confirmation page. Notice that it is not using the black and red theme you chose? It's not really a site page. Because it is one of those pages generated from an administrative setting, there is no guarantee that it will use the site theme you applied. So that is what Reader Site Group rights allow a user to do, and we know what an administrator can do on a site. Let's now add some users at the Add Users page, assign them Contributor rights, and see what that does.

1. To add more users from the Manage Users link on the Site Settings page, go to the Company Site Home page by clicking Home on the navigation bar.

2. From the Company Site Home page, click Site Settings in the navigation bar.

3. In the Site Settings page, click the Manage Users link in the Administration section.

4. Ah, did you forget that you were logged in as a Reader? It is obvious that you can see this page, because you have view rights. This means that you can see what settings are available but you can't actually use them…or can you? Click Cancel in the prompt dialog box. Then click the Back button in your browser window to go back to the Site Settings page. In the Site Settings page, scroll down to the Manage My Information section and click the Update my information link.

5. You will see that you can, in fact, see your user information from the User Information List. That means that some of the links on this page are available to people with only view item and view page rights. In the User Information page for your user, click the Go to User Information List link in the action bar. This will take you to the same place the link View Information About Site Users on the Site Settings Page does.

Readers can go to the Site Settings page and update their user information and view all other user information. This makes sense in terms of the Members List View Web Part. You can put it on a home page and have everyone see it there, so why can't you let Readers see the same information on the Site Settings page?

Unfortunately, I don't want them to know what Site Settings are, but you can't have users who *can* view pages *not* be able to view a page that has settings they are allowed to see. It is all or nothing, so SharePoint has opted for allowing all users to view the Site Settings page and even access some links. But for the most part, Readers can only affect their own data. So even if they can get into a site management page, they cannot save the settings. There are other links on the page they can't even click without being prompted for a different username and password because those settings require Manage website rights to even view their page.

So now you know. Readers, basically all users who can see a site, can see its pages. The only way to block a user from seeing the Site Settings page is to explicitly not allow them on the site at all. There is no way to set it so that no users other than Administrators can view Site Settings. This is one of the things about SharePoint that seems awfully inflexible to me.

For those of you following along, now that you have a user with Reader rights, you can see what they can or cannot do to your heart's content.

I however, would like to add some more users as Contributors (our original goal), then add users to that List Manager Site Group we created earlier, and create a Cross-site Group. Then we should be done with our overview of adding users and permissions.

Add Multiple Users at Once

You should be in the User Information List page and need to get back to Manage Users. Click the Site Settings link in the navigation bar, then click Manage Users in the Administration section.

You will be prompted for a username and password because a Reader cannot add users. In order to add users, you have to log in as someone with the right to manage this site. This will elevate the user's privileges for the page we are going to and will last for the rest of the session. To end the elevation of privilege, you will need to close out of Internet Explorer, reopen it, and log back in.

To gain access to Manage Users, use the administrative username and password you used to install Windows SharePoint Services.

1. In the Manage Users page, click Add Users in the action bar.

2. At this point we are going to add more than one user. You can add many users in Step 1 of the Manage Users page, just separate them with semicolons. In the Users text box in Step 1, add two users separated by a semicolon. I am going to add (because they have email addresses) user2@bigfirm.com; user3@bigfirm.com.

3. After typing in the usernames (separating them with semicolons), select the Contributor Site Group in Step 2 (see Figure 18.125). Realize that the boxes next to the Site Groups are check boxes. Depending on how you set up your Site Groups, it may be worthwhile to apply more than one per user.

4. After selecting Contributor, Click Next.

5. Now, because I added the users by email address, Step 3 displays the email addresses as noneditable text (as shown in Figure 18.126), and you can confirm and change SharePoint's assumption about the domain account the email addresses belong to. In my case it is correct. I am not going to bother to send them email about the site; Maybe I have sent them a note already. I am going to deselect the Send the Following Email setting in Step 4.

6. If you are finished with the settings in this page, click Finish.

FIGURE 18.125
Add multiple users

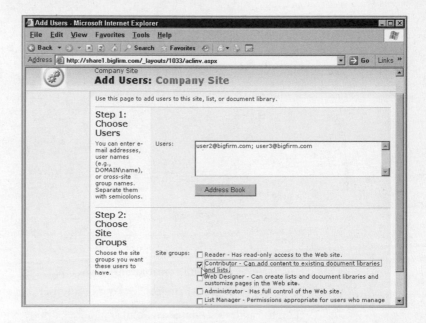

FIGURE 18.126
Add multiple users, page two

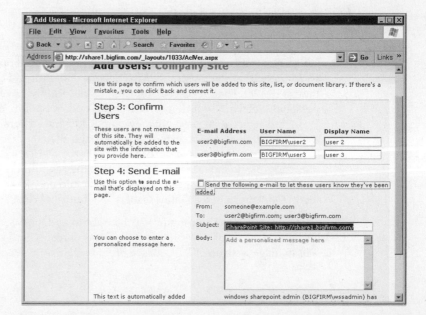

As you can see in Figure 18.127 on the Manage Users page, there are two new users with Contributor rights.

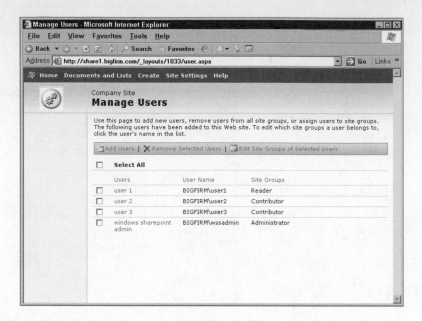

Testing a New User Account with Contributor Permissions

Now, to see what Contributors can do. Close out of Internet Explorer, then reopen it.

1. Type in the address to the SharePoint site in the address bar of Internet Explorer.

2. When prompted to log in, log in with one of the user accounts you added to the Company Site that have Contributor rights (user2 or user3). As a Contributor, you should be able to control your own personal view of Web Part pages.

3. Click the Modify My Page link. In the drop-down you'll notice that you can work in personal view (that's what Modify My Page means). But, you cannot get to shared view (see Figure 18.128). That is because Contributors can add/remove private Web Parts and update personal Web Parts, which means they can update built-in Web Parts, and add/remove Web Parts in personal view, but they cannot add and customize web pages (they don't have that right). If they cannot customize a web page, then they cannot modify the public, shared view of a page. They can see all of the Web Part galleries and use all the Web Parts because they can Add/Remove Private Web Parts. If they couldn't Update Personal Web Parts, they wouldn't be able to access the galleries and would only be able to work with the existing list view Web Parts and the Online Gallery. No built-in Web Parts for them.

Now, you know that a Contributor has the right to add, view, edit, and delete list items, mess with Web Parts in personal view, and for some reason, create Cross-site Groups. They cannot create subsites or manage websites. I'd like to see proof of that.

Figure 18.128

Contributor's view of the Company Site Home page

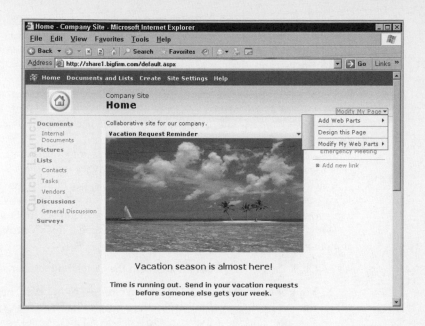

NOTE   Remember, that the Self-Service Site Creation right only refers to top-level sites and has nothing to do with subsites and workspaces.

Logged in as a Contributor, you should be on the Company Site Home page. Click Site Settings.

1. In the Site Settings page, click Manage Users.

2. You should be prompted for a username and password. Click Cancel, then click the Back button in the browser window.

   Back on the Site Settings page, we've established that Contributors are not allowed to manage a website (which is why they cannot access the Manage Users page). Now it's time to see if they can create a website.

3. In the Site Settings page, click the Manage Sites and Workspaces Link.

NOTE   Yes, I know it is counterintuitive: if a user cannot manage a site, why can they click that link? Because it is a web page that can be accessed from Documents and Lists, which all users have rights to.

4. Click the Create link in the action bar.

5. You should be able to see the New SharePoint Site page, but if you add any data and click the Create button, it will prompt you for a username and password. Curses, it looks like the Contributor can see the New SharePoint Site page but can't actually create a new subsite.

Speaking of subsites, there is a permission that the Contributor does not have. Do you remember the document-centric document workspace we created? It should not be visible to someone who did not create it.

Return to the Sites and Workspaces page. Look in the Document Workspaces section of the list. You should only see one document workspace, New Document Workspace (or your equivalent). Users with the Contributor Site Group are not part of the list of users allowed to access the document-centric document workspace (mine is called mynewdoc) because that workspace did not inherit permissions, and we didn't add any users, so only the creator can even see it in the list of document workspaces. My New Document Workspace did inherit permissions from the parent site, our newly renamed and themed Company Site. That's why our Contributor can see it. Because they can use the Company site, they should be able to use the New Document Workspace site in the same way.

To access the New Document Workspace as your Contributor Site Group user (mine is user2), click the document workspace New Document Workspace.

You should get to the New Document's Workspace Home page. It looks like inheritance works so far (see Figure 18.129), since the Contributor can get to the New Document Workspace. By the way, you might notice the Members list has more members in it now.

While in the New Document Workspace, let's see if this Contributor user can still add and edit an item in a list.

1. Click the General Discussion link in the Quick Launch bar.

2. Your boss wanted to use Discussion Groups, right? Well, here is one. You probably know how to create new list items by this point, so let's use the Contributor to add a new discussion post and see if they can add a list item. Click New Discussion.

3. You weren't prompted for a username and password (or at least you shouldn't have been), so type in a subject and some text.

4. Click Save and Close in the action bar. The new discussion should show up in the window. Therefore, you have the right to add a list item (see Figure 18.130).

FIGURE 18.129

New Document
Workspace

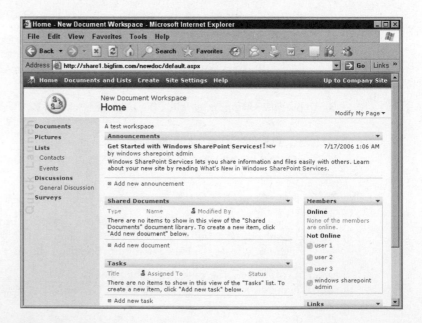

FIGURE 18.130
New post in discussion list

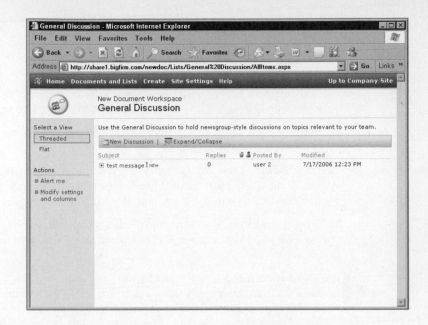

NOTE To reply to a post in a discussion list, either view the item and click Post Reply in the action bar, or move your mouse over the post's subject, click the down arrow, and select Reply from the drop-down menu.

That means that the Add Item right is available for Contributors. To check to see if Edit Item works as well, move your mouse over the discussion list post you just created and click the down arrow in the selection box.

1. Select Edit Item from the drop-down menu.

2. The Contributor account seems able to get this far, but anyone can view a page, so make a change in the text of this discussion item, and click Save and Close.

That should take you back to the list with no prompt for password, proving that a Contributor can add and edit items. It is also very likely that a Contributor can delete items too.

This also proves that workspaces that inherit permissions from a parent site allow the same access that the parent site does, and workspaces that don't inherit permissions must have permissions set up explicitly before a user can even see it listed under Sites and Workspace.

Next up is adding a user to a Site Group. Then we'll take a look at the permissions of a list. Then we will create a Cross-site Group and add them to the list. That will complete the grand tour of Windows SharePoint Services permissions.

WORK WITH A SITE GROUP

1. To get to the settings for managing Site Groups, you first need to be on the Site Settings of the Company Site, so if you are still on the New Document Workspace, click Up to Company Site in the navigation bar.

2. At the Company Site Home page, click Site Settings in the navigation bar.

3. Click Go to Site Administration (notice that a Contributor can do this).

4. Click Manage Site Groups. You will be prompted for a username and password because that's farther than a Contributor can go. Use your administrative account.

5. That will put you right into the Manage Site Groups page. Click the List Manager Site Group we created earlier.

   I know it looks like we are adding members to a Site Group. But trust me, this is going to end up exactly like adding a user and then choosing a Site Group.

6. In the Members of "List Manager" page, click Add Members in the action bar. You will be in the Add Users page (See?).

7. Then add a user. I am going to add user4@bigfirm.com and make sure she is in the List Manager Site Group (that option should already be selected). This is the part where you add a member to a Site Group (you first create the Site Group, then you add the users to it). Click Next.

8. The email address, username, and display name in Step 3 are fine (for me, make certain they work for you like any other Add User data), and I will send the mail, as is, to the user. Click Finish.

The user has been added to the Site Group (see Figure 18.131).

So, did it make a difference, adding a user to a Site Group, or adding a user through Manage Users? To find out, click Site Settings in the navigation bar.

In the Site Settings page, click the Manage Users link in the Administration section.

There is the new user we added as a member of a Site Group. As you can see, they are no different. In other words, all users that are added to SharePoint must have Site Group permissions applied to them somehow. Some people like to add users then apply Site Groups to them, other people like to go to the Site Group page and add users to the Sites Groups they just made. It's a matter of preference, but the same results occur.

FIGURE 18.131
Manage Users list

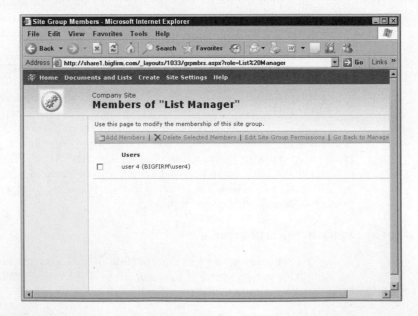

CREATE A CROSS-SITE GROUP

However, this is not the case for Cross-site Groups. A Cross-site Group is literally just a user group. That's it. If you add a user to a Cross-site Group, it does not add the user to the site itself, nor does it have any particular Site Group permissions. It's just a way to group users so that they can be added later to different Site Groups together (and then to whatever sites, libraries, or lists you'd like) as needed. Kind of like creating global groups to add them to local groups.

To create a Cross-site Group, we need to get to the Top Level Administration page (mind you, all sites can have their own Cross-site Groups, not just the top-level one. We just need to get to the site's Administration page to get to the setting). So click Site Settings in the navigation bar, then click Go to Site Administration in the Administration section.

1. Click Manage Cross-site Groups in the Users and Permissions section of the top-level site Administration page.

2. Click the New Cross-site Group link in the action bar.

3. In the New Cross-site Group page there are two sections, Name and Description, and Owner, as you can see in Figure 18.132).

   The Owner section has three settings, Yourself (which is selected by default), Allow Members of This Cross-Site Group to Add and Remove Site Users, and Someone Else (my personal favorite choice for a selection title ever). Of course, if you choose Someone Else, you have to actually select someone from the existing members of this site. Whoever you choose is going to be the person or persons who are allowed to add and remove people from this Cross-site Group. They are also going to be added to the group as a member.

4. For the Name and Description of the group, I am going to be conservative and call it Group One, and add as the description First cross-site group. I can change it later.

5. Change the owner to Allow Members of This Cross-Site Group to Add and Remove Site Users. You can always change it later. Click Create (you may have to scroll down to the bottom of the page).

FIGURE 18.132

New Cross-site Group

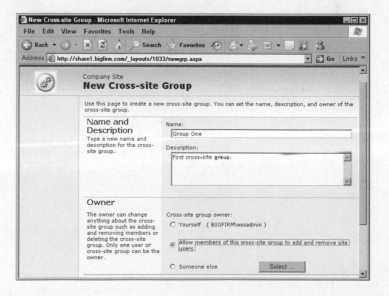

That takes you to the Members of "Group One" page. If you ever need to change the ownership, name, or description, just click the Change Cross-site Group Settings link in the action bar.

1. To add users, first click the new Cross-site Group's title (mine is Group One), then click Add Members in the action bar.

   The Add Users page should look familiar (see Figure 18.133) except for one thing: it is missing the Site Groups section that is typically required if you are adding a user to a Site, Site Group, or List.

2. Add a few users (I am going to add user5 and user6 to this group by typing **user5@big-firm.com; user6@bigfirm.com**) in the Users text box, then click Next.

3. That will bring us to Step 2, which confirms their usernames and display names. That's it. No Site Group, no permissions. Just click Finish.

Now there should be three people in this Site Group (the two users and your administrative account).

That explains what a Cross-site Group is, but let's add a Cross-site Group *to* something.

USING A CROSS-SITE GROUP TO GIVE USERS ACCESS TO A SUBSITE

Cross-site Groups, like any user group, can be added to anything that will let you type in a username in the field, so you can add Site Groups to sites that are not inheriting permissions. Yeah, you don't have to add everyone to a top-level site if they are only ever going to use a subsite. Let's do that. You may recall that document-centric workspace we created straight from a document in the Shared Documents library earlier in the chapter. You also might remember not being given the option to have the site inherit permissions from the parent site. And, because of this, it didn't.

FIGURE 18.133
Add users to a
Cross-site Group

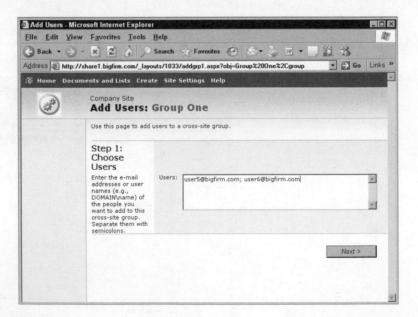

You are currently running in your administrator's context, so you can see that document-centric document workspace because you created it (otherwise you wouldn't be able to). If you can see it, you can manage it, so go to Site Settings in the navigation bar.

1. To reach that document workspace, click the Manage Sites and Workspaces in the Administration section of the Sites and Workspaces page.

2. In the Sites and Workspaces page, click mynewdoc (or whatever you called the document you generated a document workspace from) in the document workspaces section.

   That should take you to the mynewdoc document workspace. Notice how, despite all the users we have added, there are no new members in the Members List View Web Part. That is because this site only has one member, the person who built it.

3. Click Site Settings in the navigation bar.

4. In the Site Settings page, click Manage Users in the Administration section.

   You should see that there is one user, the administrative account you used to create the site.

5. Click Add Users in the action bar.

6. In Step 1 on the Add Users page, type in the Cross-site Group name in the Users text box.

7. In Step 2, choose a Site Group to apply permission to the Cross-site Group members when they are here. Notice that this site did not inherit the Site Group List Managers that we created. Choose Reader for their Site Group and click Next.

8. In the next page, Steps 3 and 4 confirm the Cross-site Group name, and the email addresses for those group members. All the data should be correct. Choose whether or not to send the email and click Finish.

Now in the Manage Users page there is a new section called Cross-site Groups with the group Group One (see Figure 18.134).

FIGURE 18.134
Added Cross-site
Group to subsite

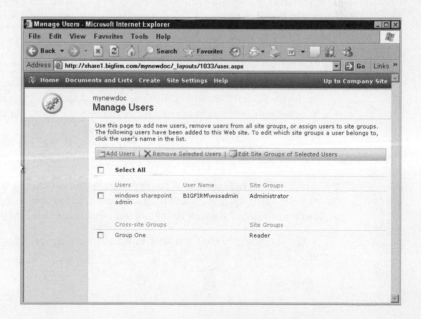

It's great that we added some users to the nynewdoc document workspace, but we managed to add users to a site that do not have any rights to the parent site. The members of Group One cannot log in to the Company Site. To prove this:

1. Select the address of the mynewdoc document workspace in the address bar of the browser and copy it (right-click and select Copy).

2. Close out of Internet Explorer and reopen it. Type the SharePoint Top-Level site address in the address bar.

3. When prompted for a username and address, use one of the users that are in the Cross-site Group. This should fail because the Cross-site Group was created at the Top-Level site, but they weren't *added* as a user at the Top-Level site, only to the mynewdocs document workspace.

   The only way for those Cross-Site Group users to get to the mynewdoc document workspace is to use the actual direct address. They can't navigate to it from the Top-Level, Company Site.

4. Select the address in the address bar of the browser. Paste the address you copied earlier over it. It should be the one that leads to the mynewdoc document workspace.

5. Hit Enter or click the Go button. Now the Cross-site Group member should be able to get into the "mynewdoc" workspace just fine.

We have covered the rights that are available in SharePoint, and where they can be set (per virtual server), what Site Groups are, how to use them and create them, how to add users to a site (and therefore the site collection, since we were using the top-level site) in several different ways, and how to create and add users to a Cross-site Group and what a Cross-site Group does. We explored what the default Site Group settings were. We then checked out what site settings and permissions were on a subsite we had created, including adding a Cross-site Group to a document workspace that did not inherit permissions.

Phew, that was a lot of permission details. Permissions can be a sticky subject with SharePoint, so I thought it might be best if I be thorough. And to that end, there is one more little thing to do. List Permissions.

List Permissions

We are finally down to the smallest thing we can apply permissions to: the List. This will be quick.
Let's work with a list we are familiar with, the Vendors list on the Company Site.
On the mynewdoc document workspace home page, click the Up to Company Site link in the navigation bar.
You will be prompted for a username and password of a user that is allowed to access the Company Site. Use the user we added to the List Manager Site Group. In my case that would be user4.

TIP A quick way to tell what user account you are logged in with on a SharePoint site is to go to Site Settings on the navigation bar and then scroll down to the Update my information link and click it. It will take you to the user information item for the user account you are logged in with.

1. After logging into the Company Site and reaching the home page, click the Vendors link in the Quick Launch bar.

2. In the Vendors list, click Modify settings and columns in the action pane.

3. In the Customize Vendors page, click Change Permissions for This List in the General Settings section. Note, the only reason that I can get into the permissions of a list without being an administrator is because the account I am using has the List Manager Site Group permissions I set up.

Right now, there are no users in the permissions for this list (see Figure 18.135). There are none in any list. They are inheriting the site's users by Site Group. Every Site Group has users in it (essentially, or users using the permissions defined by the Site Group). Any user that is in any one of the Site Groups listed here has rights of some sort (specified by their Site Group) to this list.

There are two things you can do with the Site Groups you have here. One is to change the rights of a Site Group at this level (it will not change the rights of a Site Group at the parent site). The other is to remove a Site Group's right to the list altogether.

To check out what happens when a right is removed from a Site Group at the list level, select Contributor in the list and click Edit Permissions for Selected User (in our case a Site Group, but users can be added to the permissions of this list).

In the Modify Permissions page, notice that the user is Contributor and that the Choose Permissions section has a simple list of permissions. To see the real rights behind the permissions, click the link for Standard permissions. This will take you to the real settings for this Site Group (see Figure 18.136).

This is where you go to change the rights of that Site Group, so if a user is using the permissions for that Site Group, the new rights take precedence while that user is in this list. While they are here, they play by this list's rules.

Now that you've taken a glance, remove the right to Delete List Items, and then click OK. We'll actually mess with logging out and back in a little later.

FIGURE 18.135

List Permissions

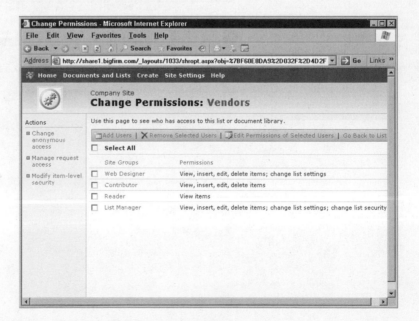

You will now find yourself on the Change Permissions page. The Contributor Site Group now has the word Custom in the permissions column with a plus sign next to it (see Figure 18.137). That means that this Site Group now no longer has one of the default set of permissions. Also, above the action bar is a new message, This List Has Unique Permissions That Are Not Inherited From the Parent Web Site. Inherit Permissions from the Parent Web Site.

FIGURE 18.136
Modify Permissions

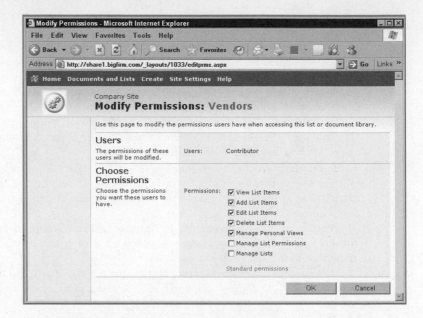

FIGURE 18.137
Custom Contributor
Site Group

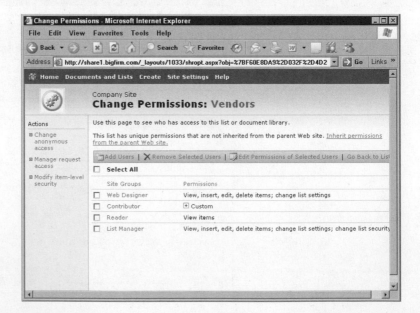

This means that this site is now no longer inheriting permissions from the parent site. If you want to change the list back to inheriting permissions, click the Inherit Permissions From the Parent Web Site link and the change you made will be undone.

The other thing you can do with the existing Site Groups in this list is to remove a Site Group from here. If you remove a Site Group from a list, the users that have that set of Site Group permissions lose rights to that list. It's a profound thing to do, a step up from just stripping a Site Group of its rights, but it is quick and effective.

Let's say that the Vendors list should not have Readers access it, not even to view the records. Put a check in the check box next to Readers in the list of permissions and click the Remove Selected Users link in the action bar.

It will ask for confirmation. Click OK.

I'd like to finish up on this page, by taking a look at three other settings here on the Change Permissions page before we go out to see what happens when we try to use this list with an account that is a Reader.

WARNING   If you restrict a user from being able to view or access a list and that list has a List View Web Part on the home page, then the user will see a warning where the Web Part is instead of the Web Part's contents.

Change anonymous access   Lists are so independent that if you enable anonymous access as an authentication method on the Virtual Server (Default Web Site in our current case) in IIS 6.0 and enabled anonymous access per site (or at the parent site level if sites are inheriting permissions) for lists and libraries, then a list can choose to allow anonymous access or it can require Windows authentication. If the site (or parent site) does not allow anonymous access, then the options will be grayed out, as they are in our case. If you want to set anonymous access, you can specify what an anonymous user can do—view, add, edit items, in any combination (see Figure 18.138). Anonymous access is what many Discussion Groups online do now. Anyone can read a discussion, but often, to contribute, you need to log in.

To see the Anonymous Access setting options (even though we know we did not allow anonymous access in IIS on this virtual server), click Change anonymous access in the action pane.

In our case, Anonymous is not available as an access choice, so it is grayed out. Click Cancel to return to the Change Permissions page.

Manage request access   Can be controlled per list, so it does not trigger if someone is denied access to this list. That way users are not able to send you repeated requests to access this list in particular if you don't want them to.

Modify item-level security   Will take you directly to the Item Level Permissions section in the Change General Settings page for this list.

I would like to disable Request Access for this list, so click the Manage request access in the action pane of the Change Permissions page and you'll see the screen shown in Figure 18.139. This page is refreshingly simple. One check box next to Allow Requests For Access and the OK and Cancel buttons. Take the check out of the check box, and click OK.

FIGURE 18.138
Anonymous List
access settings

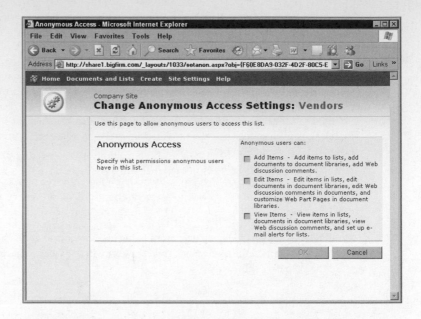

FIGURE 18.139
Manage Request
Access

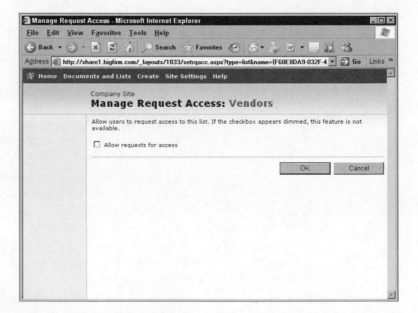

Testing List Permissions

Now let's see what the changes we made do. Log in as a Reader first and see what happens. Then we'll log in as a Contributor.

1. Close out of Internet Explorer and then reopen it. Type the SharePoint site address in the address bar.

2. At the prompt, use the username and password for a user that has Reader rights to the site. In my case it is user1.

3. At the Company Site Home page, click the Vendors link in the Quick Launch bar.

4. You should be prompted for some other username and password. You can click OK three times or just Cancel. Either way, you will find that you get an Error: Access Denied notice instead of a Request Access page (see Figure 18.140).

NOTE Have you ever noticed the Troubleshoot link in the Access Denied page? Have you ever clicked it? I have come to the realization that this link is singularly the least useful thing about SharePoint. This is why the Internet and the Windows SharePoint Services 2.0 Administrator's Guide are good things.

Congratulations, the user failed to get access to the Vendors list because that list no longer allows users with Reader rights.

Now to test the Contributor Site Group's rights on the Vendors list. Close the browser and reopen it. Use the address bar to get back to the SharePoint site.

1. When prompted for your username and password, use an account that has Contributor rights. For me that's user2.

2. Click the Vendors link in the Quick Launch bar. You will not be refused, because you still have View List as a right.

3. In the Vendors list, move your mouse over the only list item, and click the down arrow. In the drop-down list, select Delete Item.

4. You will be prompted to confirm that you really want to delete the item. This will make you feel as if you are going to be able to do it. Click OK.

FIGURE 18.140
Access denied

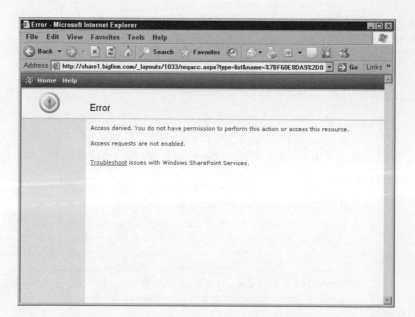

But, no. You will be prompted to enter a username and password for someone allowed to delete an item from this list. Congratulations, foiled again. Because we removed the right to delete list items from the Contributors Site Group, user2 cannot delete an item.

There are several ways to secure a list. Any change at all that you make from the defaults inherited from the site this list is attached to will break the list away from its permissions inheritance, so it doesn't take much. Basically, you can add a single user or many users and specify their permissions, you can add a Cross-site Group, you can remove a Site Group (but you can't create one specifically for the list. That's why it's called a "Site" Group), and you can modify the rights or permissions that a Site Group can use on your list. Lists can have extensively different permissions than the site that contains it if necessary.

And that's it. Those are the permissions for lists (as briefly as possible). I hope this has given you some insight into how roles, rights, Site Groups, Cross-site Groups, and permissions work in SharePoint and that it will help keep you out of trouble later when your sites start getting more complicated.

Backup and Recovery

So you've gotten a bit of an idea about administration and permissions. Now it's time to talk about what to do with your SharePoint sites and their content in case there is a disaster. I am talking about backup and recovery.

You should already be doing regular backups of your servers, that goes without saying. This means that, if necessary, you could restore the entire SharePoint server's contents if it died a nasty death due to catastrophic circumstances.

But what if you lost just one site, a site collection, or even a list of data? What if a junior administrator accidentally deleted them? How can you protect a particularly important library at the critical point in a project?

How do you back up just a site collection, site, or list? And how do you restore them?

Ahhh, let me show you.

There are three ways to do backups with SharePoint Services.

◆ If a site contains only 10MB of data or less, you can back it up as a template, then restore it by using the template. This is also true of a list, since it can be made into a template too.

TIP The 10MB limit is a hard-coded maximum size for all templates.

◆ You can back up and/or restore an entire site collection (but only an entire site collection) with the command-line tool STSADM.EXE.

◆ You can back up, move, or restore a site or site collection by using the old SMIGRATE.EXE command-line tool.

Backing up a Site Using a Template

Let's do the easiest thing first: backing up a site to a template.

When you back a site up as a template, there are some limitations. Namely, the site size limit (10MB) and the fact that permissions and user settings are not saved. That means that if a list had unique permissions that protected the data from unauthorized access, you will need to reset those permissions after the restoration. Any site can be made into a template. Right now the site with the most customization is our top-level site, so we'll back that up.

NOTE   Usually this feature is used to protect sites lower down on the list because it is the top-level site that contains the site gallery that holds the templates—so if that goes there are no templates to restore from. However, it never hurts to have a second copy. If something happens to the lists or libraries on your top-level site, you can restore them from your template and recover data from critical lists or libraries.

MAKING THE BACKUP SITE TEMPLATE

Backing up a site as a template and restoring it is really, really easy.

TIP   Site templates can even be copied to other SharePoint servers and used there. See the Windows SharePoint Services 2.0 Administrator's Guide for more.

1. Go to the site you want to back up. Let's use the Company site (since we've done so much work with it).

2. Once on the Company site, go to Site Settings on the navigation bar.

3. Once on the Site Settings page, click the Go to Site Administration link in the Administration section.

4. On the top-level site Administration page, go to the Management and Statistics section, and click Save site as template link.

5. In the Save Site as Template page (see Figure 18.141), you can see the following settings:

   File Name   Obviously, this is going to be the filename of the template file. Notice that the file extension is .stp.

   Title and Description   The title of this template is what will show up in the Template Selection list when creating a new site or workspace. As far as I know, there is no way to hide a list template so only certain users can see it in the list. Keep that in mind.

   Include Content   This setting is interesting. You can save a site, lists, surveys, libraries, theme, and all either as an empty frame or completely full of whatever data is in the site at the time you create this template.

   Type in the filename you want your site template to have. I am going to use Company1 for this example.

6. Type in a title and (if you want) a description. I am going to use Company Site Backup 1 and the description Copy of the Company site.

7. Make sure that Include Content is checked in the Include Content section. This setting is all that stands between you creating an empty copy of this site and a full one. If it is checked, then go to the bottom of the page and click OK.

You should then get the Operation Completed Successfully page (see Figure 18.142).

Note that it says you can manage this template in the Site Template Gallery. This setting is on the Site Administration page of the top-level site of a site collection only (as you may recall).

To manage this template, click the link for the site template gallery.

FIGURE 18.141
Save Site as Template

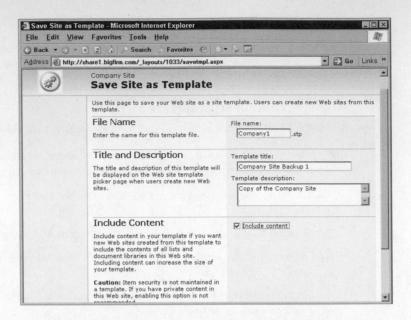

FIGURE 18.142
Operation Completed
Successfully

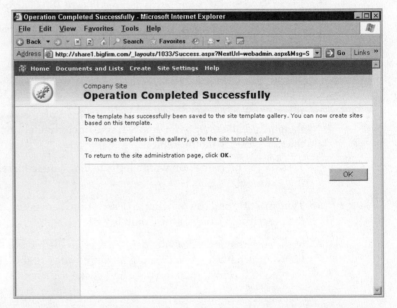

You should be able to see your new template filename listed in the Site Template Gallery page. This is where you would go to delete the template. Remember, it takes up space in your content database. To conserve space, keep the redundant templates to a minimum.

By the way, while you are here, notice that a gallery is kind of like a library of templates. You can modify settings and columns, set alerts, and even filter the list by field contents.

Click the edit icon next to the template filename.

Notice in Figure 18.144 that there is an action bar with links: Save and Close, Delete, Check Out, and Version History.

I honestly have no idea why there are links for checking out and versioning a template gallery when there is no way to actually *edit* the templates files themselves once they are made (except maybe with FrontPage, which is likely to get ugly). I have tried to check out a template and it doesn't seem to make any difference.

FIGURE 18.143

Site Template Gallery

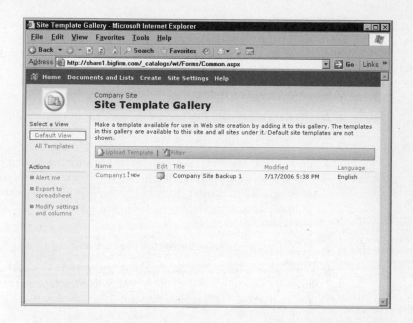

FIGURE 18.144

Template edit page

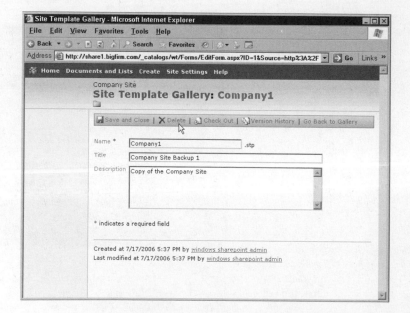

Anyway, the point of editing the template is to let you know how to delete it. When this template becomes obsolete, come to the site gallery, click the edit icon next to the template's filename, and click the delete link in the action bar.

I have had people tell me you cannot delete a template once you create it, but that's because they never tried to edit it (because they are reasonable people).

So now you know.

RESTORING A SITE FROM A TEMPLATE

To use the template, just create a new site. It will enable you to replace the original site if it got corrupted or accidentally deleted, or you can even just make a second copy to replace some files. Remember, all of your custom permissions will be gone.

1. Click Create on the navigation bar.

2. Click Web Pages under select a view in the action pane.

3. Click the link for Sites and Workspaces.

4. In the New SharePoint Site page, enter a title for the site. Since the site we are restoring exists (we are working in it), I am going to give the new site the name Company site 2, and the URL of company2 (it doesn't really need a description). You can have the site inherit or have unique permissions as you wish. Regardless, the old permissions did not carry over to the template.

5. Click Create at the bottom of the page if you have finished your settings.

6. On the Template Selection page (see Figure 18.145), select the title you gave your template (I used Company Site Backup 1). Notice that the description you gave the template is listed under the Select a Template graphic.

7. Click OK.

FIGURE 18.145
Creating a new site from backup template

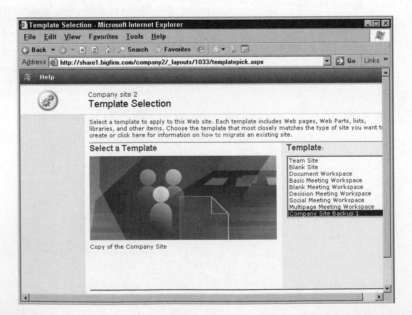

And there you are, on the home page of your new site, compliments of your new template. Notice in Figure 18.146, that all of the unique shared Web Parts, their layout, the lists in the Quick Launch bar, and the theme are all there.

You know what settings you gave your lists. Check to see if any of the permissions that you set uniquely on your lists are still there. They shouldn't be.

1. Go to the Internal Documents library by clicking its title in the Quick Launch bar. You should see that all of the documents are still there.

2. Go back to the home page, and click Contacts in the Quick Launch bar. You'll see that the data you entered earlier in the chapter is there, but the Reviews view (which was set to personal) isn't.

What does this mean? The structure and the data of the original site that you made into a template are still here. You (and the users with the rights to) will have to recreate your personalizations again (list views and personal Web Part page views) and redo all of the site's security settings.

FIGURE 18.146

Company site 2

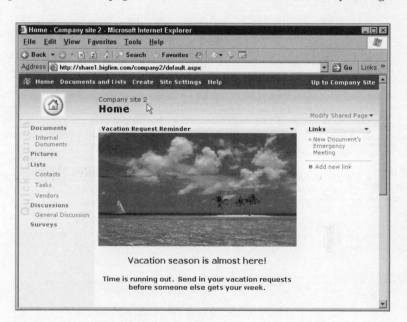

SITE TOO BIG FOR YOU? HOW TO BACK UP A LIST OR LIBRARY

By the way, the way to back up a single list (or library) is:

1. While in the list, go to Modify Settings and Columns. Click the Save This List (whatever the list name is) As Template link in the General Settings section.

2. It will bring you to a familiar Save as Template page. There will be a filename, template title and description, and include contents sections. The template will be saved in the List Template Gallery. All rules that apply to site templates also apply to list templates.

This is useful for backing up a particularly critical list or library.

And that's the story about backup and recovering sites by using templates. Remember that templates are stored as part of a site collection's inventory, so each template makes it larger, inching it closer to its quota limit. If you do use save site templates, or list templates with content, remember to regularly delete the backup templates that become obsolete.

Using STSADM.EXE Command-line Tool to Back up and Restore Site Collections

STSADM is the SharePoint command-line administrative tool, and it's a powerful and easy to use one to boot. Because it is a command-line utility, backups and other tasks can be automated with scripts. It comes with SharePoint and is usually located in the %Program Files%\Common Files\Microsoft Shared\web server extensions\60\BIN folder on the SharePoint server.

Now, STSADM has many, many uses (see Figure 18.147), but the one I am most interested in is how to use it to back up and restore site collections.

Here's a quick run down on some of STSADM's details:

◆ Very powerful and easy to use. A dangerous combination, considering it is as easy to delete sites as it is to back up a site collection or restore it (and that is really easy).

◆ Must be run locally, cannot remotely administer a SharePoint server.

◆ Backups do take up a considerable amount of resources. Like usage analysis processing, it needs to be done during the least amount of activity on the server.

◆ Creates a single flat file out of the site collection. Not something that can be done incrementally or recovered in pieces. Whole backup, whole restore, that's it.

FIGURE 18.147
An incomplete list of
STSADM's operations

◆ Does not back up or restore anything but one site collection at a time. In other words, it can't back up a single list, library, or site, nor does it have the capability of backing up or restoring several site collections at once.

◆ Backup and restore of site collections is with true fidelity. No permission data, like security and personal views, is lost.

◆ Requires administrative privilege on the local server to run (which is a good thing, considering it is such a powerful tool).

◆ Will fail to restore a site collection on a server with a different configuration database. The site collection's original configuration database must match the configuration database on the server it is restoring to. This means the site collection must be restored on the same server it was backed up from, or it can be restored to a different server in a server farm (since, by definition, servers in a server farm are sharing a common configuration database).

The command syntax is operations followed by parameters, so to do anything with STSADM, the syntax always starts with a -o switch, then the operation you want, then the parameters.

In other words, everything STSADM does starts with -o (except help, which starts with -help then parameter—use it often). In our case we are going to use three operations:

enumsites   Enumerates (lists) the site collections for the local SharePoint server. Good practice to be sure that you don't mistype the name of the site collection you want to back up. Parameters it requires are the -url of the Virtual Server that contains the site collection(s) you want to back up (remember, site collections are contained by Virtual Servers). Then it will report all the site collection URLs for use later.

backup   Backs up the site collection into a flat DAT file. Doesn't appear to do incremental backups. It's all or nothing. Requires a -url of the server and site collection, -filename of the backup file (and its path), -overwrite if you have a backup file of the same name in the location you are backing up to.

restore   Restores the backups made by STSADM. Flat restores, again all or nothing. Parameters required are -url of site collection to which the backup is being restored, -filename of the backup file, and an optional parameter of -overwrite—but I suggest you use it. I have heard of restores just stopping because there were some files that -restore was reluctant to ignore.

STSADM BACKUP

To run a STSADM backup, you should go to a command prompt and type in a painfully long path to the STSADM.EXE file. I hate doing that, so here's another option. Open Windows Explorer.

Browse to C:\Program Files\Common Files\Microsoft Shared\web server extensions\60\BIN (or wherever you keep your Program Files folder and its contents).

Once there, open a command prompt, and type **cd** and hit the spacebar at the command line. This will prep the command line for the cut and paste of the long path.

Then drag and drop the icon of the folder in Explorer's address bar (to the left of the big, long path), into the command prompt window. Then hit Enter (see Figure 18.148 for what happens next).

FIGURE 18.148
STSADM.EXE
from Explorer

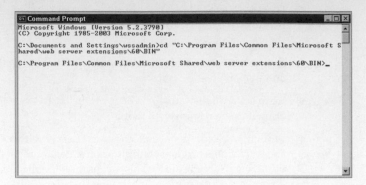

That should put you right in the folder that contains the STSADM.EXE command (and, conveniently, the SMIGRATE.EXE command as well). I prefer to drag and drop over typing a long path at the command prompt any day.

First, let's enumerate our site collections on our server. Remember that our Virtual Server is the default website in IIS, and as such, its URL is literally just the server name, so to see what site collections we have in our default website virtual server, we just need to supply the server name for the URL.

The syntax for my server would be (feel free to try this at the command prompt we just seeded with the STSADM.EXE. Use your own SharePoint server name of course):

```
STSADM.EXE -o enumsites -url http://share1
```

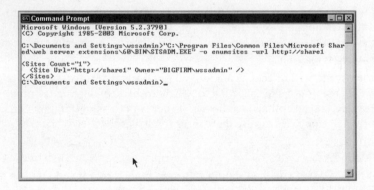

WARNING   STSADM does not use DNS, so don't use fully qualified domain names. Remember, this command runs locally, so it just needs the name of the server it is on, then, if necessary, specify the Virtual Server (if you have more than just the default Web Site) that might contain the site collection you want to back up.

Now that we are certain what our site collection is called according to STSADM, it's time to do a backup. Right now you know what state our SharePoint site is in. The theme, the permissions, the security settings, all of it. We are going to back that up, then make changes as if we were ruining our site, then we will restore the original, pristine backup.

At the command prompt, make sure that you are in the folder where STSADM.EXE is. Then use these operations and parameters (remember to use your own server name, and the filename is an example):

```
STSADM.EXE -o backup -url http://share1 -filename c:\backups\companyback.dat
```

TIP You can also end this statement with the -overwrite parameter if you are doing a backup to the same filename you used last time, as often happens in scripted, automated backups.

Now we need to mess up our site a little.

Make sure that you are on the Company Site Home (or whatever you renamed your site) page in IE and that you are logged in as your administrator.

We are going to delete Internal Documents and change the theme:

1. On the Quick Launch bar, click Internal Documents.

2. On the Internal Documents library page, click Modify Settings and Columns.

3. In the Customize Internal Documents page, click the Delete This Document Library Link Under General Settings.

4. Click OK in the This Document Library Will Be Removed, Are You Sure You Want to Do This? dialog box.

   Boom. That will put you on the Documents and Lists page; feel free to scroll through there, because Internal Documents is gone.

5. Click Home on the navigation bar.

On the Company Site Home page, notice that the Quick Launch bar doesn't have Internal Documents listed.

And finally, change the Theme of the site by going to Site Settings on the navigation bar. Scroll down to the Customization section, and click Apply Theme to Site. Choose a theme then click the Apply button. Go back to the Company Site Home page.

That's enough damage (see Figure 18.149) I think. Now let's see if we can restore the site.

FIGURE 18.149
Site damage
before restore

STSADM RESTORE

Go to the command prompt and be sure to use the full path and executable for STSADM.

Use the following operation and parameters, as shown at the bottom of Figure 18.150 (remember that you might have a different server name and backup filename if you chose to):

```
STSADM.EXE -o restore -url http://share1 -filename c:\backups\companyback.dat -
overwrite
```

The final test to see if the site was restored: open IE, go to the SharePoint site. Log in as whoever you'd like. The site should be restored to its prebackup theme, and Internal Documents should be back on the Quick Launch Bar (see Figure 18.151).

FIGURE 18.150
Restore command
and syntax

FIGURE 18.151
Restored site

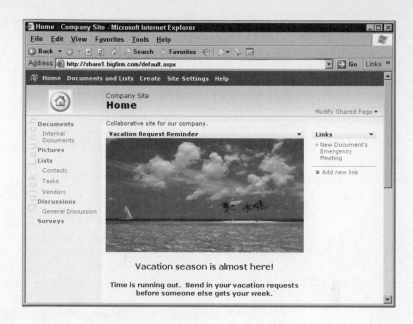

Backup and Restore using SMIGRATE.EXE

Originally this command was used to migrate SharePoint Team Services 1.0 over to SharePoint Services, but now it is great for migrating SharePoint from server to server, as well as backing up and restoring. It doesn't restore permissions or user settings like personal views; only STSADM.EXE does full fidelity backups. It does, essentially, what FrontPage does when it backs up a site. Specifically, A short list of details about SMIGRATE:

♦ Does not restore security and personalization settings.

♦ Can backup a site or site collection.

♦ Can be used remotely.

♦ Can be used by someone other than a local administrator. As long as you are an administrator of the site or site collection you don't need to be the administrator of the local server or domain.

♦ Cannot overwrite an existing location. It cannot restore to a site that has a template applied to it.

♦ However, it can restore to *any* empty site, it doesn't have to be an exact match. It doesn't have to be a restore right back to its original place.

♦ Uses the FrontPage backup file extension FWP, but unlike FrontPage, SMIGRATE can be scripted.

TIP To use SMIGRATE at the command line, take advantage of the same trick with command prompt that we did with STSADM; they are both in the same folder.

With SMIGRATE the syntax is a little different: -w means web instead of -url and -f means -filename. SMIGRATE backs up as its default function. To get it to restore, you need the -r parameter. Also, it needs you to authenticate with a valid username and password (yes, plain text, this command is old school) for the site. The parameter for user is -u and the parameter for password is -pw.

SMIGRATE BACKUP

Because SMIGRATE can back up individual sites (and their subsites too), I thought it would be a good idea to back up one of the subsites we created earlier. In order to do that, you need to know what the site's URL is.

To find a subsite's URL you can do one of two things:

◆ Go to the top-level administrative settings for the site collection that contains the site you want to back up. Once there, check the site hierarchy for the site's URL.

◆ Use the STSADM command to enumerate the site collection's subsites. To do that simply use the site collection's URL and use the -enumsubweb switch. Such as:

```
STSMADM -o enumsubweb -url http://share1
```
That will get you a list of the subsite URLs in the site collection.

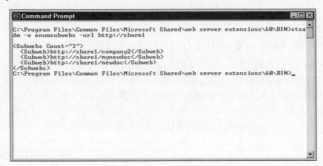

To back up the New Document Workspace we made earlier, enter at the command prompt:

```
SMIGRATE -w http://share1/newdoc -f c:\backups\companyback.fwp -u wssadmin -pw
PassW0rd
```

Once you know the name of the subsite you want to back up, go to a command prompt and use the SMIGRATE syntax just listed above (or look at the command line at the bottom of Figure 18.152). SMIGRATE is much more verbose than STSADM, but does its job.

FIGURE 18.152
SMIGRATE
site backup

SMIGRATE RESTORE

To restore a site with SMIGRATE, the location must be empty. We could delete the workspace we just backed up, then recreate it empty in order to demonstrate the recovery process. But instead, we are going to demonstrate something different about SMIGRATE: it doesn't care what site it restores a site backup to as long as it is empty.

1. In IE, go to the Company Site Home page. Click Create in the action pane.

2. In the Create page, click Web Pages in the action pane.

3. In the Web Pages view, scroll down to the Sites and Workspaces link and click it.

4. On the New SharePoint Site page, enter data in the Title, Description, and URL name for the site (particularly remember the URL, I called it "restored.").

5. Scroll down, keeping the permissions default.

6. Click the Create button at the bottom of the page.

   You will immediately go to the Template Selection page. Resist temptation: there must not be a template on this site or SMIGRATE will not be able to restore to the URL.

7. Click the Back button in the toolbar of Internet Explorer (it will take you back to the New SharePoint Site page, but that's okay. Anything is better than choosing a template).

8. In the navigation bar, click Home.

That's it, you've created a blank site. If you were to go to the Sites and Workspaces page from Documents and Settings, you would see the site listed.

Now it's time to restore the newdoc (New Document Workspace) site to the newly built, empty site.

From the command prompt, use the following syntax (see the bottom of Figure 18.153) to restore the file backup of newdoc (or whatever you backed up) to a new location:

```
SMIGRATE -r -w http://share1/restored -f c:\backups\companyback.fwp -u wssadmin
pw- PasswOrd
```

When it is done, you will have a new New Documents Workspace (complete with the Emergency Meeting subsite, how cool is that?). But if you look at the Address Bar, you'll see (in Figure 18.154) that the path in the address bar is actually pointing to my empty site restored.

FIGURE 18.153
SMIGRATE restore syntax

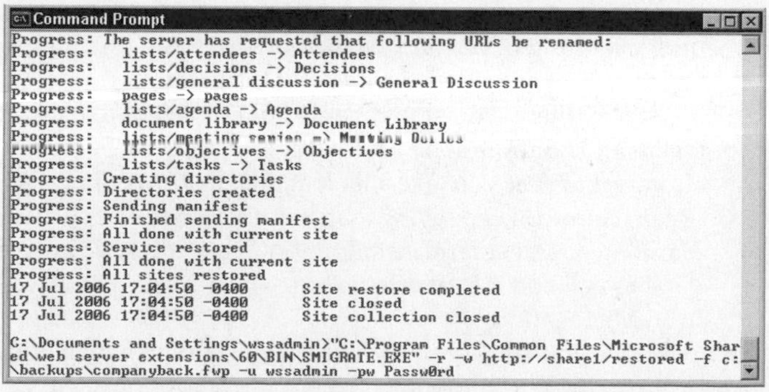

FIGURE 18.154
Restored New Document Workspace

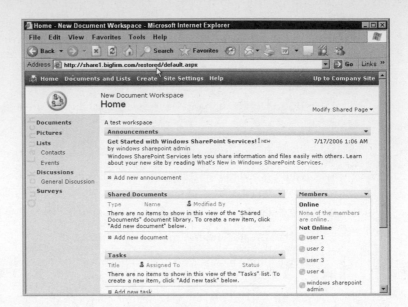

What does this mean? It means you can back up site collections, sites, and even lists and that SMIGRATE and STSADM both have their strengths and weaknesses. We have barely scratched the surface of these tools, but I hope it gave you some idea about how to back up and restore your Windows SharePoint Services sites and site collections (and lists too).

Summary

We have covered a little bit of everything in this chapter, from a typical install to lists, libraries, and workspaces to administration and permissions to, finally, backups and restores. This was just the tip of the iceberg, but I hope it has given an idea of the potential lurking underneath SharePoint Services.

To review, your boss needed you to create a collaborative solution that allowed information workers to share documents (with versioning and check out /check in capabilities), share a list of contacts, and have discussion group functionality.

In one chapter, you have learned how to give your boss what he wants and then some. In addition to what your boss wanted, you know a lot about the back end of Windows SharePoint Services, the services it requires, the databases, configuration, and design. You have more than a cursory understanding of not only what SharePoint can do, but how it does it, what it needs, and what it can't do. You are currently ahead of the game.

To stay there, you are probably going to want to move past what was covered in this simple install and configuration of Windows SharePoint Services. I tried to give you an overview, but I strongly suggest you take a look at the Windows SharePoint Services 2.0 Administrators Guide (Yeah, I know I keep saying that, but it is so darn useful). It will cover what I couldn't, like capacity planning or server farm installs or how easy it is to do an in-place upgrade to SQL on your WMSDE databases when it is time to go big. Not to mention the Configuration Analyzer, a free download from Microsoft.

I hope you take what we covered and end up with a huge server farm of your own, with dozens of Virtual Servers, holding dozens of top-level sites. At the very least, your boss should be impressed with what you can now do with a product that doesn't cost a penny. Congratulations.

Chapter 19

Unix and Windows I: Network File System

For several years, Microsoft has offered a series of tools that make it easier to run both Windows and Unix (or its cousin, Linux) on the same network. Those tools were all packaged together as something called Services for Unix (SFU), and it used to be a separate for-pay product. In January of 2004, however, Microsoft started giving it away—you can find it at Microsoft's site as Services for Unix 3.5. Several of the SFU 3.5 components are now included on the R2 CDs. One of the major pieces of SFU that R2 inherits is the ability to act both as a client and server for Network File System, or NFS. Originally developed by Sun Microsystems in 1984, NFS is a file sharing system much like the Server Message Block (SMB) file sharing service built into every copy of Windows. Like SMB, NFS is mostly an intranet, inside-the-firewall solution; most of us wouldn't employ either NFS or SMB across the Internet.

Including an NFS server module in every R2 server will simplify communicating with Unix clients; virtually every version and flavor of Unix or Linux includes an NFS client. Similarly, allowing any R2 server to be able to communicate as a client with Unix boxes hosting NFS shares makes accomplishing the Windows-Unix connection a bit simpler.

New Unix integration features include Active Directory lookup, for associating Unix accounts with Windows domain accounts, and support for the 64-bit operating system environment.

NOTE SFU 3.5 included a service (reminiscent of the NT Gateway Service for Netware, or GSNW) called Gateway for NFS, which allowed you to create client connections to NFS shares on Windows systems and then offer them to Windows clients over SMB/CIFS. This migration tool allowed Windows clients with no knowledge of Unix NFS or mount commands to connect to NFS resources as if they were shared folders on the Windows server. The Gateway for NFS has not been packaged with the R2 software. Also excluded are all of the PCNFS components that are included in SFU 3.5.

This is the first of three chapters dealing with the Unix integration tools included with R2. In this chapter, we'll discuss not only the client and components of NFS, but also how to map Unix user and group accounts to Windows user and group accounts (an important prerequisite for using the NFS components). In Chapter 20, we'll show you how an R2 domain controller can act as an NIS server. Finally, in Chapter 21, we'll talk about one-way and two-way Unix-to-Windows password synchronization.

This chapter is aimed primarily at Windows Server administrators who may not know a whole lot about Unix. A true-blue seasoned Unix admin will no doubt notice some simplification of the NFS concepts and several generalizations regarding how things usually work on Unix systems.

NFS Concepts

NFS is different from SMB (the Windows file sharing protocol) in several significant ways. If you happen to be new to NFS protocol, you may want to review the following overview of concepts before proceeding with installation and creating NFS shares.

Connecting to NFS Shares

A few years back, when Windows clients connected to shared folders on a Windows server, they would be required to map a local drive letter to that remote share so that the network resource would appear to the operating system as if it were a local drive (this would make applications that knew nothing about networking happy). Now that Windows supports direct UNC connections and most applications are network-aware, it's no longer necessary to map drives to network shares (although it's still very common).

This principle of fooling the OS into thinking it's talking to a local file system applies as well with NFS clients on Unix systems. On a Unix system, the administrator (in Unix the built-in account with powers like the Windows administrator account is called "root") account creates an empty directory at some location in the file system hierarchy and then "mounts" the NFS share from a remote server onto that directory. Usually the administrator also edits a configuration file (vfstab or nfstab) to specify that the share should be mounted whenever the system boots.

> **NOTE** One of the most common uses for NFS is home directories. On most Unix or Linux workstations, users have a home directory at /home or /export/home. By putting a user's home directory on an NFS share and mapping it to the local /home directory, NFS enables Unix admins to let their users see the same home directory no matter what system they're working from.

In the Windows world, users can make their own connections to remote shares, but in the Unix world this is typically done by the administrator and is transparent to the user.

Regular Unix users generally cannot mount or unmount NFS shares, and they may not even be aware that their home directory is remotely mounted from another server. The Microsoft Client for NFS included in R2 and in SFU 3.5 does permit individual users to map and unmap drives to NFS shares. However, for Unix clients, the mounting procedure will have to be done by someone with root access.

NFS Access and Authentication

When an administrator creates a shared folder on a Windows NT, 2000, or 2003 server, she grants or denies access to specific users or groups of users. These share-level permissions provide a network-level access control filter, and then the additional permissions on the NTFS file system permit more granular access controls.

The NFS protocol makes remote file systems available to remote client *systems* instead of to users or user groups. Unlike the SMB protocol, NFS file system sharing is based on machine-level access. When an NFS share is created, the administrator specifies read only or read-write access for remote systems, not users.

NOTE   The term *client*, used in the Services for NFS context, means "client machine." The host connecting to an NFS share on a server is a *client*. A logical group of machines permitted to connect to NFS shares is a *client group*.

The current NFS authentication protocol is based on the idea of "trusted" remote hosts. When a user accesses a file or folder on an NFS share from one of the permitted clients, the NFS server trusts that the remote client has already authenticated that user. If that user has a User ID (UID) and Group ID (GID) that also exists on the NFS server, the NFS server recognizes that user as one of its own.

Access to files and folders in the NFS share (also called an "exported directory") will be granted or denied by comparing the assigned UID and GID of the connected user with the permissions on the files and directories.

At this point, if you are scratching your head and thinking that I did not say anything about a password challenge, you are correct. The NFS server does not verify the password of the user connecting to the shared directory. The user's password on the server and the client system do not have to match at all. There are some recent implementations of NFS that do more secure user authentication (SecureNFS on Solaris, for example); however, Microsoft Services for NFS supports only NFS versions 2 and 3, which do not include any password challenge-response functions.

Instead of user password authentication, Services for NFS uses Unix-to-Windows account *mappings* Unix users and groups to associate with Windows users and groups. These associations (or maps) can be maintained in Active Directory as account attributes (after a schema extension included with R2), or in maps maintained by the User Name Mapping (UNM) service.

NOTE   The actual authentication components used by Services for NFS are Services for Users (S4U), a Kerberos extension for AD authentication; and Server for NFS Authentication, which is required for local account authentication.

This mapping of Windows to Unix accounts is critical to your success in deploying Services for NFS. Please take the time to look over the details later in the chapter.

NFS Under the Hood

NFS is based on Remote Procedure Calls (RPC) and uses a combination of UDP and TCP ports. Since Microsoft's Services for NFS supports both version 2 and 3, and everything is turned on by default, you will see multiple UDP and TCP ports open on your Windows NFS server until and unless you decide to change the default settings.

On a Unix system, NFS is implemented as several processes (or daemons) running concurrently. On your R2 box, the NFS Server is implemented as a single process (nfssvc.exe), which can be started and stopped using the Services console or the command prompt. If you look in your Task Manager or run tasklist from the command prompt, you will only see the nfssvc.exe running. However, hiding behind this single server process is a more complex structure that reveals its Unix origins. To see the separate pieces of NFS (and find out what ports are being used at the same time), run `rpcinfo -p` to list all programs registered with the RPC port mapper. If you haven't changed the default settings, which will offer NFS services on both UDP and TCP ports, you might expect to see output like this:

```
program version protocol    port
--------------------------------------------------
 100000    2    udp    111  portmapper
 100000    2    tcp    111  portmapper
 100005    1    udp   1048  mountd
 100005    2    udp   1048  mountd
 100005    3    udp   1048  mountd
 100005    1    tcp   1048  mountd
 100005    2    tcp   1048  mountd
 100005    3    tcp   1048  mountd
 100021    1    udp   1052  nlockmgr
 100021    2    udp   1052  nlockmgr
 100021    3    udp   1052  nlockmgr
 100021    4    udp   1052  nlockmgr
 100021    1    tcp   1052  nlockmgr
 100021    2    tcp   1052  nlockmgr
 100021    3    tcp   1052  nlockmgr
 100021    4    tcp   1052  nlockmgr
 100024    1    udp   1049  status
 100024    1    tcp   1049  status
 100003    2    udp   2049  nfs
 100003    3    udp   2049  nfs
 100003    2    tcp   2049  nfs
 100003    3    tcp   2049  nfs
```

In the preceding results, you see five different NFS components listening on multiple TPC and UDP ports. The portmapper process is a control process that coordinates RPC ports and RPC services. It will map RPC requests from clients for that service to the correct port. The nlockmgr and status services handle file locking and state information, respectively. The status service will work with the locking service to handle recovery functions in the case of a reboot or other service interruption. Mountd handles client mount requests, while the nfs service handles all other client file system requests. These components are roughly equivalent to their Unix daemon counterparts, which may have slight variations in names depending on the flavor or version of Unix: portmap, mountd, statd, lockd, and nfsd.

Installing and Configuring Services for NFS

Before you install Services for NFS, ensure that your Unix and Windows systems are able to communicate with each other. For example, make sure that both your Unix clients and Windows servers have records in DNS or local *hosts* files. If the Unix client systems are able to ping the R2 servers by name (and vice versa), you're probably in good shape. If there are routers or WAN links or firewalls between the systems, you'll need to ensure that the ports required for NFS communication are not being blocked. Keep in mind also that the NFS server needs to be able to do a reverse lookup of the NFS client in order to confirm its identity and permit access.

Authentication Options

Before installing and configuring Services for NFS, we should decide how to map the Unix accounts to your Windows user accounts. The approach you choose will determine which components you need to install.

Your company, Bigfirm, has an Active Directory and so you can choose to maintain the Unix user and group information in the AD database. To use this option, you'll need at least one R2 domain controller and an AD schema extension to add Unix attributes for user, group, and machine accounts. Unless you have started from scratch with an R2 DC as the first server in a new forest, you'll need to extend the schema for your Windows 2000 or 2003-based forest. If you run DCPROMO on an R2 server and make it the first DC in a new forest, the schema is automatically extended to accommodate NIS maps, although you won't see the new attributes in Active Directory Users and Computers until you install Identity Management Services for Unix (IDMU) on an R2 DC.

To implement this solution in an existing AD with Windows 2000 and 2003 DCs, you must first extend the schema by running the ADPREP tool found on R2 disc 2 on the DC that's running the schema master operations role in your forest. Log on to that domain controller as a Schema Admin, navigate to the `\cmpnents\R2\adprep` directory on Disk 2, and run the command `'ADPREP / forestprep'`.

When you've successfully extended the schema using ADPREP, you'll need to install an R2 domain controller anywhere in the forest and then install IDMU on that R2 DC. You see, although the schema has been extended, and the new Unix attributes have been created, IDMU is still required because it will add the Unix Attributes tabs to the Active Directory Users and Computers (DSA.MSC) tool on that system. You'll need to use these Unix attributes tabs in DSA.MSC to map user and group accounts between Unix and Active Directory.

NOTE   A list of all the R2 schema extensions, including the Unix/NIS extensions, is found in R2 disc 2 in `/CMPNENTS/R2/ADPREP/sch31.ldf`.

You can choose to install both Services for NFS and IDMU on an R2 domain controller, or you can keep those functions separate and install NFS on a domain member server and IDMU on a DC.

If BIGFIRM didn't already have an AD, or if you were just nervous about extending the schema, you might choose instead to install the optional User Name Mapping (UNM) component of Services for NFS. UNM can run on AD domain controllers or domain member servers.

UNM can also run on stand-alone (workgroup) servers and map Unix accounts to local machine accounts. If you choose this path, you'll also need the optional Server for NFS Authentication component of Services for NFS to handle local security authority authentication requests.

On the Unix side of the network, you have two options for providing user and group identifiers. UNM can do Network Information System (NIS) lookups to a Unix or R2 NIS server, or it can use Unix password and group files that are copied to the local system. AD lookups require an NIS domain, but you can also enter the UID/GID information directly in AD Users and Computers, as we'll discuss a bit later.

BIGFIRM has more than one Unix server, and they are not all the same OS. solaris1 is running Solaris 8, and redhatserver1 is a Linux box (Redhat version 9). As any savvy Unix admin already knows, Unix user IDs should be unique across the network. Users with accounts on more than one system must be assigned the same, unique UID on each one. Group IDs and memberships need to be consistent as well. If NIS is already available on the network, that's the preferred approach, because NIS provides a single password and group database to all Unix systems configured to use it, and also because there will be no local files to keep updated on the UNM server. If you have to use password and group files, that's a bit trickier because you'll have to worry about copying these files to the R2 server's local disk periodically or whenever there are updates. If you have multiple Unix systems, with different NFS users and groups on each server, you'll have to consolidate your password and group files into single files for the UNM Service.

If that explanation of components and dependencies has your head spinning, maybe Table 19.1 will make things clearer.

TABLE 19.1:   NFS User Mapping Options

	AD Lookup	**Map to Domain Accounts**	**Map to Machine Accounts**
Required Components	ADPREP, NFS, IDMU	NFS, UNM	NFS, UNM, Services for NFS Authentication
NIS Lookup Supported?	Yes (with an R2 NIS Master)	Yes	Yes
Password/Group Files Supported?	No	Yes	Yes

Installing Services for NFS

Now that we've discussed our options for Windows to Unix account mapping, let's review the game plan. First you're going to install and configure Services for NFS. Next, you'll need to configure user name mapping (using Active Directory lookup and/or UNM), and then you can finally configure the other NFS options and create NFS shares. Finally, you'll mount NFS shares on Unix client systems.

Let's install the Server for NFS components that you will need.

From the Control Panel, choose Add or Remove Programs and then Add/Remove Windows Components. Select Other Network File and Print Services and then highlight Microsoft Services for NFS (shown in Figure 19.1).

Select the Details button to see the various NFS components (shown in Figure 19.2).

FIGURE 19.1
Install Microsoft
Services for NFS.

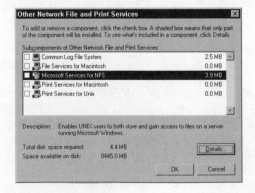

FIGURE 19.2
Services for NFS
components

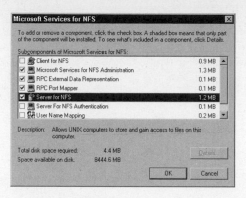

When you select Server for NFS, dependent components (RPC and Admin Tools) are automatically selected as well. If you want to install the Client for NFS now, go ahead and select it. If you're *only* going to use Active Directory lookup to manage account mappings, you don't need Server for NFS Authentication or User Name Mapping.

Select the Services for NFS components you need, click OK, and then click Next to let the Windows Component Wizard install the software. Insert R2 disc 2 when prompted.

Configuring Services for NFS

Now that you've installed the Services for NFS components, let's take a look at the NFS Server setting and discuss a few configuration options you might want to know about before exporting shares and hooking up your users. In your Administrative Tools group, locate Microsoft Services for Network File System once again and open it. Highlight Server for NFS in the console tree, right-click, and choose Properties to view and modify Server for NFS properties.

NFS SERVER SETTINGS

The Server Settings tab (shown in Figure 19.3) reveals what versions of NFS are currently running (both version 2 and 3, by default) and which network protocols are in currently use (both UDP and TCP, by default).

You may choose to disable NFS version 3 support and also choose to use only UDP or only TCP protocols for NFS. Before you just disable NFS version 3 and UDP or TCP, however, it's not a bad idea to check your Unix clients to see what NFS versions and protocols they are using.

Use the `rpcinfo` command to view version information and RPC port mappings on remote NFS servers and clients by appending the remote host name to the rpc probe command: `rpcinfo -p` *servername*. Depending on the remote server's configuration, however, you might expect to see quite a bit more than just NFS daemons and their ports running on the Unix systems. If the remote server is running NIS, for example, you might see a number of "yp" services (the service names will all start with "yp" because "yellow pages" is an old name for NIS). In the NFS concepts section, we discussed the main components of NFS protocol: portmap, mountd, statd, lockd, and nfsd. Look for these names (or variations) in the output from remote Unix systems.

FIGURE 19.3
NFS Server Settings

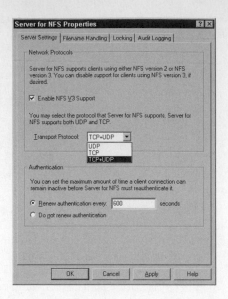

FILENAME HANDLING

Use the Filename Handling tab options (shown in Figure 19.4) to specify a character translation file, tell NFS to mark files beginning with a period (.) as hidden, and turn off or on case-sensitive searches.

Character translation is a feature to remap characters that are unsupported to permitted characters on the NTFS file system. NTFS doesn't permit any of the following characters in filenames:

    "/*?<>|:

FIGURE 19.4
NFS Filename
Handling

Unix file systems permit anything but a space or a backslash (/), which is used as a directory separator.

On Unix systems, files that begin with a period (.) are hidden from common searches. Enable this attribute in the NFS settings to also set the Windows hidden attribute so that the contents of files and directories can be presented consistently for both Windows and Unix users.

Unix clients expect the case of files and folders to be preserved and also for searches to be case-sensitive. Windows is normally "case-preservative" but case sensitivity in filename searches is enabled by default for NFS.

FILE LOCKING

Use the settings in the Locking tab (shown in Figure 19.5, below) to specify a grace period for the locking daemon (45 seconds by default). The grace period is the amount of time that clients are given after a service interruption to re-establish locks on files.

If a client system crashes and doesn't come back up right away, it is handy to be able to enumerate and release any locks that a client has on files. You can accomplish this with either the Client Locks information in this tab, or by using NFSADMIN. The command `nfsadmin server -l` will list any locks on the local NFS server system. Use `nfsadmin server -r` *client* or `nfsadmin server -r all` to release locks.

FIGURE 19.5

NFS file lock handling

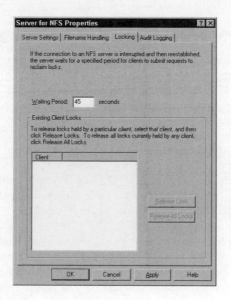

ENABLE AUDITING

Use the Audit Logging tab settings (shown in Figure 19.6) to turn on auditing of NFS actions to the Event Log or to a text file. Auditing is not enabled by default.

FIGURE 19.6
Enable NFS
Audit Logging.

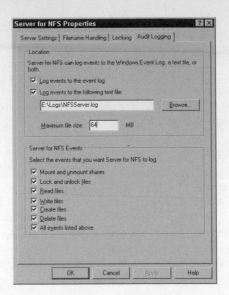

Active Directory Lookups for NFS

As we discussed in the previous section, several things are required to support Active Directory lookup for Unix accounts: the schema extension found on disk 2 of the R2 CD set, and an R2 domain controller server with IDMU installed. It's not necessary to install the IDMU components and NFS server software on the same machine. It's only necessary to install IDMU on a domain controller, in your NFS server's domain, or in a trusted domain.

From Control Panel, choose Add/Remove Windows Components to open the Windows Components Wizard. Identity Management for Unix is listed under Active Directory Services (we'll cover installation and configuration of IDMU in the next chapter).

After you run the ADPREP tool and install IDMU on your R2 DC, open the AD Users and Computers tool on the DC server. Select a user account and choose Properties. You should see a new tab labeled Unix Attributes (shown in Figure 19.7). All group and computer accounts now have a Unix attributes tab as well.

Even if you don't have an R2 NIS server running on your network, you can still "activate" the Unix attributes by selecting the NIS domain name that matches your domain (BIGFIRM.COM) from the drop-down list and fill in the Unix information manually.

Here at BIGFIRM you have only a few Unix users, in your Engineering Department, and they already have accounts on your Solaris 8 and Red Hat 9 server systems and pre-existing user accounts in AD. You do have an AD domain (BIGFIRM.COM) with two domain controllers (DC1 and DC2), a few member servers (one of which is server1), and two Unix systems for the engineers.

The Solaris and Linux systems use different default system account names and IDs, but you have unified the engineers' user IDs and groups across the two platforms. Tom Jones's user ID (1034) will be the same on all your Unix systems, and his primary group (Engineers-GID 3000) exists on all the Unix boxes as well.

FIGURE 19.7
Unix attributes of an
AD user account

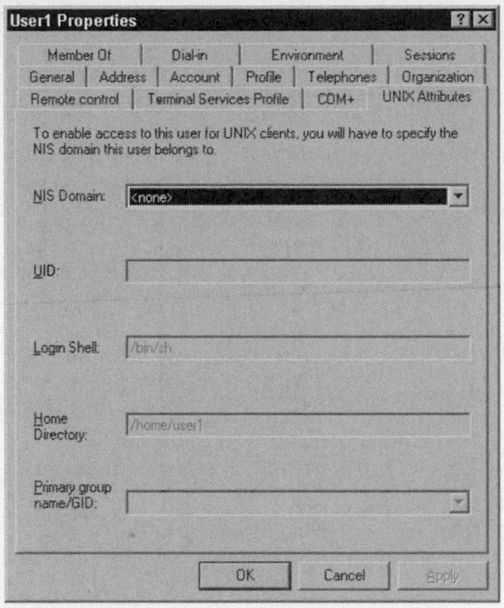

Just to make things more interesting, the Unix systems use a different naming convention than we do on the Windows side of the house. Tom Jones's user ID on solaris1 and redhatserver1 is tjones, but his Windows user name is jones_t. Likewise for Jim Smith and Ann Roberts.

A *partial* listing from our Unix /etc/passwd files shows the following:

```
tjones:x:1034:3000:Tom Jones:/export/home/tjones:/bin/sh
jsmith:x:1035:3000:Jim Smith:/export/home/jsmith:/bin/ksh
aroberts:x:1036:3000:Ann Robert:/export/home/aroberts:/bin/csh
```

The /etc/group file includes the following line:

```
engineers::3000:
```

The password and group files are made up of a single line per colon-delimited entry. In the preceding listing for the password file, the third (colon-delimited) field is the UID and the fourth is the primary GID, followed by the description, home directory, and finally login shell fields. (The x in the second field represents the absent password field, which is not included in the file at all anymore. In the group file snippet, the group name is followed by yet another vestigial and empty password field and then a GID field. The fourth field will contain a comma-delimited list of any group members for which Engineers is not the primary group.

To enable AD lookup (without a running R2 NIS server) of user accounts for access to the NFS Server, follow these steps:

1. Ensure that there are no user ID/group ID conflicts between the users on the various Unix systems.

2. Run the AD schema extension on the forest schema master domain controller and then install IDMU on an R2 domain controller.

3. For each Unix user with a pre-existing Windows account, in AD Users and Computers open the user's account properties, go to the Unix Attributes tab, and activate the Unix attributes by selecting an NIS domain. By default this will be the name of the local AD domain.

4. Once the Unix attributes are enabled, type in the UID and primary group GID for each user.

5. Map the Unix users' primary group to a Windows domain group by adding the group GID to the Unix attributes of that Windows AD group.

6. Configure Services for NFS to use AD Lookup (we'll cover that in a moment).

Figure 19.8 shows the configuration of the BIGFIRM\jones_t account's Unix attributes.

In Figure 19.9, you see an example of mapping a Windows group to a Unix group (GID 3000) using the Unix attributes in Active Directory. This is user jones_t's primary group on the Unix systems.

By the way, the Login Shell and Home Directory fields in the Unix attributes won't be used unless you actually deploy an R2 server for NIS.

FIGURE 19.8

Configure UNIX attributes in AD.

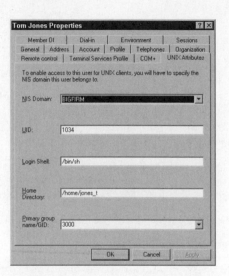

FIGURE 19.9

Configure UNIX group attributes in AD.

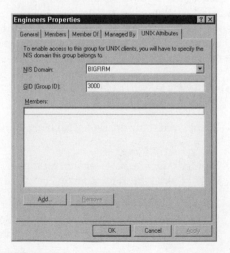

It will not matter that the user or group account names aren't the same. Specifying that BIG-FIRM/jones_t will have the UID of 1034 and GID 3000 when he connects from a Unix system will be sufficient. When he connects from solaris1, if user and group IDs are mapped correctly, any files or folders he creates will be owned by UID 1034 and GID 3000 from his perspective, and owned by BIGFIRM/tjones if a Windows administrator takes a look at the permissions. As long as the UID specified in the AD tool matches a UID on solaris1, and the GID is associated with a Windows group, everybody will be happy.

Okay, if you've specified the UID and GID for all your Unix user accounts in their corresponding Windows AD account properties, and if you've mapped their primary group accounts to pre-existing or newly created AD groups, it's time to configure Services for NFS to use AD lookup. In the NFS Admin Tool, right-click Microsoft Services for NFS. In the Properties box that opens (shown in Figure 19.10), click to enable the Active Directory Lookup check box, and type in the name of the AD domain.

AD lookup for Unix accounts is a great new feature; however, any SFU 3.5 NFS clients and servers already on your network won't be able to take advantage of it. Only R2 domain members or R2 domain controllers can use Active Directory lookup. NFS clients and servers running on top of SFU 3.5 need access to a User Name Mapping server. In the next section, we'll examine the UNM component included in R2.

FIGURE 19.10
Enable Active Directory lookup for NFS.

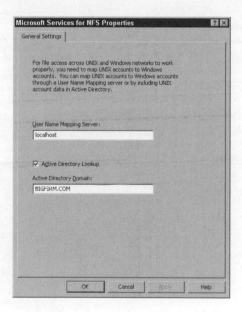

User Name Mapping

I've gone on and on about why Unix-to-Windows account mapping is so important. AD lookup is pretty cool. But there are some scenarios when you can't use AD lookup, or you just don't want to. If you have existing systems running SFU 3.5, for example, they need access to a UNM server; they can't do AD lookups. If you want to try out NFS Server on an R2 box but aren't quite ready to run the risk of doing a schema extension on your AD, you can still provide NFS using UNM.

By the way, these choices aren't mutually exclusive, as long as your R2 NFS server belongs to an AD domain. In an environment with both R2 NFS servers and SFU NFS servers, the R2 servers can use AD lookup while the SFU boxes use UNM. Supporting both means more work for the admin, but sometimes that's unavoidable.

The User Name Mapping component can be installed separately from the NFS Server component. For instance, at BIGFIRM, you'll start out by running UNM on DC1 and tell the NFS server (server1) to use DC1 for user maps.

However, when you decide to set up the NFS Server and UNM on separate machines, the UNM server must be configured to permit name mapping queries from remote systems as specified in a `.maphosts` file on the UNM server.

For environments with multiple NFS servers, it may be advisable to configure two or more UNM servers for fault tolerance or for performance reasons. It's possible to configure a second or third UNM server identical to the first and then create DNS A records to associate a single name `UNMHost` with multiple UNM server IP addresses. These are called UNM pools.

Configuring User Name Mapping

After you've installed the UNM component on your Services for NFS system, the local NFS server will automatically use the UNM server running on the local host. Figure 19.10 (in the previous section) shows the properties setting for Microsoft Services for NFS. Localhost is the default User Name Mapping Server.

To configure the User Name Mapping service properties, right-click User Name Mapping in the console tree and choose Properties. Select a source for Unix user information by clicking one of the radio buttons shown in Figure 19.11.

The choices for a Unix user source are Use Network Information Service (NIS) or Use Password and Group Files.

UNM can query multiple NIS servers and domains for account information; you'll specify which ones to use when you set up the maps.

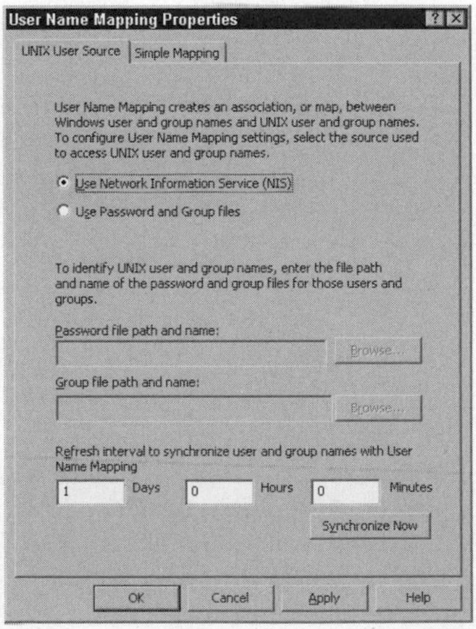

FIGURE 19.11
Select a source for
Unix user and group
names.

When NIS is not available on the network, you must choose the option for password and group files. Specify a local path on the server where UNM can read the password and group files. The local files need to be updated whenever there are changes. UNM will reread the files every day by default. In an environment where accounts change infrequently, it may only be necessary to copy the password and group files to UNM occasionally. In that case, the Synchronize Now button can be used to tell UNM to reread the files immediately.

SIMPLE MAPS AND ADVANCED MAPS

Now that you've chosen a source for Unix accounts, decide whether to use simple maps in addition to the ones you create manually (those are called *advanced maps*). Both simple and advanced maps can be used with either NIS or static password and group files.

Simple maps are Windows-Unix account pairs that are associated automatically whenever user names or group names are identical in the Unix source and in the Windows source (domain or local account). At BIGFIRM, you can't use simple maps for most users because the Windows account name is created as *lastname_firstinitial* (jones_t) while the Unix account name is tjones. However, you do have a Windows group named Engineers and a Unix Group Engineers, so these can be associated using simple maps.

To enable simple maps, go to the Simple Mapping tab in User Name Mapping Properties. Click the Use Simple Maps check box (shown in Figure 19.12).

If you specified your Unix source as password and group files, select a source Windows domain (or local machine name) for the simple map comparison. Otherwise, use the NIS configuration option in this dialog box to create one or more Windows domain to NIS domain mappings.

To create a Simple Windows domain to NIS domain mapping, click the Add button in the NIS configuration section of the Simple Mapping tab. Specify an NIS domain name, an NIS server name (optional) and select an available Windows domain, as I did in Figure 19.13.

When you've finished creating Windows to NIS domain maps, use the Move Up and Move Down buttons to manipulate the order that the maps will be evaluated. Click OK to save your changes and return to the console.

FIGURE 19.12
Enable simple maps.

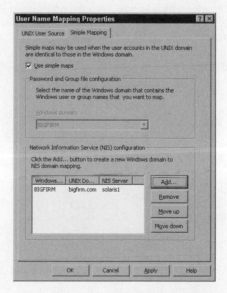

FIGURE 19.13

Create a simple NIS
to Windows domain
mapping.

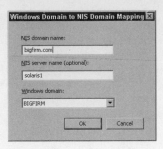

To see any simple maps that are automatically created, right-click User Maps in the console tree and click Show Simple Maps. Do the same thing for Group maps. The Type column at the far right in the details pane of User and Group Maps will distinguish between advanced maps you created and mappings discovered through simple comparisons.

Since BIGFIRM has Unix accounts without identical Windows names that need to be mapped, let's proceed to setting up advanced maps. In the console tree, right-click User Maps and choose Create Map from the context menu. In the Create Advanced User Mapping dialog box, shown in Figure 19.14, select the source Windows domain (or server) from the options listed in the Windows Domain drop-down list and click the button labeled List Windows Users to retrieve a list of user accounts.

Next, type an NIS domain name and (optionally) an NIS server name and click List Unix Users. By the way, NIS servers are located by means of a broadcast protocol, so if you don't have an NIS server on your local subnet you will definitely need to supply an NIS server name. If you are using static password and group files, you'll just click List Unix Users.

If you've successfully retrieved both lists of users, you should see something similar to Figure 19.15.

Select the Windows account and corresponding Unix account that you want to map (as shown in Figure 19.15) and click Add. Repeat as needed to create the rest of your user account mappings. When you're done, click Close. You should now see a list of Simple and Advanced user maps in the details pane, which is similar to the one shown in Figure 19.16.

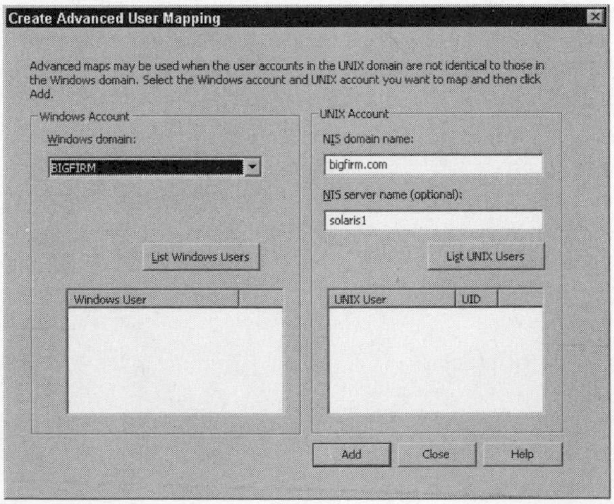

FIGURE 19.14

Create Advanced User
Mapping dialog box

FIGURE 19.15
Select Windows and
Unix accounts for
mapping.

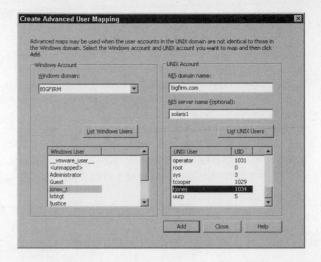

FIGURE 19.16
User Maps in
NFSMGMT tool

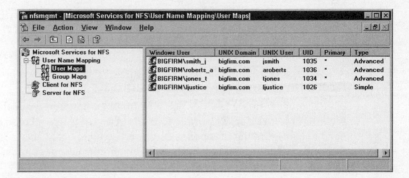

In Figure 19.16, you might note the column labeled Primary. A Unix user account can be mapped to more than one Windows account. This possibility seems most useful to the Windows NFS client: multiple Windows users could use the operator account, for example, to access NFS shares on a Unix system.

Whenever you create a second mapping for a Unix account, you'll be asked whether this is the new primary map. During authentication and access-checking, primary maps are evaluated first, and then secondary maps.

NOTE If you're using static password and group files as your source for mappings, the UNIX domain will appear as PCNFS in the User and Group Maps.

GROUP MAPS

Don't forget to set up your group maps also. The NFS server actually sets NTFS permissions based on the user and group ID of files that users create. Whenever the Unix user's primary group is not mapped to a Windows group, the NFS server will set a NULL SID permission in place of the group permission on that file or folder. Conversely, the group ID of the file on the Unix client will appear as nobody.

WARNING If you set up only user maps and no group maps, your UNIX accounts can create files with the correct UID, but the GID will be set to nobody.

Setting up group maps is similar to creating user maps. Right-click Group Maps and choose Create Map. In the Create Advanced Group Mapping Dialog box, select the Windows domain and click List Windows Groups. Now specify the NIS domain name and NIS server name and click List Unix Users (again, if you are using static password/group files, you'll just click List Unix Users since there is nothing to select).

Now highlight a Windows group and a Unix group to map, and click Add. As you add maps they will appear in the console details pane behind the active dialog box. Figure 19.17 shows a mapping of the NIS domain group staff (GID 10) to Domain Users. This is an obvious choice for a small network where you don't need complex group management.

FIGURE 19.17
Advanced
Group Maps

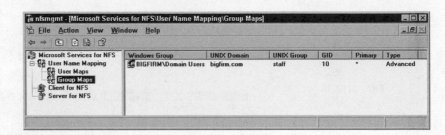

Accepting Remote Mapping Requests

An R2 server running UNM will not respond to map info requests from other NFS servers until it is configured to do so. To permit your UNM server to accept map queries from other systems, you need to configure the `.maphosts` file. You'll need to grant access to *every NFS server and NFS client* that will query the UNM server for mapping information. That includes R2 NFS servers and clients as well as SFU servers and client.

The `.maphosts` file is located in the `%windir%\msnfs` directory (usually `\WINDOWS\msnfs`). This is also the directory where all your command-line NFS tools, NFS DLL files, and the NFS Management console live.

If the file doesn't exist (it does by default), then nobody can access UNM, not even the local UNM server. If it exists and is empty (which is the default), no computer except the local UNM server can access UNM services.

There is a specific syntax for permitting and denying UNM access. Sort of like a router's access control list, the file is read line by line from the top down until a match is found, so the order of entries is very important.

Here's an example of a simple `.maphosts` file. I want to grant access to three of my NFS servers and deny access to everyone else. The `.maphosts` will read like this:

```
nfserver1 #Engineering, Building A
nfsserver2 #Development, Building A
nfsserver3 #QA, Building B
-
```

For the permitted servers, I can use hostnames, fully qualified hostnames, or IP addresses. Unfortunately, I can't specify subnets or network numbers. The text after the # is just a comment (like most Unix config files). The minus sign (–) is very important because it signifies "and deny all the rest." A plus sign (+) at the end of the file would mean "and permit everyone else." Any entries after a plus or minus will be ignored. Therefore if you use the optional plus or minus sign, it should be the last entry in the `.maphosts` file.

Here's another example. The Development folks have two NFS servers in their lab that I don't want talking to my UNM server (they should have their own UNM server and maps), but all other NFS servers should be allowed to query my UNM server.

```
Devnfs1 -
Devnfs2 -
+
```

The Development admins could get around this restriction pretty easily if they can rename a server, change DNS, or bring up another one with a different hostname/IP Address. The first example is more secure, but if you brought up a new "legit" NFS server on the network, remember that it would not automatically be able to query UNM. Whether or not that's a good thing depends on your network and operating environment.

NOTE The `.maphosts` file is a read-only file, so be sure and reset the attribute if you turned it off to edit the file or if you overwrite the file with a new version.

Configuring Multiple UNM Servers

So now you've set up your user and group maps on a UNM box and told your NFS servers to use that UNM server after permitting them access with the `.maphosts` file. Now you might want to think about making more than one UNM server available (with the same maps!) in case of a failure or if you need to take one offline for maintenance.

Here's a simple way to create a second, identical UNM server. First, install the UNM component on a second server and keep the default setting that points it to localhost for UNM server queries. Next, set the properties for the second UNM server (NIS or password and group files, simple maps) to match the properties of the first server. In other words, make sure the two servers are identically configured. Then proceed to set up identical maps on each server. If you've already set up one UNM server the way you want it, there's an easy way to do this with the Backup/Restore Maps option. This feature allows you to back up user and group maps to a single file and then restore them to the same server or to a different server running UNM.

In the NFS Management tool, right-click the User Name Mapping node and select Backup Maps. In the dialog box that follows (shown in Figure 19.18), type in (or browse to) a path and filename for the backup file and click the Backup button to write the backup map file.

FIGURE 19.18
Create a UNM
backup map file.

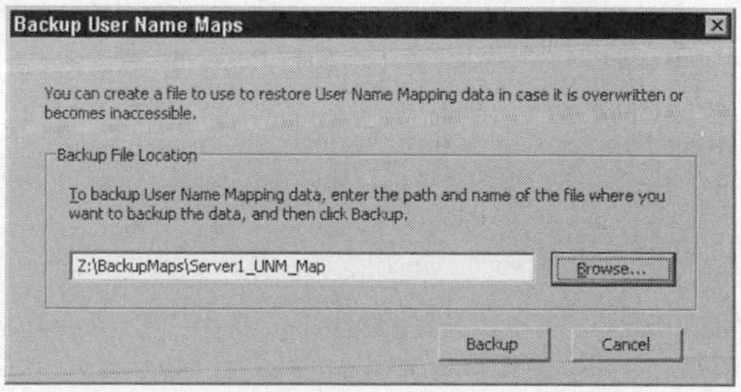

Backup User Name Maps

You can create a file to use to restore User Name Mapping data in case it is overwritten or becomes inaccessible.

Backup File Location

To backup User Name Mapping data, enter the path and name of the file where you want to backup the data, and then click Backup.

Z:\BackupMaps\Server1_UNM_Map   Browse...

Backup   Cancel

Now you have a text version of your user and group maps to restore onto another UNM server. On your target UNM server, open the NFS Management tool, right-click the User Name Mapping node, and select Restore Maps (see Figure 19.19). Browse to the location of the backup file, select it, click Open to return to the Restore User Name Maps dialog box, and then click Restore.

You may have to refresh the display to see the restored maps, but it won't be necessary to restart the UNM service. Now you should have two identical UNM servers with the same map information.

Now let's tell your R2 and SFU NFS servers to use both of your UNM servers by creating a UNM pool with DNS.

FIGURE 19.19

Restore a UNM backup map file.

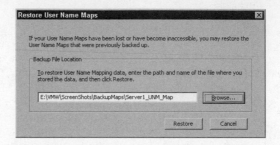

Creating a UNM Pool

UNM servers that make up *pools* should be configured identically so that NFS servers and clients will receive consistent map information regardless of which UNM server they query. We discussed how to do that in the previous section, so if you are just joining us, please review that information before proceeding.

First, create two new host (A) records in DNS, with the same name (UNMHost, in the example below). The first record will point to your first UNM server, and the second will point to your second UNM server. This is how the records might look in DNS:

```
UNMHost    Host (A)192.168.1.3
UNMHost    Host (A)192.168.1.66
```

Next, use the NFS Management tool (or Services for Unix Administration on SFU systems) to configure the R2 and SFU NFS servers and clients to use UNMHost for name mapping services.

When the NFS or SFU systems query DNS for UNMHost, DNS will return both IP addresses (192.168.1.3 and 192.168.1.66). Your NFS server will try the first address on the list and if it works, it will keep using it for a while until the record expires and it has to ask DNS for the IP address of UNMHost again. If the first address doesn't work, it will try the second IP. But here's the cool thing: just about every DNS server out there will do something called *round-robin* for host records with multiple entries. That means that it will rotate the order of the IP addresses in responses. If it gives out 192.168.1.3 first on the list to one client, when the next client queries it will list 192.168.1.66 first. Because the clients usually try the IP addresses in the order they receive them, this accomplishes a simple type of load sharing as well as fault tolerance.

Using backup and restore maps makes it simple to propagate your maps initially, but you also have to maintain a consistent configuration and identical maps. It may be easier to learn to use the command-line tool MAPADMIN to do this. Assuming you can use the same account with administrative privileges to administer all three UNM servers, you'd only have to run the same command multiple times with a different UNM server name argument.

Speaking of MAPADMIN, now that we've gotten to a point where it's actually easier to configure UNM at the command line (it does seem to be if you are going to use UNM pools), let's talk about the command-line options for administering User Name Mapping.

Command-Line UNM Administration: MAPADMIN

MAPADMIN is such a super flexible tool for administering your UNM server, I'm still trying to figure out what you *can't* do with it.

First, let's run through some information-gathering commands, and then I'll show you how to do a few administrative functions.

If you run MAPADMIN from a command line without arguments, it will return the Unix source and refresh settings for the local system running UNM. To run the command against a remote UNM server, add the remote server name:

```
C:\>mapadmin server1

The following are the settings on server1

UNIX Users and Groups Source : NIS
Refresh Interval       : 1 Days 0 Hours 0 Minutes
```

If your server is using files for mapping instead of NIS, the same command will return:

```
The following are the settings on server1

UNIX Users and Groups Source : PCNFS
NTDomain        : BIGFIRM
Password file      : e:\MAPFILES\passwd
Group file       : e:\MAPFILES\group
Refresh Interval     : 1 Days 0 Hours 0 Minutes
```

NOTE A Domain Administrator or a local administrator account is required to administer UNM on local or remote systems. If you need to supply credentials to perform an action on a remote system, all forms of MAPADMIN take a username (-u username) and password (-p password) argument.

To see what Windows domains are mapped to what NIS domains or password/group files, use the listdomainmaps argument.

```
C:\>mapadmin server1 listdomainmaps

Windows domain to UNIX domain Mappings:

 Windows Domain        UNIX Domain
 -----------------------------------------------------------
 BIGFIRM         bigfirm.com
```

To list all simple and advanced mappings on the UNM server, use the list -all argument:

```
C:\>mapadmin server1 list -all
Advanced User Mappings:
```

```
Windows user      UNIX user          Uid   Gid
------------------------------------------------------------
* BIGFIRM\jones_t    bigfirm.com\tjones 1034  10
* BIGFIRM\roberts_a  bigfirm.com\aroberts 1036  10
* BIGFIRM\smith_j    bigfirm.com\jsmith1035  10
* BIGFIRM\peters_k   bigfirm.com\operator1031  10
^ BIGFIRM\reese_k    bigfirm.com\operator1031  10

Advanced Group Mappings:
 Windows group    UNIX group          Gid
------------------------------------------------------------
* BIGFIRM\Domain Users bigfirm.com\staff       10

Simple User Mappings:
 Windows user      UNIX user          Uid   Gid
------------------------------------------------------------
- BIGFIRM\ljustice  bigfirm.com\ljustice     1026   10

Simple group Mappings:
 Windows group    UNIX group          Gid
------------------------------------------------------------
```

The three MAPADMIN commands just described will tell you most of what you need to know about a given UNM server. If you want to administer the service from the command line, Table 19.2 provides some examples of how you would accomplish many of the actions you've done using the GUI in this chapter (using server1 and BIGFIRM\jones_t as examples). Some of the commands in the table are on two lines; however, the commands should always be entered on one line.

TABLE 19.2: Common Administrative Commands Using MAPADMIN

I Want To...	Syntax
Start the UNM service	mapadmin servername stop
Stop the UNM service	mapadmin server1 start
Turn on simple maps	mapadmin server1 -i yes
Turn off simple maps	mapadmin server1 -i no
Set the synchronization interval to one hour	mapadmin server1 -r 0000.01.00
Map a domain user to an NIS user	mapadmin server1 add - wu BIGFIRM\jones_t -uu tjones@bigfirm.com
Map a domain group to an NIS group	mapadmin server1 add -wg BIGFIRM\Engineers -ug engineers@bigfirm.com

MAPADMIN also includes syntax to set maps as primary, delete maps, and backup/restore maps. For the full syntax of the MAPADMIN command, run `mapadmin /?` at the command line.

Creating NFS Shares

Now that you've set up user mapping (using AD lookup or with a UNM server) and configured the NFS server options, you are finally ready to create NFS shared folders (Unix admins often use the term *exports*, by the way, instead of 'shares' or 'shared folders'). For the purpose of this step-by-step procedure, we'll skip the part where you create a folder in the file system (E:\Development, for instance) prior to sharing it.

NOTE You should only need to set permissions on the top level folder of your NFS share. NFS server will work with the NTFS file system to set all other permissions to be Unix friendly (we'll talk more about file permissions later in this chapter).

NFS shares can be created in Explorer or using the command line. Alas, the nifty new File Server Management tool talks a big game about managing NFS shares and MAC-accessible volumes, but unless there's a magic password or something—*open NFSesame?*—at the time of this writing, that functionality hasn't appeared in the tool.

Creating NFS Shares in Explorer

Using Explorer, browse to the folder that you want to share, right-click it to open the context menu and choose Properties. Go to the tab labeled NFS Sharing. As shown in Figure 19.20, click the radio button labeled Share This Folder and accept or modify the suggested share name that R2 will provide. If necessary, select one of the available Japanese, Chinese, or Korean encoding schemes.

Anonymous access is not permitted by default on new NFS shares. To enable anonymous access, select the Allow Anonymous Access check box and specify the UID and GID for the anonymous user (the default is –2). Click Apply to create your NFS share, or click the Permissions button to set NFS share access permissions first.

NOTE Anonymous access can be permitted or denied for each share but not for individual clients.

FIGURE 19.20
Create an NFS share.

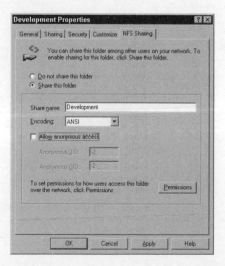

By default, any NFS client system can connect to your NFS share with read-only access. To change the default permissions, open the NFS Share Permissions dialog box (shown in Figure 19.21).

When you see this dialog box for the first time, you may try to remove the ALL MACHINES entry and then add back entries for permitted machines. You'll find that you can't remove the ALL MACHINES entry, however. Don't despair. For the ALL MACHINES entry (and only for that entry) you can set the permission to No Access. Despite the appearance that this will in effect deny all access to the NFS share for anyone, go ahead and set the ALL MACHINES entry to No Access and proceed to add permitted machines to the list. Clearly this is not the same as how NTFS ACLS work. The ALL MACHINES entry cannot be removed, and setting the ALL MACHINES entry to 'No Access' does not override all other permissions, as it would with NTFS ACLS. In this context, ALL MACHINES simply means, 'any machine not specifically listed'.

To add specific NFS client names to the permissions list, click Add. In the Add Clients and Client Groups dialog box you will see a list of client host names) and client groups already known to the NFS server.

If your client name is already on the list, highlight it and choose Add. Repeat as needed until you've added all your hosts to the Add Names list (shown in Figure 19.22).

If this is the first NFS share on this server, you probably won't see any entries in the Names list, so you'll have to type them in manually (use semicolons to separate entries). In the Add Names box, type in the hostnames of any new NFS clients. Choose OK to add them to the permissions list.

FIGURE 19.21
Default NFS share permissions

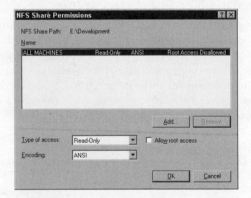

FIGURE 19.22
Add Clients to NFS share permissions.

The NFS service will try to resolve the names of all the client systems you type in. If it cannot resolve a name, you'll get an error message and you won't be able to add it.

It's possible to select the type of access (Read Only or Read-Write) in the Add Clients and Client Groups dialog box if you're only adding one host at time, but if you're adding multiple clients you might as well just add the names and then set the permissions individually back in the NFS Share Permissions dialog box. Highlight each new entry in turn and select Read-Only or Read-Write access. To permit root access for any individual host, highlight it and check the box labeled Allow Root Access.

NOTE Local root account access is not permitted to R2 NFS shares by default. However, on many UNIX systems, only the Super User (root) can use chown and chgrp to reassign group IDs and UIDs to files and folders. You may want to allow the root account on one or more UNIX systems to administer permissions on the files and folders in the NFS share. If you do permit root access, you should also map the root UID and root GID to Windows accounts.

Figure 19.23 shows a permissions list for the Development share on server1: redhatserver1 and solaris1 have Read-Write permissions, the lab servers lou and stu have Read-Only access, and all other machines will have No Access. Root access was also granted to the Super User account on solaris1.

FIGURE 19.23
NFS Share
Permissions

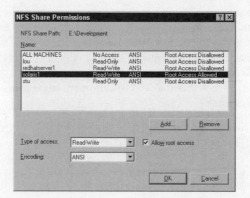

Using NFSSHARE

To create the Development NFS share using the command line, with the same permissions, type (all on one line):

```
nfsshare Development=E:\Development -o ro=lou:stu rw=redhatserver1:solaris1
root=solaris1
```

To see a simple list of all NFS shares on a given system, type **nfsshare** at the command line:

```
C:\>nfsshare

    Engineering2 = E:\Engineering
    LaughTest = E:\LaughTest
    Development = E:\Development
    QA = E:\QA
```

To see settings for individual NFS shares, use the nfsshare *<**sharename**>* syntax:

```
C:\>nfsshare Development

  Alias = Development
  Path = E:\Development
  Encoding = ansi
  ANONYMOUS access disallowed
  Anonymous UID = -2
  Anonymous GID = -2

  HOST ACCESS :
  ALL MACHINES      no access   Root Access Disallowed  ansi
  lou             read-only   Root Access Disallowed  ansi
  redhatserver1     read-write   Root Access Disallowed  ansi
  solaris1        read-write   Root Access Allowed    ansi
  stu             read-only   Root Access Disallowed  ansi
```

Creating Client Groups

Services for NFS also supports the notion of client groups. These are logical groups of clients (the documentation sometimes uses the term 'nodes' for clients) created solely for the purposes of administering NFS access permissions. Use the nfsadmin server command to create client groups and add or remove members from client groups:

In the following process I will use the creategroup, listgroups, addmembers, and listmembers arguments to create two client groups, lab and production, and add NFS clients by hostname to each group:

```
C:\>nfsadmin server creategroup lab
The settings were successfully updated.

C:\>nfsadmin server creategroup production
The settings were successfully updated.

C:\>nfsadmin server addmembers lab stu,lou
lou was successfully added to lab.
stu was successfully added to lab.

C:\>nfsadmin server addmembers production solaris1,redhatserver1
redhatserver1 was successfully added to production.
solaris1 was successfully added to production.

C:\>nfsadmin server listgroups
The following are the client groups
lab
production
```

```
C:\>nfsadmin server listmembers lab
The following are the members in the client group lab
lou
stu

C:\>nfsadmin server listmembers production
The following are the members in the client group production
redhatserver1
solaris1
```

The benefit of using client groups is that I can simply permit read-only access to the lab client group and grant read-write access to members of the production client group. Any client groups created on an NFS server become available in the permissions dialog boxes along with known hosts. Whenever the lab guys bring up a new server that needs access to the NFS shares, I can simply add it to the lab client group—I don't have to add it to the permissions list for each and every NFS share.

But first, I'll use NFSSHARE to fix the permissions on the Development share to use client groups for the lab systems instead of nodes:

```
C:\>nfsshare development -o ro=lab
Development was modified successfully

C:\>nfsshare Development -o removeclient=stu:lou
Development was modified successfully
```

NFSADMIN includes a whole bunch of options and arguments for administering your NFS servers. You should get to know this tool, because it includes several configuration options that are not available in the NFS Management console. It's the only way to create and manage client groups, for one thing.

Connecting to NFS Shares from Unix Clients

Now that you have set up name mapping for our Unix users and created NFS shares with permissions for Unix client machines, let's learn how to connect to a share from a couple of the Unix systems at BIGFIRM.

On most NFS clients (including SFU 3.5 and R2), you can run showmount -e **servername** to view a list of the shares available on remote servers. You don't have to be root or a local administrator to do this. Showmount should be located in the /usr/sbin directory on both Solaris and Linux systems:

```
% /usr/sbin/showmount -e server1
export list for server1:
/Engineering (everyone)
/Development solaris1,redhatserver1,stu,lou
/QA         redhatserver1,lou,solaris1
```

In general, mount and umount (unmount) commands have to be run by the Super User (root) account. Also, in the Unix world you have to *graft* an NFS share onto an existing empty directory in the file system. This is to make the remote file system appear to users as if it were a local file system and, since you don't have drive letters to map in Unix, you just use an empty local directory as the "mount point" instead. The following commands, run with root privilege, will create a directory, Engineering, at the root of the file system and then mount the Engineering share on R2 Server server1 on my Sun box, solaris1:

```
# mkdir /Engineering
# mount -f nfs server1:/Engineering /Engineering
```

The hash (#) sign shown in the preceding code is not typed in; it's a common prompt for a shell run by root.

The Linux mount command uses a different argument to indicate file system type, but otherwise it's identical:

```
# mount -t nfs server1:/Engineering /Engineering
```

That's it. The share is mounted and ready to use. Users need only to move to the /Engineering directory to start using the share. Unless the NFS share gives root access, the Super User won't be able to cd (change) to that directory to check it out. You (or they) will need to log off (or exit the root shell) and use an account that is mapped to a Windows account.

To enable the equivalent of "reconnect at logon," the sysadmin needs to tell the system to mount this new share when the system boots. On a Solaris system, this is done by adding an entry to the /etc/vfstab file, which specifies a list of file systems to mount during boot or whenever the mountall command is used.

The /etc/vfstab file is critical to the boot process, and you can make a system unbootable with a badly placed typo, so I don't recommend trying to edit it unless you've already earned your Unix sysadmin stripes. However, the NFS entries in the vfstab file would use this syntax:

```
filesystem - mountpoint nfs - yes options
```

To add our /Engineering share on solaris1 without specifying any particular mount options, we'd add the following entry:

```
server1:/Engineering - /Engineering nfs - yes  -
```

On a Linux or BSD system, the /etc/fstab file specifies file systems to mount at boot time. The syntax of an fstab file is

```
filesystem mountpoint nfs options
```

To add the /Engineering share to the fstab file on redhatserver1, you'd add the following line:

```
Server1:/Engineering  /Engineering  nfs rw   0 0
```

Mount options for NFS shares vary widely among the various flavors of Unix. We'll discuss mount options for Windows NFS clients in the next section.

NFS and NTFS Permissions

Let's take a closer look at how Services for NFS works with the NTFS file system to approximate Unix file permissions for client systems and users. NFS shares must be created on NTFS file systems. The NTFS file system includes the required owner and primary group attributes in the Discretionary Access Control List, or DACL (by the way, this is not a new development; the owner and primary group attributes are native to NTFS. They were used by the POSIX subsystem).

The user who creates a file is the owner and that user's primary group is the file's primary group as well. The NTFS file system uses the DACL to set access control entries (ACEs), or permission, on the file system objects.

NOTE NFS also supports sharing CD-ROM drives. Naturally, the client access is read-only and, because the file system (CDFS) has no concept of file owners, NFS Server compensates by making it appear to every user that connects that they are the owner of the directory. CDFS permissions are shown as read and execute only for the owner, group, and everyone else.

Here's where the user and group maps become important (and I use the term user map here to refer to either UNM-based or AD lookup). When a Unix user creates a file in an NFS share, the NFS server gets involved with setting the NTFS permissions.

You already know that the Windows user BIGFIRM\jones_t is mapped to NIS user tjones (UID 1034) and his primary group staff (GID 10) is mapped to BIGFIRM\Domain Users. When Tom Jones (as tjones) creates a new folder on the read-write share \Engineering, NFS works with the NTFS file system to set the DACLs and access permissions as shown in Figure 19.24.

The owner of the file (jones_t) is assigned Full Control permission, and his primary Windows group (Domain Users) is assigned Read & Execute. The Everyone group stands in for other/world and so it's assigned Read & Execute as well.

When Tom is logged on to solaris1 and navigates to the folder he created, the output of `ls -la` on that directory will appear as follows:

```
drwxr-xr-x   2 tjones   staff      64 Apr 9 20:15 .
drwx------   2 nobody   staff      64 Apr 9 20:15 ..
-rw-r--r--   1 tjones   staff    3701 Apr 9 20:15 specs
```

FIGURE 19.24
NTFS permissions on an NFS shared folder

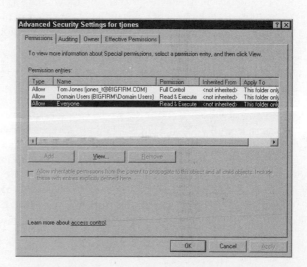

The current directory (.) in the preceding listing shows read-write-execute (rwx) permissions to the owner (tjones) and read-execute (rx) for the group (staff). Other permissions are read and execute (rx). Similarly, tjones will have read-write (rw) access to his file specs as the owner, but members of his primary group and others will have read-only (r) access.

This all seems well and good and as it should be. However, if Tom tries now to remove the folder he created (/Engineering/tjones), he will find that he cannot do so and will get a "permission denied" message for his trouble.

In Unix, as well as in Windows, the ability to remove a directory depends on the permissions of the parent directory. Notice in the preceding listing that the top-level directory (/Engineering, shown as Unix client) is owned by nobody, and the group staff and world have no permissions at all. From Tom's perspective, the question isn't, "Why can't I remove my folder?" it's, "Why was I able to create it at all?" It doesn't matter here that the owner (Administrators on the Windows side) is not mapped and therefore shows up as nobody; what matters is that the default NTFS permission on the parent directory (E:\Engineering) grants read, execute and special create files/write data, create folders/append data permissions to the Domain Users group (mapped to the Unix staff group). So, Tom Jones can create a folder but he won't be able to delete it. This combination of permissions can't be translated into Unix notation for Tom.

Thankfully, this scenario should only come into play with the top-level folders in an NFS share. NFS will work with NTFS to set permissions on subfolders and files created within the share.

One solution to this issue would be to remove the special create permissions that allows users to create folders in the root of the share (you'd need to turn off inheritance first). But if you do that, an admin will always need to create any top-level folders and set the permissions on them manually. I mention it here simply to bring it to your attention. If you decide to implement that solution, you may wish to give root access to the share from one or more client systems so that a Unix admin can manage the top-level directories. It's quite a bit simpler (in my opinion) to use chown (to change the owner) and then chmod (to set permissions) than to go through all the hoops and mouse-clicks required to configure one top-level NTFS folder in an NFS share.

NFS Clients for All: R2 and Services for Unix 3.5

Microsoft has included both the NFS Server and NFS Client components with R2; any R2 server can also be an NFS client. However this isn't much help if you need NFS client software to run on an XP or 2003 workstation. Fortunately, you can still download and install free of charge Services for Unix (SFU) Version 3.5, which includes an NFS client module. SFU 3.5 runs on Windows 2000, Windows 2003, and XP.

TIP To download SFU 3.5 from Microsoft, go to www.microsoft.com/downloads and search for SFU 3.5.

Because this book is about R2, we'll keep referring to the R2 NFS client in this section, and screen shots are from the R2 NFS client. But here's a secret: except for a slicker MMC management interface, the SFU 3.5 NFS client is pretty much the same as the R2 NFS client. With SFU, you use the Services for Unix Administration tool (an MMC 2.0–based tool) instead of NFSMGMT, which sits on top of MMC 3.0. But the configuration options are almost exactly the same. And when you use Explorer to map a drive or run the mount, showmount, nfsadmin, or rpcinfo command-line tools, you really can't tell the difference at all. So if you read this section and learn how to use the Windows 2003 R2 client for NFS, you will have mastered the SFU NFS client as well.

WARNING   Regardless of how similar they seem, Microsoft specifically warns against trying to use any of the SFU administration tools to administer Windows Server 2003 R2 NFS Clients or Servers.

Configuring the NFS Client

Let's take a look at a couple of NFS client configuration options, and then we'll proceed to mounting NFS shares.

First, make sure you are all set for User Name Mapping. Open NFSMGMT.MSC, right-click Microsoft Services for NFS in the console tree, and choose Properties (shown in Figure 19.25).

Your NFS client will need access to a UNM server, or it can be configured to use Active Directory to look up Unix to Windows account mappings (as long as it's a member of a domain). On an R2 system, both types of lookups can be enabled. Type in the name of the UNM server and/or select the Active Directory Lookup check box and supply the name of the AD domain, if necessary.

NOTE   For more information on User Name Mapping and Active Directory lookup of Unix account information, review the "User Name Mapping" section earlier in the chapter.

NOTE   With the SFU 3.5 NFS client, you will have to point it to a User Name Mapping Server using the Services for Unix Admin tool. This client doesn't know how to do AD lookups.

Now let's take a look at the client configuration options. Right-click Client for NFS in the console tree and choose Properties. The client settings for NFS (Shown in Figure 19.26) include transport protocol, mount, and buffer settings.

By default, this version of client for NFS supports both TCP and UDP (the SFU 3.5. client supports TCP *or* UDP, not both). You may choose to use the defaults, or tell the NFS client to use only UDP or only TCP for NFS communications. Your choice should depend on the protocols being used on the NFS server(s) on your network.

FIGURE 19.25
Configure the NFS client for account mappings.

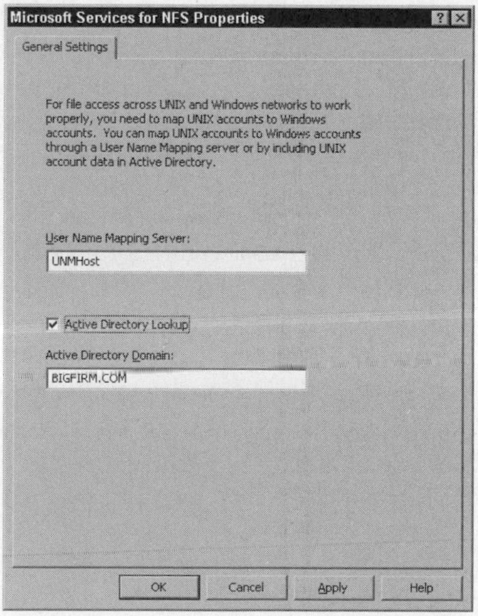

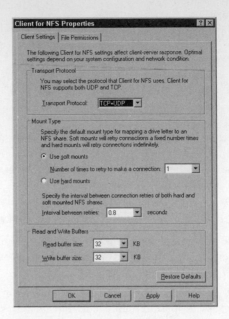

The default mount type on a SFU or R2 system is a soft mount. If a share is hard-mounted, the client assumes that the share is as available as local hard disk. If the share then becomes unavailable, applications accessing the resource will hang as the client continues to retry the connection indefinitely. If it's a soft mount, the client will eventually time out after the specified number of retry attempts and return an error. On Unix systems, however, all NFS file systems are mounted hard by default because of the risk of data corruption (the NFS protocol can't guarantee data consistency in a soft mount if the server crashes). In some situations a hanging application is more of a concern than the risk of corrupted data, so it's good to have the choice. Fortunately, you can override the default and specify hard or soft mounts on a per mount basis when you use the mount command with the `-o -mtype` option.

Click the File Permissions tab (shown in Figure 19.27) to view or modify the default file permissions that NFS client will use when creating new files and directories.

By default, new files will have read-write owner permissions, read group permission, and read-only for others. For folders, the execute permission will also permit listing of directories and traversing the folder structure. For more information on Unix permissions and user and group mappings, refer to the previous sections in this chapter.

That's about all there is to configuring the NFS client. If you need to perform configuration from the command line, check out the syntax for `nfsadmin` with the `client` argument.

Mounting NFS Shares

Connect to NFS shares using Map Network Drive in Explorer, or at the command line with `mount`.

To map a network drive in Explorer, from the menu bar, choose Tools ➤ Map Network Drive. Specify an available drive letter and either type in the NFS server and share path, or use the Browse button to locate the NFS server and its exported directories.

FIGURE 19.27
Default Unix permissions on new files and folders

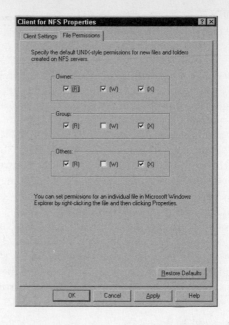

TIP Did you know that you can right-click directly on My Computer in your Start Menu and choose Map Network Drive?

If you are typing in your server name and path, both the Unix syntax and UNC syntax are supported:

```
servername:/sharename
```

or

```
\\servername\sharename
```

To connect to the /export/home share on solaris1, you might try typing:

```
solaris1:/export/home
```

or

```
\\solaris1\export\home
```

In either case, you can map directly to a subdirectory of the root NFS share, so what you might really be going for is the user's home directory on the server:

```
solaris1:/export/home/tjones
```

If you choose to browse for the NFS server and share, look for it in the NFS Network, as shown in Figure 19.28.

If all's right with the world and you locate your NFS server and share in the Browse list, highlight it and choose OK to return to the main dialog box with your server path now populated. Specify whether to reconnect at logon and whether to use a different user name and password to connect to this share.

Here's the thing about browsing for NFS shares: NFS servers on the local network are located by a broadcast. If you know the hostname of the NFS server (especially if it's on another subnet), save yourself some time and simply type the name into the Map Network Drive dialog box. If they wish, users can also add NFS LANS to the list in Network Neighborhood (oops, I mean My Network Places). This is useful if you have a number of NFS servers on other subnets.

To add an NFS LAN to My Network Places, click the Browse button in the Map Network Drive dialog box. Highlight NFS Network in My Network Places, right-click, and then choose Add/Remove NFS LANS from the context menu. In the dialog box that follows, click Add LAN and type a name for the NFS LAN, an IP address (actually any host on the target LAN), and the subnet mask of the target LAN (as shown in Figure 19.29).

Choose OK to add this NFS LAN to the list. Now you'll be able to query for NFS servers on that target subnet instead of just on your local subnet.

Here's another trick: to see a list of exported shares on a remote NFS server, expand your NFS LAN in My Network Places and select one of the NFS servers on the list. Right-click and choose Properties to see a list of exported shares (shown in Figure 19.30). Select one of the shares on the list to see what client systems are permitted access.

FIGURE 19.28
The NFS Network in
My Network Places

FIGURE 19.29
Add a broadcast
LAN for NFS.

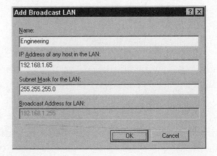

FIGURE 19.30
View NFS shares and access lists My Network Places.

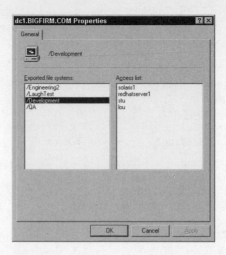

Command-Line Administration

Here's an example of using the mount command to connect to /export/home/tjones on solaris1:

```
C:/> mount solaris1.bigfirm.com:/export/home/tjones *
```

You can also use the UNC syntax:

```
C:\>mount \\solaris1.bigfirm.com\export\home\tjones Y:
```

Microsoft tells us that when we use the UNC syntax it might take longer to connect because the network software searches first for a SMB server before trying to locate a server over the NFS protocol. So the NFS syntax is preferred for performance reasons.

To override the NFS client's default settings (mount type or permissions, for example) for a particular mount point, map the drive from the command line. When a drive is mapped to an NFS share in Explorer, it's not possible to override the default settings.

Enter **mount** on the command line without arguments to see a list of mapped NFS shares and connection parameters/options:

```
C:\>mount

Local  Remote                 Properties
-------------------------------------------------------------------------
X:     \\dc1.bigfirm.com\Engineering2    UID=1026, GID=10
                          rsize=32768, wsize=32768
                          mount=soft, timeout=0.8
                          retry=1, locking=yes
                          fileaccess=755, lang=ANSI
                          casesensitive=no
```

Another nifty little tool is showmount. Use showmount to view a list of exported file systems on remote machines and find out who's connected to them. Showmount -e servername will return a list of exports and trusted clients on the specified server:

```
C:\>showmount -e dc1
Exports list on dc1:
/QA                solaris1, lou, redhatserver1
/Development          lou, stu, redhatserver1, solaris1
/LaughTest         All Machines
/Engineering2       All Machines
```

Showmount -a will return a list of connected clients on the remote server:

```
C:\>showmount -a server1
All mount points on server1:
192.168.1.65            : E:\Engineering
192.168.1.67            : E:\Engineering
192.168.1.88            : E:\Engineering
```

Summary

In this chapter we've covered the basic concepts of the NFS protocol and discussed important differences from the Windows file sharing protocol (SMB). Because NFS grants access to shared directories based on trusted client *machines* instead of users, and accepts the user ID and group ID of the user on that remote client machine, careful configuration of the mappings for Unix to Windows user and group accounts is absolutely essential.

Mapping options include Active Directory lookup, for R2 implementations of NFS in an AD environment, and the User Name Mapping (UNM) service for environments without AD, or for NFS servers and clients based on SFU 3.5. Fortunately, you don't have to create an R2 NIS environment to use the AD lookup feature for NFS, as long as you're willing to enter Unix user and group IDs manually in the AD Users and Computers console. For a pre-existing Unix-based NIS infrastructure, where migration to R2 is not planned, the UNM service should be used for name mapping. Simple maps allow you to automatically map matching user and group names between Windows and Unix, while advanced maps will accommodate situations where user names are formatted differently between platforms, or where a single account is shared by several users.

As we've seen in this chapter, once you have a solid understanding of name mapping principles and tools, creating NFS shares on a Windows R2 box and configuring access is a simple matter. Also, the robust command-line tools that Microsoft has included are similar to the Unix versions of these tools, so administrators who already know how to share and unshare, mount and unmount file systems on Unix boxes will feel right at home with Services for NFS.

Chapter 20

Unix and Windows II: Network Information Service (NIS)

Before there was Active Directory, Sun Microsystems built an application that could let a bunch of Unix systems share a centralized list of configuration files (including users, groups, and passwords) called Network Information Service, or NIS. NIS is, then, a very simple directory service. It's not used as much as it once was, mostly because it's not very scalable or secure, but in some networks it makes perfect sense. R2 supports NIS in several ways. First, a schema extension included in the R2 distribution will modify Active Directory to support NIS information. With this schema extension in place, any R2 domain controller could become an NIS server. When Services for NIS is installed on an R2 domain controller, migration tools permit admins to import NIS source files into the AD so that it can provide NIS authentication and information services to clients and subordinate NIS servers (formerly called "slaves"). An R2 DC can also be a subordinate NIS server, if the master server for the domain is an R2 NIS server. Finally, once your master NIS server is an R2 DC, when a Windows user with an associated Unix account changes his AD password, the Unix password in the NIS database can be automatically synchronized. In this way, R2 with NIS and password synchronization can provide a one-way password synchronization model without the need to install software on the Unix hosts.

NOTE   We won't cover it in any detail in this chapter, but Chapter 21 is all about using the password synchronization components of IDMU.

In the following sections, we'll examine the key NIS concepts to provide you with some background, then cover the issues involved with making your R2 system an NIS master server. Finally, we'll walk through an NIS migration to R2 and discuss care and feeding for your R2 NIS servers.

Like the previous chapter ("Unix and Windows I: Network File System"), this chapter is aimed primarily at Windows Server administrators who may not know a whole lot about Unix. I hope any seasoned Unix admins who find themselves perusing these pages will overlook my simplification of concepts and background information that must be covered as a prerequisite to the subject.

NIS Concepts

In the mid-1980s, around the time that Microsoft was releasing its first retail versions of Windows, Sun Microsystems was working on a solution to a problem that had long plagued the Unix world. Unix servers have always used text-based configuration files for user and group accounts and for just about everything else. When networking came around, a whole set of network configuration files were created to support things like resolution of hostnames to IP addresses. The main configuration files for a Unix host are almost universally stored in a directory called /etc. The /etc/passwd file contains a list of user accounts and parameters (including the user's login shell and home directory path), while /etc/hosts lists hostnames and corresponding IP addresses. Before there was a system for centralizing or distributing these files, when a new host was created on the network, the hosts file on every system had to be updated. Likewise, when a user needed accounts on multiple systems, the passwd file on every host had to be updated. System administrators quickly became overwhelmed with the task of managing all those configuration files and trying to keep them consistent.

NOTE The /etc/passwd file has a misleading name, since passwords are no longer included in the file. Modern implementations of Unix typically store encrypted passwords in the /etc/shadow file.

This is not an unfamiliar story to Windows administrators. The problem of maintaining a user account on every system was solved when NT domains came on the scene around 1992. NT 3.x and 4 domains provided a centralized set of accounts for users, groups, and computers. Similarly, NIS provides a centralized set of database files (or ""maps") for users, groups, and hosts to NIS clients. Like an NT 4 Primary Domain Controller (PDC), an NIS "master" server keeps the only writable version of the NIS "maps". NIS subordinate (or slave) servers are like NT 4 Backup Domain Controllers (BDCs) in that they have read-only copies of the NIS maps that are obtained from the NIS master and updated on a regular basis. Finally, NIS domains resemble NT domains in that the NIS clients don't care which system is the NIS master and which ones are subordinates.

Before we go too far with this analogy, however, NIS domains are different from NT and AD domains in several important ways. In this chapter, I will consistently use the term "NIS domain" to avoid any confusion with AD domains or Internet domains.

NOTE Internet domains are structures created for the hierarchical system of DNS name resolution, while NT and AD domains are made up of systems that share the same security and account information. NIS domains are groups of Unix hosts that share a common set of configuration databases (or maps) without any membership restrictions.

NIS domains are, technically speaking, not security structures. Membership is open to any NIS client, which can also query any server for any NIS domain's map information. Usually, though, an NIS client only queries for map information for its own domain.

A client becomes an NIS domain "member" when the admin runs the domainname command on the system. The NIS master and subordinate servers don't keep a list of clients or require any type of NIS client authentication, although some NIS servers use a "securenets" file, which is a list of hosts (or network numbers and masks) that are allowed to talk to NIS.

NOTE On a Solaris system, you must also add the domain name to a file, /etc/defaultdomain (or the domainname parameter doesn't survive a reboot).

Although NIS is inherently insecure in terms of membership, it is commonly used to maintain central lists of user and group accounts, so there are naturally some security considerations. For instance, while it's possible to maintain the root account information and password for all member systems in NIS, it's generally considered a no-no. It's much safer to strip out the root account (and all "system" accounts) from NIS maps and just maintain a list of users and groups that have to be consistent from machine to machine. Client systems are often configured to read their own, stripped-down, local `passwd` and group files first, and then consult NIS if an account is not found. With this strategy in place, the root password would be different on each system, but accounts and passwords for users tjones, jsmith, and aroberts would be centralized. Before you migrate NIS map information to an R2 box, you should familiarize yourself with the contents of the existing NIS databases so you'll know what to expect.

Unlike AD or DNS, NIS domains are not hierarchical. An organization or company can choose to split up NIS into more than one domain and a single NIS server (Unix or R2) can host more than one NIS domain's maps. However, a given NIS domain (such as BIGFIRM) has no knowledge of or relationship with any other NIS domain (such as DEVELOPMENT.BIGFIRM), regardless of the naming convention. There is no such thing as an NIS domain "trust relationship" to another NIS domain.

NIS maps are completely different from NT or AD domain databases. NIS maps are simply flat database files (in DBM format) created from the `/etc` configuration files or other data files; NIS maps can be used to centralize general data files, called nonstandard maps, as long as they don't contain machine-specific information. The `/etc/vfstab` file, for instance, references disk partitions for mounting file systems, which are also critical to the boot process, so it's not suitable for NIS mapping.

NOTE DBM files are indexed sequential files that only contain one key-value pair per file. These files can be searched quickly to find information based on a key value. DBM files are specific to platform architecture, so special utilities are needed to transfer the files between hosts (you can't just ftp them). Also, they are binary files that don't support direct editing, hence the need to run updates from ASCII files periodically.

Microsoft Services for NIS supports a number of standard maps, which are universally recognized, and also nonstandard maps. Nonstandard maps have to be defined separately for Services for NIS. Table 20.1 describes the standard maps that Services for NIS recognizes.

Unix source file locations will vary with the flavor of Unix. Also, alternate source file locations can be specified when the maps are built. However, NIS maps are always built from files based on and having the same format as the files listed in the table below.

Admittedly, Table 20.1 presents a simplified view of NIS maps. NIS map files provide single-key lookups for clients, so there are often two files for each type of map. For example, NIS builds two indexes from the source `hosts` file: `hosts.byname` and `hosts.byaddr`. The first index has the hostname as the key field, and the second file provides a reverse lookup on the IP address. Similarly, for the `passwd` file, NIS builds `passwd.byname` and `passwd.byuid`.

Many of these maps actually replace the local files as soon as the NIS client comes up on a Unix system. However, others (like the aliases, password, shadow, and group files) can be consulted *after* the local files are read and therefore serve to append data instead of replace it. The name service switch file (`/etc/nsswitch.conf`) on a Unix system specifies data sources as well the order in which they are consulted.

Okay, that's enough information to make you dangerous and help you ask irritating questions of your hard-core Unix admins. Now let's talk specifically about running NIS on an R2 Domain Controller. There are some important differences (and advantages) from running NIS on a Unix host.

TABLE 20.1:   Services for NIS-Standard Maps

MAP NAME	UNIX SOURCE FILE	DESCRIPTION
aliases	/etc/mail/aliases	Email aliases used by sendmail software
bootparams	/etc/bootparams	Boot information for diskless clients
ethers	/etc/ethers	Maps 48-bit MAC addresses to hostnames
hosts	/etc/hosts	Maps
group	/etc/group	Group account names and IDs
netgroup	/etc/netgroup	Network-wide user and host groups
netid	generated during ypinit; may not exist on NIS client	Network-wide names for users and hosts. Includes UID, GID for users.
netmasks	/etc/inet/netmasks	Network numbers and corresponding subnet masks
networks	/etc/inet/networks	IP network numbers and network names, network nicknames
passwd	/etc/passwd	User names and IDs, other user account parameters
protocols	/etc/inet/protocols	Internet protocol names, numbers, and aliases
rpc	/etc/rpc	RPC program numbers and service names
services	/etc/inet/services	Internet service names with ports, protocol, and aliases
ypservers	generated during ypinit	List of NIS servers
shadow	/etc/shadow	Encrypted user passwords

Services for NIS on Windows Server 2003 R2

On R2, NIS maps are supported by a schema extension to the Active Directory. This schema extension must be installed on the domain controller running the Schema Master Operations Role in the forest prior to promoting an R2 server to a domain controller. We'll step through installing the schema extension in the next section.

Services for NIS can only be installed on an R2 domain controller; the service will only consult its local copy of the AD database.

An R2 DC can become an NIS master server or a subordinate, after the maps are migrated to AD. However, the R2 DC relies on AD replication instead of the traditional NIS transfer and update processes, so it cannot be a subordinate NIS server to a Unix NIS master server. R2 subordinates must have an R2 NIS master. An R2 NIS master can have both Unix subordinates and R2 subordinate servers, though.

Because the NIS maps are stored in the AD instead of in text files, there are several efficiencies over using Unix-based NIS maps.

First, because NIS maps are synchronized using AD multi-master replication model, all domain controllers will have Unix attribute information. However, only the DCs running NIS can respond to NIS clients and subordinates. So, if an R2 NIS server dies or needs to be retired, just install services for NIS on another R2 DC to replace it. You won't have to repeat the NIS map migration.

Because of the AD replication of Unix attributes, all R2 NIS servers are actually peers (this is the same neat trick they pulled when Active DNS-AD integrated DNS zones eliminated the pain of secondary zones and zone transfers). Changes to NIS maps can be made on any R2 DC running NIS; they will be propagated to all DCs. The concepts of master and subordinate NIS servers is only preserved for the benefit of any remaining Unix subordinate servers. Just as an AD domain controller can emulate a PDC for the sake of the NT 4 domain controllers, R2 Services for NIS designates a "master" server for Unix subordinates to talk to for NIS updates.

Because Unix attributes are included in the Windows account attributes for users, groups, and machines, you can now create, delete, and modify Windows and Unix accounts for the same person at the same time. AD Users and computers can become the main tool for managing both sets of accounts. Under this system, it's possible to have a Windows account without activating a corresponding Unix NIS user, but every Unix account needs an object in AD; you can't have a Unix account in the R2 NIS without an AD object to graft it on to.

Setting up Services for NIS

In this section, we'll discuss the prerequisite schema extension using ADPREP and also the process for installing and configuring your first R2 NIS server.

Extend the Active Directory Schema

If you run DCPROMO on an R2 server and make it the first DC in a new forest, the schema is automatically extended to accommodate NIS maps, although you won't see the new attributes in AD Users and Computers until you install IDMU on an R2 DC. However, if, like most of us, you already have an existing AD with Windows 2000 and 2003 DCs, you will have to extend the schema before installing an R2 domain controller anywhere in the forest.

This forest-wide schema extension is accomplished by running an updated ADPREP tool on the DC that's running the schema master operations role in your forest.

First, log on to the DC that's running the Schema Master Operations Role as a Schema Admin.

Run ADPREP `/forestprep` from the R2 disc 2 CD (not the one on R2 disc 1). It's located in the `\cmpnents\R2\adprep` directory on disc 2. This will extend the AD schema forest-wide, including Windows 2000 and 2003 domain controllers. Your Windows 2000 and 2003 DCs do not have to be upgraded before running ADPREP.

Install an R2 DC in the Domain

The subnet where the R2 DC/NIS server is to be located is important. Although services for NIS supports clients in broadcast mode and in binding mode (in which an NIS server is specified), clients usually broadcast to find their NIS servers and so there has to be an NIS server available within shouting distance (on the same subnet). This is not true of the NIS master/slave relationship, though. NIS map propagation can and does occur over subnets, routers, and WAN links.

Install Identity Management for Unix on the R2 DC

Follow these steps to install IDMU on the R2 domain controller.

1. Open the Control Panel and select Add or Remove Programs and then Add Windows Components.

2. Locate Active Directory Services in the list of Windows Components, and click Details (shown in Figure 20.1).

3. Select Identity Management for Unix, or click the Details button to select the individual components: Administration Components, Password Synchronization, and Server for NIS, as shown in Figure 20.2. Insert the R2 disc 2 in your server's CD ROM drive when prompted. After the wizard finishes installing IDMU, you'll have to reboot.

When the server has rebooted, you'll notice that DSA.MSC has some new information. User, Group, and Computer accounts now have a new properties tab named Unix Attributes. The Unix attributes aren't turned on until you specify an NIS domain, however.

These new attributes are different for the various objects. Figure 20.3 shows the new Unix Attributes in User Properties, while Figure 20.4 shows the Unix Attributes tab for groups, and Figure 20.5 the new Attributes tab for computer accounts.

FIGURE 20.1
Install Active
Directory Services
components.

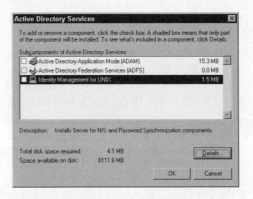

FIGURE 20.2
IDMU components

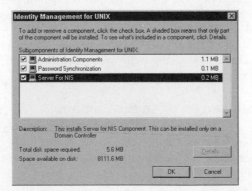

FIGURE 20.3
User Properties:
Unix Attributes

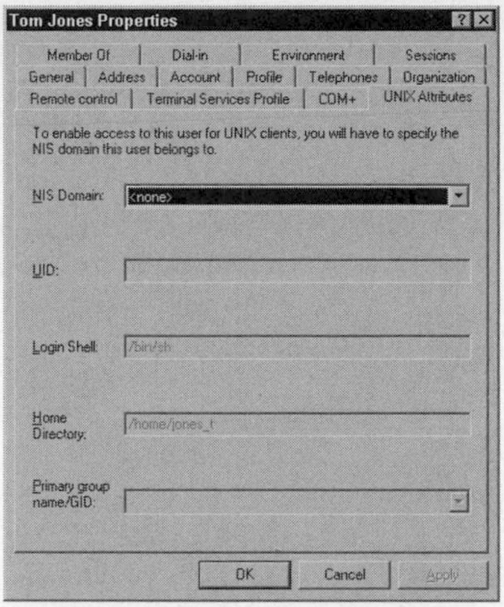

FIGURE 20.4
Group Properties:
Unix Attributes

FIGURE 20.5
Computer Properties:
Unix Attributes

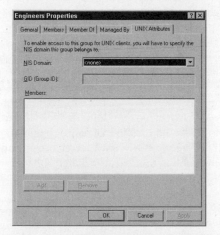

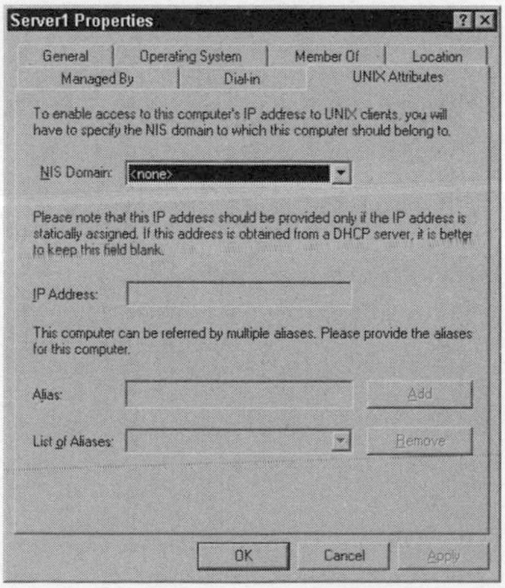

TIP Here's a little secret we touched on in Chapter 19: you don't have to migrate any NIS maps, or even start the NIS service, to start using the new UNIX attributes for NFS authentication with AD lookup. Just activate the UNIX attributes by selecting the default NIS domain (named after the AD domain, just to confuse you) from the drop down box. Now you can manually enter the Unix attributes (mainly UID and GID) that are required for NFS name mapping.

Now that you've seen the new user and group Unix attributes revealed in DSA.MSC with your own eyes, let's take a look at the IDMU management tool. Locate the tool named Microsoft Identity Management for Unix in the Administrative Tools program group, or just run IDMUMGMT.MSC from the Start/Run dialog box.

When you open IDMUMGMT, you should see two components, Password Synchronization and Server for NIS, in the console tree on the left. Selecting an item on the console tree (Server for NIS, for example) causes context-sensitive Action links to appear in the far right pane (shown in Figure 20.6).

If you click Server for NIS to expand it, you'll notice that an NIS domain named after your AD domain (BIGFIRM, in this case) has automatically been created. However, until you migrate NIS maps to the AD, there is no NIS data, so the NIS service is disabled by default. Do not start the service until you have imported NIS maps and run some tests described later in this chapter. NIS clients usually broadcast to locate NIS servers, and you don't want a rogue NIS server with no map data responding to client queries.

Before you begin migrating NIS maps, let's set a few parameters for Server for NIS.

To configure the update (or push) interval, select Server for NIS in the console tree and click the link called Map Updates in the Actions menu to open the General Properties page (see Figure 20.7). Server for NIS automatically checks for updates to maps once a day and, when it finds changes, sends a notification to any Unix subordinate NIS servers.

To enable extensive map logging for map propagation, click the Logging tab of the Properties page and select the Enable Extensive Logging check box (shown in Figure 20.8). Errors are automatically logged to the Event Viewer's Application log (look for entries with the source nissvc); however, enabling this feature will tell NIS to start logging intermediate steps and successful propagations as well.

FIGURE 20.6

Identity Management Administration tool

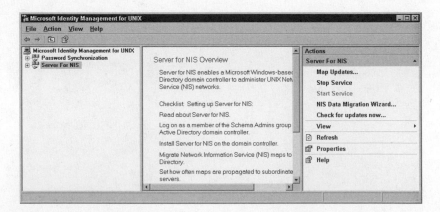

FIGURE 20.7
Server for NIS Map
update interval

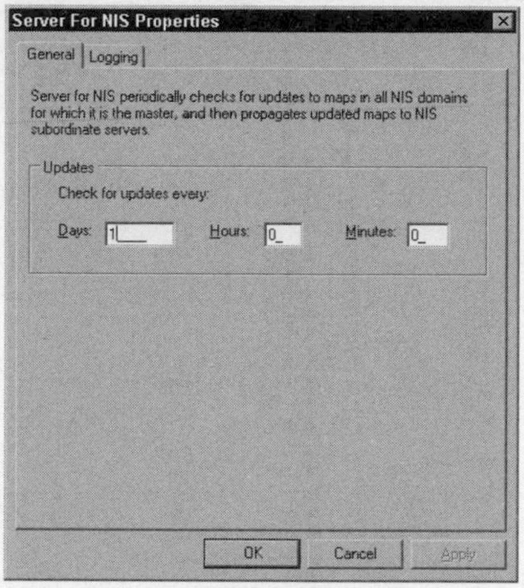

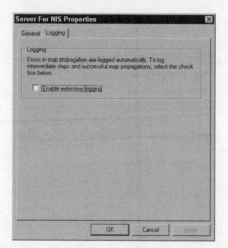

FIGURE 20.8
Enable Extensive
Logging

The last configuration option to consider is the Unix encryption method for NIS passwords. This option is configurable on a per-domain basis. The crypt algorithm is used by default and is the most widely supported by Unix systems. However, if you have an NIS domain consisting entirely of Linux boxes with Message Digest (MD5) encryption enabled, you can choose to use MD5 instead. To change the default encryption method, select the target NIS domain name in the console tree, then click the Unix Password Encryption link in the Action pane on the right. In the NIS domain's properties page (shown in Figure 20.9), select the password encryption method from the Encryption Scheme drop-down box and click OK.

FIGURE 20.9
Select the encryption
method for an NIS
domain.

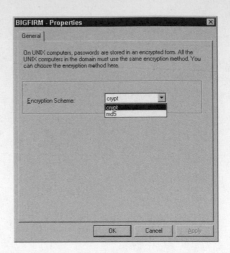

Map Migration

To perform an NIS map migration, you will need access to the Unix source files being used by the current NIS domain master server. You might also spend some time learning exactly how NIS has been implemented in your environment, so you'll know how to test it and recognize the signs if something is wrong.

If you are not also the Unix administrator, you'll need his or her assistance to access the NIS source files and understand how the various maps are being used.

Once you've done your homework and obtained copies of the NIS source files, put them in a location accessible to the R2 NIS server. You won't need to keep them around after the migration is complete.

NOTE For migration testing, the age of the map source files is not critical; however, the live migration should be performed with the most current source files, at a time when users are unlikely to change their passwords.

Here's how the migration tool works, generally speaking: if an account specified in the password or group file doesn't exist in the AD domain, an account will be created for it (user accounts will be disabled initially). If a corresponding account does exist, the migration tool can add the Unix information (UID for example) to the AD object's attributes.

NOTE If the source password file includes any of the Unix "special users" (root, daemon, or bin) that have UID of less than 20, the migration tool will create the object with a special name (*domainname*_u_root, for example).

Trial Migration with the Migration Wizard

Server for NIS provides both a Migration Wizard and a command-line tool (NIS2AD) for importing NIS source files to AD. By default, both will run only a test migration with logging so that you can identify any conflicts or problems and resolve them prior to performing the live migration.

The Migration Wizard is simply a front-end to NIS2AD that permits migration of multiple maps at once (the NIS2AD command-line tool migrates one map at a time). The programming and logic is the same for both the wizard and NIS2AD. As we discuss the underlying processes for the migration, I will sometimes use the term "NIS2AD" to mean "either the wizard or the command-line tool."

The high-level NIS map migration steps are as follows:

1. Run the Migration Wizard in trial mode (which is the default). You need to be logged on as a Domain Admin or equivalent.

2. Read the `conflict.log` and `nis2ad.log` files to see what would have happened.

3. Identify and resolve any conflicts (and test again).

4. When conflicts are resolved, proceed with the "live" map migration, perhaps using the command-line tool instead of the wizard.

Let's step through the migration of an NIS domain called production.

Before starting the Migration Wizard, copy the NIS map source files to the R2 NIS server's local hard drive (you can also make them accessible via NFS or Windows file sharing, but the share must not be read-only). If you are transferring the files to the Windows server, use a binary method like FTP. These source files should use the `/etc` files format, instead of the DBM NIS map format (`passwd.byuid`, `passwd.byname`).

On the domain controller with Server for NIS installed (DC1 at BIGFIRM) open the IDMUMGMT.MSC tool.

Server for NIS automatically creates an NIS domain with the same name (BIGFIRM.COM, in this case) but it's not mandatory to use it for migrating NIS data. Unfortunately, you can't delete this NIS domain, either.

To launch the Migration Wizard, right-click Server for NIS, and choose NIS Data Migration Wizard from the context menu. In the Welcome screen, the wizard reminds you that you will need access to the Unix NIS map source files. Click Next to continue.

In the next screen, shown in Figure 20.10, type in the name of your Unix NIS domain name (**production**, in this case).

FIGURE 20.10
Specify the UNIX NIS source domain.

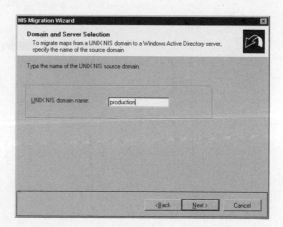

Next, the Migration Wizard wants you to verify that you are logged on as an Administrator or a member of the Domain Administrators group. If you are not currently logged on with those magical credentials, you can specify an account name and password that does qualify, as shown in Figure 20.11.

Supply your login credentials if necessary and click Next to continue.

Next, the wizard asks you to choose from a list of standard NIS maps (see Figure 20.12). Highlight a map name on the left and click Add to move it to the list of maps to migrate. Since you can migrate one map at a time or all maps at once, select all of the standard maps that you wish to test migrating now.

Nonstandard maps are any data files that are not automatically recognized by Server for NIS. The list of standard maps will vary somewhat with the implementation of NIS on different Unix platforms. For instance, the Solaris auto_home file, which specifies the locations of users' home directories for the NFS automounter daemon, is not a standard map to Server for NIS.

NOTE Server for NIS can support any nonstandard map as long as it has the necessary formatting information. You do not have to create or migrate standard maps separately from the other maps, but they do need special consideration. So we'll talk about them a little later.

FIGURE 20.11
Administrative
credentials for NIS
migration

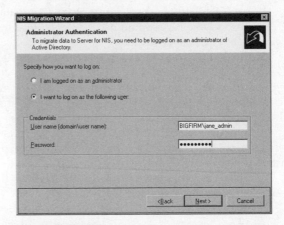

FIGURE 20.12
Select from a list of
standard NIS maps.

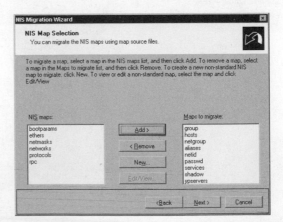

Once you've added all the maps you want to try migrating at this time, choose Next. Now the wizard asks for the location for the NIS source files (see Figure 20.13). Type in the path to the NIS source files and click Next.

The wizard will check for the existence of a file for every map you selected and return an error if it doesn't find a file. A source file must be located for every map on the migration list before the wizard can continue.

Once the Migration Wizard is satisfied that it has source files for every map you want to migrate, it asks whether to merge these maps into a previously migrated domain (like BIGFIRM, maybe) or create a new NIS domain (shown in Figure 20.14).

You also have the option to specify a different AD container for the migrated objects. Use the default container for users, groups, and hosts, or you won't see their Unix attributes in the account properties of AD users and computers. Specify the target domain and AD container for the migration (or accept the default settings) and click Next to tell the wizard how to manage any conflicts that are detected, as shown in Figure 20.15.

FIGURE 20.13

Specify the map source files location.

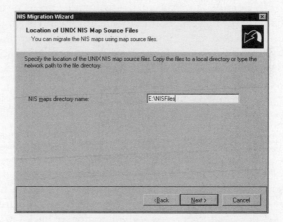

FIGURE 20.14

Choose a destination domain for migration.

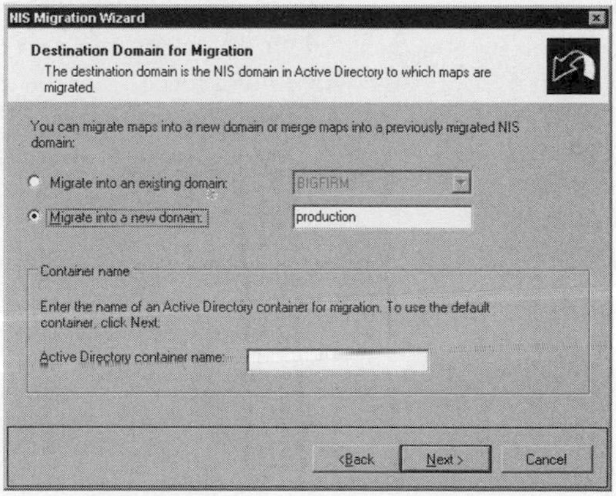

FIGURE 20.15
Select conflict man-
agement options for
migration.

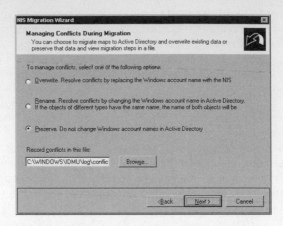

By default, NIS2AD will not overwrite or rename any accounts or objects that have the same name in the NIS map source file and in AD. It will simply log that the conflict was found and move on to the next entry. If you are migrating NIS users and groups, however, and you hope to magically add the NIS attributes for tjones to Tom's AD account, you should choose the Overwrite option. Choose the Rename option to have NIS2AD rename any objects in AD that have matching names in the NIS source files.

By default, conflicts will be recorded in the log file `\WINDOWS\IDMU\log\conflicts.log`. Specify an alternate path and filename for your conflicts log if you wish, and choose Next to continue.

As you can see in Figure 20.16, NIS2AD runs a trial migration by default and logs results to `C:\WINDOWS\IDMU\log\nis2ad.log`.

Use the radio buttons to choose whether to proceed with a trial migration or to migrate the source data to AD. Specify an alternate log file for the migration if you wish and choose Next to proceed to the final confirmation screen (shown in Figure 20.17) and review the migration settings.

Click Next to proceed with migration, or click Back to change settings if necessary.

As the NIS2AD wizard runs the trial migration, it will report on the screen about which source files are being processed, and it will stop and show an error if there is a problem with one of the files. If this happens, click OK to continue, and the wizard will move on to the next source file.

When it's done, the wizard will report that the migration log has completed (see Figure 20.18).

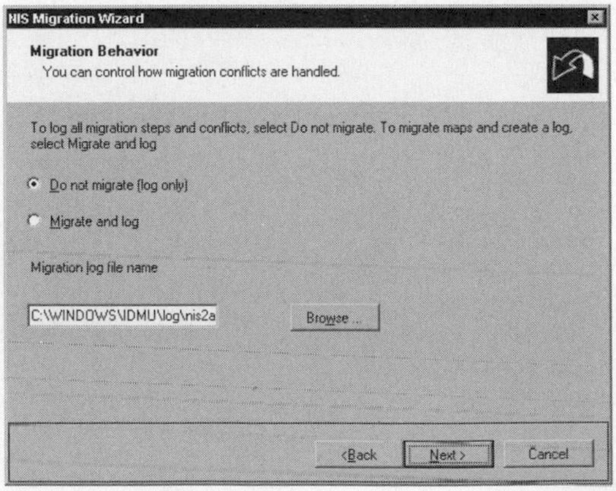

FIGURE 20.16
Perform a trial
migration with
logging.

FIGURE 20.17

The NIS migration confirmation screen

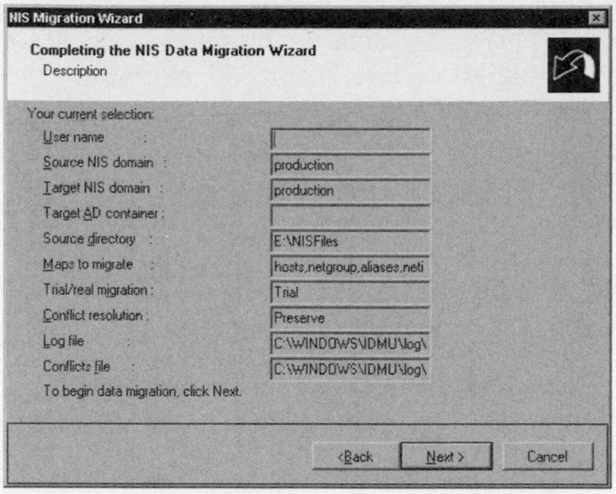

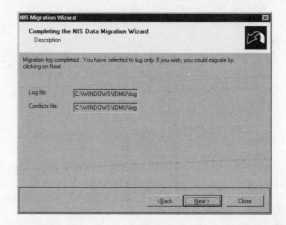

FIGURE 20.18

Completing the Data Migration Wizard

Be careful here, or you could accidentally migrate the NIS map source files before you are ready. Click Close to abort the wizard and go look at the logs. Click Next only if you are ready to go ahead and do the migration to AD!

Now let's take a look at those logs and see what might have gone wrong. Navigate to the \Windows\IDMU\log directory. There are two files, one for conflict reporting and one for the NIS2AD migration.

For the passwd source file, the conflicts.log file reports:

```
### Sun Apr 16 22:59:6 2006
: Conflict details of entries from map file and existing entries in AD. map file
= 'passwd'. ###
conflicts with  CN=Tom Jones,CN=Users,DC=BIGFIRM,DC=COM
existing data = tjones
new data      = tjones
conflicts with  CN=Taylor Cooper,CN=Users,DC=BIGFIRM,DC=COM
existing data = tcooper
new data      = tcooper
```

These entries indicate that the process found pre-existing AD accounts with logon names (tjones and tcooper) that matched names in the passwd source file. It's worth noting that if you specified that the migration should replace or overwrite existing AD information with information from the NIS map, these conflict entries will not appear in the log. For that reason, I recommend leaving off the Replace and Rename options during the trail migration.

You can expect to see conflicts in the log files for passwd or group file entries that have corresponding AD accounts already. We'll look at that more closely in the next section.

The nis2ad.log file for the trial migration first reports the exact syntax of the NIS2AD command that the wizard ran, and then it reports the details of what maps are being tested and what object names would be created in the AD:

```
nis2ad.exe -a production -y production -s localhost -c
"C:\WINDOWS\IDMU\log\conflicts.log" -f "C:\WINDOWS\IDMU\log\nis2ad.log" -d
"e:\NISFiles" passwd


*******
Started activity for map. Activity = adding NIS entries to AD  map = passwd time
= Sun Apr 16 22:59:6 2006

MESSAGE
Migrating entries.  map = 'passwd' UNIX NIS domain = 'production' AD domain =
'BIGFIRM
YES
Can migrate. object = 'tjones'. Container to migrate =
'CN=Users,DC=BIGFIRM,DC=COM'.
CONFLICT
object key = 'jsmith'
target container = 'CN=Users,DC=BIGFIRM,DC=COM'
conflicts with existing object = 'jsmith'
conflicting object location = 'CN=Jim Smith,CN=Users,DC=BIGFIRM,DC=COM'.
CONFLICT
object key = 'mjones'
target container = 'CN=Users,DC=BIGFIRM,DC=COM'
conflicts with existing object = 'mjones'
conflicting object location = 'CN=Mary Jones,CN=Users,DC=BIGFIRM,DC=COM'.
```

As you can see in the preceding listing, the NIS2AD process started by the Migration Wizard reports that (in a real migration) it would create a new object named tjones in the Users container (CN=Users,DC=BIGFIRM,DC=COM). However, the objects jsmith and mjones already exist.

As you can also see from the preceding log output, new user or group accounts will be created in the Users container. Listings in the hosts file migrate as disabled machine accounts to the Computers container. For maps that don't have equivalent objects in AD, the log reports where and how it will create the entries. If you selected the default migration container, the migrated objects will be created as follows:

```
CN=mapname,CN=NISdomain,CN=DefaultMigrationContainer,DC=ADDomain,
DC=ADDomainSuffix.
```

The NIS production domain's mail alias entries will be created as objects within
'CN=aliases,CN=production, CN=DefaultMigrationContainer30,DC=BIGFIRM,DC=COM',

while the services entry for telnet would be migrated as an object named `25/tcp` in `'CN=services,CN=production, CN=DefaultMigrationContainer30, DC=BIGFIRM,DC=COM'`.

The Map Migration Wizard is rather useful for a trial migration where all the maps are read at once and conflicts are detected. And the wizard can be used to migrate multiple maps at once, after you are satisfied that there are no remaining issues.

However, if you want to be a little more careful and deliberate after running an initial trial migration to check all the source files, use the NIS2AD command-line tool to migrate one map at a time. This is the recommended approach because of map dependencies. `Passwd` and `group` maps should be migrated before the `shadow` map, for instance. You may notice in the trial migration logs that even a trial migration of the `shadow` file will fail if the `passwd` file has not been previously migrated.

Associating AD and Unix Accounts: The Whole Story

Before proceeding with a live map migration to AD, let's discuss how to make sure that NIS2AD correctly identifies pre-existing AD user and group accounts so that the NIS attributes can be added to that object.

AD user accounts have several name attribute fields, so it's important to know what NIS2AD is going to look for as match criteria. If I refer to these using the labels that appear in DSA.MSC, there is a Name field (shown in DSA.MSC when you list all users and groups). This same field will also be called Full Name in the Rename User Dialog box (shown in Figure 20.19).

The Display Name field shown in Figure 20.19 is used by applications like Exchange. AD also stores first name and last name in separate fields. Finally, each user account has a logon name that is used during authentication.

In contrast, Unix `passwd` files have only user names and description fields:

    jsmith:x:1035:2030:Jim Smith:/export/home/jsmith:/bin/ksh

NIS2AD doesn't care about the AD Display Name, First Name, or Last Name fields, but it does look at the Full Name and Logon Name fields. In order for pre-existing AD accounts to be identified with the NIS accounts being migrated, both the full name as well as the logon name have to match with the User Name field in the `passwd` source file. The Description field in the `passwd` file is not mandatory. Even when it's used, it's not used universally for full names. The Description field is therefore not a reliable source for matching the Full Name field.

Let's look at a couple of examples. At BIGFIRM, the four employees appearing in Table 20.2 have accounts in both AD and NIS. You would like to merge these Unix accounts with the AD accounts during the NIS migration.

FIGURE 20.19
The Rename User dialog box in DSA.MSC

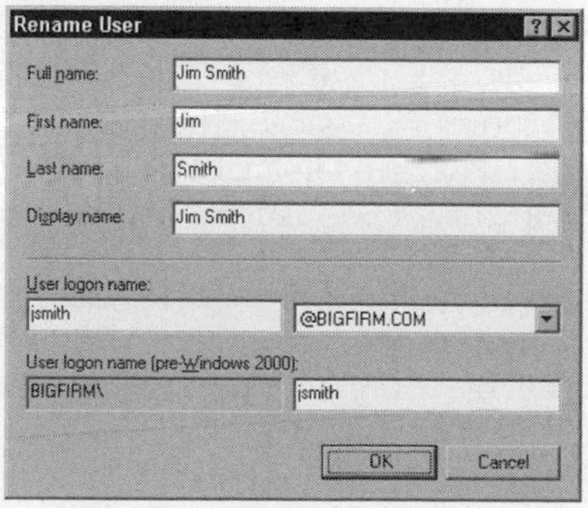

TABLE 20.2:   BIGFIRM Users with Both AD and NIS Accounts

AD FULL NAME	AD LOGON NAME	UNIX USER NAME
Tom Jones	BIGFIRM\tjones	tjones
Taylor Cooper	BIGFIRM\tcooper	tcooper
Jim Smith	BIGFIRM\smith_j	jsmith
Kathy Howard	BIGFIRM\howard_k	khoward

For all of the accounts shown in Table 20.2, the AD Full Name field (Tom Jones, for example) will not match the name that NIS2AD is looking for (tjones). In one way or another, you will not see the results you want. In the first two entries in Table 20.2, the logon name does match the Unix User Name field. If the logon name matches but the full name does not match, NIS2AD will not add the Unix attributes to that AD account even if you specify the overwrite option. In the third and fourth entries shown in Table 20.2, the logon field doesn't match either (smith_j in AD and jsmith in Unix). NIS2AD will see these as completely different accounts. When you run a live migration, NIS2AD will create new AD accounts called jsmith and khoward and give those accounts the NIS attributes instead of your pre-existing AD user objects.

In order to successfully merge the AD and NIS user accounts during the migration, the AD Full Name, AD Logon Name, and Unix User Name fields all have to be consistent, as shown in Table 20.3:

TABLE 20.3:   Consistent User Account Fields for NIS2AD Migration

AD FULL NAME	AD LOGON NAME	UNIX USER NAME
tjones	BIGFIRM\tjones	tjones
tcooper	BIGFIRM\tcooper	tcooper
jsmith	BIGFIRM\jsmith	jsmith
khoward	BIGFIRM\khoward	khoward

If you want to stick with the *lastname_firstinitial* convention, then you could alternately change the passwd source file instead. The point is, the AD Full Name, AD Logon Name, and Unix User Name fields all have to be consistent. Otherwise, NIS2AD will not recognize the AD account as a match and it will not populate the AD account with the NIS user attributes.

NOTE   For group accounts that already exist, the same principles apply, although there aren't so many fields to worry about. Group names have to match exactly, though, and they are case-sensitive. If the Unix group file has an engineering group and AD has a group named Engineers or Engineering, you will end up with two different groups in AD.

It's a pity that NIS2AD isn't a little more flexible; in my experience, it's very common to use full names in the Full Name field. Windows administrators often prefer to see real names displayed in DSA.MSC instead of logon names. If that's the case in your AD, you will not only have to resolve conflicts with NIS and AD logon names, but you may also have to change the Full Name attribute (at least temporarily) for any users who already have accounts in both worlds. It seems unwise to let NIS2AD create a new AD account and then make your Unix users start logging on with that one instead. Permissions on any files they have created on Windows file servers (not to mention any special rights) would be linked to the original accounts' SIDs.

Map Migration with NIS2AD

Before proceeding with a live migration of NIS map source files to AD, make sure all of the following requirements are met:

1. During the migration the NIS server needs access to the NIS source files. They can be located on a network drive, but the migration will fail if access permissions are read-only.

2. Resolve any conflicts reported during the trial migration by the logs.

3. Migrate the passwd file before the group or shadow files.

4. If you are migrating other maps with dependencies (netmasks depends on networks, for example), migrate the required maps first.

Let's migrate the map source files for the NIS domain production using NIS2AD, the command-line tool that migrates one map at a time.

This tool is simple to use. The basic syntax is as follows:

```
nis2ad.exe -y UNIX_NIS_Domain -a AD_NIS_Domain -d NISSourceFilesPath mapname
```

TIP If you want to cheat a little, you can just check the nis2ad.log file for the syntax of the NIS2AD commands run during the trial migration.

Run NIS2AD on the R2 NIS server with the preceding syntax to perform another trial migration using the default log file locations. When you're ready, add the -m switch to turn off the trial migration mode and add -r yes to tell NIS2AD to add (or replace) NIS attributes for any matching objects that it finds. Otherwise, NIS2AD will skip migration of objects that already exist in AD.

The following command will migrate the data in the passwd file for the production NIS domain to an NIS map in the AD NIS domain of the same name:

```
nis2ad.exe -y production -a production -d E:/NISFiles -r yes -m passwd
```

NIS2AD will read the map source files, migrate the data into AD, and report back a SUCCESS or FAILURE status. A single failure to create an object will return the FAILURE status, even if all the others succeeded; check the log to see if the failure was critical or not.

Simply repeat the command, changing the map name each time, to migrate groups, shadow, aliases, and other NIS maps.

After migrating all of the maps to AD, it's a good idea to run a few tests before starting the NIS service on the R2 system.

Post-Migration Tour and Testing

Now that you've successfully migrated the map source files to Active Directory, let's see what changed in IDMUMGMT.MSC and DSA.MSC and find out what NIS stuff is working at the command line now.

The IDMU admin tool now lists the production NIS domain under Server for NIS. Expand the production node in the console tree to reveal a list of NIS servers and NIS maps. Click NIS Servers to see a list of Unix subordinates, imported from the `ypservers` source file (shown in Figure 20.20).

Highlight NIS Maps for that domain to see a list of freshly migrated NIS maps and context-sensitive actions in the right pane (see Figure 20.21).

Now that you've migrated NIS data to AD, IDMUMGMT.MSC can be used to add and remove subordinate Unix servers, promote another R2 to master, or to propagate changes to the maps. However, it's not possible to remove a map or make changes to the map using the IDMUMGMT.MSC tool.

Now let's open Active Directory Users and Computers and see what has changed. In the Users container (shown in Figure 20.22), you see that NIS2AD has created disabled user and group accounts for entries (aroberts, for example) in the `passwd` file that did not already have AD accounts.

When matching accounts were found (jsmith and tjones, for example), NIS2AD populated the account with the NIS attributes (as you can see in Figure 20.23). NIS group entries (operators, engineering, and development) were created as global groups.

Turn on the Advanced Features (View/Advanced Features) in DSA.MSC and you can see the DefaultMigrationContainer for maps that don't have equivalent objects in AD (shown in Figure 20.24). This is interesting; you can see the name of the mail aliases and its object class, for example, but not the entire entry (in other words, members of a particular mail alias).

FIGURE 20.20

NIS production domain servers

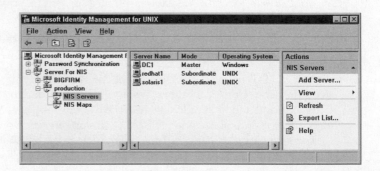

FIGURE 20.21

NIS maps in the production domain

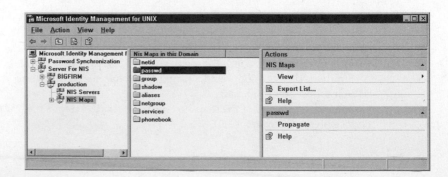

FIGURE 20.22
Migrated NIS accounts in DSA.MSC

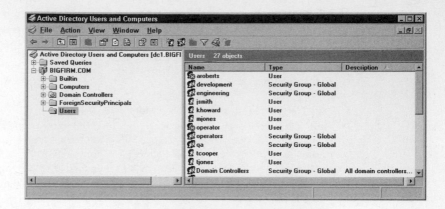

FIGURE 20.23
AD user account with imported NIS attributes

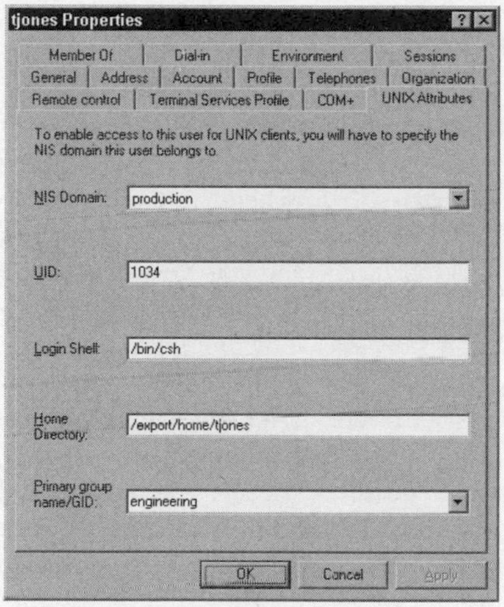

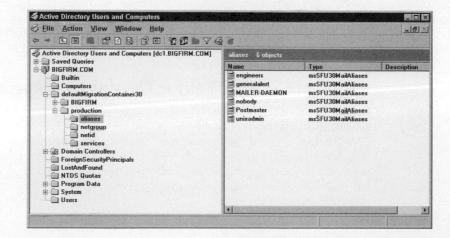

FIGURE 20.24
Use Advanced Features to view migrated maps in DSA.MSC.

The next step is to start the NIS service using IDMUMGMT.MSC or run `nisadmin start` at a command prompt. When the service has started, a probe of RPC ports using `rpcinfo -p` should show your NIS server running `ypserv` (on several ports) and `yppasswdd`, which permits users on NIS client machines to change their passwords:

```
C:/>rpcinfo -p

   program version protocol    port
---------------------------------------------------
    100000     2      udp      111   portmapper
    100000     2      tcp      111   portmapper
    100004     2      udp      772   ypserv
    100009     1      udp      773   yppasswdd
    100004     2      tcp      774   ypserv
 1073741824    1      udp      775   ypserv
```

From the R2 system, you can now test whether NIS seems to be responding to client requests. Run `ypcat -k -d` *domainname* `passwd` to see a list of `passwd` entries from NIS. If that succeeds, try `ypmatch -d` *domainname* `-k` *username* `passwd`, supplying the name of an NIS user (like tjones) to that user's `passwd` map entry. If both of those tests are successful (and the maps are accurate!), your server is ready for clients and subordinate NIS servers.

To test NIS from a Unix client, run `ypwhich` to verify that the R2 box is the NIS server that the client is talking to, and then try the `ypcat` and `ypmatch` commands described previously on the client. The syntax should be the same on most flavors of Unix.

NIS clients broadcast by default to find an NIS server on their local subnet. However, if the NIS client (`ypbind`) runs with the `-ypset` option, then a user can use the `ypset` command to tell NIS to bind with a different server (the `-ypsetme` option, which permits only the Super User account to change the binding, is considered more secure). To test the R2 NIS server from a Unix client, you may have to configure the client to run in this binding mode temporarily. To find out which NIS server is talking to your client machine, try running `ypwhich` on the Unix NIS client. If it returns the name of another NIS server, ask for permission and assistance in restarting `ypbind` with the `-ypset` option temporarily on a system that is suitable for testing.

NOTE As soon as you start the NIS service on your R2 DC, any local NIS client looking for a server (usually after a reboot) might attach to it. In other words, if you are just doing this to test NIS on R2 and you aren't going to use the most recent and accurate versions of the maps, don't do it in a production environment.

Staging the Coup: Taking Over as NIS Master

Now that you've migrated the NIS maps to a Windows Server 2003 R2 Domain Controller and run a few tests on that box and from a Unix client system, you may be ready to break the news to the Unix NIS master that there's a new sheriff in town. The Microsoft documentation on this subject (which is generally excellent) recommends that you simply configure the subordinates to use Server for NIS as the master server. To do this, run the `ypxfr` command on every slave for every NIS map, with the `-f` (force) option to tell it to retrieve the map from the R2 NIS server regardless of its configuration settings.

On Solaris1 at BIGFIRM, that process might look like this:

```
#  /usr/lib/netsvc/yp/ypxfr -d production -h dc1 -f passwd.byname
ypxfr: couldnot get dc1 address
(info) dc1 production passwd.byname ypxfrd getdbm failed (reason = -1) -- using
ypxfr
```

Ignore the irritating error messages. Server for NIS doesn't run a ypxfr service, so the NIS subordinates return an error before failing back on an older and slower transfer method (yp_all). Use ls -la to check the timestamp on the map files in /var/yp/*domainname* to see if the map updates are succeeding. The command strings *mapname* will return any human readable text strings in the map file you're trying to update, including the master server record, which should be first:

```
# strings passwd.byuid.pag
dc1YP_MASTER_NAME10002YP_LAST_MODIFIEDaroberts:VUdvv9KPfr.3I:1036:2030:Ann
Roberts:/export/home/aroberts/:/bin/sh1036
...
```

In the preceding example, you can see that the server pointer record found on the first line of the passwd.byuid file says dc1YP_MASTER, so you know that the update was successful.

If you have 12 maps on 10 different subordinate NIS servers, running ypxfr for each map on each server might become rather tedious. As an alternative, you can create an input text file listing every map name and write a script to run the commands on each subordinate.

If your file mapnames.txt contains the following entries:

```
group.bygid
group.byname
hosts.byaddr
hosts.byname
mail.aliases
mail.byaddr
netgroup.byhost
netgroup.byuser
netgroup
netid.byname
passwd.byname
passwd.byuid
services.byname
services.byservicename
ypservers
```

Then the script would look like this:

```
#!/bin/sh
# for maps in `cat mapnames.txt`
> do
> echo transferring $maps
> /usr/lib/netsvc/yp/ypxfr -h dc1 -f $maps
> done
```

Run this script on every subordinate server to tell it to get the maps from the R2 NIS server. Then you're all set to disable the NIS server process on your master (and remove old NIS maps on the master as well).

However, it's also possible to make the NIS master update its own maps with the ypxfr command shown in the preceding script and then run yppush to tell all the subordinates to get new copies of their maps. When the subordinates get their new copies from the old master, the pointer record in each map will point to DC1, the R2 NIS master. From that point on, the subordinates will look to the R2 server as the NIS master.

To do that, just add a yppush command to the preceding script (after the ypxfr command) and run it on the NIS master only:

```
#!/bin/sh
# for maps in `cat mapnames.txt`
> do
> echo transferring $maps
> /usr/lib/netsvc/yp/ypxfr -h dc1 -f $maps
> /usr/lib/netsvc/yp/yppush $maps
> done
```

A third alternative, more radical but very reliable, is to use the ypinit -s command to rebuild the NIS maps completely on the old master and on all Unix subordinates for a domain:

```
#ypinit -s DC1
```

In addition to the pain of having to touch every NIS subordinate server, an additional downside to this approach is the temporary loss of service on a given subnet while the NIS subordinate rebuilds all of its maps.

Managing Subordinate NIS Servers

When all of your NIS servers are R2 domain controllers, the NIS maps are replicated in AD, and every domain controller has the Unix attributes of users, groups, and machine accounts. Likewise, every domain controller has all of the NIS map information. However, until you install Services for NIS on an R2 DC, you won't see any Unix attributes in DSA.MSC on that system, and the DC will not respond to NIS client queries.

Once you install IDMU with Services for NIS on an R2 DC, the other NIS domain controllers will automatically detect it and add it to the list of NIS servers in the IDMUMGMT.MSC tool. Likewise, the new NIS server will be aware of the other Unix and R2 master and subordinate servers.

NOTE   Don't forget to enable and start the NIS service on a new R2 NIS server, particularly before you try to promote it to the master role for a domain. The service is disabled by default after installation.

Because of the multi-master replication model in AD, the R2 DCs running NIS don't care who the NIS master is, and changes to the NIS maps (using NISMAP, for example) can be done on any R2 DC. Only the Unix subordinates need an NIS master; they need to know what server to contact for map updates. So you designate an NIS master (by default, that's the DC you use to migrate the NIS maps, usually the first Windows 2003 server to run NIS). This is not too different from the way you designate a DC to emulate an NT4 PDC in a domain with NT4 domain controllers. Just as the PDC emulator updates the NT4 DCs and they are none the wiser, the NIS master for a given domain will respond to update requests from Unix subordinates.

Adding and Removing Subordinate NIS Servers

Add or remove Unix subordinate servers using IDMUMGMT.MSC or the command-line tool NISMAP. In IDMUMGMT.MSC, right-click the NIS servers node for the target NIS domain and choose Add Server. When prompted, type in the hostname of the new Unix subordinate. In Figure 20.25, I am adding a new subordinate named "`fedora1`" to the NIS production domain at BIGFIRM.

Server for NIS will not let you add the new subordinate if it can't contact it on the network. However, the `ypserve` daemon does not have to be running on the target system yet. To add new Unix subordinates to the NIS domain, first add the new server as a subordinate, and then configure the system as an NIS subordinate (using `ypinit -s`, for example).

To add a Unix subordinate from the command line, use NISMAP:

```
C:\ >nismap add -e "fedora1" -a production ypservers
```

To remove a Unix subordinate, use the following syntax:

```
C:\ >nismap del -k "fedora1" -a production ypservers
```

R2 NIS subordinates will automatically show up on the list when you install Server for NIS on that system. Again, because the NIS maps are stored in the AD, every R2 DC running Services for NIS will know about all NIS domains that have been migrated into your Active Directory.

Unix NIS subordinates can usually be retired by just removing the NIS maps from the `/var/yp/` directory and stopping the `ypserve` daemon.

Once you've retired one or more Unix subordinates, simply right-click their icons in IDMU and choose Delete to remove them from the list of NIS subordinates for that domain.

If you decide to retire (or demote) an R2 domain controller running Services for NIS, first uninstall Services for NIS, using Add/Remove Programs, and then run DCPROMO to demote it to a member server.

FIGURE 20.25
Adding a new UNIX
subordinate server

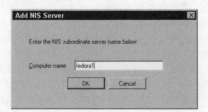

Promoting an R2 Subordinate to an NIS Master

To promote an R2 subordinate server to the master for that NIS domain, select it in the IDMUMGMT.MSC tool and click the Promote link in the Action Pane (shown in Figure 20.26).

Don't expect any bells or whistles. The update is more or less immediate.

To promote a subordinate from the command line, use NISADMIN:

```
C:\>nisadmin mkmaster -d production -m dc2
```

If the promotion is successfully, NISADMIN will simply report that 'the settings were successfully updated'.

FIGURE 20.26
Promote an R2
subordinate to
NIS master.

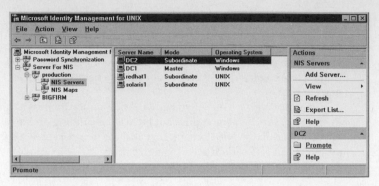

As the new master is promoted, the old master automatically becomes a subordinate.

Remember: you can only promote an R2 DC to be the master for the NIS domain. On the other hand, the master role is designated per NIS domain, so there's no reason that DC1 can't be the master for the NIS domain production while DC2 acts as the master for the NIS domain development. The decision will depend on the placement of R2 NIS servers on the network in relation to the Unix subordinates they need to update.

Propagating Maps to Unix Subordinates

There are a number of ways that map updates can be propagated to subordinates. Before describing them, permit me to emphasize once again that all of the following map propagation information pertains only to Unix subordinates. Your R2 DC NIS servers will not receive updates in any of the ways described in this section. R2 NIS servers get updates through AD replication.

Furthermore, if your environment includes more than one or two NIS servers, it's likely that the Unix folks have scheduled jobs on the NIS subordinates to automatically ask the master for updates. Ask your sysadmin if there are any cron jobs that run ypxfr scripts, which maps are updated, and how often. Offer him a cold one for the information.

While I'm on the subject, Server for NIS doesn't run ypxfr as a service. Now, that might seem troublesome, and map transfer attempts will generate errors in the logs on the Unix subordinates, but it does not prevent the subordinates from getting updates. When the Unix subordinates fail with ypxfr requests, they fall back on an older, less efficient transfer method. By the way, this news won't make the Unix admins happy; servers that use ypxfr have much faster transfer speeds (10 to 100 times faster, according to one source).

Map updates to all subordinates can be scheduled on the R2 NIS master as well, which will use yppush to propagate any changes that are detected. Server for NIS offers options in IDMUMGMT.MSC as well as command-line tools to set the update (or push) interval, update subordinates with all map changes, and force propagation of a single map to a specific subordinate or to all subordinates.

An NIS server's map update interval can be specified in the IDMU Server for NIS Properties page (shown earlier in the chapter) or at the command line:

```
nisadmin servername config pushint dd:hh:mm
```

The push interval is server-specific and will apply to all NIS domain maps on a given server.

To initialize yppush to all subordinates in all domains for all map changes, open IDMUMGMT.MSC, highlight Server for NIS, and choose the Check for Updates Now option in the Actions pane (see Figure 20.27).

A confirmation dialog box will let you know that the server has sent yppush requests to all subordinates for all domains (see Figure 20.28).

FIGURE 20.27
Check for
Map Updates

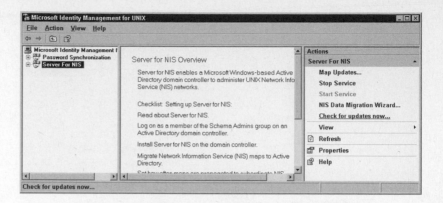

FIGURE 20.28
yppush confirmation
message

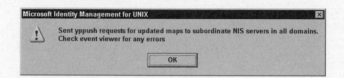

The wording of this message (and the wording of Check for Updates Now) implies that the NIS server must check something or somewhere outside of itself for changes before it can propagate them to subordinates. In fact, that's true. For performance reasons, Server for NIS maintains a map cache, located in WINDOWS\idmu\nis\MapCache*domainname*. At specific intervals, Server for NIS will check AD for changes to the NIS maps and update the map cache. If it's also an NIS master, it will then kick off the process to push map updates to subordinate servers. So the push interval is also a map cache update interval.

TIP If you are ever troubleshooting and suspect a problem with the map cache, ypcat queries the cache, while ypmatch talks directly to AD. The ypclear command can be used to clear the map cache for a particular map on a particular server.

The command-line equivalent of Check for Updates Now is nisadmin *servername* syncall, where *servername* is the name of the master server for the NIS domain; although if you are running the command on the NIS master, you can omit the *servername* argument.

To update all subordinates in a domain for changes to a specific map, in IDMUMGMT.MSC, navigate to the map name in the details pane and then choose Propagate from the Actions pane (shown in Figure 20.29).

A confirmation dialog box will warn you that this could take some time and ask if you wish to continue. If you choose to proceed, server for NIS will send yppush requests to all subordinates, asking them to check in for changes to that particular map.

To accomplish the same map-specific action using yppush at the command line, try yppush -d *domainname* -h *hostname mapname*. If you leave off the hostname argument, the map will be propagated to all subordinates. Add the -q (quiet mode) argument to tell it to go run in the background if you don't want to wait around to see the results. Otherwise, you'll watch some fascinating output from the update process as it occurs.

As long as you have Unix subordinates still running, whenever you make a change to a map, it's a good idea to use yppush (or Propagate, in IDMUMGMT.MSC) rather than waiting for the next update interval.

FIGURE 20.29
Propagate
Map Changes

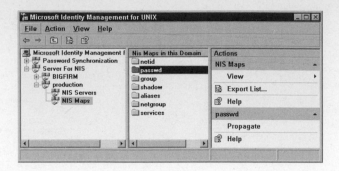

Care and Feeding of NIS Maps

Now that you have installed and configured Services for NIS, migrated NIS domain maps to AD, promoted the R2 DC NIS server to be the master server for the NIS domain, and dealt with subordinate Unix and R2 servers, it's time to discuss the care and feeding of the NIS maps themselves.

Create and Migrate Nonstandard Maps

In this context, nonstandard maps are any maps that are not recognized natively by Windows Server 2003 R2 Services for NIS. The implementation of NIS for a particular platform may include maps that are created to support platform-specific functions, such as the *automounter* daemon on Solaris. The automounter daemon permits NFS shares to be mounted and unmounted as needed on Solaris systems. Special NIS maps support this function and make NFS mappings consistent and transparent for NFS users across different systems. Automount maps are commonly used for users' home directories. By storing automount maps in NIS, a user's home directory can be NFS mounted from a central server, transparently to the user. Automounter maps (auto_master, auto_home, and so forth) are standard on Solaris implementations of NIS, but nonstandard on R2 Services for NIS.

It's also possible to create custom maps for special purposes. For example, you could create a campus directory with telephone numbers and office numbers and publish it using NIS.

The general steps to follow in setting up nonstandard maps are:

1. Use NISMAP or the migration tool to create the necessary structure in AD.

2. Import data to the map structure using NIS2AD.

Services for NIS will need to know the name of the map, where the source file is located, and the format of the source file. Specifically, it needs to know what kind of separator is used between fields and which field is the key field. Finally, it needs to know whether to include the key field as part of the value in the map entry.

So, if you wanted to create a "phonebook" map with a source file that uses the following syntax:

```
username;"Full Name";extension;bldg;room
```

individual entries would look like this:

```
tjones;"Tom Jones";4124;RE;204
jsmith;"Jim Smith";4122;RE;206
```

To create a nonstandard map for this source file with the username as the key (lookup) field, you would run the following command:

```
nismap -create -i 1 -g ; phonebook
```

The preceding NISMAP syntax instructs NIS to create a map named phonebook where the key field is the first field and subsequent fields will be separated by semicolons. Without the -y command, NISMAP will include the key field in the value.

Alternately, use the Migration Wizard to create the nonstandard map structure. At the NIS Map Selection dialog box in the wizard, select New and provide the name of the new map, the field delimiter, and the column number of the key field (see Figure 20.30).

The new map structure won't appear in the DSA.MSC Advanced View or the IDMUMGMT.MSC list of maps until map data has been imported to AD.

Once the map structure has been created in AD, you're ready to import data into the NIS map using either the Migration Wizard or NIS2AD.

To migrate the phonebook map using the wizard, open IDMUMGMT.MSC once again, right-click Server for NIS, and choose NIS Data Migration Wizard. Provide the NIS domain name and promise the wizard that you are an administrator, then select the newly created map (phonebook, in this case) from the list of NIS maps (shown in Figure 20.31) and click Add to put it on the list of maps to migrate.

FIGURE 20.30

Use the Migration Wizard to create a nonstandard map.

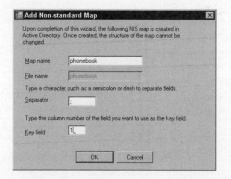

FIGURE 20.31

Migrating a nonstandard map using the Migration Wizard

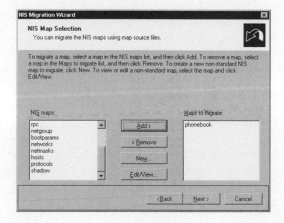

Complete the wizard as described earlier in the chapter.

To use NIS2AD to import this phonebook map to your NIS domain production where server DC1 is the master, the syntax would look like this:

```
>nis2ad.exe -a production -y production -s dc1 -m -r yes -d "E:\NISFILES" phonebook
```

The `nis2ad.log` file should report the success or failure outcome for each entry in the source file:

```
SUCCESS
Adding the object in Active Directory.
Object = 'tjones'
Object class = 'NisObject'container =
'CN=phonebook,CN=production,CN=DefaultMigrationContainer30,DC=BIGFIRM,DC=COM'.
```

After data is imported using NIS2AD or the Migration Wizard, the new map will also be viewable in the IDMUMGMT.MSC tool in the list of NIS maps for that NIS domain, as well as in DSA.MSC with Advanced Features turned on.

Now any NIS client should be able to view the entries in the phonebook map using ypcat or ypmatch:

```
>ypcat -k -d production -h dc1 phonebook

tjones  tjones;"Tom Jones";4124;RE;204
jsmith  jsmith;"Jim Smith";4122;RE;206
tcooper tcooper;"Taylor Cooper";4144;RA;310
khoward khoward;"Kathy Howard";4141;RA;311

>ypmatch -d production -h dc1 -k tjones phonebook
tjones  tjones;"Tom Jones";4124;RE;204
```

Modifying the NIS Map Data

For users, groups, and computer accounts, the Unix Attributes tabs in DSA.MSC permit admins to view and modify most things (you can't reset the Unix password in DSA.MSC, but I'll get to that in a moment). But what about editing maps that have no equivalent AD objects?

You may have noticed, as I did, that you cannot see the properties or contents of an NIS map in IDMUMGMT.MSC. Using DSA.MSC with Advanced Features turned on gets you a little further. The NIS maps appear in the default migration container, and each entry in the map is created as a separate object. However, it's not possible to modify the membership of the engineers mail alias, for example, using DSA.MSC. For that, you need the command-line tool, NISMAP.

TIP At this point, it might be helpful to set the system environment variables for DEFAULT_NIS_ DOMAIN and NIS_SERVER. Many of the command-line tools for NIS management refuse to assume that you are talking about *this server* or *this NIS domain*. Until you set these variables, you'll have to supply a domain name and server name argument in many, if not all, NIS command-line situations. If it's suitable for your environment, setting these variables will save a lot of keystrokes. System variables can be set in the Advanced tab of the System Applet in Control Panel.

USING NISMAP TO MODIFY MAP DATA

If you've been reading this chapter from start to finish, you already know that NISMAP can be used to create nonstandard map structures. It's also the only way (short of re-importing!) to update nonstandard and most other NIS maps.

Let's continue with the mail aliases (aliases) example for the purposes of this discussion. BIG-FIRM needs to make some changes to its mail aliasing structure (aliases are basically email distribution lists for the sendmail servers to use). Currently, the NIS aliases map contains the following entries (information obtained using ypcat):

```
>ypcat -k -d production aliases
Postmaster      root
MAILER-DAEMON   postmaster
nobody          /dev/null
engineers       tjones,jsmith
generalalert    tjones,jsmith,aroberts
unixadmin       tcooper,khoward
```

You need to add mjones to the engineers alias and remove aroberts from the generalalert alias. Also, you need a new alias, dev, with only aroberts on the list for now. To do this, you will have to run NISMAP three times, twice with the modify (mod) argument to modify existing entries, and once with the add argument to add a new alias entry. Ready? Here we go!

To add mjones to the engineers alias, use the following syntax:

```
C:\>nismap mod -a production -s dc1 -k
engineers -e "engineers:tjones,jsmith,mjones" aliases
```

Before we move on to the next example, let's look at the syntax a little more closely. The -a and -s arguments specify the target NIS domain and target server, respectively, for the operation. The key (-k) argument tells nismap what entry you want to modify because engineers is the key entry in that map file. The entry (-e) argument supplies the entire text string for the engineers alias as it would appear in the aliases file, not as it appears in the output of ypcat. That's important enough to say again: NISMAP entry strings are the strings from the source files, not from NIS map queries.

Now let's remove aroberts from the generalalert alias. You're not going to use NISMAP DEL, as you might think; the DEL argument would be used to delete an entire alias entry. Instead, just modify the entry by supplying a new string without the aroberts username:

```
C:\>nismap mod -a production -s dc1 -k
generalalert -e "generalalert: tjones,jsmith" aliases
```

Finally to create a new alias named dev with only aroberts as a member, use NISMAP ADD:

```
C:\ >nismap add -a production -s dc1 -e "dev:aroberts" aliases
```

For all of these commands, NISMAP will return output declaring the operation a success or a failure and telling you the path of the AD object that was created or modified. To check your work, use ypcat -k -d *domainname mapname*.

CHANGING NIS PASSWORDS

Administrators do almost all of the work of modifying and maintaining NIS map data, with one important exception: changing passwords, which users must do themselves.

There are a couple of important thing to know about password management with Services for NIS. The first thing is that the NIS and AD account passwords can be synchronized if: 1) the password is always changed in Windows first, and 2) the Password Synchronization component is installed on the domain controller that takes the change password request. If there are multiple domain controllers on the network, it's wise to install Password Synchronization on all of them. If these conditions are satisfied, then when dual-account users change their domain passwords in Windows, the password synchronization software will capture the new password, encrypt it, and store it in the Unix password attribute for that user account object in AD. We'll discuss exactly how to make that happen in Chapter 21, "Unix and Windows III: Identity Management for Unix."

On one hand, this one-way password synchronization makes good sense: it's a common pattern for a dual-account user to sit down at their Windows PC, log on to the AD domain, check email, and then fire up Exceed or Reflection or some other tool and log on to the Unix network. With Windows as the primary network logon, why not synch up your AD and NIS passwords?

On the other hand, security concerns on your network may require that NIS and AD account passwords remain separate. If that's the case, do not enable the AD to NIS password synchronization on your DCs or NIS servers. Instead, have the NIS users change their passwords using yppasswd or the equivalent on the Unix systems. Your R2 NIS servers are running a yppasswd service (it should be listed in the output of rpcinfo -p). The yppasswd command is simply an NIS-variation of passwd:

```
stu% yppasswd tjones
Enter login(NIS) password:
New password:
Re-enter new password:
NIS passwd/attributes changed on dc1
```

The user types in the old password then types the new password twice and sees confirmation that the NIS password was changed on the NIS master server.

On Solaris systems, yppasswd is simply a link to the passwd command. It is equivalent to passwd -r nis.

DISABLING UNIX AND AD ACCOUNTS

Disabling the AD account that is associated with a Unix account does not affect the Unix account, and vice versa. While an AD account can exist without a Unix counterpart, the reverse is not true. An AD user account is a prerequisite, or the Unix account cannot be managed by Services for NIS. A workaround for this is to leave the accounts created during the migration as disabled. If you actually have a separate set of human users who don't have or need AD accounts, this works very well. Even if you have an NIS tjones account and a jones_t AD account for the same person, unless there is a need for Unix-to-Windows name mapping (as there is with NFS), your users should not see any difference.

Unix admins disable user accounts by changing the password value in one of several ways, depending on the flavor of Unix and what is supported. On any platform, the password can simply be changed to a value unknown to the user. An asterisk (*) in the password field will indicate "no login" on many platforms, and LK value is often used to designate a locked account. To disable a Server for NIS user account, modify that user's passwd entry using NISMAP:

```
nismap mod -k username -e "newpasswdstring" passwd
```

Summary

In this chapter we have examined the key NIS concepts and learned how R2 NIS actually improves on Unix NIS a bit. By integrating NIS maps into the Active Directory, we can make map changes on any domain controller running Services for NIS, and they will replicate automatically to all other R2 NIS DC servers. Furthermore, this NIS/AD integration makes it possible to create Windows accounts and their corresponding Unix accounts at the same time, using a single administrative tool (DSA.MSC).

The NIS map trial migration feature includes excellent logging, which permits us to not only resolve conflicts before the actual (and irreversible) map migration, but also to gain a better understanding of the migration process. The command line tool for map migration, NIS2AD, offers more granular control of the process and is more convenient to use when migrating one map at a time, which is the recommended strategy.

Once the maps are migrated to AD, you have several options for telling Unix subordinates to start getting their updates from the R2 NIS server. If it's too much trouble to force an update using `ypxfr` for every map on every Unix subordinate, consider updating only the existing Unix NIS master and then forcing the subordinates to get the new NIS master hostname from the previous one. Another alternative, if you can tolerate a controlled service interruption, is to rebuild the NIS maps from scratch on all subordinates using `ypinit`.

After the migration, adding and removing NIS servers, promoting R2 NIS servers to the master role, and propagating updated maps to Unix subordinates are all very straightforward processes. To update map data for users, groups, and computer accounts, use the Unix Attributes tab in DSA.MSC. To modify other map data, you'll need to become familiar with the command-line tool NISMAP.

In the next chapter, we'll look at the other component of Identity Management for Unix and discover how Services for NIS and Password Synchronization can work together to achieve one-way or two-way password synchronization utopia.

Chapter 21

Unix and Windows III: Password Synchronization

The Password Synchronization service included with Windows Server 2003 R2 (and with Services for Unix) is just about the greatest thing since sliced bread.

In the real world, I support a network with 15+ Unix servers. All of the users have Windows (AD) accounts as well, but only a few people need accounts on the Unix systems. My organization has decided, for various reasons, not to implement NIS at this time. This is not the first company I've worked with that has said no to NIS. It seems rather common for administrators in this situation to decide that NIS is not very secure, it's a bit of trouble to set up and maintain, and there just aren't enough user accounts and groups to manage to justify the effort. So every Unix host keeps a separate password, group, and shadow file. Sometimes admins use an automated file copy tool like rdist to keep them synchronized, but rdist (and its cousins, rsh and rcp) are frowned upon for security reasons. So usually we just sigh and log on to every box one by one whenever we need to add, delete, or modify user accounts. It's not that bad if you don't have a lot of Unix users to manage (or a lot of account turnover). The problem occurs when we opt not to enforce password policies on the Unix systems. Why would we do that, you may ask? As much as we admins dislike touching every system to manage users and groups, asking busy stressed-out developers and database administrators to change their passwords on every single system every six weeks could invoke a mutiny. Even if they agree to such a painful procedure, there is too much room for error. Somebody always forgets to change it on one system or accidentally sets the password to something *slightly* different from what they wrote down, and you have to get involved and reset it anyway. Ultimately, in many mixed Windows and Unix environments without a centralized authentication mechanism, Unix admins may espouse an official password policy without actually enforcing it. This is essentially the same thing as not having one.

The point of this long rant is this: the Password Synchronization service will allow users to change their Windows password and *all* their corresponding Unix passwords at the same time, even without NIS. And with password synchronization in place, it's much more feasible to implement (and enforce) password expiration policies consistently between the Windows and Unix environments.

For environments where users have Unix workstations and the Windows AD or server is only a secondary connection (in other words, Windows AD is not their primary logon) it's also possible for a user to change his password on one Unix system first, and then have the Windows password and all other participating Unix systems synchronize. Now that's worth the price of admission, if you ask me.

Although this password synchronization solution sounds great, there are some general requirements to consider. First, if you want to synchronize domain accounts with Unix, every domain controller in the Unix users' AD domain needs to be running Password Synchronization, and the service has to be configured identically on every domain controller for consistent results. Each DC or Windows 2003 server runs the Password Synchronization service independently and maintains its own list of synchronization hosts and parameters. Don't worry if your domain controllers are not all running R2 yet; you can use the Password Synchronization service included with SFU 3.5 on Windows 2003 and Windows 2000 domain controllers.

If you aren't using NIS at all, you'll also need to install the Unix components (the Single Sign-On daemon, or SSOD) on every Unix box that will participate in password synchronization. Finally, if you need Unix to Windows synchronization there's another component (a pluggable authentication module, or PAM) to install on every password-changing Unix system. Fortunately, setting up the Unix components is a painless process as long as your systems are running one of the supported flavors of Unix; otherwise you're faced with compiling SSOD and PAM from source code, which is also included on the R2 CD (Disc 2) or downloadable from Microsoft.

In this chapter, we'll examine password synchronization concepts and options for your environment, review dependencies and requirements in more detail, and then provide the step-by-step procedures for installing and configuring the Windows and Unix password synchronization components.

Password Synchronization Concepts

The Password Synchronization service is actually not a service that can be stopped and started; it's a DLL (`pswdsync.dll`) that lives in the `Windows\System32` directory. PSWDSYNC can run on AD domain controllers to synchronize domain account passwords and on domain member systems or stand-alone servers to synchronize local account passwords with Unix systems.

The examples that follow use domain controllers to synchronize AD passwords with Unix systems. However, in most cases (AD NIS being the exception) and unless otherwise specified, you can substitute the term *local account* for *domain account* and *member* or *stand-alone server* for *domain controller*.

Passwords are encrypted on the source host before transmission to the Windows or Unix sync partner and decrypted on the target system before being written to the local SAM, AD, or password shadow file, as the case may be. All systems can use the same key, or a different key can be used for each Windows/Unix host pair. Additional security can be implemented by using a nonstandard port for password synchronization. Again, all systems can use the same port, or a different port can be specified for each Windows/Unix pairing.

Before we start examining the various password sync scenarios, let's discuss some guiding principles that will apply in almost every case (unless otherwise specified).

Install Password Synchronization on All DCs

Password Synchronization (PSWDSYNC) should be installed on every DC in the users' domain to ensure that the DC that receives the password change request will know to synchronize it with the Unix accounts. You may be thinking that it's unlikely that the DCs in your satellite offices will be servicing change password requests for the dual Windows-Unix users at the home office. However, it could happen, so I suggest you do your homework on that subject before deciding not to install Password Sync on the remote DCs. The official Microsoft recommendation is to install it on all DCs in the domain. For DCs that haven't been upgraded to R2 yet, use the SFU 3.5 Password Synchronization component. It runs on Windows 2000 and 2003 DCs.

The service must also be configured identically on all DCs in the domain to prevent inconsistent application of the password synching policies. If you are synching passwords between local accounts on multiple Windows members or stand-alone servers and Unix hosts, the same principle applies, except that you'll also have to create a Windows account separately for each member, stand-alone, or Unix host.

Password Policies

Before configuring password synchronization between the Windows and Unix environment, give some careful thought to your organization's password complexity requirements and expiration intervals. There are several potential problems that occur mainly in Unix to Windows synchronization scenarios.

Unix password requirements are often less restrictive than Windows passwords. For example, in Solaris 8 and 9 (by default), passwords never expire, and the minimum password length is only six characters. The first six characters of the password must contain at least two alphabetic characters and at least one special character or number. Windows 2003 default password policy requires seven characters, three out of four of upper- and lowercase characters, numbers, and special characters, and passwords expire in 42 days. In a Unix to Windows synchronization scenario it is possible to set a Solaris password to "fish99" and have the Windows domain controller reject it. If that happens, the passwords will be out of sync. So it's important to set password policies to be consistent, or at least compatible, between the Unix and Windows environments. If it's not possible for users to always change the Windows password first, then you'll need to implement stronger password requirements on your Unix boxes (which may only be partially supported) or warn users of this possibility and train them to recognize the error messages.

TIP Password complexity requirements and expiration intervals should be consistent between Windows and Unix environments for two-way synchronization. For one-way synchronization, password requirements should be at least equally restrictive on the system where the password is changed as on the system where the password is synchronized.

Ultimately, the solution you decide on will depend on whether you are doing one-way or two-way authentication, the requirements of your various systems, and your organization's needs and policies.

User Names

For successful password synchronization, user names must be consistent across Windows and Unix hosts. In every scenario described in this chapter, the process depends on corresponding Windows and Unix user names. The Windows logon name kmiles must exist as kmiles on the Unix synchronization partner, and vice versa for Unix to Windows synching. This is different from the NFS name mapping process described in Chapter 19, which uses the Unix user ID (UID) instead.

NOTE The user name mapping feature of NFS is only used by NFS. It can't be used to translate Unix to Windows account names for password synchronization.

Supported Unix Platforms

Microsoft includes on the R2 CD (Disc 2) compiled binaries for the SSOD and the PAM, along with configuration files, for the following Unix platforms:

◆ Red Hat Linux versions 8 and 9

◆ Sun Solaris (on SPARC hardware) versions 8 and 9

◆ Solaris (on x86 hardware) version 8

◆ HP-UX version 11i

◆ IBM AIX version 5L 5.2

Source code is also included on Disc 2, if you wish to compile binaries for your platform.

Windows to Unix Synchronization Options

The Password Synchronization service supports Windows to Unix synchronization with an NIS master or with stand-alone Unix hosts. For NIS domains that have been migrated to AD (and now have an R2 NIS master), the R2 version of Password Synchronization also supports AD NIS synchronization.

In this section we'll discuss scenarios for synchronizing the Unix passwords from Windows.

AD NIS Synchronization

If you've already followed the steps in Chapter 20 to migrate Unix NIS accounts to AD and now have an R2 server acting as an NIS master, Windows-to-NIS password synchronization is literally one check box away. No software has to be installed on the NIS secondaries of either platform or on NIS clients. Once you enable AD NIS synchronization, whenever a Windows/NIS user changes her password, the domain controller will also change the Unix password attribute stored in AD. Any NIS secondaries will get the new password from the R2 NIS master during propagation or AD replication. A simplified version of that process is shown in Figure 21.1.

This is the simplest option to implement because there's nothing to install on any Unix systems. However, it's only the simplest because you've already done all the work by migrating NIS accounts to AD and designating the R2 server as the NIS master.

On the downside, you will still have to install PSWDSYNC on every domain controller in the users' domain and turn on AD NIS synchronization in the IDMU console on each DC. We'll step through that procedure in the next section.

Synchronize Windows Passwords with a Unix NIS Master

The second simplest option to implement, after AD NIS synchronization, is to have your AD domain controllers sync passwords with a Unix NIS master whenever a user's Windows password is changed. As you can see in Figure 21.2, the NIS secondaries will get updates from the NIS master, and so fewer Unix systems will need the SSOD daemon installed.

To set this up, install and configure the Unix Single Sign-on daemon (or SSOD) on the NIS master server, and then add the NIS master to the list of Unix computers in the IDMU console.

If you happen to have more than one NIS domain, you'll need to install SSOD on each NIS master and add each one to the list of Unix computers in the IDMU console.

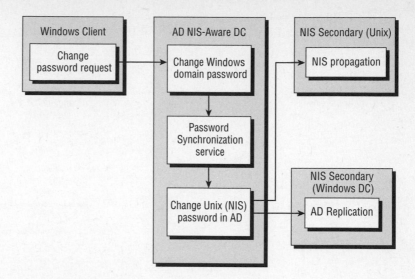

FIGURE 21.1
Windows to AD
NIS password
synchronization

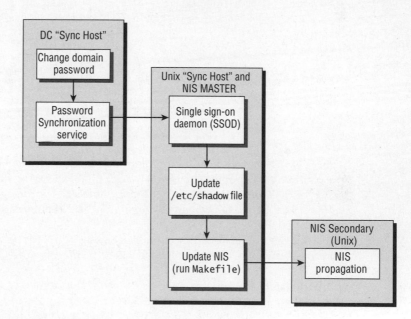

FIGURE 21.2
Windows to Unix
password synchroni-
zation: Domain
Controller to Unix
NIS Master

Synchronize Windows Passwords with Unix Hosts

If AD is used for Windows user authentication but the Unix hosts all maintain separate password
and shadow files (no NIS of any flavor, in other words), install SSOD on every Unix host that needs
to synchronize passwords with Windows and add each Unix host to the IDM console, configured
for Windows to Unix authentication (remember to do that on every DC). As you can see in the

Figure 21.3, below, when a Windows user changes his password, PSWDSYNC will contact each Unix sync host on the list and send it the new, encrypted password.

FIGURE 21.3
Windows to Unix synchronization without NIS

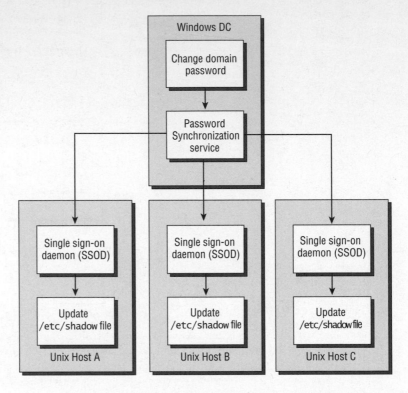

For networks based on one of the supported platforms (listed previously), this is not too terribly painful. You'll just need to install two (or three, for Linux) files, the Single Sign-on daemon (SSOD), and its configuration file. For Linux, there's also a pluggable authentication component for SSOD. Installation only involves copying the files into the correct directories and editing the configuration file.

Once you've installed and tested one host and set up a startup script to run SSOD automatically at boot, you can just TAR up the files and extract them to the correct directories on each additional Unix box.

Unfortunately, if your Unix environment isn't homogenous or they aren't all supported platforms, you might end up compiling SSOD for your unsupported flavors of Unix and copying different binaries to different machines. If every host doesn't follow the same rules, the configuration files will also vary.

Unix to Windows Synchronization Options

Configuring Unix to Windows password sync is only slightly more trouble to set up and maintain than Windows to Unix synchronization. However, the effort level (and complexity) will increase dramatically if you have a large number and variety of Unix hosts to synchronize with Windows, or in an NIS environment, which we'll discuss in a moment.

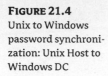

FIGURE 21.4
Unix to Windows password synchronization: Unix Host to Windows DC

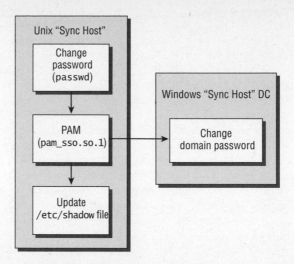

Unix to Windows synchronization relies on a pluggable authentication module (PAM) that "intercepts" the password change request on the Unix system, encrypts the new password, and sends it to the specified Windows sync hosts. The Windows sync host will accept the password change request, decrypt the password, and change the Windows password to match. This process is shown in Figure 21.4 above.

As you may have gathered from the earlier discussion of password policies, the PAM will change the Unix password and then try to update any Windows hosts listed in its configuration file. It's very possible for the change password request to update the local /etc/shadow file but fail, for any number of reasons, to update the Windows password. However, the reverse is also possible (Windows can change a domain password but fail to update Unix hosts).

Two-Way Synchronization

When two-way synching is enabled and a user changes her password in Windows, the domain password is changed, and then PSWDSYNC tries to change the password on *all* of the Windows to Unix sync partners.

On the other hand, if two-way sync is enabled and a user changes his password on a Unix system, the local password is changed, and the Unix to Windows PAM sends the encrypted password to the Windows server. When the Windows password is changed on a server or DC running PSWDSYNC, it triggers the service to initiate yet another password sync with *all* of the Unix hosts configured for Windows to Unix synchronization.

I'd like to point out two things about this redundancy. For one thing, it's not necessarily redundant. This step is necessary if you want to propagate the new password to all of the other Unix hosts on the list.

Also, don't be concerned about a password synchronization "loop of terror." The Windows to Unix synchronization bypasses the Unix to Windows PAM. At least, it does if you follow the installation instructions and copy the original system-auth file to /etc/pam.d/ssod.

Here's the payoff: if all machines are configured correctly and all Unix hosts are available at the time of the password change, a user can change her password on any Unix host or on the domain and it will be synched in AD and on every participating Unix host. Can I get an Amen?

Using Multiple Password Synchronization Options

Now that we've taken a look at the most obvious possibilities for password synchronization, I'd like to point out that these options are not mutually exclusive.

For example, at BIGFIRM, the production NIS domain has already migrated to our BIGFIRM.COM AD, but the development NIS domain is still hosted by a Linux Server (redhat1). There are also a couple of Unix systems that don't participate in either NIS domain but maintain their own password, group, and shadow files. So you can turn on the NIS AD sync for the NIS production domain users, add the development NIS master (redhat1) to the list for Windows to Unix synchronization, and add the stand-alone Unix servers (solaris2 and redhat2) to the list of computers in the IDMU-Password Synchronization console.

All of this flexibility sounds great, but there is a catch: unfortunately, you cannot specify which Windows users have accounts on the specified Unix hosts and which do not. If a Windows user account is permitted to do Unix password propagation (I'll get to that in a minute), then the password sync server has no way of knowing that tjones has an account in the NIS production domain but not the development domain. It won't know that he has a local account on redhat2 but not solaris2. PSWDSYNC will try all of the hosts on the list that are configured for Windows to Unix password synching.

Although PSWDSYNC will log every failed password sync attempt, it's not a serious issue. There would have to be a large number of Unix user accounts to synchronize, a great deal of variation between the /password files on Unix hosts, and very frequent password changes before it would cause much of a problem.

Still, it would be nice if each Unix host had an individual SYNC_USERS list in the IDMU console to tell the DC not to try to synchronize every user's password with every host on the list.

Installing and Configuring the Password Synchronization Components

Now that we've discussed the possibilities for WintoUnix and UnixtoWin synchronization, with and without an AD domain, with and without an NIS infrastructure, let's set up the PWS service on a BIGFIRM DC and install the Unix components on our Solaris and Red Hat Linux hosts.

Install and Configure PSWDSYNC

Follow these steps to install Password Synchronization on an R2 domain controller:

1. Open the Control Panel and select Add or Remove Programs and then Add Windows Components.

2. Locate Active Directory Services in the list of Windows Components and click Details (shown in Figure 21.5).

3. Select Identity Management for Unix to install all components, or click the Details button to select the individual components: Administration Components, Password Synchronization, and Server for NIS, as shown in Figure 21.6.

4. Insert the R2 Disc 2 in your server's CD-ROM drive when prompted. After the wizard finishes installing IDMU, reboot the server.

NOTE Unlike Services for NIS, which must be installed on a domain controller, you can install PSWDSYNC on a domain member or workgroup server.

FIGURE 21.5
Install Active
Directory Services
components

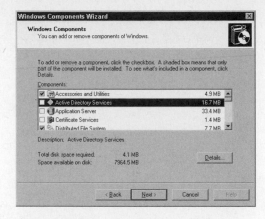

FIGURE 21.6
IDMU components

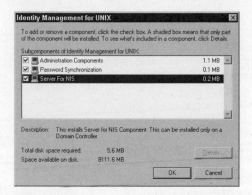

Now let's take a look at the Password Synchronization node of the IDMU Console tool.

1. Locate and open Microsoft Identity Management for Unix in the Administrative Tools Group. Highlight Password Synchronization in the console tree, and click Properties in the actions pane on the right.

2. There are only two configuration tabs for Password Synchronization, Settings and Configuration. Use the Settings dialog box, shown in Figure 21.7, to specify the default settings for PSWDSYNC: direction of password synchronization (one-way or two-way), the port to be used for communication with Unix hosts, and the default encryption key. All three of these settings can be modified for individual Unix computers but will be used if more specific options are not set.

   By the way, Figure 21.7 shows the default synchronization direction and port (6677), but not the default encryption key, which has already been changed.

3. Use the Configuration tab shown in figure 21.8 (below) to view or change the defaults for retry and attempts, logging to the Event log, and to enable Windows to (NIS) AD Password Sync. And this is the check box you use to turn on NIS AD Password Synchronization. There it is. Yep. Right there.

FIGURE 21.7
Default Password Syn-
chronization settings

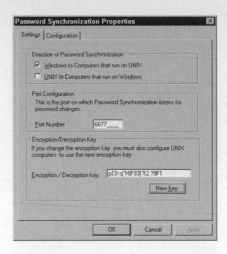

FIGURE 21.8
Default Password Syn-
chronization settings

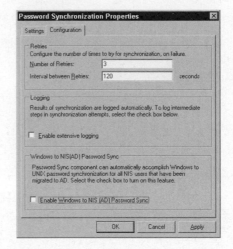

Now let's add a Unix computer to the list for synchronization.

1. Highlight Unix Computers in the console tree and click Add Computer or Properties in the actions pane on the right.

2. In the Add Computer dialog box (shown in Figure 21.9), type in the Unix host name in the Computer Name text box (you should be able to ping the host by the name you use here).

According to the system defaults, Synchronize Password Changes to the Computer Entered Above will automatically be checked. If you wish to enable Unix to Windows synchronization as well, check the box to Synchronize Password Changes from the Computer Entered Above. Synchronization must be specified in at least one direction. Change the port and encryption key from the system defaults if desired, and click OK to add this Unix host to the list.

In Figure 21.10, two Unix hosts have been added to the sync list.

FIGURE 21.9
Adding a Unix host
for synchronization

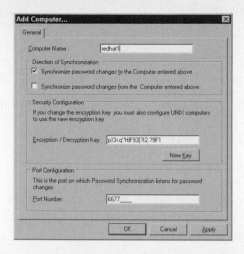

FIGURE 21.10
List of Unix hosts for
synchronization

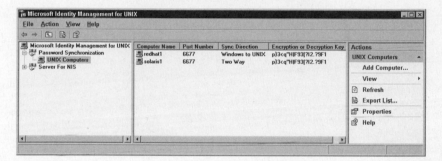

Redhat1 is set up for Windows to Unix synchronization only, while solaris1 is configured for two-way synchronization.

The port and encryption key information shown in Figure 21.10 are needed to configure the SSOD component on the Unix hosts.

Oh, by the way, now that these entries are created, when a user's password is changed on this server (DC1), it will try to contact redhat1 and solaris1 for synchronization, whether they have SSOD set up or not. It's not possible to configure PSWDSYNC and then enable it, as you can with other services like DNS or DHCP or even NIS. A workaround is to enable only Unix to Windows synchronization temporarily. Windows will wait to hear from the Unix box, and if it's not yet installed or configured to do UnixtoWin password synching, that will be the same as turning off the sync. Just remember to fix it later. The best option might be to add the Unix computer to the IDMU console after installing and configuring SSOD on the host.

The command-line tool for setting up PSWDSYNC parameters and adding Unix computers is PSADMIN. In the following examples, I use PSADMIN to view the configuration of the local system running PSWDSYNC, view the synchronization settings for redhat1, add a Unix computer named stu to the list of sync hosts, enable two-way synchronization for stu and generate a new encryption key, and finally, view the new settings for the Unix computer I just added and configured.

```
C:\>psadmin config

 Password Synchronization Settings on localhost

   Default settings
   Logging       : No
   Max Retries   : 3
   Retry Interval : 120
   Port Number   : 6677
   Sync Direction : Windows to UNIX
   Encryption Key : p}3<q"H|F93[?I2.?9F1

C:\>psadmin config -comp redhat1

 Password Synchronization Settings on localhost

   Settings for the computer redhat1
   Port Number   : 6677
   Sync Direction : Both Directions
   Encryption Key : p}3<q"H|F93[?I2.?9F1

C:\>psadmin add stu
 stu is successfully added

C:\>psadmin config -comp stu -enable BothDir -key random
 Encryption Key : ~>A~MpW7_8$#jTd1q0441
 The settings were successfully updated.

C:\>psadmin config -comp stu

 Password Synchronization Settings on localhost

   Settings for the computer stu
   Port Number   : 6677
   Sync Direction : Both Directions
   Encryption Key : ~>A~MpW7_8$#jTd1q0441
```

PSADMIN accepts remote PSWDSYNC servers as arguments and can be incorporated into a script to configure a bunch of domain controllers identically (and keep them that way).

Permitting and Denying Windows Password Propagation

Before you install the Unix components on redhat1 and solaris1, let's set up some security groups to permit or deny password propagation. As I mentioned earlier, you can't tell PSWDSYNC what accounts are on what Unix hosts, but you can specify which Windows accounts are permitted to propagate passwords using local security groups.

First, use AD Users and Computers to create two domain local groups (or a local group, if PSWDSYNC is on a domain member or stand-alone server). These groups must be named PasswordPropAllow and PasswordPropDeny. Figure 21.11 shows the PasswordPropAllow group being created.

WARNING The PasswordPropAllow and PasswordPropDeny groups must be local or domain local groups. If you accidentally create the groups as global groups, PSWDSYNC will refuse to synchronize any passwords until you fix it.

Now put all the Windows accounts that you want to propagate into the PasswordPropAllow group and all the accounts that you don't want to synchronize (Administrator, for example) into PasswordPropDeny group.

In typical Unix fashion, the Allow/Deny groups work like this:

◆ If neither group exists, then PSWDSYNC assumes that all users can sync with the Unix hosts on the list.

◆ When PasswordPropAllow exists, then users who aren't in the group cannot be synchronized. If it exists with no members, no accounts can be synchronized.

◆ When PasswordPropDeny exists, any group members will not be allowed to synchronize. This group can exist with no members.

◆ When both groups exist, then PSWDSYNC will synchronize accounts that are in PasswordPropAllow and are not in PasswordPropDeny.

Add only user accounts to the groups. Nested groups will be ignored. PSWDSYNC is only looking for the user account name and will not expand group memberships.

If you have Domain Admins (Schema Admins, Enterprise Admins) who also have Unix accounts, and you don't wish to have their domain admin account passwords synchronized over the network, you can either exclude them from propagation (they'll have to change their passwords manually), or they can use nonadministrative accounts between the Windows and Unix systems. Users with administrative responsibilities should use an unprivileged account for non-administrative activities anyway.

NOTE The PasswordPropAllow and PasswordPropDeny groups are also checked for Unix to Windows password synchronization. In fact, any rules on either the Unix or Windows hosts will apply for UnixtoWin or WintoUnix synchronization.

FIGURE 21.11
Create a group named
PasswordPropAllow.

Configure Windows to Unix Synchronization

Now that you've had an overview of password synchronization, and installed and configured PSWDSYNC on our Windows Server(s), let's step through setting up Windows to Unix (Win-toUnix) synchronization.

Let's start by enabling the NIS AD password sync, which will automatically sync passwords for the R2 NIS domain production users whenever they change their corresponding BIGFIRM.COM AD passwords.

NOTE Password synchronization will only be triggered when a password is changed by the user or by an administrator.

Next, you'll need to install and configure SSOD on redhat1 and solaris1. At BIGFIRM.COM, although you migrated the production NIS domain to AD back in Chapter 20, redhat1 is still the NIS master for another NIS domain (development). You'll need to configure it to rebuild the NIS password database (in Unix-ese: run the Makefile) whenever it gets a password sync request from a Windows PSWDSYNC server. Solaris1 will be configured as a stand-alone host, without the NIS options.

ENABLE NIS AD SYNCHRONIZATION

As you saw in the tour of the Password Synchronization components of IDMU, enabling NIS (AD) synchronization is only a couple of mouse-clicks away.

1. As a Schema Admin and Enterprise Admin, open the IDMU tool.

2. Navigate to the Password Synchronization node, right-click and choose Properties to open the Properties dialog box. Click the Configuration tab and check the Enable Windows to NIS (AD) Password Sync box, as shown in Figure 21.12.

3. You will be prompted to perform a Windows Server 2003 Service Pack 1 (SP1) compatibility check. In other words, PSWDSYNC wants to check all domain controllers to see if they are at least at Windows 2003 SP1. You can enable this feature without the compatibility check, but you have to endure a warning dialog box letting you know that the Unix password hash may be viewable to any authenticated user (see Figure 21.13)

4. Click Yes or No to perform the compatibility check. If you don't want to check all the domain controllers in the forest, click yes or no to enable the feature after you've been warned. Back in the Configuration tab, click OK, and you're done.

To test the NIS AD synch, change the Windows password for a user in the NIS domain and then try to log on with that account to a Unix NIS client machine. If you have Unix secondaries in the AD NIS domain, use the Server for NIS tool to propagate changes to the hosts. Services for NIS are discussed in the previous chapter.

Normally, you could check the Event Viewer for synchronization messages, but it will not report on NIS (AD) password sync activities; PSWDSYNC only logs information about synchronization with Unix hosts.

FIGURE 21.12
Enable NIS (AD) password synchronization.

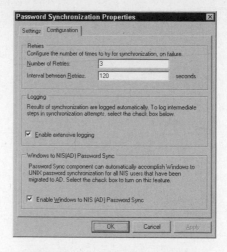

FIGURE 21.13
Bypass the compatibility check.

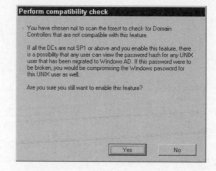

INSTALL AND CONFIGURE THE SINGLE SIGN-ON DAEMON

Now that you've enabled password sync for users in the AD-based NIS production domain, let's set up password synchronization for users in the Unix-based NIS development domain.

In this scenario, you'll only need to install the Unix Single Sign-on daemon (SSOD) on the NIS master for the development domain (redhat1). As long as you only need Windows to Unix synchronization, the secondary servers and clients for this NIS domain will not need any software installed locally and should not be added to the Unix computers in the IDMU console tool.

In a previous section (Install and Configure PSWDSYNC), you used the IDMU console tool to add redhat1 to the list of Unix computers for synchronization and selected the check box for Windows to Unix synchronization only. When you set up SSOD on redhat1, you'll need the port number and encryption key string specified it in the IDMU console tool (or it can be viewed using PSADMIN (psadmin config -comp *computername*)).

To install SSOD on redhat1, you need access to the Unix components that are to be included on the R2 release CD (under IDMU\UNIX\Bins on the Windows Server 2003 R2 CD); however, they were not included on the trial version of R2 CD and I had to download them separately from Microsoft.

If you need to download the components, go to www.microsoft.com/downloads and search on the keywords "R2," "Unix," and "ssod." The download file (ssod.tar.gz) is a 5MB gzipped tarfile (*tar* stands for *tape archive*, an old Unix-y way of archiving files to a single file, usually to tape). Download the file directly to your Unix host or download it to Windows and do a binary-mode FTP transfer to the Unix host.

On redhat1, unzip the ssod.tar.gz file and then extract the resulting tarfile:

```
[admin@redhat1]$ gunzip ssod.tar.gz
[admin@redhat1]$ tar xf ssod.tar
```

The tarfile extracts its contents into a directory named UNIX with two main subdirectories, /UNIX/bins and /UNIX/src.

These steps won't be necessary if you are copying the files directly from the CD. If you need to copy files across the network to the Unix systems, use a binary transfer method (like FTP with the bin option turned on) to avoid corrupting CR/LF (carriage-return/line-feed) pairs.

The /UNIX/bins directory includes the SSOD and PAM binaries and configuration files (sso.cfg and pam.cfg). The /UNIX/bins subdirectories are named after the OS/platform build. Table 21-1 lists the compiled platforms and corresponding directory names.

TABLE 21.1:   Table 1: Compiled Unix Platforms and Subdirectories

PLATFORM	/UNIX/bins DIRECTORY
Red Hat Linux 8	rhl_8
Red Hat Linux 9	rhl_9
Sun Solaris 8 on SPARC	sol_sparc_8
Sun Solaris 9 on SPARC	sol_sparc_9
Solaris x86 Version 8	sol_x86_8
HP-UX Version 11i	hpux_11
IBM AIX version 5L 5.2	aix_52

The /UNIX/src directory is the source code, included so that ambitious Unix admins supporting other flavors of Unix can attempt to compile the SSOD and PAM. There's no help file or README file included with the source files. When it comes to "how to compile this for your platform," apparently there are just too many variables.

Redhat1 is running on Red Hat Linux version 9, so copy the ssod.rhl binary from the UNIX/bins/rhl_9 directory to the /usr/bin or /usr/local/bin directory on redhat1 and rename it to ssod. Also copy the sso.cfg file from /UNIX/bins to /etc/sso.conf. Finally, and only because this is a Linux box, you need to copy /etc/pam.d/system-auth on the local machine to /etc/pam.d/ssod.

Copy the files as root so that root will be the owner of the files in the target directory:

```
[root@redhat1]# cp UNIX/bins/rhl_8/ssod.rhl /usr/bin/ssod
[root@redhat1]# cp UNIX/bins/sso.cfg /etc/sso.conf
[root@redhat1]# cp /etc/pam.d/system-auth /etc/pam.d/ssod
```

For other platforms, it's not necessary to copy the system-auth file to /etc/pam.d/ssod. However, you should go ahead and do it if you will also be installing the PAM for Unix to Windows synchronization.

Next, make sure that the sso.conf file is owned by root, readable and writable only by root. This configuration file will contain sensitive information, mainly the encryption/decryption key used for password synchronization. Use chmod to set the permissions if necessary (chmod 600 sso.conf).

```
[root@redhat1]# ls -la /etc/sso.conf
-rw-------    1 root     root         7675 May 27 15:08 /etc/sso.conf
```

Now use a file editor like vi to configure the /etc/sso.conf file. The default configuration parameters in the file, the lines that aren't commented out with a pound # sign at the beginning of the line, are

```
ENCRYPT_KEY=ABCDZ#efgh$12345
PORT_NUMBER=6677
SYNC_USERS=all
SYNC_HOSTS=(157.60.253.105,6677,ABCDZ#efgh$12345)
USE_SHADOW=1
FILE_PATH=/etc/shadow
USE_NIS=0
NIS_UPDATE_PATH=/var/yp/Makefile
TEMP_FILE_PATH=/etc
CASE_IGNORE_NAME=1
IGNORE_PROPAGATION_ERRORS=1
SYNC_RETRIES=3
SYNC_DELAY=30
```

The instructions and comments in the conf file are thorough, so I won't discuss everything in detail, but the parameters you will need to modify or confirm on redhat1 are ENCRYPT_KEY, SYNC_USERS, SYNC_HOSTS, USE_NIS, and NIS_UPDATE_PATH. You will need to change the default encryption key from the default to the new system default key or to the specific key assigned to that host. You're using the default port number (6677). The port number and encryption key in the sso.conf file must match the port number and encryption key shown in the Password Encryption console tool for that host (or you can see it using PSADMIN). In this case, change the encryption key from the default, but keep the default port assignment:

```
ENCRYPT_KEY=p}3<q"H|F93[?I2.?9F1
PORT_NUMBER=6677
```

Next, specify which users will be allowed to synchronize and which hosts you will accept sync requests from. It's a good idea to list only those users you wish to synchronize with Windows (this rule will apply for synchronization in either direction).

```
SYNC_USERS=+ljustice,+kmiles,+thawkins,-root
```

As you can see from the preceding example, a user name preceded by a plus sign (+) permits synchronization, and a name preceded by a minus sign (–) denies synchronization.

If you have a lot of users to permit and deny, the `sso.conf` file will accept multiple SYNC_USERS statements. However, remember that redhat1 is an NIS server and there may be many, many accounts to list. You should at least omit the Super User (root) account and any sensitive system accounts. The following alternative configuration permits everyone but root to synchronize:

```
SYNC_USERS=all,-root
```

NOTE   On some Unix systems, accounts are effectively disabled by changing the password to an unknown value or to use special characters (like *LK*) in the /etc/shadow file. On these systems, resetting a password for a disabled account will re-enable the account. If the system accounts on the Unix host don't have Windows equivalents, there's nothing to worry about, but the safest thing is to exclude every special account and accounts that must remain disabled from password synchronization.

Next, you'll list each Windows Server or DC that is permitted to pass sync requests to this host. For synching with Windows domain accounts, you'll include every domain controller that's running password synchronization.

SYNC_HOSTS statements will include the following three comma-delimited arguments for each permitted host: the name of the Windows Server or DC, the port number they will use, and the encryption key.

```
SYNC_HOSTS=(dc1,6677,p}3<q"H|F93[?I2.?9F1)
SYNC_HOSTS=(dc2,6677,p}3<q"H|F93[?I2.?9F1)
```

If you omit either the port or the encryption key in the statements, the default values will be used. Multiple hosts can be specified in one statement, so the following example is logically equivalent to the preceding one:

```
SYNC_HOSTS=(dc1,6677,p}3<q"H|F93[?I2.?9F1) (dc2,6677,p}3<q"H|F93[?I2.?9F1)
```

Also, since you are using the default encryption keys and ports, a simpler statement would be:

```
SYNC_HOSTS=(dc1)(dc2)
```

Be careful to use a name that will be resolved successfully by the system. The SSOD daemon needs to translate the IP associated with the incoming connection to the name of a trusted host. In this case, the host name dc1 should be either in the local /etc/hosts file or resolvable using DNS reverse lookup. In some cases, you may need to be more specific (dc1.bigfirm.com, for example).

Now, because redhat1 is also an NIS server, and you want it to update the password (shadow) database after a password change, you'll need to turn on NIS updates and tell SSOD where the Makefile is located using the following configuration file entries:

```
USE_NIS=1
NIS_UPDATE_PATH=/var/yp/Makefile
```

As shown in the example above, you will need to change the USE_NIS parameter to 1 (yes) but you should only change the NIS _UPDATE_PATH parameter if the Makefile directory is something other than /var/yp/Makefile. Save the modified file to `/etc/sso.conf`. Now you're ready to start the daemon (as root):

```
[root@redhat1]# /usr/bin/ssod
```

If you don't see any errors, the daemon is running. However, you can use `ps` to confirm that:

```
[root@redhat1]# ps -ef |grep ssod
root      15929     1  0 14:32 pts/2  00:00:00 /usr/bin/ssod
root      15931 15837  0 14:32 pts/2  00:00:00 grep ssod
```

To automatically start `ssod` at boot time, add a line (`/usr/bin/ssod`) to the `/etc/rc.local` file. To stop `ssod`, use `ps` to obtain the process ID of `ssod` (15929, shown in the preceding code) and use `kill` (or `pkill`):

```
[root@redhat1]# kill -9 15929
```

or

```
[root@redhat1]# pkill -9 ssod
```

Before testing SSOD by changing a user's password in Windows, confirm that redhat1 is configured in the IDMU console tool for Windows to Unix synchronization and that the port and encryption keys specified in the console are identical to the ones in the `/etc/sso.conf` file on redhat1.

Your confirmation and troubleshooting tools are the Event Viewer (it's also helpful at this point if extensive logging is turned on) and the messages file on the Unix host (`/var/log/messages` on redhat1).

In this case, you'll use DSA.MSC to reset the password for a user (thawkins). Once you see that the password has been changed successfully on Windows, you'll check the Event log for any problems.

If all goes well, you can expect to see an entry like in the one shown in Figure 21.14.

FIGURE 21.14
Successful password
synchronization

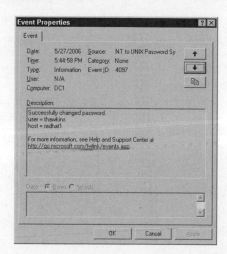

If the synchronization fails, you should see one or more helpful entries in the Event log as well. After the synchronization, redhat1 reports the following in the messages file:

```
May 27 17:45:00 redhat1 ssod:[5672]: Successfully updated password via PAM User:
thawkins
```

To ensure that the NIS Makefile ran and updated /etc/shadow successfully, you can also look in the /var/yp/development directory on redhat1 and check the timestamp for the files passwd.byname and passwd.byuid.

The final proof will be in the successful login of thawkins to an NIS client system, so don't skip that step.

The steps for installing and configuring SSOD on a Unix stand-alone host (solaris1) are identical to the steps given for an NIS master, except that you leave the USE_NIS parameter disabled (USE_NIS=0) in /etc/sso.conf.

Unix to Windows Synchronization

To set up Unix to Windows (UnixtoWin) password synchronization on a Unix host, you'll need to install the UnixtoWin PAM module for that platform and operating system and also modify the PAM configuration file on the Unix system to let it know when and how to use the UnixtoWin synchronization module.

The steps to set up SSOD are pretty much the same on any Unix platform; however, the directory location for the PAMs and their configuration files will vary somewhat from platform to platform. The Windows help file outlines the steps for all supported platforms; however, I'll include setup instructions for the two platforms at BIGFIRM, Linux (Red Hat) and Solaris, in this section. Remember, redhat1 is running on Red Hat Linux 9 (Shrike) and solaris1 is running Solaris x86 Version 8. When using the following instructions to install PAM on your Unix systems, substitute the appropriate directories and binary names for your platforms.

INSTALL THE SYNCHRONIZATION PAM ON RED HAT LINUX

To install the UnixtoWin PAM on Redhat1, follow these steps:

1. Copy pam_sso.rhl from UNIX\bins\rhl_9 to

2. /lib/security on redhat1, and rename it to pam_sso.so.1.

3. Copy /etc/pam.d/system-auth to /etc/pam.d/ssod.

   You may have copied this file previously. It's already a step required for Linux installations of SSOD.

4. Open /etc/pam.d/system-auth with a text editor, and locate the following line:

   ```
   password required /lib/security/pam_cracklib.soretry=3
   ```

5. Immediately after the line shown above, add a new line:

   ```
   password required /lib/security/pam_sso.so.1
   ```

6. Delete or comment out (with a # sign) the following line:

```
password required /lib/security/pam_deny.so
```

7. Save the modified system-auth file.

To disable UnixtoWin password synchronization later, remove the pam_sso.so.1 entry in /etc/pam.d/system-auth and uncomment the line that calls pam_deny.so.

INSTALL THE SYNCHRONIZATION PAM ON SOLARIS

We'll follow these steps to install the UnixtoWin PAM on Solaris1:

1. Copy pam_sso.sol from the UNIX\bins\sol_x86_8 to the /usr/lib/security directory, renaming it to pam_sso.so.1.

2. Open /etc/pam.conf with a text editor and locate the following line:

```
other password required /usr/lib/security/$ISA/pam_UNIX.so.1
```

3. Immediately after the preceding line, add a new line for the UnixtoWin PAM:

```
other password required /usr/lib/security/$ISA/pam_sso.so.1
```

To disable UnixtoWin password synchronization later, remove or comment out (using a # sign) the line added in step 3.

CONFIGURE THE PAM COMPONENT

The UnixtoWin PAM also uses the information in the sso.conf file. Be sure to review the sso.conf parameters (including SYNC_USERS and SYNC_HOSTS) and edit them as appropriate for Unix-toWin synchronization.

To synchronize the Unix password with an AD domain account password, add only one (reliably available) domain controller for each target domain to the sso.conf file.

That's all there is to setting up the UnixtoWin PAM; there's no service to start and no startup script to worry about. When a user invokes the passwd command on the Unix system, the PAM is invoked. It will check to make sure the user is not excluded from propagation in the SYNC_USERS list and will then attempt to synchronize with every host specified in the sso.conf file's SYNC_HOSTS list.

On the Windows side, you'll also need to add the Unix computer to the list (if it's not there already) and enable Unix to Windows Synchronization in the IDMU console.

Finally, you should run a couple of tests by changing a Unix user's password and then checking the local messages file and the Event Viewer for any problems.

If you are only setting up UnixtoWin synchronization for a single host to a Windows DC or server, you're done. If you want NIS users on client machines to be able to sync up with Windows when they change their NIS passwords, well, that's a little more complicated.

Synchronizing Password Changes from NIS to Windows

In an NIS environment, users change passwords using yppasswd instead of the usual passwd command. Yppasswd does not work with the Unix to Windows PAM. When the NIS client runs the yppasswd utility, the password will be updated in the NIS master server's database and propagated to any secondaries but not necessarily anywhere else.

This is true even if the client is talking to an R2 NIS master configured for AD NIS synchronization; when the Unix password is changed on an NIS-aware DC, the AD password is *not* automatically changed. AD NIS sync only works when the Windows password is changed first (now are you really surprised?).

On Solaris 8 or 9 systems, however, the Unix to Windows PAM *can* intercept a yppasswd request and synchronize with Windows. This is because yppasswd and nispasswd are just links to /usr/bin/passwd -r nis on Solaris 8 and 9. Don't mistake this improved NIS-aware version of passwd on Solaris for magical two-way NIS AD synchronization.

Even if you don't have a Solaris 8 or 9 system, you can set up synchronization of NIS to Windows by configuring the NIS client to sync with Windows and let the Windows sync host update the NIS master.

Once it's in place, this solution will resemble the process shown in Figure 21.15.

As you can see in Figure 21.15, the NIS user will run the passwd utility instead of yppasswd. The PAM module intercepts the request and sends it to the DC sync host. The DC sync host accepts the request and changes the Windows password. If the DC is only configured for Unix-to Windows (and not two-way) authentication, it will not send a password change request back to the NIS client. This is by design; the user account may not exist on the NIS client machine anyway. Instead, you need to tell the NIS master server that this user's password has changed. So you also include the NIS master on the list of sync hosts in the IDMU-Password Synchronization console and configure it for Windows to Unix authentication (or two-way, authentication, since it's probably also an NIS client).

FIGURE 21.15

Unix to Windows
Password Synchronization: Unix NIS client
to Windows and Unix
NIS Master

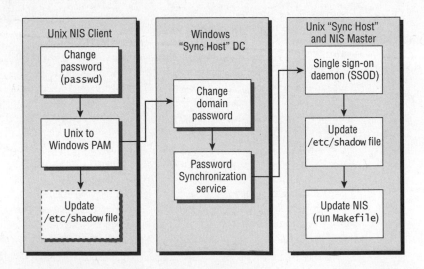

When the DC gets the change password request from the PAM module on the NIS client, it changes the Windows password in AD. Because the NIS master is on the list for Windows to Unix password synching, this in turn triggers password sync with the NIS master. The NIS master gets the new NIS password from the DC sync host instead of the NIS client and updates the NIS database.

Notice in Figure 21.15 that the NIS client's /etc/shadow is shown with a dashed line. If the account doesn't exist on the local system, passwd may return an error, but the rest of the process will not fail.

WARNING This solution also assumes that the NIS master server uses the shadow file in /etc/ shadow when it runs the Makefile. Be aware that this is not always the case. Sometimes the NIS master is configured to use database files in separate directories from the local system's /etc files. If so, the last step in the preceding solution will not work; the NIS password will not be changed on the NIS master server.

Fortunately, once you grasp this concept you already have all of the building blocks you'll need to set it up:

1. First, configure the Unix NIS master for WintoUnix synchronization. If it's also an NIS client, configure it for two-way sync.

2. Install the PAM module on every NIS client machine and configure the sso.conf file to sync with a Windows server or DC running PSWDSYNC (one domain controller running PSWDSYNC per AD domain).

3. Add all of the NIS client machines to the list of Unix computers on the Windows Server (or all domain controllers), and turn on *one-way* UnixtoWin sync for the NIS client machines. This might be a good time to use PSADMIN.

4. Train users to use passwd instead of yppasswd, or replace yppasswd with a link to the passwd utility.

After completing these steps, when the NIS user changes her password using the passwd utility, the PAM will intercept and forward a password change request to the specified Windows SYNC_ HOST(s). This in turn will trigger propagation of the new Windows password to the NIS master because it's on the list for Windows to Unix synchronization.

Summary

The password synchronization component included in R2 is extremely flexible, and can be used in domain or stand-alone server environments, with or without NIS, and even offers a welcome solution for synching passwords on multiple Unix systems that are not using NIS or another centralized authentication mechanism.

The Unix components (the single-sign-on daemon and PAM module) will be included with R2 or available from Microsoft's download site. If you are implementing them on a supported Unix platform, these are extremely simple to install and configure with just beginning or intermediate Unix systems administration skills. For unsupported platforms, however, you'll have to deal with compiling the source code, which is definitely an advanced systems administrator activity.

Remember that it's essential to install the password synchronization component on every domain controller in the 'password changing' domain and configure the service identically on all DCs for consistent results. Also, ensure that synchronizing accounts have identical usernames on Unix and Windows systems, because there is no username mapping for this service as there is for NFS. Finally, be careful to implement password complexity and expiration policies consistently between platforms wherever possible.

Chapter 22

Active Directory Federation Services (ADFS)

Active Directory provides a secure and manageable mechanism for authenticating and authorizing users within small and large organizations alike. But what happens if you want to share resources from your Active Directory Windows environment with users who are not part of your organization? This is the main job of Active Directory Federation Services (ADFS). ADFS lets you grant access to your applications—and specifically your web-based applications—to users that don't reside in your company's AD forest. In other words, you can grant access to users in another company to your web applications without creating an AD account for them in your AD forest that you have to maintain over time or without setting up forest trusts between your forest and theirs. And you can do it in a secure way that doesn't let the external user have any more access to your AD environment than they absolutely positively need to access your web application. That is the goal of ADFS.

Why would you want to do any of this? Well, let's imagine that your company, bigfirm.com, manufactures widgets. In order to produce those widgets, bigfirm.com relies on a number of different external companies to supply the parts to make the widgets. Now let's suppose bigfirm.com has an internally developed web application that shows real-time inventory and manufacturing information and you'd like to give access to some of that information to your suppliers in order to ensure that they always have enough parts available whenever you need them. Since it's an internal application, you can't really just give them an AD account and let them through your firewall to access the application. So, you need an alternative ways of granting them safe and secure access to your application environment without having to manage your partner's individual user accounts. Identity federation was specifically designed to address this problem, and ADFS lets you do this within the Windows Active Directory world. In a way, you can think of ADFS as a different kind of trust relationship between you and your partners.

In this chapter, we'll first look at some of the characteristics of identity federation in general and ADFS in particular, including the standards that Microsoft and others rely on to ensure interoperability between federation solutions. Then we'll talk conceptually about all the parts and pieces of ADFS, paying particular attention to the ones you really need to be concerned with for a basic ADFS deployment. Finally, we'll walk through a real-life example of how you can install ADFS in your environment and configure it to work with a partner organization.

The Technology behind Identity Federation

Identity federation is not an idea that started with ADFS. The notion of being able to authenticate and authorize disparate organizations in a secure way has been around for a while. In fact, there is a set of industry standards that define how software vendors can do this in a way that is both secure and interoperable (to the extent that standards are interoperable between vendors!). Why would you need standards to do this? Well, think about what Windows provides for authentication and authorization. In a typical AD environment, you sit at your Windows workstation and you authenticate to your AD domain and under the covers, Windows uses Kerberos to perform that *authentication*. Because you are a member of a number of different user groups defined in AD, you can use your group membership to *authorize* access to any number of resources running on Windows. Those resources might be files or printers or web applications running on IIS. So, between Kerberos as your authentication protocol and security groups stored in AD as a means of authorizing access, you have a complete system for ensuring that only the right users get access to the right applications.

However, other operating system platforms may and generally do use completely different mechanisms for providing authentication and authorization. For example, a Unix-based environment may use the Network Information Service (NIS) set of protocols for authentication and authorization, while still another platform may use a different implementation of Kerberos and groups than Windows does. If you're going to provide a way to federating identity across disparate organizations, then you need a "least-common denominator" way of doing that that all platforms and applications can understand. For this reason the WS-Federation and SAML (Security Assertion Markup Language) standards were born.

In fact, you could say that ADFS is all about taking the common elements of authentication and authorization that you're familiar with in Windows—stuff like Kerberos authentication and security group-based authorization—and mapping them to generic, standards-based protocols that can be used to federate organizations regardless of what platforms or application technologies they may be using.

Understanding the Web Services Federation Standards—XML, SAML, and WS-Federation

In order to understand the roles of WS-Federation and SAML, it's important to step back and talk about the notion of XML Web Services. Back in the mid-'90s, software vendors decided that it was time to come up with a better standard for letting applications talk to one another, or integrate. At the time, Extensible Markup Language (XML) technology was becoming more mainstream and seemed to provide a perfect place from which to launch a new set of application integration standards. If you're not familiar with XML, think of it as a super-set of the HTML that you see in web pages every day. Basically, HTML files are composed of tags, such as <bold></bold> or <div></div> that define how to treat text or images that appear on a web page. Those tags are predefined so that all HTML authors and software vendors that provide browsers know what to expect. However, suppose you could make up any tags that you wanted to, to represent different types of data that weren't anticipated in the HTML standard? For example, what if I created a <car model></car model> tag that let me list different models of cars within a document. That is the essence of XML. It's a way of representing almost any kind of data within a structured document. Essentially it's a free-form way of sharing data, as long as both sides know what the tags mean. XML has evolved to define "schemas" for different types of functionality. For example, the Simple Object Access

Protocol (SOAP) defines an XML schema that lets applications talk to one another. If you've heard the term SOAP-based Web Services, it's referring to the XML standard for letting one application request services from another. The advantage of Web Services is that they use protocols such as XML and HTTP (or HTTPS) to easily pass application requests over the Internet, without any special accommodations for firewalls or other network acrobatics.

So, how does WS-Federation and SAML relate to XML and SOAP-based Web Services? Well, there has been a set of standards for providing a large variety of application integration functionality over Web Services. These standards are loosely referred to as WS-* because they all begin with the Web Services (WS) moniker. Many of the WS-* standards have been put forward by Microsoft and IBM jointly and have been adopted by other vendors and standards bodies. WS-Federation is part of a larger WS-Security set of standards that defines a platform independent way for application to share information securely over the Internet. WS-Federation specifies a set of XML schemas that define an operating system–independent way of authenticating and authorizing one application to another.

Now let's talk about SAML. SAML is actually a competing federation standard to WS-Federation that provides authentication and authorization services to applications. It too is based on XML-based Web Services but chose to take a different approach to solve the problem of platform-independent authentication and authorization. The SAML standard is defined by the OASIS standards body (www.oasis-open.org) and is currently a more mature and more adopted standard. The good news for you is that you don't have to worry too much about which standard is "winning" in order to federate with your partners, because ADFS provides support for both standards! In fact, in certain scenarios, you can either use SAML-based authentication and authorization or, if you are federating between two AD forests internal to your organization, you can use good old AD Kerberos as another authentication mechanism for federation.

The key take-away for you is that ADFS implements industry-standard federation protocols that allow you to, in theory, federate between applications running on Windows and users running on different platforms. In fact, Microsoft and Sun Microsystems are already working on ensuring that each other's federation products work together. Finally, the one additional thing to know about federation standards is that there are two modes, or profiles, supported by WS-Federation. The first profile, called the passive-requestor profile, defines federation between a web server-based application and a user sitting at a web browser. The second profile, called active-requestor profile, defines federation between two applications talking to one another, where there may or may not be a user involved. ADFS in Windows Server 2003 R2, Enterprise Edition, currently only supports the passive-requestor profile for applications running on IIS 6 and ASP.Net. So, if you plan to federate with your partner with ADFS, you will only be able to support federation with web browser applications.

UNDERSTANDING CLAIMS

When you grant a user group access to a resource in Windows, you say that that group has the "right" to use that resource. Similarly, in the federation world, you need a way of specifying what right a particular user in a foreign organization has to your web applications. Such rights are typically referred to as *claims*. Claims are just a fancy way of saying to ADFS, "Tell me who you are and what groups or roles you're a member of, so that I can figure out what to authorize you access to." You will see the claims term used a lot in ADFS dialogs, so it's important to understand that a claim is almost completely analogous to a user's group membership.

Now let's look at how ADFS implements identity federation in an IIS environment.

NOTE As I mentioned in the earlier in this section, ADFS in R2 currently *only* supports the passive-requestor profile. This means that you can only federate web-based applications running on IIS/ASP.Net (or other web-based application platforms that support the federation standards). There is currently no support in ADFS in R2 for active-requestor federation, which would support client based applications (for example, client-server applications running from a GUI). The next version of ADFS should include this support.

Designing an ADFS Deployment

There are a number of different scenarios supported by ADFS for performing federation. But before we get into those, I need to introduce the concept of account partners and resource partners. This is a similar concept to account domains and resource domains that you are familiar with in AD and NT 4. Namely, whenever you have two domains, one of those domains houses the resource that users want to access and the other domain holds the user accounts that need access to those resources. In the case of ADFS, I am talking about two different organizations federating with each other, so the circumstances are a bit different, but the concepts are the same. In the case of ADFS, the account partner is the organization that has users who want access to the resources and the resource partner is the organization that has the resources—the web application that is being federated. This is illustrated in Figure 22.1.

Figure 22.1 shows an account partner that has users who wish to access a web application in the resource partner's AD domain. With ADFS, they can sit at their browser logged on as users defined in the account partner AD domain, and they can access the resource partner's web application without having to log on with different credentials. In fact, there are really three main scenarios supported by ADFS in Server 2003 R2. These scenarios are defined as follows:

Federated Web Single Sign-on (SSO) This scenario is probably the most common and supports two distinct organizations that wish to federate across the Internet in a secure fashion. This is the scenario we'll discuss in this chapter.

Federated Web SSO with Forest Trust This scenario is similar to the first one, except that account and resource partners exist within a single organization. They may be two AD forests within a single organization that don't trust each other, or they may be one AD forest where accounts are held and another forest where resources (web applications) are held and those applications are accessible to external users. For example, in this scenario the external user might be a customer sitting on an Internet connection that does not have its own federation infrastructure but wishes to access the resource partner via identity federation with the account partner.

FIGURE 22.1
Account and resource partners in ADFS

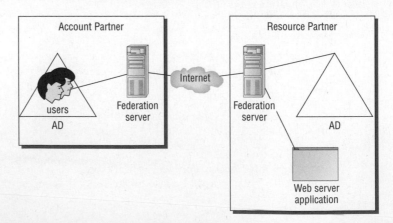

Web SSO   This scenario is not a typical federation partnership with a separate account and resource partner. In this scenario, there is only one AD domain involved that serves as both the account and resource partner, and all users accessing the web applications are external to the organization hosting the applications and are stand-alone clients on the Internet.

The Different Pieces of ADFS

The ADFS product is actually composed of a variety of server roles that can be deployed in your network in different configurations based on the federation scenario you need to support and your security and networking requirements. The different ADFS roles each have discrete functions that facilitate the identity federation of your web applications. These functions and the corresponding roles are described here:

Federation Server   The federation server role is the workhorse of ADFS. This role is where all the "action" happens. The federation server is run on both the account and resource partner sides to create a "federation trust" between the two partners. On the account partner side, the federation server is responsible for validating the user with AD and then creating the claims that will be sent to the resource partner's federation server. Remember that claims are just a way of representing who the user is and what they want to do. On the resource partner side, the federation server receives the request for access to the web application from the account partner and validates those claims against what it knows about. It also takes those claims and can transform them into something that the web application knows what to do with. For example, if your web application uses standard AD security groups to authorize access, the federation server can transform those claims coming from the account partner into security group membership. The service within the federation server that is responsible for this claims conversion is the Security Token Service, or STS. There is nothing you have to explicitly install to get the STS—it just comes as part of the federation server role—but knowing what it does when it's referenced is a good thing.

Federation Server Proxy   The federation server proxy, as the name implies, is responsible for proxying requests to and from a federation server within an account or resource partner's environment. The proxy is used if you don't want your federation server directly connected to the Internet. The proxy can sit on your DMZ (demilitarized zone) and feed requests to and from the federation server, which sits on your internal network (Figure 22.2 shows an example of this), thereby allowing your federation server to be protected from any external access other than communication with the proxy.

As you can see from the figure, the federation server proxy can be used on either side of the federation relationship, depending upon the needs of the partner. Its sole purpose is to pass authentication requests and claims back and forth between the Internet and the intranet-connected federation server.

ADFS Web Agent   The web agent is a piece of code that only gets installed on the resource partner's IIS web server. It's one of the installation options you can choose when you are installing ADFS on your Windows Server 2003 R2 servers. It is used to handle the authentication and authorization requests from the account partner to the web application that is being federated. The web agent has a relationship with the federation server running on the resource partner's website. It takes requests for access to the application and transforms those into either claims or Windows NT security tokens that can be used to authorize access to the web application. If claims are generated, then your web application must be coded to read those claims in order to grant access. If a Windows NT security token is generated, then you can use standard Windows authentication on your web application to generate access (this is the mechanism I'll use in the example in the next section). The web agent is also responsible for generating the cookies that get sent back to the client that allow for their web session with the web application to be authenticated for the period of time that they are visiting the site.

FIGURE 22.2
Deploying a federation server proxy

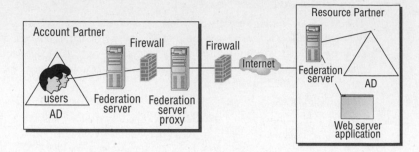

Installing and Deploying ADFS

Now let's take a look at how you can actually install and use ADFS to federate identity between two partner organizations. For the purposes of this chapter, we're going to assume the following scenario.

I have two firms, bigfirm.com and bigfirmpartner.com. They both have Active Directory and Windows Server 2003 R2 running, and they want to federate. Bigfirm.com has an IIS/ASP.Net web application that it wants to make available to users of bigfirmpartner.com, and it wants to use ADFS to make it happen. In this scenario, bigfirm.com is the resource partner and bigfirmpartner .com is the account partner. The ADFS scenario I'm going to build is shown in Figure 22.3.

The scenario I'll be deploying is the Federated Web SSO one that I described earlier. As you can see in Figure 22.3, bigfirmpartner.com will install an ADFS federation server within its network, and bigfirm.com will install a federation server and the ADFS web agent on its IIS server. I could also install a federation proxy on one or both of the partner networks if I was required to do this for security reasons. For the example, I'll assume a straight connection between the federation servers on each side of the federation trust. Before we walk through the installation, let's review the requirements for running ADFS.

FIGURE 22.3
A federation scenario involving two partner firms

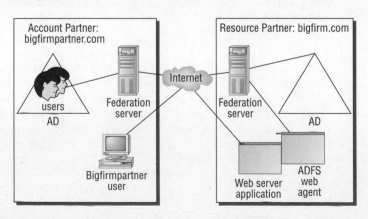

Installation Requirements for ADFS

From an OS perspective, you can only install an ADFS federation server on Windows Server 2003 R2 Enterprise or Datacenter editions. Likewise, a federation server proxy also requires these OS versions, but note that you cannot install a federation server role on the same system as a federation server proxy role. This may seem obvious, but it should be said! The ADFS web agent can run on any version of R2 server, however. For each of the three server roles, you must also have IIS installed with ASP.Net 2.0 and the .Net 2.0 Framework. And, for the federation server and any web servers running the ADFS web agent, they must support SSL and have an SSL certificate installed. If you do not have an SSL certificate for your web application, I will describe how you can create a self-signed certificate in the steps that I walk through.

NOTE ADFS relies heavily on the use of public key certificates. Certificates are used to enable SSL on ADFS-enabled web applications, which is a requirement for running ADFS. They are also required on federation servers in order to encrypt and validate communications between federation servers. In small deployments, you can use "self-signed" certificates to enable this functionality, but in larger deployments involving multiple partners, you will probably want to use Microsoft Certificate Services or purchase third-party certificates from certificate authorities such as Verisign in order to enable your federation. Step 3 in the next section describes how you can use a utility that comes with the IIS Resource Kit to create self-signed certificates for enabling SSL.

From an AD perspective, you can have AD running on any version of Windows, from Windows 2000 SP4 on up. ADFS does not require any AD schema changes to do its thing. You can also use ADAM as a credential store if the account partner does not want to use AD for this purpose. Microsoft recommends using the version of ADAM that comes with R2 if you choose this deployment path. Note that the use of AD or ADAM on the resource partner side is not necessarily required unless you plan to map claims coming from your resource partner to AD groups that are authorized for the web application. Since I'll take this approach in the example, I will install AD on the resource partner.

Installing ADFS

For the purposes of this scenario, I'm going to walk through the installation of ADFS on the resource partner side of the example—within the bigfirm.com domain. Again for the purposes of my example, I'll install both the federation server and web agent role on my bigfirm.com domain controller, called DC2. Now I'll walk through the steps for installing ADFS—remember to have the second CD from RC2 handy while you're performing the install—you will need it.

1. From the Control Panel, I run the Add/Remove Programs applet and select the Add/Remove Windows Components option on the left.

2. I double-click the Active Directory Services option to see an option for installing Active Directory Federation Services (ADFS) (Figure 22.4).

3. If I double-click the ADFS option in Figure 22.4 I can choose which of the three ADFS roles I want to install on this server. For this example, I check the ADFS Web Agents and Federation Service options and select OK.

FIGURE 22.4
Installing ADFS from the Add/Remove Programs applet

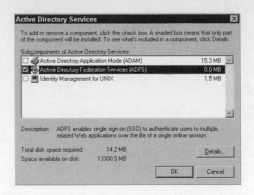

TIP At this point, when you select that you want to install ADFS, Windows will warn you if you don't have IIS and ASP.Net 2.0 installed, so I suggest installing those prior to running this install. Also, you will need an SSL certificate installed on the server, regardless of whether you are just installing a federation server or an ADFS web agent. If your web server does not already have an SSL certificate, you can download the IIS 6.0 Resource Kit Tools from Microsoft's download site (http://download.microsoft.com) and run the SelfSSL utility, which will create and install an SSL certificate on IIS for you. For my example, I ran this utility with the following syntax in order to create an SSL certificate on my default web site for bigfirm.com: selfssl /n:cn=bigfirm.com.

4. Once I click OK to install ADFS, I see the dialog box that appears in Figure 22.5.

5. This dialog box allows you to make two choices about your federation server install. The first choice asks you what kind of public key certificate you wish to use to secure communications to and from the federation server. If you have your own public key certificate, you can select it from the certificate store on your server. If not, you can have Windows create a self-signed certificate, which is perfectly valid. For my example, I choose that option. The second part of this dialog box gives you the opportunity to import a pre-existing trust policy file. A trust policy file is simply an XML file that describes a federation trust relationship that you may have with another partner or partners. Since this is the first ADFS install I am doing, I choose to create a new trust policy and then select OK to let ADFS finish installing.

FIGURE 22.5
Configuring ADFS installation options

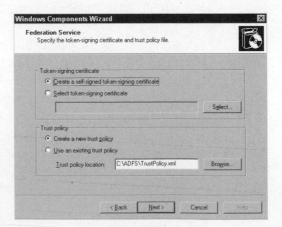

Now that ADFS is installed, I have to configure my ADFS trust policies and also configure the ADFS web agent on IIS. ADFS adds a new MMC snap-in when it installs—called the Active Directory Federation Services snap-in. If you go to Start Menu ➢ Administrative Tools, you will see the new snap-in, as show in Figure 22.6.

Now I'll configure the trust policy that will let me set up the relationship between bigfirm.com and bigfirmpartner.com.

1. From the ADFS MMC snap-in on the resource partner DC (in the example, this is DC2 in the bigfirm.com domain), I right-click the Trust Policy node and choose Properties. On the General tab, there are two text boxes—one for the federation service URI (Uniform Resource Identifier) and one for the federation service URL. The URI is a unique name that is given to my federation server and used by partner federation servers to "find" me. The URL is the IIS URL that the federation server is listening on and is how my partners will find my federation server on the Internet. In both cases, I modify these text boxes, as shown in Figure 22.7, to correspond to my domain.

FIGURE 22.6
Viewing the ADFS
MMC snap-in

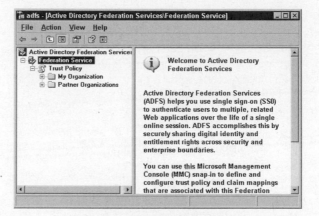

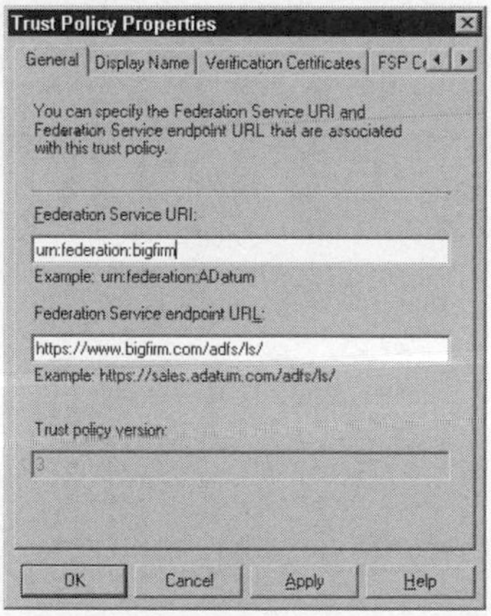

FIGURE 22.7
Modifying Trust
Policy Properties

2. As you can see, I made the URI for this federation server **urn:federation:bigfirm** and in the URL, I replaced the name of the server, DC2, with the name of my web server as it would be found on the Internet: `https://www.bigfirm.com/adfs/ls/`. Note that the `adfs/ls` path is predetermined by the ADFS installation and should not be changed unless you plan to move that virtual directory around under IIS. Once I've made the changes to the General tab, I click OK. I should not need to make any other changes to the Trust Policy properties to get started.

3. Now I need to create a claim that I can use to map to the users who are coming in from my partner organization—Bigfirmpartner.com. The way ADFS grants access to a web application for users in a different AD domain is through claims. But IIS doesn't understand claims. It only understands AD users and groups. So I need to map my claims coming from bigfirmpartner.com to a user group that exists in bigfirm.com. To do that, I right-click the Organization Claims node and choose New ➤ Organization Claim. Then I give the claim a descriptive name, like BigFirmPartner Users and select the claim type as Group Claim (see Figure 22.8).Then I click OK to accept the new claim.

4. Once the claim is created, I need to map it to an AD security group in bigfirm.com that I will use to permission my ASP.Net web application. I create a descriptive security group in AD Users and Computers—BigFirmPartner ADFS Users, in this example—and then, again from the ADFS MMC snap-in I right-click the group claim I just created under the Organization Claims node, select Properties, and focus on the Resource Group tab. From there, I check the box to map the claim to a resource group, and then I browse to the AD group I created, as in Figure 22.9. Then I click OK to complete the step.

5. Now I need to tell ADFS which web application I want to use and what types of authorization (for example, claims or NT tokens) it is expecting. To do that, I expand the My Organization node in the ADFS MMC snap-in, right-click the Applications node, and select New ➤ Application to start the Add Application wizard. ·

6. The first step of the wizard—the Application Type page—is where I tell ADFS what kind of authorization to use—claims-based or NT Token–based. I choose the latter for my example.

7. The next page—the Application Details page—asks me to identify the name and URL to the application I want to make available, as shown in Figure 22.10.

   The URL shown in this figure points to an ASP.Net web application that I have running on my server. (Note that you may need to include a trailing "/" in the URL in order to get this to work. ADFS is very finicky about this.) Once I enter this URL, choose Next to get to the next page in the wizard.

FIGURE 22.8
Creating a group claim
for Bigfirmpartner

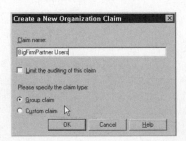

FIGURE 22.9
Mapping a claim to an
AD security group

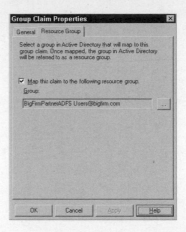

FIGURE 22.10
Entering the name
and URL to the web
application

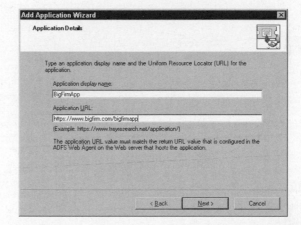

8. The next page—the Accepted Identity Claim page—asks which kinds of tokens I want the ADFS web agent to use when generating the NT token that will grant access to the application. I can use either a user principal name (UPN) in the form of user@domain or, similarly, I can use an email address instead. For my scenario, I am going to use a UPN name. Then I click Next.

9. On the Enable This Application page, I can choose to enable this application now, which I do.

10. Once the application is set up, a new application object is added under the Applications node in the ADFS MMC snap-in that represents the application I just created. When that new application is selected, there will be a list of claims shown in the right-hand pane. I see my BigFirmPartner Users group claim that I created in the previous step, but it will be gray. I want to enable that claim so that it's active for this application, so I right-click it and choose Enable.

The next step is to set up my partner account organization:

1. I begin by expanding the Partner Organizations node within the ADFS MMC snap-in, right-clicking the Account Partners node and selecting New ➤ Account Partner. The first step shows the Import Policy File Page, which lets me optionally import a policy file from my account partner, if they have one. For the purposes of my demonstration, I will select No here and choose Next.

2. The next screen—the Account Partner Details page—is where I specify the URI and URL to my account partner's federation server, as shown in Figure 22.11. This is how my big-firm.com federation server finds its partner at bigfirmpartner.com. Once I enter this information, I click Next to proceed to the next page.

3. The next screen—the Account Partner Verification Certificate page— asks me to import the x.509 verification certificate that my partner created when they set up their federation server. This is something I will have to get from my partner in order to complete this task. For my example, I export the certificate that was created on the bigfimpartner.com federation server to a .cer file and import it, then click Next to proceed.

4. The next step—the Federation Scenario page—lets me choose the federation scenario I want to support. As I mentioned earlier, since I am creating federation between two distinct organizations, I use the Federated Web SSO scenario. I then click Next to proceed.

5. The next step—the Account Partner Identity Claims page—asks me what types of claims the account partner is going to pass me. Since I already decided that my web application will accept UPN claims, I choose that option here, assuming my partner has agreed with that choice. I could also accept email claims and then decide what I want to do with them later, but for now, I'll just stick to UPN claims. Then I click Next to proceed.

6. The next step—the Accepted UPN Suffixes page— lets me select which UPN suffixes I want to accept from my partner. Since my partner's AD domain is called bigfirmpartner.com, I type that as my UPN suffix and press the Add button. If the partner had alternate UPN suffixes, I could add those here as well. Then I click Next to proceed.

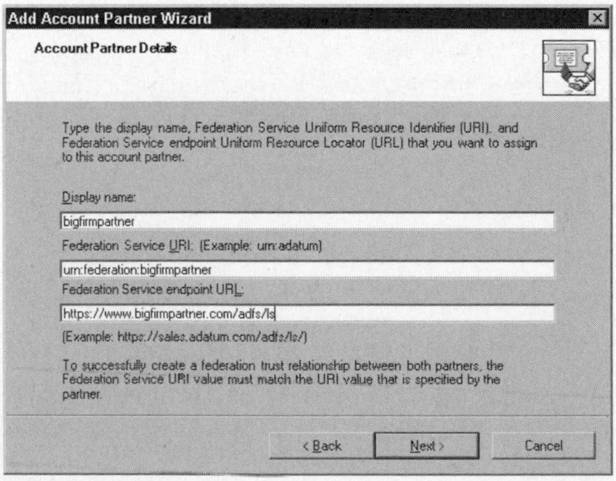

FIGURE 22.11
Specifying the account partner's federation server

7. Finally, on the Enable this Account Partner page, I enable this account partner at this time by leaving the box checked, and then selecting Next and Finish. I'm almost finished setting up my account partner.

8. Now I need to create a mapping between the claim they will send me and my own BigFirm-Partner Users group claim I set up earlier. To do this, from the ADFS MMC snap-in, I right-click the bigfirmpartner node under the Account Partners node, that I just created and select New ➤ Incoming Group Claim Mapping.

9. In the Create a New Incoming Group Claim Mapping dialog, I enter the claim name that I get from BigFirm Partners—whatever name they have specified in their outgoing claim configuration. For the purposes of this example, it is BigFirmPartner Users (see Figure 22.12). I enter that in the Incoming group claim name field and press OK.

10. The last step I need to perform on the resource partner side is to configure the ADFS web agent for my IIS web server. For that, I need to launch the IIS Manager MMC snap-in from the Administrative Tools program group. Once the IIS Manager is running, I expand the server node and right-click the Web Sites node, then choose Properties.

11. A new tab appears for this node called ADFS Web Agent. If I select this tab, I will need to enter the URL to the federation server running in my domain. If the federation server were on a different machine, I would enter the URL to that machine. The path that is entered after the service name is the default path that the federation web service application is installed to when I install ADFS, namely, `/adfs/fs/FederationServerService.asmx`. So the path I enter here is `https://www.bigfirm.com/adfs/fs/FederationServerService.asmx`. Note that this path must be defined first before I can complete the next step, which is configuring the ADFS web agent for my specific web application Then I click OK to close the screen.

12. Now let's configure the ADFS web agent for my web application, which I've called bigfirmapp (see Figure 22.13).

13. If I right-click Default Web Site and choose Properties, I once again see a new tab called ADFS Web Agent. I select that tab to enable token based authorization and configure the cookie information that will be passed back to the client browser by ADFS to enable it to access my web application (see Figure 22.14). Once I click OK, the ADFS configuration on the resource partner side is completed.

FIGURE 22.12
Mapping incoming claims to my organization claims

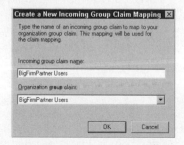

FIGURE 22.13
Viewing the
web application
to be federated

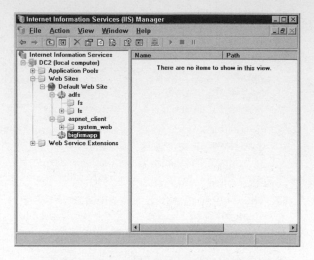

FIGURE 22.14
Enabling and
configuring the
ADFS Web Agent

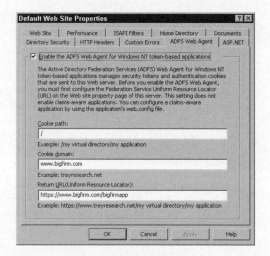

Now that I've completed the configuration of the resource partner, I'm going to set up the corresponding configuration of the resource partner on the account partner's federation server, so that if you are on that side of the fence, you know what is needed. In my example, my account partner is called bigfirmpartner.com and runs on a server called DC1.

1. From the ADFS MMC snap-in on the account partner, I going to create the outgoing claims that I want to send with every user request to bigfirm.com. So I expand the My Organization node, right-click Organization Claims and choose New ➤ Organization Claim. Just as I did on the resource partner side, I will give my claim a descriptive name—something like Big-FirmPartner Users—and then click OK. Because this is the account partner side, I don't need to map the claim to an AD user group as I did in the resource domain. I just need to create the claim.

2. Next, I once again expand the Partner Organizations node, and this time I right-click the Resource Partners node and select New ➤ Resource Partner to launch the wizard.

3. This time around, however, I'm going to make it easy on myself. I go back to the ADFS snap-in on my resource partner DC and right-click the Trust Policy node. This way, I can export the trust policy I just created to an XML file that the account partner can import and then choose Next to continue adding the resource partner.

4. Back in the Add Resource Partner wizard, once I've imported the trust policy from my resource partner, I once again choose my federation scenario (Federated Web SSO) from the Federation Scenario page, then press next.

5. On the Resource Partner Identity Claims page, I once again select the check box of the claim types I want to send (in this example, the UPN Claim) and press Next.

6. From Select UPN Suffix page, I select the radio button to "Pass through all UPN suffixes unchanged" and press Next to continue (I could map UPN suffixes to a different suffix if I wanted to do so. This would uniquely identify those users to the resource partner).

7. On the Enable this Resource Partner page, I leave the box checked to enable this new resource partner and then select Next and Finish to complete the wizard.

8. Once my resource partner organization is created, I need to map the organizational claim I created to the outgoing claim I'm going to send to bigfirm.com. To do that, from the ADFS MMC snap-in, I right-click the bigfirm.com partner organization node and select New ➤ Outgoing Claim Mapping. In the Create a New Outgoing Group Claim Mapping dialog box, I fill in the name of the outgoing claim. This name should be the same as the name I specified on the incoming claim of the resource partner's configuration, as shown in Figure 22.15.

9. The last step is to set up the Account Stores that the account partner's ADFS server will use. This tells the ADFS server whether it should accept users from either AD or an ADAM instance (or both in some cases). To do this, I simply expand the My Organization node within the ADFS MMC snap-in, right-click the Account Stores node and select New ➤ Account Store.

10. I then begin the Add Account Store wizard. I select AD as my account store from the Account Store Type page, then I press Next to proceed.

11. From the Enable this Account Store page, I leave the checkbox checked to enable it and then press Next and Finish to complete the wizard.

12. Once it's enabled, I need to modify the active claims that I use to correspond to the claims that are being expected on the resource partner side. Here is where I can tell ADFS which AD users or groups in bigfirmpartner.com can have access to the bigfirm.com application. Once I create the account store in the previous two steps, I right-click the Active Directory node under Account Stores in the ADFS MMC snap-in and choose New ➤ Group Claim Extraction.

13. In the Create a New Group Claim Extraction dialog, I can add AD users or groups that I want to map to my BigFirmPartner Users organizational claim. For this example, I just choose all users in bigfirmpartner.com, or the Authenticated Users group, as in Figure 22.16.

I have now completed my setup of ADFS, and the only thing left to do is to configure my IIS server with the proper security to enable the WebSSO feature in ADFS. To show that, I've created a simple ASP.Net web page that shows a banner and button, as shown in Figure 22.17.

FIGURE 22.15
Creating the outgoing claim mapping for the account partner

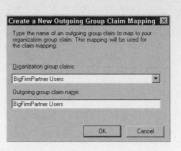

FIGURE 22.16
Associating account partner users to the organizational claim

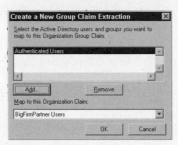

FIGURE 22.17
A simple ASP.Net page

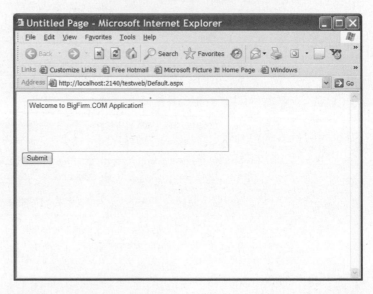

In order to ensure that the bigfirmpartner.com users who visit my ASP.Net web application are not prompted for credentials, I need to make sure that the security on my ASP.Net website in the resource partner domain (bigfirm.com) is set correctly. I follow these simple steps to do that.

1. I start up the IIS Manager MMC snap-in on the web server hosting my ASP.Net web application in bigfirm.com.

2. I right-click my bigfirmapp virtual directory that hosts the ASP.Net pages, and choose Properties ➤ Directory Security.

3. I click the Edit button on Authentication and Access Control, and, if Enable Anonymous Access is checked, I uncheck it. Then I check Integrated Windows Authentication, as shown in Figure 22.18. I click OK.

4. I right-click the bigfirmapp node one more time and select Permissions. The familiar ACL Editor dialog appears. Here, I want to add the AD user group I created earlier that is mapped from my incoming claims. That group was called BigFirmPartner ADFS Users, so I add that group to the ACL for the web application with the default permissions. Now the bigfirmpartner.com users that hit my website will have authenticated access to my ASP.Net web page. Now I'm ready to have my bigfirmpartner users access my web application without having to explicitly log on.

FIGURE 22.18
Enabling Windows authentication on my web application

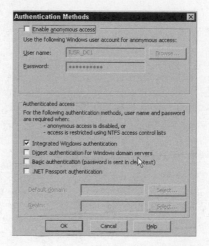

Putting ADFS to Work

After all the work you've gone through to get ADFS running, you should see very little if it's working as expected. A user in the bigfirmpartner.com domain, sitting at their desktop browser should be able to navigate to `https://www.bigfirm.com/bigfirmapp`, and behind the scenes, the ADFS server in the account domain will validate their credentials with the account partner AD domain and wrap up their request in a claim that gets sent to federation server at the resource partner, which is delivered to the ADFS web agent for validation. Then the client is passed back the page that they are requesting with a cookie that is valid for their session! Other than a short delay as the various networks and services are traversed, the user should not even know that all of that is going on in the background. The operative word here is *should*! The last step that bigfirmpartner users will want to take is configure Internet Explorer so that it does not prompt them for credentials. Even though ADFS is set up and working, when a bigfirmpartner user goes to my bigfirm web application for the first time, they will still be prompted for credentials, instead of having their bigfirmpartner user ID be passed through behind the scenes to ADFS. The reason for that is because IE's default security for the Internet Zone will always require the user to enter a username and password. The easy way around this is to configure `www.bigfirm.com` as a trusted site in IE's Internet Zone Security. Trusted sites' zone security has the option set to always pass the current username and password to the target site, as shown in Figure 22.19.

FIGURE 22.19
Setting the IE option to pass username and password behind the scenes

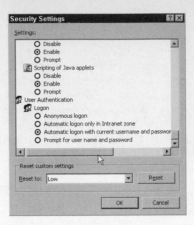

Once this option is set, a user in bigfirmpartner.com will be able to access the application shown in Figure 22.17 by simply entering in the URL, and their bigfirmpartner credentials will be passed to ADFS, translated into claims that are then translated into the BigFirmPartner ADFS Users group claim by the bigfirm.com ADFS server. The user is authenticated under the covers without ever being prompted for their credentials! That, in a nutshell, is the beauty of ADFS.

TROUBLESHOOTING

I recommend enabling all verbose ADFS logging when you are trying to get it working. You can do this by right-clicking the Federation Service node within the ADFS MMC snap-in, choosing Properties, and selecting the Troubleshooting tab. From there, you can enable all of the various kinds of logging, which are collected in text files that you can find under %systemdrive%\adfs\logs. In addition, ADFS will log events to the Application Event Log that can also be useful in troubleshooting problems. Pay attention to case and syntax as you're entering paths and configurations within ADFS. As I mentioned earlier, ADFS is very finicky when it comes to that.

Summary

ADFS is a new service in R2 that provides you with the ability to federate identity across multiple AD organizations. Whether it's providing access to IIS web applications within your own organization or across partner organizations over the Internet, ADFS provides a standards-based way to authenticate and authorize users to access your applications. And while ADFS is not trivial to set up, you can enable an ADFS partnership in a reasonable period of time and allow partner organizations access to your applications or gain access to their applications quickly and securely!

Chapter 23

Active Directory Application Mode (ADAM)

Active Directory (AD) is a great all-purpose directory for doing things like authentication and authorization and group policy, and for providing a "white pages" directory with information about your users, but there are certain circumstances where AD just doesn't fit. One example of that is when you have an application that needs to store custom information in a directory service. If you were to use AD, you may be required to extend the schema, or database structure, in order to accommodate that custom application. For example, you might have an application that wants to store shoe size with every user in your directory. If you were to put that into AD, you'd have to extend the schema to add the shoeSize attribute, and then that schema would become a permanent part of your AD database. Windows Server 2003 does allow you to deactivate schema extensions, but it does not allow you to remove them outright. So shoeSize would be forever a part of your AD. There are other examples where it may not make sense to deploy a full AD implementation, such as when you buy a third-party application that requires a directory service. In those cases, ADAM is the perfect solution. ADAM provides a "stripped-down" version of AD—essentially an AD-compatible Lightweight Directory Access Protocol (LDAP)–capable directory service that does not have the same requirements (or capabilities) that AD has, for those cases where you just need an LDAP directory service that can be replicated but that does not impact your existing AD infrastructure.

In this chapter, I'll examine the capabilities of ADAM—how it shares some characteristics of AD and how it differs. I'll walk through how to install ADAM and how you can manage it using the somewhat limited tools that Microsoft provides for this purpose. Finally, I'll look at how you can integrate ADAM into your AD environment for authentication but still maintain separate ADAM instances for all of your directory-enabled applications.

The Capabilities of ADAM

As I mentioned, ADAM is a lighter weight version of AD that can be used in cases where you need an LDAP-compatible directory service. ADAM also provides some compatibility with the industry standard X.500 directory standard, which is a superset of LDAP and is used by other vendors' directory products (for example, Sun's Directory Server or Novell's e-Directory product). ADAM now comes as part of Windows Server 2003, R2, and requires R2 (any version) to run. Earlier versions of ADAM could actually be installed on Windows XP, but for most purposes that is probably good only for testing and wouldn't fit a production environment.

ADAM is similar to AD in many ways. It supports queries, modifications, and other operations via LDAP, as AD does. It has an Access Control List (ACL)–based security model that lets you set permissions for which users and groups have access to which objects and attributes, and it supports multi-master replication—meaning that you can have multiple copies of a particular ADAM "instance" running on multiple machines on your network. An instance is essentially a unique copy of ADAM that holds directory information. ADAM has the notion of naming contexts, or partitions, and supports three different types of partitions, as described here:

Configuration Similar to the AD configuration naming context, the ADAM configuration naming context holds information about the ADAM instance's configuration, the replicas that are associated with an ADAM instance, and sites and subnets associated with the instance.

Schema The ADAM schema naming context, as the name implies, holds the schema (that is, the supported classes and attributes) for a particular ADAM instance. Like the AD schema, the ADAM schema naming context is replicated to all ADAM instances, as is the configuration naming context. The ADAM schema contains a subset of the AD schema—for example, you won't find computer objects in ADAM because ADAM's main purpose is to track information about people.

Application Directory The application directory naming context is where the actual directory data for a given ADAM instance is stored. It is analogous to AD's domain naming context and is where you define the objects (for example, people, groups, and so on) that are to be stored by ADAM. The application directory naming context can be replicated to any number of Windows Server 2003 R2 servers, closely approximating the distributed nature of AD domain controllers.

In addition to being able to replicate an instance of ADAM to multiple physical servers, you can have multiple instances of ADAM running on a single machine, and each instance can have a different schema and configuration. The schema and configuration portion of ADAM is known as a *configuration set*. When you want to replicate an application directory partition to another machine, the configuration set for that partition is replicated along with it, as shown in Figure 23.1.

As Figure 23.1 shows, I've created an ADAM instance called "A" that has a configuration set associated with it. That configuration set has an application directory partition called AppData (when you set up a new application directory partition, you need to name it, as I did here). Both the configuration set and the AppData partition get replicated to the second server, and you can configure the replication schedule, just as you can with AD.

FIGURE 23.1
Replicating an ADAM instance to a second computer

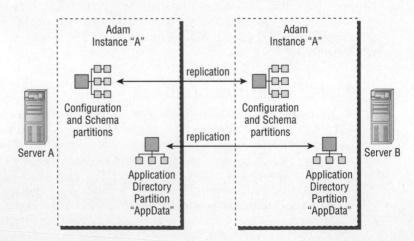

How ADAM Is Different from AD

While ADAM has many similarities to AD, it also has some important differences. The first and most important difference is that ADAM does not provide a Kerberos service for authentication, as AD does. ADAM supports a variety of non-Kerberos-based authentication mechanisms instead. When you authenticate to an ADAM instance, it's referred to as "binding" to the directory. I'll discuss these mechanisms a little bit later.

Another capability that ADAM has that AD does not is that ADAM is a restartable service. You can stop and start a particular ADAM instance just like any other service. As Figure 23.2 shows, my ADAM instance called MyLDAPAPP appears in the list of services when I type **net start** at a command prompt.

I can then stop that instance by typing **net stop myldapapp**, and then that ADAM instance will no longer be available—until it's restarted, of course.

ADAM's schema is also significantly different from that which comes with AD in Windows Server 2003 R2. ADAM is really a subset of the R2 AD schema, containing far fewer object classes and attributes than AD itself. For example, ADAM's schema does not support Group Policy Objects, DFS objects, SamAccountName, or Computer objects. If you want to add AD schema elements to an ADAM instance in order to allow both directories to support the same objects and attributes, you can run a tool called the ADSchemaAnalyzer, which comes with a standard ADAM installation and you can synchronize data between an AD domain and an ADAM instance using other tools that come with ADAM.

Now let's look at how to install ADAM on a Windows Server 2003 R2 system.

FIGURE 23.2

Viewing an ADAM instance as a Windows service

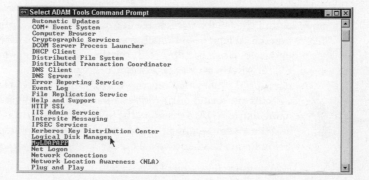

Installing ADAM

The first thing you need to know about the version of ADAM that ships with Server 2003 R2 is that it can run on any version of R2—Standard, Enterprise, or Datacenter Edition. Now let's walk through installing an ADAM instance on an R2 server in support of a directory-enabled application that needs to store shoe size information for users in an AD domain. To install ADAM, the first thing you'll need is CD 2 from the R2 installation media. With that in hand, let's begin!

1. From the R2 server, I will start the Add/Remove Programs Control Panel applet and choose the Add/Remove Windows Components button on the left.

2. Once in the Add/Remove Windows Components dialog, I'll double-click the Active Directory Services feature and check the box next to Active Directory Application Mode (ADAM). Then I'll press OK and the Next button to begin the ADAM installation.

3. Once the installation is complete, there will be a new program item in the Start Menu called ADAM. If I open this program group, I will see a number of items. The one I'm interested in is called Create an ADAM Instance—this option will let me create a new ADAM instance on this server. I choose this option to begin the Instance Creation Wizard.

4. The Setup Options screen gives me a choice of installing a new instance (unique) or a replica of an existing instance (see Figure 23.3). For this installation, I choose A Unique Instance.

5. The next screen lets me choose the name of the instance, which will also be the name of the service that appears in the Windows service manager. The default name is "instance1" but you can give your instance any meaningful name related to the application. For my example, I'm going to call my instance BigFirmApp.

6. The Ports screen lets me choose the port numbers I want to assign for communicating with my ADAM instance over LDAP. LDAP is the default protocol for communicating with ADAM (and AD). ADAM supports both LDAP and LDAP over SSL (encrypted). If I were installing this ADAM instance on a server that was not also an AD domain controller, the default ports that would be presented to me would be 389 (for LDAP) and 636 (for LDAP over SSL), but since that is not the case in my example, the ADAM Instance Wizard chooses a different set of ports for me (as shown in Figure 23.4)—in this case, 50000 and 50001.

WARNING Its very important if you are installing ADAM on an AD domain controller that you don't choose the same ports for your ADAM instance that AD is already using (TCP 389 and 636); if you do, the ADAM and AD instances will conflict.

7. Once I choose the ports to use for ADAM communication, the Application Directory Partition screen lets me optionally create the application directory partition. This is the partition within this instance that holds the directory data that my application is interested in. Why would ADAM give me the option of creating this now or waiting? Some commercial third-party applications that rely on ADAM will actually create their own ADAM application directory partition during installation. All I typically need to provide to them is the server name of my ADAM instance, the ports I've configured for it (for example, 50000 or 50001), and the instance name that I specified in the earlier step. However, for my example, I'm going to go ahead and create the application directory partition.

You'll notice that when I choose this option, I have to choose a distinguished name for the partition. The distinguished name is how I will refer to the application directory partition when I'm querying the ADAM instance. This looks very much like the distinguished name for a regular AD domain or path, with the important distinction that the partition name itself should be a container name in the form of CN=<partition name>, DC=<domain>, DC=<top level domain suffix>. For this example, I create a new application directory partition for my shoe size data called CN=bigfirmshoe, DC=bigfirm, DC=com, as shown in Figure 23.5.

NOTE When entering an application directory partition distinguished name, I can also enter an X.500 style domain name. This comes in the form of O=bigfirm,C=US, where the O= indicates an organization name and the C= indicates a country.

8. Once I enter the distinguished name for the application directory partition, I click Next to move to the next step—that of choosing the directory where I want to store the files that make up my ADAM database.

FIGURE 23.3
Choosing to install a
new ADAM instance
or a replica

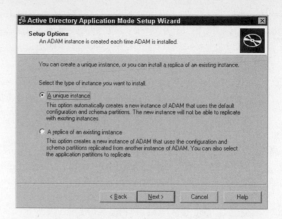

FIGURE 23.4
Choosing the LDAP
ports for a new ADAM
instance

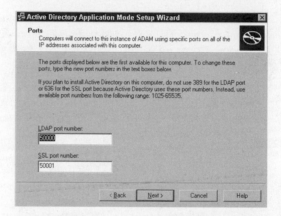

FIGURE 23.5
Entering a distin-
guished name path
to an application
directory partition

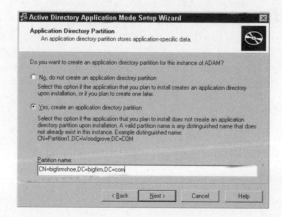

9. On the File Locations screen, I select the folder where the ADAM database files should be stored. By default, they are stored under the Program Files folder, but I can put them anywhere I want.

10. The Service Account Selection screen lets me choose the service account that the ADAM service will run under. By default, the Network Service account is used but I could use any valid security principal if desired. The Network Service is usually sufficient for most purposes, balancing the need to access other networked machines (for example, for replication of ADAM instances) with the need to limit which applications run as administrator.

11. The ADAM Administrators screen lets me choose which Windows group will be a member of the ADAM Administrators role. ADAM comes with three "roles" by default—Administrators, Readers, and Users. These roles are simply ADAM group objects that have been granted default permissions over objects that get created in an ADAM instance. By default, this dialog lets you add an AD-based (or local) user or group to the ADAM administrators role (see Figure 23.6).

   For my example, I'm going to choose the default, which is to make the currently logged on user a member of the ADAM administrators group. However, you could just as easily choose a domain-based group in an AD domain that the server running ADAM has access to (for example, it is running on a server that is a member of an AD domain).

12. The next screen—the Importing LDIF Files dialog— presents an interesting set of options. I am asked whether or not I want to import a predefined set of schema extensions into this ADAM instance. Specifically, I'm given the opportunity to choose from four different LDIF (Lightweight Directory Interchange Format) files that contain schema extensions for specific purposes. LDIF is a common format for exporting and importing LDAP-based directory data, including things like schema changes. The four LDIF files, and the reasons why you might want to include them, are listed here:

   MS-AZMan.LDF   This file has a special purpose—if I plan to use ADAM as an application directory for an application that uses Microsoft's Authorization Manager role-based authorization mechanism, then I should import this LDIF file.

   MS-InetOrgPerson.LDF   This file is used if I have an application that needs to store and use people (user) data in ADAM and that application requires X.500 compatibility. X.500-compatible directories create users of a class called InetOrgPerson, rather than the way AD creates them with the user class. If I import this LDF file, I won't import the next one, MS-User.LDF.

   MS-User.LDF   This file lets me create user objects with the same class as AD—the user class. This lets me create user objects in ADAM that are compatible with AD user objects.

   MS-UserProxy.LDF   This file lets me create a special class of object called a user proxy. The user proxy object, which I'll talk about later in the context of AD-ADAM integration, lets me create a proxy user in ADAM that corresponds to a real user ID in AD. With this proxy object, an AD user can authenticate to ADAM without having to explicitly provide credentials—the user proxy object essentially provides Single Sign-On (SSO) from AD to ADAM.

   For my example, I choose to import the MS-User.LDF and MS-UserProxy.LDF files into my ADAM instance and proceed with the next step.

13. The next dialog confirms all of the ADAM instance creation options I have chosen so far. I press Next, and the ADAM instance will be created on my system!

FIGURE 23.6
Adding users or
groups to the ADAM
Administrators role

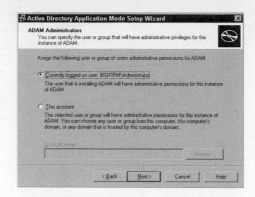

Managing ADAM

Once I've installed my ADAM instance, I need to manage it! Unfortunately, if you're used to managing AD with reasonably intuitive tools like AD Users and Computers and AD Sites and Services, you'll be disappointed with your choices for managing ADAM. If you look into the ADAM program group that gets installed on the server where you install ADAM, you will notice only one obvious tool for managing ADAM—an ADAM-specific version of ADSIEdit, which you might have used in your AD deployments for getting access to and editing raw attribute data on AD objects not exposed through AD Users and Computers. In fact, ADSIEdit for ADAM and LDP.exe are the only graphical tools provided by MS for querying, adding, modifying, and deleting objects into your ADAM application directory partitions. Let's look at how I can use ADSIEdit for ADAM to add a user object to my newly created Bigfirmshoe ADAM instance.

Using ADAM ADSIEdit to Add Objects

The first thing I do is start the ADAM ADSIEdit tool from the ADAM program group and connect to the ADAM instance. I right-click the ADAM ADSI Edit node and select Connect To. When I do that, I'll get the Connection Settings dialog shown in Figure 23.7.

1. What I want to do is give my connection a meaningful name, something like that shown in Figure 23.7, BigFirmShoe Application Directory Partition.

2. Next, I want to pick the server name where ADAM is running and the port I chose when I installed my instance—in this case 50000 (or 50001 if I'm using SSL). (If I wanted to connect to the schema or configuration naming contexts of this instance, I could have chosen the well-known naming context option instead.)

3. Finally, I choose the credentials I want to use to connect to the ADAM instance. Once I complete the connection, I'll see a tree similar to that shown in Figure 23.8.

4. From here, I can right-click any object in the tree and create a new user object (or create a container in which to store a user object). Let's go ahead and create a new user object under the root of the partition. If I right-click the CN=bigfirmshoe,DC=bigfirm,DC=com node and choose New ➢ Object, I see a dialog box with a choice of about 11 classes that I can choose from. I choose user and click Next.

5. Then I'm asked for the cn attribute for this new user object. Essentially, this is the name of the user object. I enter **Bigfirm User** in this value and click Next, as in Figure 23.9.

FIGURE 23.7
Connecting to ADAM
from ADSIEdit

FIGURE 23.8
Viewing an application directory partition through ADSIEdit

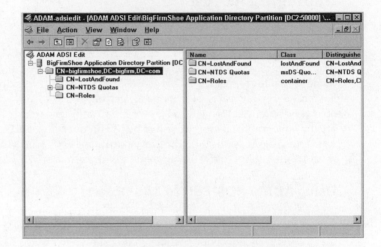

FIGURE 23.9
Modifying the cn
attribute on a new
user object

From the Create Object screen, I have the option now of filling in other attributes for this new user by pressing the More Attributes button if I want, or, alternately, I can just press Finish. Once the user is added, I can go back and edit its attributes just as if this were an AD user. The main difference here, of course, is that this user object does not yet have a password, or a SID, or anything that might be related to a real AD user object. In order to perform additional tasks like assigning a password to a user object, I need to modify additional attributes on the user object. For example, to assign a password, I need to modify the userPassword attribute. To add the user to a group, I need to double-click the group object in question and then modify the member attribute and add an ADAM or Windows security principal to the group, as shown in Figure 23.10.

As you can see, managing objects in ADAM is not as straightforward as doing it in AD. Let's look at what it takes to view and modify security permissions on ADAM objects.

FIGURE 23.10
Modifying ADAM
group membership

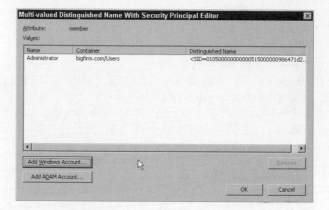

Viewing and Modifying ADAM Permissions

ADAM uses security permissions on objects to control which security principals are authorized to perform actions on objects and attributes. This is similar to AD except that, once again, ADAM doesn't provide a nice easy graphical editor tool such as the AD Users and Computers ACL Editor for viewing and modifying permissions. Instead, ADAM provides the familiar command-line utility DSACLS.exe for this purpose. DSACLS can be found by opening the ADAM Tools Command Prompt within the ADAM program group. Let's take a look at two examples. First, I'll view the permissions on the BigFirm User object I just created with ADSIEdit. Then I'll modify the permissions on that object. Figure 23.11 shows the syntax I'll use to view the permissions on the user object.

FIGURE 23.11
Using DSACLS to view
permissions on an
ADAM user object

```
ADAM Tools Command Prompt

Microsoft Windows [Version 5.2.3790]
(C) Copyright 1985-2003 Microsoft Corp.

C:\WINDOWS\ADAM>dsacls "\\dc2:50000\CN=BigFirm User, CN=BigFirmShoe, DC=bigfirm,
DC=com" /G "CN=BigFirm Managers, CN=BigFirmShoe,DC=bigfirm,DC=com":GA
Owner: CN=Administrators,CN=Roles,CN=bigfirmshoe,DC=com
Group: CN=Administrators,CN=Roles,CN=bigfirmshoe,DC=bigfirm,DC=com

Access list:
Allow CN=BigFirm Managers,CN=bigfirmshoe,DC=bigfirm,DC=com
                        FULL CONTROL
Allow CN=Readers,CN=Roles,CN=bigfirmshoe,DC=bigfirm,DC=com
                        SPECIAL ACCESS     <Inherited from parent>
                        READ PERMISSONS
                        LIST CONTENTS
                        READ PROPERTY
                        LIST OBJECT
Allow CN=Administrators,CN=Roles,CN=bigfirmshoe,DC=bigfirm,DC=com
                        FULL CONTROL     <Inherited from parent>
Allow NT AUTHORITY\SELF
                        Change Password

Permissions inherited to subobjects are:
Inherited to all subobjects
Allow CN=Readers,CN=Roles,CN=bigfirmshoe,DC=bigfirm,DC=com
                        SPECIAL ACCESS     <Inherited from parent>
```

As you can see from the command, all I need to do is enter the name and port of the ADAM server I'm connecting to (for example, \\dc2:50000) and the distinguished name of the object whose permissions I want to manage. Then I'm going to use DSACLS' /G (for grant) parameter to add a new group—the BigFirm Managers group— with Full Control permissions over my BigFirm User object. The DSACLS command I'll use for that is as follows:

```
Dsacls "\\dc2:50000\CN=BigFirm User, CN=BigFirmShoe, DC=bigfirm, DC=com"
/G "CN=BigFirm Managers, CN=BigFirmShoe, DC=bigfirm, DC=com":GA
```

This command does the following. First, I tell DSACLS which server and port to connect to. Then I tell it the object I want to operate on. Then I use the /G parameter to assign a group and per-mission. In this case, I provide the DN of my BigFirm Managers group, which is the group I want to grant the access to, and the GA (Generic All) permission to grant Full Control access to the Big-Firm User object. Again, not as easy as clicking check boxes in the ACL Editor, but nonetheless the easiest way to modify permissions in ADAM.

Querying ADAM

There are numerous ways you can query an ADAM instance to find objects and attributes. The key thing to remember about ADAM is that it uses the same LDAP query syntax as AD. So, for example, if I wanted to find all ADAM users whose display name starts with "Big", I could issue the follow-ing LDAP query against ADAM:

```
(&(objectcategory=user)(displayname=Big*))
```

ADAM provides a variety of tools for searching for objects. ADSIEdit provides support for saved queries if I right-click the application directory partition node and select New ➤ Query. LDP provides search facilities as well. Let's perform the search using LDP for all users whose displayname attribute starts with Big.

1. The first thing I do is start LDP. You can get to LDP by opening an ADAM command prompt and typing **ldp** at the command prompt.

2. Once LDP is started, I connect to my ADAM instance by choosing Connection ➤ Connect and providing the server name and port (for example, 50000).

3. Once connected, I need to bind to ADAM. Binding essentially means authenticating to ADAM—that is, providing user and password credentials. To do this, I select Connection ➤ Bind and either authenticate using my current user context or provide alternate credentials.

4. Once I bind successfully (LDP shows status of each command in the window to the right), I select View ➤ Tree and, leaving the base DN dialog blank, click OK to view each of the naming contexts of my ADAM instance, as shown in Figure 23.12.

5. Now I right-click my CN=bigfirmshoe,DC=bigfirm,DC=com partition and select Search. The Search dialog will appear, and I can choose the base DN (the point from which I'd like to start my search), and the filter, or LDAP query string, I want to search on. I can also choose the scope here. Base searches just the base DN container, One Level searches one level below the base DN, and Subtree searches all objects and containers below the base DN, regardless of how many levels they are nested. When I issue my query (by clicking the Run button), the results will appear in the right-hand results pane, as shown in Figure 23.13. As you can see, one result—Bigfirm User—was returned from my search.

FIGURE 23.12
Using LDP to bind
to and view an
ADAM instance

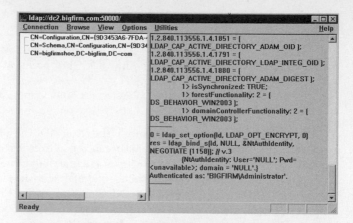

FIGURE 23.13
Using LDP to query
ADAM user objects

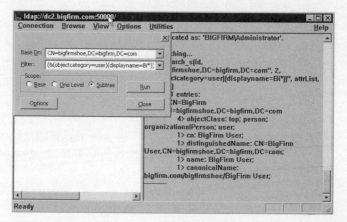

Now that you have the basics of installing and managing ADAM down, let's look at how you can implement an ADAM instance that integrates and extends Active Directory. For my example, I'm going to go back to my earlier example of adding shoe size information to my AD users. Let's look at how to implement that so that my directory-enabled application can use ADAM to discover the shoe sizes of my AD users.

Integrating AD with ADAM

Essentially what I want to accomplish is to store and be able to use shoe size information for all of my AD users. In order to do that, I need to extend my ADAM schema to include a shoeSize attribute on user objects. Next, I need to get my AD user data into ADAM so that ADAM and AD have the same data about users. This way, my application can query ADAM to get user and shoe size data. Finally, I want to do some authentication integration so that users in AD can seamlessly authenticate to ADAM to view and modify their shoe size info. Let's start by extending the ADAM schema with the shoeSize attribute.

1. To begin this process, I load the ADAM-specific schema MMC snap-in. I do this by starting a blank MMC console (type **mmc** at the Run dialog) and choosing File ➢ Add/Remove Snap-In and choosing the ADAM Schema snap-in.

2. Once I load this snap-in, I right-click the ADAM Schema node, choose Change ADAM Server, and connect to my ADAM instance using the server and port number.

3. After connecting, I right-click the Attributes node and select Create Attribute. I receive a warning about the irreversibility of schema modifications. After clicking through this by pressing the Continue button, I get to Create New Attribute dialog, which lets me set all of the properties of my new shoe size attribute. Figure 23.14 shows what this would look like when fully completed.

One thing here that is not obvious is the Object ID. The OID, as it often referred to, is a unique number assigned by an international organization to each company that has and wants to extend their X.500-compatible directory. Microsoft has a unique one, and if you look at the OID on all of AD's classes and attributes, you'll notice they start with the same set of dot-delimited digits. For my shoe size attribute, I ran a tool called OIDGen.exe from the Windows 2000 Resource Kit that lets me generate my own internal OIDs for class and attribute extensions. This is perfectly reasonable, since my ADAM instance will only be used internally. If you have an ADAM instance that may need to synchronize or share data with an external organization, then it's probably worth getting an "official" OID.

TIP You can register for an OID with Microsoft by going to `http://msdn.microsoft.com/ certification/ad-registration.asp`.

1. Once I create my new shoe size attribute, I need to associate it to user objects. I do this from the same ADAM schema snap-in by expanding the Classes node, locating the user class, double-clicking it, and choosing the Attributes tab.

2. From here I see both mandatory and optional attributes. I use the Add button to add my new shoeSize attribute to the optional attributes on the user class, and then my schema extension is complete!

I can now add shoe size to my ADAM user objects. The next step is to get my AD user data into ADAM so that ADAM becomes the definitive source for user shoe size data.

FIGURE 23.14
Adding a new attribute to ADAM

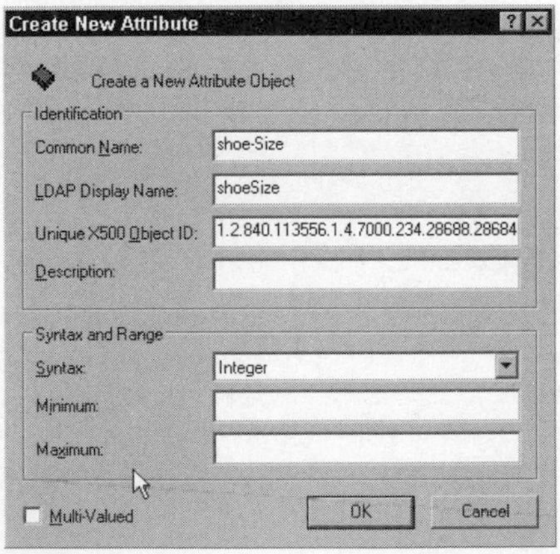

Adding AD Data to ADAM

There are any number of ways to get user data from AD to ADAM. I could use LDIFDE to export user data from AD and then reimport it into ADAM. But that would be a one-time operation and may not meet my needs for ongoing synchronization. Fortunately, ADAM provides a command-line AD-to-ADAM synchronization tool for that purpose. The tool, called ADAMSync.exe, can be rather complex to set up, but if you need ongoing synchronization, it is a good option. However, ADAMSync.exe synchronizes everything in AD to ADAM, so you need to make sure that your schemas for both ADAM and AD are exactly the same. Let's walk through the steps to use ADAM-Sync.exe to synchronize ADAM and AD data:

1. I need to extend the ADAM schema with the Server 2003 AD schema. ADAM provides an LDIF file to make this work, so I only need to run an ldifde.exe command against this LDIF file. To do this, I open up the ADAM Tool command prompt from the ADAM program group. I find a file in there called MS-ADAMSchemaW2K3.1df. I open that file in Notepad or your favorite text editor and perform a search and replace, replacing the string "DC=x" with my AD domain name. In my scenario, I replace "DC=x" with "DC=bigfirm,DC=com". This is a big file so I will see a lot of replacements!

2. Once the ldf file has been modified, I need to import it into my ADAM instance using the following command:

   ```
   Ldifde -i -s DC2:50000 -c CN=Configuration, DC=bigfirm, DC=com
   #ConfigurationNamingContext -f MS-ADAMSchemaW2K3.1df
   ```

   where DC2:50000 is the server name and port of my ADAM instance, the -c parameter specifies the DN of the configuration naming context for my AD domain, bigfirm.com, and the #ConfigurationNamingContext option refers to the configuration naming context of my ADAM instance. Once the import is completed (see Figure 23.15), when I open the ADAM Schema MMC snap-in, I see a large number of new classes and attributes.

3. Now I've imported all the base Server 2003 AD schema elements into ADAM, but I also need to import the R2-specific schema extensions. To do that, I use the AD Schema Analyzer tool that comes with ADAM. From the ADAM tools command prompt, I type **ADSchemaAnalyzer** to start the tool. From the File menu, I select Load Target Schema, and in the server field, I enter the domain name and port of my AD domain (that is, **bigfirm.com:389**).

FIGURE 23.15
Importing AD schema elements into ADAM

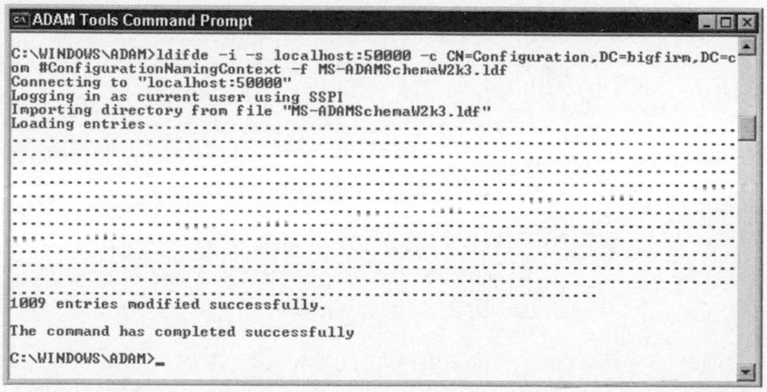

4. Next, I select File ≻ Load Base Schema and enter the server name and port of my ADAM instance (**dc2:50000**).

5. Once the two schemas are loaded, I select Schema ≻ Mark All Non-present Elements as Included from the ADSchemaAnalyzer menu.

6. Then I select File ≻ Create LDIF File and give a name to the resulting difference file (in the example, **r2-schema.ldf**). This new file represents the differences between the R2 schema in AD and my ADAM schema.

7. Once again, I need to open this LDIF file in Notepad and replace all instances of "DC=x" with "DC=bigfirm,DC=com", that is, my AD domain DN.

8. Now I import this file into ADAM using the following command:

```
Ldifde -i -s DC2:50000 -c CN=Configuration, DC=bigfirm, DC=com
#ConfigurationNamingContext -f r2-schema.ldf
```

9. I now need to import a set of schema extensions into ADAM that support the ADAMSync tool. These extensions are within the file in the ADAM Tools folder called MS-ADAMSync-Metadata.ldf. Like the LDIF file in the previous step, I need to replace the "DC=" text with the distinguished name of my AD domain. Then I can issue the following LDIFDE command to import the schema extensions:

```
ldifde -i -s DC2:50000 -c CN=Configuration,DC=bigfirm,DC=com
#ConfigurationNamingContext -f MS-AdamSyncMetadata.ldf
```

10. Once that import has completed successfully, I need to modify the ADAMSync configuration file to point to the appropriate source and target directories. This file, also in the ADAM tools folder, is called MS-ADAMSyncConf.xml. I can modify the file with Notepad or my favorite XML editor. It contains a number of tags that need to be replaced as follows:

   ◆ `<source-ad-name>fabrikam.com</source-ad-name>` should become `<source-ad-name>bigfirm.com</source-ad-name>`, that is the name of the AD domain

   ◆ `<source-ad-partition>dc=fabrikam,dc=com</source-ad-partition>` should become `<source-ad-partition>dc=bigfirm,dc=com</source-ad-partition>`, that is, the DN of the AD domain

   ◆ `<source-ad-account></source-ad-account>` should become `<source-ad-account>administrator</source-ad-account>`, that is, a domain admin account in the source AD domain

   ◆ `<account-domain></account-domain>` should become `<account-domain>bigfirm.com</account-domain>`, that is, the full DNS name of the source AD domain

   ◆ `<target-dn>dc=fabrikam,dc=com</target-dn>` should become `<target-dn>cn=bigfirmshoe,dc=bigfirm,dc=com</target-dn>`, that is, the DN of the ADAM application directory partition being synchronized into

   ◆ `<base-dn>dc=fabrikam,dc=com</base-dn>` should become `<base-dn>dc=bigfirm,dc=com</base-dn>`, that is, the DN of the AD domain that is the source of the synchronization

11. After the file has been modified, I need to import it by issuing the following command:

    ```
    Adamsync /install dc2:50000 ms-adamsyncconf.xml
    ```

12. After the ADAMSync configuration has been installed, I am ready to synchronize ADAM and AD. To perform a one-time synchronization, I issue the following command:

    ```
    Adamsync /sync dc2:50000 "cn=bigfirmshoe,dc=bigfirm,dc=com" /log
    ```

13. This command will take a while to complete, depending upon the size of the AD domain. After it does, all of the objects in the AD domain will also exist in the AD partition. I confirm this by using ADAM ADSI Edit to view the objects. If you want to synchronize ADAM and AD on a periodic basis, you can use the Windows Task Scheduler to set up a scheduled task to perform the previous Adamsync command—ensuring that your AD and ADAM data stays synchronized.

After issuing the command, your AD and ADAM instance are synchronized, and you can modify one of the recently synchronized AD users in ADAM and access their shoe size attribute. In this final part of the chapter, I'll walk through how to authenticate to ADAM using an AD user ID that makes accessing the newly available shoe size attribute seamless to those AD users.

Authenticating to ADAM

ADAM supports three forms of authentication or binding, as it's commonly called. These three forms are as follows:

Bind as Windows Principal   This method involves binding to ADAM using AD credentials (for example, bigfirm\joesmith). In order for this binding mechanism to work, the server where the ADAM instance is installed has to be in or trusting of the domain where the AD principal resides, and the user needs to be granted explicit access to the ADAM objects (for example, using DSACLS, as I described earlier).

Bind as ADAM Principal   This option involves binding to ADAM with a user account and password created in ADAM. In this case, no external AD account access is required and you are binding using the native LDAP bind process. Again, permissions will need to be granted to your ADAM user account in order to get access to ADAM objects.

Bind Using AD Proxy Object   I mentioned the AD proxy object earlier in the chapter. This is a special ADAM object that you can create that provides *pass-through authentication* to an AD user account requiring access to ADAM. This is the method I will use in the example for my seamless access from an AD account into ADAM to modify my user shoe size attribute. The one requirement to be aware of in advance is that the proxy binding approach performs what is called a *simple bind* into ADAM. A simple bind sends the user name and password in clear text over the network to the ADAM server. Since this is generally not a good thing, it is strongly recommended that you use LDAP-over-SSL to use this mechanism. LDAP-over-SSL requires a certificate for signing that can be recognized by both the client and server.

The steps I use to enable a proxy user object in ADAM are as follows:

1. I start the ADAM ADSIEdit tool and create a new user proxy object by right-clicking the container in which I want to store my proxy objects and selecting New ➤ Object. When I am prompted for a class, I select the userProxy class and click Next.

2. I need to enter a CN value for this object. It should be named something that relates to the AD user I am going to proxy. In my scenario, I want to create a proxy for the bigfirm.com user Bob so I will call this proxy object bobProxy.

3. On the final page , I have the option of editing additional attributes, which I'm going to do. When the attribute dialog appears, I select that I want to view mandatory attributes and scroll down to the objectSID attribute.

4. Here I enter the SID of the AD user I want to proxy into ADAM. I can get the SID of the AD user in a variety of ways, but perhaps the easiest is to go to www.sysinternals.com and just download the psgetsid.exe utility.

NOTE You can also go to www.microsoft.com/technet/scriptcenter/resources/qanda/ dec04/hey1203.mspx to see how you can get the user's SID using VBScript and WMI.

5. Once I have the SID of my AD user, I enter it into the proxy object's objectSID attribute to complete the proxy object.

Now that my proxy object is created, the user Bob in the AD domain bigfirm.com can access any objects and attributes in ADAM that he has been granted access to without having to explicitly authenticate to the ADAM instance—that is, Bob now has Single Sign-On access to ADAM. By default, an AD user that binds to ADAM using a proxy object is automatically placed in the ADAM Users group, which is found in the Roles container in a default ADAM installation. Therefore, any ADAM objects that are accessible to the Users group will be accessible to the proxy user. So, I could grant the Users group permissions to read and write the shoe size attribute on user objects within a specific ADAM container. Bob would then be able to edit that attribute on his ADAM user object through one of the tools I've used here (that is, LDP or ADSIEdit) or, more likely, through an application front-end that I, as an administrator, have provided for him.

Unfortunately, the proxy binding method does not provide any more granularity than as a member of the Users group, so if you plan to use this method for many AD users, you may need to choose one of the other authentication methods.

Summary

In this chapter, we looked at the role ADAM plays in the Active Directory universe, as a lightweight LDAP-compatible directory service that allows you to extend the data associated with your AD infrastructure without having to extend the AD schema. We walked through how ADAM is structured with three different naming contexts, and we looked at installing an ADAM instance on a Server 2003 R2 server. Then we looked at the tools, such as ADSIEdit and LDP, for querying and managing ADAM instances. We also looked at how you can integrate AD into ADAM from both a data and authentication perspective. ADAM provides command-line synchronization tools for performing AD-to-ADAM synchronization. ADAM also supports a variety of authentication methods, including the Single Sign-On–based proxy object for authenticating from AD user accounts into ADAM.

Index

Note to the Reader: Throughout this index **boldfaced** page numbers indicate primary discussions of a topic. *Italicized* page numbers indicate illustrations.